MORALITY AND THE GOOD LIFE

AN INTRODUCTION TO ETHICS THROUGH CLASSICAL SOURCES

MORALITY AND THE GOOD LIFE

AN INTRODUCTION TO ETHICS THROUGH CLASSICAL SOURCES

Robert C. Solomon
University of Texas at Austin

McGRAW-HILL BOOK COMPANY

New York   St. Louis   San Francisco   Auckland   Bogotá
Hamburg   London   Madrid   Mexico   Montreal   New Delhi
Panama   Paris   São Paulo   Singapore   Sydney   Tokyo   Toronto

This book was set in Times Roman and Helvetica by Black Dot, Inc. (ECU).
The editors were Anne Murphy and David Dunham;
the production supervisor was Diane Renda.
The cover was designed by Joan E. O'Connor;
the cover illustration was done by Mark Yankus.
Halliday Lithograph Corporation was printer and binder.

MORALITY AND THE GOOD LIFE

An Introduction to Ethics through Classical Sources

4567890HALHAL898

ISBN 0-07-059654-9

Library of Congress Cataloging in Publication Data

Solomon, Robert C.
    Morality and the good life.

        1. Ethics.   2. Ethics—Addresses, essays, lectures.
I. Title.
BJ1012.S57 1984   170   83-13549
ISBN 0-07-059654-9

For Paul Woodruff
and Donette Moss

CONTENTS

PREFACE

This is a textbook in ethics. It is intended as an introduction for students who have had no philosophical background but are capable of studying somewhat difficult yet indisputably important sources. The premise of this book is that the study of ethics is first of all participation in a long tradition that is based upon a (more or less) agreed-upon sequence of "great" philosophers. Of course, ethics is also an attempt to come to grips with certain perennial moral problems, but these too must be understood as part of a tradition of questions and answers as well as problems intrinsic to the human condition.

Ethics has never been a more urgent undertaking. We live at a time in which the very existence of morals—or at least any "correct" morals—has been thrown into question. But in the pedagogical attempts to capture this urgency with reference to current moral crises (the morality of abortion, the threat of nuclear war), too many introductory ethics courses have been made "relevant" only at the cost of ignoring the tradition that gives them significance. There is no disputing that questions such as "What is right and what should I do?" are utterly necessary and ought to be asked more often and with greater insight than they are in our "bottom-line"–minded society. But, on the one hand, it is not at all clear that the heavy intellectual artillery of philosophy is usually required or even suitable to answer the more usual variety of ethical queries (for example, "Why shouldn't I cheat on my test? Everyone else does."). On the other hand, it is not clear that a serious answer to such questions can be provided except *within* that long tradition that stretches from Plato and the Bible to the present.

The study of ethics is this synthesis of current problems and a long tradition of answers. It is a common error to think that ethical issues can be settled in a moral vacuum, without already shared values and a broad, if vague, general understanding of the nature of morality and the importance of being moral. But it is also an error to expect that the broad understanding of ethics—even when sharpened by the study of ethics—will provide concrete answers to pressing moral problems. (One leading American ethicist tells of the time when a student walked into his office and with obvious urgency asked, "Do you believe that suicide is ever justified?'' As a matter of fact, the ethicist did believe that suicide was justifiable in certain cases, but it was equally clear to him that this was not the time to display philosophical subtleties.)

This is not to say that ethics is irrelevant to practical problems; indeed, it would be absurd if that were so. But solving problems is not the only concern of ethics or philosophy, and there are virtues of general understanding that need not be convertible into concrete solutions. It may be that no ethical theory or viewpoint is of any interest if it does not come to grips with our everyday moral concerns, but we should not thereby expect ready-made solutions to every personal problem. Indeed, one of the lessons of the history of ethics is that difficulties enter into solving even the simplest moral dilemma. The point of learning about various ethical theories or viewpoints is not to make solving problems easier for us. In fact, it may well make problem solving harder, as we come to appreciate more and more of the implications and considerations that enter into even the simplest ethical decision.

To study ethics, with the approach assumed in this text, is to participate in that tradition which reaches back over 2500 years, a tradition we tend to trace, somewhat arbitrarily, back to Socrates. It was Socrates—at least according to his student Plato (from whom we have most of the records of Socrates's teachings) —who set in motion some of the central questions of ethics, such as What is the good? and What is justice?, as well as, Why shouldn't a person always do just what is in his or her own interest, without regard for anyone else? Studying ethics is reading and thinking through such questions and the answers provided to them by Socrates and Plato and by Plato's student Aristotle, by the medieval Christian philosopher Saint Augustine, and by such modern philosophers as David Hume, Immanuel Kant, and John Stuart Mill.

It is too often said today that students are no longer interested or willing (or sometimes able) to read original texts. But these are not so difficult as supposed, and if they seem to be, it is in part because students today are confronted less and less with original philosophy texts, which means that they have a harder time reading them, which means that they avoid them more, and so on *ad illiteratum.* At the same time, it is a pedagogical fact that students resist long tracts of original text and at least at first have considerable difficulty learning the kind of critical reading required in philosophy. Accordingly, I have tried to provide both substantial portions of original texts *and* a continuing sequence of comments and suggestions. This has the effect, however modest, of providing a tutor for each student as he or she reads through the material and encouraging him or her to participate in the process rather than just struggling with the text. It is to be hoped that the commentary will allow instructors not only more freedom in leading discussions but also more confidence that their students will have had at least some minimal exposure to a broad range of issues.

This book is composed of substantial texts coupled and broken up with background and commentary, suggestions, and study questions. The works are not complete but, given the context of an undergraduate course, more than sufficient to give the student substantial knowledge of the classical texts. This book is adequate for a full course in ethics, but it is concise enough to allow the instructor time to include other approaches—whether more contemporary authors and issues or particular moral dilemmas—in addition to the classic texts and materials presented here.

It is appropriate to comment here on the typical use of the masculine noun "man" in many of the authors included here. Aristotle, for example, develops an ethics which is literally just for men. More modern authors—Hume, Kant, and Mill, for example—use "man" as a generic term for "humanity." This grates against our contemporary sensibilities, and I have accordingly used more neutral language in the commentaries. The original language has been left in the texts as a matter of accuracy, not as a matter of approval.

I would like to express my thanks for the many useful comments and suggestions provided by colleagues who reviewed this text during the course of its development, especially to Daniel Bonevac, The University of Texas at Austin; Izchak Miller, University of Pennsylvania; John J. Stuhr, Whitman College; James J. Valone, visiting associate professor, Loyola University of Chicago; and Stephen Voss, San Jose State University. I also want to thank Kaye Pace, Anne Murphy, and David Dunham, editors at the McGraw-Hill Book Company.

Robert C. Solomon

HOW TO USE THIS BOOK

In the following pages, some of the classic texts in the history of ethics are presented with introductions and commentary to help the beginning student through the readings. It is not to be expected that most instructors will attempt to use all the readings; in fact, some may want to use only three or four of them. Several possible combinations are particularly recommended:

I. Basic Sequence
Plato, *Crito*
Augustine, *City of God*
Kant, *Groundwork*
Mill, *Utilitarianism*
(optional: Nietzsche selections)

II. Historical Survey
Plato, *Crito, Republic*
Aristotle, *Ethics,* (Book I)
Augustine, *City of God*
Hobbes, *Leviathan* (first chapter)
Hume, *Treatise, Inquiry* (Book I)
Kant, *Groundwork* (Books I and II)
Mill, *Utilitarianism* (Chapters 1 and 4)
Nietzsche (some selections)
Sartre, *Existentialism*

III. Emphasis on Justification
Aristotle, *Ethics* (Books I to III)
Augustine, *City of God*
Hobbes, *Leviathan* (first section)

Kant, *Groundwork* (Chapters 1 and 2)
Mill, *Utilitarianism* (Chapters 1 and 4)
Nietzsche, selections from *Beyond Good and Evil* and *Genealogy of Morals*
Camus, *Myth of Sisyphus*

IV. Individual and State
Plato, *Crito* and *Republic*
Aristotle, *Ethics* (Books I to III)
Hobbes, *Leviathan* (first section)
Hume, *Inquiry* (Chapters 2 and 3)
Kant, *Groundwork* (Chapters 1 and 2)
Mill, *Utilitarianism* (Chapters 1, 2, 5)
Sartre, *Existentialism* and *Bad Faith*

V. The Virtues
Plato, *Crito*
Aristotle, *Ethics* (Books I to IV)
Augustine, *City of God*
Kant, *Groundwork* (Chapters 1 and 2)
Mill, *Utilitarianism* (Chapters 1 to 3)
Nietzsche, selections
Sartre, *Existentialism*

VI. Ethos and Ethics
Plato, *Crito*
Aristotle, *Ethics* (Books I to IV)
Augustine, *City of God*
Kant, *Groundwork* (Chapter 1)
Mill, *Utilitarianism* (Chapters 1 and 4)
Nietzsche, selections
Camus, *Myth of Sisyphus*
Sartre, *Existentialism*

VII. Happiness
Aristotle, *Ethics* (Books I to III, X)
Augustine, *City of God*
Hobbes, *Leviathan* (first section)
Kant, *Groundwork* (Chapter 2)
Mill, *Utilitarianism* (Chapters 1, 2, 5)
Nietzsche, selections from *Beyond Good and Evil* and *Will to Power*
Camus, *The Stranger*

VIII. Freedom
Plato, *Crito*
Aristotle, *Ethics* (Books I to III)

Augustine, *City of God*
Hobbes, *Leviathan*
Kant, *Groundwork* (Chapters 1 and 2)
Mill, *Utilitarianism* (Chapters 1 and 2)
Nietzsche, selections from *Beyond Good and Evil* and *Will to Power*
Camus, *Myth of Sisyphus*
Sartre, *Existentialism*

Study questions are provided at the end of each chapter; thought questions appear in the discussions of the text as well. A glossary is provided at the end of the book, but new and technical terms are also explained when they are introduced in the text. The introduction is an attempt to provide a simple overview of ethics for the student who has no or little familiarity with the subject.

INTRODUCTION

Today in a wood, we heard a Voice.

We hunted for it but could not find it. Adam said he had heard it before, but had never seen it. . . . It was Lord of the Garden, he said, . . . and it had said we must not eat of the fruit of a certain tree and that if we ate of it we would surely die. . . . Adam said it was the tree of good and evil.

"Good and evil?"

"Yes."

"What is that?"

"What is what?"

"Why, those things. What is good?"

"I do not know. How should I know?"

"Well, then, what is evil?"

"I suppose it is the name of something, but I do not know what."

"But Adam, you must have some *idea of what it is." "Why* should *I have some idea? I have never seen the thing, how am I to form any conception of it? What is your own notion of it?"*

Of course I had none, and it was unreasonable of me to require him to have one. There was no way for either of us to guess what it might be. It was a new word, like the other; we had not heard them before, and they meant nothing to us.

Mark Twain[1]

[1]Mark Twain, extract from "Eve's Diary," *Letters from the Earth* (New York: Harper & Row, 1974), pp. 75–76.

1

WHAT IS ETHICS?

Ethics is the study of a way of life, *our* way of life—its values, its rules and justifications. It involves doing what Mark Twain's Adam and Eve were just beginning to do—thinking about "good" and "evil" and what they mean.

The word "ethics" refers both to a discipline—the study of our values and their justification—and to the subject matter of that discipline—the actual values and rules of conduct by which we live. The two meanings merge in the fact that we behave (and misbehave) according to a complex and continually changing set of rules, customs, and expectations; consequently, we are forced to reflect on our conduct and attitudes, to justify and sometimes to change them.

Why do we need to study ethics as a discipline? Isn't it enough that we *have* ethics, that we do (most of us, most of the time) act according to our values and rules?

In some societies, having ethics might be sufficient without the study of ethics as well. But this cannot be the case in our society, for at least four reasons:

1 Our ethics are continually changing. Consider, for example, the enormous changes that our society has experienced over just the past few decades in the realm of sexual morality; behavior is accepted today which would have been wanton immorality fifty years ago (for example, topless beachwear for men!). Only twenty years ago, many people considered it "unethical" for a wife to work, except in cases of dire family need, and it was perfectly acceptable—in fact even commendable—for a husband to spend so much time working at his career that he virtually never saw his children. Some of these changes have to do with changing economic and social conditions in our society; others are reflections of deeper ethical shifts, more emphasis on individual freedom, for example, and less emphasis on the differences between the sexes and traditional roles. Changes in ethics are always disturbing and disruptive; the study of ethics enables us to understand the nature of these changes and, just as important, to discern the stable basis of values that underlies them.

2 We live in an ethically *pluralist* society, in which there is no single code of ethics but many different values and rules. Some people in our society emphasize individual success and mobility; others emphasize the importance of group identity and stable cultural tradition. Some people insist that the ultimate value is individual freedom; others would insist that general welfare is more important, even if it interferes with individual freedom. Some people consider it absolutely wrong to take a human life—even if the life in question is that of an unborn zygote or fetus; others do not believe that such life counts as human; it should be sacrificed if necessary to the well-being of the mother. None of these differences in ethics are easily reconciled; in fact they may be unreconcilable. But that makes it all the more important that we understand the nature of these differences, and this is much of what ethical discussion and debate is about.

3 Our ethics involves *choice*. In fact, freedom of choice is one of the main values of our ethics. But to choose between alternative courses of action or opposed values requires intelligent deliberation and some sense of the *reasons* why one should choose one rather than another. This too is the function of ethical study and discussion.

We might note that the importance of choice in ethics is often confused with the idea that we "choose our own values." This is quite different however. (Jean-Paul Sartre argues for it in the final selections of this book.) Ethical choice almost always involves decisions between already established possibilities, and these we do *not* choose. A student deciding between joining the navy or going to law school does indeed have an important choice to make, but the alternatives and their values are provided by the society as a whole. Having to choose between alternatives, however, is more than enough reason to be clear about their values and implications, and this too is a central function of ethics.

4 Ethical values are often in *conflict.* Even when people agree on certain values, there will inevitably be times when two (or more) accepted values run up against one another. Conflicting goals and customs force us to reconsider continually our ethical priorities; freedom of speech sometimes threatens safety, security, or sensibilities—the proverbial yelling "fire" in a crowded theater, for example, or when newspapers publish classified military secrets or when pornographers "hide behind the first amendment." The value of free enterprise must sometimes be weighed against the tragedy of unemployment and the commercialization of society. The virtue of honesty must be balanced by concern for the consequences of telling the truth, and the virtue of courage must be measured against the danger one faces.

The key concepts of ethics define the specific values by which we live, including honesty, courage, success, money, marriage, the value of life, and the significance of death. Our ethics determines what we should want, what we should do, what we should prefer, and how we should live. But ethics also includes more abstract concepts such as the ideas of happiness and justice, the value of freedom and its sibling concept of responsibility. Such ideas do not tell us what to do in particular situations so much as they inform us of the overall goals and ideals which set the stage for our every action. More general still are the crucial concepts of *good* and *evil, right* and *wrong.* We do not do just whatever we want to do; we also want to do what is right and try to be a good person. These, accordingly, define the key questions of ethics: What actions are right? What is a good person?

It is worth noting too that asking these questions is itself an essential part of our ethics. We expect people to do what is right, but we do not value a person who unquestioningly does whatever he or she is told. Some of the most immoral acts of the century have been committed by people who unquestioningly did what they were told to do. Right action and good people, therefore, depend upon the right kinds of thinking as well as doing what is right. The study of ethics, in other words, is itself part of our ethics.

Ethics and Ethos

The word "ethics" comes from the Greek word *ethos,* meaning character or custom, and the derivative phrase *tá ēthiká,* which Plato and Aristotle used to describe their own studies of Greek values and ideals. An *ethos,* as we use that term today, is the character of a culture. Ethics, on the other hand, begins with a concern for individual character—including what we blandly call "being a good person"—but it is also the effort to understand the social rules which govern and limit our behavior, especially those ultimate rules—the rules concerning good and evil—which we call *morality.* Ethos and ethics go hand in hand.

The close connection between ethics and social customs ("mores," which shares an etymological root with the word "morality") inevitably raises the question whether morality is nothing but the customs of our particular society, our ethics nothing but the rules of our particular ethos. On the one hand, it is clear that ethics and morality are very closely tied to the laws and the customs of a particular society. Kissing in public and making a profit in a business transaction are considered immoral in some societies, not in ours. But, on the other hand, we are firmly convinced that not any laws or customs endorsed by an entire society are equably acceptable. The rules of etiquette may be merely a matter of local custom or taste, but the prohibition against cannibalism, for example, would seem to have much more universal power and justification than the simple reminder, "that just isn't done around here." Indeed, we would probably insist that cannibalism is immoral even in a society which made it permissible by law.

An *ethos* is that core of attitudes, beliefs, and feelings that gives coherence and vitality to a people (or *ethnos,* an ancient Greek word significantly similar to *ethos*). It may be spelled out explicitly in terms of laws, but much of an ethos resides in the hearts and minds of the people, in what they expect of each other and what they expect of themselves, in what they like and dislike, value and disdain, hope and fear. It is an essential part of our ethos, for example, that individual success and "standing out in the crowd" are very important to us, though there is no law or moral principle that commands that this should be so. In some societies, by way of contrast, individual ambitions and eccentricities are entirely unacceptable. "The nail that sticks out is the one that gets hammered down," reads a traditional Japanese proverb. We should not assume that all *ethê* (plural of "ethos") are the same.

Where morality is concerned, however, this dependence on the local ethos is not so obvious. Prohibitions against cannibalism and incest are not mere matters of local custom, nor, we might think, is the condemnation of lying, cheating, cruelty, and stealing. Nevertheless, some ethicists conscientiously restrict their studies to just their own societies, without even attempting to pass judgment on societies other than their own. Many ethicists insist that moral principles—at least the most basic rules—are universal and common to all societies. Others, called *relativists,* have actually argued that ethics is indeed relative to an ethos and nothing outside of that ethos. "What is moral in India can get a man hanged in France," wrote one eighteenth-century relativist, his conclusion being that morals are nothing but the local customs of a particular community.

Ethics and Morality

In modern European and American philosophy, "ethics" is often treated as a synonym for "moral philosophy" and philosophers who study ethics are called "moral philosophers." This in itself tells us a great deal about our own ethos, the fact that morality is considered so central to ethics that the one is virtually defined in terms of the other. Morality is indeed one of the central concerns of ethics, and moral principles (such as "thou shalt not kill") do comprise some of the most important restrictions and demands on our way of life. But morality is not the whole of ethics, even if it is one of the most important concerns of the ethicist. What makes morality a particularly difficult topic is the fact that moral principles at least seem to make absolute and universal claims, while many ethical rules seem to be more optional and relative to a particular society. For example, in Homer's Greece it was considered important to be brave and stand fast if an enemy came leaping after you with a sword. Today we would consider this, at most, an option which only the foolhardy would choose. But the moral principle that one should not kill the innocent just for fun is a principle that was central to Homeric Greek ethics as it is for us today. Many moral philosophers would say that the principle that one should not kill the innocent (sometimes summarized today simply as "the right to life") is a moral principle precisely because it is thought to be absolute and universal—that is, to apply to all people in all circumstances at all times without regard for particular cultural circumstances or situations.

Two Bases for Ethics: Rules and Virtues

We have been emphasizing the importance of moral principles in ethics, and, indeed, our entire ethical tradition is built around the importance of formally stated rules, from the Ten Commandments in the Old Testament to the policy of "government by laws, not men" put into law by the framers of the American Constitution. But this emphasis on principles is also a matter of ethos; the ancient Greeks, for instance, would not have understood our emphasis on rules and principles. They were far more concerned with the virtues and the character of individuals. Obeying the rules was more or less taken for granted, but a good person was not just someone who obeyed the rules. He or she had to have virtues, skills, and abilities which made society better, and this was something much more than simply abstaining from evil. (Indeed, a Homeric Greek with many warrior virtues might indulge in a great many evils and nevertheless remain an ethical hero. Agamemnon sacrificed his daughter to the gods, and Achilles often behaved like a spoiled brat.)

At the beginning of this introduction, we commented that the root of the English word "ethics" is the Greek word *ethos* and that the words are still connected in their mutual reference to the whole of a society and its life. But as we pursue the history of the subject of ethics, we can see that two very different kinds of concerns emerge, even though they are obviously connected: (1) the concern for rules and principles, in particular the principles of morality, abstract and impersonal rules which make no reference to particular persons, and (2) the character and characteristics of particular persons, which are only partially a matter of obeying the rules. (Consider the absurdity of a person trying to obey a rule to the effect that everyone ought to have a sense of humor, for example.) Moral obedience and personal virtues do not always go hand in hand; they may even conflict, as we shall hear from the great German "immoralist," Friedrich Nietzsche. Many students find, for example, that some of the characteristics they enjoy in their friends are quite different from the characteristics they list in people they admire, and some of these are quite different again from the moral characteristics they list as central to being a good person.

Ethics and Anthropology

Ethics is the attempt to understand our own ethos—the rules and principles which we take to be most important and the characteristics of people we value most in our heroes, our friends, our leaders, and—most importantly—ourselves. As such, ethics has a close affinity to anthropology (as well as to sociology and psychology and, sometimes, biology). One might say that ethics is the anthropology of our own way of life, an attempt to understand and formulate as clearly as possible our own rules and customs and expectations—why, for example, we expect a person who behaves badly to be punished, or why we think that people who work hard ought to get more than people who refuse to work at all, or why we think that modesty is a virtue and getting angry not a virtue.

The study of ethics is the attempt to come to grips with our peculiar ways of doing and valuing things, to be clear about what it is that we are doing and why it is that we value the things that we value. But in this sense, ethics is not anthropology, for it is *our* culture and *our* ethos that are under scrutiny. Philosophers often distinguish between *descriptive* statements and *prescriptive* statements; the former tell us what the facts are, but the latter tell us what ought to be. It is one thing to describe what people do and what they value; it is something more to enter into their lives and tell them what they ought to do and value. In anthropology, we can and should be content with description. In ethics, however, our descriptions are always mixed with prescriptions, for we are not simply trying to understand ourselves. We are also trying to live well and do what is right to do.

Because ethics is prescriptive as well as descriptive, there is a set of questions which do not arise for the anthropologist, such as whether at least some of the rules of our ethos should be changed or revised. As the great French anthropologist Claude Lévi-Strauss once said (in interview, 1970), concerning his own research:

> When I witness certain decisions or modes of behavior in my own society, I am filled with indignation and disgust, whereas if I observe similar behavior in a so-called primitive society, I make no attempt at a value judgment. I try to understand it.

As an anthropologist, Lévi-Strauss simply tries to understand other people, but as a citizen of France, he feels impelled to act and speak out. This is an essential difference, and it raises a difficult problem. In ethics we try to both understand and participate. But insofar as we see ourselves as one ethos among many, we realize the importance of not taking our own values as the only possible values. At the same time, we find ourselves unquestionably committed to our own values—indeed we inevitably use our own values to appraise others as well as to criticize ourselves. This is what gives ethics its peculiarities and its particular importance. It is also part of the reason for reading ethical authors from societies very different from our own.

A common but ultimately nonsensical way of interpreting the significance of the variety of values and dealing with this tension between describing and prescribing values is to dismiss ethics altogether as "ethnocentric" or merely "relative," thus appreciating the variety of ethê but utterly neglecting the all-important fact that we ourselves are inescapably part of an ethos. It is important to appreciate the variety of values and the tension between various ethics, but we also have to live and live well. Realizing the relativity of ethics to particular ethê does not undermine but underscores the need for ethics. Ethics is like anthropology in its attempt to appreciate the *context* of our values; it differs in the fact that we accept those values as our own, indeed, cannot even imagine ourselves without them.

Normative and Metaethics

Ethics includes a spectrum of issues—from very specific questions about the rightness or wrongness of certain actions (having an abortion, killing an armed intruder, refusing to register for the military draft, selling faulty merchandise, not stopping at the scene of an accident when you might possibly be of some help) to very abstract concerns such as Adam and Eve's puzzlement over the meaning of the terms "good" and "evil." In between, the spectrum includes a great many middle-level questions such as, Are moral rules the same the world over (and, if not, should they be the same)? and, Why should a person obey the rules of morality?

For simplicity's sake, philosophers who study ethics sometimes divide up this spectrum of issues into two parts; first there is *normative ethics,* which is concerned with specific questions of right and wrong, good and evil, and tries to settle on some concrete rules for correct behavior, such as "thou shalt not kill" and "do not cheat on your taxes." Second, there is *metaethics,* which is concerned with more abstract questions having to do with the meaning and justification of ethical concepts and principles, such as, What is evil?, What is a *moral* principle? and Can one prove the correctness of a position in ethics (or is it just a matter of opinion, a personal or perhaps cultural bias)? A typical normative question in ethics would be, Is it ever right to tell a lie? The metaethical question would be, What does it mean, "to tell a lie"?

In practice, the two sorts of questions cannot be separated: normative issues always involve implicit reference to some conception of the good which is their framework, and metaethical issues are vacuous and unresolvable without reference to normative issues in the light of which they are to be understood. Both normative and metaethical questions presuppose an already existing ethical context—an ethos—in which they gain their meaning and in which they must be answered. In fact, what philosophers call "metaethical questions" are to a large extent questions about the general framework of an ethical viewpoint, their ethos—questions about the way that people think and talk and justify their actions. The ethical theories developed by philosophers are, therefore, in part expressions of the most general values and concerns of their culture, spelled out in a particularly abstract way. Since the great philosophers sometimes write as if they were not themselves embedded in a particular ethos with particular values and particular ways of thinking about ethics, this is an important point to keep in mind when reading them.

The History of Ethics

It is of more than casual interest that some of the classical ethical statements which we will be studying in this book were written by philosophers who lived in cultures quite different (but not entirely different) from our own. Plato and Aristotle, most notably, wrote almost 2500 years ago, in the city-state (*polis*) of Athens. On the one hand, their ethics are sufficiently similar to ours (and often taken as an ideal by modern thinkers) so that they are traditionally treated as the originators of ethical philosophy and much of ethics since is based on them. Indeed the whole history of ethics (and philosophy in general) has been said to be the development of ideas originally suggested by Plato and Aristotle so long ago, and much of what we will see in the texts of this book will be a continuing dialogue with these two great philosophers on a number of topics of mutual interest over the years. At the same time, however, the differences between our societies are sufficiently remarkable—the differences in whom they considered to be "the good man", for example—to make us think quite seriously about our own sense of the virtues. Other writers are more modern but still quite distinctly different from ourselves and from each other. Both Immanuel Kant and Friedrich Nietzsche, for example, are German writers from the last century or so (Kant died as an old man in 1804; Nietzsche died relatively young in 1900), but even the hundred year difference that separates them is more than sufficient to display drastic differences in outlook. Kant insists that there is a universal set of absolute moral rules, while Nietzsche, heralding in the twentieth century, warns us of a breakdown in all morality and anticipates the individualistic ethical codes that have become so prevalent today. Indeed, even our two French authors, the "existentialists" Jean-Paul Sartre and Albert Camus, writing only forty years ago, give us a quite different picture of the world than most of us would recognize today. But theirs was the world of Paris under the Nazi occupation, in which the outlook was bleak but nevertheless heroic, in which individual acts of resistance could mean a great deal, and in which even the smallest gesture of defiance counted as a sign of hope.

ETHICAL QUESTIONS

What to Live for?

The Danish religious philosopher Søren Kierkegaard wrote in his *Journals,* when he was a young man of 20 or so, "I want a truth for which I can live and die." He was asking the ultimate ethical question, What is worth living for? Indeed this has been the motivating question for almost every great (and not so great) philosopher, the question of the meaning of life, the problem of choosing between a variety of alternatives, some of which (but we don't know which) will make our lives fulfilled and admirable while others will make us miserable and, perhaps, damned as well. The most dramatic presentation of this question in the history of philosophy is the dilemma of Socrates, in 399 B.C. He was already an old man of 70, and he had made a considerable reputation (and nuisance of himself) challenging the assumptions of the politicians and judges of Athens. In doing so, he made many enemies, and, finally, he was accused of "corrupting the minds" of the young students he was teaching and was sentenced to death. In prison, Socrates had a chance to escape. He also knew that he had done right and had been treated unfairly by the court. (In his own speech to the judges, he had suggested that they give him a pension instead.) He thus faced an ultimate choice—to turn down the offer to escape and face his punishment as a good (if unfairly treated) citizen, or leave Athens for sanctuary elsewhere and continue to lead his own life with its pleasures and satisfactions. He chose to stay and be executed on the grounds that honor and citizenship are more important than even life itself. That which is most worth living for may also be worth dying for. If you were in Socrates's position, what would you have done? (You will find Socrates's deliberations in Plato's *Crito,* pages 34 to 43.)

What Is the Good Life?

Somewhat more modest than the overriding question about what is worth living (or dying) for, the personal motivation behind much of ethics has been the search for the good life, a life well-lived. The problem, as Aristotle pointed out in his *Ethics* (pages 56 to 134), is that there are many different conceptions of the good life, and it is not at all clear which, if any, is the best. For example, there is the life of pleasure (also called *hedonism),* which has often been a primary candidate for the good life. But there are different kinds of pleasures and, perhaps, different "qualities" of pleasure as well (as John Stuart Mill argues in his *Utilitarianism,* pages 291 to 342). The gluttonous pleasure of stuffing oneself with fast-food hamburgers is one thing; the more ethereal pleasures of reading poetry or listening to Mozart are of quite a different nature. But then there are a great many goals in our lives that may not be aimed at pleasure at all. For example, we have ambitions and want to be successful, and though we may want success in order to give us pleasure, it is more likely for a great many people that the work required for success at least postpones, if it does not interfere with, the life of pleasure. We feel obligations and do favors for other people, often without pleasure as our reward, and we abstain from behavior which we know would give us great pleasure, just because we know that it is wrong or embarrassing. Moreover, there are conceptions of life which are antithetical to the life of pleasure; for instance, there is a conception of the good life as the religious life, in which the "pleasures of the body" are to be foregone in favor of the "purity of spirit." Questions about the good life are thus attempts to order this variety of concerns according to some sort of priorities: which is more important, a pleasant life or a successful one? Which is more important, to do what one thinks is right or to do what will advance one's own interests? To live an enjoyable life here on earth or to earn a place in Heaven? To be a respected part of the community and established in a career or to be "free"? To do work that one thinks is important or poetic or to earn as much money as possible? What is the good life? The good life is the life well lived, and every philosopher in this book has his own opinions about what that should be.

Why Be Good?

The search for the good life, whether one tends toward a life of dissolute pleasures or instead toward a religious life of self-denial and simplicity, is measured by personal satisfaction and the sense, on reflection, that one has lived as one wants to live. But there is a second set of questions which have less to do with what one personally wants out of life: these are the questions of *morality,* or what one *ought* to do. We have already anticipated that the analysis of morality will be a central topic in ethics, but it is important to ask, just by way of preliminaries, what morality is here opposed to. In the first part of our introduction, we suggested that morality might be distinguished by the fact that its principles are universal, or by the fact that moral concerns tend to be the most important concerns in an ethics. But here, let us mark off morality in a different way by noting that morality is contrasted with *prudence,* the cautious satisfaction of *one's own interests* (whether these be as basic as avoiding being hit by a truck or as ethereal as having one's soul go to heaven.) Moral considerations are *impersonal* considerations in this sense; they have to do with established rules rather than the desires of any particular person. Moral rules are not relative to personal desires and interests. Prudential considerations, on the other hand, are entirely tied up with a person's interests (whether or not he or she recognizes those interests, of course; people often want, or think they want, what is not good for them.)

Later in this introduction, we will return (again and again) to the concept of morality, first to understand what it is and what counts as moral, then to ask and answer the question, Why be moral? After all, if morality is contrasted with prudence, then we should be worried about the reasons for being moral; if we are not moral for prudential reasons (because we will be punished otherwise, or because we think it will help us get into Heaven), then what other kind of reasons might there be?

Why Should I?—The Problem of Justification

The question, Why be moral? is also a way of summing up the central quest for *justification* in ethics. To justify an action or a principle is to show that there is *good reason* for it; in fact, better reasons, perhaps, than there are for any alternatives. To justify quitting college, for example, an (ex-) student might cite such reasons as "being bored" or "wanting to see the world" or "wanting to spend more time with the working class in order to start the Revolution." Such reasons are attempted justifications, and whether or not they succeed depends on whether or not they are also *good* reasons and whether there are *better* reasons for the opposite action, staying in school.

Every attempt to order the various ingredients in the good life requires some sort of justification, some good reasons. For example, one might argue that all of our actions are aimed at pleasure anyway (Is this true?), so one might as well take pleasure explicitly as one's goal in life and not bother with the rest. (Would this be a good reason?) One might try to justify being moral by arguing that doing good makes the world a better place to live in and ultimately benefits everyone, including oneself. (Is this true?—and if so, is there a problem in justifying morality with such reasons?) Many of our actions and rules are justifiable by straightforward prudential reasons; the rule that one shouldn't drive through red traffic lights is, first of all, based on the very good reason that a person who does so is likely to get killed. Many of our actions and rules are justifiable by straightforward social or aesthetic reasons; for example, one doesn't eat chili with one's fingers because such behavior strikes most people with whom one is likely to eat as socially unacceptable and revolting. Very often a social reason consists of little more than "we just don't do it that way here (and if you don't like it, get out)." An aesthetic reason might stop with the insult, "well, then, you just have bad taste."

It is in the arena of morality and moral reasons that the problem of justification becomes acute. Morality is by its very definition not so simply justified by an appeal to one's own interests or well-being (which is not to say that one can't be happy and be moral). Moral reasons are something more than social reasons, first because we can override a social reason by showing that it is immoral (we will not be convinced by a shopkeeper in a foreign country who cheats us and then insists, "that's just the way we do things here"). Second, we expect something more by way of an anchor for justification than a sociological observation. It is for this reason that morality and moral reasons are often anchored in the word of God.

Similarly, moral reasons are much stronger than aesthetic reasons; the prohibitions against murder and treason are not based on the fact that most people find such acts distasteful or even revolting. To say that an act is immoral is to condemn it in the strongest possible terms. We expect that the reasons behind such a condemnation will be equally strong.

What justifies a course of action? Sometimes, appeal to one's own tastes or interests is sufficient (for example, when deciding to take an elective course or ordering lunch). When the interests of other people are affected, justification of our actions becomes far more complicated, since it requires a demonstration that the balance of good to harm is acceptable and proof that the action is not just in one's own interests, to the detriment of others. Sometimes (for example, in those transgressions which constitute some "victimless crimes") the prohibition of an action (gambling, homosexuality, premarital sex) includes elements that are not specifically tied to anyone's interests. These are the cases that most notoriously require more general moral principles and, ultimately, an all-encompassing moral theory for their justification. Telling lies, for example, has been a favorite example of moral philosophers for showing that justification sometimes has to look beyond the interests of those involved—and even the interests of those remotely involved—to invoke principles of a much more general nature.

How does one justify a principle such as "do not lie"? Can all justifications of moral principles—as well as particular actions—be understood in terms of people's interests and desires? (This is the position of those theorists called "utilitarians.") Or are there other kinds of justification which are independent of interests and desires (as the great German philosopher Immanuel Kant is to argue)?

Why Be Rational?—The Place of Reason in Ethics

Our discussion of justification and reasons in ethics underscores our insistence that we are not only concerned with doing right but with doing right because it is right and for the right reasons. It is not enough to be a moral hero that one foils the bank robbery inadvertently (by driving through a red light and causing an accident, for example). To do good and to be moral require doing so for reasons and for the right kind of reasons. ("Because I just felt like it" would usually not be such a reason; "because I believed that it was the right thing to do," while incomplete, would at least be the beginning of the right kind of reason.) Thus some philosophers—Aristotle and Kant, for example—take ethics to be an essentially *rational* enterprise. An act or a principle is justified by virtue of its reasons.

It is the importance of *reasons* in ethics that establishes the importance of theories in ethics as well. A moral theory is essentially an attempt to organize and ground the various sorts of reasons which justify our actions, from very particular reasons ("I did it because he had a gun") to the most general reasons ("everyone has a right to protect his or her own life"). For philosophers who insist that ethics is essentially rational, the presence of such reasons is essential to right action. Kant, for example, insists that an action has "moral worth" only if a person actually has the right reason for performing it in mind, as "respect for the law" or "because it is my duty."

There are other philosophers, however, who have challenged this primary place of reason in ethics. Some have said that reason has its limits; others have even said that reason has very little place in ethics. David Hume, for example, argued that ethics was not primarily a matter of rationality but rather of *sentiment,* emotion rather than reason. "Reason is and ought to be," he said in his *Treatise on Human Nature,* "the slave of the passions." One can justify morality in a limited way, Hume argued, by showing how it "pleases" us, but in the strong sense of rationality required by many philosophers, morality is unjustifiable and irrational. (" 'Tis not contrary to reason," Hume wrote in one of the works included here, "for me to prefer the destruction of the whole world to the scratching of my finger.") Nietzsche goes even further and argues that there has been too much emphasis on rationality in ethics and that reason, rather than being the key to the good life, is rather a symptom of failure in life, a desperate attempt to justify a life that fails to be full and satisfactory in its own terms. Camus and Sartre, in a very different way, argue that reason is mere wishful thinking and that the hard questions of ethical choice cannot be so easily and impersonally resolved.

Which Is Right?—Ethical Dilemmas

Much of the motivation of doing ethics comes from the need to resolve conflicts and put some order in one's life, from the need to order the various ingredients in the good life to the conflict of reason and the passions just mentioned. But what makes ethics so difficult, and sometimes so unsatisfying, is the fact that not all conflicts seem easily solvable, and perhaps some are not resolvable at all. For example, there is a recurrent antagonism—suggested if not exactly asserted in our introduction so far—between personal and prudential self-interests and moral, impersonal principles. Is there a general way of ordering these, giving one absolute priority over the other? Furthermore, one's own interests are often in conflict, and one can have conflicting obligations too, so that, whatever one does, one does something wrong. (Imagine that you have promised two different people that you will take them to dinner on Friday night—and taking them both out together is unthinkable.) But, most complicated of all, sometimes whole moral systems contradict one another. One society absolutely forbids sex before marriage while another encourages it. One society treats abortion as murder while another encourages abortions in the name of the general welfare. One society even condones murder as an expression of individual strength and power; another condemns any show of power and treats murder as the most heinous crime. But while a single ethical system or ethos might provide some guideline for ordering principles and priorities, a clash of ethical systems forecloses any such possibility. Thus some of the crucial questions of our time have to do not so much with the justification of one value system rather than another but with the *coexistence* of several value systems or ethê (the phenomenon we call *pluralism*). How is this possible? How can one choose among them? Are all of them equally correct relative to a particular society? Here again we face the problem of relativism—the thesis that values are correct only relative to a given culture (or subculture) and its ethos. It is one thing to point out (as an anthropologist might do) that a pluralist society has several different sets of values and opinions about what is right; it is quite different to live in that society and have to choose between these different values and opinions or justify one ethics rather than another. This again is a primary function of ethical theories—to provide us with a way of evaluating conflicting ethical viewpoints, not only with regard to particular cases but where competing ethical systems present us with very different pictures of morality and the good life.

Ethical dilemmas are particularly perplexing problems in ethics, sometimes involving whole systems of values as well as particular conflicts of values. The morality of abortion is such a dilemma because it immediately brings into question some of the most general concerns and concepts of our ethos, for example, the concern for individual right to life and the concept of what it is to be a human being. But the study of ethics is not restricted to these often dramatic dilemmas and conflicts; it is also concerned with the understanding and appreciation of the coherence and justification of our values. Ethical dilemmas bring these values into sharp focus, but the study of ethics itself is at least as concerned with what is right and essential about our ethics as it is with its difficulties and dilemmas.

ETHICAL CONCEPTS

Prudence and Morals

We have already seen that morality plays a key part in ethics and is set off from other questions about our behavior by its importance and by the form of its principles. (They are universal principles and without exceptions.) We have also suggested that morality is to be contrasted with prudence. Now it is time to look more closely at these two crucial concepts.

Prudence, in a phrase, is looking out for your own personal interests. It may be prudent "not to get involved;" it may be prudent to go to law school. In itself, prudence need not be *selfishness* (more on that later), but it does mean looking after your own interests whether or not they happen to be anyone else's interests too. It may be, as Aristotle and Mill and other philosophers suggest, that one's own interests also coincide with the interests of society.[2] But prudence refers only to one's personal interests; other people's interests are a separate question.

Morality, on the other hand, always looks beyond one's own to what is *right* or *required*. Morality will usually be concerned with other people's interests (as well as one's own), but this is not necessarily so. Morality might refer to God's interests, for example, or to a well-established moral principle which might not seem to serve

---

[2]In his *Ethics* Aristotle defines prudence as calculating one's own interests but it includes seeing "what is good for men in general."

anyone's interests. Morality, unlike prudence, is necessarily *impersonal* in this sense and *objective*. That is, morality is not determined by the *subjective* (personal) attitudes of individuals but by some authority (whether it be God's will or society or reason itself.) Moral authority does not belong to any particular person, no matter how powerful. It is concerned with rules, principles, and duties which have no reference to the desires, aspirations, interests, or power of any particular person, although particular people (for example, judges) may be guardians of morality. The moral principle "do not lie" applies to everyone, and it will not do to say, "but in my case, it's so much fun to lie" or "but when I lie to him he treats me so much better." Morality consists of impersonal demands which make no particular reference to individuals. ("John shouldn't lie" is not a moral principle; it is the application of a moral principle to John.) For this reason, contrary to a popular way of speaking, there is no such thing as a "personal morality."

We have now seen a number of characterizations of morality, but it is not evident that they all fit together or define exactly the same phenomenon. It is often said, for instance, that morality is

1 A most important set of principles
2 Principles which apply to everyone (that is, they are *universal*)
3 Principles which apply without reference to personal interests (that is, they are *objective*).

These are not equivalent. One can at least imagine a society in which the most important principles are precisely those which don't apply to everyone (many of Aristotle's ethical principles applied only to an aristocratic elite.) And one can at least imagine a society in which the most important obligations are to those people for whom we have deep personal attachments or (a case sometimes made for capitalism) in which everyone's primary obligation is to look out for his or her own interests.

But the list is incomplete. One of the primary concerns of virtually every philosopher in this book will be to characterize adequately what we call "morality" (although it is important to point out that some of the authors—Plato and Aristotle, particularly—do not have our concept at all). Not every author will say that morality is the most important set of principles in a society, and not every author will say that moral principles are impersonal or universal. Indeed, Friedrich Nietzsche will argue that the importance of morality is a historical curiosity, that despite its impersonal appearance morality does indeed serve the personal interests of a particular group and, finally, that morality is a kind of "decay" of morals and ought to be done away with. In a more moderate tone, John Stuart Mill takes morality to be a set of "rules of thumb" in the maximization of general happiness, and David Hume takes it to be a pleasing sense of general utility. Saint Augustine takes morality to be the will of God. Plato and Aristotle have no concept of morality as such, but they do have a very strong sense of social obligation and duty, such that the concept of morality and concepts of participation in the community are inextricably woven together.

The strictest characterization of morality, however, is the one we shall find in Immanuel Kant's *Groundwork of the Metaphysics of Morals*. Kant makes the separation between prudence and morality complete (which few of the other authors do). Insofar as an act is prudent, it cannot be "morally worthy" as well. Kant analyzes the principles of morality in terms of "the moral law," or what he calls "the categorical imperative." An imperative, of course, is simply a command; "categorical" is a strong way of saying what we mentioned above—the absolute and unqualified nature of moral principles. According to Kant, a moral principle is thoroughly objective, a product of reason itself ("practical reason," he calls it.) A moral principle has nothing to do with personal interests or with the particular circumstances of the case.

Morality, therefore, might be characterized in a large number of ways which are not equivalent and do not define the same phenomenon. Rules which might be moral for Plato and Aristotle (for example, "have courage") would not be moral for Kant, and the borderline that is so strictly delineated in Kant's ethics would be vague or impossible to make out for Plato and Aristotle. Moreover, the status of morality will vary from author to author as well; it is of the utmost, unquestionable importance to Kant. It is despicable and dispensable for Nietzsche. And these differences are not just differences in philosophical theories *about* morality; they also reflect differences in the nature of morality itself.

Happiness and the Good

We have just contrasted morality and prudence, but we might also contrast morality and happiness. Prudence is looking out after your own interests—whatever those interests happen to be. Happiness, however, seems at one and the same time to be both a more specific concept—happiness seems to be a single feature of life—and a more general one—happiness also seems to be the satisfaction of all (or at least a great many) of our desires in life. Happiness, of course, need not be limited to the satisfaction of one's own desires at all; one's happiness may be completely bound up in the well-being of one's family, or the success of one's business firm, or the thriving of one's community. Indeed, it might seem as if almost anything might make some people happy, which has led some authors to suggest that happiness is strictly subjective and depends only on the personal desires of the individual. On the other hand, some authors (Aristotle especially) have insisted that happiness is not merely subjective and a person can't be called "happy" unless he or she is also a good person, no matter how contented he or she might feel about life.

Whatever the scope of happiness, however, most authors seem to agree that it is one of the most important—if not the most important—thing in life. Aristotle tells us that "happiness" is the name of the ultimate goal—the *summum bonum* (literally, "greatest good")—of all of human life; it is the complete life, which could be no better. John Stuart Mill agrees (although he often conflates happiness and pleasure); it is happiness alone that moves people to act and happiness alone which can be the basis of morality and the good life. But this harmonious view of morality and happiness is broken, once again, by Kant, who insists that happiness is one thing, morality something quite different. Kant agrees that what we all *want* in life is happiness, but he also insists that what we *ought* to do need not be what makes us happy. Getting these two together (for he too agrees that ideally happiness and moral virtue should be commensurate) is one of the most difficult goals of Kant's philosophy.

What is happiness? Aristotle defines it as the Good itself, that is, "the good for man." But here we see the Good once again break into two parts, which weave in and out together throughout the history of ethics. There is the Good as in "the good life," whose aim is happiness, and there is the Good as in "a good person," whose concern is rather propriety and morality. When students are asked to draw up two lists, one in which they list the goals they would like to achieve in order to make them happy, the other a list of characteristics which they would find morally admirable, the lists are usually quite different, and one of the most troublesome questions in ethics is, Are they even compatible? In what ways are our goals and desires determined and delimited by our morals? And to what extent are our morals aimed at making us happy?

Pleasure (and Pain)

In a simple-minded way, one might say that all human activity is motivated by the pursuit of pleasure and the avoidance of pain. In an obvious sense, this is perfectly agreeable and true; we do avoid pain and we do try to do those things that are most enjoyable. But we also do much that is painful, whether the cramp-producing exercises we do to get into shape or the boredom-inducing visits to grandmother which have become obligatory. Is it so obvious that we always do so in order to avoid some greater pain? Or to produce some offsetting pleasure? Furthermore, it is not altogether clear what "the pursuit of pleasure" means; lusting for a piece of cheesecake in the store window, then rushing in to buy it, would certainly be an example; so, perhaps, would saving up the money to buy a small sailboat. But what about a person who enjoys reading theology or who enjoys playing a good, hard game of tennis? Are those activities "the pursuit of pleasure," or would it be much more accurate to say that the pleasure in some sense "accompanies" the activities one pursues? Such questions about pleasure (and pain) will pervade the texts that follow, for it is generally agreed that pleasure does have *some* role in happiness and the good life, though the exact nature of that role is not at all clear.

Egoism and Altruism

The contrast between prudence and morality is related to—but not identical to—the opposed concepts of *egoism* and *altruism*. Egoism, like prudence, means looking out for your own interests (though the word "egoism," unlike "prudence," suggests some essential antagonism between one's own interests and the interests of others). Altruism, however, means acting for the interests of others. We have already noted that morality (though often confused with altruism) need not be concerned with the interests of others (although it usually is) and that morality is by its very nature impersonal; that is, it makes reference to no particular interests. Altruism, on the other hand, is precisely this concern for the interests of other people. It may be based on some sense of attachment or compassion, but it need not be. One could be altruistic on principle, though this might still not be the same as morality. Consider, for example, a person who was routinely altruistic just because he thought himself to be worthless and other people's interests more important. Thus several authors—including Aristotle, Kant, and Nietzsche—have argued that self-respect is an essential ingredient in any ethics.

On the one hand, egoism is obviously antithetical to morality; it designates concern for one's own interests, whatever the rules and whatever one's obligations. (One can, of course, be moral and fulfill one's obligations just as a means to satisfying one's interests, but this is a complication we can postpone until later.) On the other hand, egoism has been argued by many ethicists to be the sole basis for any human behavior, moral or otherwise. This raises a very difficult question; if this is true, how is it possible to act for the sake of others (unless their interests coincide with our own) or for the sake of morality (unless our obligations also satisfy our interests)? Are we moral (when we are moral) only because it is in our interests? If I give money to a beggar and feel good that I have done so, have I in fact only given him the money in order to feel good afterward? If I act virtuously out of self-respect (because I consider myself to be a kind person, for instance), am I thereby acting selfishly?

Philosophers sometimes distinguish between *psychological* egoism and *ethical* egoism. Psychological egoism is the psychological theory that everything we do, we do for our own interests, whether or not the same act serves other people's interests or moral obligations. Ethical egoism is the view that one *ought* to act in his or her own interests. Of course, if psychological egoism is true, then one could not help but act in one's own interests. Nevertheless, the two positions are distinct. One might believe that all people are motivated by their own interests and nevertheless try to make sure that people's interests coincided with the common good and morality (for example, by inflicting punishments to offset any personal advantage in wrongdoing). And one might well believe that people are not naturally out for their own interests but that they ought to do so. Imagine a person who believes, for instance, that most of the damage done in the world is caused by "do-gooders" who "ought to leave well enough alone."

Altruism might also be divided into two parts, psychological altruism—the theory that people naturally act for the benefit of others—and ethical altruism—the view that they ought to act for the benefit of others. Regarding the first, many theorists have debated whether any of our actions are altruistically motivated, but very few have ever asserted that all of them are. The debate, therefore, centers around psychological egoism and the question whether all of our actions are self-interested. Ethical altruism, quite naturally, runs into questions about morality, and although the two concepts are different, the questions raised about their justification, for example, are essentially the same. The questions, Why should I be moral? and Why should I care about anyone else? are generally tackled together, and, for many practical purposes, they receive much the same set of answers.

According to a popular story, president Abraham Lincoln was passing a puddle in a carriage when he saw that several little piglets were drowning as the mother pig squealed helplessly. Lincoln stopped the carriage and saved the piglets. (Whether the mother pig thanked him was not recorded.) Back on the road, Lincoln's friend asked him whether that act counted as a pure case of altruism; Lincoln replied, "Why that was the very essence of selfishness. I should have had no peace of mind all day."

Selfishness

The word "egoism," unlike prudence, suggests some antagonism between one's own interests and the interests of others. Nevertheless, one can be an egoist and also be charming, morally correct, and even a philanthropist, as a number of very wealthy and ambitious people have demonstrated. The word "selfishness," however, is another matter. "Selfishness" has built into it the antagonism between one's own and others' interests, and to say that a person is selfish is to say not only that he or she is an egoist but also that he or she subverts the interests of others. "Selfishness" has an undeniable connotation of condemnation and should not be confused with the more neutral terms "egoism" and "prudence." To suggest that everyone's behavior is motivated by prudence or by their own interests is at least a plausible hypothesis; to suggest that everyone's behavior is selfish is both offensive and implausible (though nevertheless there are times when it seems to be true). Accordingly, Lincoln's reply (above) seems like nonsense.

Freedom and Responsibility

There would be little point to doing ethics if we did not believe that we are all to some extent *free* to choose one goal rather than another, to act one way rather than another way. It is one of the presuppositions of morality, according to virtually every author we will meet, that we are free beings who can make decisions and act voluntarily. We are not machines or robots who do only what we are programmed to do. Thus Aristotle includes in his ethical treatise an analysis of what it is for an action to be "voluntary" (it must not be externally compelled, and it must not be out of ignorance, he says). Kant calls freedom "a postulate of practical reason," meaning, there could be no reason—no morality—without it. But not only is freedom the presupposition of most ethical theories; some philosophers have elevated it to the highest value in ethics as well. Jean-Paul Sartre, most notably, takes freedom to be the goal as well as the basis of human consciousness, and ethics according to Sartre is primarily the realization of our freedom.

Hand in hand with freedom goes responsibility. Responsibility means, first of all, effectively bringing something about, whether or not one intended to do so. The drunken driver is responsible for hitting the dog, even if he did so out of incompetence in driving and ignorance that the dog was there. Secondly, responsibility—in the morally significant sense—includes a presumption of freedom. The driver was responsible, in part, because he was free to choose whether to drive or not to drive, to drink or not to drink, to take this road or another one, to drive faster or slower, to watch more carefully or drive as recklessly as he did. (One might say that a computer is responsible for a certain result, but only in a derivative sense. Leaving aside certain science fiction possibilities, the computer has no choice in its production of the results and is therefore not responsible.) Finally, in ethics it is usually assumed that responsibility has a moral edge to it, that one is responsible for doing—or not doing—what one ought to do. Accordingly, *praise* and *blame* are essential moral concepts having to do with responsibility. They designate responsibility (who did it, who chose to do it); at the same time, they make a moral judgment of right or wrong, good or bad (one is blamed for wrong or bad acts; one is praised for right or good acts.)

Duty, Saints, and Heroes

Most of what we have discussed under the title of "morality" has to do with fulfilling obligations, doing what one ought to do. But it is important to point out that this is not all there is to morality, although the basic conception of morality as obeying certain principles and not breaking certain rules makes this less than obvious. On this conception of morality as a set of rules to be obeyed—most of them of the "thou shalt not . . ." variety—a perfectly good person might also be an absolute bore, a moral prig whose behavior benefits no one. But then, there are also people—though very few of them—who go far beyond the rules, not breaking them but far exceeding their demands. It is significant, for example, that Aristotle's ethics turns on the crucial concept of virtue (also translatable as *excellence*). The good man for Aristotle is not just one who obeys the rules; he also excels in what he does. He is expected not only not to run in battle; he is expected to fight to the best of his ability. He is not only expected not to lie (which is easy enough if you keep silent); he is also expected to be witty and clever and informative, if not as brilliant as Socrates. Ethics and morality, in other words, need not be confined to obedient mediocrity. They can also be the demand for excellence.

This idea of going beyond moral requirements, beyond the "call of duty," is nowhere more evident than in those special people whom we designate as saints and heroes. A saint is not just someone who is perfectly good in the easy sense of not sinning (he or she may not have had any opportunities); a saint is extraordinarily good, resisting temptations that we cannot imagine resisting and doing good deeds that are far beyond the demands of duty or charity. Similarly, a hero or heroine is not just a person who does what is commanded; he or she does much more—indeed, much more than anyone could have expected. One cannot command saintliness or heroism, and it is no one's duty to be a saint or a hero or heroine. Nevertheless, our ethics would be impoverished without such concepts, and, from a somewhat different perspective, we might notice how much the whole history of western ethics is not so much the history of moral principles as it is the history of a small number of extraordinary men and women of whom we shall always stand in awe.

Virtue and the Virtues

Morality is often defined as a set of principles (of a certain sort), but ethics is not just concerned with principles. In particular, ethics is also concerned with *character* and with personal charms and achievements, whether or not these fall under moral principles. The name traditionally given to such a positive feature of a person is a *virtue*. (A negative feature, in these terms, is a *vice*.) But, unfortunately, the confused history of morals has resulted in a confusing ambiguity for this crucial term. On the one hand, there is a particular feature of a person's character—such as honesty, wittiness, generosity, or social charm. On the other hand, there is that general all-encompassing designation of a person's virtue and talk of "virtue" in general as a synonym for "morality." (Kant, for example, uses the word "virtue" in this way.)

The confusion is not so simple as the ambiguity of a single term which refers both to a general feature and to specific features as well. An ethics that focuses on the virtues has a very different emphasis than an ethics concerned with virtue (that is, morality). The first has mainly to do with character, with realizing one's potential and cultivating those habits which are most important in a particular society. The second has more to do with following certain principles and less to do with character. A person might be virtuous in the second sense, for example, by dutifully resisting temptation and painfully managing not to do anything immoral. But, in the first sense, that person would not be exemplifying the virtues at all, for a virtue is not an inner wrestling match with one's desires; it is a cultivated habit that feels entirely natural. Whether or not it also obeys some principle is not at all a part of the description of the virtue.

Aristotle, we shall see, develops an ethics based on the virtues. He insists, first of all, that a person be raised correctly so that the virtues become regular habits. Only later, in ethics, does a person learn to articulate the implicit principles which describe the goodness of such habits. In Kant, however, the very opposite is true; an action isn't moral (isn't virtuous) unless it is done *on principle,* in other words, with the principle (more or less) clearly in mind. A virtue, then, is a cultivated state of character which is deemed important by a certain society. Virtue—in the sense of obeying moral principles —is more a matter of will than of habit and only secondarily, therefore, a question of character. (Good character, in this second sense, is as much a matter of will power as good habits.)

Justice and Equality

Of all the virtues, perhaps the most prominent—certainly in the good society but also in the moral individual—is *justice*. Socrates, Plato, and Aristotle, for example, praise it more than any other virtue and devote an extraordinary amount of attention to it. Justice is sometimes considered primarily a feature of social-political philosophy—an essential concern of governments and social critics. But it is also essential to ethics, to our sense of fair play and correct behavior in personal transactions.

Justice, first of all, is that sense of wrong when someone (including ourselves) is cheated or unfairly taken advantage of. It is that sense that people who do wrong (even ourselves) should be punished and that those who do good (especially ourselves) should be rewarded. It is our belief that wealth or power should not give a person certain kinds of advantages, for example, "before the law," and it is our belief that, while hard work and accomplishment are to be encouraged, those who are afflicted by misfortune and are unable to work ought to be reasonably taken care of by someone else. Justice, ultimately, is that quality of an act or of a whole society that conforms to our highest ideals of morality and fairness.

Central to this sense of justice is the concept of equality. This is not to say that one cannot have a sense of justice without believing in equality; both Plato and Aristotle believed in a most unequal society, in which slavery was a primary economic structure. Yet they had a clear sense of justice as well as several elaborate theories about it. But our sense of justice very much includes a presupposition of equality which might be stated, "each person counts for one and for no more than one." This is not to say that everyone is the same. It is not to say, what is obviously false, that everyone has the same opportunities or abilities, and it is not to say, what seems most unjust if not nonsensical, that everyone should be treated the same, regardless of physical condition, age, abilities, ambitions, and interests. The sense of equality that is crucial here is a formal one; it means that everyone counts, and it means that, in respect to being a person, everyone should be treated the same. Thus two people accused of the same crime should expect the same considerations in court, and two people to whom we owe money should expect the same prompt payment, even if one person is a dear friend and the other a not very likable acquaintance. The formal principle of equality is that everyone is the same in certain central respects, no matter who they are or what their station in life. (It is just this that Plato and Aristotle reject; justice for them means treating someone in accordance with his or her station in life.) Justice is the demand that people be treated as they ought to be treated. [The word in Greek (*dikaiosune*) is derived from the word for "owed" and "well-ordered"; the word in Latin (*justitia*) is derived from the word for "law," a noteworthy difference of emphasis.]

Many moral virtues and many of the demands of morality refer primarily to the activities or character of the individual; justice, on the other hand, has more to do with the interchange of life, giving and taking, sharing and keeping for one's own. Justice is giving everyone his or her due, and the personal sense of justice is first of all making sure that one does not take more than one's share, as well as making sure that one is not given less.

ETHICAL JUSTIFICATION

Why Be Moral?

Morality, as opposed to prudence, is acting on the basis of principle, even at the expense of one's own interests. But why, someone is bound to ask, be moral? Why should one ever act against his or her own interests—unless, of course, doing so is also in one's interests (in the long run, for example)? What could motivate a person to be moral?

One answer to this question is that one *ought* to be moral, or that the moral way of behaving is the *right* way. But this answer just pushes the question back another step;

why should a person do what he or she ought to do instead of what he or she wants to do? Why should a person be concerned with doing what is right? Such questions motivate the ethical quest for *justification,* that is, the demonstration that certain acts or principles are right and ought to be followed. Justification, in turn, should answer the question, Why be moral? insofar as justification will provide good reasons for being moral.

Suppose a person will accept the justification of morality only if it also shows that being moral is in his or her self-interest? Or suppose a person refuses to listen to justification at all and simply insists on doing what he or she wants to do? What sorts of reasons will be ultimately convincing? What are we doing when we try to justify morality? Are we trying to convince someone who refuses to be moral? Or are we mainly trying to reassure ourselves? How can we justify morality? What kinds of reasons can we give?

Facts and Values

The first metaethical observation to be made here is the apparent gap between value judgments and facts. It is true that we often justify moral claims by citing facts: "I claim that he has done wrong because he took money that didn't belong to him," or "I was right to take the money because he promised it to me." But there is always something less than entailment in such claims; one can add up the facts indefinitely, but no value conclusion seems to follow. I can point out that Harry always brings his wife flowers, never insults or strikes her, makes love to her tenderly, and respects her career as well as makes a good living himself; but none of this entails the value judgment that Harry is a good husband. Add as many more facts as you like about Harry and the logical outcome will be the same. No number of factual statements will let you derive a value judgment.

David Hume, remarking on this logical problem, summed it up as "the impossibility of deriving an 'ought' from an 'is'."[3] In this century, the same phenomenon has been characterized by Cambridge philosopher G. E. Moore in his "Open Question Argument"; namely, no matter how many facts about a thing you add together, the question is always open, Yes, but is it a *good* thing? Lists of facts do not yield values, and value judgments, in turn, can never be completely supported by the facts. No number of deeds entail that a person is virtuous, and no number of features make a thing good. But this has led to an awkward conclusion (for example, by David Hume and others): morality, and value judgments in general, cannot be justified. They can be derived from other value judgments, of course, but there is no factual anchor which can be used to justify them all. Thus it can be argued that an ethical viewpoint—a vision of what the world ought to be—can be defended no matter what the facts. If a social reformer insists that people should be made into creatures quite different from what they are, appeals to the facts of human needs and desires and actual behavior will not change his or her mind. If a person insists that a good man is one who refuses to come out of his bedroom, there is no amount of evidence in the world which would prove him wrong.

This conclusion has not always been accepted or even seriously entertained in philosophy, no matter how frequently it is now argued. The Greek philosophers, for example, would have considered their ethical claims themselves to be factually true, and Augustine, to take a very different example, would say that a moral judgment is justified

---

[3]It is worth noting that Hume did believe that one could move from an "is" to an "ought" in one sense, however—by way of a social tradition, or what we call an ethos. The customs of a society dictate what one ought to do.

by the fact that it is based on the will of God. But even Kant—a vigorous defender of morality—accepts this harsh separation between facts and values, knowledge and morality. It is this apparent gap, accordingly, that makes the justification of morality so difficult. If solid facts won't do it, what will?

Teleology and God's Will

One way to get around the gap between facts and values is to appeal morality to a peculiar kind of fact—the fact that something has a certain purpose. Thus one can say that the value of the heart in an animal is the fact that its purpose is to pump the blood around the body. This raises a further question, What is the purpose of pumping the blood around the body? But this too can be answered in terms of a purpose (to carry food and oxygen to the body, eliminate waste, etc.). Eventually, we will reach an answer of the sort, to keep the creature alive, at which point we want to know, Is there some purpose to this? A practical if not very sentimental answer might be, Yes, we need it for food in the fall, or Yes, it has kittens which need her care. A more philosophical answer might be, Because every living thing has its place in nature. But when the creature in question is one of us, we have a very special interest in establishing some purpose for existence, and we have developed a series of powerful answers in terms of purposes—not particular purposes (such as, "because I want to finish the semester") but ultimate purposes of the sort, "because this is the way the world is supposed to be."

The philosophical term for such purposive explanations and justifications is *teleology.* The word comes from the Greek word for purpose, *telos,* and a teleological justification of morality was attempted, most famously, by Aristotle, in the work included in this book. A teleological justification appeals the basic principles of morality, or an account of the virtues, to some overriding goal, built into human nature or nature in general. We have already commented that Aristotle took this ultimate goal to be happiness, but we have not said that this goal is part of a much larger scheme of things in which Aristotle speculates upon the purpose of human existence and, ultimately, the purpose of the existence of the world. A teleological justification of morality, in other words, is a demonstration that our moral principles and behavior fit into some larger purpose. It might be an intrinsically human purpose (in response to which Sartre objects that there are no intrinsically human purposes; we make our purposes in life and make our existence purposeful). Or it might be a divine purpose, an expression of God's will (in response to which Sartre insists that there is no God and therefore no divine design which gives our lives meaning). But in Saint Augustine, for example, there is the classic statement of the view that the justification of morality depends on God. Accepting the same view, the Russian novelist Fyodor Dostoevsky has one of his characters (Ivan Karamazov) declare, "If there is no God, everything is permitted." It is a viewpoint that we shall see expressed, with a cheerful if perverse enthusiasm, by Friedrich Nietzsche. On the other hand, if there is a God, that certainly provides an ultimate purpose—and a justification—for morality.

Enlightened Egoism

A different way of justifying morality, and a more direct answer to the question, Why be moral? is to show that morality is in fact aimed at satisfying our personal interests, even if the form and scope of morality are such that no reference to personal interests is mentioned. This too is a form of teleological justification, but in the rather ordinary sense that the purposes served by morality are our interests. The argument usually takes one of a number of forms:

1 Acting morally will always lead to the satisfaction of one's own individual interests. (Not very plausible.)

2 Acting morally will usually lead to the satisfaction of one's own individual interests. (More plausible.)

3 Acting morally will usually, in the long run, lead to the satisfaction of more of one's individual interests than would be satisfied if one did not act morally. (Plausible, but hard to prove to a very clever villain.)

4 Acting morally will serve overall the greatest number of interests of the greatest number of people, including oneself. (The problem here is the slipperiness between one's own individual interests and our (collective) interests; a new tax, for example, might clearly be in our (collective) interest but not in certain people's individual interests.

5 Acting morally will, in addition to helping to satisfy some of one's own interests, set an example which will make the world a better place to live in and so satisfy other interests that may not have even been considered (such as, encouraging friendliness in the streets, making everyone more supportive and dependable, and making life generally more enjoyable). (Edifying, probably true, if only enough people believe it.)

6 Acting morally, whether or not it results in the satisfaction of one's own interest, inspires a feeling of self-righteousness and well-being which is its own satisfaction. ("Goodness is its own reward.")

There are other formulations, but these will do as representatives of a position which is sometimes called "enlightened egoism." It is egoism insofar as the basis of one's concern, and so too the basis of the justification, is an appeal to one's own interests. But it is "enlightened" insofar as it is not merely "selfish" but open to the suggestion that acting morally may serve one's own interests as well. The problem with all such justifications, however, is that they tend to fail just when they are needed most—for example, when the reward for wrongdoing is enormous and the threat of getting caught very small. One might well talk a chisler out of a small sum by raising the prospect of going to prison, but one will hardly so influence the mobster who knows the enormity of the stakes and the fact that he cannot be touched.

Utilitarianism

The most influential theory of justification of morality, in the past several centuries, has been the theory called *utilitarianism*. It is at once a metaethical theory concerning the justification of morality and at the same time a formulation of the *summum bonum*—a single principle which will tell us how we ought to act. The basic formulation of utilitarianism is simply, "the greatest good for the greatest number," or what John Stuart Mill calls "the utility principle." It is a theory that is both impersonal and objective (insofar as we consider everyone's happiness and not just our own) and answers to our personal interests (since we are included in the "everyone"). Utilitarianism begins with the view that what motivates us can only be our own happiness, but it then derives the general principle that we ought therefore to act not just for our own happiness but for "the greatest good for the greatest number."

Utilitarianism, in one sense, goes back to the beginning of ethics (thus prompting Mill to proclaim that it has been presupposed by every moral philosopher). It is no more than the generally acceptable view that morality requires that the interests of everyone should be taken into account and everyone wants to be happy. But utilitarianism as a particular ethical theory is much more specific than this; it is based upon a very particular notion of "utility" (a concept which the Greeks, and later Nietzsche, considered "vulgar") and a modern notion of justice and equality. The notion of utility—although it often masquerades under the name "happiness"—is ultimately concerned with pleasure and pain, in discrete quantities which can be measured and compared. The modern notion of justice is the view that "each person counts for one and no more than one"; in other words, everyone's pleasure (and pain) is to count equally, and it is the overall amount of pleasure that determines what one ought to do. Morality is the general maximization of pleasure and the minimization of pain.

Utilitarianism had its origins in the "enlightenment" thinking of many eighteenth-century philosophers, including David Hume, who argues for the importance of utility in his *Inquiry Concerning the Principles of Morals* (included here). The founder of the utilitarian movement proper was an English reformer named Jeremy Bentham, who developed a "happiness calculus" to evaluate every action. For every course of action, one would add up all of the various pleasures of everyone concerned, subtracting the amount of pain. One would compare that total with the amount resulting from alternative courses of action, and one would choose that course of action which maximized pleasure and minimized pain. Bentham's immediate aim was to reform the hopelessly complex and sometimes cruel English legal system by developing a schedule of punishments which would just outweigh the pleasure of the wrongful act—thus minimizing the amount of pain to the smallest amount necessary to deter crime. But the theory also had general application as an overall ethical theory.

The ultimate champion of utilitarianism was not Bentham but the son of one of his colleagues, James Mill. John Stuart Mill was one of those remarkable geniuses—like Aristotle—who made an impact on virtually every aspect of the intellectual life of his time. He was a scientist, a mathematician, a political reformer, and one of the early defenders of feminism. But he is best known for his ethical theories, particularly his defense of individual freedom [*On Liberty* (1859)] and his classic defense of utilitarianism [*Utilitarianism* (1863)]. Mill amended Bentham's calculus of sheer *quantity* of pleasure with a conception of the *quality* of pleasure. Thus Mill insisted, "It is better to be a Socrates dissatisfied, than a pig satisfied."

Although it sounds like a simple, singular theory, it is not, as we can see from this disagreement between Bentham and Mill (on quantity versus quality of pleasure.) Indeed, recent theorists have distinguished a surprisingly large number of utilitarian theories, all of them within the "greatest good for the greatest number" idea but yet significantly different. Here are two examples (both of which can be found in Mill):

1 always do that act which will bring the greatest good to the greatest number (*act* utilitarianism).

and

2 always do that kind of act (or follow the rule) which will bring the greatest good to the greatest number (*rule* utilitarianism).

If I am considering stealing a small chip of the Parthenon, for example, the act utilitarian position asks me to consider only whether this particular action will bring more pain than pleasure. Since no one else will notice (except perhaps Athena) and since having a piece of the Parthenon will bring me enormous pleasure, the act seems to be justified. On the rule utilitarian position, however, I must ask about the consequences of this type of act, namely, stealing a piece of the Parthenon. Here, the verdict seems to be quite different, and my act (whatever its consequences) is reprehensible.

The various forms of utilitarianism—all of them originating in the simple, appealing "principle of utility" formulated by Bentham and Mill—reflect a number of problems in the theory; each variation is an attempt to modify the theory to answer an objection. (The strength and influence of utilitarianism is exemplified by the number of serious revisions of it. Less compelling theories are usually just left to wither away.) The first variation to the theory was Mill's objection to Bentham's purely quantitative theory, which placed too much emphasis on bodily pleasures and not enough on the harder to quantify pleasures of the mind and spirit—the arts, friendship, philosophy. A more recent variation in utilitarian theory is the formulation of rule utilitarianism—in contrast to act utilitarianism— as a way of meeting the objection that clearly wrong acts might, in a single instance, be shown to maximize pleasure and minimize pain for everyone involved. Rule utilitarianism blocks this possibility by insisting that a *class* of actions, not just a single instance, improves the general well-being.

Utilitarianism continues to be one of the most thoroughly discussed ethical theories and strategies of moral justification, but it is not without its continuing problems too. As a theory of utility it has always been accused of being "vulgar" and devoid of more spiritual awareness. Indeed, Mill counters this objection even in *Utilitarianism,* when he answers religious critics who attack him for appealing morality to a businesslike calculation of pleasures instead of to God or the scriptures. Mill's reply is simply that God being good wants us to be happy, and so God Himself is a utilitarian and utilitarianism is just a precise way of interpreting God's will.

A more telling set of objections is aimed at the emphasis on *consequences* (whether of an action or a type of action) in utilitarian theory. When a moral principle is presented absolutely (as in the Ten Commandments, for example), it is accepted first, and the question of consequences does not arise—or arises only afterward. (Moses did not ask Jehovah, But what's so bad about people coveting their neighbor's ox?) But when every action and every rule is subject to the test of consequences, a number of objections present themselves:

1 There usually isn't time to calculate all of the consequences beforehand.

2 We usually don't know enough to calculate all of the consequences beforehand.

3 Very different kinds of consequences may be extremely difficult to compare. (Closing down the city art museum may save the taxpayers thousands of dollars, but what is the cultural "cost" of doing so?)

4 Couldn't the consequences of an act (or a class of actions) be positive and, nevertheless, the act be wrong? (Suppose it were demonstrated that adultery saves more marriages than it destroys and makes more people happy than miserable; would it then be the moral thing to do?)

Finally, the most dramatic objection to utilitarianism aims at the principle of utility itself. Mill protects the principle from abuse (for example, by a very powerful person, who makes himself happy at everyone else's expense) by insisting that "everyone counts for one and only one." But even within this principle of equality, a serious ambiguity remains. Suppose a majority of the citizens of a town pass a tax law which, in effect, takes $500 from every member of the minority and, at the same time, cuts taxes by the same amount for every member of the majority (the balance coming from the education budget, no doubt). Leaving aside the difficulty of measuring amounts of pleasure and pain merely on the basis of dollar amounts (assume that everyone has about the same income and financial status), it seems clear that this act is defensible according to utilitarianism because it maximizes pleasure (makes more people happy). And yet, we would probably all agree, the act is clearly unjust. A second, more sadistic example favored by many critics of utilitarianism is this: suppose that a rather sick society gets great joy out of the spectacle of a few innocent people being tortured to death. (Consider Rome during some of its darker days, for example.) On the utilitarian account, the great joy of the spectators—if it outweighs the suffering of the few victims—is sufficient to make their behavior moral. But this, we object, is surely unfair and immoral. What this seems to show is that utilitarianism cannot take proper account of justice. The well-being of the majority is one thing, but justice may be something else. Usually the two are commensurate, happily; but, nevertheless, as an overall theory of the justification of morality, utilitarianism has been accused of failing a crucial test; it cannot provide adequate justification for some of our most important moral convictions. We should end by noting that all of these objections have been answered by various utilitarians, but, nevertheless, many philosophers have thus been persuaded to look elsewhere for the justification of morality.

Kant and Deontology

It is in reaction to the objections to utilitarianism, particularly its apparent inadequacy in accounting for justice, that a great many philosophers have turned to an older tradition in which moral principles are not conditional on consequences but are absolute. The origins of this theory, of course, go back to the beginnings of human history, when the word of the chief, or the king, or God, was given unconditionally and without invitation to appeal on the basis of consequences. Such theories are sometimes called *deontological* theories, from the Greek root *dein* meaning "duty". In deontological theories, an act or a class of actions is justified by showing that it is right, not by showing that it has good consequences (though, again, it is usually expected that both will be the case.)

The foremost modern defender of a deontological theory is Immanuel Kant. He was reacting to the early "utility" theories of Hume and other "enlightenment" philosophers, and he anticipated the later objections to utilitarianism (Kant wrote seventy years before Mill) by insisting that what makes an act right or wrong cannot be its consequences—which are often entirely out of our hands and a matter of luck—but the principle (or "maxim") which guides the action. "Nothing . . . can be called good without qualification, except a *good will,*" he writes at the beginning of his *Groundwork of the Metaphysic of Morals.* And having a good will means acting with the right intentions, according to the right maxims or principles, doing one's duty for its own sake rather than for personal gain. This is the heart of Kant's ethics, "duty for duty's sake," not for the sake of the consequences, whether one's own good or "the greatest good for the greatest number."

What is the court of appeal for deontological theories of justification? The utilitarian, like the "enlightened" egoist and the Aristotelian teleologist, could appeal to actual human desires and aspirations. But the deontological theory, as "unconditional" or "absolute," rejects just those desires and aspirations as the ultimate court of appeal (though for Kant and almost all deontologists, they nevertheless remain important). The answer must be, they appeal to *authority.* But this does not necessarily mean that the deontologist gives up moral responsibly and passes it on to God or those in power.

Some deontologists, of course do appeal morality to the authority of God. [Thus the justification of morality by appeal to God's will has the earmarks of both a teleological and a deontological theory. It refers to purposes (God's purpose), but it is also an absolute appeal to His authority.] Other deontologists appeal to the law ("it doesn't matter what you think it's the law"). But at least one leading deontologist believes that the appeal to authority necessary to justify morality is also an appeal to one's own moral autonomy in deciding what is right and what is wrong. That deontologist is Kant, and his theory continues to be one of the two basic starting points of most modern ethical theories (the other being utilitarianism).

On Kant's theory, the court of appeal for the justification of morality is the court of reason, or what he calls "pure practical reason." Each of us is rational, which means that each of us has the ability to reason and arrive at the right way to act, by ourselves and without appeal to any "outside" authority. This capacity to reason and decide for ourselves is what Kant calls *autonomy* (opposed to *heteronomy* and being told by others). To justify morality, therefore, is to show that it is rational, and to justify any particular moral principle is to show that it is in accord with the principles of reason. Morality, we have already seen, is characterized by Kant as a system of categorical imperatives, that is, commands which are unqualified and unconditional. We can now appreciate better what this means; they are unqualified not only in the sense that they apply to everyone, without regard to their personal interests, but in the sense that they apply without regard to consequences of any kind. They are principles of reason and, as such, are not bound to the contingencies of life. (Here we can see a positive use of the gap between values and facts we spoke of; Kant takes this to be the heart of reason—that it envisions the world according to its own ideals and is not merely determined by the facts of the world.)

Because moral principles are rational principles, according to Kant, their justification must be a purely formal (or logical) justification. To prove that an act is immoral, it is not enough to show that its actual or probable consequences would be disastrous; one must demonstrate that its principle itself is "contradictory" and impossible. One of Kant's examples will serve as an illustration of what this means. Suppose I am considering borrowing money from you under false pretenses, by lying and telling you that I will pay you back next week (when in fact I will be in Hawaii, never to return). Now the utilitarian would ask for the consequences (whether of the act or of such an act); Kant asks for more. What if, he argues, I were to apply the "maxim" of my act (that is, the principle upon which I am acting) to everyone else, and urge them to act similarly? Since morality is essentially a product of reason I must be able to do this, for I cannot apply principles to myself alone. (The utilitarian would agree with this.) What would be the result? It would be to undercut the whole practice of promising to repay borrowed money, and if anyone were to ask, Can I borrow some money and pay you back next week? everyone would simply laugh, for such words would have become meaningless. Thus, Kant points out, the maxim "contradicts" itself. It not only has disastrous consequences (the concern of the utilitarian) it undercuts its own meaning and betrays a purely formal inadequacy.

Deontological theories of justification seem to succeed where utilitarian theories fail—in the demonstration of the unconditional force of moral principles. But the deontologist runs into trouble, accordingly, just where the utilitarian (and teleologists in general) succeed—in the concern for human happiness and well-being. The deontologist is not indifferent to such concerns—indeed, Kant in a curious passage even argues that we have a *duty* to be happy—but the emphasis on duty and rational, formal principles clearly relegates utility and happiness to secondary consideration. Thus Mill accuses Kant of needing utilitarianism if he is to make sense of his deontological theory, and utilitarians ever since have felt, with some justification, that no theory of the good could possibly be acceptable unless it puts in first place the concern for happiness.

Existentialism, Emotivism, and Moore

In the preceding sections, we have discussed two general strategies for justifying morality—teleological theories (including utilitarianism) which appeal to the purposes and consequences of moral behavior and deontological theories which appeal rather to the authority (including rational authority) of moral principles. We have also considered a number of particular courts of appeal, including God's will and the "design" of nature, human desires and aspirations—including utter "selfishness," reason, and the formal consistency of principles. For over two thousand years there has been debate on these strategies and appeals, and it is probable that ethicists will continue debating their various virtues and vices for the next two thousand years as well. But there is a different kind of possibility, which is that the entire enterprise of justifying morality is a mistake. Perhaps morality cannot be justified, or, perhaps, to try to justify morality already demonstrates something seriously wrong with morality, that we are not convinced of its necessity without some "proof" or "demonstration."

This doubt can be found even in the best defenders of morality. Some of the Sophists who are Socrates's interlocutors in Plato's dialogues have some frighteningly persuasive arguments, and it is not entirely clear that Socrates refutes them. Aristotle warns us at the beginning of his *Ethics* that we should not expect more precision or proof than the subject allows and insists that there is no point trying to convince someone of the importance of the virtues if he has not already been brought up correctly to accept and practice them. Mill prefaces his "proof" of utilitarianism with the similar warning that one cannot really "prove" anything in ethics.

Other authors, however, embrace the doubt that one can justify morality without hesitation. David Hume, most notably, rejects the possibility of justifying morals in any important sense (just as, in other works, he rejects the possibility of justifying our knowledge of the world). Reason, in particular, cannot justify morality, and though morals are based on our "sentiments," according to Hume, this hardly counts as justification in the strong sense demanded by philosophers. After all, if our sentiments were entirely different, so would be our morals. The question of which morals are right seems beside the point. It just happens that we are endowed by nature with certain sentiments (as it happens that we are endowed by nature with certain facilities for knowledge) and that's the end of it.

But that is not the end of it for the more radical critics of the traditional emphasis on justification. Friedrich Nietzsche accepts many of the same arguments advanced by Hume but adds some devastating arguments of his own. He asks, Why the emphasis on justification, if not that morality itself has lost its persuasiveness and we no longer believe in it? In particular, if morality depends on God and we no longer believe in God as a moral force, then couldn't we have lost our faith in the moral world order, without yet admitting it to ourselves? Why the insistence on reason, he asks, if not our fear of our own natural passions and aspirations, as if we need formal principles to keep our spirits in check. And why, he asks, this emphasis on universal principles, if not in order to impose the same set of bland demands and expectations on everyone, thus stunting the growth of those few who could excel far beyond the others? Morality, Nietzsche concludes, is not justifiable, not because philosophers haven't come up with a wholly acceptable justification, but because there is something seriously wrong with the very idea of "morality."

A similar strategy is pursued by the two French "existentialists," Camus and Sartre. They reject the attempt to justify morality on the grounds that any such justification will only serve to shift the ultimate responsibility for what we do away from our own free choice. Suppose a young man has to choose between joining the army to fight for his country or staying home with his grieving mother (who has already lost her husband and two sons in the war)? What is the "principle" he should follow in making his decision? And how will this justify the decision once he has made it? The fact is that he has to *make* a decision, and, in doing so, he might endorse a number of principles (such as, one's primary obligation is to one's mother). But both the decision and its justification are ultimately nothing other than the fact that he has made the decision and has to live with it. The problem is not justifying morality, Camus and Sartre both insist; it is rather choosing to live and living in such a manner that we can live with ourselves.

The rejection of the whole program of justifying morality has had its most radical and influential successes not in the flamboyant and passionate statements of the European existentialists, however, but in the much blander and more academic pronouncements of English and American "analytic" philosophers of this century. The most prominent figure in this development was the Cambridge philosopher G. E. Moore, whose "Open Question Argument" we met several sections ago. The consequence of that argument was that value claims could not be proved by any number of facts; one could always ask the "open question," Yes, but, is it good? Moore's own response to this conclusion was that "good" is the name of a "simple, undefinable, nonnatural property" which we know by "intuition" (thus giving rise to a theory called *"intuitionism,"* in which one knows that something is good by "seeing that it is so,". but without being able to prove it). Moore argued that one could not justify morality in the usual sense (that is, one could not prove it by appeal to reason, purposes, or consequences) but nevertheless, one could know the good and, on that basis Moore defended a version of utilitarianism. (What he rejected was the traditional "proof" of utilitarianism—exemplified by Mill—in which "good" was identified with a "natural property," namely pleasure.)

Moore's followers were not so optimistic about their ability to "intuit" the good; they accepted his "Open Question Argument" but rejected Moore's intuitionism and utilitarianism. They concluded rather that morality and ethics in general—as well as religion, aesthetics, and any number of other nonscientific disciplines—were devoid of substantial cognitive content. Attempting to justify them made no more sense than trying to justify your preference for chocolate fudge ice cream. The leading movement in this wholesale rejection of not only the attempt to justify morality but ethics as such was *logical positivism,* a movement which had its origins among a number of German and Austrian philosophers and scientists who were fighting the Nazis in the 1930s. Their view of ethics was that opinions about values were mainly matters of emotion, not knowledge, and the ethical theory developed by some of the logical positivists—notably by A. J. Ayer in England and C. L. Stevenson in the United States—was accordingly called *emotivism.* They argued (often following Hume's argument) that value judgments couldn't be based wholly on facts and that statements in ethics, therefore, were not matters of knowledge— thus "noncognitive"—and could not be justified as matters of fact could be. (Obviously the logical positivists had a theory of knowledge to back this up, but that is not our concern here.)

"Noncognitivism" has had many variants in England and America in the past fifty years. Emotivism—the view that passing a moral judgment is logically on a par with yelling "Hooray" (Ayer's formulation)—was popular for a decade or so, but it ran up against a powerful objection namely, that it left no room at all for an account of moral reasoning—that is, an account of how we deliberate and persuade ourselves and others of the rightness or wrongness of an action. Accordingly, noncognitivism moved on to other variants, including a theory of *prescriptivism* which is still being defended today by R. N. Hare of Oxford; this theory accepts the importance of moral reasoning but nevertheless rejects the idea that morality can be justified as such. We can "prescribe" certain forms of behavior to each other (as a physician "prescribes" a medicine), but we cannot prove that they are the right forms of behavior. The obvious problem facing the prescriptivist is the *fanatic,* the fellow who has his own perverted ideas about what is right and wrong and will not listen to our reasoning at all. He cannot be persuaded, and yet we want to say that his ideas are wrong. (Think of Hitler—the usual example.) Nevertheless, the prescriptivist theory—like noncognitive theories in general—strikes a sympathetic chord in most twentieth-century readers. It is a point of widespread agreement that ethics is not like science and cannot be "proved" and that—though agreement may be necessary if we are to live together in society—ethics is largely a matter of attitude and consensus, not knowledge. (Undergraduates often sum up this popular position by saying that "value judgments are subjective.")

Ethos and Justification: Morality Today

The variations on noncognitivism are plentiful today, but perhaps we can best appreciate the nature of such views if we look at them not just as metaethical theories about the justification of morality but also as expressions of a particular ethical point of view. What would that be?

In a stunning new book in ethics entitled *After Virtue* [4] Alasdair MacIntyre has analyzed emotivism and its noncognitive kin as the expression of a culture which has all but lost sight of morality and its essential nature. It is as if some grave catastrophe had destroyed our whole language and practice of morality, MacIntyre suggests, and all that are left are a few scattered words (like "ought" and "moral") and a debatable collection of principles whose point and purpose have been forgotten. Emotivism and other noncognitive theories, he then hypothesizes, are not so much metaethical theories about the nature of ethics and its language as the philosophical expressions of a culture in which moral claims actually have lost their purpose, in which it is generally agreed that we will never agree on such basic ethical issues as the right to life of unborn fetuses, the justifiability of war, and the justice of taxation and the redistribution of wealth. But if we compare this ethical confusion to the ethos which we find in Aristotle and the Greeks, for example, the difference is shocking; Aristotle regularly appeals to such general agreement among his fellow citizens, and the idea that ethical issues might be undecidable and a matter of "mere personal opinion" would have struck him and his fellows as the most dangerous kind of utter nonsense.

What is missing in our ethics, in other words, is a sense of an ethos, an already established and agreed upon way of living in which values are shared and unquestioned, in which the question of justification, therefore, is beside the point and does not arise. Of course, this does not mean that one cannot be uncritical within an ethos; quite the contrary, the established values and principles in the ethos provide a secure basis for

[4] Alasdair MacIntyre, *After Virtue* (Notre Dame: University of Notre Dame Press, 1981).

criticizing particular actions and rules. What one cannot do is to try to stand outside of the ethos and evaluate or justify *all* of its values and principles. To do so is to leave oneself without any basis at all for making the evaluation and so without any foundation for justifying the basic principles—that is, morality—of that ethos. Desires and purposes might be accepted at face value within the ethos, but they are an "open question" outside of it. The dictates and principles of reason will be "self-evident" within the ethos but arbitrary and unprovable without it. The various sentiments and emotional reactions a person has within the ethos will quite naturally be the cultivated products of one's upbringing within that ethos, but outside of any ethos all sentiments and emotional reactions will seem merely accidental and provincial. Without an ethos, in other words, there is no basis for the justification of morality. Within an ethos, however, no justification is necessary and such an exercise would seem utterly without purpose.

MacIntyre thus analyzes not just a recent movement in ethics but our entire culture as the disintegration of the communal and cultural contexts within which morality and the virtues alone make sense. The quest for justification he traces back to the enlightenment of the eighteenth century, when the European sense of ethos was already falling apart and the search for universal values and principles was taken up in earnest by way of compensation. We have already noted that Plato and Aristotle did not engage in the quest for justification which is central to modern ethics (and insofar as they did so, Nietzsche argued, it was because their Greek society too was already past its "Golden Age" and starting to decay). David Hume's rejection of the justification of morality was just part and parcel of the skeptical ethical atmosphere within which the quest for justification was being carried out, therefore, and Nietzsche, on MacIntyre's analysis, was simply the final, fatal blow to an already collapsing system of morality (an image that Nietzsche adopted for himself).

What MacIntyre suggests might too easily be mistaken for nostalgic despair and an impossible plea to return to a mythical past ("forward to the twelfth century," he half-jokingly comments). But his point is not simply a negative one (indeed, this is precisely his criticism of the whole ethical tradition from Hume to Moore and the noncognitivists). It is rather a warning about both our current attitudes toward ethics and the philosophical theories in which they are expressed. We make too much of an ideal out of being "above" any particular society and culture and so, in the name of universalism, find ourselves nowhere at all. We insist on rationally justifying our moral principles and end up wondering on what grounds we could even condemn a Hitler or a sadist. ("If there is no justification, everything is permitted.") But to have an ethics is not to have a rigid set of moral principles with an ironclad theory of justification for them; it is to be part of an ethos in which morality plays an accepted and unquestioned role and justification is unnecessary. To question everything is to be left with nothing, and attempting to justify the remnants of a morality already left behind only establishes as philosophical theory what we already feel in our everyday life—that we can't really agree about our most basic value judgments. And what is worse are the conclusions we draw from this, namely, either (1) we're hopelessly confused, swimming in a veritable sea of values, or (2) we are right and everyone else is wrong (or worse—sinful, perverted, or damned). Either way, ethics is unpleasant and the good life is an uncomfortable compromise, at best. Thus the ultimate ethical question, *What do we need to do to realize an ethos for ourselves in which morality makes sense and the good life is possible?* Reading the great ethicists of the past is like reading recipes, from which we must ultimately abstract and create our own.

Philosophy and the study of ethics are not unrelated to this need to create an ethos for ourselves in the middle of a self-consciously pluralist society. MacIntyre points out the use of moral philosophy in justifying and rationalizing a tenuous or disintegrating ethos, but discussions in ethics also function as expressions of our values and help give them form and articulation. One of the problems of a pluralist society is its inability to come to ready agreement on pressing moral issues (for example, the acceptability of nonstandard sexuality, the legitimacy of a "progressive" income tax). But this problem is in fact the other side of a virtue as well; it stimulates a degree of self-understanding that a less conflict-ridden ethos would not achieve, and it promotes the necessity of mutual understanding and tolerance that a nonpluralist would find unimaginable. This is emphatically not to say that we thereby learn to suspend ethical judgment or give up the aim of formulating a coherent and all-encompassing ethical system for ourselves. It is rather to say that articulation and argument, justification and mutual understanding are themselves among the most important virtues of our ethos, and by developing these abilities we simultaneously create and reinforce our own pluralistic ethos, however many differences and disagreements will always be found within it.

The thesis MacIntyre defends in *After Virtue* also contains a warning about the ethical enterprise which we should take very seriously in this book: it is a mistake to see every philosopher from Plato to Sartre as engaged in a single enterprise and answering a single set of questions. They are all also participants in distinctive historical epochs and different ethê and thus expressing distinctive concerns and resolving different problems. It is perfectly acceptable to compare or contrast Aristotle and Kant on certain issues or to point out certain similarities between Saint Augustine and Sartre, but this must always be done with keen historical caution and the awareness that we are not just judging a dog show with slight variations among a few classic breeds. Ethics is a curious combination of self-awareness, history, self-criticism, and anthropology. It begins with a tradition which is as old as western thought itself and ends, necessarily, in the question—OK, what do we do now?

CHAPTER 1

PLATO

A. Crito

Since Socrates himself did not write down his lectures and conversations, all that we know of his ethical views comes to us through the writings of other philosophers who either knew him and heard him discuss these matters or heard about him from others. But most of what we know of his work comes to us most directly in the form of "dialogues" written by Socrates's most illustrious student, Plato. In these dialogues, Socrates himself plays the leading role. Socrates's general strategy—which has since come to be called "the Socratic method'—is for him to feign ignorance, urging his interlocutor (the person who is going to be utterly refuted in the course of the dialogue) to state his own opinion, for example, about what one ought to do in a certain situation. Socrates then points out what is wrong with such an opinion, forcing the interlocutor to revise and restate his position in a better thought-out form, which Socrates then attacks as well. Finally, by the end of each dialogue, the fallacies and inadequacies of various positions have been displayed and Socrates presents his own view, free from the errors that have been pointed out in the others. In addition to this dialogal (sometimes called "dialectical") technique, Socrates also uses a number of dramatic techniques, for instance, taking on the role of a muse or a goddess to make a point or, in the dialogue which follows, allowing himself to be the spokesman for "the laws of Athens," which speak to us through him.

The ethical subject matter of many of Plato's Socratic dialogues is very abstract and metaethical, having to do with the meaning of such terms as "good" and "justice." (We have included such discussions in the two selections from Plato's *Republic,* which follows.) But the subject of the dialogue *Crito* could not be more down to earth and urgent in a life-and-death way. It depicts the actual scene from Socrates's own life, in which he has been tried by the court of Athens for "corrupting the youth" and sentenced to death. In the *Crito,* he is in prison, awaiting execution, when one of his good friends, Crito (the names of the Platonic dialogues are often based on the name of the interlocutor), informs Socrates that plans have been made for his escape. But Socrates, instead of being overjoyed or relieved at the news, is deeply troubled. On the one hand, he is still a healthy and vigorous man (his physical prowess and endurance were legendary). He had a family and many friends and lived what we would probably all agree was a very good life, filled with good food and wine, friends, excitement, conversation, and parties (one of which is recorded by Plato as *The Symposium,* in which the topic of the drunken evening is erotic love). Even as an old man of 70, Socrates still had much to live for. On the other hand, Socrates had made his career as a philosopher by arguing for the importance of such abstract ideals as honor and justice, and his idea of living well was not confined to the pleasures of life. Living well included doing one's duty as a citizen, which obviously included obeying and respecting the law. But in his present situation, obeying and respecting the law included accepting the (unjust) sentence of the Athenian court, which meant allowing himself to be killed. Socrates's dialogue with Crito (reported to Plato by Crito afterward) is essentially the all-important debate between the worth of life and its pleasures versus the value of duty and honor. Crito argues that Socrates should escape and go on living the good life. Socrates argues that he has an obligation to respect the law which overrides even the unjust nature of his sentence and his desire to continue to live and live well. How could he live well, he insists, if he has betrayed the principles which have made his life meaningful, if he has betrayed his own soul?

In the dialogue which follows, it is worth watching the various turns in Socrates's argument. Notice, for example, that Crito's emotional appeals to Socrates are inevitably ignored or rejected, as Socrates insists on pursuing a purely rational line of thought, free from his own feelings and as objective as possible. (This is the reason behind his dramatic device of speaking for the laws instead of just speaking for himself.) Notice too the different kinds of reasons Socrates and Crito give for their positions—arguments about duty, appeals to what the gods want, entreaties to Socrates's and Crito's personal self-interests as well as to "what people will think" and entreaties on the basis of what would be good for everyone. Socrates wins the argument, of course; but consequently, he is executed the next day, by means of a fast-acting poison derived from the hemlock plant. The execution itself is described—also second-hand—by Plato in a subsequent dialogue called the *Phaedo.*

SOCRATES

Socrates lived from 470 until 399 B.C. and spent virtually his entire life in Athens (except for various military campaigns, in which he took part). He spent most of his life in poverty, living mainly on gifts from his students. He was known to be a brilliant debater and spent much of his life debating with the "Sophists" who wandered around Greece giving lessons in philosophy and argument. But where the Sophists were cynical and pessimistic about the possibility of finding the Good in ethics (often arguing such theses as "all men are selfish" or "there is no such thing as justice"), Socrates took a positive and optimistic view. He was always confident, despite his rhetorical strategy of feigning total ignorance—that the Good could be found and taught, and it was in the name of the Good, accordingly, that he died.

PLATO

Plato lived from 427 to 347 B.C. He was a student of Socrates during the tragic period of Socrates's trial and execution, and he spent the rest of his life writing down Socrates's teachings and dialogues. He founded the famous Academy in Athens for the purpose of presenting and preserving as well as continuing Socrates's work, and he always used Socrates as the spokesman for his ideas. But what this meant was that, as his own thinking developed far beyond the relatively simple ideas of his teacher, Plato was presenting as Socrates's views ideas that were actually Plato's own. The *Crito* is probably a relatively faithful transcription of the dialogue that took place in Socrates's prison cell, but some of the other dialogues, for example the *Republic* (which follows in part), are just as much Plato as Socrates, and it is not always possible to tell which ideas belong to which philosopher.

PERSONS OF THE DIALOGUE: *Socrates, Crito*
SCENE: The Prison of Socrates
    Socrates: Why have you come at this hour Crito? It must be quite early?
    Crito: Yes, certainly.
    Soc: What is the exact time?
    Cr: The dawn is breaking.
    Soc: I wonder that the keeper of the prison would let you in.
    Cr: He knows me, because I often come, Socrates; moreover, I have done him a kindness.
    Soc: And are you only just arrived?
    Cr: No. I came some time ago.
    Soc: Then why did you sit and say nothing, instead of at once awakening me?
    Cr: I should not have liked myself. Socrates, to be in such great trouble and unrest as you are—indeed I should not: I have been watching with amazement your peaceful slumbers; and for that reason I did not awake you, because I wished to minimize the pain. I have always thought you to be of a happy disposition; but never did I see anything like the easy, tranquil manner in which you bear this calamity.
    Soc: Why, Crito, when a man has reached my age he ought not be repining at the approach of death.
    Cr: And yet other old men find themselves in similar misfortunes, and age does not prevent them from repining.
    Soc: That is true. But you have not told me why you come at this early hour.
    Cr: I come to bring you a message which is sad and painful; not, as I believe, to yourself, but to all of us who are your friends, and saddest of all to me.

From *Crito* by Plato. Translated by Benjamin Jowett (1892).

Soc: What? Has the ship come from Delos, on the arrival of which I am to die?

Cr: No, the ship has not actually arrived, but she will probably be here to-day, as persons who have come from Sunium tell me that they left her there; and therefore tomorrow, Socrates, will be the last day of your life.

Soc: Very well, Crito if such is the will of God, I am willing; but my belief is that there will be a delay of a day.

Cr: Why do you think so?

Soc: I will tell you. I am to die on the day after the arrival of the ship.

Cr: Yes; that is what the authorities say.

Soc: But I do not think that the ship will be here until to-morrow; this I infer from a vision which I had last night, or rather only just now, when you fortunately allowed me to sleep.

Cr: And what was the nature of the vision?

Soc: There appeared to me the likeness of a woman, fair and comely, clothed in bright raiment, who called to me and said: O Socrates,

"The third day hence to fertile Phthia shalt thou go."[1]

Cr: What a singular dream, Socrates!

Soc: There can be no doubt about the meaning, Crito, I think.

Cr: Yes; the meaning is only too clear. But, oh! my beloved Socrates, let me entreat you once more to take my advice and escape. For if you die I shall not only lose a friend who can never be replaced, but there is another evil: people who do not know you and me will believe that I might have saved you if I had been willing to give money, but that I did not care. Now, can there be a worse disgrace than this—that I should be thought to value money more than the life of a friend? For the many will not be persuaded that I wanted you to escape, and that you refused.

Soc: But why, my dear Crito, should we care about the opinion of the many? Good men, and they are the only persons who are worth considering, will think of these things truly as they occurred.

Cr: But you see, Socrates, that the opinion of the many must be regarded, for what is now happening shows that they can do the greatest evil to any one who has lost their good opinion.

Soc: I only wish it were so, Crito; and that the many could do the greatest evil; for then they would also be able to do the greatest good—and what a fine thing this would be! But in reality they can do neither; for they cannot make a man either wise or foolish; and whatever they do is the result of chance.

Cr: Well, I will not dispute with you; but please to tell me, Socrates, whether you are not acting out of regard to me and your other friends: are you not afraid that if you escape from prison we may get into trouble with the informers for having stolen you away, and lose either the whole or a great part of our property; or that even a worse evil may happen to us? Now, if you fear on our

[1]Homer, Il. ix. 363.

account, be at ease; for in order to save you, we ought surely to run this, or even a greater risk; be persuaded, then, and do as I say.

Soc Yes, Crito, that is one fear which you mention, but by no means the only one.

Cr: Fear not—there are persons who are willing to get you out of prison at no great cost; and as for the informers, they are far from being exorbitant in their demands—a little money will satisfy them. My means, which are certainly ample, are at your service, and if you have a scruple about spending all mine, here are strangers who will give you the use of theirs; and one of them, Simmias the Theban, has brought a large sum of money for this very purpose; and Cebes and many others are prepared to spend their money in helping you to escape. I say, therefore, do not hesitate on our account, and do not say, as you did in the court, that you will have a difficulty in knowing what to do with yourself anywhere else. For men will love you in other places to which you may go, and not in Athens only; there are friends of mine in Thessaly, if you like to go to them, who will value and protect you, and no Thessalian will give you any trouble. Nor can I think that you are at all justified, Socrates, in betraying your own life when you might be saved; in acting thus you are playing into the hands of your enemies, who are hurrying on your destruction. And further I should say that you are deserting your own children; for you might bring them up and educate them; instead of which you go away and leave them, and they will have to take their chance; and if they do not meet with the usual fate of orphans, there will be small thanks to you. No man should bring children into the world who is unwilling to persevere to the end in their nurture and education. But you appear to be choosing the easier part, not the better and manlier, which would have been more becoming in one who professes to care for virtue in all his actions, like yourself. And, indeed, I am ashamed not only of you, but of us who are your friends, when I reflect that the whole business will be attributed entirely to our want of courage. The trial need never have come on, or might have been managed differently; and this last act, of crowning folly, will seem to have occurred through our negligence and cowardice, who might have saved you, if we had been good for anything; and you might have saved yourself, for there was no difficulty at all. See now, Socrates, how sad and discreditable are the consequences, both to us and you. Make up your mind, then, or rather have your mind already made up, for the time of deliberation is over, and there is only one thing to be done, which must be done this very night, and if we delay at all will be no longer practicable or possible; I beseech you therefore, Socrates, be persuaded by me, and do as I say.

Soc: Dear Crito your zeal is invaluable, if a right one; but if wrong, the greater the zeal the greater the danger; and therefore we ought to consider whether I shall or shall not do as you say. For I am and always have been one of those natures who must be guided by reason, whatever the reason may be which upon reflection appears to me to be the best; and now that this chance has befallen me, I cannot repudiate my own words: the principles which I have hitherto honoured and revered I still honour, and unless we can at once find other and better principles, I am certain not to agree with you; no, not even if the power of the multitude could inflict many more imprisonments, confiscations, deaths, frightentng us like children with hobgoblin terrors. What will be the fairest way of considering the question? Shall I return to your old argument about the opinions of men?—we were saying that some of them are to be regarded, and others not. Now, were we right in maintaining this before I was condemned? And has the argument which was once good now proved to be talk for the sake of talking—mere childish nonsense? That is what I want to consider with your help. Crito:—whether, under my present circumstances, the argument appears to be in any way different or not; and is to be allowed by me or disallowed. That argument, which, as I believe, is maintained by many persons of authority, was to the effect, as I was saying, that the opinions of some men are to be regarded, and of other men not to be regarded. Now you, Crito, are not going to die to-morrow—at least, there is no human probability of this—and therefore you are disinterested and not liable to be deceived by the circumstances in which you are placed. Tell me, then, whether I am right in saying that some opinions, and the opinions of some men only, are to be valued, and that other opinions, and the opinions of other men, are not to be valued. I ask you whether I was right in maintaining this?

Cr: Certainly.

Soc: The good are to be regarded, and not the bad?

Cr: Yes.

Soc: And the opinions of the wise are good, and the opinions of the unwise are evil?

Cr: Certainly.

Soc: And what was said about another matter? Is the pupil who devotes himself to the practice of gymnastic supposed to attend to the praise and blame and opinion of every man, or of one man only—his physician or trainer, whoever he may be?

Cr: Of one man only.

Soc: And he ought to fear the censure and welcome the praise of that one only, and not of the many?

Cr: Clearly so.

Soc: And he ought to act and train, and eat and drink in the way which seems good to his single master who has understanding, rather than according to the opinion of all other men put together?

Cr: True.

Soc: And if he disobeys and disregards the opinion and approval of the one, and regards the opinion of the many who have no understanding, will he not suffer evil?

Cr: Certainly he will.

Soc: And what will the evil be, whither tending and what affecting, in the disobedient person?

Cr: Clearly, affecting the body; that is what is destroyed by the evil.

Soc: Very good; and is not this true, Crito, of other things which we need not separately enumerate? In questions of just and unjust, fair and foul, good and evil, which are the subjects of our present consultation, ought we to follow the opinion of the many and to fear them; or the opinion of the one man who has understanding? Ought we not to fear and reverence him more than all the rest of the world: and if we desert him shall we not destroy and injure that principle in us which may be assumed to be improved by justice and deteriorated by injustice;—there is such a principle?

Cr: Certainly there is, Socrates.

Soc: Take a parallel instance:—if, acting under the advice of those who have no understanding, we destroy that which is improved by health and is deteriorated by disease, would life be worth having? And that which has been destroyed is—the body?

Cr: Yes.

Soc: Could we live, having an evil and corrupted body?

Cr: Certainly not.

Soc: And will life be worth having, if that higher part of man be destroyed, which is improved by justice and depraved by injustice? Do we suppose that principle, whatever it may be in man, which has to do with justice and injustice, to be inferior to the body?

Cr: Certainly not.

Soc: More honourable than the body?

Cr: Far more.

Soc: Then, my friend, we must not regard what the many say of us: but what he, the one man who has understanding of just and unjust, will say, and what the truth will say. And therefore you begin in error when you advise that we should regard the opinion of the man about just and unjust, good and evil, honourable and dishonourable.—"Well, some one will say, But the many can kill us."

Cr: Yes, Socrates; that will clearly be the answer.

Soc: And it is true: but still I find with surprise that the old argument is unshaken as ever. And I should like to know whether I may say the same of another proposition—that not life, but a good life, is to be chiefly valued?

Cr: Yes, that also remains unshaken.

Soc: And a good life is equivalent to a just and honourable one—that holds also?

Cr: Yes, it does.

Soc: From these premises I proceed to argue the question whether I ought or ought not to try to escape without the consent of the Athenians: and if I am clearly right in escaping, then I will make the attempt; but if not, I will abstain. The other considerations which you mention, of money and loss of character and the duty of educating one's children, are, I fear, only the doctrines of the multitude, who would be as ready to restore people to life, if they were able, as they are to put them to death—and with as little reason. But now, since the argument has thus far prevailed, the only question which remains to be considered is, whether we shall do rightly either in escaping or in suffering others to aid in our escape and paying them in money and thanks, or whether in reality we shall not do rightly; and if the latter, then death or any other calamity which may ensue on my remaining here must not be allowed to enter into the calculation.

Cr: I think that you are right, Socrates; how then shall we proceed?

Soc: Let us consider the matter together, and do you either refute me if you can, and I will be convinced; or else cease, my dear friend, from repeating to me that I ought to escape against the wishes of the Athenians: for I highly value your attempts to persuade me to do so, but I may not be persuaded against my own better judgment. And now please to consider my first position, and try how you can best answer me.

Cr: I will

Soc: Are we to say that we are never intentionally to do wrong, or that in one way we ought and in another way we ought not to do wrong, or is doing wrong always evil and dishonourable, as I was just now saying, and as has been already acknowledged by us? Are all our former admissions which were made within a few days to be thrown away? And have we, at our age, been earnestly discoursing with one another all our life long only to discover that we are no better than children? Or, in spite of the opinion of the many, and in spite of consequences whether better or worse, shall we insist on the truth of what was then said, that injustice is always an evil and dishonour to him who acts unjustly? Shall we say so or not?

Cr: Yes.

Soc: Then we must do no wrong?

Cr: Certainly not.

Soc: Nor when injured injure in return, as the many imagine; for we must injure no one at all?

Cr: Clearly not.

Soc: Again, Crito, may we do evil?

Cr: Surely not, Socrates.

Soc: And what of doing evil in return for evil, which is the morality of the many—is that just or not?

Cr: Not just.

Soc: For doing evil to another is the same as injuring him?

Cr: Very true.

Soc: Then we ought not to retaliate or render evil for evil to any one, whatever evil we may have suffered from him. But I would have you consider, Crito, whether you really mean what you are saying. For this opinion has never been held, and never will be held, by any considerable number of persons; and those who are agreed and those who are not agreed upon this point have no common ground, and can only despise one another when they see how widely they differ. Tell me, then, whether you agree with and assent to my first principle, that neither injury nor retaliation nor warding off evil by evil is ever right. And shall that be the premise of our argument? Or do you decline and dissent from this? For so I have ever thought, and continue to think: but, if you are of another opinion, let me hear what you have to say. If, however, you remain of the same mind as formerly, I will proceed to the next step.

Cr: You may proceed, for I have not changed my mind.

Soc: Then I will go on to the next point, which may be put in the form of a question:—Ought a man to do what he admits to be right, or ought he to betray the right?

Cr: He ought to do what he thinks right.

Soc: But if this is true, what is the application? In leaving the prison against the will of the Athenians, do I wrong any? Or rather do I not wrong those whom I ought least to wrong? Do I not desert the principles which were acknowledged by us to be just—what do you say?

Cr: I cannot tell, Socrates; for I do not know.

Soc: Then consider the matter in this way:—Imagine that I am about to play truant (you may call the proceeding by any name which you like), and the laws and the government come and interrogate me: "Tell us, Socrates," they say; "what are you about? are you not going by an act of yours to overturn us—the laws, and the whole state, as far as in you lies? Do you imagine that a state can subsist and not be overthrown, in which the decisions of law have no power, but are set aside and trampled upon by individuals?" What will be our answer, Crito, to these and the like words? Any one, and especially a rhetorician, will have a good deal to say on behalf of the law which requires a sentence to be carried out. He will argue that this law should not be set aside; and shall we reply, "Yes; but the state has injured us and given an unjust sentence." Suppose I say that?

Cr: Very good, Socrates.

Soc: "And was that our agreement with you?" the law would answer; "or were you to abide by the sentence of the state?" And if I were to express my astonishment at their words, the law would probably add: "Answer, Socrates, instead of opening your eyes—you are in the habit of asking and answering questions. Tell us,—What complaint have you to make against us which justifies you in attempting to destroy us and the state? In the first place did we not bring you into existence? Your father married your mother by our aid and begat you. Say whether you have any objection to urge against those of us who regulate marriage?" None, I should reply. "Or against those of us who after birth regulate the nurture and education of children, in which you also were trained? Were not the laws, which have the charge of education, right in commanding your father to train you in music and gymnastic?" Right, I should reply. "Well, then since you were brought into the world and nurtured and educated by us, can you deny in the first place that you are our child and slave, as your fathers were before you? And if this is true, you are not on equal terms with us; nor can you think that you have a right to do to us what we are doing to you. Would you have any right to strike or revile or do any other evil to your father or your master, if you had one, because you have been struck or reviled by him, or received some other evil at his hands?—you would not say this? And because we think right to destroy you, do you think that you have any right to destroy us in return, and your country as far as in you lies? Will you, O professor of true virtue, pretend that you are justified in this? Has a philosopher like you failed to discover that our country is more to be valued and higher and holier far than mother or father or any ancestor, and more to be regarded in the eyes of the gods and of men of understanding? Also to be soothed, and gently and reverently entreated when angry, even more than a father, and either to be persuaded, or if not persuaded, to be obeyed? And when we are punished by her, whether with imprisonment or stripes, the punishment is to be endured in silence; and if she lead us to wounds or death in battle, thither we follow as is right; neither may any one yield or retreat or leave his rank, but whether in battle or in a court of law, or in any other place, he must do what his city and his country order him; or he must change their view of what is just: and if he may do no violence to his father or mother, much less may he do violence to his country." What answer shall we make to this, Crito? Do the laws speak truly, or do they not?

Cr: I think that they do.

Soc: Then the laws will say: "Consider, Socrates, if we are speaking truly that in your present attempt you are going to do us an injury. For, having brought you into the world, and nurtured and educated you, and given you and every other citizen a share in every good which we had to give, we further proclaim to any Athenian by the liberty which we allow him, that if he does not like us when he has become of age and has seen the ways of the city, and made our acquaintance, he may go where he pleases and take his goods with him. None of us laws will forbid him or interfere with him. Any one who does not like us and the city, and who wants to emigrate to a colony or to any other city, may go where he likes, retaining his property. But he who has experience of the manner in which we order justice and administer the State, and still remains, has entered into an implied contract that he will do as we command him. And he who disobeys us is, as we maintain, thrice wrong; first, because in disobeying us he is disobeying his parents; secondly, because we are the authors of his education; thirdly, because he has made an agreement with us that he will duly obey our commands; and he neither obeys them nor convinces us that our commands are unjust; and we do not rudely impose them, but give him the alternative of obeying or convincing us;—that is what we offer, and he does neither.

"These are the sort of accusations to which, as we were saying, you, Socrates, will be exposed if you accomplish your intentions; you, above all other Athenians." Suppose now I ask, why I rather than anybody else? They will justly retort upon me that I above all other men have acknowledged the agreement. "There is clear proof," they will say, "Socrates, that we and the city were not displeasing to you. Of all Athenians you have been the most constant resident in the city, which, as you never leave, you may be supposed to love. For you never went out of the city either to see the games, except once when you went to the Isthmus, or to any other place unless when you were on military service; nor did you travel as other men do. Nor had you any curiosity to know other States or their laws: your affections did not go beyond us and our State; we were your special favourites, and you acquiesced in our government of you; and here in this city you begat your children, which is a proof of your satisfaction. Moreover, you might in the course of the trial, if you had liked, have fixed the penalty at banishment; the State which refuses to let you go now would have let you go then. But you pretended that you preferred death to exile and that you were not unwilling to die. And now you have forgotten these fine sentiments, and pay no respect to us, the laws, of whom you are the destroyer; and are doing what only a miserable slave would do, running away and turning your back upon the compacts and agreements which you made as a citizen. And, first of all, answer this very question: Are we right in saying that you agreed to be governed according to us in deed, and not in word only? Is that true or not?" How shall we answer, Crito? Must we not assent?

Cr: We cannot help it, Socrates.

Soc: Then will they not say: "You, Socrates, are breaking the covenants and agreements which you made with us at your leisure, not in any haste or under any compulsion or deception, but after you have had seventy years to think of them, during which time you were at liberty to leave the city, if we were not to your mind, or if our covenants appeared to you to be unfair. You had your choice, and might have gone either to Lacedaemon or Crete, both which States are often praised by you for their good government, or to some other Hellenic or foreign State. Whereas you, above all other Athenians, seemed to be so fond of the State, or, in other words, of us, her laws (and who would care about a State which has no laws?), that you never stirred out of her; the halt, the blind, the maimed were not more stationary in her than you were. And now you run away and forsake your agreements. Not so, Socrates, if you will take our advice; do not make yourself ridiculous by escaping out of the city.

"For just consider, if you transgress and err in this sort of way, what good will you do either to yourself or to your friends? That your friends will be driven into exile and deprived of citizenship, or will lose their property, is tolerably certain; and you yourself, if you fly to one of the neighbouring cities, as, for example, Thebes or Megara, both of which are well governed, will come to them as an enemy, Socrates, and their government will be against you, and all patriotic citizens will cast an evil eye upon you as a subverter of the laws, and you will confirm in the minds of the judges the justice of their own condemnation of you. For he who is a corrupter of the laws is more than likely to be a corrupter of the young and foolish portion of mankind. Will you then flee from well-ordered cities and virtuous men? And is existence worth having on these terms? Or will you go to them without shame, and talk to them, Socrates? And what will you say to them? What you say here about virtue and justice and institutions and laws being the best things among men? Would that be decent of you? Surely not. But if you go away from well-governed States to Crito's friends in Thessaly, where there is great disorder and licence, they will be charmed to hear the tale of your escape from prison, set off with ludicrous particulars of the manner in which you were wrapped in a goatskin or some other disguise, and metamorphosed as the manner is of runaways; but will there be no one to remind you that in your old age you were not ashamed to violate the most sacred laws from a miserable desire of a little more life? Perhaps not, if you keep them in a good temper; but if they are out of temper you will hear many degrading things; you will live, but how?—as the flatterer of all men, and the servant of all men; and doing what?—eating and drinking in Thessaly, having gone abroad in order that you may get a dinner. And where will be your fine sentiments about justice and virtue? Say that you wish to live for the sake of your children—you want to bring them up and educate them—will you take them into Thessaly and deprive them of Athenian citizenship? Is this the benefit which you will confer upon them? Or are you under the impression that they will be better cared for and educated here if you are still alive, although absent from them; for your friends will take care of them? Do you fancy that if you are an inhabitant of Thessaly they will take care of them, and if you are an inhabitant of the other world that they will not take care of them? Nay; but if they who call themselves friends are good for anything, they will—to be sure they will.

"Listen, then, Socrates, to us who have brought you up. Think not of life and children first, and of justice afterwards, but of justice first, that you may be justified before the princes of the world below. For neither will you nor any that belong to you be happier or holier or juster in this life, or happier in another, if you do as Crito bids. Now you depart in innocence, a sufferer and not a doer of evil; a victim, not of the laws but of men. But if you go forth, returning evil for evil; and injury for injury, breaking the covenants and agreements which you have made with us, and wronging those whom you ought least of all to wrong, that is to say, yourself, your friends, your country, and us, we shall be angry with you while you live, and our brethren, the laws in the world below, will receive you as an enemy; for they will know that you have done your best to destroy us. Listen, then, to us and not to Crito."

This, dear Crito, is the voice which I seem to hear murmuring in my ears, like the sound of the flute in the ears of the mystic; that voice, I say, is humming in my ears, and prevents me from hearing any other. And I know that anything more which you may say will be vain. Yet speak, if you have anything to say.

Cr: I have nothing to say, Socrates.

Soc: Leave me then, Crito, to fulfil the will of God, and to follow whither he leads.

DISCUSSION

The conflict presented in the *Crito* is the life-and-death struggle between self-preservation and honor. The fact that Socrates's punishment is so unjust colors the argument even more, for one would probably feel much more righteous running away from an unjust death sentence than from a sentence which one knew one deserved. But the question can be put even in those cases in which a person rightly faces dishonor and punishment, Is life itself worth more than anything?

Death rather than dishonor has been a central ethical code of a great many societies. The naval captain has always been expected to "go down with his ship," no matter how easily he could save himself. Some of the male passengers on the ill-fated *Titanic*, which sank in 1912, felt that dying with honor was preferable to taking a seat from a woman or child (there were not nearly enough lifeboats to accommodate everyone). The multimillionaire John Jacob Astor, for example, went down with the ship in the name of his honor, leaving behind an enviable life of wealth and power.

One of the essential ethical questions of all times has been, What is worth dying for? Ask yourself this question, Under what circumstances would you be willing to give up your life? If your parents were kidnapped and your life was the ransom, would you willingly give yourself up? If your country were attacked and you were assigned a certainly fatal mission, would you willingly go? If you were caught cheating on an exam, would you—like some of the Roman heroes—kill yourself to show your remorse? Under what kinds of circumstances would you consider risking or giving up your life? Under what circumstances would you consider such action foolish or "a waste"? What is worth dying for? (which is an indirect way of asking, What is ultimately worth living for?)

A less life-and-death question raised by the *Crito* is the moral status of law. In most societies, most of the laws will be in accordance with (if not derived directly from) morality, and most judicial decisions will agree with most people's moral opinions too. But law and morality are not the same and not always in agreement. There are immoral acts which are not usually illegal (for example, lying to your friends), and there are many laws whose concern is not primarily (or even secondarily) moral (most traffic laws, for example). There are some bad laws and bad judicial decisions, and the decision against Socrates was one of the most notorious of them. Should he therefore have refused to accept the decision and escaped? Do you accept his argument that he was obliged to accept the decision, even if it was an unfair one? Can you think of a case in which you would feel obliged to break the law, in the name of morality or some higher ideal?

B. The Republic: Two Brief Selections

The idea that pervades and defines all of Plato's work—and, we may surmise, Socrates's teachings—is that of the Good. (Especially in *The Republic,* the ideas of the two men are difficult to distinguish.) Against the skeptics (doubters) of the day, Socrates and Plato continued to believe in an absolute ideal which did not depend on the whims and feelings of individuals or on the customs of particular cities or societies. One of the doubters—a Sophist named Protagoras—issued the still-familiar proclamation, "Man is the measure of all things"; it was just this that Socrates and Plato rejected. Socrates, in his life, demonstrated how a man could remain untouched by the immorality around him; Plato, in his writings, shows again and again how the ideal persists, even in the face of human ignorance and irrationality.

The idea of the Good is not, for Socrates and Plato, just an idea "in our minds." In fact, they did not have a concept of "mind" like ours such that an idea could be "in" it. Ideas (or Forms) existed in their own ideal world, a world ("the World of Being") which Socrates and Plato believed was more real than our own. Our world of everyday life ("the World of Becoming") was unstable, always changing. People grew old and died; great cities became corrupted and were destroyed. People's opinions and values seemed to change with the times and with their age. But the pure Ideas, including the pure idea of the Good, remained eternally the same. The good man, accordingly, would seek out this ideal, whatever the state of society around him. (Socrates and Plato both had ample reason to be pessimistic about finding or establishing this ideal in actuality, although both of them tried to do so, Socrates in Athens, Plato in Syracuse.) Plato's Socratic dialogue, *The Republic,* is the classic statement of this ideal, and how it would be manifested both in the good society and in the good individual.

The Republic is a dialogue about the idea of the Good, but it is also one of the most profound and disturbing blueprints for political and social organization in the history of western thought. It also introduces one of the most dramatic myths in the history of philosophy, the "Myth of the Cave," an allegory about the existence of an ideal world, over and above our everyday world. The core of *The Republic* is about the concept of *justice.* Justice is the ideal of inner harmony, both within the individual and in society. Indeed, this is the ultimate direction of all of Plato's dialogues, as exemplified in the life of Socrates: the ultimate unity of knowledge, virtue, and human happiness in the Good. The quest for knowledge of the Good at the same time makes a man virtuous and assures his happiness, whatever else may befall him.

In the following two selections from *The Republic,* Plato presents us with two of his best-known philosophical allegories. The first is purely negative and polemical; it is the "Ring of Gyges" from Book II of *The Republic.* The ring in question turns its wearer invisible and thus renders him capable of all sorts of crimes without the risk of getting caught. The story is told to Socrates by his interlocutor Glaucon, who uses it as an example of the alleged domination of self-interest over justice.

The second allegory is the famous "Myth of the Cave," from Book VII of *The Republic.* Plato (Socrates) has already introduced the grand conception of the pure Idea or the Forms, including the Idea or the Form of the Good. In Book VI he again distinguishes between the indefinitely many things in our world which we call "good" and the Good (that is, the Idea or Form of the Good) itself. The many good things are given their goodness by the single Idea, or, as Plato puts the matter, they "participate" in the Idea of the Good. Most of us, however, never see beyond the particular things to the Idea of the Good which gives them their goodness. The things may be visible, but the Idea is not; it is known only through *reason,* and it is reason alone that allows us to know the world most real, a world beyond the shadows of our everyday existence, the ideal world of the Good and its kindred ideas. It is as if, Plato (Socrates) suggests, we had spent our whole lives in a cave and had come to mistake the shadows on the wall for reality. But what would happen if someone (a philosopher, of course) were to see beyond the cave and come back to try to lead us out of it?

1. "THE RING OF GYGES"

Glaucon (to Socrates): I have never yet heard the superiority of justice to injustice maintained by anyone in a satisfactory way. I want to hear justice praised in respect of itself; then I shall be satisfied, and you are the person from whom I think that I am most likely to hear this; and therefore I will praise the unjust life to the utmost of my power and my manner of speaking will indicate the manner in which I desire to hear you too praising justice and censuring injustice. Will you say whether you approve of my proposal?

Socrates: Indeed I do; nor can I imagine any theme about which a man of sense would oftener wish to converse.

From *The Republic* by Plato. Translated by Benjamin Jowett (1892).

Glaucon: I am delighted to hear you say so, and shall begin by speaking, as I proposed, of the nature and origin of justice.

They say that to do injustice is, by nature, good; to suffer injustice, evil; but that there is more evil in the latter than good in the former. And so when men have both done and suffered injustice and have had experience of both, any who are not able to avoid the one and obtain the other, think that they had better agree among themselves to have neither; hence they began to establish laws and mutual covenants; and that which was ordained by law was termed by them lawful and just. This, it is claimed, is the origin and nature of justice;—it is a mean or compromise, between the best of all, which is to do injustice and not be punished, and the worst of all, which is to suffer injustice without the power of retaliation; and justice, being at a middle point between the two, is tolerated not as a good but as the lesser evil, and honoured where men are too feeble to do injustice. For no man who is worthy to be called a man would ever submit to such an agreement with another if he had the power to be unjust; he would be mad if he did. Such is the received account Socrates, of the nature of justice, and the circumstances which bring it into being.

Now that those who practise justice do so involuntarily and because they have not the power to be unjust will best appear if we imagine something of this kind: having given to both the just and the unjust power to do what they will, let us watch and see whither desire will lead them; then we shall discover in the very act the just and unjust man to be proceeding along the same road, following their interest, which all creatures instinctively pursue as their good; the force of law is required to compel them to pay respect to equality. The liberty which we are supposing may be most completely given to them in the form of such a power as is said to have been possessed by Gyges, the ancestor of Croesus the Lydian. According to the tradition, Gyges was a shepherd in the service of the reigning king of Lydia; there was a great storm, and an earthquake made an opening in the earth at the place where he was feeding his flock. Amazed at the sight, he descended into the opening, where, among other marvels which form part of the story, he beheld a hollow brazen horse, having doors, at which he stooping and looking in saw a dead body of stature, as appeared to him, more than human; he took from the corpse a gold ring that was on the hand, but nothing else, and so reascended. Now the shepherds met together, according to custom, that they might send their monthly report about the flocks to the king; into their assembly he came having the ring on his finger, and as he was sitting among them he chanced to turn the collet of the ring to the inside of his hand, when instantly he became invisible to the rest of the company and they began to speak of him as if he were no longer present. He was astonished at this, and again touching the ring he turned the collet outwards and reappeared; when he perceived this, he made several trials of the ring, and always with the same result—when he turned the collet inwards he became invisible, when outwards he was visible. Whereupon he contrived to be chosen one of the messengers who were sent to the court; where as soon as he arrived he seduced the queen, and with her help conspired against the king and slew him, and took the kingdom. Suppose now that there were two such magic rings, and the just put on one of them and the unjust the other; no man can be imagined to be of such an iron nature that he would stand fast in justice. No man would keep his hands off what was not his own when he could safely take what he liked out of the market, or go into houses and lie with any one at his pleasure, or kill or release from prison whom he would, and in all respects be like a god among men. Then the actions of the just would be as the actions of the unjust; they would both tend to the same goal. And this we may truly affirm to be a great proof that a man is just, not willingly or because he thinks that justice is any good to him individually, but of necessity; for wherever anyone thinks that he can safely be unjust, there he is unjust. For all men believe in their hearts that injustice is far more profitable to the individual than justice and he who argues as I have been supposing will say that they are right. If you could imagine anyone obtaining this power of becoming invisible, and never doing any wrong or touching what was another's, he would be thought by the lookers-on to be an unhappy man and a fool, although they would praise him to one another's faces, and keep up appearances with one another from a fear that they too might suffer injustice. Enough of this.

Now, if we are to form a real judgement of the two lives in these respects, we must set apart the extremes of justice and injustice; there is no other way; and how is the contrast to be effected? I answer: Let the unjust man be entirely unjust, and the just man entirely just; nothing is to be taken away from either of them, and both are to be perfectly furnished for the work of their respective lives. First, let the unjust be like other distinguished masters of craft; like the skilful pilot or physician, who knows intuitively what is possible or impossible in his art and keeps within those limits, and who, if he fails at any point, is able to recover himself. So let the unjust man attempt to do the right sort of wrongs, and let him escape detection if he is to be pronounced a master of injustice. To be found out is a sign of incompetence; for the height of injustice is to be deemed just when you are not. Therefore I say that in the perfectly unjust man we must assume the most perfect injustice; there is to be no deduction, but we must allow him, while doing the most unjust acts, to have acquired the greatest reputation for justice. If he has taken a false step he must be able to recover himself; he must be one who can speak with effect, if any of his deeds come to light, and who can force his way where force is required, by his courage and strength and command of wealth and friends. And at his side let us place the just man in his nobleness and simplicity, wishing, as Aeschylus says, to be and not to seem good. There must be no seeming, for if he seems to be just he will be honoured and rewarded, and then we shall not know whether he is just for the sake of justice or for the sake of honours and rewards; therefore, let him be clothed in justice only, and have no other covering; and he must be imagined in a state of life the opposite of the former. Let him be the best of men, and let him be reputed the worst; then he will have been put to the test and we shall see whether his justice is proof against evil reputation and its consequences. And let him continue thus to the hour of death; being just and seeming to be unjust. When both have reached the uttermost extreme, the one of justice and the other of injustice, let judgement be given which of them is the happier of the two.

Socrates: Heavens! my dear Glaucon . . . how energetically you polish them up for the decision, first one and then the other, as if they were two statues.

DISCUSSION

The distinction between virtue and prudence will be one of the central distinctions in all of ethics. Being virtuous—acting justly, for example—means acting according to an impersonal ideal that is not of one's own makng, as opposed to acting prudentially for the sake of one's own personal interests. The two are often in agreement, of course; indeed, it is part of Plato's (Socrates's) argument in *The Republic* that virtue and happiness are inextricably interwoven. The myth of Gyges is the extreme illustration of pure prudence —we would say "selfishness"—devoid of any concern for justice whatever. Glaucon uses this story to make his point that justice and individual happiness are quite distinct, to which Socrates will reply that justice must be understood in terms of an entire society, not just as a single isolated individual.

The argument here is that, although we can imagine an isolated case in which a perfectly wicked man might be quite happy and a perfectly good man utterly miserable, the case to be made for justice cannot be based upon two such unusual—if not implausible—examples. (It is very difficult to be perfectly wicked; indeed, it is as hard as it is to be perfectly good.) The argument for justice must be a *general* argument, and in the rest of Book II Socrates shifts the terms from the image of a single person who is just or unjust to the question of what it is for the whole society to be just. Again, this is a form of argument which we will see in different guises throughout the history of ethics: the move from individual, personal concerns to more general, impersonal considerations. Why should we be just? Not because, in each individual case, it will necessarily make us happier but rather because—thinking prudentially—if we want to live in a livable society in which we will all be happier in general, justice is better than injustice. But Socrates will introduce another argument, which is not a prudential argument but what we will later call a "moral" consideration. (Plato does not use this concept.) This is the insistence that a "noble" person will be just for justice's sake and not because of the usual rewards of having a good reputation. But it is notable that Plato does not make much of this distinction, except to acknowledge it as a possibility; for him, justice and well-being go hand in hand, and Socrates criticizes Glaucon precisely for artificially forcing them apart ("polish(ing) them . . . as if they were two statues").

2. "THE MYTH OF THE CAVE"

Socrates: And now, let me show in a figure how far our nature is enlightened or unenlightened:—Behold! human beings housed in an underground cave, which has a long entrance open towards the light and as wide as the interior of the cave; here they have been from their childhood, and have their legs and necks chained, so that they cannot move and can only see before them, being

From *The Republic* by Plato. Translated by Benjamin Jowett (1892).

prevented by the chains from turning round their heads. Above and behind them a fire is blazing at a distance, and between the fire and the prisoners there is a raised way; and you will see, if you look, a low wall built along the way, like the screen which marionette players have in front of them, over which they show the puppets.

Glaucon: I see.

Soc: And do you see, men passing along the wall carrying all sorts of vessels, and statues and figures of animals made of wood and stone and various materials, which appear over the wall? While carrying their burdens, some of them, as you would expect, are talking, others silent.

Gl: You have shown me a strange image, and they are strange prisoners.

Soc: Like ourselves; for in the first place do you think they have seen anything of themselves, and of one another, except the shadows which the fire throws on the opposite wall of the cave?

Gl: How could they do so, if throughout their lives they were never allowed to move their heads?

Soc: And of the objects which are being carried in like manner they would only see the shadows?

Gl: Yes.

Soc And if they were able to converse with one another, would they not suppose that the things they saw were the real things?

Gl: Very true.

Soc: And suppose further that the prison had an echo which came from the other side, would they not be sure to fancy when one of the passers-by spoke that the voice which they heard came from the passing shadow?

Gl: No question.

Soc: To them, the truth would be literally nothing but the shadows of the images.

Gl: That is certain.

Soc: And now look again, and see in what manner they would be released from their bonds, and cured of their error, whether the process would naturally be as follows. At first, when any of them is liberated and compelled suddenly to stand up and turn his neck round and walk and look towards the light, he will suffer sharp pains; the glare will distress him, and he will be unable to see the realities of which in his former state he had seen the shadows; and then conceive someone saying to him that what he saw before was an illusion, but that now, when he is approaching nearer to being and his eye is turned towards more real existence, he has a clearer vision,—what will be his reply? And you may further imagine that his instructor is pointing to the objects as they pass and requiring him to name them,—will he not be perplexed? Will he not fancy that the shadows which he formerly saw are truer than the objects which are now shown to him?

Gl: Far truer.

Soc: And if he is compelled to look straight at the light, will he not have a pain in his eyes which will make him turn away to take refuge in the objects of vision which he can see, and which he will conceive to be in reality clearer than the things which are now being shown to him?

Gl: True.

Soc: And suppose once more, that he is reluctantly dragged up that steep and rugged ascent, and held fast until he is forced into the presence of the sun himself, is he not likely to be pained and irritated? When he approaches the light his eyes will be dazzled, and he will not be able to see anything at all of what are now called realities.

Gl: Not all in a moment.

Soc: He will require to grow accustomed to the sight of the upper world. And first he will see the shadows best, next the reflections of men and other objects in the water, and then the objects themselves; and when he turned to the heavenly bodies and the heaven itself, he would find it easier to gaze upon the light of the moon and the stars at night than to see the sun or the light of the sun by day?

Gl: Certainly.

Soc: Last of all he will be able to see the sun, not turning aside to the illusory reflections of him in the water, but gazing directly at him in his own proper place, and contemplating him as he is.

Gl: Certainly.

Soc: He will then proceed to argue that this is he who gives the seasons and the years, and is the guardian of all that is in the visible world, and in a certain way the cause of all things which he and his fellows have been accustomed to behold?

Gl: Clearly, he would arrive at this conclusion after what he had seen.

Soc: And when he remembered his old habitation, and the wisdom of the cave and his fellow-prisoners, do you not suppose that he would felicitate himself on the change, and pity them?

Gl: Certainly, he would.

Soc: And if they were in the habit of conferring honours among themselves on those who were quickest to observe the passing shadows and to remark which of them went before and which followed after and which were together, and who were best able from these observations to divine the future, do you think that he would be eager for such honours and glories, or envy those who attained honour and sovereignty among those men? Would he not say with Homer,

'Better to be a serf, labouring for a landless master',

and to endure anything, rather than think as they do and live after their manner?

Gl: Yes, I think that he would consent to suffer anything rather than live in this miserable manner.

Soc: Imagine once more such a one coming down suddenly out of the sunlight, and being replaced in his old seat; would he not be certain to have his eyes full of darkness?

Gl: To be sure.

Soc: And if there were a contest, and he had to compete in measuring the shadows with the prisoners who had never moved out of the cave, while his sight was still weak, and before his eyes had become steady (and the time which would be needed to acquire this new habit of sight might be very considerable), would he not make himself ridiculous? Men would say of him that he had returned from the place above with his eyes ruined; and that it was better not even to think of ascending; and if anyone tried to loose another and lead him up to the light, let them only catch the offender, and they would put him to death.

Gl: No question.

Soc: This entire allegory, you may now append, dear Glaucon, to the previous argument; the prison-house is the world of sight, the light of the fire is the power of the sun, and you will not misapprehend me if you interpret the journey upwards to be the ascent of the soul into the intellectual world according to my surmise, which, at your desire, I have expressed—whether rightly or wrongly God knows. But, whether true or false, my opinion is that in the world of knowledge the Idea of good appears last of all, and is seen only with an effort; although when seen, it is inferred to be the universal author of all things beautiful and right, parent of light and of the lord of light in the visible world, and the immediate and supreme source of reason and truth in the intellectual; and that this is the power upon which he who would act rationally either in public or private life must have his eye fixed.

Gl: I agree, as far as I am able to understand you.

Soc: Moreover, you must agree once more, and not wonder that those who attain to this vision are unwilling to take any part in human affairs; for their souls are ever hastening into the upper world where they desire to dwell; which desire of theirs is very natural, if our allegory may be trusted.

Gl: Yes, very natural.

Soc: And is there anything surprising in one who passes from divine contemplations to the evil state of man, appearing grotesque and ridiculous; if, while his eyes are blinking and before he has become accustomed to the surrounding darkness, he is compelled to fight in courts of law, or in other places, about the images or the shadows of images of justice, and must strive against some rival about opinions of these things which are entertained by men who have never yet seen the true justice?

Gl: Anything but surprising.

Soc: Anyone who has common sense will remember that the bewilderments of the eyes are of two kinds and arise from two causes, either from coming out of the light or from going into the light, and, judging that the soul may be affected in the same way, will not give way to foolish laughter when he sees anyone whose vision is perplexed and weak; he will first ask whether that soul of man has come out of the brighter life and is unable to see because unaccustomed to the dark, or having turned from darkness to the day is dazzled by excess of light. And he will count the one happy in his condition and state of being, and he will pity the other; or, if he have a mind to laugh at the soul which comes from below into the light, this laughter will not be quite so laughable as that which greets the soul which returns from above out of the light into the cave.

Gl: That is a very just distinction.

Soc: But then, if I am right, certain professors of education must be wrong when they say that they can put a knowledge into the soul which was not there before, like sight into blind eyes.

Gl: They undoubtedly say this.

Soc: Whereas our argument shows that the power and capacity of learning exists in the soul already; and that just as if it were not possible to turn the eye from darkness to light without the whole body, so too the instrument of knowledge can only by the movement of the whole soul be turned from the world of becoming to that of being, and learn by degrees to endure the sight of being, and of the brightest and best of being, or in other words, of the good.

Gl: Very true.

DISCUSSION

In the "Myth of the Cave" and in his theory of "Ideas" or "the Forms," Plato provides us with a spectacular answer to some of the most troubling and perennial problems in philosophy. One of the central questions of metaethics might simply be stated, What does the word "good" mean? There are various answers, some of them more or less "objective" (that is, that goodness is a property of the "object" itself). Others are more "subjective" (that is, that it is the attitude of the person who calls something good that makes it good). Advocates of the latter, more subjective position often argue that the word "good" is a sign of approval or recommendation (for example, "I approve of this and you should too"). Advocates of the more objective position insist that goodness is a real property of the object, whether or not it is recognized by any number of subjects. The disadvantage of the former position is that it leaves us with no way of finding out what is really good, except perhaps by way of consensus and what people agree is good. The difficulty of the latter theory is trying to describe this property of "goodness." It is here that Plato's theory enters the picture.

Plato's theory of Ideas or the Forms is even more than an objective theory. Not only is the property goodness a real property of the object, goodness is an object itself, an ideal object which is even more real than the things that are good. Why does Plato believe this? First of all, he firmly believes that goodness is objective and not dependent on individuals or social consensus. He utterly rejects Protagoras, in other words, who insists that "man is the measure of all things." But not only this, Plato also realizes that, if goodness is to be a real property of things, then it must have a definable set of characteristics, like other real properties. An animal has the property of being a dog, for example, because it has certain characteristics—four legs, fur, teeth, it barks, and so on. So too all good things have something in common, but what would this be? Could it be a simple property, like redness? But what simple such property would all good things have in common? A good paperweight is heavy; a good crepe is light. Don't we have to say that goodness is a different property in different good things, depending on the kind of things that they are? Plato doesn't think so. Indeed, his theory is that, if all good things didn't share some property in common, then we would have no right calling them all "good."

This property is participation in the Good; it is not a property of things but an Idea or Form which good things "imitate." The reasons behind Plato's metaphysical speculations on the independent reality of such Ideas or Forms are beyond the scope of ethics, but the basic principle is clear enough: if good things are really good, and if they all deserve to be called by the same name, then they must have something in common, namely, that they all resemble the Idea of the Good. The "Myth of the Cave" is Plato's extremely dramatic way of suggesting to us the existence of an ideal world other than our own imperfect world—a vision that would later influence the development of Christianity. But the theory behind the myth is based on a metaethical concern—to try to account for our use of the word "good" and to explain how it is that we can call so many things good, including, not least, the good man and the good life for man.

STUDY QUESTIONS

1 What is the argument in "The Ring of Gyges"? How would you answer Glaucon?

2 What are Socrates's arguments against running away and for staying to be executed? Are they convincing arguments? What kinds of reasons appear in these arguments (for example, Crito's appeal to the good times that Socrates will still have if he lives)?

3 Does being born and staying and living in a community give a person an absolute obligation to obey the laws of that community?

4 What is wrong with the concept of justice which says, in effect, "might makes right"? Why is it not just that a person should get what he or she can, without further qualificatiion or restrictions?

5 Is being good simply obeying the law? Why or why not?

6 Why does Socrates (Plato) introduce the idea of the Form of the Good (and Justice) in his argument? Why not restrict attention to actual good acts? What philosophical power does the introduction of the Forms give the Socratic argument? What alternative positions is Socrates (Plato) attempting to cut off?

7 What does Plato's "Myth of the Cave" represent? What is the cave? What are the Sun and the Shadows? What is it that will allow us to "see the light," in more literal terms?

8 Define the word "good." Now take the role of Socrates and criticize your own definition. In what ways is it too broad? In what ways too narrow? Try again. (Then try the same with "justice.")

CHAPTER 2

ARISTOTLE

Aristotle was a student in Plato's academy, and, not surprisingly, his ethical philosophy is deeply indebted to his mentor. But, like all good philosophy students, Aristotle disagreed with his teacher almost as much as he agreed with him, and the difference in style as well as in substance between them is enormous. Plato's Socratic dialogues are literary as well as philosophical masterpieces, dramatic plays which could be performed as well as studied. Aristotle, on the other hand, wrote ponderous and technical philosophical treatises, brilliant but—unlike the Platonic dialogues—not much fun to read. (Actually, this is misleading; Aristotle supposedly wrote dialogues too, but none of them have ever been found.) Many of Plato's (Socrates's) ethical investigations, furthermore, were mainly concerned with the most metaethical questions, the definition of the Good and Justice and the structure of the ideal society (namely, the republic). Aristotle, on the other hand, was more interested in the details of everyday normative ethics—how a good person should behave and what goes wrong when someone knows what should be done but doesn't do it (or knows what should not be done and does it anyway.) *The Nicomachean Ethics* covers the entire spectrum of ethical issues, from the most general metaethical concerns about the nature of the Good to the most specific questions about the value of certain emotions (pride, for example) and the way one ought to act toward friends. Indeed, there has probably never been a book more complete on the subject of ethics than Aristotle's *Ethics*. (In fact Aristotle wrote at least two treatises in ethics. The "Nicomachean" treatise—edited by Aristotle's son Nicomachus and later named for him—is by far the better known. The other treatise, the "Eudemian Ethics" differs in some significant ways from *The Nicomachean Ethics,* but these differences will not concern us here and we will simply refer to the better-known treatise as the *Ethics.*[1])

---

[1] See Anthony Kenny, *The Aristotelian Ethics* (Oxford, 1978).

The stated purpose of the *Ethics* is to describe "the good for man." The emphasis on description here is extremely important, for Aristotle often appeals his views to "what most men think" and begins a point by saying "all agree that. . . ." (This too was a major difference between Aristotle and Socrates/Plato, who refused to concern themselves with common opinion.) Aristotle's *Ethics* is not just an ethical theory but a detailed description of an *ethos*—life and attitudes in Athens in the fourth century B.C. As a self-satisfied description of his society, Aristotle's *Ethics* is less involved than many modern ethical treatises in the justification of the values and institutions described. It seemed sufficient to simply describe them, for their virtues seemed to speak for themselves. [In Aristotle's *Politics* many modern readers have been deeply offended that he matter-of-factly introduces slavery as an institution essential to the just society, with only the most minimal and obviously unsatisfactory (to us) arguments.]

The effort to describe "the good for man" also points to a very different emphasis in Aristotle (from what we saw in Plato); whereas Plato was most concerned with the Good and "the laws" and Justice, Aristotle always bases his arguments on human interests and what he describes as "the function of man." (The term "man" here is *not* used in the innocent grammatical sense covering both men and women. Aristotle intended his ethics to apply literally to men, but in thinking through his viewpoint in our own terms, we can apply most of his descriptions just as well to modern women.) The emphasis on *function* is typical of Aristotle's overall biological view of the world; he was also an accomplished scientist who was always asking, What is it *for?*—whether the organ in question was the tongue of an insect, the gills on a fish, or the mind of man. The philosopher's word for this biological way of thinking is *teleology* (from the Greek word for "purpose," *telos*) and the overall framework of Aristotle's ethics is distinctively teleological. All ethical questions are appealed to this concept of the function—or purpose—of human existance.

In the first book of the *Ethics,* Aristotle makes the general point that the Good must be the good for man, which in turn means that toward which all human activities ultimately aim. This ultimate good (or *summum bonum*) has a name—we call it "happiness," or in Greek, *eudaimonia.* (A more literal translation of the Greek word, however, would be "doing well," with an emphasis on activity and accomplishment rather than a mere feeling of contentment or satisfaction.) But this is only a name, Aristotle points out, and people are not in agreement as to what kind of life is most happy. Some say happiness is wealth, some say it is pleasure, and some say it is honor, but Aristotle rejects all of these. The function of man, he argues—what makes him biologically unique among the animals—is *reason,* and therefore—according to the teleological viewpoint that dominates the *Ethics*— the good for man (or *eudaimonia*) must be the life of reason. But whereas we might think that the life of reason is a sedentary academic life—just sitting around thinking about Truth and Beauty and the Good—Aristotle is quite clear that the rational life is also the active life, the life of "rational activity." Thus one of the central concepts of Aristotle's *Ethics*—the concept of *virtue*—is defined simply as "rational activity, activity in accordance with a rational principle." A man with courage, according to Aristotle, is not only braver but also more rational than a coward.

In subsequent books of the *Ethics,* Aristotle goes on to describe the central concepts of happiness *(eudaimonia)* and virtue *(arete)* and to list and describe the various virtues. He also spends considerable effort attacking the hedonist who argues that the good for man is pleasure and analyzing various pitfalls that plague our attempts to be good. Two full books are devoted to describing the virtues of friendship—an emphasis lacking in many ethical treatises that should make us stop and think about the usual neglect of this very important part of life. ("No one would choose to live without friends," he says.)

Because of the complexity and difficulty of the material which follows, we will frequently interrupt the flow of the text with notes and reference guides.

ARISTOTLE

Aristotle was born in 384 B.C. in northern Greece (in Stagira). His father was the physician to the king (Philip of Macedonia), and Aristotle later became tutor to Philip's son Alexander (later to become Alexander the Great). Aristotle studied with Plato for eighteen years, but when Plato died, Aristotle turned much more to the sciences—biology in particular—and his various theories ruled western science for almost two thousand years. He set up his own school in Athens; but, when Alexander died and his empire started to fall apart, anti-Macedonian feeling in Athens was such that Aristotle beat a hasty retreat, supposedly remarking that the Athenians would not have a second chance to sin against philosophy.

A. The Goal of Human Activity

Aristotle begins his *Ethics* by clearly stating his teleological premise: everything aims at some good, and there must be some ultimate good. Notice that, for Aristotle, ethics and politics are part of the same discipline, and the good of the individual and the good of the society (the state) go hand in hand.

BOOK I

1. Every art and every kind of inquiry, and likewise every act and purpose, seems to aim at some good; and so it has been well said that the good is that at which everything aims. But a difference is observable among these aims or ends. What is aimed at is sometimes the exercise of a faculty, sometimes a certain result beyond that exercise. And where there is an end beyond that act, there the result is better than the exercise of the faculty. Now since there are many kinds of actions and many arts and sciences, it follows that there are many ends also; *e.g.* health is the end of medicine, ships of shipbuilding, victory of the art of war, and wealth of economy. But when several of these are subordinated to some one art or science,—as the making of bridles and other trappings to the art of horsemanship, and this in turn, along with all else that the soldier does, to the art of war, and so on,—then the end of the master art is always more desired than the end of the subordinate arts, since these are pursued for its sake. And this is equally true whether the end in view be the mere exercise of a faculty or something beyond that, as in the above instances.

Aristotle, *The Nicomachean Ethics* translated by F. H. Peters, 8th edition (1901), with some revisions and changes in the paragraphing.

2. If then in what we do there be some end which we wish for on its own account, choosing all the others as means to this, but not every end without exception as a means to something else (for so we should go on *ad infinitum*, and desire would be left void and objectless),—this evidently will be the good or the best of all things. And surely from a practical point of view it much concerns us to know this good; for then, like archers shooting at a definite mark, we shall be more likely to attain what we want. If this be so, we must try to indicate roughly what it is, and first of all to which of the arts or sciences it belongs. It would seem to belong to the supreme art or science, that one which most of all deserves the name of master-art or master-science. Now Politics seems to this description. For it prescribes which of the sciences a state needs, and which each man shall study, and up to what point; and to it we see subordinated even the highest arts, such as economy, rhetoric, and the art of war. Since then it makes use of the other practical sciences, and since it further ordains what men are to do and from what to refrain, its end must include the ends of the others, and must be the proper good of man. For though this good is the same for the individual and the state, yet the good of the state seems a grander and more perfect thing both to attain and to secure; and glad as one would be to do this service for a single individual, to do it for a people and for a number of states is nobler and more divine.

This then is the aim of the present inquiry, which is a sort of political inquiry.

---

3. Aristotle now warns his readers:

1 Ethics cannot be an exact science. Good things may yet be harmful, and so we must not expect unqualified general principles about what is good.
2 Much of ethics has to do with "good judgment" *(phronesis)* which requires a good upbringing. It is no good trying to learn ethics if one does not already know, in some sense, what is good.
3 Young people (presumably college students) have not had enough experience in life to know what is good. Besides, they are too easily distracted by their desires and emotions. (The word "incontinent" means knowing what is right but not doing it.)

---

3. We must be content if we can attain to so much precision in our statement as the subject before us admits of; for the same degree of accuracy is no more to be expected in all kinds of reasoning than in all kinds of handicraft. Now the things that are noble and just (with which Politics deals) are so various and so uncertain, that some think these are merely conventional and not natural distinctions. There is a similar uncertainty also about what is good, because good things often do people harm: men have before now been ruined by wealth, and have lost their lives through courage. Our subject, then, and our data being of this nature, we must be content if we can indicate the truth roughly and in outline, and if, in dealing with matters that are not amenable to immutable laws, and reasoning from premises that are but probable, we can arrive at probable conclusions. The reader, on his part, should take each of my statements in the same spirit; for it is the mark of an educated man to require, in each kind of inquiry, just so much exactness as the subject admits of: it is equally absurd to

accept probable reasoning from a mathematician, and to demand scientific proof from an orator.

But each man can form a judgment about what he knows, and is called "a good judge" of that—of any special matter when he has received a special education therein, "a good judge" (without any qualifying epithet) when he has received a universal education. And hence a young man is not qualified to be a student of Politics; for he lacks experience of the affairs of life, which form the data and the subject-matter of Politics. Further, since he is apt to be swayed by his feelings, he will derive no benefit from a study whose aim is not speculative but practical. But in this respect young in character counts the same as young in years; for the young man's disqualification is not a matter of time, but is due to the fact that feeling rules his life and directs all his desires. Men of this character turn the knowledge they get to no account in practice, as we see with those we call incontinent; but those who direct their desires and actions by reason will gain much profit from the knowledge of these matters.

So much then by way of preface as to the student and the spirit in which he must accept what we say, and the object which we propose to ourselves.

---

4. Aristotle now returns to his main theme, the ultimate good. Everyone (the "masses" as well as "men of culture") agrees that it is happiness or *eudaimonia* (more accurately "doing or living well"). But most people ("the masses") take this happiness to be something very specific, such as pleasure, wealth, health, or fame, while the philosophers ("men of culture," mainly Plato) take the ultimate good to be something outside of human life (Plato's Form of the Good). After a brief poetic digression, Aristotle then looks at three examples of the good life, two of which he rejects (pleasure and honor); the third, the life of contemplation (living as a philosopher)—which he accepts— he postpones for future discussion. He then takes a fast slap at the idea that the good life means making a lot of money (money is only a means to something else, never an end in itself) and spends a few paragraphs politely (more or less) attacking Plato's idea that the Good is something outside of ordinary human life, a Form or Idea which all good things share. Aristotle rejects this in favor of his own teleological approach, which looks for the good in the goals of things, in what they are and what they try to be.

---

4. Since—to resume—all knowledge and all purpose aims at some good, what is this which we say is the aim of Politics; or, in other words, what is the highest of all realizable goods? As to its name, I suppose nearly all men are agreed; for the masses and the men of culture alike declare that it is happiness, and hold that to "live well" or to "do well" is the same as to be "happy." But they differ as to what this happiness is, and the masses do not give the same account of it as the philosophers. The former take it to be something palpable and plain, as pleasure or wealth or fame; one man holds it to be this, and another that, and often the same man is of different minds at different times,—after sickness it is health, and in poverty it is wealth; while when they are impressed with the consciousness of their ignorance, they admire most those who say grand things that are above their comprehension. Some philosophers, on the other hand, have thought that, beside these several good things, there is an "absolute" good which is the cause of their goodness. As it would hardly be worth while to review all the opinions

that have been held, we will confine ourselves to those which are most popular, or which seem to have some foundation in reason.

But we must not omit to notice the distinction that is drawn between the method of proceeding from your starting-points or principles, and the method of working up to them. Plato used with fitness to raise this question, and to ask whether the right way is from or to your starting-points, as in the race-course you may run from the judges to the boundary, or *vice versa*. Well, we must start from what is known. But "what is known" may mean two things: "what is known to us," which is one thing, or "what is known" simply, which is another. I think it is safe to say that *we* must start from what is known to *us*. And on this account nothing but a good moral training can qualify a man to study what is noble and just—in a word, to study questions of Politics. For the undemonstrated fact is here the starting-point, and if this undemonstrated fact be sufficiently evident to a man, he will not require a "reason why." Now the man who has had a good moral training either has already arrived at starting-points or principles of action, or will easily accept them when pointed out. But he who neither has them nor will accept them may hear what Hesiod says—

The best is he who of himself doth know;
Good too is he who listens to the wise;
But he who neither knows himself nor heeds
The words of others, is a useless man.

5. Aristotle again returns to his main point, having digressed once more. (Remember that these were originally lectures, not written down as a book,) What is happiness? It is to be found in terms of the function of man, that is, the ultimate end which is not just one good thing among others but the goal of all good things in life. Here Aristotle's biological teleology is fully evident: our function cannot be simply "to live," for this we share even with plants. It cannot be just to move around and experience the world, for even cows can do this. The one thing that is uniquely human (and note that our function must be unique in this sense) is our reason. Our function, then, is to be rational. This does not exclude other human activities, such as physical prowess, nor does it exclude pleasure (more on this later); indeed, Aristotle is even willing to insist that a person can't be happy without being (by his standards) relatively rich, and also good-looking and born into an aristocratic family. But all of this is not yet happiness, though these are the preconditions of happiness. One of the most substantial differences between Aristotle's ethics and what most of us believe is his unabashed *elitism;* happiness is not for everyone, but only for the lucky few.

5. It seems that men not unreasonably take their notions of the good or happiness from the lives actually led, and that the masses who are the least refined suppose it to be pleasure, which is the reason why they aim at nothing higher than the life of enjoyment. For the most conspicuous kinds of life are three: this life of enjoyment, the life of the statesman, and, thirdly, the contemplative life. The mass of men show themselves utterly slavish in their preference for the life of brute beasts, but their views receive consideration because many of those in high places have the tastes of Sardanapalus. Men of refinement with a practical turn prefer honour; for I suppose we may say that

honour is the aim of the statesman's life. But this seems too superficial to be the good we are seeking; for it appears to depend upon those who give rather than upon those who receive it; while we have a presentiment that the good is something that is peculiarly a man's own and can scarce be taken away from him. Moreover, these men seem to pursue honour in order that they may be assured of their own excellence,—at least, they wish to be honoured by men of sense, and by those who know them, and on the ground of their virtue or excellence. It is plain, then, that in their view, at any rate, virtue or excellence is better than honour; and perhaps we should take this to be the end of the statesman's life, rather than honour. But virtue or excellence also appears too incomplete to be what we want; for it seems that a man might have virtue and yet be asleep or be inactive all his life, and, moreover, might meet with the greatest disasters and misfortunes; and no one would maintain that such a man is happy, except for argument's sake. But we will not dwell on these matters now, for they are sufficiently discussed in the popular treatises. The third kind of life is the life of contemplation: we will treat of it further on. As for the money-making life, it is something quite contrary to nature; and wealth evidently is not the good of which we are in search, for it is merely useful as a means to something else. So we might rather take pleasure and virtue or excellence to be ends than wealth; for they are chosen on their own account. But it seems that not even they are the end, though much breath has been wasted in attempts to show that they are. . . .

7. Leaving these matters, then, let us return once more to the question, what this good can be of which we are in search. It seems to be different in different kinds of action and in different arts,—one thing in medicine and another in war, and so on. What then is the good in each of these cases? Surely that for the sake of which all else is done. And that in medicine is health, in war is victory, in building is a house,—a different thing in each different case, but always, in whatever we do and in whatever we choose, the end. For it is always for the sake of the end that all else is done. If then there be one end of all that man does, this end will be the realizable good,—or these ends, if there be more than one.

By this generalization our argument is brought to the same point as before. This point we must try to explain more clearly. We see that there are many ends. But some of these are chosen only as means, as wealth, flutes, and the whole class of instruments. And so it is plain that not all ends are final. But the best of all things must, we conceive, be something final. If then there be only one final end, this will be what we are seeking,—or if there be more than one, then the most final of them. Now that which is pursued as an end in itself is more final than that which is pursued as means to something else, and that which is never chosen as means than that which is chosen both as an end in itself and as means, and that is strictly final which is always chosen as an end in itself and never as means.

Happiness seems more than anything else to answer to this description: for we always choose it for itself, and never for the sake of something else; while honour and pleasure and reason, and all virtue or excellence, we choose partly indeed for themselves (for, apart from any result, we should choose each of them), but partly also for the sake of happiness, supposing that they will help to make us happy. But no one chooses happiness for the sake of these things, or as a means to anything else at all. We seem to be led to the same conclusion when we start from the notion of self-sufficiency. The final good is thought to be self-sufficing [or all-sufficing]. In applying this term we do not regard a man as an individual leading a solitary life, but we also take account of parents, children, wife, and, in short, friends and fellow-citizens generally, since man is naturally a social being. Some limit must indeed be set to this; for if you go on to parents and descendants and friends of friends, you will never come to a stop. But this we will consider further on: for the present we will take self-sufficing to mean what by itself makes life desirable and in want of nothing. And happiness is believed to answer to this description. And further, happiness is believed to be the most desirable thing in the world, and that not merely as one among other good things: if it were merely one among other good things [so that other things could be added to it], it is plain that the addition of the least of other goods must make it more desirable; for the addition becomes a surplus of good, and of two goods the greater is always more desirable. Thus it seems that happiness is something final and self-sufficing, and is the end of all that man does.

But perhaps the reader thinks that though no one will dispute the statement that happiness is the best thing in the world, yet a still more precise definition of it is needed. This will best be gained, I think, by asking, What is the function of man? For as the goodness and the excellence of a piper or a sculptor, or the practiser of any art, and generally of those who have any function or business to do, lies in that funciton, so man's good would seem to lie in his function, if he has one. But can we suppose that, while a carpenter and a cobbler has a function and a business of his own, man has no business and no function assigned him by nature? Nay, surely as his several members, eye and hand and foot, plainly have each his own function, so we must suppose that man also has some function over and above all these.

What then is it? Life evidently he has in common even with the plants, but we want that which is peculiar to him. We must exclude, therefore, the life of mere nutrition and growth. Next to this comes the life of sense; but this too he plainly shares with horses and cattle and all kinds of animals. There remains then the life whereby he acts—the life of his rational nature, with its two sides or divisions, one rational as obeying reason, the other rational as having and exercising reason. But as this expression is ambiguous, we must be understood to mean thereby the life that consists in the exercise [not the mere possession] of the faculties; for this seems to be more properly entitled to the name.

The function of man, then, is exercise of his vital faculties [or soul] on one side in obedience to reason, and on the other side with reason. But what is called the function of a man of any profession and the function of a man who is good in that profession are, generically the same, *e.g.* of a harper and of a good harper; and this holds in all cases without exception, only that in the case of the latter his superior excellence at his work is added; for we say a harper's function is to harp, and a good harper's to harp well. Man's function then being, as we say, a kind of life—that is to say, exercise of his faculties and action of various kinds with reason—the good man's function is to do this well and beautifully [or nobly]. But the function of anything is done well when it is done in accordance with the proper excellence of that thing. If this be so the result is that the good of man is exercise of his faculties in accordance with excellence or virtue, or, if there be more than one, in accordance with the best and most complete virtue. But there must also be a full term of years for this exercise; for one swallow or one fine day does not make a spring, nor does one day or any small space of time make a blessed or happy man.

This, then, may be taken as a rough outline of the good; for this, I think, is the proper method,—first to sketch the outline, and then to fill in the details. But it would seem that, the outline once fairly drawn, any one can carry on the work and fit in the several items which time reveals to us or helps us to find. And this indeed is the way in which the arts and sciences have grown; for it requires no extraordinary genius to fill up the gaps. We must bear in mind, however, what was said above, and not demand the same degree of accuracy in all branches of study, but in each case so much as the subject-matter admits of and as is proper to that kind of inquiry. The carpenter and the geometer both look for the right angle, but in different ways: the former only wants such an approximation to it as his work requires, but the latter wants to know what constitutes a right angle, or what is its special quality; his aim is to find out the truth. And so in other cases we must follow the same course, lest we spend more time on what is immaterial than on the real business in hand. Nor must we in all cases alike demand the reason why; sometimes it is enough if the undemonstrated fact be fairly pointed out, as in the case of the starting–points or principles of a science. Undemonstrated facts always form the first step or starting–point of a science; and these starting–points or principles are arrived at some in one way, some in another—some by induction, others by perception, others again by some kind of training. But in each case we must try to apprehend them in the proper way, and do our best to define them clearly; for they have great influence upon the subsequent course of an inquiry. A good start is more than half the race, I think, and our starting–point of principle, once found, clears up a num–ber of our difficulties.

8. We must not be satisfied, then, with examining this starting-point or principle of ours as a conclusion from our data, but must also view it in its relation to current opinions on the subject; for all experience harmonizes with a true principle, but a false one is soon found to be incompatible with the facts. Now, good things have been divided into three classes, external goods on the one hand, and on the other goods of the soul and goods of the body; and the goods of the soul are commonly said to be goods in the fullest sense, and more good than any other. But "actions and exercises of the vital faculties may be said to be of the soul." So our account is confirmed by this opinion, which is both of

long standing and approved by all who busy themselves with philosophy. But, indeed, we secure the support of this opinion by the mere statement that certain actions and exercises are the end; for this implies that it is to be ranked among the goods of the soul, and not among external goods. Our account, again, is in harmony with the common saying that the happy man lives well and does well; for we may say that happiness, according to us, is living well and doing well. And, indeed, all the characteristics that men expect to find in happiness seem to belong to happiness as we define it. Some hold it to be virtue or excellence, some prudence, others a kind of wisdom; others, again, held it to be all or some of these, with the addition of pleasure, either as an ingredient or as a necessary accompaniment; and some even include external prosperity in their account of it. Now, some of these views have the support of many voices and of old authority; others have few voices, but those of weight; but it is probable that neither the one side nor the other is entirely wrong, but that in some one point at least, if not in most, they are both right.

First, then, the view that happiness is excellence or a kind of excellence harmonizes with our account; for "excercise of faculties in accordance with excellence" belongs to excellence. But I think we may say that it makes no small difference whether the good be conceived as the mere possession of something, or as its use—as a mere habit or trained faculty, or as the exercise of that faculty. For the habit or faculty may be present, and yet issue in no good result, as when a man is asleep, or in any other way hindered from his function; but with its exercise this is not possible, for it must show itself in acts and in good acts. And as at the Olympic games it is not the fairest and strongest who receive the crown, but those who contend (for among these are the victors), so in life, too, the winners are those who not only have all the excellences, but manifest these in deed.

And, further, the life of these men is in itself pleasant. For pleasure is an affection of the soul, and each man takes pleasure in that which he is said to love,—he who loves horses in horses, he who loves sight-seeing in sight-seeing, and in the same way he who loves justice in acts of justice, and generally the lover of excellence or virtue in virtuous acts or the manifestation of excellence. And while with most men there is a perpetual conflict between the several things in which they find pleasure, since these are not naturally pleasant, those who love what is noble take pleasure in that which is naturally pleasant. For the manifestations of excellence are naturally pleasant, so that they are both pleasant to them and pleasant in themselves. Their life, then, does not need pleasure to be added to it as an appendage, but contains pleasure in itself.

Indeed, in addition to what we have said, a man is not good at all unless he takes pleasure in noble deeds. No one would call a man just who did not take pleasure in doing justice, nor generous who took no pleasure in acts of generosity, and so on. If this be so, the manifestations of excellence will be pleasant in themselves. But they are also both good and noble, and that in the highest degree—at least, if the good man's judgment about them is right, for this is his judgment. Happiness, then, is at once the best and noblest and pleasantest thing in the world, and these are not separated, as the Delian inscription would have them to be:

What is most just is noblest, health is best,
Pleasantest is to get your heart's desire.

For all these characteristics are united in the best exercises of our faculties; and these, or some one of them that is better than all the others, we identify with happiness.

But nevertheless happiness plainly requires external goods too, as we said; for it is impossible, or at least not easy, to act nobly without some furniture of fortune. There are many things that can only be done through instruments, so to speak, such as friends and wealth and political influence: and there are some things whose absence takes the bloom off our happiness, as good birth, the blessing of children, personal beauty; for a man is not very likely to be happy if he is very ugly in person, or of low birth, or alone in the world, or childless, and perhaps still less if he has worthless children or friends, or has lost good ones that he had. As we said, then, happiness seems to stand in need of this kind of prosperity; and so some identify it with good fortune, just as others identify it with excellence.

---

9. Plato had asked (in his dialogue *Meno*) whether virtue and happiness should be learned by way of principles or rather engrained in children as a habit or perhaps granted by the gods. Aristotle sidesteps the question but insists again that happiness presupposes a good upbringing and a "good character," but it also requires understanding and reason. (Thus no animal is ever happy, in Aristotle's sense, and children are happy only in the sense that we hope that they will do well as adults.)

---

9. This has led people to ask whether happiness is attained by learning, or the formation of habits, or any other kind of training, or comes by some divine dispensation or even by chance. Well, if the Gods do give gifts to men, happiness is likely to be among the number, more likely, indeed, than anything else, in proportion as it is better than all other human things. This belongs more properly to another branch of inquiry; but we may say that even if it is not heaven-sent, but comes as a consequence of virtue or some kind of learning or training, still it seems to be one of the most divine things in the world; for the prize and aim of virtue would appear to be better than anything else and something divine and blessed. Again, if it is thus acquired it will be widely accessible; for it will then be in the power of all except those who have lost the capacity for excellence to acquire it by study and diligence. And if it be better that men should attain happiness in this way rather than by chance, it is reasonable to suppose that it is so, since in the sphere of nature all things are arranged in the best possible way, and likewise in the sphere of art, and of each mode of causation, and most of all in the sphere of the noblest mode of causation. And indeed it would be too absurd to leave what is noblest and fairest to the dispensation of chance.

But our definition itself clears up the difficulty; for happiness was defined as a certain kind of exercise of the vital faculties in accordance with excellence or virtue. And of the remaining goods [other than happiness itself], some must be present as necessary conditions, while others are aids and useful instruments to happiness. And this agrees with what we said at starting. We then laid down that the end of the art political is the best of all ends; but the chief business of that art is to make the citizens of a certain character—that is, good and apt to do what is noble. It is not without reason, then, that we do not call an ox, or a horse, or any brute happy; for none of them is able to share in this kind of activity. For the same reason also a child is not happy; he is as yet, because of his age, unable to do such things. If we ever call a child happy, it is because we hope he will do them. For, as we said, happiness requires not only perfect excellence or virtue, but also a full term of years for its exercise. For our circumstances are liable to many changes and to all sorts of chances, and it is possible that he who is now most prosperous will in his old age meet with great disasters, as is told of Priam in the tales of Troy; and a man who is thus used by fortune and comes to a miserable end cannot be called happy.

---

10. We tend to think of happiness as a feeling or sense of contentment. For Aristotle, it is "doing well," and not just for a while (one's freshman year of college) but for a whole lifetime. Indeed, the insistence that one can be happy only after having lived a full life leads Aristotle to a curious question which would not even make sense to our more fleeting sense of happiness:

---

10. Are we, then, to call no man happy as long as he lives, but to wait for the end, as Solon said? And, supposing we have to allow this, do we mean that he actually is happy after he is dead? Surely that is absurd, especially for us who say that happiness is a kind of activity or life. But if we do not call the dead man happy, and if Solon meant not this, but that only then could we safely apply the term to a man, as being now beyond the reach of evil and calamity, then here too we find some ground for objection. For it is thought that both good and evil may in some sort befall a dead man (just as they may befall a living man, although he is unconscious of them), *e.g.* honours rendered to him, or the reverse of these, and again the prosperity or the misfortune of his children and all his descendants. But this, too, has its difficulties; for after a man has lived happily to a good old age, and ended as he lived, it is possible that many changes may befall him in the persons of his descendants, and that some of them may turn out good and meet with the good fortune they deserve, and others the reverse. It is evident too that the degree in which the descendants are related to their ancestors may vary to any extent. And it would be a strange thing if the dead man were to change with these changes and become happy and miserable by turns. But it would also be strange to suppose that the dead are not affected at all, even for a limited time, by the fortunes of their posterity.

But let us return to our former question; for its solution will, perhaps, clear up this other difficulty. The saying of Solon may mean that we ought to look for the end and then call a man happy, not because he now is, but because he once was happy. But surely it is strange that when he is happy we should refuse to say what is true of him, because we do not like to apply the term to living men in view of the changes to which they are liable, and because we hold happiness to be something that endures and is little liable to change, while the fortunes of one and the same man often undergo many revolutions: for, it is argued, it is plain that, if we follow the changes of fortune, we shall call the same man happy and miserable many times over, making the happy man "a sort of chameleon and one who rests on no sound foundation." We reply that it cannot be right thus to follow fortune. For it is not in this that our weal or woe lies; but, as we said, though good fortune is needed to complete man's life, yet it is the excellent employment of his powers that constitutes his happiness, as the reverse of this constitutes his misery.

But the discussion of this difficulty leads to a further confirmation of our account. For nothing human is so constant as the excellent exercise of our faculties. The sciences themselves seem to be less abiding. And the highest of these exercises are the most abiding, because the happy are occupied with them most of all and most continuously (for this seems to be the reason why we do not forget how to do them). The happy man, then, as we define him, will have this required property of permanence, and all through life will preserve his character; for he will be occupied continually, or with the least possible interruption, in excellent deeds and excellent speculations; and, whatever his fortune be, he will take it in the noblest fashion, and bear himself always and in all things suitably, since he is truly good and "foursquare without a flaw."

But the dispensations of fortune are many, some great, some small. The small ones, whether good or evil, plainly are of no weight in the scale; but the great ones, when numerous, will make life happier if they be good; for they help to give a grace to life themselves, and their use is noble and good; but, if they be evil, will enfeeble and spoil happiness; for they bring pain, and often impede the exercise of our faculties. But nevertheless true worth shines out even here, in the calm endurance of many great misfortunes, not through insensibility, but through nobility and greatness of soul. And if it is what a man does that determines the character of his life, as we said, then no happy man will become miserable; for he will never do what is hateful and base. For we hold that the man who is truly good and wise will bear with dignity whatever fortune sends, and will always make the best of his circumstances, as a good general will turn the forces at his command to the best account, and a good shoemaker will make the best shoe that can be made out of a given piece of leather, and so on with all other crafts. If this be so, the happy man will never become miserable, though he will not be truly happy if he meets with the fate of Priam.

But yet he is not unstable and lightly changed: he will not be moved from his happiness easily, nor by any ordinary misfortunes, but only by many heavy ones; and after such, he will not recover his happiness again in a short time, but if at all, only in a considerable period, which has a certain completeness, and in which he attains to great and noble things.

We shall meet all objections, then, if we say that a happy man is "one who exercises his faculties in accordance with perfect excellence, being duly furnished with external goods, not for any chance time, but for a full term of years": to which perhaps we should add, "and who shall continue to live so, and shall die as he lived," since the future is veiled to us, but happiness we take to be the end and in all ways perfectly final or complete. If this be so, we may say that those living men are blessed or perfectly happy who both have and shall continue to have these characteristics, but happy as men only.

11. Passing now from this question to that of the fortunes of descendants and of friends generally, the doctrine that they do not affect the departed at all seems too cold and too much opposed to popular opinion. But as the things that happen to them are many and differ in all sorts of ways, and some come home to them more and some less, so that to discuss them all separately would be a long, indeed an endless task, it will perhaps be enough to speak of them in general terms and in outline merely. Now, as of the misfortunes that happen to a man's self, some have a certain weight and influence on his life, while others are of less moment, so is it also with what happens to any of his friends. And, again, it always makes much more difference whether those who are affected by an occurrence are alive or dead than it does whether a terrible crime in a tragedy be enacted on the stage or merely supposed to have already taken place. We must therefore take these differences into account, and still more, perhaps, the fact that it is a doubtful question whether the dead are at all accessible to good and ill. For it appears that even if anything that happens, whether good or evil, does come home to them, yet it is something unsubstantial and slight to them if not in itself; or if not that, yet at any rate its influence is not of that magnitude or nature that it can make happy those who are not, or take away their happiness from those that are. It seems then—to conclude—that the prosperity, and likewise the adversity, of friends does affect the dead, but not in such a way or to such an extent as to make the happy unhappy, or to do anything of the kind. . . .

---

13. What is happiness? Happiness is an activity of the soul, in accordance with virtue. We now have to see what virtue is (the main topic of the next several books), with the preliminary understanding that virtue is primarily of the soul. Furthermore, there are two kinds of virtues, *intellectual* virtues (which have to do with rational principles and the ability to think) and *moral* virtues, which have to do with acting correctly in accordance with reason (for example, being courageous). Note that "moral" here has nothing particularly to do with what we call "morality"—an impersonal set of principles which we are all bound to obey.

---

13. Since happiness is an exercise of the vital faculties in accordance with perfect virtue or excellence, we will now inquire about virtue or excellence; for this will probably help us in our inquiry about happiness. And indeed the true statesman seems to be especially concerned with virtue, for he wishes to make the citizens good and obedient to the laws. Of this we have an example in the Cretan and the Lacedaemonian lawgivers, and any others who have resembled them. But if the inquiry belongs to Politics or the science of the state, it is plain that it will be in accordance with our original purpose to pursue it.

The virtue or excellence that we are to consider is, of course, the excellence of man; for it is the good of man and the happiness of man that we started to seek. And by the excellence of man I mean excellence not of body, but of soul; for happiness we take to be an activity of the soul. If this be so, then it is evident that the statesman must have some knowledge of the soul, just as the man who is to heal the eye or the whole body must have some knowledge of them, and that the more in proportion as the science of the state is higher and better than medicine. But all educated physicians take much pains to know about the body. As statesmen and students of Politics, then, we must inquire into the nature of the soul, but in so doing we must keep our special purpose in view and go only so far as that requires; for to go into minuter detail would be too laborious for the present undertaking.

Now, there are certain doctrines about the soul which are stated elsewhere with sufficient precision, and these we will adopt. Two parts of the soul are distinguished, an irrational and a rational part. Whether these are separated as are the parts of the body or any divisible thing, or whether they are only distinguishable in thought but in fact inseparable, like concave and convex in the circumference of a circle, makes no difference for our present purpose.

Of the irrational part, again, one division seems to be common to all things that live, and to be possessed by plants—I mean that which causes nutrition and growth; for we must assume that all things that take nourishment have a faculty of this kind, even when they are embryos, and have the same faculty when they are full grown; at least, this is more reasonable than to suppose that they then have a different one. The excellence of this faculty, then, is plainly one that man shares with other beings, and not specifically human. And this is confirmed by the fact that in sleep this part of the soul, or this faculty, is thought to be most active, while the good and the bad man are undistinguishable when they are asleep (whence the saying that for half their lives there is no difference between the happy and the miserable; which indeed is what we should expect; for sleep is the cessation of the soul from those functions in respect of which it is called good or bad), except that they are to some slight extent roused by what goes on in their bodies, with the result that the dreams of the good man are better than those of ordinary people. However, we need not pursue this further, and may dismiss the nutritive principle, since it has no place in the excellence of man.

But there seems to be another vital principle that is irrational, and yet in some way partakes of reason. In the case of the continent and of the incontinent man alike we praise the reason or the rational part, for it exhorts them rightly and urges them to do what is best; but there is plainly present in them another principle besides the rational one, which fights and struggles against the reason. For just as a paralyzed limb, when you will to move it to the right, moves on the contrary to the left, so is it with the soul; the incontinent man's impulses run counter to his reason. Only whereas we see the refractory member in the case of the body, we do not see it in the case of the soul. But we must nevertheless, I think, hold that in the soul too there is something beside the reason, which opposes and runs counter to it (though in what sense it is distinct from the reason does not matter here). It seems, however, to partake of reason also, as we said: at least, in the continent man it submits to the reason; while in the temperate and courageous man we may say it is still more obedient; for in him it is altogether in harmony with the reason.

The irrational part, then, it appears, is twofold. There is the vegetative faculty, which has no share of reason; and the faculty of appetite or of desire in general, which in a manner partakes of reason or is rational as listening to reason and submitting to its sway,—rational in the sense in which we speak of rational obedience to father or friends, not in the sense in which we speak of rational apprehension of mathematical truths. But all advice and all rebuke and exhortation testify that the irrational part is in some way amenable to reason. If then we like to say that this part, too, has a share of reason, the rational part also will have two divisions: one rational in the strict sense as possessing reason in itself, the other rational as listening to reason as a man listens to his father. Now, on this division of the faculties is based the division of excellence; for we speak of intellectual excellences and of moral excellences; wisdom and understanding and prudence we call intellectual, liberality and temperance we call moral virtues or excellences. When we are speaking of a man's moral character we do not say that he is wise or intelligent, but that he is gentle or temperate. But we praise the wise man, too, for his habit of mind or trained faculty; and a habit or trained faculty that is praiseworthy is what we call an excellence or virtue.

DISCUSSION

In Book I, Aristotle has set out his central question and his general strategy for answering it. The question is, "What is the good life for man?" by which he means, "What is our ultimate goal in life?" What do we really want? What will really make us happy? The strategy, already partially determined by the teleological form of this main question, is to examine various aspects of human life and put them in a kind of logical order. Thus such different sides of our personalities as emotions, habits, intelligence, and skills are considered, and in each case their place in the overall scheme of the good life is determined.

The logical framework Aristotle has set up, then, is an overall teleological scheme. Everything we do has a goal, and all of the things that we do have an ultimate goal. This is called "happiness." The question then becomes, "What is Happiness?" Aristotle's answer is in terms of our "function," our unique characteristic, which is reason. Happiness is therefore living according to reason. But what does this mean? It does not mean just thinking (although, in the contemplative life, Aristotle gives great importance to thinking): happiness is a life of *activity* in accordance with reason. But activity in accordance with reason is called *virtue* or *excellence,* which is habitual as well as understandable in terms of rational principles. Thus we have our middle term between abstract happiness and particular activities; happiness is the virtuous life, and with this general outline, Aristotle turns to the concept of virtue and the particular kinds of virtue.

As matter-of-fact as Aristotle makes all of this seem, his framework can be questioned in a number of ways. First of all, one can ask why we should accept the teleological scheme that he gives us. A person who believes that the purpose of life is to serve God and do His bidding, for example, will not accept Aristotle's strictly humanistic framework in which all human activity is aimed at satisfying *our* goals and functions. (It is worth noting, however, that St. Thomas Aquinas later turned Aristotle's arguments into a very Christian conception of morality.) Second, even if one does accept the teleological humanistic framework, does it follow that there is a single goal ("happiness") that is the "end" of all of our activities? Can you think of other goals? Third, must one accept the argument that happiness is necessarily tied to reason (again, even if one accepts the teleological scheme)? What problems are there with Aristotle's conception of "reason" so far? Finally, why consider virtue so important? Important for whom? If a person can enjoy a life of slovenly but harmless vice, or can be content with a life of mediocrity and comfort, devoid of "excellence," why should we deny that person his or her conception of the good life? What kinds of arguments can you raise at this point for and against Aristotle's framework for "the good for man"?

B. Moral Virtue

The second book of the *Ethics*—and several chapters to follow—is concerned with "the moral virtues," those "excellences" which have to do with correct behavior. (The word "virtue" and the word "excellence" are used interchangeably as translations of *arete.*) It is in the list of moral virtues, perhaps more than anywhere else, that the vast differences between Aristotle's Athens and our modern society are most evident. Aristotle's society was only a few generations removed from comparatively primitive tribal times, and during his lifetime Greece was constantly involved in wars (both among the city-states and with other nations). Thus military virtues such as courage are of primary importance. Moreover, many Christian virtues are absent from the list: faith is not to be found, nor hope, humility, or charity. Indeed some of these would be *vices* for an Aristotelian Greek. Athens was an elitist society with a privileged class of male citizens, and it was for them alone that Aristotle was writing. The moral virtues, therefore, are specific to an aristocratic, wealthy, and politically powerful brotherhood. In studying Aristotle's account of them, it would be a good idea to write up your own list of virtues, marking the similarities and differences.

Aristotle begins the second book by repeating his distinction between the moral and intellectual virtues and characterizing the latter by reference to "habit or custom." Indeed, this is a most important concept for Aristotle which we will find to be quite absent from some later ethicists (Kant, for example). Being a good person is first of all doing the right things without even thinking about it. Aristotle would consider the plight of a person who has to "wrestle with his conscience" all the time to be absurd and not at all good (much less happy), even if, in the end, he did the right thing. Being virtuous is, first of all, having good habits, which means having had the luck to be brought up in the right way.

BOOK II

1. Excellence, then, being of these two kinds, intellectual and moral, intellectual excellence owes its birth and growth mainly to instruction, and so requires time and experience, while moral excellence is the result of habit or custom and has accordingly in our language received a name formed by a slight

change from the word for custom. From this it is plain that none of the moral excellences or virtues is implanted in us by nature; for that which is by nature cannot be altered by training. For instance, a stone naturally tends to fall downwards, and you could not train it to rise upwards, though you tried to do so by throwing it up ten thousand times, nor could you train fire to move downwards, nor accustom anything which naturally behaves in one way to behave in any other way. The virtues, then, come neither by nature nor against nature, but nature gives the capacity for acquiring them, and this is developed by training.

Again, where we do things by nature we get the power first, and put this power forth in act afterwards: as we plainly see in the case of the senses; for it is not by constantly seeing and hearing that we acquire those faculties, but, on the contrary, we had the power first and then used it, instead of acquiring the power by the use. But the virtues we acquire by doing the acts, as is the case with the arts too. We learn an art by doing that which we wish to do when we have learned it; we become builders by building, and harpers by harping. And so by doing just acts we become just, and by doing acts of temperance and courage we become temperate and courageous. This is attested, too, by what occurs in states; for the legislators, make their citizens good by training; *e.g.* this is the wish of all legislators, and those who do not succeed in this miss their aim, and it is this that distinguishes a good from a bad constitution.

Again, both the moral virtues and the corresponding vices result from and are formed by the same acts; and this is the case with the arts also. It is by harping that good harpers and bad harpers alike are produced: and so with builders and the rest; by building well they will become good builders, and bad builders by building badly. Indeed, if it were not so, they would not want anybody to teach them, but would all be born either good or bad at their trades. And it is just the same with the virtues also. It is by our conduct in our intercourse with other men that we become just or unjust, and by acting in circumstances of danger, and training ourselves to feel fear or confidence, that we become courageous or cowardly. So, too, with our animal appetites and the passion of anger; for by behaving in this way or in that on the occasions with which these passions are concerned, some become temperate and gentle, and others profligate and ill-tempered. In a word, acts of any kind produce habits or characters of the same kind. Hence we ought to make sure that our acts be of a certain kind; for the resulting character varies as they vary. It makes no small difference, therefore, whether a man be trained from his youth up in this way or in that, but a great difference, or rather all the difference.

---

2. Aristotle now seeks a general test for virtue. He has already defined a virtue as activity in accordance with reason and said that virtue must be manifested in us as habit, as part of our character. But now, he asks, how can we tell what activities and habits are the rational ones? And how can we test to see whether someone has a virtue or not? The fact that a person does a virtuous act does not necessarily mean that he or she is virtuous. A soldier might not run in battle because he is more afraid of his commanding officer than he is of the enemy. This is not courage, even though he does what the

courageous man does—stays in battle. A student who does not cheat on an exam because he or she is afraid of getting caught is not virtuous, even though he or she has done what virtuous students do, namely, not cheated on an exam.

Aristotle's theory of virtue is this: a virtue is neither too much nor too little, a "mean between the extremes." Too much perseverence in the face of an enemy isn't courage, but foolhardiness. Too little perseverence is cowardice. Having too much to drink is vulgar and ruinous but, Aristotle insists, refusing to drink altogether is not virtuous either. Virtue is having the right amount (of perseverence, of drink, of money, of humor, of strength, of pleasure). It is worth noting how Aristotle does not consider abstention itself to be a virtue; a man who does not enjoy himself he calls a "boor." Virtue is a kind of moderation, and this is cultivated, as we have seen, by habitually putting ourselves (or being put) in circumstances in which moderation must be practiced.

2. But our present inquiry has not, like the rest, a merely speculative aim; we are not inquiring merely in order to know what excellence or virtue is, but in order to become good; for otherwise it would profit us nothing. We must ask therefore about these acts, and see of what kind they are to be; for, as we said, it is they that determine our habits or character. First of all, then, that they must be in accordance with right reason is a common characteristic of them, which we shall here take for granted, reserving for future discussion the question what this right reason is, and how it is related to the other excellences.

But let it be understood, before we go on, that all reasoning on matters of practice must be in outline merely, and not scientifically exact: for, as we said at starting, the kind of reasoning to be demanded varies with the subject in hand; and in practical matters and questions of expediency there are no invariable laws, any more than in questions of health. And if our general conclusions are thus inexact, still more inexact is all reasoning about particular cases; for these fall under no system of scientifically established rules or traditional maxims, but the agent must always consider for himself what the special occasion requires, just as in medicine or navigation. But though this is the case we must try to render what help we can.

First of all, then, we must observe that, in matters of this sort, to fall short and to exceed are alike fatal. This is plain (to illustrate what we cannot see by what we can see) in the case of strength and health. Too much and too little exercise alike destroy strength; and to take too much meat and drink, or to take too little, is equally ruinous to health, but the fitting amount produces and increases and preserves them. Just so, then, is it with temperance also, and courage, and the other virtues. The man who shuns and fears everything and never makes a stand, becomes a coward; while the man who fears nothing at all, but will face anything, becomes foolhardy. So, too, the man who takes his fill of any kind of pleasure, and abstains from none, is a profligate, but the man who shuns all (like him whom we call a "boor") is devoid of sensibility. Thus temperance and courage are destroyed both by excess and defect, but preserved by moderation. But habits or types of character are not only produced and preserved and destroyed by the same occasions and the same means, but they will also manifest themselves in the same circumstances. This is the case with palpable things like strength. Strength is produced by taking plenty of nourishment and doing plenty of hard work, and the strong man, in turn, has the greatest capacity for these. And the case is the same with the virtues: by abstaining from pleasure we become temperate, and when we have become temperate we are best able to abstain. And so with courage: by habituating ourselves to despise danger, and to face it, we become courageous; and when we have become courageous, we are best able to face danger.

---

3. The test of virtue is this: a man who is virtuous *enjoys* being virtuous. A person is not more virtuous because he or she is in great pain, having been deprived of some desired goal [the regret of having said "no" or desperately wanting one (too many) more martini]. The virtuous person prefers being virtuous and does not regret it. The courageous man enjoys being courageous (which is not to say, of course, that he has to enjoy the danger of battle). And again, this is a matter of upbringing; a person must be educated to enjoy virtue and not enjoy vice. (What would Aristotle say about a society such as ours, where entertainment for youths consists in the glorification of clever bank heists and attempts to bring off the perfect crime?)

---

3. The pleasure or pain that accompanies the acts must be taken as a test of the formed habit or character. He who abstains from the pleasures of the body and rejoices in the abstinence is temperate, while he who is vexed at having to abstain is profligate; and again, he who faces danger with pleasure, or, at any rate, without pain, is courageous, but he to whom this is painful is a coward. For moral virtue or excellence is closely concerned with pleasure and pain. It is pleasure that moves us to do what is base, and pain that moves us to refrain from what is noble. And therefore, as Plato says, man needs to be so trained from his youth up as to find pleasure and pain in the right objects. This is what sound education means.

Another reason why virtue has to do with pleasure and pain, is that it has to do with actions and passions or affections; but every affection and every act is accompanied by pleasure or pain. The fact is further attested by the employment of pleasure and pain in correction; they have a kind of curative property, and a cure is effected by administering the opposite of the disease.

Again, as we said before, every type of character [or habit or formed faculty] is essentially relative to, and concerned with, those things that form it for good or for ill; but it is through pleasure and pain that bad characters are formed— that is to say, through pursuing and avoiding the wrong pleasures and pains, or pursuing and avoiding them at the wrong time, or in the wrong manner, or in any other of the various ways of going wrong that may be distinguished. And hence some people go so far as to define the virtues as a kind of impassive or neutral state of mind. But they err in stating this absolutely, instead of qualifying it by the addition of the right and wrong manner, time, etc. We may lay down, herefore, that this kind of excellence [*i.e.* moral excellence] makes us do what is best in matters of pleasure and pain, while vice or badness has the contrary effect. But the following considerations will throw additional light on the point.

There are three kinds of things that move us to choose, and three that move us to avoid them: on the one hand, the beautiful or noble, the advantageous, the pleasant; on the other hand, the ugly or base, the hurtful, the painful. Now, the good man is apt to go right, and the bad man to go wrong, about them all, but especially about pleasure: for pleasure is not only common to man with animals, but also accompanies all pursuit or choice; since the noble, and the advantageous also, are pleasant in idea. Again, the feeling of pleasure has been fostered in us all from our infancy by our training, and has thus become so engrained in our life that it can scarce be washed out. And, indeed, we all more or less make pleasure our test in judging of actions. For this reason too, then, our whole inquiry must be concerned with these matters; since to be pleased and pained in the right or the wrong way has great influence on our actions. Again, to fight with pleasure is harder than to fight with wrath (which Heraclitus says is hard), and virtue, like art, is always more concerned with what is harder; for the harder the task the better is success. For this reason also, then, both [moral] virtue or excellence and the science of the state must always be concerned with pleasures and pains; for he that behaves rightly with regard to them will be good, and he that behaves badly will be bad. We will take it as established, then, that [moral] excellence or virtue has to do with pleasures and pains; and that the acts which produce it develop it, and also, when differently done, destroy it; and that it manifests itself in the same acts which produced it.

4. Aristotle now pursues this idea, that virtue requires habituation of right activity. In order for an act to be virtuous,

1 One must know what he is doing
2 One must deliberately choose to do it, and
2a One must do it for its own sake
3 It must be a manifestation of a state of character and not just an isolated incident

4. But here we may be asked what we mean by saying that men can become just and temperate only by doing what is just and temperate: surely, it may be said, if their acts are just and temperate, they themselves are already just and temperate, as they are grammarians and musicians if they do what is grammatical and musical. We may answer, I think, firstly, that this is not quite the case even with the arts. A man may do something grammatical [or write something correctly] by chance, or at the prompting of another person: he will not be grammatical till he not only does something grammatical, but also does it grammatically [or like a grammatical person], *i.e.* in virtue of his own knowledge of grammar. But, secondly, the virtues are not in this point analogous to the arts. The products of art have their excellence in themselves, and so it is enough if when produced they are of a certain quality; but in the case of the virtues, a man is not said to act justly or temperately [or like a just or temperate man] if what he does merely be of a certain sort—he must be in a certain state of mind when he does it; *i.e.*, first of all, he must know what he is doing; secondly, he must choose it, and choose it for itself; and, thirdly, his act must be the expression of a formed and stable character. Now, of these conditions, only one, the knowledge, is necessary for the possession of any art; but for the possession

of the virtues knowledge is of little or no avail, while the other conditions that result from repeatedly doing what is just and temperate are not a little important, but all-important.

The thing that is done, therefore, is called just or temperate when it is such as the just or temperate man would do; but the man who does it is not just or temperate, unless he also does it in the spirit of the just or the temperate man. It is right, then, to say that by doing what is just a man becomes just, and temperate by doing what is temperate, while without doing thus he has no chance of ever becoming good. But most men, instead of doing thus, fly to theories, and fancy that they are philosophizing and that this will make them good, like a sick man who listens attentively to what the doctor says and then disobeys all his orders. This sort of philosophizing will no more produce a healthy habit of mind than this sort of treatment will produce a healthy habit of body.

---

5. What is a virtue? So far we have seen that it is (1) activity, (2) in accordance with reason, (3) the mean between the extremes, (4) a matter of habit, (5) and gives pleasure to the virtuous person. Aristotle now approaches this question again, asking whether a virtue is

1 A passion or an emotion
2 A power or faculty
3 A habit or trained faculty

We already know the answer (number 3), but Aristotle gives us his reasons for rejecting the first two possibilities. (Why is it important to him that a virtue is not simply an emotion? What would follow if virtues were emotions?)

---

5. We have next to inquire what excellence or virtue is. A quality of the soul is either (1) a passion or emotion, or (2) a power or faculty, or (3) a habit or trained faculty; and so virtue must be one of these three. By (1) a passion or emotion we mean appetite, anger, fear, confidence, envy, joy, love, hate, longing, emulation, pity, or generally that which is accompanied by pleasure or pain; (2) a power or faculty is that in respect of which we are said to be capable of being affected in any of these ways, as, for instance, that in respect of which we are able to be angered or pained or to pity; and (3) a habit or trained faculty is that in respect of which we are well or ill regulated or disposed in the matter of our affections; as, for instance, in the matter of being angered, we are ill regulated if we are too violent or too slack, but if we are moderate in our anger we are well regulated. And so with the rest.

Now, the virtues are not emotions, nor are the vices—(1) because we are not called good or bad in respect of our emotions, but are called so in respect of our virtues or vices; (2) because we are neither praised nor blamed in respcet of our emotions (a man is not praised for being afraid or angry, nor blamed for being angry simply, but for being angry in a particular way), but we are praised or blamed in respect of our virtues or vices; (3) because we may be angered or frightened without deliberate choice, but the virtues are a kind of deliberate choice, or at least are impossible without it; and (4) because in respect of our emotions we are said to be moved, but in respect of our virtues and vices we are not said to be moved, but to be regulated or disposed in this way or in that.

For these same reasons also they are not powers or faculties; for we are not called either good or bad for being merely capable of emotion, nor are we either praised or blamed for this. And further, while nature gives us our powers or faculties, she does not make us either good or bad. (This point, however, we have already treated.) If, then, the virtues be neither emotions nor faculties, it only remains for them to be habits or trained faculties.

---

6. Aristotle now pursues his analysis of moral virtue as habitual rational activity and a mean between extremes. But not all activities or motives can be moderated. One can drink just so much, not more or less, and one can stay in battle just so long. But one cannot commit just the right amount of adultery or theft, for any amount of such activities is wrong. Similarly, although a person can have a right amount of anger and be angry at the right things (which is a virtue), he or she cannot have a virtuous amount of envy, for envy is one of those emotions which are degrading in any amounts.

---

6. We have thus found the genus to which virtue belongs; but we want to know, not only that it is a trained faculty, but also what species of trained faculty it is. We may safely assert that the virtue or excellence of a thing causes that thing both to be itself in good condition and to perform its function well. The excellence of the eye, for instance, makes both the eye and its work good; for it is by the excellence of the eye that we see well. So the proper excellence of the horse makes a horse what he should be, and makes him good at running, and carrying his rider, and standing a charge. If, then, this holds good in all cases, the proper excellence or virtue of man will be the habit or trained faculty that makes a man good and makes him perform his function well.

How this is to be done we have already said, but we may exhibit the same conclusion in another way, by inquiring what the nature of this virtue is. Now, if we have any quantity, whether continuous or discrete, it is possible to take either a larger [or too large], or a smaller [or too small], or an equal [of fair] amount, and that either absolutely or relatively to our own needs. By an equal or fair amount I understand a mean amount, or one that lies between excess and deficiency. By the absolute mean, or mean relatively to the thing itself, I understand that which is equidistant from both extremes, and this is one and the same for all. By the mean relatively to us I understand that which is neither too much nor too little for us; and this is not one and the same for all. For instance, if ten be too large and two too small, six is the mean relatively to the thing itself; for it exceeds one extreme by the same amount by which it is exceeded by the other extreme: and this is the mean in arithmetical proportion. But the mean relatively to us cannot be found in this way. If ten pounds of food is too much for a given man to eat, and two pounds too little, it does not follow that the trainer will order him six pounds: for that also may perhaps be too much for the man in question, or too little; too little for Milo, too much for the beginner. The same holds true in running and wrestling. And so we may say generally that a master in any art avoids what is too much and what is too little, and seeks for the mean and chooses it—not the absolute but the relative mean.

If, then, every art or science perfects its work in this way, looking to the mean and bringing its work up to this standard (so that people are wont to say of a good work that nothing could be taken from it or added to it, implying that excellence is destroyed by excess or deficiency, but secured by observing the mean; and good artists, as we say, do in fact keep their eyes fixed on this in all that they do), and if virtue, like nature, is more exact and better than any art, it follows that virtue also must aim at the mean—virtue of course meaning moral virtue or excellence; for it has to do with passions and actions, and it is these that admit of excess and deficiency and the mean. For instance, it is possible to feel fear, confidence, desire, anger, pity, and generally to be affected pleasantly and painfully, either too much or too little, in either case wrongly; but to be thus affected at the right times, and on the right occasions, and towards the right persons, and with the right object, and in the right fashion, is the mean course and the best course, and these are characteristics of virtue. And in the same way our outward acts also admit of excess and deficiency, and the mean or due amount. Virtue, then, has to deal with feelings or passions and with outward acts, in which excess is wrong and deficiency also is blamed, but the mean amount is praised and is right—both of which are characteristics of virtue. Virtue, then, is a kind of moderation inasmuch as it aims at the mean.

Again, there are many ways of going wrong (for evil is infinite in nature, to use a Pythagorean figure, while good is finite), but only one way of going right; so that the one is easy and the other hard—easy to miss the mark and hard to hit. On this account also, then, excess and deficiency are characteristic of vice, hitting the mean is characteristic of virtue.

Virtue, then, is a habit or trained faculty of choice, the characteristic of which lies in moderation or observance of the mean relatively to the persons concerned, as determined by reason, *i.e.* by the reason by which the prudent man would determine it. And it is a moderation, firstly, inasmuch as it comes in the middle or mean between two vices, one on the side of excess, the other on the side of defect; and, secondly, inasmuch as, while these vices fall short of or exceed the due measure in feeling and in action, it finds and chooses the mean, middling, or moderate amount. Regarded in its essence, therefore, or according to the definition of its nature, virtue is a moderation or middle state, but viewed in its relation to what is best and right it is the extreme of perfection.

But it is not all actions nor all passions that admit of moderation; there are some whose very names imply badness, as malevolence, shamelessness, envy, and, among acts, adultery, theft, murder. These and all other like things are blamed as being bad in themselves, and not merely in their excess or deficiency. It is impossible therefore to go right in them; they are always wrong: rightness and wrongness in such things (*e.g.* in adultery) does not depend upon whether it is the right person and occasion and manner, but the mere doing of any one of them is wrong. It would be equally absurd to look for moderation or excess or deficiency in unjust cowardly or profligate conduct; for then there would be moderation in excess or deficiency, and excess in excess, and deficiency in deficiency. The fact is that just as there can be no excess or deficiency in temperance or courage because the mean or moderate amount is, in a sense, an extreme, so in these kinds of conduct also there can be no moderation or excess or deficiency, but the acts are wrong however they be done. For, to put it generally, there cannot be moderation in excess or deficiency, nor excess or deficiency in moderation.

___

7. Aristotle now gives us his list of the virtues, and it is here that the reader would be well advised—if he or she has not done so already—to make out a comparable list of our own virtues, to see how it compares. Here is Aristotle's list:

- Courage (particularly, but not only, in battle).
- Temperance (self-control in such pleasant activities as eating, drinking, sex).
- Liberality [spending money; notice that charity itself is not a virtue, and giving away all of one's money (like some of the saints) would be considered not only excessive but insane].
- Magnificence [living well materially, driving a substantial but not too flashy chariot, living in a big (but not too big) house, giving good (but not too ridiculously lavish) parties].
- Pride (taking public pleasure in one's accomplishments and status. Notice that, for Aristotle, not doing so, being humble, is a vice.)
- High-mindedness (not being petty).
- "Aspiration" (being ambitious but not too ambitious. Notice that Aristotle says that this virtue has no name in Greek and that what we call "ambition" is taken by him to be a vice. Why?)
- Gentleness (not wimpiness—Athens was a very "macho" society—but charm and concern for others, sensitivity).
- Truthfulness (not being a liar, particularly with regard to one's own accomplishments).
- Wittiness (having a sense of humor).
- Friendliness (properly pleasant and outgoing; this is different from having friends, which is much more than a moral virtue; it is one of the absolute necessities of the good life, whatever one's virtues).
- Modesty (not the same as humility, just not thinking too much of oneself).
- Righteous indignation [getting angry about the right things, and in proportion to the offense in question. Not getting angry at all (a Christian virtue) is considered a vice, if something is worth being angry about.]

___

7. But it is not enough to make these general statements [about virtue and vice]: we must go on and apply them to particulars [*i.e.* to the several virtues and vices]. For in reasoning about matters of conduct general statements are too vague, and do not convey so much truth as particular propositions. It is with particulars that conduct is concerned: our statements, therefore, when applied to these particulars, should be found to hold good. These particulars then [*i.e.* the several virtues and vices and the several acts and affections with which they deal], we will take from the following list.

Moderation in the feelings of fear and confidence is courage: of those that exceed, he that exceeds in fearlessness has no name (as often happens), but he that exceeds in confidence is foolhardy, while he that exceeds in fear, but is deficient in confidence, is cowardly. Moderation in respect of certain pleasures and also (though to a less extent) certain pains is temperance, while excess is profligacy. But defectiveness in the matter of these pleasures is hardly ever found, and so this sort of people also have as yet received no name: let us put them down as "void of sensibility." In the matter of giving and taking money, moderation is liberality, excess and deficiency are prodigality and illiberality. But both vices exceed and fall short in giving and taking; while the illiberal man exceeds in taking, but falls short in spending. (For the present we are but giving an outline or summary, and aim at nothing more; we shall afterwards treat these points in greater detail.) But, besides these, there are other dispositions in the matter of money: there is a moderation which is called magnificence (for the magnificent is not the same as the liberal man: the former deals with large sums, the latter with small), and an excess which is called bad taste or vulgarity, and a deficiency which is called meanness; and these vices differ from those which are opposed to liberality: how they differ will be explained later. With respect to honour and disgrace, there is a moderation which is pride, an excess which may be called vanity, and a deficiency which is humility.

But just as we said that liberality is related to magnificence, differing only in that it deals with small sums, so here there is a virtue related to high-mindedness, and differing only in that it is concerned with small instead of great honours. A man may have a due desire for honour, and also more or less than a due desire: he that carries this desire to excess is called ambitious, he that has not enough of it is called unambitious, but he that has the due amount has no name. There are also no abstract names for the characters, except "ambition," corresponding to ambitious. And on this account those who occupy the extremes lay claim to the middle place. And in common parlance, too, the moderate man is sometimes called ambitious and sometimes unambitious, and sometimes the ambitious man is praised and sometimes the unambitious. Why this is we will explain afterwards; for the present we will follow out our plan and enumerate the other types of character. In the matter of anger also we find excess and deficiency and moderation. The characters themselves hardly have recognized names, but as the moderate man is here called gentle, we will call his character gentleness; of those who go into extremes, we may take the term wrathful for him who exceeds, with wrathfulness for the vice, and wrathless for him who is deficient, with wrathlessness for his character.

Besides these, there are three kinds of moderation, bearing some resemblance to one another, and yet different. They all have to do with intercourse in speech and action, but they differ in that one has to do with the truthfulness of this intercourse, while the other two have to do with its pleasantness—one of the two with pleasantness in matters of amusement, the other with pleasantness in all the relations of life. We must therefore speak of these qualities also in order that we may the more plainly see how, in all cases, moderation is praiseworthy, while the extreme courses are neither right nor praiseworthy, but blamable. In these cases also names are for the most part wanting, but we must try, here as elsewhere, to coin names ourselves, in order to make our argument clear and easy to follow.

In the matter of truth, then, let us call him who observes the mean a true [or truthful] person, and observance of the mean truth [or truthfulness]: pretence, when it exaggerates, may be called boasting, and the person a boaster; when it understates, let the names be irony and ironical. With regard to pleasantness in amusement, he who observes the mean may be called witty, and his character wittiness; excess may be called buffoonery, and the man a buffoon; while boorish may stand for the person who is deficient, and boorishness for his character. With regard to pleasantness in the other affairs of life, he who makes himself properly pleasant may be called friendly, and his moderation friendliness; he that exceeds may be called obsequious if he have no ulterior motive, but a flatterer if he has an eye to his own advantage; he that is deficient in this respect, and always makes himself disagreeable, may be called a quarrelsome or peevish fellow.

Moreover, in mere emotions and in our conduct with regard to them, there are ways of observing the mean; for instance, shame is not a virtue, but yet the modest man is praised. For in these matters also we speak of this man as observing the mean, of that man as going beyond it (as the shame-faced man whom the least thing makes shy), while he who is deficient in the feeling, or lacks it altogether, is called shameless; but the term modest is applied to him who observes the mean. Righteous indignation, again, hits the mean between envy and malevolence. These have to do with feelings of pleasure and pain at what happens to our neighbours. A man is called righteously indignant when he feels pain at the sight of undeserved prosperity, but your envious man goes beyond him and is pained by the sight of any one in prosperity, while the malevolent man is so far from being pained that he actually exults in the misfortunes of his neighbours. But we shall have another opportunity of discussing these matters. As for justice, the term is used in more senses than one; we will, therefore, after disposing of the above questions, distinguish these various senses, and show how each of these kinds of justice is a kind of moderation. And then we will treat of the intellectual virtues in the same way.

8. There are, as we said, three classes of disposition, viz. two kinds of vice, one marked by excess, the other by deficiency, and one kind of virtue, the observance of the mean. Now, each is in a way opposed to each, for the extreme dispositions are opposed both to the mean or moderate disposition and to one another, while the moderate disposition is opposed to both the extremes. Just as a quantity which is equal to a given quantity is also greater when compared with a less, and less when compared with a greater quantity, so the mean or moderate dispositions exceed as compared with the defective dispositions, and fall short as compared with the excessive dispositions, both in feeling and in action; *e.g.* the

courageous man seems foolhardy as compared with the coward, and cowardly as compared with the foolhardy; and similarly the temperate man appears profligate in comparison with the insensible, and insensible in comparison with the profligate man; and the liberal man appears prodigal by the side of the illiberal man, and illiberal by the side of the prodigal man. And so the extreme characters try to displace the mean or moderate character, and each represents him as falling into the opposite extreme, the coward calling the courageous man foolhardy, the foolhardy calling him coward, and so on in other cases. But while the mean and the extremes are thus opposed to one another, the extremes are strictly contrary to each other rather than to the mean; for they are further removed from one another than from the mean, as that which is greater than a given magnitude is further from that which is less, and that which is less is further from that which is greater, than either the greater or the less is from that which is equal to the given magnitude.

Sometimes, again, an extreme, when compared with the mean, has a sort of resemblance to it, as foolhardiness to courage, or prodigality to liberality; but there is the greatest possible dissimilarity between the extremes. Again, "things that are as far as possible removed from each other" is the accepted definition of contraries, so that the further things are removed from each other the more contrary they are.

In comparison with the mean, however, it is sometimes the deficiency that is the more opposed, and sometimes the excess; *e.g.* foolhardiness, which is excess, is not so much opposed to courage as cowardice, which is deficiency; but insensibility, which is lack of feeling, is not so much opposed to temperance as profligacy, which is excess.

The reasons for this are two. One is the reason derived from the nature of the matter itself: since one extreme is, in fact, nearer and more similar to the mean, we naturally do not oppose it to the mean so strongly as the other; *e.g.* as foolhardiness seems more similar to courage and nearer to it, and cowardice more dissimilar, we speak of cowardice as the opposite rather than the other: for that which is further removed from the mean seems to be more opposed to it. This, then, is one reason, derived from the nature of the thing itself. Another reason lies in ourselves: and it is this—those things to which we happen to be more prone by nature appear to be more opposed to the mean: *e.g.* our natural inclination is rather towards indulgence in pleasure, and so we more easily fall into profligate than into regular habits: those courses, then, in which we are more apt to run to great lengths are spoken of as more opposed to the mean; and thus profligacy, which is an excess, is more opposed to temperance than the deficiency is.

9. We have sufficiently explained, then, that moral virtue is moderation or observance of the mean, and in what sense, viz. (1) as holding a middle position between two vices, one on the side of excess, and the other on the side of deficiency, and (2) as aiming at the mean or moderate amount both in feeling

and in action. And on this account it is a hard thing to be good; for finding the middle or the mean in each case is a hard thing, just as finding the middle or centre of a circle is a thing that is not within the power of everybody, but only of him who has the requisite knowledge. Thus any one can be angry—that is quite easy; any one can give money away or spend it: but to do these things to the right person, to the right extent, at the right time, with the right object, and in the right manner, is not what everybody can do, and is by no means easy; and that is the reason why right doing is rare and praiseworthy and noble. He that aims at the mean, then, should first of all strive to avoid that extreme which is more opposed to it, as Calypso bids Ulysses—

Clear of these smoking breakers keep thy ship.

For of the extremes one is more dangerous, the other less. Since then it is hard to hit the mean precisely, we must "row when we cannot sail," as the proverb has it, and choose the least of two evils; and that will be best effected in the way we have described. And secondly we must consider, each for himself, what we are most prone to—for different natures are inclined to different things—which we may learn by the pleasure or pain we feel. And then we must bend ourselves in the opposite direction; for by keeping well away from error we shall fall into the middle course, as we straighten a bent stick by bending it the other way.

But in all cases we must be especially on our guard against pleasant things, and against pleasure; for we can scarce judge her impartially. And so, in our behaviour towards her, we should imitate the behaviour of the old counsellors

---

ARISTOTLE'S VIRTUES AND VICES

Virtue (mean)	Vices (extremes)
Courage	Foolhardiness, cowardice
Temperance	Licentiousness, "insensibility"
Liberality	Prodigality, illiberality (miserliness)
Magnificence	Vulgarity, meanness
Pride	Vanity, humility, high-mindedness, snobbishness, pettiness
"Aspiration"	Ambition, laziness
Gentleness	Obsequiousness, wimpishness
Truthfulness	Boastfulness, irony[2]
Wittiness	Buffoonery, boorishness
Friendliness	Obsequiousness or too flattering, quarrelsome
Modesty	Bashfulness, shamelessness
Righteous indignation	Envy, malice
Justice	Injustice (more complex than the others)

---

[2]What would Aristotle say about Socrates's famed "irony" (insisting that he was most ignorant)? Does this help explain the fact that Socrates was not considered an ideal by most of his contemporaries?

towards Helen, and in all cases repeat their saying: if we dismiss her we shall be less likely to go wrong.

This then, in outline, is the course by which we shall best be able to hit the mean. But it is a hard task, we must admit, especially in a particular case. It is not easy to determine, for instance, how and with whom one ought to be angry, and upon what grounds, and for how long; for public opinion sometimes praises those who fall short, and calls them gentle, and sometimes applies the term mainly to those who show a harsh temper. In fact, a slight error, whether on the side of excess or deficiency, is not blamed, but only a considerable error; for then there can be no mistake. But it is hardly possible to determine by reasoning how far or to what extent a man must err in order to incur blame; and indeed matters that fall within the scope of perception never can be so determined. Such matters lie within the region of particulars, and can only be determined by perception. So much then is plain, that the middle character is in all cases to be praised, but that we ought to incline sometimes towards excess, sometimes towards deficiency; for in this way we shall most easily hit the mean and attain to right doing.

DISCUSSION

The alternative translation for the word for "virtue" *(arete)* as "excellence" points to an extremely important feature of Aristotle's ethics. The good for Aristotle is defined not so much in terms of obeying certain laws or "being moral" as excelling as human beings. We have several times emphasized Aristotle's elitism—the fact that his ethics is aimed at an aristocratic, mainly male Athenian class. But because of this, Aristotle's conception of virtue is not at all concerned with the good life or the virtues of people who are not in this privileged class. Unlike Christian ethics, for example, Aristotle's ethics is not concerned with that form of goodwill that is possible for everyone. The ordinary citizen and his or her virtues do not enter into his considerations. It is assumed that a shoemaker should be a good shoemaker and a baker should be a good baker and, of course, husbands, wives, and children should be good husbands, wives, and children. But there is nothing in Aristotle that would generally count as "being a good person," without reference to role or rank, and Aristotle would have found such an idea (despite his own phrase, "the good for man") to be unintelligible. The virtues, accordingly, are tailored for men of leisure and considerable status and responsibility in the community. They are excellences in the sense that they measure a particular kind of social achievement and recognition ("honor"), and they demand of these privileged, accomplished, and already "noble" men that they not only exercise the virtues peculiar to their rank (social magnificence, for example) but also excel in those special skills (such as statesmanship and justice) appropriate for the leadership of society. Many of Aristotle's virtues would hardly apply to poor people (liberality—as well as stinginess and waste—refer to quite different traits and concerns in the poor). Let us note again that a number of Aristotle's virtues would not count as virtues for us at all, but, furthermore, let us note that Aristotle calls these "moral" virtues. How many of them would count as "moral" in our terms (as opposed to merely pleasant or charming traits, such as wittiness and friendliness)? What important moral virtues—in our sense of that term—have been left off of Aristotle's list?

C. Questions about Action

Since virtue is activity, it is important that Aristotle give us an account of activity. What sorts of actions can be virtuous? When is an action voluntary, and when involuntary? When do we praise and blame people; when do we pardon what they do? When can we properly blame our misdeeds or mistakes on external circumstances? These are the questions of the first eight chapters of Book III. (The last chapters of Book III more properly belong with the discussion of the particular virtues in Book IV.)

BOOK III

1. Virtue, as we have seen, has to do with feelings and actions. Now, praise or blame is given only to what is voluntary; that which is involuntary receives pardon, and sometimes even pity. It seems, therefore, that a clear distinction between the voluntary and the involuntary is necessary for those who are investigating the nature of virtue, and will also help legislators in assigning rewards and punishments.

That is generally held to be involuntary which is done under compulsion or through ignorance. "Done under compulsion" means that the cause is external, the agent or patient contributing nothing towards it; as, for instance, if he were carried somewhere by a whirlwind or by men whom he could not resist.

But there is some question about acts done in order to avoid a greater evil, or to obtain some noble end; *e.g.* if a tyrant were to order you to do something disgraceful, having your parents or children in his power, who were to live if you did it, but to die if you did not—it is a matter of dispute whether such acts are involuntary or voluntary. Throwing a cargo overboard in a storm is a somewhat analogous case. No one voluntarily throws away his property if nothing is to come of it, but any sensible person would do so to save the life of himself and the crew. Acts of this kind, then, are of a mixed nature, but they more nearly resemble voluntary acts. For they are desired or chosen at the time when they are done, and the end or motive of an act is that which is in view at the time. In applying the terms voluntary and involuntary, therefore, we must consider the state of the agent's mind at the time. Now, he wills the act at the time; for the cause which sets the limbs going lies in the agent in such cases and where the cause lies in the agent, it rests with him to do or not to do.

Such acts, then, are voluntary, though in themselves [or apart from these qualifying circumstances] we may allow them to be involuntary; for no one would choose anything of this kind on its own account. And, in fact, for actions of this sort men are sometimes praised, *e.g.* when they endure something disgraceful or painful in order to secure some great and noble result: but in the contrary case they are blamed; for no worthy person would endure the extremity of disgrace when there was no noble result in view, or but a trifling one.

But in some cases we do not praise, but pardon, *i.e.* when a man is induced to do a wrong act by pressure which is too strong for human nature and which no one could bear. Though there are some cases of this kind, I think, where the plea of compulsion is inadmissible, and where, rather than do the act, a man ought to suffer death in its most painful form; for instance, the circumstances which "compelled" Alcmaeon in Euripides to kill his mother seem absurd.

It is sometimes hard to decide whether we ought to do this deed to avoid this evil, or whether we ought to endure this evil rather than do this deed; but it is still harder to abide by our decisions: for generally the evil which we wish to avoid is something painful, the deed we are pressed to do is something disgraceful; and hence we are blamed or praised according as we do or do not suffer ourselves to be compelled.

And now, a crucial claim:

What kinds of acts, then, are to be called compulsory? I think our answer must be that, in the first place, when the cause lies outside and the agent has no part in it, the act is called, without qualification, "cumpulsory" [and therefore involuntary]; but that, in the second place, when an act that would not be voluntarily done for its own sake is chosen now in preference to this given alternative, the cause lying in the agent, such an act must be called "involuntary in itself," or "in the abstract," but "now, and in preference to this alternative, voluntary." But an act of the latter kind is rather of the nature of a voluntary act: for acts fall within the sphere of particulars; and here the particular thing that is done is voluntary. It is scarcely possible, however, to lay down rules for determining which of two alternatives it to be preferred; for there are many differences in the particular cases.

It might, perhaps, be urged that acts whose motive is something pleasant or something noble are compulsory, for here we are constrained by something outside us. But if this were so, all our acts would be compulsory; for these are the motives of every act of every man.

Again, acting under compulsion and against one's will is painful, but action whose motive is something pleasant or noble involves pleasure. It is absurd, then, to blame things outside us instead of our own readiness to yield to their allurements, and, while we claim our noble acts as our own, to set down our disgraceful actions to "pleasant things outside us." Comoulsory, then, it appears, is that of which the cause is external, the person compelled contributing nothing thereto.

What is done through ignorance is always "not-voluntary," but is "involuntary" when the agent is pained afterwards and sorry when he finds what he has done. For when a man, who has done something through ignorance, is not vexed at what he has done, you cannot indeed say that he did it voluntarily, as he did not know what he was doing, but neither can you say that he did it involuntarily or unwillingly, since he is not sorry. A man who has acted through ignorance, then, if he is sorry afterwards, is held to have done the deed involuntarily or unwillingly; if he is not sorry afterwards we may say (to mark the distinction) he did the deed "not-voluntarily"; for, as the case is different, it is better to have a distinct name. Acting *through* ignorance, however, seems to be different from acting *in* ignorance. For instance, when a man is drunk or in a rage he is not thought to act *through* ignorance, but through intoxication or rage, and yet not knowingly, but *in* ignorance.

Every vicious man, indeed, is ignorant of what ought to be done and what ought not to be done, and it is this kind of error that makes men unjust and bad generally. But the term "involuntary" is not properly applied to cases in which a man is ignorant of what is fitting. The ignorance that makes an act involuntary is not this ignorance of the principles which should determine preference (this constitutes vice),—not, I say, this ignorance of the universal (for we blame a man for this), but ignorance of the particulars, of the persons and things affected by the act. These are the grounds of pity and pardon; for he who is ignorant of any of these particulars acts involuntarily.

It may be as well, then, to specify what these particulars are, and how many. They are—first, the doer; secondly, the deed; and, thirdly, the object or person affected by it; sometimes also that wherewith (*e.g.* the instrument with which) it is done, and that for the sake of which it is done (*e.g.* for protection), and the way in which it is done (*e.g.* gently or violently). Now, a man cannot (unless he be mad) be ignorant of all these particulars; for instance, he evidently cannot be ignorant of the doer: for how can he not know himself? But a man may be ignorant of what he is doing; *e.g.* a man who has said something will sometimes plead that the words escaped him unawares, or that he did not know that the subject was forbidden (as Aeschylus pleaded in the case of the Mysteries); or a man might plead that when he discharged the weapon he only intended to show the working of it, as the prisoner did in the catapult case. Again, a man might mistake his son for an enemy, as Merope does, or a sharp spear for one with a button, or a heavy stone for a pumice-stone. Again, one might kill a man with a drug intended to save him, or hit him hard when one wished merely to touch him (as boxers do when they spar with open hands). Ignorance, then, being possible with regard to all these circumstances, he who is ignorant of any of them is held to have acted involuntarily, and especially when he is ignorant of the most important particulars; and the most important seem to be the persons affected and the result. Besides this, however, the agent must be grieved and sorry for what he has done, if the act thus ignorantly committed is to be called involuntary.

But now, having found that an act is involuntary when done under compulsion or through ignorance, we may conclude that a voluntary act is one which is originated by the doer with knowledge of the particular circumstances of the act. For I venture to think that it is incorrect to say that acts done through anger or desire are involuntary. In the first place, if this be so we can no longer allow that any of the other animals act voluntarily, nor even children. Again, does the saying mean that none of the acts which we do through desire or anger are voluntary, or that the noble ones are voluntary and the disgraceful ones involuntary? Interpreted in the latter sense, it is surely ridiculous, as the cause of both is the same. If we take the former interpretation, it is absurd, I think, to say that we ought to desire a thing, and also to say that its pursuit is involuntary; but, in fact, there are things at which we ought to be angry, and things which we ought to desire, *e.g.* health and learning. Again, it seems that what is done unwillingly is painful, while what is done through desire is pleasant. Again, what difference is there, in respect of involuntariness, between wrong deeds done upon calculation and wrong deeds done in anger? Both alike are to be avoided, but the unreasoning passions or feelings seem to belong to the man just as much as does the reason, so that the acts that are done under the impulse of anger or desire are also the man's acts. To make such actions involuntary, therefore, would be too absurd.

---

2. Since it is essential to virtuous action that it be voluntary and a choice, rather than an accident, Aristotle now proceeds to discuss the important notion of choice. It might be worth noting that, both in this and in the preceding discussion of voluntary action, Aristotle does not raise the now central philosophical question of "free will." In fact, given the enormous amount of knowledge and theory in psychology which we all take for granted, Aristotle shows little concern for the troublesome questions of motivation and the possibility of unconscious compulsions which, for us, present some of the most difficult questions in ascertaining blame and responsibility (for example, in crimes of passion and in which there is a plea of insanity).

---

2. Now that we have distinguished voluntary from involuntary acts, our next task is to discuss choice or purpose. For it seems to be most intimately connected with virtue, and to be a surer test of character than action itself.

It seems that choosing is willing, but that the two terms are not identical, willing being the wider. For children and other animals have will, but not choice or purpose; and acts done upon the spur of the moment are said to be voluntary, but not to be done with deliberate purpose.

Those who say that choice is appetite, or anger, or wish, or an opinion of some sort, do not seem to give a correct account of it. In the first place, choice is not shared by irrational creatures, but appetite and anger are. Again, the incontinent man acts from appetite and not from choice or purpose, the continent man from purpose and not from appetite. Again, appetite may be contrary to purpose, but one appetite cannot be contrary to another appetite. Again, the object of appetite [or aversion] is the pleasant or the painful, but the object of purpose [as such] is neither painful nor pleasant. Still less can purpose be anger; for acts done in anger seem to be least of all done of purpose or deliberate choice.

Nor yet is it wish, though it seem very like; for we cannot purpose or deliberately choose the impossible, and a man who should say that he did would be thought a fool; but we may wish for the impossible, *e.g.* to escape death. Again, while we may wish what never could be effected by our own agency (*e.g.* the success of a particular actor or athlete), we never purpose or deliberately choose such things, but only those that we think may be effected by our own agency. Again, we are more properly said to wish the end, to choose the means; *e.g.* we wish to be healthy, but we choose what will make us healthy: we wish to be happy, and confess the wish, but it would not be correct to say we purpose or deliberately choose to be happy; for we may say roundly that purpose or choice deals with what is in our power.

Now can it be opinion; for, in the first place, anything may be matter of opinion—what is unalterable and impossible no less than what is in our power; and, in the second place, we distinguish opinion according as it is true or false, not according as it is good or bad, as we do with purpose or choice. We may say, then, that purpose is not the same as opinion in general; nor, indeed, does any one maintain this. But, further, it is not identical with a particular kind of opinion. For one choice of good or evil makes us morally good or bad, holding certain opinions does not. Again, we choose to take or to avoid a good or evil thing; we opine what its nature is, or what it is good for, or in what way; but we cannot opine to take or to avoid. Again, we commend a purpose for its rightness or correctness, an opinion for its truth. Again, we choose a thing when we know well that it is good; we may have an opinion about a thing of which we know nothing. Again, it seems that those who are best at choosing are not always the best at forming opinions, but that some who have an excellent judgment fail, through depravity, to choose what they ought. It may be said that choice or purpose must be preceded or accompanied by an opinion or judgment; but this makes no difference: our question is not that, but whether they are identical.

What, then, is choice or purpose, since it is none of these? It seems, as we said, that what is chosen or purposed is willed, but that what is willed is not always chosen or purposed. The required differentia, I think, is "after previous deliberation." For choice or purpose implies calculation and reasoning. The name itself, too, seems to indicate this, implying that something is chosen before or in preference to other things.

---

3. One manifestation of choosing an alternative is preliminary *deliberation* about it, that is, thinking about the alternatives. What is deliberation? About what do or can we deliberate? Could a person deliberate about obeying the law of gravity? Could we deliberate about the laws regarding female dress in Iran? (Under what circumstances could we do so?)

---

3. Now, as to deliberation, do we deliberate about everything, and may anything whatever be matter for deliberation, or are there some things about which deliberation is impossible? By "matter for deliberation" we should understand, I think, not what a fool or a maniac, but what a rational being would deliberate about. Now, no one deliberates about eternal or unalterable things, *e.g.* the system of the heavenly bodies, or the incommensurability of the side and the diagonal of a square. Again, no one deliberates about things which change, but always change in the same way (whether the cause of change be necessity, or nature, or any other agency), *e.g.* the solstices and the sunrise; nor about things that are quite irregular, like drought and wet; nor about matters of chance, like the finding of a treasure. Again, even human affairs are not always matter of deliberation; *e.g.* what would be the best constitution for Scythia is a question that no Spartan would deliberate about. The reason why we do not deliberate about these things is that none of them are things that we can ourselves effect.

But the things that we do deliberate about are matters of conduct that are within our control. And these are the only things that remain; for besides nature and necessity and chance, the only remaining cause of change is reason and human agency in general. Though we must add that men severally deliberate about what they can themselves do. A further limitation is that where there is exact and absolute knowledge, there is no room for deliberation; *e.g.* writing: for there is no doubt how the letters should be formed. We deliberate, then, about things that are brought about by our own agency, but not always in the same way; *e.g.* about medicine and money-making, and about navigation more than about gymnastic, inasmuch as it is not yet reduced to so perfect a system, and so on; but more about matters of art than matters of science, as there is more doubt about them. Matters of deliberation, then, are matters in which there are rules that generally hold good, but in which the result cannot be predicted, *i.e.* in which there is an element of uncertainty. In important matters we call in advisers, distrusting our own powers of judgment.

It is not about ends, but about means that we deliberate. A physician does not deliberate whether he shall heal, nor an orator whether he shall persuade, nor a statesman whether he shall make a good system of laws, nor a man in any other profession about his end; but, having the proposed end in view, we consider how and by what means this end can be attained; and if it appear that it can be attained by various means, we further consider which is the easiest and best; but if it can only be attained by one means, we consider how it is to be attained by this means, and how this means itself is to be secured, and so on, until we come to the first link in the chain of causes, which is last in the order of discovery. For in deliberation we seem to inquire and to analyze in the way described, just as we analyze a geometrical figure in order to learn how to construct it (and though inquiry is not always deliberation— mathematical inquiry, for instance, is not—deliberation is always inquiry); that which is last in the analysis coming first in the order of construction. If we come upon something impossible, we give up the plan; *e.g.* if it needs money, and money cannot be got: but if it appear possible, we set to work. By possible I mean something that can be done by *us;* and what can be done by our friends can in a manner be done by us; for it is we who set our friends to work. Sometimes we have to find out instruments, sometimes how to use them; and so on with the rest: sometimes we have to find out what agency will produce the desired effect, sometimes how or through whom this agency is to be set at work.

It appears, then, that a man, as we have already said, originates his acts; but that he deliberates about that which he can do himself, and that what he does is done for the sake of something else. For he cannot deliberate about the end, but about the means to the end; nor, again, can he deliberate about particular tacts, *e.g.* whether this be a leaf, or whether it be properly baked: these are matters of immediate perception. And if he goes on deliberating for ever he will never come to a conclusion.

But the object of deliberation and the object of choice or purpose are the same, except that the latter is already fixed and determined; when we say, "this is chosen" or "purposed," we mean that it has been selected after deliberation. For we always stop in our inquiry how to do a thing when we have traced back the chain of causes to ourselves, and to the commanding part of ourselves; for this is the part that chooses. This may be illustrated by the ancient constitutions which Homer describes; for there the kings announce to the people what they have chosen. Since, then, a thing is said to be chosen or purposed when, being in our power, it is desired after diliberation, choice or purpose may be defined as deliberate desire for something in our power; for we first deliberate, and then, having made our decision thereupon, we desire in accordance with deliberation.

Let this stand, then, for an account in outline of choice or purpose, and of what it deals with, viz. means to ends. . . .

5. Finally, Aristotle raises the question, When is a person to be held responsible for what he or she does? Sometimes we have to distinguish between an action and the conditions in which an action takes place; a person who is immoral because he or she is drunk may act involuntarily but is still responsible for having gotten drunk. Action out of ignorance may sometimes excuse a person, but, just as often, a person is responsible for being ignorant. ("Ignorance of the law is no excuse.") A person who has bad habits may be responsible for having cultivated those bad habits (though a person cannot be responsible for the facts of his or her birth and the way he or she was reised). In general, Aristotle urges us to look for the causes of action in the responsibility of the agent rather than blame our actions on "external circumstances."

5. We have seen that, while we wish for the end, we deliberate upon and choose the means thereto. Actions that are concerned with means, then, will be guided by choice, and so will be voluntary. But the acts in which the virtues are manifested are concerned with means. Therefore virtue depends upon ourselves: and vice likewise. For where it lies with us to do, it lies with us not to do. Where we can say no, we can say yes. If then the doing a deed, which is noble, lies with us, the not doing it, which is disgraceful, lies with us; and if the not doing, which is noble, lies with us, the doing, which is disgraceful, also lies with us. But if the doing and likewise the not doing of noble or base deeds lies with us, and if this is, as we found, identical with being good or bad, then it follows that it lies with us to be worthy or worthless men.

And so the saying—

None wills to be wicked, none wills not to be blessed,

seems partly false and partly true: no one indeed is blessed against his will; but vice is voluntary. If we deny this, we must dispute the statements made just now, and must contend that man is not the originator and the parent of his actions, as of his children. But if those statements commend themselves to us, and if we are unable to trace our acts to any other sources than those that depend upon ourselves, then that whose source is within us must itself depend upon us and be voluntary.

This seems to be attested, moreover, by each one of us in private life, and also by the legislators; for they correct and punish those that do evil (except when it is done under compulsion, or through ignorance for which the agent is not responsible), and honour those that do noble deeds, evidently intending to encourage the one sort and discourage the other. But no one encourages us to do that which does not depend on ourselves, and which is not voluntary: it would be useless to be persuaded not to feel heat or pain or hunger and so on, as we should feel them all the same.

I say "ignorance for which the agent is not responsible," for the ignorance itself is punished by the law, if the agent appear to be responsible for his ignorance, *e.g.* for an offence committed in a fit of drunkenness the penalty is doubled: for the origin of the offence lies in the man himself; he might have avoided the intoxication, which was the cause of his ignorance. Again, ignorance of any of the ordinances of the law, which a man ought to know and easily can know, does not avert punishment. And so in other cases, where ignorance seems to be the result of negligence, the offender is punished, since it lay with him to remove this ignorance; for he might have taken the requisite trouble.

It may be objected that it was the man's character not to take the trouble. We reply that men are themselves responsible for acquiring such a character by a dissolute life, and for being unjust or profligate in consequence of re–peated acts of wrong, or of spending their time in drinking and so on. For it is repeated acts of a particular kind that give a man a particular character. This is shown by the way in which men train themselves for any kind of contest or performance: they practise continually. Not to know, then, that repeated acts of this or that kind produce a corresponding character or habit, shows an utter want of sense. Moreover, it is absurd to say that he who acts unjust–ly does not wish to be unjust, or that he who behaves profligately does not wish to be profligate.

But if a man knowingly does acts which must make him unjust, he will be voluntarily unjust; though it does not follow that, if he wishes it, he can cease to be unjust and be just, any more than he who is sick can, if he wishes it, be whole. And it may be that he is voluntarily sick, through living incontinently and disobeying the doctor. At one time, then, he had the option not to be sick, but he no longer has it now that he has thrown away his health. When you have discharged a stone it is no longer in your power to call it back; but nevertheless the throwing and casting away of that stone rests with you; for the beginning of its flight depended upon you. Just so the unjust or the profligate man at the beginning was free not to acquire this character, and therefore he is voluntarily unjust or profligate; but now that he has acquired it, he is no longer free to put it off.

But it is not only our mental or moral vices that are voluntary; bodily vices also are sometimes voluntary, and then are censured. We do not censure natural ugliness, but we do censure that which is due to negligence and want of exercise. And so with weakness and infirmity: we should never reproach a man who was born blind, or had lost his sight in an illness or by a blow—we should rather pity him, but we should all censure a man who had blinded himself by excessive drinking or any other kind of profligacy. We see, then, that of the vices of the body it is those that depend on ourselves that are censured, while those that do not depend on ourselves are not censured. And if this be so, then in other fields also those vices that are blamed must depend upon ourselves.

Some people may perhaps object to this. "All men," they may say, "desire that which appears good to them, but cannot control this appearance; a man's character, whatever it be, decides what shall appear to him to be the end." If, I answer, each man be in some way responsible for his habits or character, then in some way he must be responsible for this appearance also. But if this be not the case, then a man is not responsible for, or is not the cause of, his own evil doing, but it is through ignorance of the end that he does evil, fancying that thereby he will secure the greatest good: and the striving towards the true end does not depend on our own choice, but a man must be born with a gift of sight, so to speak, if he is to discriminate rightly and to choose what is really good: and he is truly well-born who is by nature richly endowed with this gift; for, as it is the greatest and the fairest gift, which we cannot acquire or learn from another, but must keep all our lives just as nature gave it to us, to be well and nobly born in this respect is to be well-born in the truest and completest sense.

Now, granting this to be true, how will virtue be any more voluntary than vice? For whether it be nature or anything else that determines what shall appear to be the end, it is determined in the same way for both alike, for the good man as for the bad, and both alike refer all their acts of whatever kind to it. And so whether we hold that it is not merely nature that decides what appears to each to be the end (whatever that be), but that the man himself contributes something; or whether we hold that the end is fixed by nature, but that virtue is voluntary, inasmuch as the good man voluntarily takes the steps to that end—in either case vice will be just as voluntary as virtue; for self is active in the bad man just as much as in the good man, in choosing the particular acts at least, if not in determining the end. If then, as is generally allowed, the virtues are voluntary (for we do, in fact, in some way help to make our character, and, by being a certain character, give a certain complexion to our idea of the end), the vices also must be voluntary; for all this applies equally to them.

We have thus described in outline the nature of the virtues in general, and have said that they are forms of moderation or modes of observing the mean, and that they are habits or trained faculties, and that they show themselves in the performance of the same acts which produce them, and that they depend on ourselves and are voluntary, and that they follow the guidance of right reason. But our particular acts are not voluntary in the same sense as our habits: for we are masters of our acts from beginning to end when we know the particular circumstances; but we are masters of the beginnings only of our habits or characters, while their growth by gradual steps is imperceptible, like the growth of disease. Inasmuch, however, as it lay with us to employ or not to employ our faculties in this way, the resulting characters are on that account voluntary.

Now let us take up each of the virtues again in turn, and say what it is, and what its subject is, and how it deals with it; and in doing this, we shall at the same time see how many they are. And, first of all, let us take courage.

DISCUSSION

Why is an account of voluntary action and the nature of deliberation so crucial to Aristotle's theory? It is essential because he insists that the good life consists of activity and what a man *does,* not just what happens to him (though good fortune plays a large role in Aristotle's theory). A man would not be virtuous if he accidentally did what virtuous men do (for example, if he tried to run from a battle but ran in the wrong direction and ended up inspiring and leading a charge). And it would hardly count as a virtuous action if a person gave a generous party for all of his friends, but only because a slighted acquaintence had threatened to burn down his house if he did not. Thus Aristotle insists that a virtuous action must be done knowingly (as opposed to our "hero" who ran in the wrong direction) and without compulsion, that is, without being forced. But notice again how limited this definition of voluntary action is from our modern viewpoint. There is no discussion of the ignorance we sometimes have of our own motives or intentions, such that an act which seems voluntary or involuntary may be just the opposite. Freud documents many cases, for example, in which a person feels compelled to do some ridiculous ritual, but it turns out that, with understanding, one sees the purpose and why one did it. Are such actions involuntary just because we don't know what we're doing, in an important sense? By the same token, what about all of those impulses and influences which affect our every action, which (whether or not they are known) are a powerful set of external determinants of our behavior? Do these modify our conception of the voluntary? It is evident that Aristotle did not even consider the free will problem which is so central to so much modern philosophy. That problem begins with the recognition— stated loosely above—that every action is completely determined by any number of causal factors—in our heredity, our upbringing, our peer relationships, the stars, the weather, the immediate neurochemistry of our brains. But if this is so, then there could not be any action which is voluntary in Aristotle's sense since every act would be compelled by external forces. And if this is so, can we even talk of virtuous activity? Or should we be limited to just describing the behavior of individuals as simply "well, that's the sort of things he does." Indeed, Aristotle himself insists that the good man must be raised to be good; does this undermine his insistence on the voluntariness of virtuous activity? And couldn't deliberation, too, just be the product of a certain kind of upbringing, a fully determined preliminary to virtuous action? Would these considerations bother Aristotle? Why or why not?

D. The Intellectual Virtues, the Practical Syllogism, and the Problem of Incontinence

In Book III, Aristotle gave us a brief analysis of deliberation as an essential prelude to rational and voluntary action. In Book VI, he once again turns to the importance of deliberation and the relationship between thought and action. His overall concern here is "the intellectual virtues," that is, those virtues or "excellences" which are special to the "rational" (opposed to the "irrational") part of the soul. This is not to say that Aristotle firmly distinguishes between thought and action; quite the contrary, he is continually at considerable pains to show their interdependence (for instance, in his insistence that ethics can be "useful" and in his treatment of "incontinence," which we shall discuss shortly). But much of Aristotle's philosophizing consists in drawing cautious distinctions, even when he then goes on to argue that the parts distinguished cannot really be separated. Here too, therefore, he begins by once again dividing up his subject matter.

BOOK VI

1. We said above that what we should choose is neither too much nor too little, but "the mean," and that "the mean" is what "right reason" prescribes. This we now have to explain.

Each of the virtues we have discussed implies (as every mental habit implies) some aim which the rational man keeps in view when he is regulating his efforts; in other words, there must be some standard for determining the several modes of moderation, which we say lie between excess and deficiency, and are in accordance with "right reason." But though this is quite true, it is not sufficiently precise. In any kind of occupation which can be reduced to rational principles, it is quite true to say that we must brace ourselves up and relax ourselves neither too much nor too little, but "in moderation," "as right reason orders;" but this alone would not tell one much; *e.g.* a man would hardly learn how to treat a case by being told to treat it as the art of medicine prescribes, and as one versed in that art would treat it. So in the case of mental habits or types of character also it is not enough that the rule we have laid down is correct; we need further to know precisely what this right reason is, and what is the standard which it affords.

The virtues or excellences of the mind or soul, it will be remembered, we divided into two classes, and called the one moral and the other intellectual. The moral excellences or virtues we have already discussed in detail; let us now examine the other class, the intellectual excellences, after some preliminary remarks about the soul. We said before that the soul consists of two parts, the rational and the irrational part. We will now make a similar division of the former, and will assume that there are two rational faculties: (1) that by which we know those things that depend on invariable principles, (2) that by which we know those things that are variable. For to generically different objects must correspond generically different faculties, if, as we hold, it is in virtue of some kind of likeness or kinship with their objects that our faculties are able to know them. Let us call the former the scientific or demonstrative, the latter the calculative or deliberative faculty. For to deliberate is the same as to calculate, and no one deliberates about things that are invariable. One division then of the rational faculty may be fairly called the calculative faculty. Our problem, then, is to find what each of these faculties becomes in its full development, or in its best state; for that will be its excellence or virtue. But its excellence will bear direct reference to its proper function. . . .

In the next chapters, Aristotle discusses the "means by which the soul arrives at the truth", namely, art, science, prudence, wisdom, and intuitive reason *(nous)*. His discussions of art and science are of no special relevance to what we call ethics (though it is worth noting that they were to him); prudence and wisdom, however, are clearly essential to ethics.

What is prudence? Notice, first of all, that Aristotle's use of this term is significantly different from ours. We mean by "prudence" watching out for one's own interests; Aristotle includes judging what is "good for men in general" as well (for example, in a statesman like Pericles). Once again, Aristotle does not distinguish sharply as we do between one's own interests and the interests of one's general community.

5. In order to ascertain what prudence is, we will first ask who they are whom we call prudent. It seems to be characteristic of a prudent man that he is able to deliberate well about what is good or expedient for himself, not with a view to some particular end, such as health or strength, but with a view to well-being or living well. This is confirmed by the fact that we apply the name sometimes to those who deliberate well in some particular field, when they calculate well the means to some particular good end, in matters that do not fall within the sphere of art. So we may say, generally, that a man who can deliberate well is prudent.

But no one deliberates about that which cannot be altered, nor about that which it is not in his power to do. Now science, we saw, implies demonstration; but things whose principles or causes are variable do not admit of demonstration; for everything that depends upon these principles or causes is also variable; and, on the other hand, things that are necessarily determined do not admit of deliberation. It follows, therefore, that prudence cannot be either a science or an art: it cannot be a science, because the sphere of action is that which is alterable; it cannot be an art, because production is generically different from action. It follows from all this that prudence is a formed faculty that apprehends truth by reasoning or calculation, and issues in action, in the domain of human good and ill; for while production has another end than itself, this is not so with action, since good action or well doing is itself the end.

For this reason Pericles and men who resemble him are considered prudent, because they are able to see what is good for themselves and for men in general; and this we take to be the character of those who are able to manage a household or a state. This, too, is the reason for the term "temperance," which signifies [in Greek] that it is the virtue which preserves prudence. But what temperance preserves is this particular kind of judgment. For it is not *any* kind of judgment that is destroyed or perverted by the presentation of pleasant or painful objects (not such a judgment, for instance, as that the angles of a triangle are equal to two right angles), but only judgments about matters of practice. For the principles of practice [or the causes which originate action] are the ends for the sake of which acts are done; but when a man is corrupted by pleasure or pain, he straightway loses sight of the principle, and no longer sees that this is the end for the sake of which, and as a means to which, each particular act should be chosen and done; for vice is apt to obliterate the principle. Our conclusion then is that prudence is a formed faculty which apprehends truth by reasoning or calculation, and issues in action, in the field of human good.

Moreover, the artistic faculty has its perfect development in something other than itself, but this is not so with prudence. Again, in the domain of art voluntary error is not so bad as involuntary, but it is worse in the case of prudence, as it is in the case of all the virtues or excellences. It is plain, then, that prudence is a virtue or excellence, and not an art. And the rational parts of the soul or the intellectual faculties being two in number, prudence will be the virtue of the second, the faculty of opinion; for opinion deals with that which is variable, and so does prudence. But it is something more than a formed state of apprehending truth by reasoning or calculation; as we see from the fact that such a state may be forgotten, but prudence, once acquired, can never be lost. . . .

7. Now, what is wisdom?

7. The term wisdom is sometimes applied in the domain of the arts to those who are consummate masters of their art; *e.g.* it is applied to Phidias as a master of sculpture, and to Polyclitus for his skill in portrait-statues; and in this application it means nothing else than excellence of art or perfect development of the artistic faculty. But there are also men who are considered wise, not in part nor in any particular thing (as Homer says in the Margites—

> Him the gods gave no skill with spade or plough,
> Nor made him wise in aught),

but generally wise. In this general sense, then, wisdom plainly will be the most perfect of the sciences.

The wise man, then, must not only know what follows from the principles of knowledge, but also know the truth about the principles. Wisdom, therefore, will be the union of [intuitive] reason with [demonstrative] scientific knowledge, or scientific knowledge of the noblest objects with its crowning perfection, so to speak, added to it. For it would be absurd to suppose that the political faculty or prudence is the highest of our faculties, unless indeed man is the best of all things in the universe.

Now, as the terms wholesome and good mean one thing in the case of men and another in the case of fishes, while white and straight always have the same meaning, we must all allow that wise means one thing always, while prudent means different things; for we should all say that those who are clear-sighted in their own affairs are prudent, and deem them fit to be entrusted with those affairs. (And for this reason we sometimes apply the term prudent even to animals, when they show a faculty of foresight in what concerns their own life.) Moreover, it is plain that wisdom cannot be the same as statesmanship. If we apply the term wisdom to knowledge of what is advantageous to ourselves, there will be many kinds of wisdom; for the knowledge of what is good will not be one and the same for all animals, but different for each species. It can no more be one than the art of healing can be one and the same for all kinds of living things.

Man may be superior to all other animals, but that will not make any difference here; for there are other things of a far diviner nature than man, as—to take the most conspicuous instance—the heavenly bodies.

It is plain, then, after what we have said, that wisdom is the union of scientific [or demonstrative] knowledge and [intuitive] reason about objects of the noblest nature. And on this account people call Anaxagoras and Thales and men of that sort wise, but not prudent, seeing them to be ignorant of their own advantage;

and say that their knowledge is something out of the common, wonderful, hard of attainment, nay super-human, but useless, since it is no human good that they seek.

Prudence, on the other hand, deals with human affairs, and with matters that admit of deliberation: for the prudent man's special function, as we conceive it, is to deliberate well; but no one deliberates about what is invariable, or about matters in which there is not some end, in the sense of some realizable good. But a man is said to deliberate well (without any qualifying epithet) when he is able, by a process of reasoning or calculation, to arrive at what is best for man in matters of practice. Prudence, moreover, does not deal in general propositions only, but implies knowledge of particular facts also; for it issues in action, and the field of action is the field of particulars. This is the reason why some men that lack [scientific] knowledge are more efficient in practice than others that have it, especially men of wide experience; for if you know that light meat is digestible and wholesome, but do not know what meats are light, you will not be able to cure people so well as a man who only knows that chicken is light and wholesome. But prudence is concerned with practice; so that it needs knowledge both of general truths and of particular facts, but more especially the latter. But here also [*i.e.* in the domain of practice] there must be a supreme form of the faculty [which we will now proceed to consider]. . . .

In the final passage here, Aristotle introduces one of his most important technical suggestions; he calls it "the practical syllogism."

Aristotle is often called the father of logic, and he is credited with inventing many of the basic forms of deduction which have defined the core of formal logic ever since. Best known among these basic forms is the *syllogism,* and the best-known example is

All men are mortal.
   Socrates is a man.
   Therefore, Socrates is mortal.

The first statement of such a syllogism is called *the major premise,* and it has *universal* form ("All a's are b"). The second statement is *the minor premise,* and it has a particular subject (Socrates). The term "man(men)" is called *the middle term.* As a valid deductive argument, the conclusion will be true if the premises are both true. We might call this a "theoretical syllogism," because it is concerned with deriving true statements. A "practical syllogism," on the other hand, results in an action. The practical syllogism, in other words, is the form of deliberation.

Using the example Aristotle gives us here, we can construct the following practical syllogism:

All light meats are digestible and wholesome.
   This chicken is light meat.
   Therefore, (eat this chicken)

Once again, we have a universal major premise ("All a's are b) and a minor premise with a particular subject (the piece of chicken sitting on our plate in front of us), but the conclusion, in a practical syllogism, is an action, namely, eating the chicken. (Here "light meat" is the middle term; see Aristotle's comment on the "false syllogism" in chapter 9.)

This simple device allows Aristotle to offer several interesting analyses of the nature of deliberate action and what can go wrong with it. It is a model of how one ought to deliberate, from general principles and particular facts; it shows why one must have both general knowledge (in the form of universal principles) and experience and knowledge of particular facts, which are recognized by "perception" or "correctness in judging" (Chapter 9). It also shows us at least two ways in which deliberation can go wrong: one can be ignorant of the universal principle, or one can have poor judgment and not recognize the facts of the case. Suppose, for example, a person begins to act obnoxiously after a third drink. Here he or she is, standing in front of the bar, deliberating whether or not to have another martini. One possibility:

"Drinking is good for social poise; it relaxes you and makes you more charming."
Wrong major premise.
Another possibility:

"I know drinking causes obnoxiousness (right major premise), but these martinis aren't very strong and I've had a lot to eat." (Wrong minor premise.)

What about the link between the two premises and the conclusion (the action)—couldn't a person have all the requisite knowledge of both facts and principles and yet not do the action? But this is the problematic phenomenon of "incontinence" (knowing what is right but doing what is wrong); it requires separate treatment. (Aristotle's essential answer is, No, it is not possible to have the knowledge and not do the act in question.)

9. Before, Aristotle gave us an analysis of what deliberation is; now, he gives us an analysis of what it is to deliberate well.

9. Inquiry and deliberation are not the same; for deliberation is a particular kind of inquiry. But we must ascertain what good deliberation is—whether it is a kind of science or opinion, or happy guessing, or something quite different. It is not science; for we do not inquire about that which we know: but good deliberation is a kind of deliberation, and when we deliberate we inquire and calculate. Nor is it happy guessing; for we make happy guesses without calculating and in a moment, but we take time to deliberate, and it is a common saying that execution should be swift, but deliberation slow. Good deliberation, again, is different from sagacity, which is a kind of happy guessing. Nor is it any kind of opinion. But since in deliberating ill we go wrong, and in deliberating well we go right, it is plain that good deliberation is a kind of rightness, but a rightness or correctness neither of science nor opinion; for science does not admit of correctness (since it does not, admit of error), and correctness of opinion is simply truth; and, further, that concerning which we have an opinion is always something already settled. Good deliberation, however, is impossible without calculation. We have no choice left, then, but to say that it is correctness of reasoning; for reasoning is not yet assertion: and whereas opinion is not an inquiry, but already a definite assertion, when we are deliberating, whether well or ill, we are inquiring and calculating.

But as good deliberation is a kind of correctness in deliberation, we must first inquire what deliberation means, and what its field is [Cf. Book III, 3].

Now, there are various kinds of correctness, and it is plain that not every kind of correctness in deliberation is good deliberation; for the incontinent man or the vicious man may duly arrive, by a process of calculation, at the end which he has in view, so that he will have deliberated correctly, though what he gains is a great evil. But to have deliberated well is thought to be a good thing; for it is only a particular kind of correctness in deliberation that is called good deliberation—that, namely, which arrives at what is good.

But, further, what is good may be arrived at by a false syllogism; I mean that a right conclusion as to what is to be done may be arrived at in a wrong way or upon wrong grounds—the middle term being wrong; so that what leads to a right conclusion as to what should be done is not good deliberation, unless the grounds also be right. A further difference is that one may arrive at the right conclusion slowly, another rapidly. So we must add yet another condition to the above, and say that good deliberation means coming to a right conclusion as to what is expedient or ought to be done, and coming to it in the right manner and at the right time. Again, we speak of deliberating well simply, and of deliberating well with a view to a particular kind of end. So good deliberation simply [or without any qualifying epithet] is that which leads to right conclusions as to the means to the end simply; a particular kind of good deliberation is that which leads to right conclusions as to the means to a particular kind of end. And so, when we say that prudent men must deliberate well, good deliberation in this case will be correctness in judging what is expedient to that end of which prudence has a true conception. . . .

---

12. Finally, he answers the skeptics (the Sophists in his day) who are interested only in what is practical, not in the abstract speculations of philosophy or the concerns of ethics. Prudence and wisdom are not only good according to the philosopher, they are useful too. Furthermore, he argues that prudence is the means to wisdom.

---

12. But here an objection may be raised. "What is the use of them?" it may be asked. "Wisdom does not consider what tends to make man happy (for it does not ask how anything is brought about). Prudence indeed does this, but why do we need it? Prudence is the faculty which deals with what is just and noble and good for man, *i.e.* with those things which it is the part of the good man to do; but the knowledge of them no more makes us apter to do them, if (as has been said) the [moral] virtues are habits, than it does in the case of what is healthy and wholesome—healthy and wholesome, that is, not in the sense of conducing to, but in the sense of issuing from, a healthy habit; for a knowledge of medicine and gymnastics does not make us more able to do these things. But if it be meant that a man should be prudent, not in order that he may do these acts, but in order that he may become able to do them, then prudence will be no use to those who *are* good, nor even to those who are not. For it will not matter whether they have prudence themselves, or take the advice of others who have it. It will be enough to do in these matters as we do in regard to health; for if we wish to be in health, we do not go and learn medicine. Again, it seems to be a strange thing that prudence, though inferior to wisdom, must yet govern it, since in every field the practical faculty bears away and issues orders."

We must now discuss these points; for hitherto we have been only stating objections.

First, then, we may say that both prudence and wisdom must be desirable in themselves, since each is the virtue of one of the parts of the soul, even if neither of them produces anything.

Next, they *do* produce something. On the one hand, wisdom produces happiness, not in the sense in which medicine produces health, but in the sense in which health produces health; that is to say, wisdom being a part of complete virtue, its possession and exercise make a man happy. On the other hand [in the sphere of action], man performs his function perfectly when he acts in accordance with both prudence and moral virtue; for while the latter ensures the rightness of the end aimed at, the former ensures the rightness of the means thereto. The fourth[3] part of the soul, the vegetative part, or the faculty of nutrition, has no analogous excellence; for it has no power to act or not to act.

But as to the objection that prudence makes us no more apt to do what is noble and just, let us take the matter a little deeper, beginning thus: We allow, on the one hand, that some who do just acts are not yet just; *e.g.* those who do what the laws enjoin either unwillingly or unwittingly, or for some external motive and not for the sake of the acts themselves (though they do that which they ought and all that a good man should do). And, on the other hand, it seems that when a man does the several acts with a certain disposition he is good; *i.e.* when he does them of deliberate purpose, and for the sake of the acts themselves. Now, the rightness of the purpose is secured by [moral] virtue, not to [moral] virtue, but to another faculty. But we must dwell a little on this point and try to make it quite clear.

There is a faculty which we call cleverness, the power of carrying out the means to any proposed end, and so achieving it. If then the end be noble, the power merits praise; but if the end be base, the power is the power of the villain. So we apply the term clever both to the prudent man and the villain. Now, this power is not identical with prudence, but is its necessary condition. But this power, the "eye of the soul" as we may call it, does not attain its perfect development without moral virtue, as we said before, and as may be shown thus: All syllogisms or deductive reasonings about what is to be done have for their starting point "the end or the supreme good is so and so" (whatever it be; any definition of the good will do for the argument). But it is only to the good man that this presents itself as the good; for vice perverts us and causes us to err about the principles of action. So it is plain, as we said, that it is impossible to be prudent without being morally good.

13. This suggests a further consideration of moral virtue; for the case is closely analogous to this—I mean that just as prudence is related to cleverness, being not identical with it, but closely akin to it, so is fully developed moral virtue related to natural virtue. All admit that in a certain sense the several kinds of character are bestowed by nature. Justice, a tendency to temperance, courage, and the other types of character are exhibited from the moment of birth. Nevertheless, we look for developed goodness as something different

---

[3]The other three are sense, reason, desire.

from this, and expect to find these same qualities in another form. For even in children and brutes these natural virtues are present, but without the guidance of reason they are plainly hurtful. So much at least seems to be plain—that just as a strong-bodied creature devoid of sight stumbles heavily when it tries to move, because it cannot see, so is it with this natural virtue; but when it is enlightened by reason it acts surpassingly well; and the natural virtue (which before was only like virtue) will then be fully developed virtue.

We find, then, that just as there are two forms of the calculative faculty, viz. cleverness and prudence, so there are two forms of the moral qualities, viz. natural virtue and fully developed virtue, and that the latter is impossible without prudence. On this account some people say that all the virtues are forms of prudence, and in particular Socrates held this view, being partly right in his inquiry and partly wrong—wrong in thinking that all the virtues are actually forms of prudence, but right in saying that they are impossible without prudence. This is corroborated, by the fact that nowadays every one in defining virtue would, after specifying its field, add that it is a formed faculty or habit in accordance with right reason, "right" meaning "in accordance with prudence." Thus it seems that every one has a sort of inkling that a formed habit or character of this kind (*i.e.* in accordance with prudence) is virtue. Only a slight change is needed in this expression. Virtue is not simply a formed habit in accordance with right reason, but a formed habit *implying the use of* right reason. But right reason in these matters is prudence. So whereas Socrates held that the [moral] virtues are forms of reason (for he held that they are all modes of knowledge), we hold that they imply the use of reason.

It is evident, then, from what has been said that it is impossible to be good in the full sense without prudence, or to be prudent without moral virtue. And in this way we can meet an objection which may be urged. "The virtues," it may be said, "are found apart from each other; a man who is strongly predisposed to one virtue has not an equal tendency towards all the others, so that he will have acquired this virtue while he still lacks that." We may answer that though this may be the case with the natural virtues, yet it cannot be the case with those virtues for which we call a man good without any qualifying epithet. The presence of the single virtue of prudence implies the presence of all the moral virtues. And thus it is plain, in the first place, that, even if it did not help practice, we should yet need prudence as the virtue or excellence of a part of our nature; and, in the second place, that purpose cannot be right without both prudence and moral virtue; for the latter makes us desire the end, while the former makes us adopt the right means to the end.

Nevertheless, prudence is not the mistress of wisdom and of the better part of our nature [the reason], any more than medicine is the mistress of health. Prudence does not employ wisdom in her service, but provides means for the attainment of wisdom—does not rule it, but rules in its interests. To assert the contrary would be like asserting that statesmanship rules the gods, because it issues orders about all public concerns [including the worship of the gods.]

BOOK VII: INCONTINENCE *(AKRASIA)*

According to the practical syllogism, right action follows correct knowledge as a true conclusion follows from a sound argument. So, if a person acts wrongly, it follows that he or she must not have correct knowledge in the same way that, if a person draws a false conclusion from a valid argument, it must be because one of the premises is false. But behind this technical analogy lies a deep and continuing ethical concern—how it is that being rational and knowing what is good necessitates right action. Just knowing what is good, Socrates had argued, is sufficient to lead a person to do the right thing. Two thousand years later, Immanuel Kant also argued that reason has its own motivating force, quite independent of our other desires and passions. But what then are we to make of those cases in which a person seems to know what is right but doesn't do it—or what we call "incontinence"? Aristotle begins by raising this objection against Socrates's rejection of incontinence but, finally, ends up agreeing with him that a person cannot knowingly do wrong.

2. In what sense, it may be objected, can a man judge rightly when he acts incontinently? Some people maintain that he cannot act so if he really knows what is right; for it would be strange, thought Socrates, if, when real knowledge were in the man, something else should master him and hale him about like a slave. Socrates, indeed, contested the whole position, maintaining that there is no such thing as incontinence: when a man acts contrary to what is best, he never, according to Socrates, has a right judgment of the case, but acts so by reason of ignorance. Now, this theory evidently conflicts with experience; and with regard to the passion which sways the incontinent man, if it really is due to ignorance, we must ask what kind of ignorance it is due to. For it is plain that, at any rate, he who acts incontinently does not fancy that the act is good till the passion is upon him.

There are other people who in part agree and in part disagree with Socrates. They allow that nothing is able to prevail against knowledge, but do not allow that men never act contrary to what *seems* best; and so they say that the incontinent man, when he yields to pleasure, has not knowledge, but only opinion. But if, in truth, it be only opinion and not knowledge, and if it be not a strong but a weak belief or judgment that opposes the desires (as is the case when a man is in doubt), we pardon a man for not abiding by it in the face of strong desires; but, in fact, we do not pardon vice nor anything else that we call blamable.

Are we, then, to say that it is prudence that opposes desire? For it is the strongest form of belief. Surely that would be absurd: for then the same man would be at once prudent and incontinent; but no one would maintain that a prudent man could voluntarily do the vilest acts. Moreover, we have already shown that prudence is essentially a faculty that issues in act; for it is concerned with the ultimate thing [the thing to be done], and implies the possession of all the moral virtues. Again, if a man cannot be continent without having strong and bad desires, the temperate man will not be continent, nor the continent man temperate; for it is incompatible with the temperate character to have either very violent or bad desires.

They must, however, be both strong and bad in the continent man: for if they were good, the habit that hindered from following them would be bad, so that continence would not be always good; if they were weak and not bad, it would be nothing to respect; and if they were bad, but at the same time weak, it would be nothing to admire.

Again, if continence makes a man apt to abide by any opinion whatsoever, it is a bad thing—as, for instance, if it makes him abide by a false opinion: and if incontinence makes a man apt to abandon any opinion whatsoever, there will be a kind of incontinence that is good, an instance of which is Neoptolemus in the Philoctetes of Sophocles; for he merits praise for being prevented from persevering in the plan which Ulysses had persuaded him to adopt by the pain which he felt at telling a lie.

Again, the well-known argument of the sophists, though fallacious, makes a difficulty: for, wishing to establish a paradoxical conclusion, so that they may be thought clever if they succeed, they construct a syllogism which puzzles the hearer; for his reason is fettered, as he is unwilling to rest in the conclusion, which is revolting to him, but is unable to advance, since he cannot find a flaw in the argument. Thus it may be argued that folly combined with incontinence is virtue:—by reason of his incontinence a man does the opposite of that which he judges to be good; but he judges that the good is bad and not to be done; the result is that he will do the good and not the bad.

Again, he who pursues and does what is pleasant from conviction, and deliberately chooses these things, would seem [if this doctrine be true] to be better than he who does so, not upon calculation, but by reason of incontinence. For the former is more curable, as his convictions might be changed; but to the incontinent man we may apply the proverb which says, "If water chokes you, what will you wash it down with?" For if he were convinced that what he does is good, a change in his convictions might stop his doing it; but, as it is, though he is convinced that something else is good, he nevertheless does this.

Again, if incontinence and continence may be displayed in *anything*, who is the man whom we call incontinent simply? For though no one man unites all the various forms of incontinence, there yet are people to whom we apply the term without any qualification.

Something of this sort, then, are the objections that suggest themselves; and of these we must remove some and leave others; for the resolution of a difficulty is the discovery of the truth.

3. We have, then, to inquire (1) whether the incontinent man acts with knowledge or not, and what knowledge means here; then (2) what is to be regarded as the field in which continence and incontinence manifest themselves —I mean whether their field be all pleasures and pains, or certain definite classes of these; then (3) with regard to the continent and the hardy man, whether they

are the same or different; and so on with the other points that are akin to this inquiry.

(But we ought to begin by inquiring whether the species of continence and the species of incontinence of which we are here speaking are to be distinguished from other species by the field of their manifestation or by their form or manner—I mean whether a man is to be called incontinent in this special sense merely because he is incontinent or uncontrolled by reason in certain things, or because he is incontinent in a certain manner, or rather on both grounds; and in connection with this we ought to determine whether or no this incontinence and this continence may be displayed in all things. And our answer to these questions will be that the man who is called simply incontinent, without any qualification, does not display his character in all things, but only in those things in which the profligate manifests himself; nor is it simply an uncontrolled disposition with regard to them that makes him what he is (for then incontinence would be the same as profligacy), but a particular kind of uncontrolled disposition. For the profligate is carried along of his own deliberate choice or purpose, holding that what is pleasant at the moment is always to be pursued; while the incontinent man thinks otherwise, but pursues it all the same.) [Let us now turn to question (1).]

As to the argument that it is true opinion and not knowledge against which men act incontinently, it really makes no difference here; for some of those who merely have opinions are in no doubt at all, but fancy that they have exact knowledge. If then it be said that those who have opinion more readily act against their judgment because of the weakness of their belief, we would answer that there is no such difference between knowledge and opinion; for some people have just as strong a belief in their opinions as others have in what they really know, of which Heraclitus is an instance.

But we use the word know in two different senses: he who has knowledge which he is not now using is said to know a thing, and also he who is now using his knowledge. Having knowledge, therefore, which is not now present to the mind, about what one ought not to do, will be different from having knowledge which is now present. Only in the latter sense, not in the former, does it seem strange that a man should act against his knowledge.

Again, since these reasonings involve two kinds of premises [a universal proposition for major and a particular for minor], there is nothing to prevent a man from acting contrary to his knowledge though he has both premises, if he is now using the universal only, and not the particular; for the particular is the thing to be done.

Again, different kinds of universal propositions may be involved: one may concern the agent himself, another the thing; for instance, you may reason (1) "all men are benefited by dry things, and I am a man"; and (2) "things of this kind are dry"; but the second minor, "this thing is of this kind," may be unknown or the knowledge of it may be dormant.

These distinctions, then, will make a vast difference, so much so that it does not seem strange that a man should act against his knowledge if he knows in one way, though it does seem strange if he knows in another way.

But again, it is possible for a man to "have knowledge" in yet another way than those just mentioned: we see, I mean, that "having knowledge without using it" includes different modes of having, so that a man may have it in one sense and in another sense not have it; for instance, a man who is asleep, or mad, or drunk. But people who are under the influence of passion are in a similar state; for anger, and sexual desire and the like do evidently alter the condition of the body, and in some cases actually produce madness. It is plain, then, that the incontinent man must be allowed to have knowledge in the same sort of way as those who are asleep, mad, or drunk.

But to repeat the words of knowledge is no proof that a man really has knowledge [in the full sense of having an effective knowledge]; for even when they are under the influence of these passions people repeat demonstrations and sayings of Empedocles, just as learners string words together before they understand their meaning—the meaning must be ingrained in them, and that requires time. So we must hold that the incontinent repeat words in the same sort of way that actors do.

Again, one may inquire into the cause of this phenomenon [of incontinence] by arguments based upon its special nature, as follows:—You may have (1) a universal judgment, (2) a judgment about particular facts which fall at once within the province of sense or perception; but when the two are joined together, the conclusion must in matters of speculation be assented to by the mind, in matters of practice be carried out at once into act; for instance, if you judge (1) "all sweet things are to be tasted," (2) "this thing before me is sweet"—a particular fact,—then, if you have the power and are not hindered, you cannot but at once put the conclusion ["this is to be tasted"] into practice.

Now, when you have on the one side the universal judgment forbidding you to taste, and on the other side the universal judgment, "all sweet things are pleasant," with the corresponding particular, "this thing before me is sweet" (but it is the particular judgment which is effective), and appetite is present— then, though the former train of reasoning bids you avoid this, appetite moves you [to take it]; for appetite is able to put the several bodily organs in motion. And thus it appears that it is in a way under the influence of reason, that is to say of opinion, that people act incontinently— opinion, too, that is, not in itself, but only accidentally, opposed to right reason. For it is the desire, not the opinion, that is opposed to right reason. And this is the reason why brutes cannot be incontinent; they have no universal judgments, but only images and memories of particular facts.

As to the process by which the incontinent man gets out of this ignorance and recovers his knowledge, the account of it will be the same as in the case of a man who is drunk or asleep, and will not be peculiar to this phenomenon; and for such an account we must go to the professors of natural science. But since the minor premise is an opinion or judgment about a fact of perception, and determines action, the incontinent man, when under the influence of passion, either has it not, or has it in a sense in which, as we explained, having is equivalent, not to knowing in the full sense, but to repeating words as a drunken man repeats the sayings of Empedocles. And thus, since the minor premise is not universal, and is thought to be less a matter of knowledge than the universal judgment [or major premise], it seems that what Socrates sought to establish really is the case; for when passion carries a man away, what is present to his mind is not what is regarded as knowledge in the strict sense, nor is it such knowledge that is perverted by his passion, but sense knowledge merely.

4. So much, then, for the question whether the incontinent man knows or not, and in what sense it is possible to act incontinently with knowledge. We next have to consider whether a man can be incontinent simply, or only incontinent in some particular way, and, if the former be the case, what is the field in which the character is manifested.

It is evident that it is in the matter of pleasures and pains that both continent and hardy and incontinent and soft men manifest their characters. Of the sources of pleasure, some are necessary, and others are desirable in themselves but admit of excess: "necessary" are the bodily processes, such as nutrition, the propagation of the species, and generally those bodily function with which we said that profligacy and temperance have to do; others, though not necessary, are in themselves desirable, such as victory, honour, wealth, and other things of the kind that are good and pleasant. Now, those who go to excess in these latter in spite of their own better reason are not called incontinent simply, but with a qualifying epithet, as incontinent with respect to money, or gain, or honour, or anger—not simply, since they are different characters, and only called incontinent in virtue of a resemblance—just as the victor in the last Olympic games was called a man; for though the meaning of the name as applied to him was but slightly different from its common meaning, still it was different. And this may be proved thus: incontinence is blamed, not simply as a mistake, but as a kind of vice, either of vice simply, or of some particular vice; but those who are thus incontinent [in the pursuit of wealth, etc.] are not thus blamed.

But of the characters that manifest themselves in the matter of bodily enjoyments, with which we say the temperate and the profligate are concerned, he who goes to excess in pursuing what is pleasant and avoiding what is painful, in the matter of hunger and thirst, and heat and cold, and all things that affect us by touch or taste, and who does this not of deliberate choice, but contrary to his deliberate choice and reasoning, is called incontinent—not with the addition that he is incontinent with respect to this particular thing, as anger, but simply incontinent. A proof of this is that people are also called soft in these latter matters, but not in any of the former [honour, gain, etc.]. And on this account we group the incontinent with the profligate and the continent and the temperate (but do not class with them any of those who are metaphorically called continent and incontinent), because they are in a way concerned with the same pleasures and pains. They are, in fact, concerned with the same matters, but their behaviour is different; for whereas the other three deliberately choose what they do, the incontinent man does not. And so a man who, without desire, or with only a moderate desire, pursues excess of pleasure, and avoids even slight pains, would more properly be called profligate than one who is impelled so to act by violent desires; for what would the former do if the violent passions of youth were added, and if it were violent pain to him to forego the satisfaction of his natural appetites?

But some of our desires and pleasures are to be classed as noble and good (for some of the things that please us are naturally desirable), while others are the reverse of this, and others are intermediate between the two, as we explained before,—such things as money, gain, victory, and honour falling within the first class. With regard both to these, then, and to the intermediate class, men are blamed not for being affected by them, or desiring them, or caring for them, but only for doing so in certain ways and beyond the bounds of moderation. So we blame those who are moved by, or pursue, some good and noble object to an unreasonable extent, as, for instance, those who care too much for honour, or for their children or parents: for these, too, are noble objects, and men are praised for caring about them; but still one might go too far in them also, if one were to fight even against the gods, like Niobe, or to do as did Satyrus, who was nicknamed Philopator from his affection for his father—for he seemed to carry his affection to the pitch of folly.

In these matters, then, there is no room for vice or wickedness for the reason mentioned, viz. that all these are objects that are in themselves desirable, though excess in them is not commendable, and is to be avoided. Similarly, in these matters there is no room for incontinence strictly so called (for incontinence is not only to be avoided, but is actually blamable), but because of the similarity of the state of mind we do here use the term incontinence with a qualification, saying "incontinent in this or in that," just as we apply the term "bad physician" or "bad actor" to a man whom we should not call bad simply or without a qualifying epithet. Just as in the latter case, then, the term badness or vice is applied, not simply, but with a qualification, because each of these qualities is not a vice strictly, but only analogous to a vice, so in this case also it is plain that we must understand that only to be strictly incontinence (or continence) which is manifested in those matters with which temperance and profligacy are concerned, while that which is manifested with regard to anger is only metaphorically called so; and therefore we call a man "incontinent in anger," as "in honour" or "in gain," adding a qualifying epithet.

DISCUSSION

The intellectual virtues seem to be of two related kinds, those that are involved with and support the moral virtues (through deliberation, for example) and those which are activities with excellences of their own, notably thinking for its own sake (philosophy). Although he distinguishes them (in accordance with the various parts of the soul), Aristotle also stresses their interconnection. But notice that the distinction between the "rational" and "irrational" parts of the soul is none too clear either, in part because what is "rational" seems to include aspects of habits and feeling (which are defined as irrational) and what is "irrational" (for example, emotions) has a clearly rational element for Aristotle. (For example, he analyzes the emotion anger in his *Rhetoric* on the basis of a number of "reasonable" judgments and desires.) Sometimes, Aristotle makes the distinction between rational and irrational on the basis of the mind and body, but elsewhere (*De Anima,* notably) he rejects any such distinction. Thus, despite the distinctions that define the structure of the *Ethics,* one would probably be most accurate to say that Aristotle is arguing a view of ethics which is a unified whole, in contrast to those authors (for instance, Kant) whose ethical theories are based on a comparatively sharp division of the human psyche into a number of at least potentially antagonistic compartments.

The practical syllogism is an analysis of the "calculative faculty" regarding action. It is a model of deliberation, the process by which we come to act voluntarily, through choice rather than ignorance or compulsion. But is the practical syllogism an adequate model of deliberation? Is that how we actually think about our potential actions? Consider yourself about to ask a new friend for a date. What goes through your mind? What sort of model would seem to capture the logic involved? What happens when you have gone through this procedure and come out with the conclusion, "make the date," but then you find yourself unable to do it (incontinent)? What would Aristotle say about your case?

E. Friendship

Aristotle's discussion of friendship occupies the single greatest portion of the *Ethics*—two full chapters, or almost a quarter of the book. The extensiveness of the discussion attests to the importance of this most necessary component of the good life, "for no one would want to live without friends." Aristotle's ethics is first of all a *social* ethics in which it is all-important for people to get along with one another, help one another, and inspire one another to be even more virtuous. (Aristotle defends many of the virtues by commenting that one's friends will approve of and appreciate virtuous action but will disdain vice.) Friendship, as something more than a single virtue, is the best manifestation of all of these concerns. Friends not only get along, they *like* (even *love*) each other. They help each other, and they also—ideally—inspire one another to ever-new heights of virtue. You will notice that Aristotle considers friendship much more than mere companionship and mutual help; it is a kind of love *(philia)* and is one of the most important determinants of character.

In Chapters 1 to 6 of Book VIII, Aristotle discusses the necessity of friendship for the good life and delineates three distinct kinds of friendship, from the merely useful to the ideal.

BOOK VIII

1. After what we have said, a discussion of friendship would naturally follow, since it is a virtue or implies virtue, and is besides most necessary with a view to living. For without friends no one would choose to live, though he had all other goods; even rich men and those in possession of office and of dominating power are thought to need friends most of all; for what is the use of such prosperity without the opportunity of beneficence, which is exercised chiefly and in its most

laudable form towards friends? Or how can prosperity be guarded and preserved without friends? The greater it is, the more exposed is it to risk. And in poverty and in other misfortunes men think friends are the only refuge. It helps the young, too, to keep from error; it aids older people by ministering to their needs and supplementing the activities that are failing from weakness; those in the prime of life it stimulates to noble actions—'two going together'—for with friends men are more able both to think and to act. Again, parent seems by nature to feel it for offspring and offspring for parent, not only among men but among birds and among most animals; it is felt mutually by members of the same race, and especially by men, whence we praise lovers of their fellowmen. We may see even in our travels how near and dear every man is to every other. Friendship seems too to hold states together, and lawgivers to care more for it than for justice; for unanimity seems to be something like friendship, and this they aim at most of all, and expel faction as their worst enemy; and when men are friends they have no need of justice, while when they are just they need friendship as well, and the truest form of justice is thought to be a friendly quality.

But it is not only necessary but also noble; for we praise those who love their friends, and it is thought to be a fine thing to have many friends; and again we think it is the same people that are good men and are friends.

Not a few things about friendship are matters of debate. Some define it as a kind of likeness and say like people are friends, whence come the sayings 'like to like', 'birds of a feather flock together', and so on; others on the contrary say 'two of a trade never agree'. On this very question they inquire for deeper and more physical causes, Euripides saying that 'parched earth loves the rain, and stately heaven when filled with rain loves to fall to earth', and Heraclitus that 'it is what opposes that helps' and 'from different tones comes the fairest tune' and 'all things are produced through strife'; while Empedocles, as well as others, expresses the opposite view that like aims at like. The physical problems we may leave alone (for they do not belong to the present inquiry); let us examine those which are human and involve character and feeling, *e.g.* whether friendship can arise between any two people or people cannot be friends if they are wicked, and whether there is one species of friendship or more than one. Those who think there is only one because it admits of degrees have relied on an inadequate indication; for even things different in species admit of degree. We have discussed this matter previously.

2. The kinds of friendship may perhaps be cleared up if we first come to know the object of love. For not everything seems to be loved but only the lovable, and this is good, pleasant, or useful; but it would seem to be that by which some good or pleasure is produced that is useful, so that it is the good and the useful that are lovable as ends. Do men love, then, *the* good, or what is good for *them?* These sometimes clash. So too with regard to the pleasant. Now it is thought that each loves what is good for himself, and that the good is without qualification lovable, and what is good for each man is lovable for him; but each man loves not what is good for him but what seems good. This however will make no

difference; we shall just have to say that this is 'that which seems lovable'. Now there are three grounds on which people love; of the love of lifeless objects we do not use the word 'friendship'; for it is not mutual love, nor is there a wishing of good to the other (for it would surely be ridiculous to wish wine well; if one wishes anything for it, it is that it may keep, so that one may have it oneself); but to a friend we say we ought to wish what is good for his sake. But to those who thus wish good we ascribe only goodwill, if the wish is not reciprocated; goodwill when it *is* reciprocal being friendship. Or must we add 'when it is recognized'? For many people have goodwill to those whom they have not seen but judge to be good or useful; and one of these might return this feeling. These people seem to bear goodwill to each other; but how could one call them friends when they do not know their mutual feelings? To be friends, then, they must be mutually recognized as bearing goodwill and wishing well to each other for one of the aforesaid reasons.

3. Now these reasons differ from each other in kind; so, therefore, do the corresponding forms of love and friendship. There are therefore three kinds of friendship, equal in number to the things that are lovable; for with respect to each there is a mutual and recognized love, and those who love each other wish well to each other in that respect in which they love one another. Now those who love each other for their utility do not love each other for themselves but in virtue of some good which they get from each other. So too with those who love for the sake of pleasure; it is not for their character that men love ready-witted people, but because they find them pleasant. Therefore those who love for the sake of utility love for the sake of what is good for *themselves,* and those who love for the sake of pleasure do so for the sake of what is pleasant to *themselves,* and not in so far as the other is the person loved but in so far as he is useful or pleasant. And thus these friendships are only incidental; for it is not as being the man he is that the loved person is loved, but as providing some good or pleasure. Such friendships, then, are easily dissolved, if the parties do not remain like themselves; for if the one party is no longer pleasant or useful the other ceases to love him.

Now the useful is not permanent but is always changing. Thus when the motive of the friendship is done away, the friendship is dissolved, inasmuch as it existed only for the ends in question. This kind of friendship seems to exist chiefly between old people (for at that age people pursue not the pleasant but the useful) and, of those who are in their prime or young, between those who pursue utility. And such people do not live much with each other either; for sometimes they do not even find each other pleasant; therefore they do not need such companionship unless they are useful to each other; for they are pleasant to each other only in so far as they rouse in each other hopes of something good to come. Among such friendships people also class the friendship of host and guest. On the other hand the friendship of young people seems to aim at pleasure; for they live under the guidance of emotion, and pursue above all what is pleasant to themselves and what is immediately before them; but with increasing age their pleasures become different. This is why they quickly become friends and quickly cease to be so; their friendship changes with the object that is found pleasant, and such pleasure alters quickly. Young people are amorous too; for the greater part of the friendship of love depends on emotion and aims at pleasure; this is why they fall in love and quickly fall out of love, changing often within a single day. But these people do wish to spend their days and lives together; for it is thus that they attain the purpose of their friendship.

Perfect friendship is the friendship of men who are good, and alike in virtue; for these wish well alike to each other *qua* good, and they are good in themselves. Now those who wish well to their friends for their sake are most truly friends; for they do this by reason of their own nature and not incidentally; therefore their friendship lasts as long as they are good—and goodness is an enduring thing. And each is good without qualification and to his friend, for the good are both good without qualification and useful to each other. So too they are pleasant; for the good are pleasant both without qualification and to each other, since to each his own activities and others like them are pleasurable, and the actions of the good *are* the same or like. And such a friendship is as might be expected permanent, since there meet in it all the qualities that friends should have. For all friendship is for the sake of good or of pleasure—good or pleasure either in the abstract or such as will be enjoyed by him who has the friendly feeling—and is based on a certain resemblance; and to a friendship of good men all the qualities we have named belong in virtue of the nature of the friends themselves; for in the case of this kind of friendship the other qualities also are alike in both friends, and that which is good without qualification is also without qualification pleasant, and these are the most lovable qualities. Love and friendship therefore are found most and in their best form between such men.

But it is natural that such friendships should be infrequent; for such men are rare. Further, such friendship requires time and familiarity; as the proverb says, men cannot know each other till they have 'eaten salt together'; nor can they admit each other to friendship or be friends till each has been found lovable and been trusted by each. Those who quickly show the marks of friendship to each other wish to be friends, but are not friends unless they both are lovable and know the fact; for a wish for friendship may arise quickly, but friendship does not.

4. This kind of friendship, then, is perfect both in respect of duration and in all other respects, and in it each gets from each in all respects the same as, or something like what, he gives; which is what ought to happen between friends. Friendship for the sake of pleasure bears a resemblance to this kind; for good people too *are* pleasant to each other. So too does friendship for the sake of utility; for the good are also useful to each other. Among men of these inferior sorts too, friendships are most permanent when the friends get the same thing from each other (e.g. pleasure), and not only that but also from the same source, as happens between ready-witted people, not as happens between lover and beloved. For these do not take pleasure in the same things, but the one in seeing

the beloved and the other in receiving attentions from his lover; and when the bloom of youth is passing the friendship sometimes passes too (for the one finds no pleasure in the sight of the other, and the other gets no attentions from the first); but many lovers on the other hand are constant, if familiarity has led them to love each other's characters, these being alike. But those who exchange not pleasure but utility in their amour are both less truly friends and less constant. Those who are friends for the sake of utility part when the advantage is at an end; for they were lovers not of each other but of profit.

For the sake of pleasure or utility, then, even bad men may be friends of each other, or good men of bad, or one who is neither good nor bad may be a friend to any sort of person, but for their own sake clearly only good men can be friends; for bad men do not delight in each other unless some advantage come of the relation.

The friendship of the good too and this alone is proof against slander; for it is not easy to trust any one's talk about a man who has long been tested by oneself; and it is among good men that trust and the feeling that 'he would never wrong me' and all the other things that are demanded in true friendship are found. In the other kinds of friendship, however, there is nothing to prevent evils arising.

For men apply the name of friends even to those whose motive is utility, in which sense states are said to be friendly (for the alliances of states seem to aim at advantage), and to those who love each other for the sake of pleasure, in which sense children are called friends. Therefore we too ought perhaps to call such people friends, and say that there are several kinds of friendship—firstly and in the proper sense that of good men *qua* good, and by analogy the other kinds; for it is in virtue of something good and something akin to what is found in true friendship that they are friends, since even the pleasant is good for the lovers of pleasure. But these two kinds of friendship are not often united, nor do the same people become friends for the sake of utility and of pleasure; for things that are only incidentally connected are not often coupled together.

Friendship being divided into these kinds, bad men will be friends for the sake of pleasure or of utility, being in this respect like each other, but good men will be friends for their own sake, i.e. in virtue of their goodness. These, then, are friends without qualification; the others are friends incidentally and through a resemblance to these.

5. As in regard to the virtues some men are called good in respect of a state of character, others in respect of an activity, so too in the case of friendship; for those who live together delight in each other and confer benefits on each other, but those who are asleep or locally separated are not performing, but are disposed to perform, the activities of friendship; distance does not break off the friendship absolutely, but only the activity of it. But if the absence is lasting, it seems actually to make men forget their friendship; hence the saying 'out of sight, out of mind'. Neither old people nor sour people seem to make friends easily; for there is little that is pleasant in them, and no one can spend his days with one whose company is painful, or not pleasant, since nature seems above all

to avoid the painful and to aim at the pleasant. Those, however, who approve of each other but do not live together seem to be well-disposed rather than actual friends. For there is nothing so characteristic of friends as living together (since while it is people who are in need that desire benefits, even those who are supremely happy desire to spend their days together; for solitude suits such people least of all); but people cannot live together if they are not pleasant and do not enjoy the same things, as friends who are companions seem to do.

The truest friendship, then, is that of the good, as we have frequently said; for that which is without qualification good or pleasant seems to be lovable and desirable, and for each person that which is good or pleasant to him; and the good man is lovable and desirable to the good man for both these reasons. Now it looks as if love were a feeling, friendship a state of character; for love may be felt just as much towards lifeless things, but mutual love involves choice and choice springs from a state of character; and men wish well to those whom they love, for their sake, not as a result of feeling but as a result of a state of character. And in loving a friend men love what is good for themselves; for the good man in becoming a friend becomes a good to his friend. Each, then, both loves what is good for himself, and makes an equal return in goodwill and in pleasantness; for friendship is said to be equality, and both of these are found most in the friendship of the good.

6. Between sour and elderly people friendship arises less readily, inasmuch as they are less good-tempered and enjoy companionship less; for these are thought to be the greatest marks of friendship and most productive of it. This is why, while young men become friends quickly, old men do not; it is because men do not become friends with those in whom they do not delight; and similarly sour people do not quickly make friends either. But such men may bear goodwill to each other; for they wish one another well and aid one another in need; but they are hardly *friends* because they do not spend their days together nor delight in each other, and these are thought the greatest marks of friendship.

One cannot be a friend to many people in the sense of having friendship of the perfect type with them, just as one cannot be in love with many people at once (for love is a sort of excess of feeling, and it is the nature of such only to be felt towards one person); and it is not easy for many people at the same time to please the same person very greatly, or perhaps even to be good in his eyes. One must, too, acquire some experience of the other person and become familiar with him, and that is very hard. But with a view to utility or pleasure it is possible that many people should please one; for many people are useful or pleasant, and these services take little time.

Of these two kinds that which is for the sake of pleasure is the more like friendship, when both parties get the same things from each other and delight in each other or in the same things, as in the friendships of the young; for generosity is more found in such friendships. Friendship based on utility is for the commercially minded. People who are supremely happy, too, have no need of useful friends, but do need pleasant friends: for they wish to live with *some one* and, though they can endure for a short time what is painful, no one could put up with it continuously, nor even with the Good itself if it were painful to him; this is why they look out for friends who are pleasant. Perhaps they should look out for friends who, being pleasant, are also good, and good for them, too; for so they will have all the characteristics that friends should have.

People in positions of authority seem to have friends who fall into distinct classes; some people are useful to them and others are pleasant, but the same people are rarely both; for they seek neither those whose pleasantness is accompanied by virtue nor those whose utility is with a view to noble objects, but in their desire for pleasure they seek for ready-witted people, and their other friends they choose as being clever at doing what they are told, and these characteristics are rarely combined. Now we have said that the *good* man *is* at the same time pleasant and useful; but such a man does not become the friend of one who surpasses him in station, unless he is surpassed also in virtue; if this is not so, he does not establish equality by being proportionally exceeded in both respects. But people who surpass him in both respects are not so easy to find.

However that may be, the aforesaid friendships involve equality; for the friends get the same things from one another and wish the same things for one another, or exchange one thing for another, e.g. pleasure for utility; we have said, however, that they are both less truly friendships and less permanent. But it is from their likeness and their unlikeness to the same thing that they are thought both to be and not to be friendships. It is by their likeness to the friendship of virtue that they seem to be friendships (for one of them involves pleasure and the other utility, and these characteristics belong to the friendship of virtue as well); while it is because the friendship of virtue is proof against slander and permanent, while these quickly change (besides differing from the former in many other respects), that they appear *not* to be friendships; i.e. it is because of their unlikeness to the friendship of virtue. . . .

In Book IX, Aristotle continues his discussion of the dynamics of friendship, including questions of motivation and obligation. Crucial to this discussion is that perennial ethical debate between those who insist that all of our actions—including acts of friendship—are ultimately motivated by self-interest and those who insist that there are genuine acts of altruism and friendship in which self-interest is not a motive. In Chapter 4 of the *Ethics,* Book IX, Aristotle finds a position between these two extremes and insists that friendship is based on "self-love". In Chapter 8, he then goes on to discuss the nature of true self-love.

BOOK IX

4. Friendly relations to others, and all the characteristics by which friendship is defined, seem to be derived from our relations towards ourselves. A friend is sometimes described as one who wishes and does to another what is good or seems good for that other's sake, or as one who wishes his friend to exist and to live for his (the friend's) sake. (This is what mothers feel towards their children, and what friends who have had a difference feel for one another.) Others

describe a friend as one who lives with another and chooses what he chooses, or as one who sympathizes with the griefs and joys of his friend. (This, also, is especially the case with mothers.) And, similarly, friendship is usually defined by some one or other of these characteristics.

Now, every one of these characteristics we find in the good man's relations to himself (and in other men just so far as they suppose themselves to be good; but it seems, as we have said, that virtue and the good man are in everything the standard): for the good man is of one mind with himself, and desires the same things with all his soul, and wishes for himself what both is and seems good, and does that (for it is characteristic of him to work out that which is good) for his own sake—for the sake, that is to say, of the rational part of him, which seems to be a man's self. And he wishes his self to live and be preserved, and especially that part of his self by which he thinks: for existence is good to the good man. But it is for himself that each wishes the good; no one would choose to have all that is good (as *e.g.* God is in complete possession of the good) on condition of becoming someone else, but only on condition of still being just himself. But his reason would seem to be a man's self, or, at least, to be so in a truer sense than any other of his faculties.

Such a man also wishes to live with himself; for his own company is pleasant to him. The memory of his past life is sweet, and for the future he has good hopes; and such hopes are pleasant. His mind, moreover, is well stored with matter for contemplation: and he sympathizes with himself in sorrow and in joy; for at all seasons the same things give him pain and pleasure, not this thing now, and then another thing,—for he is, so to speak, not apt to change his mind.

Since, then, all these characteristics are found in the good man's relations to himself, and since his relations to his friend are the same as his relations to himself (for his friend is his second self), friendship is described by one or other of these characteristics, and those are called friends in whom these characteristics are found. The question whether friendship towards one's self is or is not possible may be dismissed at present; but that it is possible so far as one has two or more selves would seem to follow from what has been already said, and also from the fact that the extreme of friendship for another is likened to friendship for one's self.

But the characteristics we have mentioned appear to be found in the generality of men, though they are not good. Perhaps we may say that so far as they are agreeable to themselves, and believe they are good, so far do they share these characteristics. People who are utterly worthless and impious never have them, nor do they even seem to have them. But we might almost say roundly that they are wanting in all who are not good; for such men are not at one with themselves: they desire one thing while they wish another, as the incontinent do, for instance (for, instead of what they hold to be good, they choose what is pleasant though injurious). Others, again, through cowardice or laziness, shrink from doing that which they believe is the best for them; while those who have done many terrible things out of wickedness, hate life, and wish to get rid of it, and sometimes actually destroy themselves. Bad men try to find people with whom to spend their time, and eschew their own company; for there is much that is painful in the past on which they look back and in the future to which they look forward when they are by themselves, but the company of others diverts them from these thoughts. As there is nothing lovable in them, they have no friendly feelings towards themselves.

He who is not good, then, cannot sympathize with himself in joy or sorrow; for his soul is divided against itself: one part of him, by reason of its viciousness, is pained at being deprived of something, while another part of him is pleased; one part pulls this way, another that, tearing him to pieces, as it were, between them. Or if it be impossible to be pained and pleased at the same time, yet, at any rate, after a short interval he is pained that he was pleased, and wishes that he had never partaken of this pleasure; for those who are not good are full of remorse. Thus we may say roundly that he who is not good has no friendly feelings even for himself, as there is nothing lovable in him. If, then, to be in this state is utterly miserable, we ought to strain every nerve to avoid vice, and try to be good; for thus we may be friendly disposed towards ourselves, and make friends with others. . . .

8. Another question which is raised is, whether we ought most to love ourselves or others. We blame, it is said, those who love themselves most, and apply the term self-loving to them as a term of reproach: and, again, he who is not good is thought to have regard to himself in everything that he does, and the more so the worse he is; and so we accuse him of doing nothing disinterestedly. The good man on the other hand, it is thought, takes what is noble as his motive, and the better he is the more is he guided by this motive, and by regard for his friend, neglecting his own interest.

But this theory disagrees with facts, nor is it surprising that it should. For it is allowed that we ought to love him most who is most truly a friend, and that he is most truly a friend who, in wishing well to another, wishes well to him for his (the other's) sake, and even though no one should ever know. But all these characteristics, and all the others which go to make up the definition of a friend, are found in the highest degree in a man's relations to himself; for we have already seen how it is from our relations to ourselves that all our friendly relations to others are derived. Moreover, all the proverbs point to the same conclusion—such as "Friends have one soul," "Friends have all things in common," "Equality makes friendship," "The knee is nearer than the shin." All these characteristics are found in the highest degree in a man's relations to himself; for he is his own best friend: and so he must love himself better than any one else.

People not unnaturally are puzzled to know which of these two statements to adopt, since both appeal to them. Perhaps the best method of dealing with conflicting statements of this kind is first to make out the difference between them, and then to determine how far and in what sense each is right. So here, if we first ascertain what self-loving means in each statement, the difficulty will perhaps be cleared up. Those who use self-loving as a term of reproach apply the name to those who take more than their due of money, and honour, and bodily pleasures; for the generality of men desire these things, and set their hearts upon them as the best things in the world, so that they are keenly competed for. Those, then, who grasp at more than their share of these things indulge their animal appetites and their passions generally—in a word, the irrational part of their nature. But this is the character of the generality of men; and hence the term self-loving has come to be used in this bad sense from the fact that the greater part of mankind are not good. It is with justice, then, that we reproach those who are self-loving in this sense. That it really is to those who take more than their due of these things that the term is usually applied by the generality of men, may easily be shown; for if what a man always set his heart upon were that he, rather than another, should do what is just or temperate, or in any other way virtuous—if, in a word, he were always claiming the noble course of conduct, no one would call him self-loving and no one would reproach him.

And yet such a man would seem to be more truly self-loving. At least, he takes for himself that which is noblest and most truly good, and gratifies the ruling power in himself, and in all things obeys it. But just as the ruling part in a state or in any other system seems, more than any other part, to be the state or the system, so also the ruling part of a man seems to be most truly the man's self. He therefore who loves and gratifies this part of himself is most truly self-loving. Again, we call a man continent or incontinent, according as his reason has or has not the mastery, implying that his reason is his self; and when a man has acted under the guidance of his reason he is thought, in the fullest sense, to have done the deed himself, and of his own will. It is plain, then, that this part of us is our self, or is most truly our self, and that the good man more than any other loves this part of himself. He, then, more than any other, will be self-loving, in another sense than the man whom we reproach as self-loving, differing from him by all the difference that exists between living according to reason and living according to passion, between desiring what is noble and desiring what appears to be profitable.

Those who beyond other men set their hearts on noble deeds are welcomed and praised by all; but if all men were vieing with each other in the pursuit of what is noble, and were straining every nerve to act in the noblest possible manner, the result would be that both the wants of the community would be perfectly satisfied, and at the same time each individually would win the greatest of all good things—for virtue is that.

The good man, therefore, ought to be self-loving; for by doing what is noble he will at once benefit himself and assist others: but the bad man ought not; for he will injure both himself and his neighbours by following passions that are not good. Thus, with the bad man there is a discrepancy between what he ought to do and what he does: but with the good man what he ought to do is what he does; for reason always chooses that which is best for itself; and the good man obeys the voice of reason. Again, it is quite true to say of the good man that he does many things for the sake of his friends and of his country, and will, if need be, even die for them. He will throw away money and honour, and, in a word, all the good things for which men compete, claiming for himself that which is noble; for he will prefer a brief period of intense pleasure to a long period of mild pleasure, one year of noble life to many years of ordinary life, one great and noble action to many little ones. This, we may perhaps say, is what he gets who gives his life for others: and so he chooses for himself something that is noble on a grand scale.

Such a man will surrender wealth to enrich his friend: for while his friend gets the money, he gets what is noble; so he takes the greater good for himself. His conduct will be the same with regard to honours and offices: he will give up all to his friend; for this he deems noble and praiseworthy. Such a man, then, is not unreasonably considered good, as he chooses what is noble in preference to everything else. But, again, it is possible to give up to your friend an opportunity for action, and it may be nobler to cause your friend to do a deed than to do it yourself.

It is plain, then, that in all cases in which he is praised the good man takes for himself a larger share of what is noble. And in this sense, as we have said, a man ought to be self-loving, but not in the sense in which the generality of men are self-loving.

F. Pleasure and Happiness

The notion that pleasure is the good life ("hedonism") was one of the first positions Aristotle considered in Book I (Chapters 4 and 5), where he simply dismisses this view as "slavish" and the life of "brute beasts." In Chapter 7 he says that we do not choose pleasure entirely for itself but partly for the sake of happiness (which is the aim of all our activities). In Chapter 8 he insists that the life of the virtuous is "in itself pleasant; . . . for the manifestations of excellence are naturally pleasant, so that they are both pleasant to them and pleasant in themselves. Their life, then, does not need pleasure added to it as an appendage, but contains pleasure itself." Throughout Aristotle's discussion of the moral virtues, moreover, he has insisted that taking such pleasure in virtue is the test of being virtuous. The life of virtue and the life of pleasure are not, therefore, incompatible, but the life of pleasure without virtue, according to Aristotle, is not the good life.

In Book VII (after the discussion of incontinence) Aristotle comes back to the role of pleasure in the good life and debates three competing opinions about pleasure, which he will reject,

1 That no pleasure is good.
2 That some pleasures are good, but most are bad.
3 That even if every pleasure is good, the highest good still cannot be pleasure.

Regarding opinion 1, Aristotle states the argument that pleasure is not ever good because it is never an end but a mere sensory phenomenon. Pleasure may be pleasant (a trivial truth, except for a masochist), but pleasure is not an activity and cannot be worked for (as one builds a house, for example). Moreover, the definition of temperance is avoiding too much pleasure which suggests that pleasure cannot be good in itself (or else one could not get too much of it). He adds that the prudent man seeks painlessness, not pleasure; he notes that pleasure interferes with thinking and "in the pleasure of love, e.g. thought is out of the question, while it lasts." He once again states glibly that pleasure is for children and brute beasts, thus concluding that, while pleasure need not be bad, it is never good in itself.

Regarding opinion 2, Aristotle repeats the popular argument that there are pleasures which are disgraceful and disreputable as well as being injurious. (One must choose one's pleasures carefully.)

For opinion 3, Aristotle presents the argument that pleasure cannot be the highest good because it is not a process (compare with opinion 1).

But having stated the arguments for the three positions, Aristotle then undercuts them all, insisting that it does not follow that pleasure is not good, or even the supreme good. He rejects opinion 1 by denying that pleasure is merely sensory, insisting that, in some cases, there may be no end distinct from the pleasures themselves (as when a person says he or she is "just enjoying myself"). Moreover, Aristotle points out that one can and does work for pleasure, and he counters the "pleasure is distraction" thesis by pointing out that one is not distracted by the pleasure of the activity itself (for example, the pleasure of thinking). Furthermore, he distinguishes between absolute and more limited pleasures and points out that children and brutes may pursue the latter but not the former. The mistake is thinking of pleasure simply in terms of bodily pleasures. Aristotle agrees that some pleasures may be injurious, but it does not follow that all or even most pleasures are bad. And finally, since pain is an absolute evil and happiness is pleasurable unimpeded activity, Aristotle argues, pleasure of some kind must be the supreme good.

What Aristotle is doing is to create some middle ground between the hedonists—who think that pleasure in itself is the only good—and those who deny that pleasure is a good. While deemphasizing the bodily pleasures (which Aristotle agrees are pursued by people too vulgar to enjoy the higher pleasures[4]), he wants to in some sense identify pleasure with happiness and the good life. But he finally does this in Book X, where he brings together these various thoughts on pleasure and defines the good life, which is—as anticipated—the philosophical life of contemplation.

BOOK X

Pleasure

1. Our next business, I think, should be to treat of pleasure. For pleasure seems, more than anything else, to have an intimate connection with our nature; which is the reason why, in educating the young, we use pleasure and pain as the rudders of their course. Moreover, delight in what we ought to delight in, and hatred of what we ought to hate, seem to be of the utmost importance in the formation of a virtuous character; for these feelings pervade the whole of life, and have power to draw a man to virtue and happiness, as we choose what pleases, and shun what pains us.

And it would seem that the discussion of these matters is especially incumbent on us, since there is much dispute about them. There are people who say that the

[4]Compare with John Stuart Mill, pages 295 to 310.

good is pleasure, and there are people who say, on the contrary, that pleasure is altogether bad—some, perhaps, in the conviction that it is really so, others because they think it has a good effect on men's lives to assert that pleasure is a bad thing, even though it be not; for the generality of men, they say, incline this way, and are slaves to their pleasures, so that they ought to be pulled in the opposite direction: for thus they will be brought into the middle course. . . .

4. Aristotle begins his own account with the claim that pleasure is complete and perfect, in that (like vision) it is not any better by being longer (which is not to say, of course, that we don't want it to continue). Then, the heart of the analysis: "pleasure completes the exercise of a faculty." It is a "sort of super-added completeness, like the grace of youth." Pleasure is the completion of good activity; it is not an end in itself, but neither is it something other than the activity enjoyed.

4. As to the nature of quality of pleasure, we shall more readily discover it if we make a fresh start as follows: Vision seems to be perfect or complete at any moment; for it does not lack anything which can be added afterwards to make its nature complete. Pleasure seems in this respect to resemble vision; for it is something whole and entire, and it would be impossible at any moment to find a pleasure which would become complete by lasting longer. Therefore pleasure is not a motion; for every motion requires time and implies an end (*e.g.* the motion of building), and is complete when the desired result is produced— either in the whole time therefore, or in this final moment of it. But during the progress of the work all the motions are incomplete, and specifically different from the whole motion and from each other; the fitting together of the stones is different from the fluting of the pillar, and both from the building of the temple. The building of the temple is complete; nothing more is required for the execution of the plan. But the building of the foundation and of the triglyph are incomplete; for each is the building of a part only. These motions, then, are specifically different from one another, and it is impossible to find a motion whose nature is complete at any moment—it is complete, if at all, only in the whole time.

It is the same also with walking and the other kinds of locomotion. For though all locomotion is a motion from one place to another, yet there are distinct kinds of locomotion, as flying, walking, leaping, etc. Nay, not only so, but even in walking itself there are differences, for the whence and whither are not the same in the entire course and in a portion of the course, or in this portion and in that, nor is crossing this line the same as crossing that; for you do not cross a line simply, but a line that is in a given place, and this line is in a different place from that. I must refer to my other works for a detailed discussion of motion; but it seems that it is not complete at any moment, but that its several parts are incomplete, and that they are specifically different from one another, the whence and whither being a specific difference. Pleasure, on the other hand, is complete in its nature at any moment. It is evident, therefore, that these two must be distinct from each other, and that pleasure must be one of the class of whole and complete things. And this would also seem to follow from the fact that though duration is necessary for motion, it is not necessary for pleasure—for a momentary pleasure is something whole and entire.

From these considerations it is plain that they are wrong in saying that pleasure is a motion or a coming into being. For these terms are not applied to every thing, but only to those things that are divisible into parts and are not wholes. We cannot speak of the coming into being of vision, or of a mathematical point, or of unity; nor is any one of them a motion or a coming into being. And these terms are equally inapplicable to pleasure; for it is something whole and entire.

Every sense exercises itself upon its proper object, and exercises itself completely when it is in good condition and the object is the noblest of those that fall within its scope (for the complete exercise of a faculty seems to mean this; and we may assume that it makes no difference whether we speak of the sense, or of the sensitive subject as exercising itself): of each sense, then, we may say that the exercise is best when on the one side you have the finest condition, and on the other the highest of the objects that fall within the scope of this faculty. But this exercise of the faculty will be not only the most complete, but also the pleasantest: for the exercise of every sense is attended with pleasure, and so is the exercise of reason and the speculative faculty; and it is pleasantest when it is most complete, and it is most complete when the faculty is well-trained and the object is the best of those that fall under this faculty. And, further, the pleasure completes the exercise of the faculty. But the pleasure completes it in a different way from that in which the object and the faculty of sense complete it, when both are as they should be; just as health causes healthy activities in a different way from that in which the physician causes them. (That the exercise of every sense is accompanied by pleasure is evident: we speak of pleasant sights and pleasant sounds. It is evident also that the pleasure is greatest when both faculty and that upon which it is exercised are as good as they can be: when this is the case both with the object of sense and the sentient subject, there will always be pleasure, so long, that is, as you have the subject to act and the object to be acted upon.) Now, the pleasure makes the exercise complete not as the habit or trained faculty does, being already present in the subject, but as a sort of super-added completeness, like the grace of youth. So long, then, as both the object of thought or of sense and the perceptive or contemplative subject are as they ought to be, so long will there be pleasure in the exercise; for so long as the object to be acted upon the subject that is able to act remain the same, and maintain the same relation to each other, the result must be the same.

How is it, then, that we are incapable of continuous pleasure? Perhaps the reason is that we become exhausted; for no human faculty is capable of continuous exercise. Pleasure, then, also cannot be continuous; for it is an accompaniment of the exercise of faculty. And for the same reason some things please us when new, but afterwards please us less. For at first the intellect is stimulated and exercises itself upon them strenuously, just as we strain our eyes to look hard at something; but after a time the exertion ceases to be so intense, and becomes relaxed; and so the pleasure also loses its keenness.

The desire for pleasure we should expect to be shared by all men, seeing that all desire to live. For life is an exercise of faculties, and each man exercises the faculties he most loves upon the things he most loves; e.g. the musical man exercises his hearing upon melodies, and the studious man exercises his intellect upon matters of speculation, and so on with the rest. But pleasure completes the exercise of faculties, and therefore life, which men desire. Naturally, therefore, men desire pleasure too; for each man finds in it the completion of his life, which is desirable. But whether we desire life for the sake of pleasure, or pleasure for the sake of life, is a question which we may dismiss for the present. For the two seem to be joined together, and not to admit of separation: without exercise of faculties there is no pleasure, and every such exercise is completed by pleasure.

---

5. Finally (like John Stuart Mill centuries later) Aristotle insists on dividing the pleasures into various kinds.

---

5. And from this it seems to follow that pleasures differ in kind, since specifically different things we believe to be completed by specifically different things. For this seems to be the case with the products both of nature and of art, as animals and trees, paintings, sculptures, houses, and furniture. Similarly, then, we believe that exercises of faculty which differ in kind are completed by things different in kind.

But the exercises of the intellectual faculties are specifically different from the exercises of the senses, and the several kinds of each from one another; therefore the pleasures which complete them are also different.

The same conclusion would seem to follow from the close connection that exists between each pleasure and the exercise of faculty which it completes. For the exercise is increased by its proper pleasure; *e.g.* people are more likely to understand any matter, and to go to the bottom of it, if the exercise is pleasant to them. Thus, those who delight in geometry become geometricians, and understand all the propositions better than others; and similarly, those who are fond of music, or of architecture, or of anything else, make progress in that kind of work, because they delight in it. The pleasures, then, help to increase the exercise; but that which helps to increase it must be closely connected with it: but when things are specifically different from one another, the things that are closely connected with them must also be specifically different.

The same conclusion follows perhaps still more clearly from the fact that the exercise of one faculty is impeded by the pleasure proper to another; *e.g.* a lover of the flute is unable to attend to an argument if he hears a man playing, since he takes more delight in flute-playing than in his present business; the pleasure of the flute-player, therefore, hinders the exercise of the reason. The same result follows in other cases, too, whenever a man is exercising his faculties on two things at a time; the pleasanter business thwarts the other, and, if the difference in pleasantness be great, thwarts it more and more, even to the extent of suppressing it altogether. Thus, when anything gives us intense delight, we cannot do anything else at all, and when we do a second thing, we do not very much care about the first; and so people who eat sweetmeats in the theatre do this most of all when the actors are bad. Since its proper pleasure heightens the exercise of a faculty, making it both more prolonged and better, while pleasure from another source spoils it, it is evident that there is a great difference between these two pleasures. Indeed, pleasure from another source has almost the same effect as pain from the activity itself. For the exercise of a faculty is spoilt by pain arising from it; as happens, for instance, when a man finds it disagreeable and painful to write or to calculate; for he stops writing in the one case and calculating in the other, since the exercise is painful. The exercise of a faculty, then, is affected in opposite ways by its proper pleasure and its proper pain; and by "proper" I mean that which is occaisioned by the exercise itself. But pleasure from another source, we have already said, has almost the same effect as its proper pain; *i.e.* it interferes with the exercise of the faculty, though not to the same extent.

Again, as the exercises of our faculties differ in goodness and badness, and some are to be desired and some to be shunned, while some are indifferent, so do the several pleasures differ; for each exercise has its proper pleasure. The pleasure which is proper to a good activity, then, is good, and that which is proper to one that is not good is bad: for the desire of noble things is laudable, and the desire of base things is blamable; but the pleasures which accompany the exercises of our faculties belong to them even more than the·desires do, since the latter are distinct both in time and in nature, while the former are almost coincident in time, and so hard to distinguish from them that it is a matter of debate whether the exercise be not identical with the pleasure. (It seems, however, that the pleasure is not the same as the act of thinking or of feeling; that is impossible: but the fact that the two are inseparable makes some people fancy that they are identical.) As, then, the exercises of the faculties vary, so do their respective pleasures. Sight is purer than touch, hearing and smell than taste: there is a corresponding difference, therefore, between their pleasures; and the pleasures of the intellect are purer than these pleasures of sense, and some of each kind are purer than others.

Each kind of being, again, seems to have its proper pleasure, as it has its proper function,—viz. the pleasure which accompanies the exercise of its faculties or the realization of its nature. And a separate consideration of the several kinds of animals will confirm this: the pleasures of a horse, a dog, and a man are all different—as Heraclitus says, a donkey would prefer hay to gold; for there is more pleasure in fodder than in gold to a donkey. The pleasures of specifically different beings, then, are specifically different; and we might naturally suppose that there would be no specific difference between the pleasures of beings of the same species. And yet there is no small difference, in the pleasures of men at least: what pleases this man pains that; what is grievous and hateful to one is pleasant and lovable to another. This occurs in the case of sweet things, too: a man in a fever has a different notion of what is sweet from a man in health; and a feeble man's notion of what is hot is different from that of a robust man. And the like occurs in other matters also.

But in all matters of this kind we hold that things *are* what they appear to be to the perfect man. Now, if this opinion is correct, as we hold it to be—if, that is, in every case the test is virtue, or the good man as such—then what appears to him to be pleasure will be pleasure, and what he delights in will be pleasant. If what is disagreeable to him appears pleasant to another, we need not be astonished; for there are many ways in which men are corrupted and perverted: such things, however, are not pleasant, but only pleasant to these men with their disposition. It is plain, then, that we must not allow the confessedly base pleasures to be pleasures at all, except to corrupt men.

But of the pleasures that are considered good, which or what kind are to be called the proper pleasures of man? We cannot be in doubt if we know what are the proper exercises of his faculties; for the proper pleasures are their accompaniments. Whether, then the exercise of faculties proper to the complete and happy man be one or many, the pleasures that complete that exercise will be called pleasures of man in the full meaning of the words, and the others in a secondary sense and with a fraction of that meaning, just as is the case with the exercises of the faculties.

Happiness

Aristotle ends his *Ethics* with a discussion of the central concept with which it began, happiness, or *eudaimonia*. Happiness, he reiterates, is not a moral state but an activity. It is not merely enjoyment or relaxation but virtuous activity. But there are many virtues—the moral as well as the intellectual virtues. Which of these are best? In accordance with Aristotle's teleological scheme, it must be the "highest virtue" which is, in turn, the exercise of our "best" faculty—namely reason. In fact Aristotle even calls reason "the divine part of us," and reason is best exercised—where else?—in speculation and theorizing, in other words, in philosophy. (Of course, "philosophy" for Aristotle included all of the sciences and most of the liberal arts as well, so we should not think him too narrow.) This emphasis on thinking does not exclude pleasure and activities of other kinds, however. The good life is still the full life and, besides, one needs ample experience to think about. Here again, however, Aristotle displays his unabashed aristocratic outlook; the good life demands leisure—the life of a gentleman. It may be most noble to be a statesman or a soldier, but such lives are too busy to allow for sufficient thinking, and so are inferior. Moreover, the virtues of thinking are superior to the others, because, unlike almost any other human activity, our thinking is entierly our own; it requires no equipment, no help, no social arrangements. Of course, one can't think all the time, though Aristotle sometimes sounds as if that would be preferable. (In his other ethical treatise, this tendency is even more pronounced.) He does say (Chapter 8) that the moral virtues and their exercise yield merely a "secondary" happiness and that the "higher" happiness of pure reason is quite distinct from "the lower nature" (that is, morally virtuous life). Indeed, he argues that the virtues of the gods would surely be of the contemplative sort (rather than the everyday commercial activities of trading and such, which Aristotle despised). This idea of the gods thinking eventually turns into one of Aristotle's most celebrated theses in his *Metaphysics,* the idea of the ultimate purpose (teleology) of the universe being "thought thinking itself."

Happiness, then, is the life of contemplation. Moreover, because this is so, the philosophical activity of studying ethics is not just a matter of theorizing rather than doing, it is also actually doing. In thinking, at least, thinking and doing are one and the same, and talking about the good life is the essential part of living it.

6. Now that we have discussed the several kinds of virtue and friendship and

pleasure, it remains to give a summary account of happiness, since we assume that it is the end of all that man does. And it will shorten our statement if we first recapitulate what we have said above.

We said that happiness is not a habit or trained faculty. If it were, it would be within the reach of a man who slept all his days and lived the life of a vegetable, or of a man who met with the greatest misfortunes. As we cannot accept this conclusion, we must place happiness in some exercise of faculty, as we said before. But as the exercises of faculty are sometimes necessary (*i.e.* desirible for the sake of something else), sometimes desirable in themselves, it is evident that happiness must be placed among those that are desirable in themselves, and not among those that are desirable for the sake of something else: for happiness lacks nothing; it is sufficient in itself.

Now, the exercise of faculty is desirable in itself when nothing is expected from it beyond itself. Of this nature are held to be (1) the manifestations of excellence; for to do what is noble and excellent must be counted desirable for itself: and (2) those amusements which please us; for they are not chosen for the sake of anything else,—indeed, men are more apt to be injured than to be benefited by them, through neglect of their health and fortunes. Now, most of those whom men call happy have recourse to pastimes of this sort. And on this account those who show a ready wit in such pastimes find favour with tyrants; for they make themselves pleasant in that which the tyrant wants, and what he wants is pastime. These amusements, then, are generally thought to be elements of happiness, becuase princes employ their leisure in them. But such persons, we may venture to say, are no criterion. For princely rank does not imply the possession of virtue or of reason, which are the sources of all excellent exercise of faculty. And if these men, never having tasted pure and refined pleasure, have recourse to the pleasures of the body, we should not on that account think these more desirable; for children also fancy that the things which they value are better than anything else. It is only natural, then, that as children differ from men in their estimate of what is valuable, so bad men should differ from good.

As we have often said, therefore, that is truly valuable and pleasant which is so to the perfect man. Now, the exercise of those trained faculties which are proper to him is what each man finds most desirable; what the perfect man finds most desirable, therefore, is the exercise of virtue. Happiness, therefore, does not consist in amusement; and indeed it is absurd to suppose that the end is amusement, and that we toil and moil all our life long for the sake of amusing ourselves. We may say that we choose everything for the sake of something else, excepting only happiness; for it is the end. But to be serious and to labour for the sake of amusement seems silly and utterly childish; while to amuse ourselves in order that we may be serious, as Anacharsis says, seems to be right; for amusement is a sort of recreation, and we need recreation because we are unable to work continuously. Recreation, then, cannot be the end; for it is taken as a means to the exercise of our faculties.

Again, the happy life is thought to be that which exhibits virtue; and such a life must be serious and cannot consist in amusement. Again, it is held that things of serious importance are better than laughable and amusing things, and that the better the organ or the man, the more important is the function; but we have already said that the function or exercise of that which is better is higher and more conducive to happiness. Again, the enjoyment of bodily pleasures is within the reach of anybody, of a slave no less the best of men; but no one supposes that a slave can participate in happiness, seeing that he cannot participate in the proper life of man. For indeed happiness does not consist in pastimes of this sort, but in the exercise of virtue, as we have already said.

7. But if happiness be the exercise of virtue, it is reasonable to suppose that it will be the exercise of the highest virtue; and that will be the virtue or excellence of the best part of us. Now, that part or faculty—call it reason or what you will—which seems naturally to rule and take the lead, and to apprehend things noble and divine—whether it be itself divine, or only the divinest part of us—is the faculty the exercise of which, in its proper excellence, will be perfect happiness. That this consists in speculation or theorizing we have already said.

This conclusion would seem to agree both with what we have said above, and with known truths. This exercise of faculty must be the highest possible; for the reason is the highest of our faculties and of all knowable things those that reason deals with are the highest. Again, it is the most continuous; for speculation can be carried on more continuously than any kind of action whatsoever. We think too that pleasure ought to be one of the ingredients of happiness; but of all virtuous exercises it is allowed that the pleasantest is the exercise of wisdom. At least philosophy is thought to have pleasures that are admirable in purity and steadfastness; and it is reasonable to suppose that the time passes more pleasantly with those who possess, than with those who are seeking knowledge. Again, what is called self-sufficiency will be most of all found in the speculative life. The necessaries of life, indeed, are needed by the wise man as well as by the just man and the rest; but, when these have been provided in due quantity, the just man further needs persons towards whom, and along with whom, he may act justly; and so does the temperate and the courageous man and the rest; while the wise man is able to speculate even by himself, and the wiser he is the more is he able to do this. He could speculate better, we may confess, if he had others to help him, but nevertheless he is more self-sufficient than anybody else. Again, it would seem that this life alone is desired solely for its own sake; for it yeilds no result beyond the contemplation, but from the practical activities we get something more or less besides action.

Again, happiness is thought to imply leisure; for we toil in order that we may have leisure, as we make war in order that we may enjoy peace. Now, the practical virtues are exercised either in politics or in war; but these do not seem to be leisurely occupations. War, indeed, seems to be quite the reverse of leisurely; for no one chooses to fight for fighting's sake, or arranges a war for that purpose: he would be deemed a bloodthirsty villain who should set friends at enmity in order that battles and slaughter might ensue. But the politician's life also is not a leisurely occupation, and, beside the practice of politics itself, it brings power and honours, or happiness, to himself and his fellow-citizens, which is something different from politics; for we [who are asking what happiness is] also ask what politics is, evidently implying that it is something different from happiness. If, then, the life of the statesman and the soldier, though they surpass all other virtuous exercises in nobility and grandeur, are not leisurely occupations, and aim at some ulterior end, and are not desired merely for themselves, but the exercise of the reason seems to be superior in seriousness (since it contemplates truth), and to aim at no end beside itself, and to have its proper pleasure (which also helps to increase the exercise), and further to be self-sufficient, and leisurely, and inexhaustible (as far as anything human can be), and to have all the other characteristics that are ascribed to happiness, it follows that the exercise of reason will be the complete happiness of man, *i.e.* when a complete term of days is added; for nothing incomplete can be admitted into our idea of happiness.

But a life which realized this idea would be something more than human; for it would not be the expression of man's nature, but of some divine element in that nature—the exercise of which is as far superior to the exercise of the other kind of virtue, as this divine element is superior to our compound human nature. If then reason be divine as compared with man, the life which consists in the exercise of reason will also be divine in comparison with human life. Nevertheless, instead of listening to those who advise us as men and mortals not to lift our thoughts above what is human and mortal, we ought rather, as far as possible, to put off our mortality and make every effort to live in the exercise of the highest of our faculties; for though it be but a small part of us, yet in power and value it far surpasses all the rest. And indeed this part would even seem to constitute our true self, since it is the sovereign and the better part. It would be strange, then, if a man were to prefer the life of something else to the life of his true self. Again, we may apply here what we said above—for every being that is best and pleasantest which is naturally proper to it. Since, then, it is the reason that in the truest sense is the man, the life that consists in the exercise of the reason is the best and pleasantest for man—and therefore the happiest.

8. The life that consists in the exercise of the other kind of virtue is happy in a secondary sense; for the manifestations of moral virtue are emphatically human [not divine]. Justice, I mean, and courage, and the other moral virtues are displayed in our relations towards one another by the observance, in every case, of what is due in contracts and services, and all sorts of outward acts, as well as in our inward feelings. And all these seem to be emphatically human affairs. Again, moral virtue seems, in some points, to be actually a result of physical constitution, and in many points to be closely connected with the passions. Again, prudence is inseparably joined to moral virtue, and moral virtue to prudence, since the moral virtues determine the principles of prudence, while prudence determines what is right in morals. But the moral virtues, being bound up with the passions, must belong to our compound nature; and the virtues of the compound nature are emphatically human. Therefore the life which

manifests them, and the happiness which consists in this, must be emphatically human.

But the happiness which consists in the exercise of the reason is separate from the lower nature. (So much we may be allowed to assert about it; a detailed discussion is beyond our present purpose.) Further, this happiness would seem to need but a small supply of external goods, certainly less than the moral life needs. Both need the necessaries of life to the same extent, let us say; for though, in fact, the politician takes more care of his person than the philosopher, yet the difference will be quite inconsiderable. But in what they need for their activities there will be a great difference. Wealth will be needed by the liberal man, that he may act liberally; by the just man, that he may discharge his obligations (for a mere wish cannot be tested,—even unjust people pretend a wish to act justly); the courageous man will need strength if he is to execute any deed of courage; and the temperate man liberty of indulgence,—for how else can he, or the possessor of any other virtue, show what he is?

Again, people dispute whether the intent or the action be more essential to virtue, virtue being understood to imply both. It is plain, then, that both are necessary to completeness. But many things are needed for action, and the greater and nobler the action, the more is needed. On the other hand, he who is engaged in speculation needs none of these things for his *work;* nay, it may even be said that they are a hindrance to speculation: but as a man living with other men, he chooses to act virtuously; and so he will need things of this sort to enable him to behave like a man.

That perfect happiness is some kind of speculative activity may also be shown in the following way: It is always supposed that the gods are, of all beings, the most blessed and happy; but what kind of actions shall we ascribe to them? Acts of justice? Surely it is ridiculous to conceive the gods engaged in trade and restoring deposits, and so on. Or the acts of the courageous character who endures fearful things and who faces danger because it is noble to do so? Or acts of liberality? But to whom are they to give? And is it not absurd to suppose that they have money or anything of that kind? And what could acts of temperance mean with them? Surely it would be an insult to praise them for having no evil desires. In short, if we were to go through the whole list, we should find that all action is petty and unworthy of the gods. And yet it is universally supposed that they live, and therefore that they exert their powers; for we cannot suppose that they lie asleep like Endymion. Now, if a being lives, and action cannot be ascribed to him, still less production, what remains but contemplation? It follows, then, that the divine life, which surpasses all others in blessedness, consists in contemplation. Of all modes of human activity, therefore, that which is most akin to this will be capable of the greatest happiness.

And this is further confirmed by the fact that the other animals do not participate in happiness, being quite incapable of this kind of activity. For the life of the gods is entirely blessed, and the life of man is blessed just so far as he attains to some likeness of this kind of activity; but none of the other animals are happy, since they are quite incapable of contemplation.

Happiness, then, extends just so far as contemplation, and the more contemplation the more happiness is there in a life,—not accidentally, but as a necessary accompaniment of the contemplation; for contemplation is precious in itself. Our conclusion, then, is that happiness is a kind of speculation or contemplation.

But as we are men we shall need external good fortune also: for our nature does not itself provide all that is necessary for contemplation; the body must be in health, and supplied with food, and otherwise cared for. We must not, however, suppose that because it is impossible to be happy without external good things, therefore, a man who is to be happy will want many things or much. It is not the superabundance of good things that makes a man independent, or enables him to act; and a man may do noble deeds, though he be not ruler of land and sea. A moderate equipment may give you opportunity for virtuous action (as we may easily see, for private persons seem to do what is right not less, but rather more, than princes), and so much as gives this opportunity is enough; for that man's life will be happy who has virtue and exercises it.

Solon too, I think, gave a good description of the happy man when he said that, in his opinion, he was a man who was moderately supplied with the gifts of fortune, but had done the noblest deeds, and lived temperately; for a man who has but modest means may do his duty. Anaxagoras also seems to have held that the happy man was neither a rich man nor a prince; for he said that he should not be surprised if the happy man were one whom the masses could hardly believe to be so; for they judge by the outside, which is all they can appreciate. The opinions of the wise, then, seem to agree with our theory. But though these opinions carry some weight, the test of truth in matters of practice is to be found in the facts of life; for it is in them that the supreme authority resides. The theories we have advanced, therefore, should be tested by comparison with the facts of life; and if they agree with the facts they should be accepted, but if they disagree they should be accounted mere theories.

But, once more, the man who exercises his reason and cultivates it, and has it in the best condition, seems also to be the most beloved of heaven. For if the gods take any care for men, as they are thought to do, it is reasonable to suppose that they delight in that which is best in man and most akin to themselves (*i.e.* the reason), and that they requite those who show the greatest love and reverence for it, as caring for that which is dear to themselves and doing rightly and nobly. But it is plain that all these points are found most of all in the wise man. The wise man, therefore, is the most beloved of heaven; and therefore, we may conclude, the happiest. In this way also, therefore, the wise man will be happier than any one else.

9. Now that we have treated (sufficiently, though summarily) of these matters, and of the virtues, and also of friendship and pleasure, are we to suppose that we have attained the end we proposed? Nay, surely the saying holds good, that in practical matters the end is not a mere speculative knowledge of what is to be done, but rather the doing of it. It is not enough to know about

virtue, then, but we must endeavour to possess it and to use it, or to take any other steps that may make us good.

Now, if theories had power of themselves to make us good, "many great rewards would they deserve" as Theognis says, and such ought we to give; but in fact it seems that though they are potent to guide and to stimulate liberal-minded young men, and though a generous disposition, with a sincere love of what is noble, may by them be opened to the influence of virtue, yet they are powerless to turn the mass of men to goodness. For the generality of men are naturally apt to be swayed by fear rather than by reverence, and to refrain from evil rather because of the punishment that it brings than because of its own foulness. For under the guidance of their passions they pursue the pleasures that suit their nature and the means by which those pleasures may be obtained, and avoid the opposite pains, while of that which is noble and truly pleasant they have not even a conception, as they have never tasted it. What theories or arguments, then, can bring such men as these to order? Surely it is impossible, or at least very difficult, to remove by any argument what has long been ingrained in the character. For my part, I think we must be well content if we can get some modicum of virtue when all the circumstances are present that seem to make men good.

Now, what makes men good is held by some to be nature, by others habit [or training], by others instruction. As for the goodness that comes by nature, it is plain that it is not within our control, but is bestowed by some divine agency on certain people who truly deserve to be called fortunate. As for theory or instruction, I fear that it cannot avail in all cases, but that the hearer's soul must be prepared by training it to feel delight and aversion on the right occasions, just as the soil must be prepared if the seed is to thrive. For if he lives under the sway of his passions, he will not listen to the arguments by which you would dissuade him, nor even understand them. And when he is in this state, how can you change his mind by argument? To put it roundly, passion seems to yield to force only, and not to reason. The character, then, must be already formed, so as to be in some way akin to virtue, loving what is noble and hating what is base.

But to get right guidance from youth up in the road to virtue is hard, unless we are brought up under suitable laws; for to live temperately and regularly is not pleasant to the generality of men, especially to the young. Our nurture, then, should be prescribed by law, and our whole way of life; for it will cease to be painful as we get accustomed to it. And I venture to think that it is not enough to get proper nurture and training when we are young, but that as we ought to carry on the same way of life after we are grown up, and to confirm these habits, we need the intervention of the law in these matters also, and indeed, to put it roundly, in our whole life. For the generality of men are more readily swayed by compulsion than by reason, and by fear of punishment than by desire for what is noble.

For this reason, some hold that the legislator should, in the first instance, invite the people and exhort them to be virtuous because of the nobility of virtue, as those who have been well trained will listen to him; but that when they will not listen, or are of less noble nature, he should apply correction and punishment, and banish utterly those who are incorrigible. For the good man, who takes what is noble as his guide, will listen to reason, but he who is not good, whose desires are set on pleasure, must be corrected by pain like a beast of burden. And for this reason, also, they say the pains to be applied must be those that are most contrary to the pleasures which the culprit loves.

As we have said, then, he who is to be good must be well nurtured and trained, and thereafter must continue in a like excellent way of life, and must never, either voluntarily or involuntarily, do anything vile; and this can only be effected if men live subject to some kind of reason and proper regimen, backed by force.

Now, the paternal rule has not the requisite force or power of compulsion, nor has the rule of any individual, unless he be a king or something like one; but the law has a compulsory power, and at the same time is a rational ordinance proceeding from a kind of prudence or reason. And whereas we take offence at individuals who oppose our inclinations, even though their opposition is right, we do not feel aggrieved when the law bids us do what is right.

But Sparta is the only, or almost the only, state where the legislator seems to have paid attention to the nurture and mode of life of the citizens. In most states these matters are entirely neglected, and each man lives as he likes, ruling wife and children in Cyclopean fashion. It would be best, then, that the regulation of these matters should be undertaken and properly carried out by the state; but as the state neglects it, it would seem that we should each individually help our own children or friends on the road to virtue, and should have the power or at least the will to do this.

Now, it would seem from what has been said that to enable one to do this the best plan would be to learn how to legislate. For state training is carried on by means of laws, and is good when the laws are good; but it would seem to make no difference whether the laws be written or unwritten, nor whether they regulate the education of one person or many, any more than it does in the case of music, or gymnastics, or any other course of training. For as in the state that prevails which is ordained by law and morality, so in the household that which is ordained by the word of the father of the family and by custom prevails no less, or even more, because of the ties of kinship and of obligation; for affection and obedience are already implanted by nature in the members of the family. Moreover, in spite of what has just been said, individual treatment is better than treatment by masses, in education no less than in medicine. As a general rule, repose and fasting are good for a fever patient, but in a particular case they may not be good. A teacher of boxing, I suppose, does not recommend every one to adopt the same style. It would seem, then, that individuals are educated more perfectly under a system of private education; for then each gets more precisely what he needs.

But you will best be able to treat an individual case (whether you are a doctor, or a trainer, or anything else) when you know the general rule, "Such and such a thing is good for all men," or "for all of a certain temperament;" for science is said to deal, and does deal, with that which is common to a number of individuals. I do not mean to deny that it may be quite possible to treat an individual well, even without any scientific knowledge, if you know precisely by experience the effect of particular causes upon him, just as some men seem to be able to treat themselves better than any doctor, though they would be quite unable to prescribe for another person. But, nevertheless, I venture to say that if a man wishes to master any art, or to gain a scientific knowledge of it, he must advance to its general principles, and make himself acquainted with them in the proper method; for, as we have said, it is with universal propositions that the sciences deal.

And so I think that he who wishes to make men better by training (whether many or few) should try to acquire the art or science of legislation, supposing that men may be made good by the agency of law. For fairly to mould the character of any person that may present himself is not a thing that can be done by anybody, but (if at all) only by him who has knowledge, just as is the case in medicine and other professions where careful treatment and prudence are required.

Our next business, then, I think, is to inquire from whom or by what means we are to learn the science or art of legislation. "As we learn the other arts." it will be said,—"*i.e.* from the politicians who practise it: for we found that legislation is a part of politics." But I think the case is not quite the same with politics as with the other sciences and arts. For in other cases it is plain that the same people communicate the art and practise it, as physicians and painters do. But in the case of politics, while the sophists profess to teach the art, it is never they that practise it, but the statesmen. And the statesmen would seem to act by some instinctive faculty, proceeding empirically rather than by reasoning. For it is plain that they never write or speak about these matters (though perhaps that were better than making speeches in the courts or the assembly), and have never communicated the art to their sons or to any of their friends. And yet we might expect that they would have done so if they could; for they could have left no better legacy to their country, nor have chosen anything more precious than this power as a possession for themselves, and, therefore, for those dearest to them. Experience, however, seems, we must allow, to be of great service here; for otherwise people would never become statesmen by familiarity with politics. Those who wish for a knowledge of statesmanship, then, seem to need experience [as well as theory].

But those sophists who profess to teach statesmanship seem to be ludicrously incapable of fulfilling their promises; for, to speak roundly, they do not even know what it is or what it deals with. If they did know, they would not make it identical with rhetoric, or inferior to it, nor would they think it was easy to legislate by collecting the laws that are thought well of; they say it is possible to select the best laws, as though even the selection did not demand intelligence and as though right judgement were not the greatest thing, as in matters of music. For while people experienced in any department judge rightly the works produced in it, and understand by what means or how they are achieved, and what harmonizes with what, the inexperienced must be content if they do not fail to see whether the work has been well or ill made—as in the case of painting. Now laws are as it were the 'works' of the political art; how then can one learn from them to be a legislator, or judge which are best? Even medical men do not seem to be made by a study of text-books. Yet people try, at any rate, to state not only the treatments, but also how particular classes of people can be cured and should be treated—distinguishing the various habits of body; but while this seems useful to experienced people, to the inexperienced it is valueless. Surely, then, while collections of laws, and of constitutions also, may be serviceable to those who can study them and judge what is good or bad and what enactments suit what circumstances, those who go through such collections without a practised faculty will not have right judgement (unless it be as a spontaneous gift of nature), though they may perhaps become intelligent in such matters.

DISCUSSION

This is the time to look again at Aristotle's conception of happiness *eudaimonia* and reemphasize some important differences between his ethics and our own. First of all, his concept of *eudaimonia* is not, like our notion of happiness, concerned with what we feel. Feeling happy, we would argue, is being happy, at least if it lasts long enough. It wouldn't even make sense, without a very dramatic story to go along with it, that a person felt he was happy and thought that he was happy for forty years, but then realized that he hadn't been. But for Aristotle, this would make perfectly good sense, if, that is, he would understand what "feeling happy" meant in the first place. *Eudaimonia* means "doing well," and though one should presumably not feel miserable or malcontent, the feeling of happiness is not at issue. By contrast, even our example of a person who realized after forty years that he had not been happy requires some account of how he was wrong about his private feelings, not about the publically observable details of his life. But for Aristotle, the observable details of life are all. He did not even have a conception of "feeling" in our sense. (Thus the German philosopher Heidegger once said, tongue in cheek, that no Greek ever "had an experience.") The emphasis on the "inner man" is a modern invention, and Aristotle would not have understood a word of it.

This objective, observable emphasis, as opposed to the subjective, inner emphasis of our own conception of the good life, parallels other differences between Aristotle's ethics and politics, for instance, but saw them as both continuous and isomorphic. The good life for an individual was necessarily the life of participation in and contribution to a good community. (It was an ancient Áthenian saying, "to be happy means to live in a great city.") Happiness was public and entirely interpersonal and observable. The American ideal of the rugged individualist, making it on his or her own, would have made no sense. Indeed, to be exiled from one's polis was tantamount to, or worse than, death. In an important sense, exile was death, for one's whole identity and the grounds for the good life—in fact, any life at all—were in the polis. Aristotle's virtues are thus public virtues—traits that make a person better to be with (wittiness, friendliness, and so on)—and his conception of happiness is similarly a public happiness, dependent just as much upon one's role and reputation in the community as upon one's own individual self. In fact, one's individual self was itself defined by the polis, and one would be no one without it.

The ideal of happiness is often contrasted with the moral ideal of virtue. (Kant makes this contrast the basis of his entire ethics.) One's virtue is sometimes measured, therefore, by the sacrifices one is willing to make, the amount of happiness one is willing to give up in order to do what is morally right. It is worth noting one more time that this conflict between happiness and virtue—although the Greeks certainly knew about personal sacrifice—would have been all but incomprehensible, for not only are the virtues identified by their contribution to happiness but the test for virtuous action is whether one enjoys doing it. There is no conflict, accordingly, between what a virtuous person ought to do and what he wants to do. Resisting temptation is not the mark of virtue but that of a lack of virtue. Happiness, accordingly, has the virtues built right into it (in fact, is even defined in terms of them).

The same must be said of Aristotle's view of pleasure and the good life. These two are often conflated and treated the same, as simply "happiness" (in John Stuart Mill, for example), or else they are set against one another as opposites, the one referring only to the pleasures of the body and the other referring to more spiritual, idealistic matters. But for Aristotle, pleasure is neither identical to, nor distinct from happiness and the good life. It is essential to happiness; indeed one cannot conceive of happiness without it. It is the test of virtue—one cannot be virtuous without enjoying being so. And yet pleasure is neither happiness nor virtue as such but rather their "completion," their essential accompaniment. Pleasure is thus not cut off from virtuous and other "higher" activities that would give it respectability and ethical status, nor is it too simply identified with the good life, rendering the status of "higher" activities suspect. The good life for Aristotle is a whole life, in which these various components are ultimately inseparable.

Aristotle's polis was a relatively small community, still warriorlike and militaristic, in which a small aristocracy (whether or not they were democratic among themselves) reaped the advantages of leisure and wealth provided, in part, by a large slave population. The Greeks themselves—at least those to whom and of whom Aristotle is speaking—did not work, and Aristotle accordingly thought very little of the virtues of labor—whether toiling the fields or skilled carpentry, or, for that matter, what we today would call white-collar work—trading and marketing and business of various kinds. The Greek (that is, Athenian) conception of the Good, accordingly, was very specific and, given Aristotle's own aristocratic status, wholly concerned with the most desirable traits of that small privileged class. (A few centuries later, when ethics would be written by slaves, the virtues would be predictably very different.) There was little attention to rules and universal principles, much more attention to custom and mutual agreement. Happiness was defined in terms of the good for this certain group of people, and their advantages and good fortunes were taken for granted as a precondition for happiness. The Christian-Kantian question, whether one deserved such advantages, was not asked and would not arise, except for a few routine comments about "fate" and "the natural order of society." The idea of a moral code concerned primarily with dealing with strangers (as ours is) would have seemed useless if not stupid. One did not talk of honor with barbarians; their opinions didn't count and their own behavior and customs marked them as not even human. The idea of an ethics in which everyone has some equal status "as a human being" would have seemed pointless too, for what could be more obvious than the fact that we are *not* all equal and that no single set of rules—no matter how vague or how minimal—would apply to all of us.

How different all this is from those single codes of morality (for example, the Ten Commandments) which we think of as universal and applicable to everyone everywhere.

STUDY QUESTIONS

1 What is "teleology," and what is a teleological approach to ethics? How is Aristotle a teleologist, in this sense?

2 Is it valid to infer from the statement that "every act and inquiry aims at some good (some goal)" that there is a single Good (or Goal) at which everything aims? Why or why not? What is the ethical advantage of accepting this idea of a single goal for all human behavior?

3 What does Aristotle mean by "happiness" *(eudaimonia)?* In what significant ways does his term radically differ from our own notion of happiness.

4 Why should we not look for "too much precision" in ethics? Is it because every rule has its exceptions? Or because of the complicated variety of human behavior? Why can ethics not be an exact science—like mathematics or geometry (Aristotle's models)?

5 Why is ethics wasted on the young? Isn't that where moral exhortation is most important, as a way of building character and conscience?

6 Why is *eudaimonia* not for everybody? What is wrong with being "happy as a clam"? (Could clams be *eudaimon?*) What are the necessary material and social conditions for happiness?

7 Why is making a lot of money not in itself the good life?

8 Why does Aristotle keep stressing the connection between ethics and politics? What would he say about the current belief that personal morality is one thing, public and political ethics something quite different?

9 Why is the good life necessarily a *rational* life? What does Aristotle mean by "reason" here? In what sense is an activity rational? Why are the virtues rational?

10 Aristotle attacks his teacher Plato's view that, over and above all particular good things, there is also the Form of the Good. In what way(s) is Aristotle presenting an alternative to that view here? In what ways does Aristotle continue to accept certain aspects of the theory of Forms?

11 What does it mean to say that something is "good-in-itself" (or intrinsically good)? What sorts of things might be good-in-themselves? What is good-in-itself for Aristotle?

12 Aristotle keeps appealing to the fact that "everyone agrees" or "all men call this '. . .'." Is this a valid form of ethical argument? What does it presuppose? What are its limitations?

13 Why does Aristotle insist (following Solon) that "no man can be called happy while he is still alive." What does this show about Aristotle's notion of happiness? Does it make any sense to call a man happy *after* he is dead? Why or why not?

14 Why should our goal in life not be simply to stay healthy and grow? How does Aristotle's teleology help him make this point? What contemporary examples of these same arguments can you find?

15 What is a "virtue"? Do we still have the concept of virtue—or has our notion of virtue changed drastically since Aristotle's time? What is a virtuous person—for us? What is a virtuous person—for Aristotle?

16 Why is the good life not the life of pleasure? Why is the good life inconceivable without pleasure? How do these two theses fit together in Aristotle's ethics? (In other words, what is the proper place of pleasure in the good life?)

17 In what sense is virtue the "mean between the extremes"? Is this the same as saying "everything in moderation"? Give an example of a virtue, and explain how it is a mean between extremes. What are the extremes? What is the motive or activity of which these are extremes?

18 Why is a person painfully following his or her conscience not thereby virtuous, according to Aristotle?

19 If you have had the misfortune to be brought up vulgar and inconsiderate, is there any hope for you?

20 Can a person knowingly do wrong? Give seeming examples and show how according to Aristotle (or Plato) such actions are in fact born of ignorance. Are there any acts for which you cannot do this?

21 Why is *pride* a virtue? Why is it not a vice?—or at least an emotion to be ignored in ethics? What is the difference between pride and *vanity*?

22 What is courage?

23 What are Aristotle's two conditions for *voluntary* action? Can you think of others? Could an act fulfill both of Aristotle's conditions and still not be voluntary? Give examples.

24 What is deliberation? Can one deliberate over an action and not do it? What is the difference between deliberation and simply "mulling over various possibilities"?

25 What is the "practical syllogism"? Give an example of such a syllogism. Why are practical syllogisms so important for the overall point of Aristotle's ethics? What do they have to do with virtuous behavior and good character?

26 What is so good about the life of contemplation? What *is* the life of contemplation?

27 Do friends inevitably "use" one another? Explain. If you want very much to play a game of tennis and join up with an acquaintance to be able to do so, are you using him or her? Why or why not?

28 Could a person be happy without any friends at all? Explain.

CHAPTER 3

SAINT AUGUSTINE

Questions of ethics are, among other things, concerned with ideals, the ideal of the Good, the ideal of Justice. But ideals are, by their very nature, not readily attainable in the complexities, confusions, and unexpected tragedies of life. Many philosophers would say that these ideals are unattainable, that they are to be striven for, but, in this life, it is not possible to achieve them (except, perhaps, in a tiny number of extremely exceptional cases). Accordingly, one can take the ultimate question of the Good in ethics—the *summum bonum*—in either of two directions: one can remain within the sphere of the secular and refocus the quest as the search for "the good for man," as Aristotle did; or one can continue to defend the pure ideals themselves, which our worldly performances, at best, approximate, as Plato did. Of course, Aristotle still believed in ideals, and Plato staunchly defended the importance of the secular manifestations of virtue. Nevertheless, the difference between them, albeit one of ethical emphasis, set the stage for the most dramatic single development in the whole history of ethics, the separation of the secular and the "transcendent" values, best known to us through Christianity.

Although Christian ethics clearly places its emphasis upon the transcendent and the divine, this is not to the neglect of the secular. Few Christian spokesmen, for example, have ever suggested that worldly virtue is unimportant. Nevertheless, the core of Christian ethics is the existence of a sphere of pure ideals which transcends the secular worldly stage of human action, which our worldly performances at best approximate. This neo-Platonic vision is nowhere more powerfully developed than in the writings of the Christian Saint Augustine. In the midst of the fall of the mighty Roman Empire, he distinguished two "cities"—the city of man and the city of God. The first was the worldly social and political life of the flesh, the search for a purely secular happiness celebrated and given ethical articulation by Aristotle. The second, reminiscent of Plato's world of ideal froms ("World of Being"), was the Christian heaven, the domain of the Almighty, the realm of the Spirit and of true happiness and true virtue, the *summum bonum*.

Saint Augustine's two cities did not exist in the pagan harmony of Plato and Aristotle, who would not have understood. Augustine's cities were wholly antagonistic, he even refers to them as the city of God versus the city of the devil. Nor was human life simply the quest for virtue; it was undermined by original sin which could not be undone by any human effort but only by the grace of God. Indeed, one of the major battles of Augustine's career was the dispute with the British monk Pelagius and his followers (Pelagians), who denied original sin and emphasized good works (worldly virtues) as well as the grace of God. In Augustine's harsh ethics, we are essentially corrupt and helpless and God is our only salvation. Aristotle's quest for happiness through virtuous activity is, therefore, only a delusion.

In *The City of God,* Augustine attacks the pagan philosophers and defends Christian ethics against them. The central idea is that the *summum bonum* is neither happiness nor worldly virtue but faith in God and salvation. The goal to be sought is not the good life but acceptance into heaven, and much of *The City of God* is concerned with describing just what heaven will be.

SAINT AUGUSTINE

Augustine was born in 354, in Africa. He was raised in Carthage and learned Christianity as a child, but he was also steeped in paganism and spent an admittedly wild youth in "the pleasures of the flesh." Eventually, he earned his living in Rome by teaching rhetoric. At the age of 30, however, he was deeply troubled and unhappy both with his life and with the pagan view of life. After two years of study and contemplation, he rather suddenly decided to embrace Christianity and was baptized on Easter, 387. He returned to Carthage and spent the rest of his life in Hippo, where he died during a siege in 430. He is generally recognized as the founder of Christian theology and, after only Saint Paul, the second most powerful influence on the development of Christianity. His discussion of Christian ethics, while extreme, is the classic statement of the separation of the secular and the divine (in contrast to the more Aristotelian and synthetic teachings of Saint Thomas Aquinas, nearly nine hundred years later).

The City of God

In the following passages, Augustine distinguishes between his two "cities" and attacks the pagan philosophers—Aristotle and his followers ("peripatetics")—in particular—for their belief that the highest good (the *summum bonum*) is to be found in this life rather than in the city of God.

THE TWO CITIES (From Book XIV)

God, desiring not only that the human race might be able by their similarity of nature to associate with one another, but also that they might be bound together in harmony and peace by the ties of relationship, was pleased to derive all men

Saint Augustine, From *The City of God,* translated and edited by Marcus Dods (1872).

from one individual, and created man with such a nature that the members of the race should not have died, had not the two first (of whom the one was created out of nothing, and the other out of him) merited this by their disobedience; for by them so great a sin was committed, that by it the human nature was altered for the worse, and was transmitted also to their posterity, liable to sin and subject to death. And the kingdom of death so reigned over men that the deserved penalty of sin would have hurled all headlong even into the second death, of which there is no end, had not the undeserved grace of God saved some therefrom. And thus it has come to pass, that though there are very many and great nations all over the earth, whose rites and customs, speech, arms, and dress, are distinguished by marked differences, yet there are no more than two kinds of human society, which we may justly call two cities, according to the language of our Scriptures. The one consists of those who wish to live after the flesh, the other of those who wish to live after the spirit; and when they severally achieve what they wish, they live in peace, each after their kind.

WHAT THE CHRISTIANS BELIEVE REGARDING THE SUPREME GOOD AND EVIL, IN OPPOSITION TO THE PHILOSOPHERS, WHO HAVE MAINTAINED THAT THE SUPREME GOOD IS IN THEMSELVES (Book XIX)

If, then, we be asked what . . . the supreme good and evil is, [we] will reply that life eternal is the supreme good, death eternal the supreme evil, and that to obtain the one and escape the other we must live rightly. And thus it is written, "The just lives by faith," for we do not as yet see our good, and must therefore live by faith; neither have we in ourselves power to live rightly, but can do so only if He who has given us faith to believe in His help do help us when we believe and pray (Hab. 2:4). As for those who have supposed that the sovereign good and evil are to be found in this life, and have placed it either in pleasure or in virtue, or in both; in repose or in virtue, or in both; in pleasure and repose, or in virtue, or in all combined; in the primary objects of nature, or in virtue, or in both,—all these have, with a marvellous shallowness, sought to find their blessedness in this life and in themselves. Contempt has been poured upon such ideas by the Truth, saying by the prophet, "The Lord knoweth the thoughts of men" (or, as the Apostle Paul cites the passage, "The Lord knoweth the thoughts of the *wise* ") "that they are vain" (Ps. XCIV: 11; 1 Cor. 3:20).

For what flood of eloquence can suffice to detail the miseries of this life? Cicero, in the *Consolation* on the death of his daughter, has spent all his ability in lamentation; but how inadequate was even his ability here? For when, where, how, in this life can these primary objects of nature be possessed so that they may not be assailed by unforeseen accidents? Is the body of the wise man exempt from any pain which may dispel pleasure, from any disquietude which may banish repose? The amputation or decay of the members of the body puts an end to its integrity, deformity blights its beauty, weakness its health, lassitude its vigour, sleepiness or sluggishness its activity,—and which of these is it that may not assail the flesh of the wise man? Comely and fitting attitudes and movements of the body are numbered among the prime natural blessings; but what if some sickness makes the members tremble? What if a man suffers from curvature of the spine to such an extent that his hands reach the ground, and he goes upon all-fours like a quadruped? Does not this destroy all beauty and grace in the body, whether at rest or in motion? What shall I say of the fundamental blessings of the soul, sense and intellect, of which the one is given for the perception, and the other for the comprehension of truth? But what kind of sense is it that remains when a man becomes deaf and blind? Where are reason and intellect when disease makes a man delirious? We can scarcely, or not at all, refrain from tears, when we think of or see the actions and words of such frantic persons, and consider how different from and even opposed to their own sober judgment and ordinary conduct their present demeanour is. And what shall I say of those who suffer from demoniacal possession? Where is their own intelligence hidden and buried while the malignant spirit is using their body and soul according to his own will? And who is quite sure that no such thing can happen to the wise man in this life? Then, as to the perception of truth, what can we hope for even in this way while in the body, as we read in the true book of Wisdom, "The corruptible body weigheth down the soul, and the earthly tabernacle presseth down the mind that museth upon many things?" (Wisdom, 4:15). And eagerness, or desire of action, if this is the right meaning to put upon the Greek λλρμ is also reckoned among the primary advantages of nature; and yet is it not this which produces those pitiable movements of the insane, and those actions which we shudder to see, when sense is deceived and reason deranged?

In fine, virtue itself, which is not among the primary objects of nature, but succeeds to them as the result of learning, though it holds the highest place among human good things, what is its occupation save to wage perpetual war with vices,—not those that are outside of us, but within; not other men's, but our own,—a war which is waged especially by that virtue which the Greeks call σωφροσύνη and we temperance, and which bridles carnal lusts, and prevents them from winning the consent of the spirit to wicked deeds? For we must not fancy that there is no vice in us, when, as the apostle says, "The flesh lusteth against the spirit" (Gal. 5:17); for to this vice there is a contrary virtue, when, as the same writer says, "The spirit lusteth against the flesh." "For these two," he says, "are contrary one to the other, so that you cannot do the things which you would." But what is it we wish to do when we seek to attain the supreme good, unless that the flesh should cease to lust against the spirit, and that there be no vice in us against which the spirit may lust? And as we cannot attain to this in the present life, however ardently we desire it, let us by God's help accomplish at least this, to preserve the soul from succumbing and yielding to the flesh that lusts against it, and to refuse our consent to the perpetration of sin. Far be it from us, then, to fancy that while we are still engaged in this intestine war, we have already found the happiness which we seek to reach by victory. And who is there so wise that he has no conflict at all to maintain against his vices?

What shall I say of that virtue which is called prudence? Is not all its vigilance spent in the discernment of good from evil things, so that no mistake may be admitted about what we should desire and what avoid? And thus it is itself a proof that we are in the midst of evils, or that evils are in us; for it teaches us that it is an evil to consent to sin, and a good to refuse this consent. And yet this evil, to which prudence teaches and temperance enables us not to consent, is removed from this life neither by prudence nor by temperance. And justice, whose office it is to render to every man his due, whereby there is in man himself a certain just order of nature, so that the soul is subjected to God, and the flesh to the soul, and consequently both soul and flesh to God,—does not this virtue demonstrate that it is as yet rather labouring towards its end than resting in its finished work? For the soul is so much the less subjected to God as it is less occupied with the thought of God; and the flesh is so much the less subjected to the spirit as it lusts more vehemently against the spirit. So long, therefore, as we are beset by this weakness, this plague, this disease, how shall we dare to say that we are safe? And if not safe, then how can we be already enjoying our final beatitude? Then that virtue which goes by the name of fortitude is the plainest proof of the ills of life, for it is these ills which it is compelled to bear patiently. And this holds good, no matter though the ripest wisdom co-exists with it. And I am at a loss to understand how the Stoic philosophers can presume to say that these are no ills, though at the same time they allow the wise man to commit suicide and pass out of this life if they become so grievous that he cannot or ought not to endure them. But such is the stupid pride of these men who fancy that the supreme good can be found in this life, and that they can become happy by their own resources, that their wise man, or at least the man whom they fancifully depict as such, is always happy, even though he become blind, deaf, dumb, mutilated, racked with pains, or suffer any conceivable calamity such as may compel him to make away with himself; and they are not ashamed to call the life that is beset with these evils happy. O happy life, which seeks the aid of death to end it! If it is happy, let the wise man remain in it; but if these ills drive him out of it, in what sense is it happy? Or how can they say that these are not evils which conquer the virtue of fortitude, and force it not only to yield, but so to rave that it in one breath calls life happy and recommends it to be given up? For who is so blind as not to see that if it were happy it would not be fled from? And if they say we should flee from it on account of the infirmities that beset it, why then do they not lower their pride and acknowledge that it is miserable? Was it, I would ask, fortitude or weakness which prompted Cato to kill himself? For he would not have done so had he not been too weak to endure Caesar's victory. Where, then, is his fortitude? It has yielded, it has succumbed, it has been so thoroughly overcome as to abandon, forsake, flee this happy life. Or was it no longer happy? Then it was miserable. How, then, were these not evils which made life miserable, and a thing to be escaped from?

And therefore those who admit that these are evils, as the Peripatetics do, and the Old Academy, the sect which Varro advocates, express a more intelligible doctrine; but theirs also is a surprising mistake, for they contend that this is a happy life which is beset by these evils, even though they be so great that he who endures them should commit suicide to escape them. "Pains and anguish of body," says Varro, "are evils, and so much the worse in proportion to their severity; and to escape them you must quit this life." What life, I pray? This life, he says, which is oppressed by such evils. Then it is happy in the midst of these very evils on account of which you say we must quit it? Or do you call it happy because you are at liberty to escape these evils by death? What, then, if by some secret judgment of God you were held fast and not permitted to die, nor suffered to live without these evils? In that case, at least, you would say that such a life was miserable. It is soon relinquished, no doubt, but this does not make it not miserable; for were it eternal, you yourself would pronounce it miserable. Its brevity, therefore, does not clear it of misery; neither ought it to be called happiness because it is a brief misery. Certainly there is a mighty force in these evils which compel a man—according to them, even a wise man—to cease to be a man that he may escape them, though they say, and say truly, that it is as it were the first and strongest demand of nature that a man cherish himself, and naturally therefore avoid death, and should so stand his own friend as to wish and vehemently aim at continuing to exist as a living creature, and subsisting in this union of soul and body. There is a mighty force in these evils to overcome this natural instinct by which death is by every means and with all a man's efforts avoided, and to overcome it so completely that what was avoided is desired, sought after, and if it cannot in any other way be obtained, is inflicted by the man on himself. There is a mighty force in these evils which make fortitude a homicide,—if indeed, that is to be called fortitude which is so thoroughly overcome by these evils, that it not only cannot preserve by patience the man whom it undertook to govern and defend, but is itself obliged to kill him. The wise man, I admit, ought to bear death with patience, but when it is inflicted by another. If, then, as those men maintain, he is obliged to inflict it on himself, certainly it must be owned that the ills which compel him to this are not only evils, but intolerable evils. The life, then, which is either subject to accidents, or environed with evils so considerable and grievous, could never have been called happy, if the men who give it this name had condescended to yield to the truth, and to be conquered by valid arguments, when they inquired after the happy life, as they yield to unhappiness, and are overcome by overwhelming evils, when they put themselves to death, and if they had not fancied that the supreme good was to be found in this mortal life; for the very virtues of this life, which are certainly its best and most useful possessions, are all the more telling proofs of its miseries in proportion as they are helpful against the violence of its dangers, toils, and woes. For if these are true virtues,—and such cannot exist save in those who have true piety,—they do not profess to be able to deliver the men who possess them from all miseries; for true virtues tell no such lies, but they profess that by the hope of the future world this life, which is miserably involved in the many and great evils of this world, is happy as it is also safe. For if not yet safe, how could it be happy? And therefore the Apostle Paul, speaking not of men without prudence, temperance, fortitude, and justice, but of those whose lives were regulated by true piety, and whose virtues were therefore true, says,

"For we are saved by hope: now hope which is seen is not hope; for what a man seeth, why doth he yet hope for? But if we hope for that we see not, then do we with patience wait for it" (Rom. 8:24). As, therefore, we are saved, so we are made happy by hope. And as we do not as yet possess a present, but look for a future salvation, so is it with our happiness, and this "with patience"; for we are encompassed with evils, which we ought patiently to endure, until we come to the ineffable enjoyment of unmixed good; for there shall be no longer anything to endure. Salvation, such as it shall be in the world to come, shall itself be our final happiness. And this happiness these philosophers refuse to believe in, because they do not see it, and attempt to fabricate for themselves a happiness in this life, based upon a virtue which is as deceitful as it is proud.

In other chapters, Augustine goes on to remind us of the inevitable unhappiness of (this) life, and, finally, he contrasts this to the eternal happiness of Heaven (the city of God), which he compares to an endless "Sabbath"—the day of rest, free from toil and the hardships of life.

NO PEACE OF MIND IN THIS LIFE (From Book XIV)

According to the sacred Scriptures and sound doctrine, the citizens of the holy city of God, who live according to God in the pilgrimage of this life, both fear and desire, and grieve and rejoice. And because their love is rightly placed, all these affections of theirs are right. They fear eternal punishment, they desire eternal life; they grieve because they themselves groan within themselves, waiting for the adoption, the redemption of their body (Rom. 8:23); they rejoice in hope, because there "shall be brought to pass the saying that is written, Death is swallowed up in victory" (1 Cor. 15:54). In like manner they fear to sin, they desire to persevere; they grieve in sin, they rejoice in good works. . . .

If these emotions and affections, arising as they do from the love of what is good and from a holy charity, are to be called vices, then let us allow these emotions which are truly vices to pass under the name of virtues. But since these affections, when they are exercised in a becoming way, follow the guidance of right reason, who will dare to say that they are diseases or vicious passions. . . . So long as we wear the infirmity of this life, we are rather worse men than better if we have none of these emotions at all. For the apostle vituperated and abominated some who, as he said, were "without natural affection" (Rom. 1:31). The sacred Psalmist also found fault with those of whom he said, "I looked for some to lament with me, and there was none" (Ps. 69:30). For to be quite free from pain while we are in this place of misery is only purchased, as one of this world's literati perceived and remarked, at the price of blunted sensibilities both of mind and body. And therefore that which the Greeks call *apátheia,* and what the Latins call, if their language would allow them, *impassibilitas,* if it be taken to mean an impassibility of spirit and not of body, or, in other words, a freedom from those emotions which are contrary to reason and disturb the mind, then it is obviously a good and most desirable quality, but it is not one which is attainable in this life. For the words of the apostle are the confession, not of the common herd, but of the eminently pious, just, and holy men: "If we say we have no sin, we deceive ourselves, and the truth is not in us" (1 John 1:8). When there shall be no sin in a man, then there shall be this *apátheia*. At present it is enough if we live without crime; and he who thinks he lives without sin puts aside not sin, but pardon. And if that is to be called apathy, where the mind is the subject of no emotion, then who would not consider this insensibility to be worse than all vices? It may, indeed, reasonably be maintained that the perfect blessedness we hope for shall be free from all sting of fear or sadness; but who that is not quite lost to truth would say that neither love nor joy shall be experienced there? But if by apathy a condition be meant in which no fear terrifies nor any pain annoys, we must in this life renounce such a state if we would live according to God's will, but may hope to enjoy it in that blessedness which is promised as our eternal condition.

And since this is so,—since we must live a good life in order to attain to a blessed life,—a good life has all these affections right, a bad life has them wrong. But in the blessed life eternal there will be love and joy, not only right, but also assured; but fear and grief there will be none. Whence it already appears in some sort what manner of persons the citizens of the city of God must be in this their pilgrimage, who live after the spirit, not after the flesh,—that is to say, according to God, not according to man,—and what manner of persons they shall be also in that immortality whither they are journeying. And the city or society of the wicked, who live not according to God, but according to man, and who accept the doctrines of men or devils in the worship of a false and contempt of the true divinity, is shaken with those wicked emotions as by diseases and disturbances. And if there be some of its citizens who seem to restrain and, as it were, temper those passions, they are so elated with ungodly pride, that their disease is as much greater as their pain is less. And if some, with a vanity monstrous in proportion to its rarity, have become enamoured of themselves because they can be stimulated and excited by no emotion, moved or bent by no affection, such persons rather lose all humanity than obtain true tranquillity. For a thing is not necessarily right because it is inflexible, nor healthy because it is insensible.

WHAT THE RIGHTEOUS WISH FOR (From Book XIV)

We see that no one lives as he wishes but the blessed, and that no one is blessed but the righteous. But even the righteous himself does not live as he wishes, until he has arrived where he cannot die, be deceived, or injured, and until he is assured that this shall be his eternal condition. For this nature demands; and nature is not fully and perfectly blessed till it attains what it seeks. But what man is at present able to live as he wishes, when it is not in his power so much as to live? He wishes to live, he is compelled to die. How, then, does he live as he wishes who does not live as long as he wishes? Or if he wishes to die, how can he live as he wishes, since he does not wish even to live? Or if he wishes to die, not because he dislikes life, but that after death he may live better, still he is not yet living as he wishes, but only has the prospect of so living when, through death, he reaches that which he wishes. But admit that he lives as he wishes, because he has done violence to himself, and forced himself not to wish what he cannot obtain, and to wish only what he can (as Terence has it, "Since you cannot do what you will, will what you can"), is he therefore blessed because he is patiently wretched? For a blessed life is possessed only by the man who loves it. If it is loved and possessed, it must necessarily be more ardently loved than all besides; for whatever else is loved for the sake of the blessed life. And if it is loved as it deserves to be,—and the man is not blessed who does not love the blessed life as it deserves,—then he who so loves it but wish it to be eternal. Therefore it shall then only be blessed when it is eternal.

HELL UPON EARTH (From Book XXII)

That the whole human race has been condemned in its first origin, this life itself, if life it is to be called, bears witness by the host of cruel ills with which it is filled. Is not this proved by the profound and dreadful ignorance which produces all the errors that enfold the children of Adam, and from which no man can be delivered without toil, pain, and fear? Is it not proved by his love of so many vain and hurtful things, which produces gnawing cares, disquiet, griefs, fears, wild joys, quarrels, law-suits, wars, treasons, angers, hatreds, deceit, flattery, fraud, theft, robbery, perfidy, pride, ambition, envy, murders, parricides, cruelty, ferocity, wickedness, luxury, insolence, impudence, shamelessness, fornications, adulteries, incests, and the numberless uncleannesses and unnatural acts of both sexes, which it is shameful so much as to mention; sacrileges, heresies, blasphemies, perjuries, oppression of the innocent, calumnies, plots, falsehoods, false witnessings, unrighteous judgments, violent deeds, plunderings, and whatever similar wickedness has found its way into the lives of men, though it cannot find its way into the conception of pure minds? These are indeed the crimes of wicked men, yet they spring from that root of error and misplaced love which is born with every son of Adam. . . .

Who can conceive the number and severity of the punishments which afflict the human race,—pains which are not only the accompaniment of the wickedness of godless men, but are a part of the human condition and the common misery,—what fear and what grief are caused by bereavement and mourning, by losses and condemnations, by fraud and falsehood, by false suspicions, and all the crimes and wicked deeds of other men? For at their hands we suffer robbery, captivity, chains, imprisonment, exile, torture, mutilation, loss of sight, the violation of chastity to satisfy the lust of the oppressor, and many other dreadful evils. What numberless casualties threaten our bodies from without,— extremes of heat and cold, storms, floods, inundations, lightning, thunder, hail, earthquakes, houses falling; or from the stumbling, or shying, or vice of horses; from countless poisons in fruits, water, air, animals; from the painful or even deadly· bites of wild animals; from the madness which a mad dog communicates, so that even the animal which of all others is most gentle and friendly to its own master, becomes an object of intenser fear than a lion or dragon, and the man whom it has by chance infected with this pestilential contagion becomes so rabid, that his parents, wife, children, dread him more than any wild beast! What disasters are suffered by those who travel by land or sea! What man can go out of his own house without being exposed on all hands to unforeseen accidents? Returning home sound in limb, he slips on his own door-step, breaks his leg, and never recovers. What can seem safer than a man sitting in his chair? Eli the priest fell from his, and broke his neck. How many accidents do farmers, or rather all men, fear that the crops may suffer from the weather, or the soil, or the ravages of destructive animals? Commonly they feel safe when the crops are gathered and housed. Yet, to my certain knowledge, sudden floods have driven the labourers away, and swept the barns clean of the finest harvest. Is innocence a sufficient protection against the various assaults of demons? That no man might think so, even baptized infants, who are certainly unsurpassed in innocence, are some-times so tormented, that God, who permits it, teaches us hereby to bewail the calamities of this life, and to desire the felicity of the life to come. As to bodily diseases, they are so numerous that they cannot all be contained even in medical books. And in very many, or almost all of them, the cures and remedies are themselves tortures, so that men are delivered from a pain that destroys by a cure that pains. Has not the madness of thirst driven men to drink human urine, and even their own? Has not hunger driven men to eat human flesh, and that the flesh not of bodies found dead, but of bodies slain for the purpose? Have not the fierce pangs of famine driven mothers to eat their own children, incredibly savage as is seems? In fine, sleep itself, which is justly called repose, how little of repose there sometimes is in it when disturbed with dreams and visions; and with what terror is the wretched mind overwhelmed by the appearances of things which are so presented, and which, as it were, so stand out before the senses, that we cannot distinguish them from realities! How wretchedly do false appearances distract men in certain diseases! With what astonishing variety of appearances are even healthy men sometimes deceived by evil spirits, who produce these delusions for the sake of perplexing the senses of their victims, if they cannot succeed in seducing them to their side!

From this hell upon earth there is no escape, save through the grace of the Saviour Christ, our God and Lord. The very name Jesus shows this, for it means Saviour; and He saves us especially from passing out of this life into a more wretched and eternal state, which is rather a death than a life. For in this life, though holy men and holy pursuits afford us great consolations, yet the blessings which men crave are not invariably bestowed upon them, lest religion should be cultivated for the sake of these temporal advantages, while it ought rather to be cultivated for the sake of that other life from which all evil is excluded. . . .

THE BLESSINGS OF THIS LIFE (From Book XXII)

But we must now contemplate the rich and countless blessings with which the goodness of God, who cares for all He has created, has filled this very misery of the human race, which reflects His retributive justice. That first blessing which He pronounced before the fall, when He said, "Increase, and multiply, and replenish the earth" (Gen. 1:28), He did not inhibit after man had sinned, but the fecundity originally bestowed remained in the condemned stock; and the vice of sin, which has involved us in the necessity of dying, has yet not deprived us of that wonderful power of seed, or rather of that still more marvellous power by which seed is produced, and which seems to be as it were inwrought and inwoven in the human body. But in this river, as I may call it, or torrent of the human race, both elements are carried along together,—both the evil which is derived from him who begets, and the good which is bestowed by Him who creates us. In the original evil there are two things, sin and punishment; in the original good, there are two other things, propagation and conformation. But of the evils, of which the one, sin, arose from our audacity, and the other, punishment from God's judgment, we have already said as much as suits our present purpose. I mean now to speak of the blessings which God has conferred or still confers upon our nature, vitiated and condemned as it is. For in condemning it He did not withdraw all that He had given it, else it has been annihilated; neither did He, in penally subjecting it to the devil, remove it beyond His own power; for not even the devil himself is outside of God's government, since the devil's nature subsists only by the supreme Creator, who gives being to all that in any form exists.

Of these two blessings, then, which we have said flow from God's goodness, as from a fountain, towards our nature, vitiated by sin and condemned to punishment, the one, propagation, was conferred by God's benediction when He made those first works, from which He rested on the seventh day. But the other, conformation, is conferred in that work of His wherein "He worketh hitherto" (John 5:17). For were He to withdraw His efficacious power from things, they should neither be able to go on and complete the periods assigned to their measured movements, nor should they even continue in possession of that nature they were created in. God, then, so created man that He gave him what we may call fertility, whereby he might propagate other men, giving them a congenital capacity to propagate their kind, but not imposing on them any necessity to do so. This capacity God withdraws at pleasure from individuals, making them barren: but from the whole race He has not withdrawn the blessing of propagation once conferred. But though not withdrawn on account of sin, this power of progagation is not what it would have been had there been no sin. For since "man placed in honour fell, he has become like the beasts" (Ps. 69:20), and generates as they do, though the little spark of reason, which was the image of God in him, has not been quite quenched. But if conformation were not added to propagation, there would be no reproduction of one's kind. For even though there were no such thing as copulation, and God wished to fill the earth with human inhabitants, He might create all these as He created one without the help of human generation. And, indeed, even as it is, those who copulate can generate nothing save by the creative energy of God. As, therefore, in respect of that spiritual growth whereby a man is formed to piety and righteousness, the apostle says, "Neither is he that planteth anything, neither he that watereth, but God that giveth the increase" (1 Cor. 3:7), so also it must be said that it is not he that generates that is anything, but God that giveth the essential form; that it is not the mother who carries and nurses the fruit of her womb that is anything, but God that giveth the increase. For He alone, by that energy wherewith "He worketh hitherto," causes the seed to develope, and to evolve from certain secret and invisible folds into the visible forms of beauty which we see. He alone, coupling and connecting in some wonderful fashion the spiritual and corporeal natures, the one to command, the other to obey, makes a living being. And this work of His is so great and wonderful, that not only man, who is a rational animal, and consequently more excellent than all other animals of the earth, but even the most diminutive insect, cannot be considered attentively without astonishment and without praising the Creator.

It is He, then, who has given to the human soul a mind, in which reason and understanding lie as it were asleep during infancy, and as if they were not, destined, however, to be awakened and exercised as years increase, so as to become capable of knowledge and of receiving instruction, fit to understand what is true and to love what is good. It is by this capacity the soul drinks in wisdom, and becomes endowed with those virtues by which, in prudence, fortitude, temperance, and righteousness, it makes war upon error and the other inborn vices, and conquers them by fixing its desires upon no other object than the supreme and unchangeable Good. And even though this be not uniformly the result, yet who can competently utter or even conceive the grandeur of this work of the Almighty, and the unspeakable boon He has conferred upon our rational nature, by giving us even the capacity of such attainment? For over and above those arts which are called virtues, and which teach us how we may spend our life well, and attain to endless happiness,—arts which are given to the children of the promise and the kingdom by the sole grace of God which is in Christ,—has not the genius of man invented and applied countless astonishing arts, partly the result of necessity, partly the result of exuberant invention, so that this vigour of mind, which is so active in the discovery not merely of superfluous but even of dangerous and destructive things, betokens an inexhaustible wealth in the nature which can invent, learn, or employ such arts? What wonderful—one might say stupefying—advances has human industry made in the arts of weaving and building, of agriculture and navigation! With what endless variety are designs in pottery, painting, and sculpture produced, and with what skill executed! What wonderful spectacles are exhibited in the theatres, which those who have not seen them cannot credit! How skillful the contrivances for catching, killing, or taming wild beasts! And for the injury of men, also, how many kinds of poisons, weapons, engines of destruction, have been invented, while for the preservation or restoration of health the appliances and remedies are infinite! To provoke appetite and please the palate, what a variety of seasonings have been concocted! To express and gain entrance for thoughts, what a multitude and variety of signs there are, among which speaking and writing hold the first place! What ornaments has eloquence at command to delight the mind! What wealth of song is there to captivate the ear! How many musical instruments and strains of harmony have been devised! What skill has been attained in measures and numbers! With what sagacity have the movements and connections of the stars been discovered! Who could tell the thought that has been spent upon nature, even though, despairing of recounting it in detail, he endeavoured only to give a general view of it? In fine, even the defence of errors and misapprehensions, which has illustrated the genius of heretics and philosophers, cannot be sufficiently declared. For at present it is the nature of the human mind which adorns this mortal life which we are extolling, and not the faith and the way of truth which lead to immortality. And since this great nature has certainly been created by the true and supreme God, who administers all things He has made with absolute power and justice, it could never have fallen into these miseries, nor have gone out of them to miseries eternal,—saving only those who are redeemed,—had not an exceeding great sin been found in the first man from whom the rest have sprung.

Moreover, even in the body, though it dies like that of the beasts, and is in many ways weaker than theirs, what goodness of God, what providence of the great Creator, is apparent! The organs of sense and the rest of the members, are not they so placed, the appearance, and form, and stature of the body as a whole, is it not so fashioned, as to indicate that it was made for the service of a reasonable soul? Man has not been created stooping towards the earth, like the irrational animals; but his bodily form, erect and looking heavenwards, admonishes him to mind the things that are above. Then the marvellous nimbleness which has been given to the tongue and the hands, fitting them to speak, and write, and execute so many duties, and practise so many arts, does it not prove the excellence of the soul for which such an assistant was provided? And even apart from its adaptation to the work required of it, there is such a symmetry in its various parts, and so beautiful a proportion maintained, that one is at a loss to decide whether, in creating the body, greater regard was paid to utility or to beauty. Assuredly no part of the body has been created for the sake of utility which does not also contribute something to its beauty. And this would be all the more apparant, if we knew more precisely how all its parts are connected and adapted to one another, and were not limited in our observations to what appears on the surface; for as to what is covered up and hidden from our view, the intricate web of veins and nerves, the vital parts of all that lies under the skin, no one can discover it. For although, with a cruel zeal for science, some medical men, who are called anatomists, have dissected the bodies of the dead, and sometimes even of sick persons who died under their knives, and have inhumanly pried into the secrets of the human body to learn the nature of the disease and its exact seat, and how it might be cured, yet those relations of which I speak, and which form the concord, or, as the Greeks call it, "harmony," of the whole body outside and in, as of some instrument, no one has been able to discover, because no one has been audacious enough to seek for them. But if these could be known, then even the inward parts, which seem to have no beauty, would so delight us with their exquisite fitness, as to afford a profounder satisfaction to the mind—and the eyes are but its ministers—than the obvious beauty which gratifies the eye. There are some things, too, which have such a place in the body, that they obviously serve no useful purpose, but are solely for beauty, as *e.g.* the teats on a man's breast, or the beard on his face; for that this is for ornament, and not for protection, is proved by the bare faces of women, who ought rather, as the weaker sex, to enjoy such a defence. If, therefore, of all those members which are exposed to our view, there is certainly not one in which beauty is sacrificed to utility, while there are some which serve no purpose but only beauty, I think it can readily be concluded that in the creation of the human body comeliness was more regarded than necessity. In truth, necessity is a transitory thing; and the time is coming when we shall enjoy one another's beauty without any lust,—a condition which will specially redound to the praise of the Creator, who, as it is said in the psalm, has "put on praise and comeliness" (Ps. 104:1).

How can I tell of the rest of creation, with all its beauty and utility, which the divine goodness has given to man to please his eye and serve his purposes, condemned though he is, and hurled into these labours and miseries? Shall I speak of the manifold and various loveliness of sky, and earth, and sea; of the plentiful supply and wonderful qualities of the light; of sun, moon, and stars; of the shade of trees; of the colours and perfume of flowers; of the multitude of birds, all differing in plumage and in song; of the variety of animals, of which the smallest in size are often the most wonderful,—the works of ants and bees astonishing us more than the huge bodies of whales? Shall I speak of the sea, which itself is so grand a spectacle, when it arrays itself as it were in vestures of various colours, now running through every shade of green, and again becoming purple or blue? Is it not delightful to look at it in storm, and experience the soothing complacency which it inspires, by suggesting that we ourselves are not tossed and shipwrecked? What shall I say of the numberless kinds of food to alleviate hunger, and the variety of seasonings to stimulate appetite which are scattered everywhere by nature, and for which we are not indebted to the art of cookery? How many natural appliances are there for preserving and restoring health! How grateful is the alternation of day and night! How pleasant the breezes that cool the air! How abundant the supply of clothing furnished us by trees and animals! Who can enumerate all the blessings we enjoy? If I were to attempt to detail and unfold only these few which I have indicated in the mass, such an enumeration would fill a volume. And all these are but the solace of the wretched and condemned, not the rewards of the blessed. What then shall these rewards be, if such be the blessings of a condemned state? What will He give to those whom He has predestined to life, who has given such things even to those whom He has predestined to death? What blessings will He in the blessed life shower upon those for whom, even in this state of misery, He has been willing that His only-begotten Son should endure such sufferings even to death? Thus the apostle reasons concerning those who are predestined to that kingdom: "He that spared not His own Son, but delivered Him up for us all, how shall He not with Him also give us all things (Rom. 8:32)? When this promise is fulfilled, what shall we be? What blessings shall we receive in that kingdom, since already we have received as the pledge of them Christ's dying? In what condition shall the spirit of man be, when it has no longer any vice at all; when it neither yields to any, nor is in bondage to any, nor has to make war against any, but is perfected, and enjoys undisturbed peace with itself? Shall it not then know all things with certainty, and without any labour or error, when unhindered and joyfully it drinks the wisdom of God at the fountainhead? What shall the body be, when it is in every respect subject to the spirit, from which it shall draw a life so sufficient, as to stand in need of no other nutriment? For it shall no longer be animal, but spiritual, having indeed the substance of flesh, but without any fleshly corruption.

OF THE ETERNAL FELICITY OF THE CITY OF GOD, AND OF THE PERPETUAL SABBATH (From Book XXII)

How great shall be that felicity, which shall be tainted with no evil, which shall lack no good, and which shall afford leisure for the praises of God, who shall be all in all! For I know not what other employment there can be where no lassitude shall slacken activity, nor any want stimulate to labour. I am admonished also by the sacred song, in which I read or hear the words, "Blessed are they that dwell in Thy house, O Lord; they will be still praising Thee." All the members and organs of the incorruptible body, which now we see to be suited to various necessary uses, shall contribute to the praises of God; for in that life necessity shall have no place, but full, certain, secure, everlasting felicity. For all those parts of the bodily harmony, which are distributed through the whole body, within and without, and of which I have just been saying that they at present elude our observation, shall then be discerned; and, along with the other great and marvellous discoveries which shall then kindle rational minds in praise of the great Artificer, there shall be the enjoyment of a beauty which appeals to the reason. What power of movement such bodies shall possess, I have not the audacity rashly to define, as I have not the ability to conceive. Nevertheless I will say that in any case, both in motion and at rest, they shall be, as in their appearance, seemly; for into that state nothing which is unseemly shall be admitted. One thing is certain, the body shall forthwith be wherever the spirit wills, and the spirit shall will nothing which is unbecoming either to the spirit or to the body. True honour shall be there, for it shall be denied to none who is worthy, nor yielded to any unworthy; neither shall any unworthy person so much as sue for it, for none but the worthy shall be there. True peace shall be there, where no one shall suffer opposition either from himself or any other. God Himself, who is the Author of virtue, shall there be its reward; for, as there is nothing greater or better, He has promised Himself. What else was meant by His word through the prophet, "I will be your God, and ye shall be my people" (Lev. 26:12), than, I shall be their satisfaction, I shall be all that men honourably desire,—life, and health, and nourishment, and plenty, and glory, and honour, and peace, and all good things? This, too, is the right interpretation of the saying of the apostle, "That God may be all in all" (1 Cor. 15:28). He shall be the end of our desires who shall be seen without end, loved without cloy, praised without weariness. This outgoing of affection, this employment, shall certainly be, like eternal life itself, common to all.

But who can conceive, not to say describe, what degrees of honour and glory shall be awarded to the various degrees of merit? Yet it cannot be doubted that there shall be degrees. And in that blessed city there shall be this great blessing, that no inferior shall envy any superior, as now the archangels are not envied by the angels, because no one will wish to be what he has not received, though bound in strictest concord with him who has received; as in the body the finger does not seek to be the eye, though both members are harmoniously included in the complete structure of the body. And thus, along with his gift, greater or less, each shall receive this further gift of contentment to desire no more than he has.

Neither are we to suppose that because sin shall have no power to delight them, free will must be withdrawn. It will, on the contrary, be all the more truly free, because set free from delight in sinning to take unfailing delight in not sinning. For the first freedom of will which man received when he was created upright consisted in an ability not to sin, but also in an ability to sin; whereas this last freedom of will shall be superior, inasmuch as it shall not be able to sin. This, indeed, shall not be a natural ability, but the gift of God. For it is one thing to be God, another thing to be a partaker of God. God by nature cannot sin, but the partaker of God receives this inability from God. And in this divine gift there was to be observed this gradation, that man should first receive a free will by which he was able not to sin, and at last a free will by which he was not able to sin,—the former being adapted to the acquiring of merit, the latter to the enjoying of the reward. But the nature thus constituted, having sinned when it had the ability to do so, it is by a more abundant grace that is delivered so as to reach that freedom in which it cannot sin. For as the first immortality which Adam lost by sinning consisted in his being able not to die, while the last shall consist in his not being able to die, so the first free will consisted in his being able not to sin, the last in his not being able to sin. And thus piety and justice shall be as indefeasible as happiness. For certainly by sinning we lost both piety and happiness; but when we lost happiness, we did not lose the love of it. Are we to say that God Himself is not free because He cannot sin? In that city, then, there shall be free will, one in all the citizens, and indivisible in each, delivered from all ill, filled with all good, enjoying indefeasibly the delights of eternal joys, oblivious of sins, oblivious of sufferings, and yet not so oblivious of its deliverance as to be ungrateful to its Deliverer.

The soul, then, shall have an intellectual remembrance of its past ills; but, so far as regards sensible experience, they shall be quite forgotten. For a skillful physician knows, indeed, professionally almost all diseases; but experimentally he is ignorant of a great number which he himself has never suffered from. As, therefore, there are two ways of knowing evil things,—one by mental insight, the other by sensible experience, for it is one thing to understand all vices by the wisdom of a cultivated mind, another to understand them by the foolishness of an abandoned life,—so also there are two ways of forgetting evils. For a well-instructed and learned man forgets them one way, and he who has experimentally suffered from them forgets them another,—the former by neglecting what he has learned, the latter by escaping what he has suffered. And in this latter way the saints shall forget their past ills, for they shall have so thoroughly escaped them all, that they shall be quite blotted out of their experience. But their intellectual knowledge, which shall be great, shall keep them acquainted not only with their own past woes, but with the eternal sufferings of the lost. For if they were not to know that they had been miserable, how could they, as the Psalmist says, for ever sing the mercies of God? Certainly that city shall have no greater joy than the celebration of the grace of Christ, who redeemed us by His blood. There shall be accomplished the words of the psalm, "Be still, and know that I am God" (Ps. 66:10). There shall be the great Sabbath which has no evening, which God celebrated among His first works, as it is written, "And God rested on the seventh day from all His works which He had made. And God blessed the seventh day, and sanctified it; because that in it He had rested from all His work which God began to make" (Gen. 2:2,3). For we shall ourselves be the seventh day, when we shall be filled and replensihed with God's blessing and sanctification. There shall we be still, and know that He is God; that He is that which we ourselves aspired to be when we fell away from Him, and listened to the voice of the seducer, "Ye shall be as Gods" (Gen. 3:5), and so abandoned God, who would have made us as gods, not by deserting Him, but by participating in Him. For without Him what have we accomplished, save to perish in His anger? But when we are restored by Him, and perfected with greater grace, we shall have eternal leisure to see that He is God, for we shall be full of Him when He shall be all in all. For even our good works, when they are understood to be rather His than ours, are imputed to us that we may enjoy this Sabbath rest. For if we attribute them to ourselves, they shall be servile; for it is said of the Sabbath, "Ye shall do no servile work in it." Wherefore also it is said by Ezekiel the prophet, "And I gave them my Sabbaths to be a sign between me and them, that they might know that I am the Lord who sanctify them." This knowledge shall be perfected when we shall be perfectly at rest, and shall perfectly know that He is God.

This Sabbath shall appear still more clearly if we count the ages as days, in accordance with the periods of time defined in Scripture, for that period will be found to be the seventh. The first age, as the first day, extends from Adam to the deluge; the second from the deluge to Abraham, equalling the first, not in length of time, but in the number of generations, there being ten in each. From Abraham to the advent of Christ there are, as the evangelist Matthew calculates, three periods, in each of which are fourteen generations—one period from Abraham to David, a second from David to the captivity, a third from the captivity to the birth of Christ in the flesh. There are thus five ages in all. The sixth is now passing, and cannot be measured by any number of generations, as it has been said, "It is not for you to know the times, which the Father hath put in His own power." After this period God shall rest as on the seventh day, when

He shall give us (who shall be the seventh day) rest in Himself. But there is not now space to treat of these ages; suffice it to say that the seventh shall be our Sabbath, which shall be brought to a close, not by evening, but by the Lord's day, as an eighth and eternal day, consecrated by the resurrection of Christ, and prefiguring the eternal repose not only of the spirit, but also of the body. There we shall rest and see, see and love, love and praise. This is what shall be in the end without end. For what other end do we propose to ourselves than to attain to the kingdom of which there is no end?

DISCUSSION

For Augustine, faith is the most important virtue. But faith alone is not sufficient to account for the details of ethical life. What is good, and what is evil? Appealing all values to God and holding God Himself as the highest Good *(summum bonum)* still leaves open the question that also plagued Augustine, What should one do in this life? How should one live? How does one do God's will, in addition to having faith in him? Augustine may have disagreed with Pelagius about the importance of good works, but nevertheless the way one behaves in the details of life is as important to Augustine as to Aristotle. Where does our knowledge of these details—our knowledge of the Christian virtues—come from?

In one of his early dialogues—*Euthyphro*—Plato has Socrates debating the suggestion that "the Good is what the gods find pious." In Augustine's neo-Platonic Christian ethics, we might simply translate this as "the Good is what God wills." But this suggestion contains an essential ambiguity; it might mean: Whatever God wills (whatever the gods find pious) is good. Or it might mean: God always wills the Good (the gods always find the Good to be pious). In the first case, it is the fact that God wills something (for example, chastity or charity) that makes it good. In the second case, something is already good, and God wills it because it is good and, just as important, because He is (infinitely) good.

This distinction makes an enormous practical difference to us, however. If the Good is appealed to God's will, it is of the utmost importance that we can know God's will. Where God gives us explicit commands (for example, in the scriptures, or through Moses, or, occasionally, through the direct communication to some saintly figure), God's will is presumably straightforward (though serious problems of interpretation remain—as the whole history of Christianity has demostrated in an often violent way). But where there are no explicit commandments, the question of the Good is left to secular reflection as well as religious speculation, and the question of the Good cannot be answered solely on the appeal to God's will. But even where God's will is seemingly explicit and straightforward—for example, in the Ten Commandments—the problem remains that we must interpret those commandments and understand their qualifications (for example, understand in what circumstances one can kill, despite the clarity of the commandment, "Thou shalt not kill"). And is killing wrong because God prohibits it (except in certain circumstances)? Or does God prohibit killing because killing is wrong? In the *Euthyphro,* Plato makes Socrates's (and his own) position clear—the gods find certain acts pious because they are good. And Augustine too holds that God loves the Good because He is Good. But this means that the appeal to God's will for the determination of the Good has an essential limitation; God may love the Good, but we must still ask ourselves what is good. The essential concerns of ethics are not resolved by religion;

they are only given an infinitely larger stage on which to play their crucial roles in our lives and a divine realm of judgment, rewards, and punishments to give them even more weight and significance.

STUDY QUESTIONS

1 Does good mean "what God wills"? Is this what Augustine is arguing? What problems are there with such a definition? What would happen if God willed evil (for example, commanding Abraham to kill his son)?

2 Does the evil and injustice in the world contradict our faith in God? Should it do so? How is it possible to believe in a God who is all-powerful, all-knowing, and good in the face of all the needless suffering in the world?

3 Why can "happiness" *not* be the "good for man," according to Augustine?

4 What are the "two cities?" In what way are these parallel to Plato's "two worlds" (of everyday life and the Forms, respectively)?

5 What is "original sin"? What importance does it have for ethics? Why would the theology of good works (advanced by the monk Pelagius, for example) contradict the concept of original sin?

6 What would Augustine have to say about those modern American theologians who claim that God will show his grace to those who believe by making them rich? What changes in Christianity are necessary in order to even condone—much less encourage — business activity (making a profit, selling one's skills or inventions to the highest bidder, lending money at the highest allowable interest rate)?

7 What is salvation? What are we saved *from*? Why believe in it? What is desirable about it?

8 The French philosopher Pascal advanced a "wager" which he thought demonstrated the rationality of believing in God. He argued, briefly, that one could choose to believe or not believe; not believing, he acknowledged, had certain secular advantages. Believing "paid off" spectacularly if God actually did exist. In graphic form, here is the bet—with odds—that Pascal is setting out for us:

	God Exists	God Does Not Exist
Believe	Infinite reward	Wasted piety
Not Believe	Infinite punishment	No wasted piety

What would Augustine say about this line of reasoning?

9 How do we know what God wills? Do we have to know that God willed it to know that it is good?

CHAPTER 4

THOMAS HOBBES

For Plato and for Augustine, the Good in ethics had to be defined through metaphysics—by reference to a transcendent Idea or Form of "the Good" or by appeal to a transcendent almighty God. For Aristotle, the Good was identified as "the good for man," by appeal to human happiness. But not even Aristotle wholly made the move that has become the basis of much of modern ethics and moral philosophy—the appeal to human *psychological* nature, the actual springs and impulses that drive us and determine our goals and desires. Both Plato and Augustine were psychologically insightful, even brilliantly so. Aristotle certainly delved into the logic of deliberation and action as deeply as any philosopher before or since. But the idea of basing ethics wholly on psychology is a distinctively modern idea, and one of its first and foremost proponents was the English philosopher Thomas Hobbes.

Hobbes was not an optimist on questions of human nature. He believed that our primary passion is *fear* and our natural tendencies are selfishness and violence. He famously suggested that without the controlling force of government and society our lives would be "nasty, brutish and short" and there would be a "war of everyone against everyone." But though he was a proponent of strong government as an antidote to our less than benevolent natures, Hobbes was also a progressive thinker who rejected the still-prevalent divine right of kings conception of government and advocated the then radical theory that the power of the sovereign is derived from the people (for which he got himself into considerable trouble).

Hobbes's main work is a monumental treatise appropriately entitled *Leviathan* (1651). (A leviathan is a medieval sea monster, often conceived as a snake or a whale. Hobbes uses it to refer to the whole of society.) It begins as a treatise on psychology—the nature of the mind and the nature of human nature; it then turns to ethics and, ultimately, to politics. Hobbes's view of people as primarily selfish and, more than anything else, afraid for their lives, dictated the ultimate principles of his ethics, which is that people must get together and form a society with a strong government in order to protect themselves from enemies and each other. This in turn sets up the basis of his political theory, that society is based upon a *social contract* in which everyone gives up certain rights and privileges in return for the protection and advantages of society. (Other social contract theories were developed in the following century by John Locke and Jean-Jacques Rousseau, from which evolved our own social contract—so evident in our Declaration of Independence, for example—"to secure these rights, Governments are instituted among Men, deriving their Just powers from the consent of the governed . . . ". His psychology developed as part of a larger view of the universe as essentially mechanical in its workings, as "matter in motion." (Isaac Newton developed his own mechanical theory of the universe only a few years later.) His ethics is one of the great examples of *psychological egoism,* the theory that all of our actions—good or bad, noble or vicious—are motivated by our own self-interest, especially the fear of violent death. His politics provided at one and the same time the justification of a strong central government and the more radical parliamentarianism that was becoming influential at the time. (The Glorious Revolution in England was only thirty-seven years later.)

THOMAS HOBBES

Hobbes was born in 1588, graduated from Oxford University, and entered into a lifetime of study in the sciences and mathematics. He earned his living as a tutor (for a while he was tutor to Prince Charles, later Charles II of England). He often traveled to Europe and became friendly with Galileo and Gassendi, the leading scientists of the time. His early political writings had already gotten him into trouble, and so he prudently left England in the 1640s for France. But his politics also endangered him in France, and his irreligious materialism caused him to be condemned by the French church as well. Accordingly, he went back to England in 1651, when he published *Leviathan,* and lived relatively peacefully until his death in 1679.

Leviathan

In the following excerpts from *Leviathan,* Hobbes first outlines for us the mechanical basis of his psychology in terms of "motions," in particular, actions (or "endeavors") moved by "appetite or desire." He then provides us with a brief catalog of the reigning human passions and gives us his definition of that all-important ethical word, "good." According to Hobbes, "good" means "the object of any man's appetite or desire," and it is clearly a "subjective" matter whether something is good or not ("there being nothing simply and absolutely so").

OF THE INTERIOR BEGINNINGS OF VOLUNTARY MOTIONS COMMONLY CALLED THE PASSIONS AND THE SPEECHES BY WHICH THEY ARE EXPRESSED

There be in animals, two sorts of *motions* peculiar to them: one called *vital;* begun in generation, and continued without interruption through their whole

Thomas Hobbes, *Leviathan,* from Molesworth edition (1839).

life; such as are the *course* of the *blood,* the *pulse,* the *breathing,* the *concoction, nutrition, excretion,* etc. to which motions there needs no help of imagination: the other is *animal motion,* otherwise called *voluntary motion;* as to *go,* to *speak,* to *move* any of our limbs, in such manner as is first fancied in our minds. That sense is motion in the organs and interior parts of man's body, caused by the action of the things we see, hear, etc.; and that fancy is but the relics of the same motion, remaining after sense, has been already said in the first and second chapters. And because *going, speaking,* and the like voluntary motions, depend always upon a precedent thought of *whither, which way,* and *what;* it is evident, that the imagination is the first internal beginning of all voluntary motion. And although unstudied men do not conceive any motion at all to be there, where the thing moved is invisible; or the space it is moved in is, for the shortness of it, insensible; yet that doth not hinder, but that such motions are. For let a space be never so little, that which is moved over a greater space, whereof that little one is part, must first be moved over that. These small beginnings of motion, within the body of man, before they appear in walking, speaking, striking, and other visible actions, are commonly called ENDEAVOUR.

This endeavour, when it is toward something which causes it, is called APPETITE, or DESIRE; the latter, being the general name; and the other oftentimes restrained to signify the desire of food, namely *hunger* and *thirst.* And when the endeavour is fromward something, it is generally called AVERSION. These words, *appetite* and *aversion,* we have from the Latins; and they both of them signify the motions, one of approaching, the other of retiring. So also do the Greek words for the same, which are ορμὴ and αφορμὴ. For nature itself does often press upon men those truths, which afterwards, when they look for somewhat beyond nature, they stumble at. For the Schools find in mere appetite to go, or move, no actual motion at all: but because some motion they must acknowledge, they call it metaphorical motion; which is but an absurd speech: for though words may be called metaphorical; bodies and motions can not.

That which men desire, they are also said to LOVE: and to HATE those things for which they have aversion. So that desire and love are the same thing; save that by desire, we always signify the absence of the object; by love, most commonly the presence of the same. So also by aversion, we signify the absence; and by hate, the presence of the object.

Of appetites and aversions, some are born with men; as appetite of food, appetite of excretion, and exoneration, which may also and more properly be called aversions, from somewhat they feel in their bodies; and some other appetites, not many. The rest, which are appetites of particular things, proceed from experience, and trial of their effects upon themselves or other men. For of things we know not at all, or believe not to be, we can have no further desire, than to taste and try. But aversion we have for things, not only which we know have hurt us, but also that we do not know whether they will hurt us, or not.

Those things which we neither desire, nor hate, we are said to *contemn;* CONTEMPT being nothing else but an immobility, or contumacy of the heart, in resisting the action of certain things; and proceeding from that the heart is already moved otherwise, by other more potent objects; or from want of experience of them.

And because the constitution of a man's body is in continual mutation, it is impossible that all the same things should always cause in him the same appetites, and aversions: much less can all men consent, in the desire of almost any one and the same object.

But whatsoever is the object of any man's appetite or desire, that is it which he for his part calleth *good:* and the object of his hate and aversion, *evil;* and of his contempt, *vile* and *inconsiderable.* For these words of good, evil, and contemptible, are ever used with relation to the person that useth them: there being nothing simply and absolutely so; nor any common rule of good and evil, to be taken from the nature of the objects themselves; but from the person of the man, where there is no commonwealth; or, in a commonwealth, from the person that representeth it; or from an arbitrator or judge, whom men disagreeing shall by consent set up, and make his sentence the rule thereof. . . .

As, in sense, that which is really within us, is, as I have said before, only motion, caused by the action of external objects, but in apparence; to the sight light and colour; to the ear, sound; to the nostril, odour, &c.: so, when the action of the same object is continued from the eyes, ears, and other organs to the heart, the real effect there is nothing but motion, or endeavour; which consisteth in appetite, or aversion, to or from the object moving. But the apparence, or sense of that motion, is that we either call *delight,* or *trouble of mind.* . . .

Pleasure therefore, or *delight,* is the apparence, or sense of good; and *molestation,* or *displeasure,* the apparence, or sense of evil. And consequently all appetite, desire, and love, is accompanied with some delight more or less; and all hatred and aversion, with more or less displeasure and offence.

Of pleasures or delights, some arise from the sense of an object present; and those may be called *pleasure of sense;* the word *sensual* as it is used by those only that condemn them, having no place till there be laws. Of this kind are all onerations and exonerations of the body; as also all that is pleasant, in the *sight, hearing, smell, taste, or touch.* Others arise from the expectation, that proceeds from foresight of the end, or consequence of things; whether those things in the sense please or displease. And these are *pleasures of the mind* of him that draweth those consequences, and are generally called JOY. In the like manner, displeasures are some in the sense, and called PAIN; others in the expectation of consequences, and are called GRIEF.

These simple passions called *appetite, desire, love, aversion, hate, joy,* and *grief,* have their names for divers considerations diversified. As first, when they one succeed another, they are diversely called from the opinion men have of the likelihood of attaining what they desire. Secondly, from the object loved or hated. Thirdly, from the consideration of many of them together. Fourthly, from the alteration or succession itself.

For *appetite,* with an opinion of attaining, is called HOPE.

The same, without such opinion, DESPAIR.

Aversion, with opinion of HURT from the object, FEAR. . . .

The "natural condition" of man, we have anticipated, is one of misery. Not only are we essentially selfish, but we are all more or less equal—whatever the obvious differences between us—at least in the sense that almost everyone has the power to make life miserable—and dangerous—for everyone else. We do not enjoy each other so much as we interfere with one another; we quarrel constantly, because we are competitive, because we are insecure, because we are vain. All in all, it is not a pretty portrait of ourselves. But because there is only selfishness and conflict, there is no such thing as natural justice—or injustice either. There is no right and wrong, there is only the power of *force* and, if you are clever, the trickery of fraud. This is not to say that we wouldn't like things otherwise, but it is no noble sentiment that so moves us; it is the simple fear of death.

OF THE NATURAL CONDITION OF MANKIND AS CONCERNING THEIR FELICITY AND MISERY

Nature hath made men so equal, in the faculties of the body, and mind; as that though there be found one man sometimes manifestly stronger in body, or of quicker mind than another; yet when all is reckoned together, the difference between man, and man, is not so considerable, as that one man can thereupon claim to himself any benefit, to which another may not pretend, as well as he. For as to the strength of body, the weakest has strength enough to kill the strongest, either by secret machination, or by confederacy with others, that are in the same danger with himself.

And as to the faculties of the mind, setting aside the arts grounded upon words, and especially that skill of proceeding upon general, and infallible rules, called science; which very few have, and but in few things; as being not a native faculty, born with us; nor attained, as prudence, while we look after somewhat else, I find yet a greater equality amongst men, than that of strength. For prudence, is but experience; which equal time, equally bestows on all men, in those things they equally apply themselves unto. That which may perhaps make such equality incredible, is but a vain conceit of one's own wisdom, which almost all men think they have in a greater degree, than the vulgar; that is, than all men but themselves, and a few others, whom by fame, or for concurring with themselves, they approve. For such is the nature of men, that howsoever they may acknowledge many others to be more witty, or more eloquent, or more learned; yet they will hardly believe there be many so wise as themselves; for they see their own wit at hand, and other men's at a distance. But this proveth rather that men are in that point equal, than unequal. For there is not ordinarily a greater sign of the equal distribution of any thing, than that every man is contented with his share.

From this equality of ability, ariseth equality of hope in the attaining of our ends. And therefore if any two men desire the same thing, which nevertheless they cannot both enjoy, they become enemies; and in the way to their end, which is principally their own conservation, and sometimes their delectation only, endeavour to destroy, or subdue one another. And from hence it comes to pass, that where an invader hath no more to fear, than another man's single power; if one plant, sow, build, or possess a convenient seat, others may probably be expected to come prepared with forces united, to dispossess, and deprive him, not only of the fruit of his labour, but also of his life, or liberty. And the invader again is in the like danger of another.

And from this diffidence of one another, there is no way for any man to secure himself, so reasonable, as anticipation; that is, by force, or wiles, to master the persons of all men he can, so long, till he see no other power great enough to endanger him: and this is no more than his own conservation requireth, and is generally allowed. Also because there be some, that taking pleasure in contemplating their own power in the acts of conquest, which they pursue farther than their security requires; if others, that otherwise would be glad to be at ease within modest bounds, should not by invasion increase their power, they would not be able, long time, by standing only on their defence, to subsist. And by consequence, such augmentation of dominion over men being necessary to a man's conservation, it ought to be allowed him.

Again, men have no pleasure, but on the contrary a great deal of grief, in keeping company, where there is no power able to over-awe them all. For every man looketh that his companion should value him, at the same rate he sets upon himself: and upon all signs of contempt, or undervaluing, naturally endeavours, as far as he dares, (which amongst them that have no common power to keep them in quiet, is far enough to make them destroy each other), to extort a greater value from his contemners, by damage; and from others, by the example.

So that in the nature of man, we find three principal causes of quarrel. First, competition; secondly, diffidence; thirdly, glory.

The first, maketh men invade for gain; the second, for safety; and the third, for reputation. The first use violence, to make themselves masters of other men's persons, wives, children, and cattle; the second, to defend them; the third, for trifles, as a word, a smile, a different opinion, and any other sign of undervalue, either direct in their persons, or by reflection in their kindred, their friends, their nation, their profession, or their name.

Hereby it is manifest, that during the time men live without a common power to keep them all in awe, they are in that condition which is called war; and such a war, as is of every man, against every man. For WAR, consisteth not in battle only, or the act of fighting; but in a tract of time, wherein the will to contend by the battle is sufficiently known: and therefore the notion of *time,* is to be considered in the nature of war; as it is in the nature of weather. For as the nature of foul weather, lieth not in a shower or two of rain; but in an inclination thereto of many days together: so the nature of war, consisteth not in actual fighting; but in the known disposition thereto, during all the time there is no assurance to the contrary. All other time is PEACE.

Whatsoever therefore is consequent to a time of war, where every man is enemy to every man; the same is consequent to the time, wherein men live without other security, than what their own strength, and their own invention shall furnish them withal. In such condition, there is no place for industry; because the fruit thereof is uncertain: and consequently no culture of the earth;

no navigation, nor use of the commodities that may be imported by sea; no commodious building; no instruments of moving, and removing, such things as require much force; no knowledge of the face of the earth; no account of time; no arts; no letters; no society; and which is worst of all, continual fear, and danger of violent death; and the life of man, solitary, poor, nasty, brutish, and short.

It may seem strange to some man, that has not well weighed these things; that nature should thus dissociate, and render men apt to invade, and destroy one another: and he may therefore, not trusting to this inference, made from the passions, desire perhaps to have the same confirmed by experience. Let him therefore consider with himself, when taking a journey, he arms himself, and seeks to go well accompanied; when going to sleep, he locks his doors; when even in his house he locks his chests; and this when he knows there be laws, and public officers, armed, to revenge all injuries shall be done him; what opinion he has of his fellow-subjects, when he rides armed; of his fellow citizens, when he locks his doors; and of his children, and servants, when he locks his chests. Does he not there as much accuse mankind by his actions, as I do by my words? But neither of us accuse man's nature in it. The desires, and other passions of man, are in themselves no sin. No more are the actions, that proceed from those passions, till they know a law that forbids them: which till laws be made they cannot know: nor can any law be made, till they have agreed upon the person that shall make it.

It may peradventure be thought, there was never such a time, nor condition of war as this; and I believe it was never generally so, over all the world: but there are many places, where they live so now. For the savage people in many places of America, except the government of small families, the concord whereof dependeth on natural lust, have no government at all; and live at this day in that brutish manner, as I said before. Howsoever, it may be perceived what manner of life there would be, where. there were no common power to fear, by the manner of life, which men that have formerly lived under a peaceful govern-ment, use to degenerate into, in a civil war.

But though there had never been any time, wherein particular men were in a condition of war one against another; yet in all times, kings, and persons of sovereign authority, because of their independency, are in continual jealousies, and in the state and posture of gladiators; having their weapons pointing, and their eyes fixed on one another; that is, their forts, garrisons, and guns upon the frontiers of their kingdoms; and continual spies upon their neighbours; which is a posture of war. But because they uphold thereby, the industry of their subjects; there does not follow from it, that misery, which accompanies the liberty of particular men.

To this war of every man, against every man, this also is consequent; that nothing can be unjust. The notions of right and wrong, justice and injustice have there no place. Where there is no common power, there is no law: where no law, no injustice. Force, and fraud, are in war the two cardinal virtues. Justice, and injustice are none of the faculties neither of the body, nor mind. If they were, they might be in a man that were alone in the world, as well as his senses, and passions. They are qualities, that relate to men in society, not in solitude. It is consequent also to the same condition, that there be no propriety, no diminion, no *mine* and *thine* distinct; but only that to be every man's that he can get; and for so long, as he can keep it. And thus much for the ill condition, which man by mere nature is actually placed in; though with a possibility to come out of it, consisting partly in the passions, partly in his reason.

The passions that incline men to peace, are fear of death; desire of such things as are necessary to commodious living; and a hope by their industry to obtain them. And reason suggesteth convenient articles of peace, upon which men may be drawn to agreement. These articles, are they, which otherwise are called the Laws of Nature: whereof I shall speak more particularly, in the following chapters.

Hobbes spells out for us the nature of "natural law" and the origin of "the social contract." The ultimate law of nature is "the right to life," not in any religious or metaphysical sense but in the strictly secular sense that each of us, "by instinct," fights for our own survival and cannot do otherwise. Indeed, Hobbes argues that not even the law can take away this primary right, although—also by right—society may take the life of a person who threatens its well-being. But because of this instinct for self-preservation, it follows that each of us wants—in our own interest—a general peace. The second law, accordingly, is that we are willing—out of self-interest—to give up our claims to everything (since there is no ownership or rights unless there is also a law or custom) in return for this peace. Accordingly, we do give up and transfer our rights in what we call a "contract."

OF THE FIRST AND SECOND NATURAL LAWS AND OF CONTRACTS

The right of nature, which writers commonly call *jus naturale,* is the liberty each man hath, to use his own power, as he will himself, for the preservation of his own nature; that is to say, of his own life; and consequently, of doing any thing, which in his own judgment, and reason, he shall conceive to be the aptest means thereunto.

By liberty, is understood, according to the proper signification of the word, the absence of external impediments: which impediments, may oft take away part of a man's power to do what he would; but cannot hinder him from using the power left him, according as his judgment, and reason shall dictate to him.

A law of nature, *lex naturalis,* is a precept or general rule, found out by reason, by which a man is forbidden to do that, which is destructive of his life, or taketh away the means of preserving the same; and to omit that, by which he thinketh it may be best preserved. For though they that speak of this subject, use to confound *jus,* and *lex, right* and *law:* yet they ought to be distinguished; because RIGHT, consisteth in liberty to do, or to forbear; whereas LAW, determineth, and bindeth to one of them: so that law, and right, differ as much, as obligation, and liberty, which in one and the same matter are inconsistent.

And because the condition of man, as hath been declared in the precedent chapter, is a condition of war of every one against every one: in which case every one is governed by his own reason; and there is nothing he can make use of, that may not be a help unto him, in preserving his life against his enemies; it followeth, that in such a condition, every man has a right to every thing; even to one another's body. And therefore, as long as this natural right of every man to every thing endureth, there can be no security to any man, how strong or wise soever he be, of living out the time, which nature ordinarily alloweth men to live. And consequently it is a precept, or general rule of reason, *that every man, ought to endeavour peace, as far as he has hope of obtaining it; and when he cannot obtain it, that he may seek, and use, all helps, and advantages of war.* The first branch of which rule, containeth the first, and fundamental law of nature; which is, to *seek peace, and follow it.* The second, the sum of the right of nature; which is, *by all means we can, to defend ourselves.*

From this fundamental law of nature, by which men are commanded to endeavour peace, is derived this second law; *that a man be willing, when others are so too, as far-forth, as for peace, and defence of himself he shall think it necessary, to lay down this right to all things; and be contented with so much liberty against other men, as he would allow other men against himself.* For as long as every man holdeth this right, of doing any thing he liketh; so long are all men in the condition of war. But if other men will not lay down their right, as well as he; then there is no reason for any one, to divest himself of his: for that were to expose himself to prey, which no man is bound to, rather than to dispose himself to peace. This is that law of the Gospel; *whatsoever you require that others should do to you, that do ye to them.* And that law of all men, *quod tibi fieri non vis, alteri ne feceris.*

To *lay down* a man's *right* to any thing, is to *divest* himself of the *liberty,* of hindering another of the benefit of his own right to the same. For he that renounceth, or passeth away his right, giveth not to any other man a right which he had not before; because there is nothing to which every man had not right by nature: but only standeth out of his way, that he may enjoy his own original right, without hindrance from him; not without hindrance from another. So that the effect which redoundeth to one man, by another man's defect of right, is but so much diminution of impediments to the use of his own right original.

Right is laid aside, either by simply remouncing it; or by transferring it to another. By *simply* RENOUNCING; when he cares not to whom the benefit therof redoundeth. By TRANSFERRING; when he intendeth the benefit thereof to some certain person, or persons. And when a man hath in either manner abandoned, or granted away his right; then is he said to be OBLIGED, OR BOUND, not to hinder those, to whom such right is granted, or abandoned, from the benefit of it: and that he *ought,* and it is his DUTY, not to make void that voluntary act of his own: and that such hindrance is INJUSTICE, and INJURY, as being *sine jure;* the right being before renounced, or transferred. So that *injury,* or *injustice,* in the controversies of the world, is somewhat like to that, which in the disputations of scholars is called *absurdity.* For as it is there called an absurdity, to contradict what one maintained in the beginning: so in the world, it is called injustice, and injury, voluntarily to undo that, which from the beginning he had voluntarily done. The way by which a man either simply renounceth, or transferreth his right, is a declaration, or signification, by some voluntary and sufficient sign, or signs, that he doth so renounce, or transfer; or hath so renounced, or transferred the same, to him that accepteth it. And these signs are either words only, or actions only; or, as it happeneth most often, both words, and actions. And the same are the BONDS, by which men are bound, and obliged: bonds, that have their strength, not from their own nature, for nothing is more easily broken than a man's word, but from fear of some evil consequence upon the rupture.

Whensoever a man transferreth his right, or renounceth it; it is either in consideration of some right reciprocally transferred to himself; or for some other good he hopeth for thereby. For it is a voluntary act: and of the voluntary acts of every man, the object is some *good to himself.* And therefore there be some rights, which no man can be understood by any words, or other signs, to have abandoned, or transferred. As first a man cannot lay down the right of resisting them, that assault him by force, to take away his life; because he cannot be understood to aim thereby, at any good to himself. The same may be said of wounds, and chains, and imprisonment; both because there is no benefit consequent to such patience; as there is to the patience of suffering another to be wounded, or imprisoned: as also because a man cannot tell, when he seeth men proceed against him by violence, whether they intend his death or not. And lastly the motive, and end for which this renouncing, and transferring of right is introduced, is nothing else but the security of a man's person, in his life, and in the means of so preserving life, as not to be weary of it. And therefore if a man by words, or other signs, seem to despoil himself of the end, for which those signs were intended; he is not to be understood as if he meant it, or that it was his will; but that he was ignorant of how such words and actions were to be interpreted.

The mutual transferring of right, is that which men call CONTRACT.

There is difference between transferring of right to the thing: and transferring, or tradition, that is delivery of the thing itself. For the thing may be delivered together with the translation of the right; as in buying and selling with ready-money; or exchange of goods, or lands: and it may be delivered some time after.

Again, one of the contractors, deliver the thing contracted for on his part, and leave the other to perform his part at some determinate time after, and in the mean time be trusted; and then the contract on his part, is called PACT, or COVENANT: or both parts may contract now, to perform hereafter: in which cases, he that is to perform in time to come, being trusted, his performance is called *keeping of promise,* or faith: and the failing of performance, if it be voluntary, *violation of faith. . . .*

As the result of the social contract, we bond together to form a society for the well-being of all, a "commonwealth," in which the rights and powers which we once had alone (and ineffectively) are now concentrated in the hands of "the sovereign," who can use that power very effectively to make us behave for our own good.

CHAPTER XVII—OF THE CAUSES, GENERATION, AND DEFINITION OF A COMMONWEALTH

The final cause, end, or design of men, who naturally love liberty, and dominion over others, in the introduction of that restraint upon themselves, in which we see them live in commonwealths, is the foresight of their own preservation, and of a more contented life thereby; that is to say, of getting themselves out from that miserable condition of war, which is necessarily consequent, as hath been shown in chapter XIII, to the natural passions of men, when there is no visible power to keep them in awe, and tie them by fear of punishment to the performance of their covenants, and observation of those laws of nature set down in the fourteenth and fifteenth chapters.

For the laws of nature, as *justice, equity, modesty, mercy,* and, in sum, *doing to others, as we would be done to,* of themselves, without the terror of some power, to cause them to be observed, are contrary to our natural passions, that carry us to partiality, pride, revenge, and the like. And covenants, without the sword, are but words, and of no strength to secure a man at all. Therefore notwithstanding the laws of nature, which every one hath then kept, when he has the will to keep them, when he can do it safely, if there be no power erected, or not great enough for our security; every man will, and may lawfully rely on his own strength and art, for caution against all other men. And in all places, where men have lived by small families, to rob and spoil one another, has been a trade, and so far from being reputed against the law of nature, that the greater spoils they gained, the greater was their honour; and men observed no other laws therein, but the laws of honour; that is, to abstain from cruelty, leaving to men their lives, and instruments of husbandry. And as small families did then; so now do cities and kingdoms which are but greater families, for their own security, enlarge their dominions, upon all pretences of danger, and fear of invasion, or assistance that may be given to invaders, and endeavour as much as they can, to subdue, or weaken their neighbours, by open force, and secret arts, for want of other caution, justly; and are remembered for it in after ages with honour. . . .

The only way to erect such a common power, as may be able to defend them from the invasion of foreigners, and the injuries of one another, and thereby to secure them in such sort, as that by their own industry, and by the fruits of the earth, they may nourish themselves and live contentedly; is, to confer all their power and strength upon one man, or upon one assembly of men, that may reduce all their wills, by plurality of voices, unto one will: which is as much as to say, to appoint one man, or assembly of men, to bear their person; and every one to own, and acknowledge himself to be author of whatsoever he that so beareth their person, shall act, or cause to be acted, in those things which concern the common peace and safety; and therein to submit their wills, every one to his will, and their judgments, to his judgment. This is more than consent, or concord; it is a real unity of them all, in one and the same person, made by covenant of every man with every man, in such manner, as if every man should say to every man, *I authorize and give up my right of governing myself, to this man, or to this assembly of men, on this condition, that thou give up thy right to him, and authorize all his actions in like manner.* This done, the multitude so united in one person, is called a COMMONWEALTH, in Latin CIVITAS. This is the generation of that great LEVIATHAN, or rather, to speak more reverently, of that *mortal god,* to which we owe under the *immortal God,* our peace and defence. For by this authority, given him by every particular man in the commonwealth, he hath the use of so much power and strength conferred on him, that by terror thereof, he is enabled to perform the wills of them all, to peace at home, and mutual aid against their enemies abroad. And in him consisteth the essence of the commonwealth; which, to define it, is *one person, of whose acts a great multitude, by mutual covenants one with another, have made themselves every one the author, to the end he may use the strength and means of them all, as he shall think expedient, for their peace and common defence.*

And he that carrieth this person, is called SOVEREIGN, and said to have *sovereign power;* and every one besides, his SUBJECT.

The attaining to this sovereign power, is by two ways. One, by natural force; as when a man maketh his children, to submit themselves, and their children to his government, as being able to destroy them if they refuse; or by war subdueth his enemies to his will, giving them their lives on that condition. The other, is when men agree amongst themselves, to submit to some man, or assembly of men, voluntarily, on confidence to be protected by him against all others. This latter, may be called a political commonwealth, or commonwealth by *institution;* and the former, a commonwealth by *acquisition. . . .*

The problem with any theory in which fear and force are primary motives is the role of *freedom* (or liberty). In a commonwealth (a society), what is a person free to do, or not to do? Does a person thereby give up a substantial amount of freedom or could it be argued that we are much freer within the restrictions of society than outside of it in our "natural condition"?

CHAPTER XXI—OF THE LIBERTY OF SUBJECTS

LIBERTY, or FREEDOM, signifieth, properly, the absence of opposition; by opposition, I mean external impediments of motion; and may be applied no less to irrational, and inanimate creatures, than to rational. For whatsoever is so tied, or environed, as it cannot move but within a certain space, which space is determined by the opposition of some external body, we say it hath not liberty to go further. And so of all living creatures, whilst they are imprisoned, or restrained, with walls, or chains; and of the water whilst it is kept in by banks, or vessels, that otherwise would spread itself into a larger space, we use to say, they are not at liberty, to move in such manner, as without those external impediments they would. But when the impediment of motion, is in the constitution of the thing itself, we use not to say; it wants the liberty; but the power to move; as when a stone lieth still, or a man is fastened to his bed by sickness.

And according to this proper, and generally received meaning of the word, a FREEMAN, *is he, that in those things, which by his strength and wit he is able to do, is not hindered to do what he has a will to.* But when the words *free,* and *liberty,* are applied to any thing but *bodies,* they are abused; for that which is not subject to motion, is not subject to impediment: and therefore, when it is said, for example, the way is free, no liberty of the way is signified, but of those that walk in it without stop. And when we say a gift is free, there is not meant any liberty of the gift, but of the giver, that was not bound by any law or covenant to give it. So when we *speak freely,* it is not the liberty of voice, or pronunciation, but of the man, whom no law hath obliged to speak otherwise than he did. Lastly, from the use of the word *free-will,* no liberty can be inferred of the will, desire, or inclination, but the liberty of the man; which consisteth in this, that he finds no stop, in doing what he has the will, desire, or inclination to do.

Fear and liberty are consistent; as when a man throweth his goods into the sea for *fear* the ship should sink, he doth it nevertheless very willingly, and may refuse to do it if he will: it is therefore the action of one that was *free:* so a man sometimes pays his debt, only for *fear* of imprisonment, which because nobody hindered him from detaining, was the action of a man at *liberty.* And generally all actions which men do in commonwealths, for *fear* of the law, are actions, which the doers had *liberty* to omit.

Liberty, and *necessity* are consistent: as in the water, that hath not only *liberty,* but *a necessity* of descending by the channel; so likewise in the actions which men voluntarily do: which, because they proceed from their will, proceed from *liberty;* and yet, because every act of man's will, and every desire, and inclination proceedeth from some cause, and that from another cause, in a continual chain, whose first link is in the hand of God the first of all causes, proceed from *necessity.* So that to him that could see the connexion of those causes, the *necessity* of all men's voluntary actions, would appear manifest. And therefore God, that seeth, and disposeth all things, seeth also that the *liberty* of man in doing what he will, is accompanied with the *necessity* of doing that which God will, and no more, nor less. For though men may do many things, which God does not command, nor is therefore author of them; yet they can have no passion, nor appetite to anything, of which appetite God's *liberty,* which only is properly called *liberty.*

But as men, for the attaining of peace, and conservation of themselves thereby, have made an artificial man, which we call a commonwealth; so also have they made artificial chains, called *civil laws,* which they themselves, by mutual convenants, have fastened at one end, to the lips of that man, or assembly, to whom they have given the sovereign power; and at the other end to their own ears. These bonds, in their own nature but weak, may nevertheless he made to hold, by the danger, though not by the difficulty of breaking them.

In relation to these bonds only it is, that I am to speak now, of the *liberty* of *subjects.* For seeing there is no commonwealth in the world, wherein there be rules enough set down, for the regulating of all the actions, and words of men; as being a thing impossible: to followeth necessarily, that in all kinds of actions by the laws praetermitted, men have the liberty, of doing what their own reasons shall suggest, for the most profitable to themselves. For if we take liberty in the proper sense, for corporal liberty; that is to say, freedom from chains and prison; it were very absurd for men to clamour as they do, for the liberty they so manifestly enjoy. Again, if we take liberty, for an exemption from laws, it is no less absurd, for men to demand as they do, that liberty, by which all other men may be masters of their lives. And yet, as absurd as it is, this is it they demand; not knowing that the laws are of no power to protect them, without a sword in the hands of a man, or men, to cause those laws to be put in execution. The liberty of a subject, lieth therefore only in those things, which in regulating their actions, the sovereign hath praetermitted: such as is the liberty to buy, and sell, and otherwise contract with one another; to choose their own abode, their own diet, their own trade of life, and institute their children as they themselves think fit; and the like.

Nevertheless we are not to understand, that by such liberty, the sovereign power of life and death, is either abolished, or limited. For it has been already shown, that nothing the sovereign representative can do to a subject, on what pretence soever, can properly be called injustice, or injury; because every subject is author of every act the sovereign doth; so that he never wanteth right to anything, otherwise, than as he himself is the subject of God, and bound thereby to observe the laws of nature. And therefore it may, and doth often happen in commonwealths, that a subject may be put to death, by the command of the sovereign power; and yet neither do the other wrong: as when Jephtha caused his daughter to be sacrificed: in which, and the like cases, he that so dieth, had liberty to do the action, for which he is nevertheless, without injury put to death. And the same holdeth also in a sovereign prince, that putteth to death an innocent subject. For though the action be against the law of nature, as being contrary to equity, as was the killing of Uriah, because the right to do what he pleased was given him by Uriah himself: and yet to God, because David was God's subject, and prohibited all iniquity by the law of nature: which distinction, David himself, when he repented the fact, evidently confirmed, saying, *To thee only have I sinned.* In the same manner, the people of Athens, when they banished the most potent of their commonwealth for ten years, thought they committed no injustice; and yet they never questioned what crime he had done; but what hurt he would do: nay they commanded the banishment of they knew not whom; and every citizen bringing his oystershell into the market place, written with the name of him he desired should be banished, without actually accusing him, sometimes banished an Aristides, for his reputation of justice; and sometimes a scurrilous jester, as Hyperbolus, to make a jest of it. And yet a man cannot say, the sovereign people of Athens wanted right to banish them; or an Athenian the liberty to jest, or to be just.

The liberty, whereof there is so frequent and honourable mention, in the histories, and philosophy of the ancient Greeks, and Romans, and in the writings, and discourse of those that from them have received all their learning in the politics, is not the liberty of particular men; but the liberty of the commonwealth: which is the same with that which every man then should have, if there were no civil laws, nor commonwealth at all. And the effects of its also be the same. For as amongst masterless men, there is perpetual war, of every man against his neighbour; no inheritance, to transmit to the son, nor to expect from the father; no propriety of goods, or lands; no security; but a full and absolute liberty in every particular man: so in states, and commonwealths not dependent on one another, every commonwealth, not every man, has an absolute liberty, to do what it shall judge, that is to say, what that man, or assembly that representeth it, shall judge most conducing to their benefit. But withal, they live in the condition of a perpetual war, and upon the confines of battle, with their frontiers armed, and cannons planted against their neighbours round about. The Athenians, and Romans were free; that is, free commonwealths: not that any particular men had the liberty to resist their own representative; but that their representative had the liberty to resist, or invade other people. There is written on the turrets of the city of Lucca in great characters at this day, the word LIBERTAS; yet no man can thence infer, that a particular man has more liberty, or immunity from the service of the commonwealth there, than in Constantinople. Whether a commonwealth be monarchical, or popular, of commonwealths, from Aristotle, Cicero, and other men, Greeks and Romans, that living under popular states, derived those rights, not from the principles of nature, but transcribed them into their books, out of the practice of their own commonwealths, which were popular; as the grammarians describe the rules of language, out of the practice of the time; or the rules of poetry, out of the poems of Homer and Virgil. And because the Athenians were taught, to keep them from desire of changing their government, that they were freemen, and all that lived under monarchy were slaves; therefore Aristotle puts it down in his *Politics*, *(lib. 6. cap. ii). In democracy,* LIBERTY *is to be supposed: for it is commonly held, that no man is* FREE *in any other government.* And as Aristotle; so Cicero, and other writers have grounded their civil doctrine, on the opinions of the Romans, who were taught to hate monarchy, at first, by them that having deposed their sovereign, shared amongst them these Greek, and Latin authors, men from their childhood have gotten a habit, under a false show of liberty, of favouring tumults, and of licentious controlling the actions of their sovereigns, and again of controlling those controllers; with the effusion of so much blood, as I think I may truly say, there was never any thing so dearly bought, as these western parts have bought the learning of the Greek and Latin tongues.

To come now to the particulars of the true liberty of a subject; that is to say, what are the things, which though commanded by the sovereign, he may nevertheless, without injustice, refuse to do; we are to consider, what rights we pass away, when we make a commonwealth; or, which is all one, what liberty we deny ourselves, by owning all the actions, without exception, of the man, or assembly we make our sovereign. For in the act of our *submission,* consisteth both our *obligation,* and our *liberty;* which must therefore be inferred by arguments taken from thence; there being no obligation on any man, which ariseth not from some act of his own; for all men equally, are by nature free. And because such arguments, must either be drawn from the express words, *I authorize all his actions,* or from the intention of him that submitteth himself to his power, which intention is to be understood by the end for which he so submitteth; the obligation, and liberty of the subject, is to be derived, either from those words, or others equivalent; or else from the end of the institution of sovereignty, namely, the peace of the subjects within themselves, and their defence against a common enemy.

First therefore, seeing sovereignty by institution, is by covenant of every one to everyone; and sovereignty by acquisition, by covenants of the vanquished to the victor, or child to the parent; it is manifest, that every subject has liberty in all those things, the right whereof cannot by covenant be transferred. I have shown before in the 14th chapter, that covenants, not to defend a man's own body, are void. Therefore,

If the sovereign command a man, though justly condemned, to kill, wound, or maim himself; or not to resist those that assault him; or to abstain from the use of food, air, medicine, or any other thing, without which he cannot live; yet hath that man the liberty to disobey.

If a man be interrogated by the sovereign, or his authority, concerning a crime done by himself, he is not bound, without assurance of pardon, to confess it; because no man, as I have shown in the same chapter, can be obliged by covenant to accuse himself.

Again, the consent of a subject to sovereign power, is contained in these words, *I authorize, or take upon me, all his actions;* in which there is no restriction at all, of his own former natural liberty: for by allowing him to *kill me,* I am not bound to kill myself when he commands me. It is one thing to say, *kill me, or my fellow, if you please;* another thing to say, *I will kill myself, or my fellow.* It followeth therefore, that

No man is bound by the words themselves, either to kill himself, or any other man; and consequently, that the obligation a man may sometimes have, upon the command of the severign to execute any dangerous, or dishonourable office, dependeth not on the words of our submission; but on the intention, which is to be understood by the end thereof. When therefore our refusal to obey, frustrates the end for which the sovereignty was ordained; then there is no liberty to refuse: otherwise there is.

Upon this ground, a man that is commanded as a soldier to fight against the enemy, though his sovereign have right enough to punish his refusal with death, may nevertheless in many cases refuse, without injustice; as when he substituteth a sufficient soldier in his place: for in this case he deserteth not the service of the commonwealth. And there is allowance to be made for natural timorousness; not only to women, of whom no such dangerous duty is expected, but also to men of feminine courage. When armies fight, there is on one side, or both, a running away; yet when they do it not out of treachery, but fear, they are not esteemed to do it unjustly, but dishonourably. For the same reason, to avoid battle, is not injustice, but cowardice. But he that inrolleth himself a soldier, or taketh imprest money, taketh away the excuse of a timorous nature; and is obliged, not only to go to the battle, but also not to run from it, without his captain's leave. And when the defence of the commonwealth, requireth at once the help of all that are able to bear arms, every one is obliged; because otherwise the institution of the commonwealth, which they have not the purpose, or courage to preserve, was in vain.

To resist the sword of the commonwealth, in defence of another man, guilty, or innocent, no man hath liberty; because such liberty, takes away from the sovereign, the means of protecting us; and is therefore destructive of the very essence of government. But in case a great many men together, have already resisted the sovereign power unjustly, or committed some capital crime, for which every one of them expecteth death, whether have they not the liberty then to join together, and assist, and defend one another? Certainly they have: for they but defend their lives, which the guilty man may as well do, as the innocent. There was indeed injustice in the first breach of their duty; their bearing of arms subsequent to it, though it be to maintain what they have done, is no new unjust act. And if it be only to defend their persons, it is not unjust at all. But the offer of pardon taketh from them, to whom it is offered, the plea of self-defence, and maketh their perseverance in assisting, or defending the rest, unlawful.

As for other liberties, they depend on the silence of the law. In cases where the sovereign has prescribed no rule, there the subject hath the liberty to do, or forbear, according to his own discretion. And therefore such liberty is in some places more, and in some less; and in some times more, in other times less, according as they that have the sovereignty shall think most convenient. As for example, there was a time, when in England a man might enter into his own land, and dispossess such as wrongfully possessed it, by force. But in aftertimes, that liberty of forcible entry, was taken away by a statute made, by the king, in parliament. And in some places of the world, men have the liberty of many wives: in other places, such liberty is not allowed.

If a subject have a controversy with his sovereign, of debt, or of right of possession of lands or goods, or concerning any service required at his hands, or concerning any penalty, corporal, or pecuniary, grounded on a precedent law; he hath the same liberty to sue for his right, as if it were against a subject; and before such judges, as are appointed by the sovereign. For seeing the sovereign demandeth by force of a former law, and not by virtue of his power; he declareth thereby, that he requireth no more, than shall appear to be due by that law. The suit therefore is not contrary to the will of the sovereign: and consequently the subject hath the liberty to demand the hearing of his cause; and sentence, according to that law. But if he demand, or take anything by pretence of his power; there lieth, in that case, no action of law; for all that is done by him in virtue of his power, is done by the authority of every subject, and consequently he that brings an action against the sovereign, brings it against himself.

If a monarch, or sovereign assembly, grant a liberty to all, or any of his subjects, which grant standing, he is disabled to provide for their safety, the grant is void; unless he directly renounce, or transfer the sovereignty to another. For in that he might openly, if it had been his will, and in plain terms, have renounced, or transferred it, and did not: it is to be understood it was not his will, but that the grant proceeded from ignorance of the repugnancy between such a liberty and the sovereign power; and therefore the sovereignty is still retained; and consequently all those powers, which are necessary to the exercising thereof; such as are the power of war, and peace, of judicature, of appointing officers, and councillors, of levying money, and the rest named in the 18th chapter.

The obligation of subjects to the sovereign, is understood to last as long, and no longer, than the power lasteth, by which he is able to protect them. For the right men have by nature to protect themselves, when none else can protect them, can by no covenant be relinquished. The sovereignty is the soul of the commonwealth; which once departed from the body, the members do no more receive their motion from it. The end of obedience is protection; which, wheresoever a man seeth it, either in his own, or in another's sword, nature applieth his obedience to it, and his endeavour to maintain it. And though sovereignty, in the intention of them that make it, be immortal; yet is it in its own nature not only subject to violent death, by foreign war; but also through the ignorance and passions of men, it hath in it, from the very institution, many seeds of a natural mortality, by intestine discord.

If a subject be taken prisoner in war; or his person, or his means of life be within the guards of the enemy, and hath his life and corporal liberty given him, on condition to be subject to the victor, he hath liberty to accept the condition; and having accepted it, is the subject of him that took him; because he had no other way to preserve himself. The case is the same, if he be detained on the same terms, in a foreign country. But if a man be held in prison, or bonds, or is not trusted with the liberty of his body; he cannot be understood to be bound by covenant to subjection; and therefore may, if he can, make his escape by any means whatsoever.

If a monarch shall relinquish the sovereignty, both for himself, and his heirs, his subjects return to the absolute liberty of nature; because, though nature may declare who are his sons, and who are the nearest of his kin; yet it dependeth on his own will, as hath been said in the precedent chapter, who shall be his heir. If therefore he will have no heir, there is no sovereignty, nor subjection. The case is the same, if he die without known kindred, and without declaration of his heir. For then there can no heir be known, and consequently no subjection be due.

If the sovereign banish his subject; during the banishment, he is not subject. But he that is sent on a message, or hath leave to travel, is still subject; but it is, by contract between sovereigns, not by virtue of the covenant of subjection. For whosoever entereth into another's dominion, is subject to all the laws thereof, unless he have a privilege by the amity of the sovereigns, or by special licence.

If a monarch subdued by war, render himself subject to the victor; his subjects are delivered from their former obligation, and become obliged to the victor. But if he be held prisoner, or have not the liberty of his own body; he is not understood to have given away the right of sovereignty; and therefore his subjects are obliged to yield obedience to the magistrates formerly placed, governing not in their own name, but in his. For, his right remaining, the question in only of the administration; that is to say, of the magistrates and officers; which, if he have not means to name, he is supposed to approve those, which he himself had formerly appointed.

DISCUSSION

In these excerpts from *Leviathan,* Hobbes presents us with (at least) two theses that are radically at odds with the accounts of virtue we found in Plato and Aristotle (and, of course, in Augustine). First, Hobbes gives us a psychological account of human nature in which self-interest—even selfishness—is the sole motive for every action. In Plato and Aristotle's account of virtuous action, on the other hand, it is quite clear that—whether or not virtuous action is also in one's self-interest—it is action which is motivated just by the fact that it is virtuous and certainly not—as in Hobbes—out of fear or defensiveness. (The Greek virtue of courage, for instance, becomes unintelligible on Hobbes's account.) Second, Hobbes gives us an account of the formation of society and social bonds out of a "state of nature" in which each of us is a miserable, independent but defensive animal, coming together for mutual protection and peace. In Plato and Aristotle, it is assumed from the outset that our natural condition *is* to be social and in society. (Aristotle famously defines man as "the social animal".) Societies are not created by individuals; individuals are born into and, in an important sense, created by society.

These two differences mark a series of debates which have characterized ethics since ancient times. We can find a straightforward version of Hobbes's egoism, for example, in Plato's *Republic,* in his telling of "the ring of Gyges"—about a ring which allows a person to be invisible and thus immune from capture and punishment for whatever crimes and selfish actions. Glaucon's argument, when he presents this story, is that people are just only because they are afraid of being caught and punished. They are wary of the sanctions of society, but they do not act justly for the sake of being virtuous. Plato (Socrates) rejects this account, though not on psychological grounds, because it fails to account for the importance of justice in society in general. The more psychological answer would be that we do not, in fact, act out of selfish motives alone and that we do act out of consideration for other people's welfare, for the good of society, and for the sake of impersonal principles. Plato and Aristotle would have taken this for granted, but in modern ethics, beginning with Hobbes, the very possibility of altruism has become a major issue. Do we ever act unselfishly, however seemingly noble our motives?

This issue is *psychological egoism.* (It has sometimes been suggested that Hobbes is also an *ethical egoist*—arguing that we ought to act in our own selfish interests. He says, for example, "It is natural, *and so reasonable,* for each individual to aim solely at his own preservation or pleasure" [emphasis added].) It is true, of course, that people in society often act for the benefit of others; indeed, Hobbes even allows that they ought to do so because of the rules to which they have (tacitly) agreed because of the social contract. But such behavior is nevertheless motivated by selfish motives, by the desire to protect oneself and maximize security and power in society. Thus the egoist need not argue that every act in itself must be carried out for purely selfish motives; it is enough that one's overall behavior in society is motivated by the desire for personal peace and well-being.

Egoism has been attacked vigorously ever since it became popular. One of the classic attacks on the egoist position was launched soon after Hobbes's death by Bishop Joseph Butler in England. In *Fifteen Sermons* (1726), he rejected Hobbes's psychological egoism on several grounds; he began by accepting the distinction between (1) "private good and a person's own preservation and happiness" and (2) "respect to society and the promotion of public good and happiness of society." But these are not always in conflict, as the egoist too easily presumes; harking back to Plato and Aristotle, Butler argues that, to the contrary, they are almost always in harmony.

Butler's arguments might be condensed to three main points, all of which are still being debated today (for example, in Thomas Nagel's recent book, *The Possibility of Altruism*). First, he says, the disposition to compassion and benevolence is just as natural in us as our motives of self-interest. Moreover, so much of our self-interest depends upon the good will and approval (if not also affection) of other people that the two motives—egoism and altruism—are almost always in agreement. Second, most of our interests in personal gain also (whether we intend them to or not) benefit the rest of society. (This is a position that economist Adam Smith would also argue, fifty years later, in his suggestion that capitalism works, because, even though every person pursues only his or her financial interest, there is nonetheless "an invisible hand" which coordinates these interests for the good of all and "the wealth of the nation.") Third, Butler argues, the egoist neglects the important influence of what he calls "conscience" (many psychologists today would call it "the superego") in correcting our behavior and leading us to do the right thing. Butler agrees that there are occasional villains in the world who do in fact seem to be actual egoists, but they should not be taken as examples, rather as exceptions. Most of us are not egoists, though not perfect altruists either. Acting on our desires does not make us selfish, since, as Plato and Aristotle simply assumed, most of those desires are cultivated by and for the good of society as a whole. Virtue is as natural to us as prudence, and the desire to be good as important (if not as traumatic) as the fear of death.

Hobbes's theory of the formation of society (the "Leviathan") goes far beyond the scope of ethics, but the basic concern is clearly central to every ethical theory. Whether or not one agrees with Hobbes's egoism (and by no means are all social contract theorists egoists), the idea that society is formed by already preexisting individuals (whether this is taken as literal history or only as a theoretical fiction) is one of those fundamental frameworks within which all the rest of ethics gets formed. If one accepts any such theory, it becomes inevitable that the individual and his or her desires and needs will be the primary consideration in ethics. (Our Declaration of Independence is again an example: "We hold these truths to be self-evident, that all men are created equal and endowed by their creator with certain inalienable rights. . . .") On the other hand, if one conceives of society itself as primary—as Plato and Aristotle do—then the significance of the individual is determined by society, and the good of society—not the desires and needs of the individual—becomes primary. This is emphatically not to say that, on the latter view, the desires and needs of the individual do not count; indeed, proponents of the socially oriented theory would answer that this conception of ethics provides a much better way of fulfilling people's real desires and needs. Nor is it the case that the individualist conception necessarily cares more for the individual; Hobbes, because of his deeply pessimistic view of human nature, gives much less credit to sympathy and compassion than Aristotle, who sees virtue and nobleness as natural human traits.

STUDY QUESTIONS

1 What is "the state of nature"? Is it important for Hobbes's argument that there ever actually existed such a presocietal state? What theory of human nature underlies

Hobbes's view that the state of nature is a "war of all against all"? Do you accept this? Why or why not?

2 What is the basis of the state, according to Hobbes? What alternative conceptions of the foundation of society can you think of? Does society need a "foundation," in this sense?

3 What is the "leviathan"? Why does Hobbes use this image?

4 What is the "social contract"? Who signed it? Give examples of real historical social contracts and explain what they do.

5 Why is there no justice in the state of nature? What does this say about the nature of justice? Would it make a difference if God looked over (and created) the state of nature?

6 Why does Hobbes begin a treatise on ethics and politics with a discussion of the passions? Why not just start out discussing what is good and what is bad?

7 What is pleasure, according to Hobbes? Is pleasure necessarily good?

8 In what sense are we all equal, according to Hobbes? Why is this essential to his theory of society, human nature, and the social contract?

9 Are we all basically selfish? Are our actions basically founded on fear and insecurity? Does Hobbes mean that literally *every* act is selfish?

10 What is a "right"? How does one have a right? Under what circumstances can a right be taken away? Can a person *give* a right away? When and how?

11 What is a "commonwealth". How is it formed? Is every state a commonwealth?

12 What does Hobbes mean by "liberty" ("freedom")? Would a person be freer if there were no laws and no state restricting his or her actions?

Chapter 5

DAVID HUME

David Hume commands an impressive but curious position in the world of philosophy. On the one hand, he has often been admired—for example, by the great twentieth-century philosopher Bertrand Russell—as the outstanding genius of British philosophy; on the other hand, he has just as often been denounced as the ultimate skeptic who reduced all philosophical inquiry to nonsense and thus confirmed the tragic divorce between philosophy and our practical, everyday beliefs and affairs. Historically, Hume was a prominent spokesman for the Enlightenment, that largely eighteenth-century intellectual movement which celebrated reason and critical thinking. But in his conclusions, Hume seriously challenged the abilities of reason and critical thinking to provide us with justifications of even the most basic beliefs and so undermined precisely that movement in which he was widely known as the ultimate spokesman and befriended as "le bon David." But by rejecting reason, Hume proposed a shift in ethics (and philosophy in general) from abstract thinking to concrete experience. Ethics, in other words, was to become something of a *science* (which was very much in accord with Enlightenment thinking).

The key to Hume's philosophical method is *empiricism*—the appeal to the facts of experience to justify all knowledge; his primary conclusion, however, is *skepticism*—the denial that ultimate justification is possible. We cannot prove that we know anything about the world; we cannot even prove that there is in fact an external world beyond our senses. But whatever the limitations of philosophical reason, "nature," Hume assures us, gives us the good sense to live in the world and believe what we must believe— whether or not the philosophers can prove it true. He finishes his great book—his *Treatise of Human Nature*—exclaiming,

> Most fortunately it happens, that since reason is incapable of dispelling these clouds
> nature herself suffices to that purpose, and cures me of this philosophical mel⌐
> and delirium, either by relaxing this bent of mind, or by some avocatio⌐

impression of my senses, which obliterate all these chimeras. I dine, I play a game of backgammon, I converse, and am merry with my friends; and when after three or four hours' amusement, I would return to these speculations they appear so cold, and strained, and ridiculous, that I cannot find in my heart to enter into them any farther.

Nevertheless, Hume's arguments for skepticism were so powerful that Bertand Russell wrote of him, in 1945, that

Hume's skeptical conclusions . . . are equally difficult to refute and to accept. The result was a challenge to philosophers, which, in my opinion, has still not been adequately met.

In the realm of morality, Hume's skepticism takes a similar form; we cannot know that the moral principles which govern our actions are right; indeed, Hume suggests (like his perverse contemporary in France, the Marquis de Sade)[1], that what is morally right in one society could be equally wrong in another. The ends of human action

can never, in any case, be accounted for by *reason,* but recommend themselves entirely to the sentiments and affections of mankind, without any dependence on the intellectual faculties.

Accordingly, Hume even goes so far as to argue that, "Tis not contrary to reason to prefer the destruction of the whole world to the scratching of my finger" (*Treatise,* p. 416).

Moral skepticism is the view that we cannot know what is right, that there is no rational justification of our ethical opinions. But as in his skeptical views about knowledge, Hume offers us an escape from this troubling conclusion; "nature," once again, provides us with the good sense to live well and act rightly, even if the Good and the Right are beyond the reach of reason. Our "sentiments and affections" guide our actions, not the deliberations of reason. Indeed, in his most famous phrase, Hume tell us that "reason is, and ought to be the slave of the passions." He may be a moral skeptic, but morals still have a basis, not in reason, perhaps, but in our emotions and our desires.

It would not be either wrong or insulting to call Hume a pagan in his moral philosophy. He was a vehement atheist and wrote polemical treatises against Christianity (especially his *Dialogues on Natural Religion,* which were published only after his death). He was a great admirer of the ancient Greeks and was steeped in the study of classical literature. Most importantly, his ethics was far more concerned with the nature of a person's character than with the abstract rules which make up morality. Hume far more resembles Aristotle in his moral philosophy than he does many modern-day moralists, especially the greatest of them, his German successor, Immanuel Kant (who was reacting in part *against* Hume's moral views). It is good character and the virtues that provide us with the elements of ethics, not abstract and absolute principles. It is not morality but morals that are crucial to Hume, the concern for "personal merit" and agreeable "qualities"—such as a good sense of humor and trustworthiness. Hume, like Aristotle, begins with a view of people as social and sociable beings. Unlike Hobbes, he does not see human nature in terms of selfishness and the need for laws to keep us from murdering one another. Our basic instincts are rather those of sympathy and fellow-feeling, and morals are

---

[1]"I ask you now, if, after these reflections, I can still retain any feeling of guilt for having committed, either for the sake of pleasure or self-interest, a crime in France which is nothing but a virtue in China? Or if I ought to make myself very miserable or be prodigiously troubled about practicing actions in France which would have me burned in Siam?" (*Justine,* p. 696).

essentially those useful and agreeable characteristics that make it not only possible but necessary and even delightful for us to live together.

How does Hume's moral skepticism tie into his pagan ethics? First, it must be pointed out that skepticism for Hume is a limited doctrine; it denies the possibility of a rational justification of morals, but it does not reject their importance or necessity. Indeed, Hume was very much a conservative in both his politics and ethics, emphasizing the importance of tradition and continuity. Furthermore, it should be emphasized that Hume is much more skeptical in his early *Treatise of Human Nature* (1739) than he is in his later *Inquiry* (presented here). The emphasis in the *Treatise* is on the distinctions between reason and sentiment and between judgments of value and judgments of fact, with the conclusion that morals are matters of sentiment and value and cannot be rationally justified. The emphasis in the *Inquiry,* however, is on the positive substance of ethics, an investigation into those sentiments and qualities which make up morals, including especially our sense of benevolence and justice and those qualities of character which are most agreeable to ourselves and others. The early skepticism purges moral philosophy of what Hume considered an excessive emphasis on rationality; the later ethical inquiry replaces the proper emphasis on moral character and our more sociable feelings about one another. The two works are not opposed but complement one another; Hume's skepticism and his paganism are of a single piece—however unthinkable the former·might have been to Aristotle.

We began by saying that Hume was, in his method, an *empiricist,* appealing all knowledge to experience. His empiricism helps give substance to his skepticism, for experience deals in facts, whereas ethics is concerned with values, which Hume sharply distinguishes from facts. Nevertheless, Hume's empiricism also provides him with the "experimental" method that is evident throughout the *Inquiry*—as it was so evident in Aristotle's *Ethics*—a descriptive method which relies heavily on what ordinary people in fact do feel rather than a rational discourse on what they ought to feel. It is the fact that we are benevolent creatures, concerned with others as well as for ourselves, that provides the starting point of Hume's ethics. Nevertheless, this undeniable fact does not constitute a justification of morals. It only means that this is the way we do act and do think, not that we ought to do so. In another of Hume's famous phrases, there is no deriving an "ought" from an "is."

The body of Hume's *Inquiry* is a detailed exploration of the variety and complexity of human behavior, with the intent to "deduce general maxims from a comparison of particular instances." These general maxims (which are not the same as moral principles) essentially include the concept of a virtue, which is "a quality of the mind agreeable to or approved of by everyone who considers or contemplates it." This emphasis on what is "agreeable" and "approved of" in turn forms the basic quest of Hume's ethics, which is to discover "those universal principles from which all censure and approbation is ultimately derived." These principles can be summarized in two words, "happiness" and "utility." Like Aristotle, Hume insists that happiness is the end of all human activity. And like John Stuart Mill and the utilitarians who succeed Hume in English philosophy, he takes the usefulness of certain qualities to be their sole basis in ethics. Justice, for instance, is often defended in part by appeal to public utility, but Hume goes much further and insists that utility is "the sole foundation of its [justice's] merit."

Hume's "experimental" method was derived most immediately from his empiricist predecessor John Locke, but his real intellectual hero was the great British scientist, Sir Isaac Newton. In the *Treatise,* Hume tried self-consciously to derive a theory of human nature on a par with Newton's grand theory of nature. The aim of the *Inquiry* is more modest, but it is still directed at the reduction of the variety of human behavior to a single principle. Agreeableness and approval are the basis of ethical judgments, but they are not yet its ultimate principle. Happiness and utility are primary considerations, but they too are not yet ultimate. What is the ultimate principle for Hume? It is the simple fact of "social sympathy in human nature" (Section V, part ii). There is no need and no point to "push our researches" beyond this, for there is no rational justification or divine design behind this simple fact. We are social and sociable creatures "by nature," and that is the end (and the beginning) of our ethical inquiries.

DAVID HUME

Hume was born in 1711, in Scotland, where he spent most of his life. But he also traveled extensively as a popular spokesman for the Enlightenment, and he was as well known in Paris and London as he was in his home city of Edinburgh. He confessed that the ruling passion of his life was the desire for "literary fame," but his first book, the *Treatise,* "fell stillborn from the press," as he put it, and his later philosophical works did not fare much better. Because of his atheism, Hume was never able to secure a university position, and his published works earned him the title of "the great infidel." His literary fame in his lifetime was based on his ambitious *History of England* rather than on his philosophical writings, and it was only later that he received his recognition as one of the greatest minds in the history of philosophy. Hume died in 1776, the year of a colonial revolution of which, as a conservative, he could not wholly approve.

A. Reason, Feelings, and Morals: An Excerpt from *Treatise of Human Nature*

In the following selection from Hume's *Treatise* of 1739, he draws his sharp distinctions between reason and sentiment and judgments of value and of fact; he concludes that morals cannot be based upon reason and the there is no deriving "an 'ought' from an 'is.' "

OF VIRTUE AND VICE IN GENERAL

Section I. Moral Distinctions Not Derived From Reason

It has been observed that nothing is ever present to the mind but its perceptions; and that all the actions of seeing, hearing, judging, loving, hating, and thinking, fall under this denomination. The mind can never exert itself in any action which we may not comprehend under the term of *perception;* and consequently that term is no less applicable to those judgments by which we distinguish moral good and evil, than to every other operation of the mind. To approve of one character, to condemn another, are only so many different perceptions.

David Hume, *Treatise of Human Nature* (London, 1739).

Now, as perceptions resolve themselves into two kinds, viz., *impressions* and *ideas,* this distinction gives rise to a question, with which we shall open up our present inquiry concerning morals, whether it is by means of our *ideas* or *impressions* we distinguish betwixt vice and virtue, and pronounce an action blamable or praiseworthy? This will immediately cut off all loose discourses and declamations, and reduce us to something precise and exact on the present subject.

Those who affirm that virtue is nothing but a conformity to reason; that there are eternal fitnesses and unfitnesses of things which are the same to every rational being that considers them; that the immutable measure of right and wrong imposes an obligation, not only on human creatures, but also on the Deity himself: all these systems concur in the opinion that morality, like truth, is discerned merely by ideas, and by their juxtaposition and comparison. In order, therefore, to judge of these systems, we need only consider whether it be possible from reason alone to distinguish betwixt moral good and evil, or whether there must concur some other principles to enable us to make that distinction.

If morality had naturally no influence on human passions and actions, it were in vain to take such pains to inculcate it; and nothing would be more fruitless than that multitude of rules and precepts with which all moralists abound. Philosophy is commonly divided into *speculative* and *practical;* and as morality is always comprehended under the latter division, it is supposed to influence our passions and actions, and to go beyond the calm and indolent judgments of the understanding. And this is confirmed by common experience, which informs us that men are often governed by their duties, and are deterred from some actions by the opinion of injustice, and impelled to others by that of obligation.

Since morals, therefore, have an influence on the actions and affections, it follows that they cannot be derived from reason. . . . Morals excite passions, and produce or prevent actions. Reason of itself is utterly impotent in this particular. The rules of morality, therefore, are not conclusions of our reason.

No one, I believe, will deny the justness of this inference; nor is there any other means of evading it than by denying that principle on which it is founded. As long as it is allowed that reason has no influence on our passions and actions, it is in vain to pretend that morality is discovered only by a deduction of reason. An active principle can never be founded on an inactive; and if reason be inactive in itself, it must remain so in all its shapes and appearances, whether it exerts itself in natural or moral subjects, whether it considers the powers of external bodies or the actions of rational beings. . . .

Reason is the discovery of truth or falsehood. Truth or falsehood consists in an agreement or disagreement either to the *real* relations of ideas, or to *real* existence and matter of fact. Whatever, therefore, is not susceptible of this agreement or disagreement is incapable of being true or false, and can never be an object of our reason. Now, it is evident our passions, volitions, and actions, are not susceptible of any such agreement or disagreement; being original facts and realities, complete in themselves, and implying no reference to other passions, volitions, and actions. It is impossible, therefore, they can be pronounced either true or false, and be either contrary or conformable to reason.

This argument is of double advantage to our present purpose. For it proves *directly* that actions do not derive their merit from a conformity to reason, nor their blame from a contrariety to it; and it proves the same truth more *indirectly,* by showing us that as reason can never immediately prevent or produce any action by contradicting or approving of it, it cannot be the source of moral good and evil, which are found to have that influence. Actions may be laudable or blamable, but they cannot be reasonable or unreasonable: laudable or blamable, therefore, are not the same with reasonable or unreasonable. The merit and demerit of actions frequently contradict, and sometimes control our natural propensities. But reason has no such influence. Moral distinctions, therefore, are not the offspring of reason. Reason is wholly inactive, and can never be the source of so active a principle as conscience, or a sense of morals. . . .

It has been observed that reason, in a strict and philosophical sense, can have an influence on our conduct only after two ways: either when it excites a passion by informing us of the existence of something which is a proper object of it; or when it discovers the connection of causes and effects so as to afford us means of exerting any passion. These are the only kinds of judgment which can accompany our actions, or can be said to produce them in any manner; and it must be allowed that these judgments may often be false and erroneous. A person may be affected with passion, by supposing a pain or pleasure to lie in an object which has no tendency to produce either of these sensations, or which produces the contrary to what is imagined. A person may also take false measures for the attaining of his end, and may retard by his foolish conduct instead of forwarding the execution of any object. These false judgments may be thought to affect the passions and actions, which are connected with them, and may be said to render them unreasonable, in a figurative and improper way of speaking. But though this be acknowledged, it is easy to observe that these errors are so far from being the source of all immorality that they are commonly very innocent, and draw no manner of guilt upon the person who is so unfortunate as to fall into them. They extend not beyond a mistake of *fact,* which moralists have not generally supposed criminal, as being perfectly involuntary. I am more to be lamented than blamed if I am mistaken with regard to the influence of objects in producing pain or pleasure, or if I know not the proper means of satisfying my desires. No one can ever regard such errors as a defect in my moral character. A fruit, for instance, that is really disagreeable appears to me at a distance, and, through mistake, I fancy it to be pleasant and delicious. Here is one error. I choose certain means of reaching this fruit which are not proper for my end. Here is a second error; nor is there any third one which can ever possibly enter into our reasonings concerning actions. I ask, therefore, if a man in this situation, and guilty of these two errors, is to be regarded as vicious and criminal, however unavoidable they might have been? Or if it be possible to imagine that such errors are the sources of all immorality? . . .

Thus, upon the whole, it is impossible that the distinction betwixt moral good and evil can be made by reason; since that distinction has an influence upon our actions, of which reason alone is incapable. Reason and judgment may, indeed, be the mediate cause of an action, by prompting or by directing a passion; but it is not pretended that a judgment of this kind, either in its truth or falsehood, is attended with virtue or vice. And as to the judgments which are caused by our judgments, they can still less bestow those moral qualities on the actions which are their causes.

But, to be more particular, and to show that those eternal immutable fitnesses and unfitnesses of things cannot be defended by sound philosophy, we may weigh the following considerations.

If the thought and understanding were alone capable of fixing the boundaries of right and wrong, the character of virtuous and vicious either must lie in some relations of objects, or must be a matter of fact which is discovered by our reasoning. This consequence is evident. As the operations of human understanding divide themselves into two kinds—the comparing of ideas and the inferring of matter of fact—were viture discovered by the understanding, it must be an object of one of these operations; nor is there any third operation of the understanding which can discover it. There has been an opinion very industriously propagated by certain philosophers that morality is susceptible of demonstration; and though no one has ever been able to advance a single step in those demonstrations, yet it is taken for granted that this science may be brought to an equal certainty with geometry or algebra. Upon this supposition vice and virtue must consist in some relations, since it is allowed on all hands that no matter of fact is capable of being demonstrated. Let us therefore begin with examining this hypothesis. . . .

Of all crimes that human creatures are capable of committing, the most horrid and unnatural is ingratitude, especially when it is committed against parents, and appears in the more flagrant instances of wounds and death. This is acknowledged by all mankind, philosophers as well as the people. The question only arises among philosophers, whether the guilt or moral deformity of this action be discovered by demonstrative reasoning, or be felt by an internal sense and by means of some sentiment which the reflecting on such an action naturally occasions. This question will soon be decided against the former opinion, if we can show the same relations in other objects without the notion of any guilt or iniquity attending them. Reason or science is nothing but the comparing of ideas, and the discovery of their relations; and if the same relations have different characters it must evidently follow that those characters are not discovered merely by reason. To put the affair, therefore, to this trial, let us choose any inanimate object, such as an oak or elm, and let us suppose that by the dropping of its seed it produces a sapling below it which, springing up by degrees, at last overtops and destroys the parent tree: I ask if in this instance there be wanting any relation which is discoverable in parricide or ingratitude? Is not the one tree the cause of the other's existence; and the latter the cause of the destruction of the former in the same manner as when a child murders his parent? It is not sufficient to reply that a choice or will is wanting. For in the case of parricide, a will does not give rise to any *different* relations, but is only the cause from which the action is derived; and consequently produces the *same* relations that in the oak or elm arise from some other principles. It is a will or choice that determines a man to kill his parent; and they are the laws of matter and motion that determine a sapling to destroy the oak from which it sprung. Here then the same relations have different causes; but still the relations are the same; and as their discovery is not in both cases attended with a notion of immorality, it follows that that notion does not arise from such a discovery.

But to choose an instance still more resembling; I would fain ask anyone why incest in the human species is criminal, and why the very same action and the same relations in animals have not the smallest moral turpitude and deformity? If it be answered that this action is innocent in animals, because they have not reason sufficient to discover its turpitude, but that man being endowed with that faculty which *ought* to restrain him to his duty, the same action instantly becomes criminal to him. Should this be said, I would reply that this is evidently arguing in a circle. For before reason can perceive this turpitude, the turpitude must exist, and consequently is independent of the decisions of our reason, and is their object more properly than their effect. According to this system, then, every animal that has sense, and appetite, and will, that is, every animal must be susceptible of all the same virtues and vices for which we ascribe praise and blame to human creatures. All the difference is that our superior reason may serve to discover the vice or virtue, and by that means may augment the blame or praise; but still this discovery supposes a separate being in these moral distinctions, and a being which depends only on the will and appetite, and which, both in thought and reality, may be distinguished from reason. Animals are susceptible of the same relations with respect to each other as the human species, and therefore would also be susceptible of the same morality if the essence of morality consisted in these relations. Their want of a sufficient degree of reason may hinder them from perceiving the duties and obligations of morality; but can never hinder these duties from existing; since they must antecedently exist in order to their being perceived. Reason must find them, and can never produce them. This argument deserves to be weighed as being, in my opinion, entirely decisive.

Nor does this reasoning only prove that morality consists not in any relations that are the objects of science; but, if examined, will prove with equal certainty that it consists not in any *matter of fact* which can be discovered by the understanding. This is the *second* part of our argument; and if it can be made evident, we may conclude that morality is not an object of reason. But can there be any difficulty in proving that vice and virtue are not matters of fact whose existence we can infer by reason? Take any action allowed to be vicious—willful murder, for instance. Examine it in all lights, and see if you can find that matter of fact or real existence which you call *vice*. In whichever way you take it, you find only certain passions, motives, volitions, and thoughts. There is no other matter of fact in the case. The vice entirely escapes you, as long as you consider the object. You never can find it till you turn your reflection into your own breast and find a sentiment of disapprobation which arises in you towards this action. Here is a matter of fact; but it is the object of feeling, not of reason. It lies in yourself, not in the object. So that when you pronounce any action or character to be vicious, you mean nothing, but that from the constitution of your nature you have a feeling or sentiment of blame from the contemplation of it. Vice and virtue, therefore, may be compared to sounds, colours, heat, and cold, which, according to modern philosophy, are not qualities in objects but perceptions in the mind: and this discovery in morals, like that other in physics, is to be regarded as a considerable advancement of the speculative sciences; though, like that too, it has little or no influence on practice. Nothing can be more real, or concern us more, than our own sentiments of pleasure and uneasiness; and if these be favourable to virtue, and unfavourable to vice, no more can be requisite to the regulation of our conduct and behaviour.

I cannot forbear adding to these reasonings an observation which may, perhaps, be found of some importance. In every system of morality which I have hitherto met with, I have always remarked that the author proceeds for some time in the ordinary way of reasoning, and establishes the being of a god, or makes observations concerning human affairs; when of a sudden I am surprised to find that instead of the usual copulations of propositions *is* and *is not,* I meet with no proposition that is not connected with an *ought* or an *ought not.* This change is imperceptible, but is, however, of the last consequence. For as this *ought* or *ought not* expresses some new relation or affirmation, it is necessary that it should be observed and explained; and at the same time that a reason should be given for what seems altogether inconceivable, how this new relation can be a deduction from others which are entirely different from it. But as authors do not commonly use this precaution, I shall presume to recommend it to the readers; and am persuaded that this small attention would subvert all the vulgar systems of morality and let us see that the distinction of vice and virtue is not founded merely on the relations of objects, nor is perceived by reason.

Section II. Moral Distinctions Derived from a Moral Sense

Thus the course of the argument leads us to conclude that since vice and virtue are not discoverable merely by reason, or the comparison of ideas, it must be by means of some impression or sentiment they occasion, that we are able to mark the difference betwixt them. Our decisions concerning moral rectitude and depravity are evidently perceptions; and as all perceptions are either impressions or ideas, the exclusion of the one is a convincing argument for the other. Morality, therefore, is more properly felt than judged of; though this feeling or sentiment is commonly so soft and gentle that we are apt to confound it with an idea, according to our common custom of taking all things for the same which have any near resemblance to each other.

The next question is of what nature are these impressions, and after what manner do they operate upon us? Here we cannot remain long in suspense, but must pronounce the impression arising from virtue to be agreeable, and that proceeding from vice to be uneasy. Every moment's experience must convince us of this. There is no spectacle so fair and beautiful as a noble and generous action; nor any which gives us more abhorrence than one that is cruel and treacherous. No enjoyment equals the satisfaction we receive from the company of those we love and esteem; as the greatest of all punishments is to be obliged to pass our lives with those we hate or contemn. A very play or romance may afford us instances of this pleasure which virtue conveys to us; and pain which arises from vice.

Now, since the distinguishing impressions by which moral good or evil is known are nothing but *particular* pains or pleasures, it follows that in all inquiries concerning these moral distinctions it will be sufficient to show the principles which make us feel a satisfaction or uneasiness from the survey of any character, in order to satisfy us why the character is laudable or blamable. An action, or sentiment, or character, is virtuous or vicious; why? Because its view causes a pleasure or uneasiness of a particular kind. In giving a reason, therefore, for the pleasure or uneasiness, we sufficiently explain the vice or virtue. To have the sense of virtue is nothing but to *feel* a satisfaction of a particular kind from the contemplation of a character. The very *feeling* constitutes our praise or admiration. We go no further; nor do we inquire into the cause of the satisfaction. We do not infer a character to be virtuous because it pleases; but in feeling that it pleases after such a particular manner we in effect feel that it is virtuous. The case is the same as in our judgments concerning all kinds of beauty, and tastes, and sensations. Our approbation is implied in the immediate pleasure they convey to us.

I have objected to the system, which establishes eternal rational measures of right and wrong, that 'tis impossible to shew, in the actions of reasonable creatures, any relations, which are not found in external objects; and therefore, if morality always attended these relations, 'twere possible for inanimate matter to become virtuous or vicious. Now it may, in like manner, be objected to the present system, that if virtue and vice be determin'd by pleasure and pain, these qualities must, in every case, arise from the sensations; and consequently any object, whether animate or inanimate, rational or irrational, might become morally good or evil, provided it can excite a satisfaction or uneasiness. But tho' this objection seems to be the very same, it has by no means the same force, in the one case as in the other. For, *first,* 'tis evident, that under the term *pleasure* we comprehend sensations, which are very different from each other, and which have only such a distant resemblance, as is requisite to make them be express'd by the same abstract term. A good composition of music and a bottle of good wine equally produce pleasure; and what is more, their goodness is determin'd merely by the pleasure. But shall we say upon that account, that the wine is harmonious, or the music of a good flavour? In like manner an inanimate object, and the character or sentiments of any person may, both of them, give satisfaction; but as the satisfaction is different, this keeps our sentiments concerning them from being confounded, and makes us ascribe virtue to the one, and not to the other. Nor is every sentiment of pleasure or pain, which arises from characters and actions, of that *peculiar* kind, which makes us praise or condemn. The good qualities of an enemy are hurtful to us; but may still command our esteem and respect, 'Tis only when a character is considered in general, without reference to our particular interest, that it causes such a feeling or sentiment, as denominates it morally good or evil. 'Tis true, those sentiments, from interest and morals, are apt to be confounded, and naturally run into one another. It seldom happens, that we do not think an enemy vicious, and can distinguish betwixt his opposition to our interest and real villainy or baseness. But this hinders not, but that the sentiments are, in themselves, distinct; and a man of temper and judgment may preserve himself from these illusions. In like manner, tho' 'tis certain a musical voice is nothing but one that naturally gives a *particular* kind of pleasure; yet 'tis difficult for a man to be sensible, that the voice of an enemy is agreeable, or to allow it to be musical. But a person of a fine ear, who has the command of himself, can separate these feelings, and give praise to what deserves it. . . .

Thus we are still brought back to our first position that virtue is distinguished by the pleasure, and vice by the pain, that any action, sentiment, or character, gives us by the mere view and contemplation. This decision is very commodious; because it reduces us to this simple question, *why any action or sentiment, upon the general view or survey, gives a certain satisfaction or uneasiness,* in order to show the origin of its moral rectitude or depravity, without looking for any incomprehensible relations and qualities which never did exist in nature, nor even in our imagination, by any clear and distinct conception? I flatter myself I have executed a great part of my present design by a statement of the question which appears to me so free from ambiguity and obscurity.

We may begin with considering anew the nature and force of *sympathy.* The minds of all men are similar in their feelings and operations, nor can any one be actuated by any affection, of which all others are not, in some degree susceptible. As in strings equally wound up, the motion of one communicates itself to the rest; so all the affections readily pass from one person to another, and beget correspondent movements in every human creature. When I see the *effects* of passion in the voice and gesture of any person, my mind immediately passes from these effects to their causes, and forms such a lively idea of the passion, as is presently converted into the passion itself. In like manner, when I perceive the *causes* of any emotion, my mind is convey'd to the effects, and is actuated with a like emotion. Were I present at any of the more terrible operations of surgery, 'tis certain, that even before it begun, the preparation of the instruments, the laying of the bandages in order, the heating of the irons, with all the signs of anxiety and concern in the patients and assistants, would have a great effect upon my mind, and excite the strongest sentiments of pity and terror. No passion of another discovers itself immediately to the mind. We are only sensible of its causes or effects. From *these* we infer the passion: And consequently *these* give rise to our sympathy. . . .

Thus it appears, *that* sympathy is a very powerful principle in human nature, . . . and *that* it produces our sentiment of morals in all the artificial virtues. From thence we may presume, that it also gives rise to many of the other virtues; and that qualities acquire our approbation, because of their tendency to the good of mankind. This presumption must become a certainty, when we find that most of those qualities, which we *naturally* approve of, have actually that tendency, and render a man a proper member of society: While the qualities, which we *naturally* disapprove of, have a contrary tendency, and render any intercourse with the person dangerous or disagreeable. For having found, that such tendencies have force enough to produce the strongest sentiment of morals, we can never reasonably, in these cases, look for any other cause of approbation or blame; it being an inviolable maxim in philosophy, that where any particular cause is sufficient for an effect, we ought to rest satisfied with it, and ought not to multiply causes without necessity. . . .

There have been many systems of morality advanc'd by philosophers in all ages; but if they are strictly examin'd, they may be reduc'd to two, which alone merit our attention. Moral good and evil are certainly distinguish'd by our *sentiments,* not by *reason:* But these sentiments may arise either from the mere species or appearance of characters and passions, or from reflexions on their tendency to the happiness of mankind, and of particular persons. My opinion is, that both these causes are intermix'd in our judgments of morals; after the same manner as they are in our decisions concerning most kinds of external beauty: Tho' I am also of opinion, that reflexions on the tendencies of actions have by far the greatest influence, and determine all the great lines of our duty. There are, however, instances, in cases of less moment, wherein this immediate taste or sentiment produces our approbation. Wit, and a certain easy and disengag'd behaviour, are qualities *immediately agreeable* to others, and command their love and esteem. Some of these qualities produce satisfaction in others by particular *original* principles of human nature, which cannot be accounted for: Others may be resolv'd into principles, which are more general. This will best appear upon a particular enquiry.

DISCUSSION

At the end of another book (*An Inquiry Concerning Human Understanding,* 1748) Hume also announces "Morals and criticism are not so properly objects of the understanding as of taste and sentiment. Beauty, whether moral or natural, is felt more properly than perceived." (p. 173) This sharp distinction between judgments of fact (by way of "understanding") and judgments of value (through taste and sentiment) is the key to Hume's moral philosophy. It is, first of all, a kind of psychological theory about the origins and motivation of value judgments, but it is, much more importantly, a logical thesis about their nature and justification. In the *Treatise,* "sentiment" is sharply distinguished from "reason," which Hume continuously dismisses as "impotent" and incapable of "producing any action or volition." "Reason is, and ought to be, the slave of the passions, and can never pretend to any other office than to serve and obey them," he insists (*Treatise,* pp. 414–415). Morals and actions are motivated by our emotions, desires, and instincts; reason is mere calculation of connections between ideas. No fact or mere idea can motivate us to do or want to do anything, Hume claims. At most, reason may be called in to deliberate the *means* to get what we want; it cannot (as Aristotle, for example, believed) establish our *ends*.

Hume's central logical argument in the *Treatise* (and his opening argument in the *Inquiry*) turns on the essential and often neglected distinction between judgments of fact and judgments of value. It is one thing to know that a thing has a certain quality (for example, that the fish has rotted or that Mr. Pickwick has an acute sense of humor), something quite different to be repulsed or attracted to that thing because of that quality. Virtue and vice are not the same as—and cannot be deduced from—the qualities themselves. This difference can be demonstrated too in a logical distinction which, according to Hume, has been ignored by even the greatest moral philosophers.

> In every system of morality, which I have hitherto met with, . . . the author proceeds for some time in the ordinary way of reasoning . . . when all of a sudden I am surprised to find that, instead of the usual copulations of propositions *is* and *is not,* I meet with no proposition that is not connected with an *ought* or an *ought not.* This change is imperceptible; but it is, however, of the last consequence. For as this *ought* or *ought not* expresses some new relation or affirmation it is necessary that it should be observed and explained; and that at the same time a reason should be given, for what seems altogether inconceivable, how this new relation can be a deduction from others which are entirely different from it. (*Treatise,* p. 469)

The *Inquiry* does not reiterate this point, but nevertheless the distinction between fact and value continues to be central to Hume's position. The argument—recently dubbed "the naturalistic fallacy"—is that no statement that something is good or bad, right or wrong, follows logically from a purely descriptive statement about what something is. Even the most extreme case—a description of the massacre of a defenseless village by bandits—does not yet warrant the conclusion that this is bad or wrong. (Imagine the same basic description supplied by a household exterminator, reporting to a homeowner on the treatment of a termite colony.) Psychologically, what must be added to the factual description to move us to repulsion are our feelings of human sympathy; logically, what must be added to the description is at least one premise that connects the "is" of description to the "ought" of morals, such as,

> (Factual premise) Three thousand creatures were killed.
> (Value premise) Killing is wrong.
> (Conclusion) Something wrong has been done.

But many moral philosophers commit the *naturalistic fallacy* with arguments such as the following (which are usually sufficiently complex so that the fallacy isn't so obvious):

> (Factual premise) The Bible says "thou shalt not kill."
> (Value conclusion) Therefore, do not kill.

or,

> (Factual premise) People are basically selfish.
> (Value conclusion) Therefore, people ought to do what is in their own best interests.

Sometimes, this "fallacy" is the core of an entire ethics, for example, in Aristotle (and Kant). Aristotle begins with certain "facts" about human nature and deduces, in just the way forbidden by Hume, conclusions about what is good and right and what one ought to do. (Kant begins with a factual premise about our rational faculties and similarly deduces that what we ought to do is to act rationally.) But is this "fallacy" really a fallacy? Or is Hume too strictly enforcing a too-narrow distinction and ignoring the *context* in which "is" and "ought" claims are made? Could we save the traditional arguments with an added premise, for example, which says that we *ought* to do what is *natural,* thus undercutting the so-called naturalistic fallacy by introducing nature into the argument itself (the teleological position, in effect). Or consider the following sequence of statements, formulated by the American philosopher John Searle as a counterexample to Hume's "is-ought" argument:

1 Jones uttered the words "I hereby promise to pay you, Smith, five dollars."
2 Jones promised to pay Smith five dollars.
3 Jones placed himself under an obligation to pay Smith five dollars.
4 Jones is under an obligation to pay Smith five dollars.
5 Jones ought to pay Smith five dollars.

Searle claims that this sequence moves from purely factual statements to a conclusion that is clearly an "ought" type judgment of value. How is this possible? Is there a concealed evaluative premise somewhere in the argument, for instance, the value judgment that one ought to keep one's promises? (Searle claims that this is merely a tautology—a purely trivial statement.) Are there implicit conditions (for example, our own cultural expectations and understanding of promises) which provide unspoken premises? Indeed, how many other such arguments can you formulate, in which the facts about certain institutions or established behavior seem to yield clear "ought" type value judgments? How defensible is Hume's "is-ought" distinction? And what does this imply about the general distinction between facts and values?

B. Virtue and Utility: An Inquiry Concerning the Principles of Morals

1. OF THE GENERAL PRINCIPLES OF MORALS: BENEVOLENCE AND JUSTICE

Hume begins his *Inquiry* of 1751, as he began his earlier *Treatise,* by marking the distinction between reason and sentiment, and he again insists that the basis of morals can only be our feelings, not reason. On this basis, he again insists that virtually the whole of moral philosophy has been mistaken; but here in the *Inquiry* his emphasis is primarily on the positive, on the "scientific" approach to ethics and a study of "the estimable [and] blamable qualities of men" (Section I). He begins with two of the most estimable qualities—benevolence and justice (Sections II and III). Justice, Hume claims, is founded solely on *utility,* a claim that is calculated to challenge the whole history of the subject, from Plato until the present. Finally, Hume corrects his British compatriot Hobbes, who argued that political society is based on the force of *law,* originating with "the social contract;" but political society is rather based, like justice, on the foundation of utility.

Section I. Of the General Principles of Morals

Disputes with men pertinaciously obstinate in their principles are, of all others, the most irksome, except, perhaps, those with persons entirely disingenuous, who really do not believe the opinions they defend, but engage in the controversy from affectation, from a spirit of opposition, or from a desire of showing wit and ingenuity superior to the rest of mankind. The same blind adherence to their own arguments is to be expected in both: the same contempt of their antagonists, and the same passionate vehemence in enforcing sophistry and falsehood. And as reasoning is not the source whence either disputant derives his tenets, it is in vain to expect that any logic which speaks not to the affections will ever engage him to embrace sounder principles.

Those who have denied the reality of moral distinctions may be ranked among the disingenuous disputants; nor is it conceivable that any human creature could ever seriously believe that all characters and actions were alike entitled to the affection and regard of everyone. The difference which nature has placed between one man and another is so wide, and this difference is still so much further widened by education, example, and habit that, where the opposite extremes come at once under our apprehension, there is no skepticism so scrupulous, and scarce any assurance so determined, as absolutely to deny all distinction between them. Let a man's insensibility be ever so great, he must often be touched with the images of *right* and *wrong;* and let his prejudices be ever so obstinate, he must observe that others are susceptible of like impressions. The only way, therefore, of converting an antagonist of this kind is to leave him to himself. For, finding that nobody keeps up the controversy with him, it is probable he will at last of himself, from mere weariness come over to the side of common sense and reason.

There has been a controversy started of late, much better worth examination, concerning the general foundation of *morals;* whether they be derived from *reason* or from *sentiment;* whether we attain the knowledge of them by a chain of argument and induction or by an immediate feeling and finer internal sense; whether, like all sound judgment of truth and falsehood, they should be the same to every rational, intelligent being, or whether, like the perception of beauty and deformity, they be founded entirely on the particular fabric and constitution of the human species.

The ancient philosophers, though they often affirm that virtue is nothing but conformity to reason, yet, in general, seem to consider morals as deriving their existence from taste and sentiment. On the other hand, our modern inquirers, though they also talk much of the beauty of virtue and deformity of vice, yet have commonly endeavored to account for these distinctions by metaphysical reasonings and by deductions from the most abstract principles of the understanding. Such confusion reigned in these subjects that an opposition of the greatest consequence could prevail between one system and another, and even in the parts of almost each individual system, and yet nobody, till very lately,

David Hume, *An Inquiry Concerning the Principles of Morals* (1751).

was ever sensible of it. The elegant Lord Shaftesbury, who first gave occasion to remark this distinction, and who, in general, adhered to the principles of the ancients, is not himself entirely free from the same confusion.

It must be acknowledged that both sides of the question are susceptible of specious arguments. Moral distinctions, it may be said, are discernible by pure *reason:* else, whence the many disputes that reign in common life, as well as in philosophy, with regard to this subject; the long chain of proofs often produced on both sides, the examples cited, the authorities appealed to, the analogies employed, the fallacies detected, the inferences drawn, and the several conclusions adjusted to their proper principles? Truth is disputable, not taste: what exists in the nature of things is the standard of our judgment; what each man feels within himself is the standard of sentiment. Propositions in geometry may be proved, systems in physics may be controverted, but the harmony of verse, the tenderness of passion, the brilliancy of wit must give immediate pleasure. No man reasons concerning another's beauty, but frequently concerning the justice or injustice of his actions. In every criminal trial, the first object of the prisoner is to disprove the facts alleged and deny the actions imputed to him; the second, to prove that, even if these actions were real, they might be justified as innocent and lawful. It is confessedly by deductions of the understanding that the first point is ascertained: how can we suppose that a different faculty of the mind is employed in fixing the other?

On the other hand, those who would resolve all moral determinations into *sentiments* may endeavor to show that it is impossible for reason ever to draw conclusions of this nature. To virtue, say they, it belongs to be *amiable,* and vice *odious.* This forms their very nature or essence. But can reason or argumentation distribute these different epithets to any subjects and pronounce beforehand that this must produce love, and that hatred? Or what other reason can we ever assign for these affections but the original fabric and formation of the human mind, which is naturally adapted to receive them?

The end of all moral speculations is to teach us our duty, and, by proper representations of the deformity of vice and beauty of virtue, beget correspondent habits, and engage us to avoid the one, and embrace the other. But is this ever to be expected from inferences and conclusions of the understanding, which of themselves have no hold of the affections or set in motion the active powers of men? They discover truths. But where the truths which they discover are indifferent and beget no desire or aversion, they can have no influence on conduct and behavior. What is honorable, what is fair, what is becoming, what is noble, what is generous takes possession of the heart and animates us to embrace and maintain it. What is intelligible, what is evident, what is probable, what is true procures only the cool assent of the understanding, and, gratifying a speculative curiosity, puts an end to our researches.

Extinguish all the warm feelings and prepossessions in favor of virtue, and all disgust or aversion to vice; render men totally indifferent toward these distinctions; and morality is no longer a practical study, nor has any tendency to regulate our lives and actions.

These arguments on each side (and many more might be produced) are so plausible that I am apt to suspect they may, the one as well as the other, be solid and satisfactory, and that *reason* and *sentiment* concur in almost all moral determinations and conclusions. The final sentence, it is probable, which pronounces characters and actions amiable or odious, praiseworthy or blamable; that which stamps on them the mark of honor or infamy, approbation or censure; that which renders morality an active principle and constitutes virtue our happiness, and vice our misery—it is probable, I say, that this final sentence depends on some internal sense or feeling which nature has made universal in the whole species. For what else can have an influence of this nature? But in order to pave the way for such a sentiment and give a proper discernment of its object, it is often necessary, we find, that much reasoning should precede, that nice distinctions be made, just conclusions drawn, distant comparisons formed, complicated relations examined, and general facts fixed and ascertained. Some species of beauty, especially the natural kinds, on their first appearance command our affection and approbation; and where they fail of this effect, it is impossible for any reasoning to redress their influence or adapt them better to our taste and sentiment. But in many orders of beauty, particularly those of the finer arts, it is requisite to employ much reasoning in order to feel the proper sentiment; and a false relish may frequently be corrected by argument and reflection. There are just grounds to conclude that moral beauty partakes much of this latter species and demands the assistance of our intellectual faculties in order to give it a suitable influence on the human mind.

But though this question concerning the general principles of morals be curious and important, it is needless for us at present to employ further care in our researches concerning it. For if we can be so happy, in the course of this inquiry, as to discover the true origin of morals, it will then easily appear how far either sentiment or reason enters into all determinations of this nature. In order to attain this purpose, we shall endeavor to follow a very simple method: we shall analyze that complication of mental qualities which form what, in common life, we call "personal merit"; we shall consider every attribute of the mind which renders a man an object either of esteem and affection or of hatred and contempt; every habit or sentiment or faculty which, if ascribed to any person, implies either praise or blame and may enter into any panegyric or satire of his character and manners. The quick sensibility, which, on this head, is so universal among mankind, gives a philosopher sufficient assurance that he can never be considerably mistaken in framing the catalogue or incur any danger of misplacing the objects of his contemplation: he needs only enter into his own breast for a moment and consider whether or not he should desire to have this or that quality ascribed to him, and whether such or such an imputation would proceed from a friend or an enemy. The very nature of language guides us almost infallibly in forming a judgment of this nature; and as every tongue possesses one set of words which are taken in a good sense, and another in the opposite, the least acquaintance with the idiom suffices, without any reasoning, to direct us in collecting and arranging the estimable or blamable qualities of men. The only

object of reasoning is to discover the circumstances on both sides which are
common to these qualities—to observe that particular in which the estimable
qualities agree, on the one hand, and the blamable, on the other; and thence to
reach the foundation of ethics and find those universal principles from which all
censure or approbation is ultimately derived. As this is a question of fact, not of
abstract science, we can only expect success by following the experimental
method and deducing general maxims from a comparison of particular instances.
The other scientifical method, where a general abstract principle is first
established, and is afterwards branched out into a variety of inferences and
conclusions, may be more perfect in itself, but suits less the imperfection of
human nature and is a common source of illusion and mistake, in this as well as
in other subjects. Men are now cured of their passion for hypotheses and systems
in natural philosophy, and will hearken to no arguments but those which are
derived from experience. It is full time they should attempt a like reformation in
all moral disquisitions and reject every system of ethics, however subtle or
ingenious, which is not founded on fact and observation.

We shall begin our inquiry on this head by the consideration of the social
virtues; Benevolence and Justice. The explication of them will probably give us
an opening by which the others may be accounted for.

Section II. Of Benevolence

Part I   It may be esteemed, perhaps, a superfluous task to prove that the
benevolent or softer affections are *estimable* and, wherever they appear, engage
the approbation and good will of mankind. The epithets, *sociable, good-natured,
humane, merciful, grateful, friendly, generous, beneficent,* or their equivalents,
are known in all languages, and universally express the highest merit which
human nature is capable of attaining. Where these amiable qualities are
attended with birth and power and eminent abilities, and display themselves in
the good government or useful instruction of mankind, they seem even to raise
the possessors of them above the rank of *human nature* and make them
approach, in some measure, to the divine. Exalted capacity, undaunted courage,
prosperous success—these may only expose a hero or politician to the
envy and ill will of the public. But as soon as the praises are added of
humane and beneficent, when instances are displayed of lenity, tenderness,
or friendship, envy itself is silent or joins the general voice of approbation
and applause.

When Pericles, the great Athenian statesman and general, was on his
deathbed, his surrounding friends, deeming him now insensible, began to
indulge their sorrow for their expiring patron by enumerating his great qualities
and successes, his conquests and victories, the unusual length of his administration, and his nine trophies erected over the enemies of the republic. *You forget,*
cries the dying hero who had heard all, *you forget the most eminent of my praises,
while you dwell so much on those vulgar advantages in which fortune had a
principal share. You have not observed that no citizen has ever yet worn mourning
on my account.*

In men of more ordinary talents and capacity, the social virtues become, if possible, still more essentially requisite, there being nothing eminent, in that case, to compensate for the want of them, or preserve the person from our severest hatred as well as contempt. A high ambition, an elevated courage is apt, says Cicero, in less perfect characters, to degenerate into a turbulent ferocity. The more social and softer virtues are there chiefly to be regarded. These are always good and amiable.

The principal advantage which Juvenal discovers in the extensive capacity of the human species is that it renders our benevolence also more extensive and gives us larger opportunities of spreading our kindly influence than what are indulged to the inferior creation. It must, indeed, be confessed that by doing good only can a man truly enjoy the advantages of being eminent. His exalted station, of itself, but the more exposes him to danger and tempest. His sole prerogative is to afford shelter to inferiors who repose themselves under his cover and protection.

But I forget that it is not my present business to recommend generosity and benevolence, or to paint in their true colors all the genuine charms of the social virtues. These, indeed, sufficiently engage every heart, on the first apprehension of them; and it is difficult to abstain from some sally or panegyric, as often as they occur in discourse or reasoning. But our object here being more the speculative than the practical part of morals, it will suffice to remark (what will readily, I believe, be allowed) that no qualities are more entitled to the general good will and approbation of mankind than beneficence and humanity, friendship and gratitude, natural affection and public spirit, or whatever proceeds from a tender sympathy with others and a generous concern for our kind and species. These, wherever they appear, seem to transfuse themselves, in a manner, into each beholder, and to call forth, in their own behalf, the same favorable and affectionate sentiments which they exert on all around.

Part II We may observe that in displaying the praises of any humane, beneficent man there is one circumstance which never fails to be amply insisted on—namely, the happiness and satisfaction derived to society from his intercourse and good offices. To his parents, we are apt to say, he endears himself by his pious attachment and duteous care still more than by the connections of nature. His children never feel his authority but when employed for their advantage. With him, the ties of love are consolidated by beneficence and friendship. The ties of friendship approach, in a fond observance of each obliging office, to those of love and inclination. His domestics and dependents have in him a sure resource, and no longer dread the power of fortune but so far as she exercises it over him. From him the hungry receive food, the naked clothing, the ignorant and slothful skill and industry. Like the sun, an inferior minister of Providence, he cheers, invigorates, and sustains the surrounding world.

If confined to private life, the sphere of his activity is narrower, but his influence is all benign and gentle. If exalted into a higher station, mankind and posterity reap the fruit of his labors.

As these topics of praise never fail to be employed, and with success, where we would inspire esteem for anyone, may it not thence be concluded that the *utility* resulting from the social virtues forms, at least, a *part* of their merit, and is one source of that approbation and regard so universally paid to them?

When we recommend even an animal or a plant as *useful* and *beneficial,* we give it an applause and recommendation suited to its nature. As, on the other hand, reflection on the baneful influence of any of these inferior beings always inspires us with the sentiment of aversion. The eye is pleased with the prospect of cornfields and loaded vineyards, horses grazing, and flocks pasturing; but flies the view of briars and brambles affording shelter to wolves and serpents.

A machine, a piece of furniture, a vestment, a house well contrived for use and convenience is so far beautiful and is contemplated with pleasure and approbation. An experienced eye is here sensible to many excellences which escape persons ignorant and uninstructed.

Can anything stronger be said in praise of a profession, such as merchandise or manufacture, than to observe the advantages which it procures to society? And is not a monk and inquisitor enraged when we treat his order as useless or pernicious to mankind?

The historian exults in displaying the benefit arising from his labors. The writer of romance alleviates or denies the bad consequences ascribed to his manner of composition.

In general, what praise is implied in the simple epithet "useful"! What reproach in the contrary!

Your gods, says Cicero, in opposition to the Epicureans, cannot justly claim any worship or adoration with whatever imaginary perfections you may suppose them endowed. They are totally useless and inactive. Even the Egyptians, whom you so much ridicule, never consecrated any animal but on account of its utility.

The skeptics assert, though absurdly, that the origin of all religious worship was derived from the utility of inanimate objects, as the sun and moon to the support and well-being of mankind. This is also the common reason assigned by historians for the deification of eminent heroes and legislators.

To plant a tree, to cultivate a field, to beget children—meritorious acts, according to the religion of Zoroaster.

In all determinations of morality, this circumstance of public utility is ever principally in view; and wherever disputes arise, either in philosophy or common life, concerning the bounds of duty, the question cannot, by any means, be decided with greater certainty than by ascertaining, on any side, the true interests of mankind. If any false opinion, embraced from appearances, has been found to prevail, as soon as further experience and sounder reasoning have given us juster notions of human affairs, we retract our first sentiment and adjust anew the boundaries of moral good and evil.

Giving alms to common beggars is naturally praised, because it seems to carry relief to the distressed and indigent. But when we observe the encouragement thence arising to idleness and debauchery, we regard that species of charity rather as a weakness than a virtue.

Tyrannicide, or the assassination of usurpers and oppressive princes, was highly extolled in ancient times, because it both freed mankind from many of these monsters and seemed to keep the others in awe whom the sword or poniard could not reach. But history and experience having since convinced us that this practice increases the jealousy and cruelty of princes, a Timoleon and a Brutus, though treated with indulgence on account of the prejudices of their times, are now considered as very improper models for imitation.

Liberality in princes is regarded as a mark of beneficence. But when it occurs that the homely bread of the honest and industrious is often thereby converted into delicious cakes for the idle and the prodigal, we soon retract our heedless praises. The regrets of a prince for having lost a day were noble and generous; but had he intended to have spent it in acts of generosity to his greedy courtiers, it was better lost than misemployed after that manner.

Luxury, or a refinement on the pleasures and conveniences of life, had long been supposed the source of every corruption in government, and the immediate cause of faction, sedition, civil wars, and the total loss of liberty. It was therefore universally regarded as a vice, and was an object of declamation to all satirists and severe moralists. Those who prove, or attempt to prove, that such refinements rather tend to the increase of industry, civility, and arts regulate anew our *moral* as well as *political* sentiments and represent as laudable or innocent what had formerly been regarded as pernicious and blamable.

Upon the whole, then, it seems undeniable that nothing can bestow more merit on any human creature than the sentiment of benevolence in an eminent degree, and that a *part,* at least, of its merit arises from its tendency to promote the interests of our species and bestow happiness on human society. We carry our view into the salutary consequences of such a character and disposition; and whatever has so benign an influence and forwards so desirable an end is beheld with complacency and pleasure. The social virtues are never regarded without their beneficial tendencies, nor viewed as barren and unfruitful. The happiness of mankind, the order of society, the harmony of families, the mutual support of friends are always considered as the result of the gentle dominion over the breasts of men.

How considerable a *part* of their merit we ought to ascribe to their utility will better appear from future disquisitions as well as the reason why this circumstance has such a command over our esteem and approbation (Section V).

Section III. Of Justice

Part I That Justice is useful to society, and consequently that *part* of its merit, at least, must arise from that consideration, it would be a superfluous undertaking to prove. That public utility is the *sole* origin of Justice, and that reflections on the beneficial consequences of this virtue are the *sole* foundation of its merit, this proposition, being more curious and important, will better deserve our examination and inquiry.

Let us suppose that nature has bestowed on the human race such profuse *abundance* of all *external* conveniences that, without any uncertainty in the event, without any care or industry on our part, every individual finds himself fully provided with whatever his most voracious appetites can want or luxurious imagination wish or desire. His natural beauty, we shall suppose, surpasses all acquired ornaments: the perpetual clemency of the seasons renders useless all clothes or covering; the raw herbage affords him the most delicious fare; the clear fountain the richest beverage. No laborious occupation required: no tillage, no navigation. Music, poetry, and contemplation form his sole business; conversation, mirth, and friendship, his sole amusement.

It seems evident that in such a happy state every other social virtue would flourish and receive tenfold increase; but the cautious, jealous virtue of justice would never once have been dreamed of. For what purpose make a partition of goods where everyone has already more than enough? Why give rise to property where there cannot possibly be any injury? Why call this object *mine* when, upon the seizing of it by another, I need but stretch out my hand to possess myself of what is equally valuable? Justice, in that case, being totally *useless*, would be an idle ceremonial and could never possibly have place in the catalogue of virtues.

We see, even in the present necessitous condition of mankind, that, wherever any benefit is bestowed by nature in an unlimited abundance, we leave it always in common among the whole human race and make no subdivisions of right and property. Water and air, though the most necessary of all objects, are not challenged as the property of individuals; nor can any man commit injustice by the most lavish use and enjoyment of these blessings. In fertile, extensive countries, with few inhabitants, land is regarded on the same footing. And no topic is so much insisted on, by those who defend the liberty of the seas, as the unexhausted use of them in navigation. Were the advantages procured by' navigation as inexhaustible, these reasoners had never had any adversaries to refute, nor had any claims ever been advanced of a separate, exclusive dominion over the ocean.

It may happen in some countries, at some periods, that there be established a property in water, none in land, if the latter be in greater abundance than can be used by the inhabitants, and the former be found with difficulty and in very small quantities.

Again: suppose that, though the necessities of the human race continue the same as at present, yet the mind is so enlarged and so replete with friendship and generosity that every man has the utmost tenderness for every man, and feels no more concern for his own interest than for that of his fellows: It seems evident that the *use* of Justice would, in this case, be suspended by such an extensive benevolence, nor would the divisions and barriers of property and obligation have ever been thought of. Why should I bind another, by a deed or promise, to do me any good office when I know that he is already prompted by the strongest inclination to seek my happiness and would of himself perform the desired service, except the hurt he thereby receives be greater than the benefit accruing to me; in which case he knows that, from my innate humanity and friendship, I should be the first to oppose myself to his imprudent generosity? Why raise landmarks between my neighbor's field and mine when my heart has made no division between our interests, but shares all his joys and sorrows with the same force and vivacity as if originally my own? Every man, upon this supposition, being a second self to another, would trust all his interests to the discretion of every man without jealousy, without partition, without distinction. And the whole human race would form only one family where all would lie in common and be used freely, without regard to property; but cautiously too, with an entire regard to the necessities of each individual, as if our own interests were most intimately concerned.

In the present disposition of the human heart, it would perhaps be difficult to find complete instances of such enlarged affections; but still we may observe that the case of families approaches toward it; and the stronger the mutual benevolence is among the individuals, the nearer it approaches, till all distinction of property be, in a great measure, lost and confounded among them. Between married persons, the cement of friendship is by the laws supposed so strong as to abolish all division of possessions, and has often, in reality, the force ascribed to it. And it is observable that, during the ardor of new enthusiasms, when every principle is inflamed into extravagance, the community of goods has frequently been attempted; and nothing but experience of its inconveniences, from the returning or disguised selfishness of men, could make the imprudent fanatics adopt anew the ideas of justice and of separate property. So true is it that this virtue derives its existence entirely from its necessary *use* to the intercourse and social state of mankind.

To make this truth more evident, let us reverse the foregoing suppositions and, carrying everything to the opposite extreme, consider what would be the effect of these new situations. Suppose a society to fall into such want of all common necessaries that the utmost frugality and industry cannot preserve the greater number from perishing and the whole from extreme misery: it will readily, I believe, be admitted that the strict laws of justice are suspended in such a pressing emergency and give place to the stronger motives of necessity and self-preservation. Is it any crime, after a shipwreck, to seize whatever means or instrument of safety one can lay hold of, without regard to former limitations of property? Or if a city besieged were perishing with hunger, can we imagine that men will see any means of preservation before them and lose their lives from a scrupulous regard to what, in other situations, would be the rules of equity and justice? The *use* and *tendency* of that virtue is to procure happiness and security, by preserving order in society. But where the society is ready to perish from extreme necessity, no greater evil can be dreaded from violence and injustice, and every man may now provide for himself by all the means which prudence can dictate or humanity permit. The public, even in less urgent necessities, opens granaries without the consent of proprietors, as justly supposing that the authority of magistracy may, consistent with equity, extend so far. But were any number of men to assemble without the tie of laws or civil jurisdiction, would an equal partition of bread in a famine, though effected by power and even violence, be regarded as criminal or injurious?

Suppose, likewise, that it should be a virtuous man's fate to fall into the society of ruffians, remote from the protection of laws and government, what conduct must he embrace in that melancholy situation? He sees such a desperate rapaciousness prevail, such a disregard to equity, such contempt of order, such stupid blindness to future consequences, as must immediately have the most tragical conclusion and must terminate in destruction to the greater number and in a total dissolution of society to the rest. He, meanwhile, can have no other expedient than to arm himself, to whomever the sword he seizes, or the buckler, may belong; to make provision of all means of defense and security. And his particular regard to justice being no longer of *use* to his own safety or that of others, he must consult the dictates of self-preservation alone, without concern for those who no longer merit his care and attention.

When any man, even in political society, renders himself by his crimes obnoxious to the public, he is punished by the laws in his goods and person; that is, the ordinary rules of justice are, with regard to him, suspended for a moment, and it becomes equitable to inflict on him, for the *benefit* of society, what otherwise he could not suffer without wrong or injury.

The rage and violence of public war, what is it but a suspension of justice among the warring parties who perceive that this virtue is now no longer of any *use* or advantage to them? The laws of war, which then succeed to those of equity and justice, are rules calculated for the *advantage* and *utility* of that particular state in which men are now placed. And were a civilized nation engaged with barbarians who observed no rules even of war, the former must also suspend their observance of them where they no longer serve to any purpose, and must render every action or rencounter as bloody and pernicious as possible to the first aggressors.

Thus the rules of equity or justice depend entirely on the particular state and condition in which men are placed, and owe their origin and existence to that *utility* which results to the public from their strict and regular observance. Reverse, in any considerable circumstance, the condition of men: produce extreme abundance or extreme necessity, implant in the human breast perfect moderation and humanity or perfect rapaciousness and malice; by rendering justice totally *useless,* you thereby totally destroy its essence and suspend its obligation upon mankind.

The common situation of society is a medium amidst all these extremes. We are naturally partial to ourselves and to our friends, but are capable of learning the advantage resulting from a more equitable conduct. Few enjoyments are given us from the open and liberal hand of nature; but by art, labor, and industry we can extract them in great abundance. Hence the ideas of property become necessary in all civil society; hence justice derives its usefulness to the public; and hence alone arises its merit and moral obligation.

These conclusions are so natural and obvious that they have not escaped even the poets in their descriptions of the felicity attending the golden age or the reign of Saturn. The seasons in that first period of nature were so temperate, if we credit these agreeable fictions, that there was no necessity for men to provide themselves with clothes and houses, as a security against the violence of heat and cold: the rivers flowed with wine and milk; the oaks yielded honey; and Nature spontaneously produced her greatest delicacies. Nor were these the chief advantages of that happy age. Tempests were not alone removed from nature, but those most furious tempests were unknown to human breasts which now cause such uproar and engender such confusion. Avarice, ambition, cruelty, selfishness were never heard of; cordial affection, compassion, sympathy were the only movements with which the mind was yet acquainted. Even the punctillious distinction of *mine* and *thine* was banished from among that happy race of mortals and carried with it the very notion of property and obligation, justice and injustice.

This *poetical* fiction of the *golden age* is, in some respects, of a piece with the *philosophical* fiction of the *state of nature;* only that the former is represented as the most charming and most peaceable condition which can possibly be imagined, whereas the latter is painted out as a state of mutual war and violence attended with the most extreme necessity. On the first origin of mankind, we are told, their ignorance and savage nature were so prevalent that they could give no mutual trust, but must each depend upon himself and his own force or cunning for protection and security. No law was heard of; no rule of justice known; no distinction of property regarded; power was the only measure of right; and a perpetual war of all against all was the result of men's untamed selfishness and barbarity.[2]

Whether such a condition of human nature could ever exist or, if it did, could continue so long as to merit the appellation of a state may justly be doubted. Men are necessarily born in a family society at least and are trained up by their parents to some rule of conduct and behavior. But this must be admitted, that, if such a state of mutual war and violence was ever real, the suspension of all laws of justice, from their absolute inutility, is a necessary and infallible consequence.

---

[2]This fiction of a state of nature as a state of war was not first started by Mr. Hobbes, as is commonly imagined. Plato endeavors to refute a hypothesis very like it in the 2d, 3d, and 4th books *de Republica.* Cicero, on the contrary, supposes it certain and universally acknowledged in the following passage, "For is there anyone among you, gentlemen of the jury, who does not know that nature brought it about that there was a time when neither natural nor civil law was yet defined and men roamed scattered and dispersed over the fields and only had what they were able to seize and keep with violent hands through slaughter and wounds? Accordingly, those who first were eminent by reason of their outstanding virtue and judgment recognized the kind of teachability and intelligence inherent in man, gathered the dispersed in one place, and transformed them from savagery into justice and gentleness. Then affairs were organized to the common advantage, which we call public affairs; then associations came into being, which were later called states; then dwelling places were joined together, to which we give the name of 'cities,' and enclosed with walls, after divine and human law had been invented. Nothing so marks the difference between this highly civilized life of ours and that early monstrous way of life as 'law' and 'violence.' If we refuse to employ one of them, we have to use the other. If we want violence to be extirpated, we must of necessity let law prevail, that is, the verdicts in which all law is contained. If we dislike the verdicts or they are not enforced, violence must necessarily rule. That is clear to all." *Pro P. Sextio* [*For Publius Sextius*), 1. 42.]

The more we vary our views of human life, and the newer and more unusual the lights are in which we survey it, the more shall we be convinced that the origin here assigned for the virtue of justice is real and satisfactory.

Were there a species of creatures intermingled with men which, though rational, were possessed of such inferior strength, both of body and mind, that they were incapable of all resistance and could never, upon the highest provocation, make us feel the effects of their resentment, the necessary consequence, I think, is that we should be bound, by the laws of humanity, to give gentle usage to these creatures, but should not, properly speaking, lie under any restraint of justice with regard to them, nor could they possess any right or property exclusive of such arbitrary lords. Our intercourse with them could not be called society, which supposes a degree of equality, but absolute command on the one side, and servile obedience on the other. Whatever we covet, they must instantly resign. Our permission is the only tenure by which they hold their possessions, our compassion and kindness the only check by which they curb our lawless will; and as no inconvenience ever results from the exercise of a power so firmly established in nature, the restraints of justice and property, being totally *useless,* would never have place in so unequal a confederacy.

This is plainly the situation of men with regard to animals; and how far these may be said to possess reason I leave it to others to determine. The great superiority of civilized Europeans above barbarous Indians tempted us to imagine ourselves on the same footing with regard to them and made us throw off all restraints of justice, and even of humanity, in our treatment of them. In many nations, the female sex are reduced to like slavery and are rendered incapable of all property, in opposition to their lordly masters. But though the males, when united, have in all countries bodily force sufficient to maintain this severe tyranny, yet such are the insinuations, address, and charms of their fair companions that women are commonly able to break the confederacy and share with the other sex in all the rights and privileges of society.

Were the human species so framed by nature as that each individual possessed within himself every faculty requisite both for his own preservation and for the propagation of his kind, were all society and intercourse cut off between man and man by the primary intention of the Supreme Creator, it seems evident that so solitary a being would be as much incapable of justice as of social discourse and conversation. Where mutual regards and forbearance serve to no manner of purpose, they would never direct the conduct of any reasonable man. The headlong course of the passions would be checked by no reflection on future consequences. And as each man is here supposed to love himself alone and to depend only on himself and his own activity for safety and happiness, he would on every occasion, to the utmost of his power, challenge the preference above every other being, to none of which he is bound by any ties, either of nature or of interest.

But suppose the conjunction of the sexes to be established in nature, a family immediately arises, and particular rules being found requisite for its subsistence, these are immediately embraced, though without comprehending the rest of mankind within their prescriptions. Suppose that several families unite together into one society which is totally disjoined from all others, the rules which preserve peace and order enlarge themselves to the utmost extent of that society, but, becoming then entirely useless, lose their force when carried one step farther. But again, suppose that several distinct societies maintain a kind of intercourse for mutual convenience and advantage, the boundaries of justice still grow larger, in proportion to the largeness of men's views and the force of their mutual connections. History, experience, reason sufficiently instruct us in this natural progress of human sentiments and in the gradual enlargement of our regards to justice, in proportion as we become acquainted with the extensive utility of that virtue.

Part II   If we examine the *particular* laws by which justice is directed and property determined, we shall still be presented with the same conclusions. The good of mankind is the only object of all these laws and regulations. Not only is it requisite for the peace and interest of society that men's possessions should be separated, but the rules which we follow in making the separation are such as can best be contrived to serve further the interests of society.

We shall suppose that a creature possessed of reason, but unacquainted with human nature, deliberates with himself what *rules* of justice or property would best promote public interest and establish peace and security among mankind: his most obvious thought would be to assign the largest possessions to the most extensive virtue and give everyone the power of doing good, proportioned to his inclination. In a perfect theocracy, where a being infinitely intelligent governs by particular volitions, this rule would certainly have place and might serve to the wisest purposes. But were mankind to execute such a law, so great is the uncertainty of merit, both from its natural obscurity and from the self-conceit of each individual, that no determinate rule of conduct would ever result from it; and the total dissolution of society must be the immediate consequence. Fanatics may suppose *that dominion is founded on grace,* and *that saints alone inherit the earth;* but the civil magistrate very justly puts these sublime theorists on the same footing with common robbers and teaches them, by the severest discipline, that a rule which in speculation may seem the most advantageous to society may yet be found in practice totally pernicious and destructive.

That there were *religious* fanatics of this kind in England during the civil wars, we learn from history; though it is probable that the obvious *tendency* of these principles excited such horror in mankind, as soon obliged the dangerous enthusiasts to renounce, or at least conceal, their tenets. Perhaps the *levellers,* who claimed an equal distribution of property, were a kind of *political* fanatics which arose from the religious species, and more openly avowed their pretensions; as carrying a more plausible appearance, of being practicable in themselves as well as useful to human society.

It must, indeed, be confessed that nature is so liberal to mankind that, were all her presents equally divided among the species and improved by art and industry, every individual would enjoy all the necessaries and even most of the comforts of life, nor would ever be liable to any ills but such as might accidentally arise from the sickly frame and constitution of his body. It must also be confessed that wherever we depart from this equality we rob the poor of more satisfaction than we add to the rich, and that the slight gratification of a frivolous vanity in one individual frequently costs more than bread to many families, and even provinces. It may appear withal that the rule of equality, as it would be highly *useful,* is not altogether *impracticable,* but has taken place, at least in an imperfect degree, in some republics, particularly that of Sparta, where it was attended, it is said, with the most beneficial consequences. Not to mention that the *agrarian* laws, so frequently claimed in Rome, and carried into execution in many Greek cities, proceeded, all of them, from the general idea of the utility of this principle.

But historians, and even common sense, may inform us that, however specious these ideas of *perfect* equality may seem, they are really at bottom *impracticable;* and were they not so, would be extremely *pernicious* to human society. Render possessions ever so equal, men's different degrees of art, care, and industry will immediately break that equality. Or if you check these virtues, you reduce society to the most extreme indigence and, instead of preventing want and beggary in a few, render it unavoidable to the whole community. The most rigorous inquisition, too, is requisite to watch every inequality on its first appearance; and the most severe jurisdiction to punish and redress it. But besides that so much authority must soon degenerate into tyranny and be exerted with great partialities: who can possibly be possessed of it in such a situation as is here supposed? Perfect equality of possessions, destroying all subordination, weakens extremely the authority of magistracy and must reduce all power nearly to a level, as well as property.

We may conclude, therefore, that, in order to establish laws for the regulation of property, we must be acquainted with the nature and situation of man, must reject appearances which may be false, though specious; and must search for those rules which are, on the whole, most *useful* and *beneficial:* vulgar sense and slight experience are sufficient for this purpose, where men give not way to too selfish avidity or too extensive enthusiasm.

Who sees not, for instance, that whatever is produced or improved by a man's art or industry ought forever to be secured to him in order to give encouragement to such *useful* habits and accomplishments? That the property ought also to descend to children and relations, for the same *useful* purpose? That it may be alienated by consent in order to beget that commerce and intercourse which is so *beneficial* to human society? And that all contracts and promises ought carefully to be fulfilled in order to secure mutual trust and confidence, by which the general *interest* of mankind is so much promoted?

Examine the writers on the laws of nature and you will always find that, whatever principles they set out with, they are sure to terminate here at last and to assign, as the ultimate reason for every rule which they establish, the convenience and necessities of mankind. A concession thus extorted, in opposition to systems, has more authority than if it had been made in prosecution of them.

What other reason, indeed, could writers ever give why this must be *mine* and that *yours,* since uninstructed nature, surely, never made any such distinction? The objects which receive those appellations are of themselves foreign to us; they are totally disjoined and separated from us; and nothing but the general interests of society can form the connection.

Sometimes the interests of society may require a rule of justice in a particular case, but may not determine any particular rule, among several which are all equally beneficial. In that case the *slightest* analogies are laid hold of in order to prevent that indifference and ambiguity which would be the source of perpetual dissension. Thus possession alone, and first possession, is supposed to convey property where nobody else has any preceding claim and pretension. Many of the reasonings of lawyers are of this analogical nature and depend on very slight connections of the imagination.

Does anyone scruple, in extraordinary cases, to violate all regard to the private property of individuals and sacrifice to public interest a distinction which had been established for the sake of that interest? The safety of the people is the supreme law: all other particular laws are subordinate to it and dependent on it; and if, in the *common* course of things, they be followed and regarded, it is only because the public safety and interest *commonly* demand so equal and impartial an administration.

Sometimes both *utility* and *analogy* fail and leave the laws of justice in total uncertainty. Thus it is highly requisite that prescription or long possession should convey property; but what number of days or months or years should be sufficient for that purpose it is impossible for reason alone to determine. *Civil laws* here supply the place of the natural *code* and assign different terms for prescription, according to the different *utilities* proposed by the legislature. Bills of exchange and promissory notes, by the laws of most countries, prescribe sooner than bonds and mortgages and contracts of a more formal nature.

In general, we may observe that all questions of property are subordinate to the authority of civil laws, which extend, restrain, modify, and alter the rules of natural justice, according to the particular *convenience* of each community. The laws have, or ought to have, a constant reference to the constitution of government, the manners, the climate, the religion, the commerce, the situation of each society. A late author of genius, as well as learning, has prosecuted this subject at large, and has established from these principles a system of political knowledge which abounds in ingenious and brilliant thoughts, and is not wanting in solidity (Montesquieu).

What is a man's property? Anything which it is lawful for him, and for him alone, to use. *But what rule have we by which we can distinguish these objects?* Here we must have recourse to statutes, customs, precedents, analogies, and a hundred other circumstances—some of which are constant and inflexible, some variable and arbitrary. But the ultimate point, in which they all professedly terminate, is the interest and happiness of human society. Where this enters not into consideration, nothing can appear more whimsical, unnatural, and even superstitious than all or most of the laws of justice and of property.

Those who ridicule vulgar superstitions and expose the folly of particular regards to meats, days, places, postures, apparel have an easy task, while they consider all the qualities and relations of the objects and discover no adequate cause for that affection or antipathy, veneration or horror, which have so mighty an influence over a considerable part of mankind. A Syrian would have starved rather than taste pigeons; an Egyptian would not have approached bacon; but if these species of food be examined by the senses of sight, smell, or taste, or scrutinized by the sciences of chemistry, medicine, or physics, no difference is ever found between them and any other species, nor can that precise circumstance be pitched on which may afford a just foundation for the religious passion. A fowl on Thursday is lawful food; on Friday abominable: eggs, in this house and in this diocese, are permitted during Lent; a hundred paces farther, to eat them is a damnable sin. This earth or building yesterday was profane; today, by the muttering of certain words, it has become holy and sacred. Such reflections as these, in the mouth of a philosopher, one may safely say, are too obvious to have any influence, because they must always, to every man, occur at first sight; and where they prevail not of themselves, they are surely obstructed by education, prejudice, and passion, not by ignorance or mistake.

It may appear to a careless view, or rather a too abstracted reflection, that there enters a like superstition into all the sentiments of justice; and that, if a man expose its object, or what we call property, to the same scrutiny of sense and science, he will not, by the most accurate inquiry, find any foundation for the difference made by moral sentiment. I may lawfully nourish myself from this tree; but the fruit of another of the same species, ten paces off, it is criminal for me to touch. Had I worn this apparel an hour ago, I had merited the severest punishment; but a man, by pronouncing a few magical syllables, has now rendered it fit for my use and service. Were this house placed in the neighboring territory, it had been immoral for me to dwell in it; but being built on this side the river, it is subject to a different municipal law, and by its becoming mine I incur no blame or censure. The same species of reasoning, it may be thought, which so successfully exposes superstition is also applicable to justice; nor is it possible, in the one case more than in the other, to point out in the object that precise quality or circumstance which is the foundation of the sentiment.

But there is this material difference between *superstition* and *justice,* that the former is frivolous, useless, and burdensome; the latter is absolutely requisite to the well-being of mankind and existence of society. When we abstract from this circumstance (for it is too apparent ever to be overlooked), it must be confessed that all regards to right and property seem entirely without foundation, as much as the grossest and most vulgar superstition. Were the interests of society nowise concerned, it is as unintelligible why another's articulating certain sounds, implying consent, should change the nature of my actions with regard to a particular object, as why the reciting of a liturgy by a priest, in a certain habit and posture, should dedicate a heap of brick and timber and render it thenceforth and forever sacred.

These reflections are far from weakening the obligations of justice, or diminishing anything from the most sacred attention to property. On the contrary, such sentiments must acquire new force from the present reasoning. For what stronger foundation can be desired or conceived for any duty than to observe that human society, or even human nature, could not subsist without the establishment of it, and will still arrive at greater degrees of happiness and perfection, the more inviolable the regard is which is paid to that duty?

The dilemma seems obvious: as justice evidently tends to promote public utility and to support civil society, the sentiment of justice is either derived from our reflecting on that tendency or, like hunger, thirst, and other appetites, resentment, love of life, attachment to offspring, and other passions, arises from a simple original instinct in the human breast, which nature has implanted for like salutary purposes. If the latter be the case, it follows that property, which is the object of justice, is also distinguished by a simple, original instinct, and is not ascertained by any argument or reflection. But who is there that ever heard of such an instinct? Or is this a subject in which new discoveries can be made? We may as well expect to discover in the body new senses which had before escaped the observation of all mankind.

But further, though it seems a very simple proposition to say that nature, by an instinctive sentiment, distinguishes property, yet in reality we shall find that there are required for that purpose ten thousand different instincts, and these employed about objects of the greatest intricacy and nicest discernment. For when a definition of *property* is required, that relation is found to resolve itself into any possession acquired by occupation, by industry, by prescription, by inheritance, by contract, etc. Can we think that nature, by an original instinct, instructs us in all these methods of acquisition?

These words, too, inheritance and contract, stand for ideas infinitely complicated; and to define them exactly a hundred volumes of laws, and a thousand volumes of commentators have not been found sufficient. Does nature, whose instincts in men are all simple, embrace such complicated and artificial objects and create a rational creature without trusting anything to the operation of his reason?

But even though all this were admitted, it would not be satisfactory. Positive laws can certainly transfer property. Is it by another original instinct that we recognize the authority of kings and senates and mark all the boundaries of their jurisdiction? Judges, too, even though their sentence be erroneous and illegal, must be allowed, for the sake of peace and order, to have decisive authority and ultimately to determine property. Have we original, innate ideas of praetors, and chancellors, and juries? Who sees not that all these institutions arise merely from the necessities of human society?

All birds of the same species, in every age and country, build their nests alike: in this we see the force of instinct. Men, in different times and places, frame their houses differently: here we perceive the influence of reason and custom. A like inference may be drawn from comparing the instinct of generation and the institution of property.

How great soever the variety of municipal laws, it must be confessed that their chief outlines pretty regularly concur, because the purposes to which they tend are everywhere exactly similar. In like manner, all houses have a roof and walls, windows and chimneys, though diversified in their shape, figure, and materials. The purposes of the latter, directed to the conveniences of human life, discover not more plainly their origin from reason and reflection than do those of the former, which point all to a like end.

I need not mention the variations which all the rules of property receive from the finer turns and connections of the imagination, and from the subtleties and abstractions of law topics and reasonings. There is no possibility of reconciling this observation to the notion of original instincts.

What alone will beget a doubt concerning the theory on which I insist is the influence of education and acquired habits, by which we are so accustomed to blame injustice that we are not, in every instance, conscious of any immediate reflection on the pernicious consequences of it. The views the most familiar to us are apt, for that very reason, to escape us; and what we have very frequently performed from certain motives we are apt likewise to continue mechanically, without recalling, on every occasion, the reflections which first determined us. The convenience, or rather necessity, which leads to justice is so universal and everywhere points so much to the same rules that the habit takes place in all societies; and it is not without some scrutiny that we are able to ascertain its true origin. The matter, however, is not so obscure but that, even in common life, we have every moment recourse to the principle of public utility and ask, *What must become of the world, if such practices prevail? How could society subsist under such disorders?* Were the distinction or separation of possessions entirely useless, can anyone conceive that it ever should have obtained in society?

Thus we seem, upon the whole, to have attained a knowledge of the force of that principle here insisted on, and can determine what degree of esteem or moral approbation may result from reflections on public interest and utility. The necessity of justice to the support of society is the *sole* foundation of that virtue; and since no moral excellence is more highly esteemed, we may conclude that this circumstance of usefulness has, in general, the strongest energy and most entire command over our sentiments. It must therefore be the source of a considerable part of the merit ascribed to humanity, benevolence, friendship, public spirit, and other social virtues of that stamp; as it is the *sole* source of the moral approbation paid to fidelity, justice, veracity, integrity, and those other estimable and useful qualities and principles. It is entirely agreeable to the rules of philosophy, and even of common reason, where any principle has been found to have a great force and energy in one instance, to ascribe to it a like energy in all similar instances. This indeed is Newton's chief rule of philosophizing.

Section IV. Of Political Society

Had every man sufficient *sagacity* to perceive, at all times, the strong interest which binds him to the observance of justice and equity, and *strength of mind* sufficient to persevere in a steady adherence to a general and a distant interest, in opposition to the allurements of present pleasure and advantage, there had never, in that case, been any such thing as government or political society; but each man, following his natural liberty, had lived in entire peace and harmony with all others. What need of positive law where natural justice is of itself a sufficient restraint? Why create magistrates where there never arises any disorder or iniquity? Why abridge our native freedom when, in every instance, the utmost exertion of it is found innocent and beneficial? It is evident that, if government were totally useless, it never could have place, and that the *sole* foundation of the duty of *allegiance* is the *advantage* which it procures to society by preserving peace and order among mankind. . . .

Even in societies which are established on principles the most immoral, and the most destructive to the interests of the general society, there are required certain rules which a species of false honor, as well as private interest, engages the members to observe. Robbers and pirates, it has often been remarked, could not maintain their pernicious confederacy did they not establish a new distributive justice among themselves and recall those laws of equity which they have violated with the rest of mankind.

I hate a drinking companion, says the Greek proverb, who never forgets. The follies of the last debauch should be buried in eternal oblivion in order to give full scope to the follies of the next.

Among nations where an immoral gallantry, if covered with a thin veil of mystery, is in some degree authorized by custom, there immediately arises a set of rules calculated for the convenience of that attachment. The famous court or parliament of love in Provence formerly decided all difficult cases of this nature.

In societies for play there are laws required for the conduct of the game; and these laws are different in each game. The foundation, I own, of such societies is frivolous, and the laws are in a great measure, though not altogether, capricious and arbitrary. So far is there a material difference between them and the rules of justice, fidelity, and loyalty. The general societies of men are absolutely requisite for the subsistence of the species; and the public convenience, which regulates morals, is inviolably established in the nature of man, and of the world in which he lives. The comparison, therefore, in these respects is very imperfect. We may only learn from it the necessity of rules wherever men have any intercourse with each other.

They cannot even pass each other on the road without rules. Wagoners, coachmen, and postilions have principles by which they give the way; and these are chiefly founded on mutual ease and convenience. Sometimes also they are arbitrary, at least dependent on a kind of capricious analogy, like many of the reasonings of lawyers.

To carry the matter further, we may observe that it is impossible for men so much as to murder each other without statutes and maxims, and an idea of justice and honor. War has its laws as well as peace; and even that sportive kind of war, carried on among wrestlers, boxers, crudgel players, gladiators, is regulated by fixed principles. Common interest and utility beget infallibly a standard of right and wrong among the parties concerned.

DISCUSSION

Hume begins his *Inquiry* by distinguishing once again the roles of reason and sentiment in morals, but his treatment here is much less polemical than in the *Treatise* and reason is given a more generous role in the ascertaining of utility, at least. Nevertheless, he tells us right away that "truth is disputable, not taste." The method of the *Inquiry,* however, is not to pursue this central distinction so much as to study in detail the particular sentiments that motivate our actions. Always the scientist, Hume conscientiously abstains from moralizing:

> But I forget that it is not my present business to recommend generosity and benevolence, or to paint in their true colors all the genuine charms of the social virtues. . . . Our object here being more speculative than the practical part of morals, it will suffice to remark (what will readily, I believe, be allowed) that no qualities are more entitled to the general good will and approbation of mankind than beneficence and humanity, friendship and gratitude, natural affection and public spirit, or whatever proceeds from a tender sympathy with others and a generous concern for our kind and our species.

The *Inquiry,* in other words, is a description of our moral feelings rather than an attempt to praise and evoke them. Like Aristotle, he bases his argument on what people generally agree to, rather than his own moral arguments or feelings. Nevertheless, the writing of the *Inquiry* makes it quite obvious that Hume is also doing the latter, encouraging these good feelings as well as describing them. Again, like Aristotle.

The analysis of the key sentiments of benevolence and justice involve a somewhat troublesome circle; benevolence is explained in terms of its utility, but then later (in Section V) it is made quite clear to us that utility pleases us because it serves our general feeling of benevolence. The thrust of Hume's analysis, however, is clearly pointed; morals is first of all a question of good character, "personal merit," and most of the virtues Hume praises are not what we would usually call "moral" virtues but rather *social* virtues—those which allow us to get along and enjoy each other's company. In this, again, he most resembles Aristotle and least resembles the Christian moralists of his own day, against whom Hume was vigorously reacting. Benevolence, of course, is an essential ingredient in Christian ethics as well. But Hume makes it clear that it is not "loving thy neighbor" as a divine duty, but rather as a natural affection, that is the key to morals.

Hume's heavy emphasis on utility becomes much more problematic when he turns to the virtue of justice. "Justice," Hume begins, "is useful to society." That much is beyond dispute. But Hume then goes on to say that "utility is the *sole* origin [and foundation] of Justice," which he insists is a "more curious and important" claim, deserving of our attention. If the world were more generous and if we all had everything that we wanted, Hume says, there would be no need for justice. Furthermore—again harking back to Aristotle—Hume suggests that if there were universal benevolence, for instance, if all of us were friends, there would be no use for justice either. Justice and benevolence are thereby distinguished; justice comes in when benevolence runs out. But can justice be attributed solely to utility?

The utility of justice is directed in every instance (though not always successfully) to "the good of mankind." But the argument, that justice is necessary to the support of society (which Hume demonstrates through a large variety of considerations), does not demonstrate his polemical claim that utility is the *sole* foundation of justice. What he shows persuasively is the importance of justice and the wide variety of arrangements that might be just—because they are practical or convenient—in different societies and different circumstances. But he makes no mention of the problem of justice that dominates modern discussions of justice—and ancient discussions of justice too—the question of *rights*. Hume rejects the ideal of universal equality as "impractical," and he points to the utility of considerations of *merit*. But he does not consider those cases where justice demands a respect for rights which is clearly against the general utility, perhaps even destructive to the whole society. He could argue that respect for such rights will, in the long run, prove to be useful, but this is an argument that he does not make for himself and that has often been disputed. And, in any case, it would seem that justice sometimes demands respect for such rights, *whatever the effects on general utility.* Justice consists of a number of competing claims, among them claims to rights, an insistence on some kind of equality (before the law, for example), demands of merit and desert, contractual obligations, and a number of other, related concerns. To suggest that justice is solely a matter of utility is either to ignore these complications or to so stretch the concept of "utility" that it no longer means that singular concern around which Hume builds his ethics.

Why is Hume so adamant about this? His last sentence (in Section III) gives it away, "This indeed is Newton's chief rule of philosophizing." It is the scientific elegance of a single explanatory principle that leads Hume to his single-mindedness.

2. WHY UTILITY PLEASES

Having reduced morality to "utility," Hume now faces the critical question of how to explain the desirability of utility itself. After remarking on the curiosity that this principle has so often been ignored in morals, he goes on to assert the importance of *self-love.* (See also Appendix II, pages 231 to 235.) But self-love does not mean selfishness, and Hume takes great care to emphasize that hand in hand with self-love goes our natural sentiments of sympathy and benevolence. It is our approval and repulsion of other people's behavior (for example, in studying the heroic and evil figures in history) that determine much of our feelings about ourselves, and it is a concern for the public good that motivates many of our actions, as part of our own good too:

> It appears that a tendency to public good and to the promoting of peace, harmony and order in society does always, by affecting the benevolent principles of our frame, engage us on the side of the social virtues. And it appears, as an additional confirmation, that these principles of humanity and sympathy enter so deeply into all our sentiments and have so powerful an influence as may enable them to excite the strongest censure and applause.

Section V. Why Utility Pleases

Part I   It seems so natural a thought to ascribe to their utility the praise which we bestow on the social virtues that one would expect to meet with this principle everywhere in moral writers as the chief foundation of their reasoning and inquiry. In common life we may observe that the circumstance of utility is always appealed to, nor is it supposed that a greater eulogy can be given to any man than to display his usefulness to the public and enumerate the services which he has performed to mankind and society. What praise, even of an inanimate form, if the regularity and elegance of its parts destroy not its fitness for any useful purpose! And how satisfactory an apology for any disproportion or seeming deformity if we can show the necessity of that particular construction for the use intended! A ship appears more beautiful to an artist, or one moderately skilled in navigation, where its prow is wide and swelling beyond its poop, than if it were framed with a precise geometrical regularity, in contradiction to all the laws of mechanics. A building whose doors and windows were exact squares would hurt the eye by that very proportion as ill-adapted to the figure of a human creature, for whose service the fabric was intended. What wonder then that a man whose habits and conduct are hurtful to society and dangerous or pernicious to everyone who has an intercourse with him should, on that account, be an object of disapprobation and communicate to every spectator the strongest sentiment of disgust and hatred?

But perhaps the difficulty of accounting for these effects of usefulness, or its contrary, has kept philosophers from admitting them into their systems of ethics, and has induced them rather to employ any other principle in explaining the origin of moral good and evil. But it is no just reason for rejecting any principle confirmed by experience that we cannot give a satisfactory account of its origin, nor are able to resolve it into other, more general principles. And if we would employ a little thought on the present subject we need be at no loss to account for the influence of utility and to deduce it from principles the most known and avowed in human nature.

From the apparent usefulness of the social virtues it has readily been inferred by skeptics, both ancient and modern, that all moral distinctions arise from education, and were at first invented, and afterwards encouraged, by the art of politicians in order to render men tractable and subdue their natural ferocity and selfishness, which incapacitated them for society. This principle, indeed, of precept and education must so far be owned to have a powerful influence that it may frequently increase or diminish, beyond their natural standard, the sentiments of approbation or dislike; and may even, in particular instances, create, without any natural principle, a new sentiment of this kind, as is evident in all superstitious practices and observances. But that *all* moral affection or dislike arises from this origin will never surely be allowed by any judicious inquirer. Had nature made no such distinction, founded on the original constitution of the mind, the words *honorable* and *shameful, lovely* and *odious, noble* and *despicable* had never had place in any language, nor could politicians, had they invented these terms, ever have been able to render them intelligible or make them convey any idea to the audience. So that nothing can be more superficial than this paradox of the skeptics; and it were well if, in the abstruser studies of logic and metaphysics, we could as easily obviate the cavils of that sect as in the practical and more intelligible sciences of politics and morals.

The social virtues must, therefore, be allowed to have a natural beauty and amiableness, which at first, antecedent to all precept or education, recommends them to the esteem of uninstructed mankind and engages their affections. And as the public utility of these virtues is the chief circumstance whence they derive their merit, it follows that the end which they have a tendency to promote must be some way agreeable to us and take hold of some natural affection. It must please either from considerations of self-interest or from more generous motives and regards.

It has often been asserted that as every man has a strong connection with society and perceives the impossibility of his solitary subsistence, he becomes, on that account, favorable to all those habits or principles which promote order in society and insure to him the quiet possession of so inestimable a blessing. As much as we value our own happiness and welfare, as much must we applaud the practice of justice and humanity by which alone the social confederacy can be maintained and every man reap the fruits of mutual protection and assistance.

This deduction of morals from self-love, or a regard to private interest, is an obvious thought and has not arisen wholly from the wanton sallies and sportive assaults of the skeptics. To mention no others, Polybius, one of the gravest and most judicious as well as most moral writers of antiquity, has assigned this selfish origin of all our sentiments of virtue. But though the solid, practical sense of that author and his aversion to all vain subtleties render his authority on the present subject very considerable, yet is not this an affair to be decided by authority; and the voice of nature and experience seems plainly to oppose the selfish theory.

We frequently bestow praise on virtuous actions performed in very distant ages and remote countries, where the utmost subtlety of imagination would not discover any appearance of self-interest or find any connection of our present happiness and security with events so widely separated from us.

A generous, a brave, a noble deed performed by an adversary commands our approbation, while, in its consequences, it may be acknowledged prejudicial to our particular interest.

When private advantage concurs with general affection for virtue, we readily perceive and avow the mixture of these distinct sentiments, which have a very different feeling and influence on the mind. We praise, perhaps, with more alacrity where the generous, humane action contributes to our particular interest; but the topics of praise, which we insist on, are very wide of this circumstance. And we may attempt to bring over others to our sentiments, without endeavoring to convince them that they reap any advantage from the actions which we recommend to their approbation and applause.

Frame the model of a praiseworthy character consisting of all the most amiable moral virtues: give instances in which these display themselves after an eminent and extraordinary manner; you readily engage the esteem and approbation of all your audience, who never so much as inquire in what age and country the person lived who possessed these noble qualities—a circumstance, however, of all others the most material to self-love, or a concern for our own individual happiness.

Once on a time a statesman, in the shock and contest of parties, prevailed so far as to procure by his eloquence the banishment of an able adversary; whom he secretly followed, offering him money for his support during his exile and soothing him with topics of consolation in his misfortunes. *Alas!* cries the banished statesman, *with what regret must I leave my friends in this city where even enemies are so generous!* Virtue, though in an enemy, here pleased him; and we also give it the just tribute of praise and approbation; nor do we retract these sentiments when we hear that the action passed at Athens about two thousand years ago, and that the persons' names were Aeschines and Demosthenes.

What is that to me? There are few occasions when this question is not pertinent; and had it that universal, infallible influence supposed, it would turn into ridicule every composition, and almost every conversation, which contained any praise or censure of men and manners.

It is but a weak subterfuge, when pressed by these facts and arguments, to say that we transport ourselves, by the force of imagination, into distant ages and countries and consider the advantage which we should have reaped from these characters had we been contemporaries and had any commerce with the persons. It is not conceivable how a *real* sentiment or passion can ever arise from a known *imaginary* interest, especially when our *real* interest is still kept in view and is often acknowledged to be entirely distinct from the imaginary, and even sometimes opposite to it.

A man brought to the brink of a precipice cannot look down without trembling; and the sentiment of *imaginary* danger actuates him, in opposition to the opinion and belief of *real* safety. But the imagination is here assisted by the presence of a striking object, and yet prevails not, except it be also aided by novelty and the unusual appearance of the object. Custom soon reconciles us to heights and precipices, and wears off these false and delusive terrors. The reverse is observable in the estimates which we form of characters and manners; and the more we habituate ourselves to an accurate scrutiny of morals, the more delicate feeling do we acquire of the most minute distinctions between vice and virtue. Such frequent occasion, indeed, have we in common life to pronounce all kinds of moral determinations that no object of this kind can be new or unusual to us, nor could any *false* views or prepossessions maintain their ground against an experience so common and familiar. Experience being chiefly what forms the associations of ideas, it is impossible that any association could establish and support itself in direct opposition to that principle.

Usefulness is agreeable and engages our approbation. This is a matter of fact confirmed by daily observation. But *useful?* For what? For somebody's interest surely. Whose interest then? Not our own only, for our approbation frequently extends further. It must therefore be the interest of those who are served by the character or action approved of; and these, we may conclude, however remote, are not totally indifferent to us. By opening up this principle we shall discover one great source of moral distinctions.

Part II   Self-love is a principle in human nature of such extensive energy, and the interest of each individual is in general so closely connected with that of the community, that those philosophers were excusable who fancied that all our concern for the public might be resolved into a concern for our own happiness and preservation. They saw, every moment, instances of approbation or blame, satisfaction or displeasure toward characters and actions; they denominated the objects of these sentiments *virtues* or *vices;* they observed that the former had a tendency to increase the happiness, and the latter the misery of mankind; they asked whether it were possible that we could have any general concern for society or any disinterested resentment of the welfare or injury of others; they found it simpler to consider all these sentiments as modifications of self-love, and they discovered a pretense at least for this unity of principle in that close union of interest which is so observable between the public and each individual.

But notwithstanding this frequent confusion of interests, it is easy to attain what natural philosophers, after Lord Bacon, have affected to call the *experimentum crucis,* or that experiment which points out the right way in any doubt or ambiguity. We have found instances in which private interest was separate from public in which it was even contrary, and yet we observed the moral sentiment to continue, notwithstanding this disjunction of interests. And wherever these distinct interests sensibly concurred, we always found a sensible increase of the sentiment and a more warm affection to virtue and detestation of vice, or what we properly call "gratitude" and "revenge." Compelled by these instances we must renounce the theory which accounts for every moral sentiment by the principle of self-love. We must adopt a more public affection and allow that the interests of society are not, even on their own account, entirely indifferent to us. Usefulness is only a tendency to a certain end; and it is a contradiction in terms that anything pleases as means to an end where the end itself nowise affects us. If usefulness, therefore, be a source of moral sentiment, and if this usefulness be not always considered with a reference to self, it follows that everything which contributes to the happiness of society recommends itself directly to our approbation and good will. Here is a principle which accounts, in great part, for the origin of morality: and what need we seek for abstruse and remote systems when there occurs one so obvious and natural?[3]

Have we any difficulty to comprehend the force of humanity and benevolence? Or to conceive that the very aspect of happiness, joy, prosperity gives pleasure; that of pain, suffering, sorrow communicates uneasiness? The human countenance, says Horace, borrows smiles or tears from the human countenance. Reduce a person to solitude and he loses all enjoyment, except either of the sensual or speculative kind; and that because the movements of his heart are

---

[3]It is needless to push our researches so far as to ask, why we have humanity or a fellow-feeling with others? It is sufficient that this is experienced to be a principle in human nature. We must stop somewhere in our examination of causes; and there are, in every science, some general principles beyond which we cannot hope to find any principle more general. No man is absolutely indifferent to the happiness and misery of others. The first has a natural tendency to give pleasure, the second pain. This everyone may find in himself. It is not probable that these principles can be resolved into principles more simple and universal, whatever attempts may have been made to that purpose. But if it were possible, it belongs not to the present subject; and we may here safely consider these principles as original—happy if we can render all the consequences sufficiently plain and perspicuous!

not forwarded by correspondent movements in his fellow creatures. The signs of sorrow and mourning, though arbitrary, affect us with melancholy, but the natural symptoms, tears and cries and groans, never fail to infuse compassion and uneasiness. And if the effects of misery touch us in so lively a manner, can we be supposed altogether insensible or indifferent toward its causes when a malicious or treacherous character and behavior are presented to us?

We enter, I shall suppose, into a convenient, warm, well-contrived apartment: we necessarily receive a pleasure from its very survey because it presents us with the pleasing ideas of ease, satisfaction, and enjoyment. The hospitable, good-humored, humane landlord appears. This circumstance surely must embellish the whole, nor can we easily forbear reflecting, with pleasure, on the satisfaction which results to everyone from his intercourse and good offices.

His whole family, by the freedom, ease, confidence, and calm enjoyment diffused over their countenances, sufficiently express their happiness. I have a pleasing sympathy in the prospect of so much joy, and can never consider the source of it without the most agreeable emotions.

He tells me that an oppressive and powerful neighbor had attempted to dispossess him of his inheritance and had long disturbed all his innocent and social pleasures. I feel an immediate indignation arise in me against such violence and injury.

But it is no wonder, he adds, that a private wrong should proceed from a man who had enslaved provinces, depopulated cities, and made the field and scaffold stream with human blood. I am struck with horror at the prospect of so much misery and am actuated by the strongest antipathy against its author.

In general, it is certain that wherever we go, whatever we reflect on or converse about, everything still presents us with the view of human happiness or misery and excites in our breast a sympathetic movement of pleasure or uneasiness. In our serious occupations, in our careless amusements, this principle still exerts its active energy.

A man who enters the theater is immediately struck with the view of so great a multitude participating of one common amusement, and experiences, from their very aspect, a superior sensibility or disposition of being affected with every sentiment which he shares with his fellow creatures.

He observes the actors to be animated by the appearance of a full audience and raised to a degree of enthusiasm which they cannot command in any solitary or calm moment.

Every movement of the theater, by a skillful poet, is communicated, as it were, by magic to the spectators, who weep, tremble, resent, rejoice, and are inflamed with all the variety of passions which actuate the several personages of the drama.

Where any event crosses our wishes and interrupts the happiness of the favorite characters, we feel a sensible anxiety and concern. But where their sufferings proceed from the treachery, cruelty, or tyranny of an enemy, our breasts are affected with the liveliest resentment against the author of these calamities.

It is here esteemed contrary to the rules of art to represent anything cool and indifferent. A distant friend, or a confidant, who has no immediate interest in the catastrophe ought, if possible, to be avoided by the poet, as communicating a like indifference to the audience and checking the progress of the passions.

Few species of poetry are more entertaining than *pastoral;* and everyone is sensible that the chief source of its pleasure arises from those images of a gentle and tender tranquillity which it represents in its personages, and of which it communicates a like sentiment to the reader. Sannazarius, who transferred the scene to the seashore, though he presented the most magnificent object in nature, is confessed to have erred in his choice. The idea of toil, labor, and danger suffered by the fisherman is painful, by an unavoidable sympathy which attends every conception of human happiness or misery.

When I was twenty, says a French poet, Ovid was my favorite. Now I am forty, I declare for Horace. We enter, to be sure, more readily into sentiments which resemble those we feel every day; but no passion, when well represented, can be entirely indifferent to us, because there is none of which every man has not within him at least the seeds and first principles. It is the business of poetry to bring every affection near to us by lively imagery and representation, and make it look like truth and reality; a certain proof that, wherever the reality is found, our minds are disposed to be strongly affected by it.

Any recent event or piece of news by which the fate of states, provinces, or many individuals is affected is extremely interesting even to those whose welfare is not immediately engaged. Such intelligence is propagated with celerity, heard with avidity, and inquired into with attention and concern. The interest of society appears, on this occasion, to be in some degree the interest of each individual. The imagination is sure to be affected, though the passions excited may not always be so strong and steady as to have great influence on the conduct and behavior.

The perusal of a history seems a calm entertainment, but would be no entertainment at all did not our hearts beat with correspondent movements to those which are described by the historian.

Thucydides and Guicciardin support with difficulty our attention while the former describes the trivial rencounters of the small cities of Greece and the latter the harmless wars of Pisa. The few persons interested, and the small interest, fill not the imagination and engage not the affections. The deep distress of the numerous Athenian army before Syracuse, the danger which so nearly threatens Venice—these excite compassion; these move terror and anxiety.

The indifferent, uninteresting style of Suetonius, equally with the masterly pencil of Tacitus, may convince us of the cruel depravity of Nero or Tiberius; but what a difference of sentiment! While the former coldly relates the facts, the latter sets before our eyes the venerable figures of a Soranus and a Thrasea, intrepid in their fate and only moved by the melting sorrows of their friends and kindred. What sympathy then touches every human heart! What indignation against the tyrant whose causeless fear or unprovoked malice gave rise to such detestable barbarity!

If we bring these subjects nearer, if we remove all suspicion of fiction and deceit, what powerful concern is excited, and how much superior, in many instances, to the narrow attachments of self-love and private interest! Popular sedition, party seal, a devoted obedience to factious leaders—these are some of the most visible, though less laudable, effects of this social sympathy in human nature.

The frivolousness of the subject, too, we may observe, is not able to detach us entirely from what carries an image of human sentiment and affection.

When a person stutters and pronounces with difficulty, we even sympathize with this trivial uneasiness and suffer for him. And it is a rule in criticism that every combination of syllables or letters which gives pain to the organs of speech in the recital appears also, from a species of sympathy, harsh and disagreeable to the ear. Nay, when we run over a book with our eye, we are sensible of such unharmonious composition, because we still imagine that a person recites it to us and suffers from the pronunciation of these jarring sounds. So delicate is our sympathy!

Easy and unconstrained postures and motions are always beautiful: an air of health and vigor is agreeable; clothes which warm, without burdening the body, which cover, without imprisoning the limbs, are well fashioned. In every judgment of beauty the feelings of the person affected enter into consideration and communicate to the spectator similar touches of pain or pleasure. What wonder, then, if we can pronounce no judgment concerning the character and conduct of men without considering the tendencies of their actions and the happiness or misery which thence arises to society? What association of ideas would ever operate were that principle here totally inactive?[4]

If any man, from a cold insensibility or narrow selfishness of temper, is unaffected with the images of human happiness or misery, he must be equally indifferent to the images of vice and virtue; as, on the other hand, it is always found that a warm concern for the interests of our species is attended with a delicate feeling of all moral distinctions—a strong resentment of injury done to men, a lively approbation of their welfare. In this particular, though great superiority is observable of one man above another, yet none are so entirely indifferent to the interests of their fellow creatures as to perceive no distinctions of moral good and evil, in consequence of the different tendencies of actions and principles. How, indeed, can we suppose it possible in anyone who wears a

[4]In proportion to the station which a man possesses, according to the relations in which he is placed, we always expect from him a greater or less degree of good, and, when disappointed, blame his inutility; and much more do we blame him, if any ill or prejudice arises from his conduct and behavior. When the interests of one country interfere with those of another, we estimate the merits of a statesman by the good or ill which results to his own country from his measures and counsels, without regard to the prejudice which he brings on its enemies and rivals. His fellow citizens are the objects which lie nearest the eye while we determine his character. And as nature has implanted in everyone a superior affection to his own country, we never expect any regard to distant nations where a competition arises. Not to mention that while every man consults the good of his own community, we are sensible that the general interest of mankind is better promoted than by any loose indeterminate views to the good of a species, whence no beneficial action could ever result for want of a duly limited object on which they could exert themselves.

human heart that, if there be subjected to his censure one character or system of conduct which is beneficial, and another which is pernicious to his species or community, he will not so much as give a cool preference to the former or ascribe to it the smallest merit or regard? Let us suppose a person ever so selfish, let private interest have engrossed ever so much his attention, yet in instances where that is not concerned he must unavoidably feel *some* propensity to the good of mankind and make it an object of choice, if everything else be equal. Would any man who is walking alone tread as willingly on another's gouty toes, whom he has no quarrel with, as on the hard flint and pavement? There is here surely a difference in the case. We surely take into consideration the happiness and misery of others in weighing the several motives of action, and incline to the former where no private regards draw us to seek our own promotion or advantage by the injury of our fellow creatures. And if the principles of humanity are capable, in many instances, of influencing our actions, they must, at all times, have *some* authority over our sentiments and give us a general approbation of what is useful to society, and blame of what is dangerous or pernicious. The degrees of these sentiments may be the subject of controversy, but the reality of their existence, one should think, must be admitted in every theory or system.

A creature absolutely malicious and spiteful, were there any such in nature, must be worse than indifferent to the images of vice and virtue. All his sentiments must be inverted, and directly opposite to those which prevail in the human species. Whatever contributes to the good of mankind, as it crosses the constant bent of his wishes and desires, must produce uneasiness and disapprobation; and, on the contrary, whatever is the source of disorder and misery in society must, for the same reason, be regarded with pleasure and complacency. Timon, who, probably from his affected spleen more than any inveterate malice, was denominated the man-hater, embraced Alcibiades with great fondness. *Go on, my boy!* cried he, *acquire the confidence of the people: you will one day, I foresee, be the cause of great calamities to them.* Could we admit the two principles of the Manichaeans [good and evil], it is an infallible consequence that their sentiments of human actions, as well as of everything else, must be totally opposite, and that every instance of justice and humanity, from its necessary tendency, must please the one deity and displease the other. All mankind so far resemble the good principle that where interest or revenge or envy perverts not our disposition, we are always inclined, from our natural philanthropy, to give the preference to the happiness of society and, consequently, to virtue above its opposite. Absolute, unprovoked, disinterested malice has never, perhaps, place in any human breast; or if it had, must there pervert all the sentiments of morals as well as the feelings of humanity. If the cruelty of Nero be allowed entirely voluntary, and not rather the effect of constant fear and resentment, it is evident that Tigellinus, preferably to Seneca or Burrhus, must have possessed his steady and uniform approbation.

A statesman or patriot who serves our own country in our own time has always a more passionate regard paid to him than one whose beneficial influence operated on distant ages or remote nations, where the good resulting from his generous humanity, being less connected with us, seems more obscure and affects us with a less lively sympathy. We may own the merit to be equally great, though our sentiments are not raised to an equal height in both cases. The judgment here corrects the inequalities of our internal emotions and perceptions, in like manner as it preserves us from error in the several variations of images presented to our external senses. The same object, at a double distance, really throws on the eye a picture of but half the bulk, yet we imagine that it appears of the same size in both situations; because we know that, on our approach to it, its image would expand on the eye, and that the difference consists not in the object itself, but in our position with regard to it. And indeed, without such a correction of appearances, both in internal and external sentiment, men could never think or talk steadily on any subject while their fluctuating situations produce a continual variation on objects and throw them into such different and contrary lights and positions.[5]

The more we converse with mankind, and the greater social intercourse we maintain, the more shall we be familiarized to these general preferences and distinctions without which our conversation and discourse could scarcely be rendered intelligible to each other. Every man's interest is peculiar to himself, and the aversions and desires which result from it cannot be supposed to affect others in a like degree. General language, therefore, being formed for general use, must be molded on some more general views and must affix the epithets of praise or blame in conformity to sentiments which arise from the general interests of the community. And if these sentiments, in most men, be not so strong as those which have a reference to private good, yet still they must make some distinction, even in persons the most depraved and selfish, and must attach the notion of good to a beneficent conduct, and of evil to the contrary. Sympathy, we shall allow, is much fainter than our concern for ourselves, and sympathy with persons remote from us much fainter than that with persons near and contiguous; but for this very reason it is necessary for us, in our calm judgments and discourse concerning the characters of men, to neglect all these differences and render our sentiments more public and social. Besides that we ourselves often change our situation in this particular; we every day meet with persons who are in a situation different from us, and who could never converse with us were we to remain constantly in that position and point of view which is peculiar to ourselves. The intercourse of sentiments, therefore, in society and

---

[5]For a like reason, the tendencies of actions and characters, not their real accidental consequences, are alone regarded in our moral determinations or general judgments, though in our real feeling or sentiment we cannot help paying greater regard to one whose station, joined to virtue, renders him really useful to society, than to one who exerts the social virtues only in good intentions and benevolent affections. Separating the character from the fortune by an easy and necessary effort of thought, we pronounce these persons alike, and give them the same general praise. The judgment corrects, or endeavors to correct, the appearance, but is not able entirely to prevail over sentiment.

Why is this peach tree said to be better than that other, but because it produces more or better fruit? And would not the same praise be given it, though snails or vermin had destroyed the peaches before they came to full maturity? In morals, too, is not *the tree known by the fruit?* And cannot we easily distinguish between nature and accident, in the one case as well as in the other?

conversation makes us form some general unalterable standard by which we may approve or disapprove of characters and manners. And though the heart takes not part entirely with those general notions, nor regulates all its love and hatred by the universal, abstract differences of vice and virtue without regard to self or the persons with whom we are more intimately connected, yet have these moral differences a considerable influence; and being sufficient, at least, for discourse, serve all our purposes in company, in the pulpit, in the theater, and in the schools.[6]

Thus, in whatever light we take this subject, the merit ascribed to the social virtues appears still uniform and arises chiefly from that regard which the natural sentiment of benevolence engages us to pay to the interests of mankind and society. If we consider the principles of the human make, such as they appear to daily experience and observation, we must, *a priori,* conclude it impossible for such a creature as man to be totally indifferent to the well or ill-being of his fellow creatures, and not readily, of himself, to pronounce, where nothing gives him any particular bias, that what promotes their happiness is good, what tends to their misery is evil, without any further regard or consideration. Here then are the faint rudiments at least, or outlines, of a *general* distinction between actions, and in proportion as the humanity of the person is supposed to increase, his connection with those who are injured or benefited, and his lively conception of their misery or happiness, his consequent censure or approbation acquires proportionable vigor. There is no necessity that a generous action, barely mentioned in an old history or remote gazette, should communicate any strong feelings of applause and admiration. Virtue, placed at such a distance, is like a fixed star which, though to the eye of reason it may appear as luminous as the sun in his meridian, is so infinitely removed as to affect the senses neither with light nor heat. Bring this virtue nearer, by our acquaintance or connection with the persons, or even by an eloquent recital of the case, our hearts are immediately caught, our sympathy enlivened, and our cool approbation converted into the warmest sentiments of friendship and regard. These seem necessary and infallible consequences of the general principles of human nature, as discovered in common life and practice.

Again, reverse these views and reasonings: consider the matter *a posteriori;* and, weighing the consequences, inquire if the merit of social virtue be not, in a great measure, derived from the feelings of humanity with which it affects the spectators. It appears to be matter of fact that the circumstance of *utility,* in all subjects, is a source of praise and approbation; that it is constantly appealed to in all moral decisions concerning the merit and demerit of actions; that it is the *sole* source of that high regard paid to justice, fidelity, honor, allegiance, and chastity; that it is inseparable from all the other social virtues, humanity,

[6]It is wisely ordained by nature that private connections should commonly prevail over universal views and considerations, otherwise our affections and actions would be dissipated and lost for want of a proper limited object. Thus a small benefit done to ourselves, or our near friends, excites more lively sentiments of love and approbation than a great benefit done to a distant commonwealth; but still we know here, as in all the senses, to correct these inequalities by reflection, and retain a general standard of vice and virtue, founded chiefly on general usefulness.

generosity, charity, affability, lenity, mercy, and moderation; and, in a word, it is a foundation of the chief part of morals which has a reference to mankind and our fellow creatures.

It appears also that in our general approbation of characters and manners the useful tendency of the social virtues moves us not by any regards to self-interest, but has an influence much more universal and extensive. It appears that a tendency to public good and to the promoting of peace, harmony, and order in society does always, by affecting the benevolent principles of our frame, engage us on the side of the social virtues. And it appears, as an additional confirmation, that these principles of humanity and sympathy enter so deeply into all our sentiments and have so powerful an influence as may enable them to excite the strongest censure and applause. The present theory is the simple result of all these inferences, each of which seems founded on uniform experience and observation.

Were it doubtful whether there were any such principle in our nature as humanity or a concern for others, yet when we see, in numberless instances, that whatever has a tendency to promote the interest of society is so highly approved of, we ought thence to learn the force of the benevolent principle, since it is impossible for anything to please as means to an end where the end is totally indifferent. On the other hand, were it doubtful whether there were implanted in our nature any general principle of moral blame and approbation, yet when we see, in numberless instances, the influence of humanity, we ought thence to conclude that it is impossible, but that everything which promotes the interests of society must communicate pleasure, and what is pernicious give uneasiness. But when these different reflections and observations concur in establishing the same conclusion, must they not bestow an undisputed evidence upon it?

It is, however, hoped that the progress of this argument will bring a further confirmation of the present theory, by showing the rise of other sentiments of esteem and regard from the same or like principles.

DISCUSSION

The concept of utility is clearly central to Hume's analysis, and he envisions it as a moral analog to the concept of force in Newton's physics—a singular explanatory concept which will explain a wide variety of diverse phenomena. But Newton's concept of force is precisely defined (in terms of mass and movement); Hume's concept of utility is not. Sometimes, he appeals to utility in the most obvious sense—as "usefulness." Education is useful, for example, in training people to do certain jobs. Sometimes he refers to a broad sense of social function, in which society is more efficient, or more harmonious, or better able to defend itself against enemies. He finally appeals the concept of utility to "self-love" and the satisfaction of individual desires, though the connection with the broader senses of utility is not obvious. (Does the general utility consist of the satisfaction of individual desires, as the later utilitarians argued? If everyone cannot be equally satisfied, what principle determines whose interests should be satisfied and whose should not?) But then Hume also refers to the less obvious utility of beautiful and noble things and the satisfaction of our "more generous motives and regards." The

French novelist Stendhal later said that "beauty is the promise of happiness," but is this true, or even plausible in many cases? We cannot disagree with Hume that a person's sense of humor and sociability are extremely desirable characteristics, but in what sense do they serve utility? Is there a way to define utility as precisely as Newton define force?

Force = Mass × Acceleration

In what sense are such virtues as generosity and mercy useful? How would Hume show that mere utility is not best served by an extremely efficient and orderly totalitarian society (for example, as depicted in George Orwell's *1984* or Aldous Huxley's drug-numbed *Brave New World*)?

Why does utility please us? Because it serves our self-interests, Hume suggests, but also because it serves our general sense of benevolence. But by Hume's own account so far, it would seem that these are quite different and sometimes opposed, and the appeal of utility would seem to depend quite heavily on what kind of utility is in question. The appeal of utility, in other words, would seem to be as varied and imprecise as the concept of utility itself.

3. VIRTUE, APPROVAL, AND SELF-LOVE

The final chapters of the *Inquiry* are detailed discussions of the various virtues. Hume concludes the *Inquiry* by once again emphasizing the importance of personal merit and its relation to utility. In the Appendixes he further analyzes his critical notion of the "moral sentiments" (a view that he shared with many philosophers of his time, most notably Frances Hutcheson before him and later Adam Smith, who wrote his *Theory of the Moral Sentiments* before he began his great economic treatise, *Wealth of Nations*).

Section IX. Conclusion

Part I It may justly appear surprising that any man in so late an age should find it requisite to prove, by elaborate reasoning, that *personal merit* consists altogether in the possession of mental qualities, *useful* or *agreeable* to the *person himself* or to *others*. It might be expected that this principle would have occurred even to the first, rude, unpracticed inquirers concerning morals, and been received from its own evidence without any argument or disputation. Whatever is valuable in any kind, so naturally classes itself under the division of *useful* or *agreeable,* the *utile* or the *dulce,* that it is not easy to imagine why we should ever seek further, or consider the question as a matter of nice research or inquiry. And as everything useful or agreeable must possess these qualities with regard either to the *person himself* or to *others,* the complete delineation or description of merit seems to be performed as naturally as a shadow is cast by the sun, or an image is reflected upon water. If the ground on which the shadow is cast be not broken and uneven, nor the surface from which the image is reflected disturbed and confused, a just figure is immediately presented without any art or attention. And it seems a reasonable presumption that systems and hypotheses have perverted our natural understanding when a theory so simple and obvious could so long have escaped the most elaborate examination. . . .

And as every quality which is useful or agreeable to ourselves or others is, in common life, allowed to be a part of personal merit, so no other will ever be received where men judge of things by their natural, unprejudiced reason, without the delusive glosses of superstition and false religion. Celibacy, fasting, penance, mortification, self-denial, humility, silence, solitude, and the whole train of monkish virtues—for what reason are they everywhere rejected by men of sense but because they serve to no manner of purpose; neither advance a man's fortune in the world, nor render him a more valuable member of society; neither qualify him for the entertainment of company nor increase his power of self-enjoyment? We observe, on the contrary, that they cross all these desirable ends, stupefy the understanding and harden the heart, obscure the fancy and sour the temper. We justly, therefore, transfer them to the opposite column and place them in the catalogue of vices; nor has any superstition force sufficient among men of the world to pervert entirely these natural sentiments. A gloomy, hair-brained enthusiast, after his death, may have a place in the calendar, but will scarcely ever be admitted when alive into intimacy and society, except by those who are as delirious and dismal as himself.

It seems a happiness in the present theory that it enters not into that vulgar dispute concerning the *degrees* of benevolence or self-love which prevail in human nature—a dispute which is never likely to have any issue, both because men who have taken part are not easily convinced, and because the phenomena which can be produced on either side are so dispersed, so uncertain, and subject to so many interpretations that it is scarcely possible accurately to compare them or draw from them any determinate inference or conclusion. It is sufficient for our present purpose, if it be allowed, what surely, without the greatest absurdity, cannot be disputed, that there is some benevolence, however small, infused into our bosom; some spark of friendship for humankind; some particle of the dove kneaded into our frame, along with the elements of the wolf and serpent. Let these generous sentiments be supposed ever so weak, let them be insufficient to move even a hand or finger of our body, they must still direct the determinations of our mind and, where everything else is equal, produce a cool preference of what is useful and serviceable to mankind above what is pernicious and dangerous. A *moral distinction,* therefore, immediately arises; a general sentiment of blame and approbation; a tendency, however faint, to the objects of the one, and a proportionable aversion to those of the other. Nor will those reasoners who so earnestly maintain the predominant selfishness of humankind be anywise scandalized at hearing of the weak sentiments of virtue implanted in our nature. On the contrary, they are found as ready to maintain the one tenet as the other; and their spirit of satire (for such it appears, rather than of corruption) naturally gives rise to both opinions, which have, indeed, a great and almost an indissoluble connection together.

Avarice, ambition, vanity, and all passions vulgarly, though improperly, comprised under the denomination of *self-love* are here excluded from our theory concerning the *origin* of morals, not because they are too weak, but because they have not a proper direction for that purpose. The notion of morals implies some sentiment common to all mankind, which recommends the same object to general approbation and makes every man, or most men, agree in the same opinion or decision concerning it. It also implies some sentiment so universal and comprehensive as to extend to all mankind, and render the actions and conduct, even of the persons the most remote, an object of applause or censure, according as they agree or disagree with that rule of right which is established. These two requisite circumstances belong alone to the sentiment of humanity here insisted on. The other passions produce, in every breast, many strong sentiments of desire and aversion, affection and hatred, but these neither are felt so much in common nor are so comprehensive as to be the foundation of any general system and established theory of blame or approbation.

When a man denominates another his *enemy,* his *rival,* his *antagonist,* his *adversary,* he is understood to speak the language of self-love and to express sentiments peculiar to himself and arising from his particular circumstances and situation. But when he bestows on any man the epithets of *vicious* or *odious* or *depraved,* he then speaks another language and expresses sentiments in which he expects all his audience are to concur with him. He must here, therefore, depart from his private and particular situation and must choose a point of view common to him with others: he must move some universal principle of the human frame and touch a string to which all mankind have an accord and symphony. If he mean, therefore, to express that this man possesses qualities whose tendency is pernicious to society, he has chosen this common point of view and has touched the principle of humanity in which every man, in some degree, concurs. While the human heart is compounded of the same elements as at present, it will never be wholly indifferent to public good, nor entirely unaffected with the tendency of characters and manners. And though this affection of humanity may not generally be esteemed so strong as vanity or ambition, yet being common to all men, it can alone be the foundation of morals or of any general system of blame or praise. One man's ambition is not another's ambition, nor will the same event or object satisfy both; but the humanity of one man is the humanity of everyone; and the same object touches this passion in all human creatures.

But the sentiments which arise from humanity are not only the same in all human creatures and produce the same approbation or censure, but they also comprehend all human creatures; nor is there anyone whose conduct or character is not, by their means, an object, to everyone, of censure or approbation. On the contrary, those other passions, commonly denominated selfish, both produce different sentiments in each individual, according to his particular situation, and also contemplate the greater part of mankind with the utmost indifference and unconcern. Whoever has a high regard and esteem for me flatters my vanity; whoever expresses contempt, mortifies and displeases me. But as my name is known but to a small part of mankind there are few who come within the sphere of this passion, or excite, on its account, either my affection or disgust. But if you represent a tyrannical, insolent, or barbarous behavior, in any country or in any age of the world, I soon carry my eye to the pernicious tendency of such a conduct and feel the sentiment of repugnance and displeasure toward it. No character can be so remote as to be, in this light, wholly indifferent to me. What is beneficial to society or to the person himself must still be preferred. And every quality or action of every human being must by this means be ranked under some class or denomination expressive of general censure or applause.

What more, therefore, can we ask to distinguish the sentiments dependent on humanity from those connected with any other passion, or to satisfy us why the former are the origin of morals, not the latter? Whatever conduct gains my approbation, by touching my humanity, procures also the applause of all mankind by affecting the same principle in them; but what serves my avarice or ambition pleases these passions in me alone and affects not the avarice and ambition of the rest of mankind. There is no circumstance of conduct in any man, provided it have a beneficial tendency, that is not agreeable to my humanity, however remote the person; but every man, so far removed as neither to cross nor serve my avarice and ambition, is regarded as wholly indifferent by those passions. The distinction, therefore, between these species of sentiment being so great and evident, language must soon be molded upon it and must invent a peculiar set of terms in order to express those universal sentiments of censure or approbation which arise from humanity, or from views of general usefulness and its contrary. *Virtue* and *vice* become then known: morals are recognized; certain general ideas are framed of human conduct and behavior; such measures are expected from men in such situations: this action is determined to be conformable to our abstract rule; that other, contrary. And by such universal principles are the particular sentiments of self-love frequently controlled and limited.[7]

Another spring of our constitution that brings a great addition of force to moral sentiment is the love of fame, which rules with such uncontrolled authority in all generous minds, and is often the grand object of all their designs and undertakings. By our continual and earnest pursuit of a character, a name, a reputation in the world, we bring our own deportment and conduct frequently in review and consider how they appear in the eyes of those who approach and

---

[7]It seems certain, both from reason and experience, that a rude, untaught savage regulates chiefly his love and hatred by the ideas of private utility and injury, and has but faint conceptions of a general rule or system of behavior. The man who stands opposite to him in battle he hates heartily, not only for the present moment, which is almost unavoidable, but forever after; nor is he satisfied without the most extreme punishment and vengeance. But we, accustomed to society, and to more enlarged reflections, consider that this man is serving his own country and community; that any man, in the same situation, would do the same; that we ourselves, in like circumstances, observe a like conduct; that, in general, human society is best supported on such maxims. And by these suppositions and views, we correct, in some measure, our ruder and narrower passions. And though much of our friendship and enmity be still regulated by private considerations of benefit and harm, we pay at least this homage to general rules, which we are accustomed to respect, that we commonly pervert our adversary's conduct by imputing malice or injustice to him, in order to give vent to those passions which arise from self-love and private interest. When the heart is full of rage, it never wants pretenses of this nature, though sometimes as frivolous as those from which Horace, being almost crushed by the fall of a tree, affects to accuse of parricide the first planter of it.

regard us. This constant habit of surveying ourselves, as it were in reflection, keeps alive all the sentiments of right and wrong, and begets in noble natures a certain reverence for themselves as well as others, which is the surest guardian of every virtue. The animal conveniences and pleasures sink gradually in their value, while every inward beauty and moral grace is studiously acquired and the mind is accomplished in every perfection which can adorn or embellish a rational creature.

Here is the most perfect morality with which we are acquainted; here is displayed the force of many sympathies. Our moral sentiment is itself a feeling chiefly of that nature and our regard to a character with others seems to arise only from a care of preserving a character with ourselves; and in order to attain this end, we find it necessary to prop our tottering judgment on the correspondent approbation of mankind.

But that we may accommodate matters and remove, if possible, every difficulty, let us allow all these reasonings to be false. Let us allow that, when we resolve the pleasure which arises from views of utility into the sentiments of humanity and sympathy, we have embraced a wrong hypothesis. Let us confess it necessary to find some other explication of that applause which is paid to objects, whether inanimate, animate, or rational, if they have a tendency to promote the welfare and advantage of mankind. However difficult it be to conceive that an object is approved of on account of its tendency to a certain end, while the end itself is totally indifferent, let us swallow this absurdity and consider what are the consequences. The preceding delineation or definition of *personal merit* must still retain its evidence and authority: It must still be allowed that every quality of the mind which is *useful* or *agreeable* to the *person himself* or to *others* communicates a pleasure to the spectator, engages his esteem, and is admitted under the honorable denomination of virtue or merit. Are not justice, fidelity, honor, veracity, allegiance, chastity esteemed solely on account of their tendency to promote the good of society? Is not that tendency inseparable from humanity, benevolence, lenity, generosity, gratitude, moderation, tenderness, friendship, and all the other social virtues? Can it possibly be doubted that industry, discretion, frugality, secrecy, order, perseverance, forethought, judgment, and this whole class of virtues and accomplishments of which many pages would not contain the catalogue—can it be doubted, I say, that the tendency of these qualities to promote the interest and happiness of their possessor is the sole foundation of their merit? Who can dispute that a mind which supports a perpetual serenity and cheerfulness, a noble dignity and undaunted spirit, a tender affection and good will to all around, as it has more enjoyment within itself, is also a more animating and rejoicing spectacle than if dejected with melancholy, tormented with anxiety, irritated with rage, or sunk into the most abject baseness and degeneracy? And as to the qualities immediately *agreeable to others,* they speak sufficiently for themselves; and he must be unhappy indeed, either in his own temper, or in his situation and company, who has never perceived the charms of a facetious wit or flowing affability, of a delicate modesty or decent genteelness of address and manner.

I am sensible that nothing can be more unphilosophical than to be positive or dogmatical on any subject, and that, even if *excessive* skepticism could be maintained, it would not be more destructive to all just reasoning and inquiry. I am convinced that where men are the most sure and arrogant, they are commonly the most mistaken, and have there given reins to passion without that proper deliberation and suspense which can alone secure them from the grossest absurdities. Yet I must confess that this enumeration puts the matter in so strong a light that I cannot, *at present,* be more assured of any truth which I learn from reasoning and argument, than that personal merit consists entirely in the usefulness or agreeableness of qualities to the person himself possessed of them, or to others who have any intercourse with him. But when I reflect that though the bulk and figure of the earth have been measured and delineated, though the motions of the tides have been accounted for, the order and economy of the heavenly bodies subjected to their proper laws, and *infinite* itself reduced to calculation yet men still dispute concerning the foundation of their moral duties—when I reflect on this, I say, I fall back into diffidence and skepticism, and suspect that an hypothesis so obvious, had it been a true one, would long ere now have been received by the unanimous suffrage and consent of mankind.

Part II   Having explained the moral *approbation* attending merit or virtue, there remains nothing but briefly to consider our interested *obligation* to it, and to inquire whether every man who has any regard to his own happiness and welfare will not best find his account in the practice of every moral duty. If this can be clearly ascertained from the foregoing theory, we shall have the satisfaction to reflect that we have advanced principles which not only, it is hoped will stand the test of reasoning and inquiry, but may contribute to the amendment of men's lives and their improvement in morality and social virtue. And though the philosophical truth of any proposition by no means depends on its tendency to promote the interests of society, yet a man has but a bad grace who delivers a theory, however true, which he must confess leads to a practice dangerous and pernicious. Why rake into those corners of nature which spread a nuisance all around? Why dig up the pestilence from the pit in which it is buried? The ingenuity of your researches may be admired, but your systems will be detested, and mankind will agree, if they cannot refute them, to sink them at least in eternal silence and oblivion. Truths which are *pernicious* to society, if any such there be, will yield to errors which are salutary and *advantageous.*

But what philosophical truths can be more advantageous to society than those here delivered, which represent virtue in all her genuine and most engaging charms and make us approach her with ease, familiarity, and affection? The dismal dress falls off, with which many divines and some philosophers have covered her, and nothing appears but gentleness, humanity, beneficence, affability, nay, even at proper intervals, play, frolic, and gaiety. She talks not of useless austerities and rigors, suffering, and self-denial. She declares that her sole purpose is to make her votaries, and all mankind, during every instant of their existence, if possible, cheerful and happy; nor does she ever willingly part with any pleasure but in hopes of ample compensation in some other period of their lives. The sole trouble which she demands is that of just calculation and a steady preference of the greater happiness. And if any austere pretenders approach her, enemies to joy and pleasure, she either rejects them as hypocrites and deceivers, or, if she admit them in her train, they are ranked, however, among the least favored of her votaries.

And, indeed, to drop all figurative expression, what hopes can we ever have of engaging mankind to a practice which we confess full of austerity and rigor? Or what theory of morals can ever serve any useful purpose unless it can show, by a particular detail, that all the duties which it recommends are also the true interest of each individual? The peculiar advantage of the foregoing system seems to be that it furnishes proper mediums for that purpose.

That the virtues which are immediately *useful* or *agreeable* to the person possessed of them are desirable in a view to selfinterest, it would surely be superfluous to prove. Moralists, indeed, may spare themselves all the pains which they often take in recommending these duties. To what purpose collect arguments, to evince that temperance is advantageous and the excesses of pleasure hurtful? When it appears that these excesses are only denominated such because they are hurtful, and that if the unlimited use of strong liquors, for instance, no more impaired health or the faculties of mind and body, than the use of air or water, it would not be a whit more vicious or blamable.

It seems equally superfluous to prove that the *companionable* virtues of good manners and wit, decency and genteelness are more desirable than the contrary qualities. Vanity alone, without any other consideration, is a sufficient motive to make us wish for the possession of these accomplishments. No man was ever willingly deficient in this particular. All our failures here proceed from bad education, want of capacity, or a perverse and unpliable disposition. Would you have your company coveted, admired, followed rather than hated, despised, avoided? Can anyone seriously deliberate in the case? As no enjoyment is sincere without some reference to company and society, so no society can be agreeable, or even tolerable, where a man feels his presence unwelcome and discovers all around him symptoms of disgust and aversion.

But why, in the greater society or confederacy of mankind, should not the case be the same as in particular clubs and companies? Why is it more doubtful that the enlarged virtues of humanity generosity, beneficence are desirable, with a view to happiness and self-interest than the limited endowments of ingenuity and politeness? Are we apprehensive lest those social affections interfere in a greater and more immediate degree than any other pursuits with private utility, and cannot be gratified without some important sacrifice of honor and advantage? If so, we are but ill instructed in the nature of the human passions, and are more influenced by verbal distinctions than by real differences.

Whatever contradiction may vulgarly be supposed between the *selfish* and *social* sentiments or dispositions, they are really no more opposite than selfish and ambitious, selfish and revengeful, selfish and vain. It is requisite that there be an original propensity of some kind, in order to be a basis to self-love, by giving a relish to the objects of its pursuit; and none more fit for this purpose than benevolence or humanity. The goods of fortune are spent in one gratification or another: the miser who accumulates his annual income and lends it out at interest has really spent it in the gratification of his avarice. And it would be difficult to show why a man is more a loser by a generous action than by any other method of expense, since the utmost which he can attain by the most elaborate selfishness is the indulgence of some affection.

Now if life without passion must be altogether insipid and tiresome, let a man suppose that he has full power of modeling his own disposition and let him deliberate what appetite or desire he would choose for the foundation of his happiness and enjoyment. Every affection, he would observe, when gratified by success, gives a satisfaction proportioned to its force and violence; but besides this advantage, common to all, the immediate feeling of benevolence and friendship, humanity and kindness is sweet, smooth, tender, and agreeable, independent of all fortune and accidents. These virtues are, besides, attended with a pleasing consciousness or remembrance and keep us in humor with ourselves as well as others, while we retain the agreeable reflection of having done our part toward mankind and society. And though all men show a jealousy of our success in the pursuits of avarice and ambition, yet are we almost sure of their good will and good wishes so long as we persevere in the paths of virtue and employ ourselves in the execution of generous plans and purposes. What other passion is there where we shall find so many advantages united: an agreeable sentiment a pleasing consciousness, a good reputation? But of these truths, we may observe, men are of themselves pretty much convinced; nor are they deficient in their duty to society because they would not wish to be generous, friendly, and humane, but because they do not feel themselves such.

Treating vice with the greatest candor and making it all possible concessions, we must acknowledge that there is not, in any instance, the smallest pretext for giving it the preference above virtue with a view to self-interest, except, perhaps, in the case of justice where a man, taking things in a certain light, may often seem to be a loser by his integrity. And though it is allowed that, without a regard to property, no society could subsist, yet, according to the imperfect way in which human affairs are conducted, a sensible knave, in particular incidents, may think that an act of iniquity or infedelity will make a considerable addition to his fortune without causing any considerable breach in the social union and confederacy. That *honesty is the best policy* may be a good general rule, but is liable to many exceptions. And he, it may perhaps be thought, conducts himself with most wisdom who observes the general rule and takes advantage of all the exceptions.

I must confess that if a man think that this reasoning much requires an answer, it will be a little difficult to find any which will to him appear satisfactory and convincing. If his heart rebel not against such pernicious maxims, if he feel no reluctance to the thoughts of villany or baseness he has indeed lost a considerable motive to virtue; and we may expect that his practice will be answerable to his speculation. But in all ingenuous natures the antipathy to treachery and roguery is too strong to be counterbalanced by any views of profit or pecuniary advantage. Inward peace of mind, consciousness of integrity, a satisfactory review of our own conduct—these are circumstances very requisite to happiness and will be cherished and cultivated by every honest man who feels the importance of them.

Such a one has, besides, the frequent satisfaction of seeing knaves, with all their pretended cunning and abilities, betrayed by their own maxims; and while they purpose to cheat with moderation and secrecy, a tempting incident occurs—nature is frail—and they give in to the snare, whence they can never extricate themselves without a total loss of reputation and the forfeiture of all future trust and confidence with mankind.

But were they ever so secret and successful, the honest man, if he has any tincture of philosophy, or even common observation and reflection, will discover that they themselves are, in the end, the greatest dupes, and have sacrificed the invaluable enjoyment of a character with themselves at least, for the acquisition of worthless toys and gewgaws. How little is requisite to supply the *necessities* of nature? And in a view to *pleasure,* what comparison between the unbought satisfaction of conversation, society, study, even health and the common beauties of nature, but above all, the peaceful reflection on one's own conduct? What comparison, I say, between these and the feverish, empty amusements of luxury and expense? These natural pleasures, indeed, are really without price, both because they are below all price in their attainment and above it in their enjoyment.

Appendix II. Of Self-Love

There is a principle, supposed to prevail among many, which is utterly incompatible with all virtue or moral sentiment; and as it can proceed from nothing but the most depraved disposition, so in its turn it tends still further to encourage that depravity. This principle is that all *benevolence* is mere hypocrisy, friendship a cheat, public spirit a farce, fidelity a snare to procure trust and confidence; and that, while all of us, at bottom, pursue only our private interest, we wear these fair disguises in order to put others off their guard and expose them the more to our wiles and machinations. What heart one must be possessed of who professes such principles, and who feels no internal sentiment that belies so pernicious a theory, it is easy to imagine; and also, what degree of affection and benevolence he can bear to a species whom he represents under such odious colors and supposes so little susceptible of gratitude or any return of affection. Or, if we should not ascribe these principles wholly to a corrupted heart, we must at least account for them from the most careless and precipitate examination. Superficial reasoners, indeed, observing many false pretenses among mankind, and feeling, perhaps, no very strong restraint in their own disposition, might draw a general and a hasty conclusion that all is equally corrupted, and that men, different from all other animals, and indeed from all other species of existence, admit of no degrees of good or bad, but are, in every instance, the same creatures under different disguises and appearances.

There is another principle somewhat resembling the former, which has been much insisted on by philosophers, and has been the foundation of many a system—that, whatever affection one may feel, or imagine he feels for others, no passion is, or can be, disinterested; that the most generous friendship, however sincere, is a modification of self-love; and that, even unknown to ourselves, we seek only our own gratification while we appear the most deeply engaged in schemes for the liberty and happiness of mankind. By a turn of imagination, by a refinement of reflection, by an enthusiasm of passion, we seem to take part in the interests of others and imagine ourselves divested of all selfish considerations. But, at bottom, the most generous patriot, and most niggardly miser, the bravest hero, and most abject coward have, in every action, an equal regard to their own happiness and welfare.

Whoever concludes from the seeming tendency of this opinion that those who make profession of it cannot possibly feel the true sentiments of benevolence, or have any regard for genuine virtue, will often find himself, in practice, very much mistaken. Probity and honor were no strangers to Epicurus and his sect. Atticus and Horace seem to have enjoyed from nature, and cultivated by reflection, as generous and friendly dispositions as any disciple of the austerer schools; and among the modern, Hobbes and Locke, who maintained the selfish system of morals, lived irreproachable lives, though the former lay not under any restraint of religion which might supply the defects of his philosophy. An Epicurean or a Hobbist readily allows that there is such a thing as friendship in the world without hypocrisy or disguise, though he may attempt, by a philosophical chemistry, to resolve the elements of this passion, if I may so speak, into those of another and explain every affection to be self-love twisted and molded by a particular turn of imagination into a variety of appearances. But as the same turn of imagination prevails not in every man, nor gives the same direction to the original passion, this is sufficient, even according to the selfish system, to make the widest difference in human characters and denominate one man virtuous and humane, another vicious and meanly interested. I esteem the man whose self-love, by whatever means, is so directed as to give him a concern for others and render him serviceable to society, as I hate or despise him who has no regard to anything beyond his own gratifications and enjoyments. In vain would you suggest that these characters, though seemingly opposite, are at bottom the same, and that a very inconsiderable turn of thought forms the whole difference between them. Each character, notwithstanding these inconsiderable differences, appears to me, in practice, pretty durable and untransmutable; and I find not in this more than in other subjects that the natural sentiments, arising from the general appearances of things, are easily destroyed by subtle reflections concerning the minute origin of these appearances. Does not the lively, cheerful color of a countenance inspire me with complacency and pleasure, even though I learn from philosophy that all difference of complexion arises from the most minute differences of thickness in the most minute parts of the skin, by means of which a superficies is qualified to reflect one of the original colors of light, and absorb the others?

But though the question concerning the universal or partial selfishness of man be not so material, as is usually imagined, to morality and practice, it is certainly of consequence in the speculative science of human nature, and is a proper object of curiosity and inquiry. It may not, therefore, be unsuitable, in this place, to bestow a few reflections upon it.[8]

The most obvious objection to the selfish hypothesis is that as it is contrary to common feeling and our most unprejudiced notions, there is required the highest stretch of philosophy to establish so extraordinary a paradox. To the most careless observer there appear to be such dispositions as benevolence and generosity, such affections as love, friendship, compassion, gratitude. These sentiments have their causes, effects, objects, and operations marked by common language and observation, and plainly distinguished from those of the selfish passions. And as this is the obvious appearance of things, it must be admitted till some hypothesis be discovered which, by penetrating deeper into human nature, may prove the former affections to be nothing but modifications of the latter. All attempts of this kind have hitherto proved fruitless, and seem to have proceeded entirely from that love of *simplicity* which has been the source of much false reasoning in philosophy. I shall not here enter into any detail on the present subject. Many able philosophers have shown the insufficiency of these systems; and I shall take for granted what, I believe, the smallest reflection will make evident to every impartial inquirer.

But the nature of the subject furnishes the strongest presumption that no better system will ever, for the future, be invented in order to account for the origin of the benevolent from the selfish affections, and reduce all the various emotions of the human mind to a perfect simplicity. The case is not the same in this species of philosophy as in physics. Many a hypothesis in nature, contrary to first appearances, has been found on more accurate scrutiny solid and satisfactory. Instances of this kind are so frequent that a judicious as well as witty philosopher has ventured to affirm, if there be more than one way in which any phenomenon may be produced, that there is a general presumption for its arising from the causes which are the least obvious and familiar. But the presumption always lies on the other side in all inquiries concerning the origin of our passions and of the internal operations of the human mind. The simplest and most obvious cause which can there be assigned for any phenomenon is probably the true one. When a philosopher, in the explication of his system, is obliged to have recourse to some very intricate and refined reflections, and to suppose them essential to the production of any passion or emotion, we have reason to be

[8]Benevolence naturally divides into two kinds, the *general* and the *particular*. The first is where we have no friendship, or connection, or esteem for the person, but feel only a general sympathy with him, or a compassion for his pains, and a congratulation with his pleasures. The other species of benevolence is founded on an opinion of virtue, on services done us, or on some particular connections. Both these sentiments must be allowed real in human nature; but whether they will resolve into some nice considerations of self-love is a question more curious than important. The former sentiment, to wit, that of general benevolence, or humanity, or sympathy, we shall have occasion frequently to treat of in the course of this inquiry; and I assume it as real from general experience, without any other proof.

extremely on our guard against so fallacious a hypothesis. The affections are not susceptible of any impression from the refinements of reason or imagination; and it is always found that a vigorous exertion of the latter faculties, necessarily from the narrow capacity of the human mind, destroys all activity in the former. Our predominant motive or intention is, indeed, frequently concealed from ourselves when it is mingled and confounded with other motives which the mind, from vanity or self-conceit, is desirous of supposing more prevalent. But there is no instance that a concealment of this nature has ever arisen from the abstruseness and intricacy of the motive. A man that has lost a friend and patron may flatter himself that all his grief arises from generous sentiments, without any mixture of narrow or interested considerations; but a man that grieves for a valuable friend who needed his patronage and protection—how can we suppose that his passionate tenderness arises from some metaphysical regards to a self-interest which has no foundation or reality? We may as well imagine that minute wheels and springs, like those of a watch, give motion to a loaded wagon, as account for the origin of passion from such abstruse reflections.

Animals are found susceptible of kindness, both to their own species and to ours; nor is there, in this case, the least suspicion of disguise or artifice. Shall we account for all *their* sentiments, too, from refined deductions of self-interest? Or if we admit a disinterested benevolence in the inferior species, by what rule of analogy can we refuse it in the superior?

Love between the sexes begets a complacency and good will very distinct from the gratification of an appetite. Tenderness to their offspring in all sensible beings, is commonly able alone to counterbalance the strongest motives of self-love, and has no manner of dependence on that affection. What interest can a fond mother have in view who loses her health by assiduous attendance on her sick child, and afterwards languishes and dies of grief when freed, by its death, from the slavery of that attendance?

Is gratitude no affection of the human breast, or is that a word merely without any meaning or reality? Have we no satisfaction in one man's company above another's, and no desire of the welfare of our friend even though absence or death should prevent us from all participation in it? Or what is it commonly that gives us any participation in it, even while alive and present, but our affection and regard to him?

These and a thousand other instances are marks of a general benevolence in human nature, where no *real* interest binds us to the object. And how an *imaginary* interest, known and avowed for such, can be the origin of any passion or emotion seems difficult to explain. No satisfactory hypothesis of this kind has yet been discovered, nor is there the smallest probability that the future industry of men will ever be attended with more favorable success.

But further, if we consider rightly of the matter, we shall find that the hypothesis which allows of a disinterested benevolence, distinct from self-love, has really more *simplicity* in it and is more conformable to the analogy of nature than that which pretends to resolve all friendship and humanity into this latter principle. There are bodily wants or appetites acknowledged by everyone, which

necessarily precede all sensual enjoyment and carry us directly to seek possession of the object. Thus hunger and thirst have eating and drinking for their end;
and from the gratification of these primary appetites arises a pleasure which may
become the object of another species of desire or inclination that is secondary
and interested. In the same manner, there are mental passions by which we are
impelled immediately to seek particular objects, such as fame, or power, or
vengeance, without any regard to interest; and when these objects are attained,
a pleasing enjoyment ensues as the consequence of our indulged affections.
Nature must, by the internal frame and constitution of the mind, give an original
propensity to fame ere we can reap any pleasure from that acquisition or pursue
it from motives of self-love and a desire of happiness. If I have no vanity, I take
no delight in praise; if I be void of ambition, power gives me no enjoyment; if I
be not angry, the punishment of an adversary is totally indifferent to me. In all
these cases there is a passion which points immediately to the object and
constitutes it our good or happiness, as there are other secondary passions which
afterwards arise and pursue it as a part of our happiness when once it is
constituted such by our original affections. Were there no appetite of any kind
antecedent to self-love, that propensity could scarcely ever exert itself, because
we should, in that case, have felt few and slender pains or pleasures, and have
little misery or happiness to avoid or to pursue.

Now, where is the difficulty in conceiving that this may likewise be the case
with benevolence and friendship, and that, from the original frame of our
temper, we may feel a desire of another's happiness or good, which, by means of
that affection, becomes our own good and is afterwards pursued from the
combined motives of benevolence and self-enjoyment? Who sees not that
vengeance, from the force alone of passion, may be so eagerly pursued as to
make us knowingly neglect every consideration of ease, interest, or safety, and,
like some vindictive animals, infuse our very souls into the wounds we give an
enemy? And what a malignant philosophy must it be that will not allow to
humanity and friendship the same privileges which are indisputably granted to
the darker passions of enmity and resentment? Such a philosophy is more like a
satire than a true delineation or description of human nature, and may be a good
foundation for paradoxical wit and raillery, but is a very bad one for any serious
argument or reasoning.

DISCUSSION

Throughout the *Inquiry,* benevolence is juxtaposed with self-love, and, in the conclusion,
Hume explicitly plays them against one another, concerned to show that there is at least
"some benevolence, however small, infused into our bosom." But this contrast threatens
the intended unity of Hume's moral philosophy, and he therefore takes considerable
pains to minimize the conflict. He does this through a rather extensive discussion of
self-love, which permeates the whole of the *Inquiry,* but finally becomes the focus of
attention only in the conclusion and a special appendix. At the same time, Hume is
concerned to further explain his conception of the moral sentiments, such as benevo-

lence, in order to show that these are not to be construed as *against* our self-interest but rather in agreement with it.

It is worth making one short comment on Hume's list of virtues (in the omitted Sections VI to VIII). Hume makes it quite clear that those qualities "useful and agreeable to ourselves" are virtually identical to those qualities "useful and agreeable to others;" thus having a sense of humor, being honest and generous, being courteous and reasonable are all advantageous to the person who has such qualities and to those around him or her. But along with this list of virtues Hume also gives us a list of *false* virtues—the cardinal virtues of Christianity. He lists, for instance, celibacy, penance, self-denial, and humility (which receives extended treatment in Book II of the *Treatise*). These "monkish virtues" are "everywhere rejected by men of sense" because "they serve no manner or purpose." Hume excludes from his account of the qualities of self-love the "vulgar" passions of avarice, ambition, and vanity, precisely because they are not "common to all mankind" and agreeable to everyone. In other words, the mutual agreeableness of the virtues to ourselves and others functions as something of a critierion for Hume. A virtue is not a virtue unless it is useful or agreeable both to the person who has that virtue and to others. Thus self-love becomes more and more a sense of feeling good about oneself in society rather than the satisfaction of selfish interests and the moral sentiments and social virtues become more and more the qualities which most satisfy our self-interest.

As self-love is made more sociable, the moral sentiments are defended too. Hume rejects that "depraved" view that "all benevolence is mere hypocrisy, friendship a cheat, public spirit a farce, fidelity a snare to procure trust and confidence." If the distinction between our own interests and the interests of others becomes exaggerated, then there is always the danger that—because in fact our motives are typically an amalgam of both—a cynic can plausibly argue that even our most generous and altruistic actions are in fact motivated by self-interest, and thus (in terms of their altruistic facade) hypocritical and fraudulent. But benevolence is real, Hume argues, precisely because it is not so sharply opposed to our self-love. Indeed, it is our benevolence that provides us with one of the most important sources of our self-love. Self-love is not that greedy selfishness that has always been condemned by moralists; it is rather feeling good about oneself for the qualities one has and the sentiments one feels. And it is the limits of self-love, not in humility or self-denial but simply in indifference, that makes benevolence so readily understandable. Few people may be wholly satisfied with what they have, but few people are out for themselves in the unbridled way suggested by some cynical philosophers. The proponents of selfishness (egoism) are not only advancing a dubious theory of human motivation, they are also seriously misperceiving the simple facts of human behavior.

How does reason fit into all of this? In the *Treatise*, Hume is largely concerned with emphasizing reason's impotence; here in the *Inquiry* he corrects that antagonism by pointing out how important reason is, for example, in fixing the laws of justice. Accurate reason and good judgment (Plato and Aristotle's *phronesis*) thus become virtues in their own right. He continues to reject the idea that reason is the "sole source of morals," but he no longer excludes it from the center of the moral stage.

STUDY QUESTIONS

1 What is "moral skepticism"? In what ways is Hume a moral skeptic? In what ways is he not?

2 Hume claims (in the *Treatise*) that reason is "impotent"? Does he really deny reason any place in ethics? What does he mean when he says (also in the *Treatise*) that "reason is, and ought to be, the slave of the passions"?

3 Does it matter that Hume is an atheist—as far as his moral philosophy is concerned? Does he believe, as Dostoevsky wrote in the following century, "If there is no God, then everything is permitted"?

4 Why does Hume insist that "sentiment" is the basis of morality? What problems can you see with basing morals on sentiment?

5 What does it mean to say that "you can't derive an 'ought' from an 'is' "? Can you? Why or why not?

6 The basis of Hume's ethics is the sense of "fellow-feeling" and our need to get along well with one another. How does this differ and how is it similar to Aristotle? To Hobbes?

7 What does Hume mean by his "experimental method"? What kind of ethical inquiry is he thereby rejecting?

8 What does Hume mean by "utility"? Why is utility desirable? ("Why utility pleases.")

9 What is the connection between utility and fellow-feeling, for Hume? Which concept is the more fundamental?

10 Is Hume a utilitarian? In what ways? In what ways not? (See Chapter VII, John Stuart Mill, *Utilitarianism*.)

11 Hume often said that his intellectual model was Isaac Newton. In what ways is his moral philosophy similar to Newton's philosophy of physics?

12 What is Hume's vision of "human nature"? Do you agree with it? How would Hume explain the existence of wickedness and evil? What would he urge us to do about it?

13 What is the link between utility and benevolence? Is benevolence based on utility, or is utility based on benevolence? What considerations does Hume offer for each?

14 Is justice based on utility? Why does Hume think that the sole foundation of justice is utility? What problems do you see in this?

15 Is society based on a "social contract" according to Hume? Was there such a thing as justice before the formation of a legal (law-governed) society?

16 Is it irrational for me to prefer the destruction of the whole world to the scratching of my little finger? Why or why not?

17 If people in another society feel differently about an activity that we find repulsive (for example, cannibalism or human sacrifice), is it *right for them*? What does this mean?

18 What are the "moral" sentiments? Are all emotions moral sentiments? What distinguishes those which are from those which are not?

19 What is "self-love"? Is it the same as selfishness? What is Hume saying when he insists that all actions—including what we would call "altruistic" actions—are based first of all on self-love?

CHAPTER 6

IMMANUEL KANT

Immanuel Kant is considered by many philosophers to be the greatest thinker since Plato and Aristotle. He stands at the beginning of virtually every modern movement in philosophy both in America and in Europe, and his ethical theories are still the basis for much of the debate in contemporary moral philosophy. The heart of Kant's ethics is his emphasis on the importance of *reason* and the unqualified *rational* nature of moral principles. Morality is not to be confused with self-interest—no matter how "enlightened" —and the dictates of reason are not to be conflated with the pangs of Humean "sentiment" or with mere utility. The meaning of morality is *duty,* and duty for the sake of duty. It is a strict, hard-headed, and uncompromising view of morality, but Kant's ambition was to set morality on a rational basis and establish a single set of moral principles "for all rational beings," once and for all. ("Oh Duty,/ why hast thou not the visage/ of a sweetie or a cutie," wrote the popular American poet Ogden Nash.)

Kant's philosophical work and reputation are based upon three voluminous critiques (*The Critique of Pure Reason, The Critique of Practical Reason,* and *The Critique of Judgment*), all written in the last two decades of the eighteenth century. It is the second critique, *The Critique of Practical Reason,* which contains his ethics (although this presumes the theory of knowledge in the first book and anticipates the teleological view of the third). But before he published the second critique itself, Kant wrote a brief, more clearly written pamphlet on ethics—which serves as an introduction to the *Critique*— entitled *The Groundwork of the Metaphysics of Morals.* It is this shorter work which we have included here; in its essential features it is the same as the much larger volume.

Kant once described the critical moment in his own philosophical education as a debt to Hume, "who awakened me from my philosophical slumbers." It was Hume's doubts about the justifiability of both knowledge and morality that prompted Kant onto the path that resulted in the three critiques, and the first two volumes are in part a refutation of Hume's doubts, first with regard to knowledge, then with regard to morality. Hume's doubts about knowledge (his *skepticism*) were drawn from the question whether we that morality is also *autonomous*—that is, presupposes the ability of every rational being to ascertain for him- or herself the rightness or wrongness of a principle or an action. Morality is made up of rational principles that are arrived at through practical reason.

Since morality is a matter of reason, the "moral worth" of a person's behavior cannot depend on the contingencies of fate that dictate the success or failure of an action or, for that matter, on the fortune or misfortune of birth, talent, social status, and abilities. Thus Kant could not be more opposed to Plato and Aristotle in this, for they believed that "the good man" included a very definite set of restrictions in terms of sex, birth, citizenship, health, and good fortune of all kinds. If I try to save a baby from drowning, according to Kant, but I am tripped on the wharf by a clumsy sailor and drown the baby by accident, the consequences of my act may have been disastrous but, nonetheless, I behaved in a moral way. Contrary to the utilitarians, Kant argues that it is never the consequences of an action that determine its "moral worth" but always the intentions and principles ("the maxim") which lie behind it. Thus Kant begins,

> Nothing can be conceived in the world, or even out of it, which can be called good without qualification, except a *good will.*

He thus dismisses out of hand all of those features which the Greeks called happiness and turns instead to the characterization of the rational will as the basis of ethical theory.

Kant's ethics, as you can easily tell from his three metaphysical postulates, is essentially a formalization of Christian ethics, but with a number of startling variations. First and foremost, notice in the above quotation that Kant includes the curious phrase, "or even out of it." Elsewhere he speaks of "any rational creature." What he has in mind is the *primacy* of morality, that is, the rational justifiability of morality independent of God or divine commandments. Traditional Judeo-Christian morality presented morality as the commandments of God and that was their justification (as well as their ultimate sanction). But Kant is arguing the other way around—that God is moral and gave us moral commandments *because he is rational.* Kant never hesitates in his piety, but this reversal of God and morality will have momentous consequences in the future of moral thinking.

Other aspects of Kant's ethics display dramatically the central features of the Judeo-Christian tradition, however. His rejection of all "external" factors in determining moral worth and—ultimately—happiness is essential to the biblical emphasis on the goodness of one's soul as opposed to the gifts and punishments of fortune. His insistence on the autonomy and equality of every individual, while not in accordance with some traditional church teachings, is certainly in line with the Lutheran Pietism Kant learned at his mother's knee, and, of course, the final appeal to divine judgment and Heaven and Hell marks Kant's ethics as prototypically Christian—as opposed to Aristotle's paganism or Hume's enlightenment emphasis on the purely secular. And yet, Kant too defends a conception of morality which is wholly self-contained and not dependent on God or gods or, in one sense, on anything outside of the human will. Indeed, that is the ultimate challenge for Kant's philosophy—whether a theory so restricted and pure can capture the rich complexity of our daily moral life.

IMMANUEL KANT

Immanuel Kant was a Prussian, and a pious Lutheran, who lived through most of the eighteenth century (1724–1804). He was a lifelong bachelor who was reputedly so

could ever prove that our "ideas" corresponded to reality; Kant's elaborate res
developed the "revolutionary" view that we could know that we know reality pro
because we "constitute" reality through the concepts of our understanding. In
Hume had doubted that reason could ever justify morality, for morality was based
passions and "reason is, and ought to be, the slave of the passions." Kant's reply,
we shall study here, is that Hume misunderstood the nature of morality, that mor
based on reason, not passion, and the correctness of our moral principles is i
provable by reason.

What is wrong with a view of morality based on passion or sentiments? Hume h
had pointed out that such a view not only precludes the proper justification of mc
but it also leaves open the possibility that people with very different sentiments
have very different morals, equally correct. It was this relativist view that Kant
unthinkable. Killing is wrong, and it is wrong everywhere; it does not matter if
perverse people somewhere enjoy killing and mutually approve of it. Lying is wron
just as a matter of social consensus or feeling but because the suggestion that ly
permissible is itself *incomprehensible*. Kant's ethical theory, therefore, is aimed f
all at providing a rational basis for morality which will be correct for all people at all
and in all circumstances.

Second, however, Kant wanted to provide a general criterion for moral principl
test which could be used to determine which principles were indeed morally correct
at the same time, prove rationally that they were correct. It is to this end that he deve
his theory of *the categorical imperative,* not only to stress the unconditional natu
moral principles, but also to establish a way of proving them as well. Finally, Kant
wants to establish the *presuppositions* of morality—those conditions without which t
could be no morality and which themselves *must* be believed in the moral life. Kant
such presuppositions "the postulates of practical reason" and summarizes them witl
triad, "God, Freedom and Immortality." That is, the three beliefs which are necessar
the moral life are

1 That there is a God, who is all-powerful, all-knowing, and just, who is the judg
our actions and our virtue
2 That our actions are free and we are responsible for what we do
3 That the soul is immortal, that there is an afterlife with a Heaven and a Hell
divine rewards and punishments for those who are good and evil respectively

Since these three beliefs are also the substance of what Kant calls "metaphysics,"
short treatise on ethics which sets up the foundation for them is called "the groundw
of the metaphysics of morals."

The three parts of the pamphlet correspond to Kant's three ambitions.

• To establish morality on a universal, rational basis
• To provide the categorical imperative as a test for moral principles
• To set the basis for a proof of the three metaphysical principles, "God, Freedo
and Immortality."

In Kant's ethics, morality consists of the dictates of practical reason. This means th
morality does not depend on particular circumstances or the facts of a situation, and
means that morality does not depend on the customs of a particular society or t
feelings engendered in its members. Kant's theory is what we have called a *deontolog
cal* theory, and so its central concept is that of *duty*. And yet, it is crucial to Kant's ethi

regular in his habits that his neighbors set their clocks by his daily three o'clock walks. He lived his entire life in the east Prussian port city of Königsberg, but the city was sufficiently cosmopolitan that Kant could claim, late in his life, that he had seen "every type of humanity" at one time or another. And yet, from his safe distance, he was enthusiastic about the French Revolution, and he was no less of a revolutionary himself in the realm of the intellect. (The German poet Heine compared him to Robespierre.) He published the first volume of his monumental philosophical system, *The Critique of Pure Reason,* in 1781, followed by *The Critique of Practical Reason* in 1788 and *The Critique of Judgment* in 1790. *The Groundwork of the Metaphysics of Morals* was published in 1785. By the time he died, nearly 80 years old, he had set the tone of German philosophy for a century or more to come.

A. Empirical and A Priori Ethics

In the short preface to the *Groundwork,* Kant distinguishes two parts to ethics, based on a central distinction from his work in the theory of knowledge. The distinction, which will also be important for his ethics, is between

1 Empirical—based on experience
2 And a priori—literally "before" experience; a priori principles are those which provide the framework within which all experience is to be understood

In ethics, the distinction between the two parts is thus,

1 Empirical, which has to do with the details of our practical life, the circumstances in which we find ourselves and the skills we develop to cope with them. Kant suggests that the empirical part of ethics might be called "practical anthropology."
2 The a priori, which has to do with the strictly *rational* part of ethics, that is, the principles provided by practical reason which form the framework for all of our practical behavior. Kant calls this a priori part of ethics *morality.*

Kant adds that the two parts of ethics are almost always mixed together, but, nevertheless, it is possible and important to construct a "pure moral philosophy, perfectly cleared of everything which is only empirical and which belongs to anthropology." This philosophy will be based on the everyday concept of duty and moral laws. Thus the commandment, "Thou shalt not steal," like the rule, "don't lie," is a priori insofar as it is the basis of obligations which we do not find in situations but rather bring to them (thus "before" experience or "a priori"). Only such principles can properly be called *moral laws.*

Morality, Kant then continues, is action in obedience to moral principles. But, because morality is a priori, it is not enough that an action should happen to conform to the law (for example, when a person doesn't cheat because he or she didn't know how or forgot to do it). The action must be done for the sake of the law; in other words, one must have the moral principle in some sense "in mind" as the basis for action. The other motives which go into every action (and Kant never denies their influence) are not part of morality or moral philosophy. So far as the a priori part of ethics is concerned, Kant is analyzing a "pure rational will," though, of course, none of us has such a pure will.

The *Groundwork* is the "popular" introduction to this conception of moral philosophy, but it is also the search for a practical test, "the supreme principle of morality," which is the singular key to every moral decision.

PREFACE

Ancient Greek philosophy was divided into three sciences: Physics, Ethics, and Logic. This division is perfectly suitable to the nature of the thing; and the only improvement that can be made in it is to add the principle on which it is based, so that we may both satisfy ourselves of its completeness, and also be able to determine correctly the necessary subdivisions.

All rational knowledge is either *material* or *formal:* the former considers some object, the latter is concerned only with the form of the understanding and of the reason itself, and with the universal laws of thought in general without distinction of its objects. Formal philosophy is called Logic. Material philosophy, however, which has to do with determinate objects and the laws to which they are subject, is again two-fold; for these laws are either laws of *nature* or of *freedom.* The science of the former is Physics, that of the latter, Ethics; they are also called *natural philosophy* and *moral philosophy* respectively.

Logic cannot have any empirical part; that is, a part in which the universal and necessary laws of thought should rest on grounds taken from experience; otherwise it would not be logic, *i.e.* a canon for the understanding or the reason, valid for all thought, and capable of demonstration. Natural and moral philosophy, on the contrary, can each have their empirical part, since the former has to determine the laws of nature as an object of experience; the latter the laws of the human will, so far as it is affected by nature: the former, however, being laws according to which everything does happen; the latter, laws according to which everything ought to happen. Ethics, however, must also consider the conditions under which what ought to happen frequently does not.

We may call all philosophy *empirical,* so far as it is based on grounds of experience: on the other hand, that which delivers its doctrines from *à priori* principles alone we may call *pure* philosophy. When the latter is merely formal, it is *logic;* if it is restricted to definite objects of the understanding, it is *metaphysic.*

In this way there arises the idea of a twofold metaphysic—a *metaphysic of nature* and a *metaphysic of morals.* Physics will thus have an empirical and also a rational part. It is the same with Ethics; but here the empirical part might have the special name of *practical anthropology,* the name *morality* being appropriated to the rational part.

All trades, arts, and handiworks have gained by division of labour, namely, when, instead of one man doing everything, each confines himself to a certain kind of work distinct from others in the treatment it requires, so as to be able to perform it with greater facility and in the greatest perfection. Where the

From *Kant's Critique of Practical Reason and Other Works on the Theory of Ethics,* translated by Thomas Kingsmill Abbott, (1873).

different kinds of work are not so distinguished and divided, where everyone is a jack-of-all-trades, there manufactures remain still in the greatest barbarism. It might deserve to be considered whether pure philosophy in all its parts does not require a man specially devoted to it, and whether it would not be better for the whole business of science if those who, to please the tastes of the public, are wont to blend the rational and empirical elements together, mixed in all sorts of proportions unknown to themselves, and who call themselves independent thinkers, giving the name of minute philosophers to those who apply themselves to the rational part only—if these, I say, were warned not to carry on two employments together which differ widely in the treatment they demand, for each of which perhaps a special talent is required, and the combination of which in one person only produces bunglers. But I only ask here whether the nature of science does not require that we should always carefully separate the empirical from the rational part, and prefix to Physics proper (or empirical physics) a metaphysic of nature, and to practical anthropology a metaphysic of morals, which must be carefully cleared of everything empirical, so that we may know how much can be accomplished by pure reason in both cases, and from what sources it draws this its *à priori* teaching, and that whether the latter inquiry is conducted by all moralists (whose name is legion), or only by some who feel a calling thereto.

As my concern here is with moral philosophy, I limit the question suggested to this: Whether it is not of the utmost necessity to construct a pure moral philosophy, perfectly cleared of everything which is only empirical, and which belongs to anthropology? For that such a philosophy must be possible is evident from the common idea of duty and of the moral laws. Everyone must admit that if a law is to have moral force, *i.e.* to be the basis of an obligation, it must carry with it absolute necessity; that, for example, the precept, "Thou shalt not lie," is not valid for men alone, as if other rational beings had no need to observe it; and so with all the other moral laws properly so called; that, therefore, the basis of obligation must not be sought in the nature of man, or in the circumstances in the world in which he is placed, but *à priori* simply in the conceptions of pure reason; and although any other precept which is founded on principles of mere experience may be in certain respects universal, yet in as far as it rests even in the least degree on an empirical basis, perhaps only as to a motive, such a precept, while it may be a practical rule, can never be called a moral law.

Thus not only are moral laws with their principles essentially distinguished from every other kind of practical knowledge in which there is anything empirical, but all moral philosophy rests wholly on its pure part. When applied to man, it does not borrow the least thing from the knowledge of man himself (anthropology), but gives laws *à priori* to him as a rational being. No doubt these laws require a judgment sharpened by experience, in order on the one hand to distinguish in what cases they are applicable, and on the other to procure for them access to the will of the man, and effectual influence on conduct; since man is acted on by so many inclinations that, though capable of the idea of a practical pure reason, he is not so easily able to make it effective *in concreto* in his life.

A metaphysic of morals is therefore indispensably necessary, not merely for speculative reasons, in order to investigate the sources of the practical principles which are to be found *à priori* in our reason, but also because morals themselves are liable to all sorts of corruption, as long as we are without that clue and supreme canon by which to estimate them correctly. For in order that an action should be morally good, it is not enough that it *conform* to the moral law, but it must also be done *for the sake of the law,* otherwise that conformity is only very contingent and uncertain; since a principle which is not moral, although it may now and then produce actions conformable to the law, will also often produce actions which contradict it. Now it is only in a pure philosophy that we can look for the moral law in its purity and genuineness (and, in a practical matter, this is of the utmost consequence): we must, therefore, begin with pure philosophy (metaphysic), and without it there cannot be any moral philosophy at all. That which mingles these pure principles with the empirical does not deserve the name of philosophy (for what distinguishes philosophy from common rational knowledge is, that it treats in separate sciences what the latter only comprehends confusedly); much less does it deserve that of moral philosophy, since by this confusion it even spoils the purity of morals themselves, and counteracts its own end.

Let it not be thought, however, that what is here demanded is already extant in the propaedeutic prefixed by the celebrated Wolf to his moral philosophy, namely, his so-called *general practical philosophy,* and that, therefore, we have not to strike into an entirely new field. Just because it was to be a general practical philosophy, it has not taken into consideration a will of any particular kind—say one which should be determined solely from *à priori* principles without any empirical motives, and which we might call a pure will, but volition in general, with all the actions and conditions which belong to it in this general signification. By this it is distinguished from a metaphysic of morals, just as general logic, which treats of the acts and canons of thought *in general,* is distinguished from transcendental philosophy, which treats of the particular acts and canons of *pure* thought, *i.e.* that whose cognitions are altogether *à priori.* For the metaphysic of morals has to examine the idea and the principles of a possible *pure* will, and not the acts and conditions of human volition generally, which for the most part are drawn from psychology. It is true that moral laws and duty are spoken of in the general practical philosophy (contrary indeed to all fitness). But this is no objection, for in this respect also the authors of that science remain true to their idea of it; they do not distinguish the motives which are prescribed as such by reason alone altogether *à priori,* and which are properly moral, from the empirical motives which the understanding raises to general conceptions merely by comparison of experiences; but without noticing the difference of their sources, and looking on them all as homogeneous, they consider only their greater or less amount. It is in this way they frame their notion of *obligation,* which, though anything but moral, is all that can be asked for in a philosophy which passes no judgment at all on the origin of all possible practical concepts, whether they are *à priori,* or only *à posteriori.*

Intending to publish hereafter a metaphysic of morals, I issue in the first instance these fundamental principles. Indeed there is properly no other foundation for it than the *critical examination of a pure practical reason;* just as that of metaphysics is the critical examination of the pure speculative reason, already published. But in the first place the former is not so absolutely necessary as the latter, because in moral concerns human reason can easily be brought to a high degree of correctness and completeness, even in the commonest understanding, while on the contrary in its theoretic but pure use it is wholly dialectical; and in the second place if the critique of a pure practical reason is to be complete, it must be possible at the same time to show its identity with the speculative reason in a common principle, for it can ultimately be only one and the same reason which has to be distinguished merely in its application. I could not, however, bring it to such completeness here, without introducing considerations of a wholly different kind, which would be perplexing to the reader. On this account I have adopted the title of *Fundamental Principles of the Metaphysic of Morals* instead of that of a *Critical Examination of the pure practical reason.*

But in the third place, since a metaphysic of morals, in spite of the discouraging title, is yet capable of being presented in a popular form, and one adapted to the common understanding, I find it useful to separate from it this preliminary treatise on its fundamental principles, in order that I may not hereafter have need to introduce these necessarily subtle discussions into a book of a more simple character.

The present treatise is, however, nothing more than the investigation and establishment of *the supreme principle of morality,* and this alone constitutes a study complete in itself, and one which ought to be kept apart from every other moral investigation. No doubt my conclusions on this weighty question, which has hitherto been very unsatisfactorily examined, would receive much light from the application of the same principle to the whole system, and would be greatly confirmed by the adequacy which it exhibits throughout; but I must forego this advantage; which indeed would be after all more gratifying than useful, since the easy applicability of a principle and its apparent adequacy give no very certain proof of its soundness, but rather inspire a certain partiality, which prevents us from examining and estimating it strictly in itself, and without regard to consequences.

I have adopted in this work the method which I think most suitable, proceeding analytically from common knowledge to the determination of its ultimate principle, and again descending synthetically from the examination of this principle and its sources to the common knowledge in which we find it employed. The division will, therefore, be as follows:

1 *First section.*—Transition from the common rational knowledge of morality to the philosophical.

2 *Second section.*—Transition from popular moral philosophy to the metaphysic of morals.

3 *Third section.*—Final step from the metaphysic of morals to the critique of the pure practical reason.

DISCUSSION

In his preface, Kant admits that while the distinction between a priori and empirical elements is essential to ethics, the distinction is virtually impossible to make out in practice. Furthermore, from a more personal viewpoint, we would consider overly harsh this separation of moral (a priori principled) considerations from immediate questions of consequences and interpersonal relationships. The very idea of deciding what one ought to do in the absence of any particular circumstances, personal feelings, or local customs or rules seems to us impossible, or at least peculiar. Why, then, does Kant so insist on it?

The answer has two parts, one of them, appropriately, abstract and philosophical— though not a priori—the other strictly historical and cultural. The philosophical answer is that our concept of morality—as Kant himself points out—is an idealistic and "pure" concept which, it may be admitted, few if any of us ever achieve, though most of us make some effort to do so, at least some of the time. The analysis of the ideal is therefore necessarily distinct from the empirical details of our actual behavior, for, as Kant also points out, one can never get a clear picture of an ideal by trying to abstract from the confusion of actual examples. One must have a clear picture of the concept itself, and, in this instance, the concept of morality is the subject for analysis. The question is not whether anyone has ever been perfectly moral, anymore than, in physics, the question is whether there actually is an "ideal gas" or whether a person could travel at the speed of light. Nevertheless, our abstract understanding of an ideal can make an enormous difference to our actual behavior.

The historical-cultural explanation of Kant's hard-headed conception of morality takes us back to that period we keep referring to as the Enlightenment (or, in Germany, the *Aufklärung*). This powerful movement preoccupied European intellectual and cultural life during most of the seventeenth and eighteenth centuries. Its foremost concept—and weapon—was *criticism* (thus Kant's three great books were all called "critiques"). The Enlightenment was to a large extent the expression of a newly prospering and increasingly powerful middle class (between the royalty and the aristocracy on top, and the peasants and workers on the bottom). The members of the middle class were for the most part professionals—lawyers, doctors, teachers, clerks, bankers, businesspeople— and they held jobs in which they generally served the public (which meant, vaguely, society in general). Thus they came to think of themselves as "the universal class" (an expression later picked up by Hegel and then Marx, who called the working class "the universal class"). The speakers for the Enlightenment—in part because they were professionals and critical of the inefficiency and inequity of the older regimes—made every attempt to break down class and national barriers to better government and better business, attacking every belief that seemed to them to be an inefficient relic of the past as "superstition" and rejecting everything provincial in favor of what was universal or "cosmopolitan" (literally, of the universal city). With this in mind, we can easily understand that Kant—who was one of the foremost spokesmen of the Enlightenment in Germany—was trying to capture in his ethics just that universal sense that the Enlightenment was promoting. His attempt to bypass everything circumstantial and get to the heart of morality for all of humanity was part and parcel of the Enlightenment program, and we might add, very much in tune with Kant's French enlightenment predecessor and intellectual hero—Jean-Jacques Rousseau. Several years before, Rousseau had stunned Europe with his intriguing theory of an "inherent natural goodness" in everyone, which modern society had "corrupted." It was Rousseau who invoked the image of "the noble savage," and, although Kant would not follow him quite that far, he too sought that "inner goodness" in all people, not in the realm of sentiment (which Rousseau defended, with his one-time friend Hume) but in the more rigorous realm of reason and the will.

B. The Rational Basis of Morality

The first part of the *Groundwork* begins with the sentence we have already quoted, "Nothing can possibly be conceived in the world, or out of it, which can be called good without qualification, except a *good will.*" In this single sentence, Kant captures the heart of his a priori conception of morals, the fact that it is our intentions that are moral or immoral, not the empirical fortunes of our lives, our abilities, and our successes and failures. It is what we *try* to do that counts. Indeed, what Aristotle called the essence of moral virtue, namely *character,* is dismissed immediately by Kant as not being morally good at all. Character is desirable, of course, but character like all other abilities and talents involves too much luck—having been born into the right family and with a good disposition and so on, not a matter of will. A good will is thus contrasted with good fortune, which altogether we call "happiness." But here Kant makes an important qualification, that although good will (morality) is wholly distinct from good fortune (happiness), we naturally expect that the two will go together; indeed, we are repulsed by the very idea of a person who has no good intentions enjoying prosperity. "Thus," Kant concludes, "a good will appears to constitute the indispensable condition even of being *worthy* of happiness" (emphasis added).

FIRST SECTION. TRANSITION FROM THE COMMON RATIONAL KNOWLEDGE OF MORALITY TO THE PHILOSOPHICAL

Nothing can possibly be conceived in the world, or even out of it, which can be called good without qualification, except a *good will.* Intelligence, wit, judgment, and other *talents* of the mind, however they may be named, or courage, resolution, perseverance, as qualities of temperament, are undoubtedly good and desirable in many respects; but these gifts of nature may also become extremely bad and mischievous if the will which is to make use of them, and which, therefore, constitutes what is called *character,* is not good. It is the same with the *gifts of fortune.* Power, riches, honor, even health, and the general well-being and contentment with one's condition which is called *happiness,* inspire pride, and often presumption, if there is not a good will to correct the influence of these on the mind, and with this also to rectify the whole principle of acting, and adapt it to its end. The sight of a being who is not adorned with a single feature of a pure and good will, enjoying unbroken prosperity, can never give pleasure to an impartial rational spectator. Thus a good will appears to constitute the indispensable condition even of being worthy of happiness.

There are even some qualities which are of service to this good will itself, and may facilitate its action, yet which have no intrinsic unconditional value, but always presuppose a good will, and this qualifies the esteem that we justly have for them, and does not permit us to regard them as absolutely good. Moderation in the affections and passions, self-control, and calm deliberation are not only good in many respects, but even seem to constitute part of the intrinsic worth of the person; but they are far from deserving to be called good without qualification, although they have been so unconditionally praised by the ancients. For without the principles of a good will, they may become extremely bad; and the coolness of a villain not only makes him far more dangerous, but also directly makes him more abominable in our eyes than he would have been without it.

A good will is good not because of what it performs or effects, not by its aptness for the attainment of some proposed end, but simply by virtue of the volition—that is, it is good in itself, and considered by itself is to be esteemed much higher than all that can be brought about by it in favor of any inclination, nay, even of the sum-total of all inclinations. Even if it should happen that, owing to special disfavor of fortune, or the niggardly provision of a stepmotherly nature, this will should wholly lack power to accomplish its purpose, if with its greatest efforts it should yet achieve nothing, and there should remain only the good will (not, to be sure, a mere wish, but the summoning of all means in our power), then, like a jewel, it would still shine by its own light, as a thing which has its whole value in itself. Its usefulness or fruitlessness can neither add to nor take away anything from this value. It would be, as it were, only the setting to enable us to handle it the more conveniently in common commerce, or to attract to it the attention of those who are not yet connoisseurs, but not to recommend it to true connoisseurs, or to determine its value.

There is, however, something so strange in this idea of the absolute value of the mere will, in which no account is taken of its utility, that notwithstanding the thorough assent of even common reason to the idea, yet a suspicion must arise that it may perhaps really be the product of mere high-flown fancy, and that we may have misunderstood the purpose of nature in assigning reason as the governor of our will. Therefore we will examine this idea from this point of view.

Although Kant is a deontologist in his ethical theory (that is, his ethics is based upon duty and the rational authority of morality rather than the consequences of our actions), he is also a teleologist in his vision of the world, much like Aristotle. This is a view that he defends mainly in his third critique, *The Critique of Judgment,* but it is manifested here in his ethics too. The teleological view of the world is simply, in Kant's words (from the third critique), that "nature does nothing in vain." Thus when he refers to "the purpose of nature in assigning reason as governor of our will" in the preceding paragraph, he is not just waxing poetic. He does see in all of nature a purpose, and he assumes that whatever nature does is done for a reason. The argument which follows is almost identical to the one employed by Aristotle: if we are rational creatures, it must be for a reason. Nature must have intended us to use our reason for a purpose. What purpose? Reason cannot have the job of making us happy, since our ability to reason and calculate and plot and brood has obviously caused more of us to be unhappy than happy. Indeed, who could be happier than a "dumb" animal, a dog romping in the woods or a kitten playing with a ball of yarn. Therefore reason must have some more exalted purpose, distinct from happiness. This is, of course, morality.

In the physical constitution of an organized being, that is, a being adapted suitably to the purposes of life, we assume it as a fundamental principle that no organ for any purpose will be found but what is also the fittest and best adapted for that purpose. Now in a being which has reason and a will, if the proper object of nature were its *conservation*, its *welfare*, in a word, its *happiness*, then nature would have hit upon a very bad arrangement in selecting the reason of the creature to carry out this purpose. For all the actions which the creature has to perform with a view to this purpose, and the whole rule of its conduct, would be far more surely prescribed to it by instinct, and that end would have been attained thereby much more certainly than it ever can be by reason. Should reason have been communicated to this favored creature over and above, it must only have served it to contemplate the happy constitution of its nature, to admire it, to congratulate itself thereon, and to feel thankful for it to the beneficent cause, but not that it should subject its desires to that weak and delusive guidance, and meddle bunglingly with the purpose of nature. In a word, nature would have taken care that reason should not break forth into *practical exercise,* nor have the presumption, with its weak insight, to think out for itself the plan of happiness and of the means of attaining it. Nature would not only have taken on herself the choice of the ends but also of the means, and with wise foresight would have entrusted both to instinct.

And, in fact, we find that the more a cultivated reason applies itself with deliberate purpose to the enjoyment of life and happiness, so much the more does the man fail of true satisfaction. And from this circumstance there arises in many, if they are candid enough to confess it, a certain degree of *misology,* that is, hatred of reason, especially in the case of those who are most experienced in the use of it, because after calculating all the advantages they derive—I do not say from the invention of all the arts of common luxury, but even from the sciences (which seem to them to be after all only a luxury of the understanding) —they find that they have, in fact, only brought more trouble on their shoulders rather than gained in happiness; and they end by envying rather than despising the more common stamp of men who keep closer to the guidance of mere instinct, and do not allow their reason much influence on their conduct. And this we must admit, that the judgment of those who would very much lower the lofty eulogies of the advantages which reason gives us in regard to the happiness and satisfaction of life, or who would even reduce them below zero, is by no means morose or ungrateful to the goodness with which the world is governed, but that there lies at the root of these judgments the idea that our existence has a different and far nobler end, for which, and not for happiness, reason is properly intended, and which must, therefore, be regarded as the supreme condition to which the private ends of man must, for the most part, be postponed.

For as reason is not competent to guide the will with certainty in regard to its objects and the satisfaction of all our wants (which it to some extent even multiplies), this being an end to which an implanted instinct would have led with much greater certainty; and since, nevertheless, reason is imparted to us as a practical faculty, that is, as one which is to have influence on the *will,* therefore, admitting that nature generally in the distribution of her capacities has adapted the means to the end, its true destination must be to produce a *will,* not merely good as a *means* to something else, but *good in itself,* for which reason was absolutely necessary. This will then, though not indeed the sole and complete good, must be the supreme good and the condition of every other, even of the desire of happiness. Under these circumstances, there is nothing inconsistent with the wisdom of nature in the fact that the cultivation of the reason, which is requisite for the first and unconditional purpose, does in many ways interfere, at least in this life, with the attainment of the second, which is always conditional— namely, happiness. Nay, it may even reduce it to nothing, without nature thereby failing of her purpose. For reason recognizes the establishment of a good will as its highest practical destination, and in attaining this purpose is capable only of a satisfaction of its own proper kind, namely, that from the attainment of an end, which end again is determined by reason only, notwithstanding that this may involve many a disappointment to the ends of inclination.

Kant now repeats his all-important distinction between acting in conformity with duty versus acting for the sake of duty. A grocer, for example, might abstain from cheating his customers, but only because he is afraid of getting caught and losing business. He acts in conformity with duty; his action "agrees" with the moral principle "don't steal," but his reason for obeying is not that stealing is wrong, which would be acting for the sake of duty. Morality consists of the latter, not the former.

Contrasted with duty, which is rational, are the *inclinations;* that is, all of our desires, instincts, emotions, ambitions, compulsions—in short what we *want.* These are strictly empirical, and so of no moral worth. This phrase, "moral worth," is critical in Kant. When he says that an act "has no moral worth," he is not saying that it is a bad act. The grocer who does not cheat his customers because he is afraid of getting caught is not doing wrong; he is just not morally praiseworthy, which is Kant's concern.

A great many actions are motivated by both duty and inclination. For example, Kant suggests that self-preservation is both a duty and one of our most basic instincts. Usually, we stay alive because we want to (from "inclination"), but sometimes, if we are very depressed and considering suicide, we might stay alive out of duty. Then our staying alive has "moral worth," but not otherwise. So too, being kind ("beneficent") is often a matter of sympathy (and thus an inclination), but it is when one does not feel kindly that kindness has moral worth. This is where Kant's notion of "moral worth" starts bothering many people's intuitions. Is a philanthropist who gives to charity out of duty morally superior to one who gives just because he wants to?

We have then to develop the notion of a will which deserves to be highly esteemed for itself, and is good without a view to anything further, a notion which exists already in the sound natural understanding, requiring rather to be cleared up than to be taught, and which in estimating the value of our actions always takes the first place and constitutes the condition of all the rest. In order to do this, we will take the notion of duty, which includes that of a good will, although implying certain subjective restrictions and hindrances. These, however, far from concealing it or rendering it unrecognizable, rather bring it out by contrast and make it shine forth so much the brighter.

I omit here all actions which are already recognized as inconsistent with duty, although they may be useful for this or that purpose, for with these the question whether they are done *from duty* cannot arise at all, since they even conflict with it. I also set aside those actions which really conform to duty, but to which men have *no* direct *inclination,* performing them because they are impelled thereto by some other inclination. For in this case we can readily distinguish whether the action which agrees with duty is done *from duty* or from a selfish view. It is much harder to make this distinction when the action accords with duty, and the subject has besides a *direct* inclination to it. For example, it is always a matter of duty that a dealer should not overcharge an inexperienced purchaser and wherever there is much commerce the prudent tradesman does not overcharge, but keeps a fixed price for everyone, so that a child buys of him as well as any other. Men are thus *honestly* served; but this is not enough to make us believe that the tradesman has so acted from duty and from principles of honesty; his own advantage required it; it is out of the question in this case to suppose that he might besides have a direct inclination in favor of the buyers, so that, as it were, from love he should give no advantage to one over another. Accordingly the action was done neither from duty nor from direct inclination, but merely with a selfish view.

On the other hand, it is a duty to maintain one's life; and, in addition, everyone has also a direct inclination to do so. But on this account the often anxious care which most men take for it has no intrinsic worth, and their maxim has no moral import. They preserve their life as *duty requires,* no doubt, but not *because duty requires.* On the other hand, if adversity and hopeless sorrow have completely taken away the relish for life, if the unfortunate one, strong in mind, indignant at his fate rather than desponding or dejected, wishes for death, and yet preserves his life without loving it—not from inclination or fear, but from duty—then his maxim has a moral worth.

To be beneficent when we can is a duty; and besides this, there are many minds so sympathetically constituted that without any other motive of vanity or self-interest, they find a pleasure in spreading joy around them, and can take delight in the satisfaction of others so far as it is their own work. But I maintain that in such a case an action of this kind, however proper, however amiable it may be, has nevertheless no true moral worth, but is on a level with other inclinations, for example, the inclination to honor, which, if it is happily directed to that which is in fact of public utility and accordant with duty, and consequently honorable, deserves praise and encouragement, but not esteem. For the maxim lacks the moral import, namely, that such actions be done *from duty,* not from inclination. Put the case that the mind of that philanthropist was clouded by sorrow of his own, extinguishing all sympathy with the lot of others, and that while he still has the power to benefit others in distress, he is not touched by their trouble because he is absorbed with his own; and now suppose that he tears himself out of his dead insensibility and performs the action without any inclination to it, but simply from duty, then first has his action its genuine moral worth. Further still, if nature has put little sympathy in the heart of this or that man, if he, supposed to be an upright man, is by temperament cold and indifferent to the sufferings of others, perhaps because in respect of his own he is provided with the special gift of patience and fortitude, and supposes, or even requires, that others should have the same—and such a man would certainly not be the meanest product of nature—but if nature had not specially framed him for a philanthropist, would he not still find in himself a source from whence to give himself a far higher worth than that of a good-natured temperament could be? Unquestionably. It is just in this that the moral worth of the character is brought out which is incomparably the highest of all, namely, that he is beneficent, not from inclination, but from duty.

In what follows, Kant gives us his curious argument that, though duty and happiness are distinct, a person has a duty to be happy. The reason (which is not clearly compatible with the above account of moral worth) is that people who are miserable are less likely to do their duty.

To secure one's own happiness is a duty, at least indirectly; for discontent with one's condition, under a pressure of many anxieties and amidst unsatisfied wants, might easily become a great *temptation to transgression of duty.* But here again, without looking to duty, all men have already the strongest and most intimate inclination to happiness, because it is just in this idea that all inclinations are combined in one total. But the precept of happiness is often of such a sort that it greatly interferes with some inclinations, and yet a man cannot form any definite and certain conception of the sum of satisfaction of all of them which is called happiness. It is not then to be wondered at that a single inclination, definite both as to what it promises and as to the time within which it can be gratified, is often able to overcome such a fluctuating idea, and that a gouty patient, for instance, can choose to enjoy what he likes, and to suffer what he may, since, according to his calculation, on this occasion at least, he has [only] not sacrificed the enjoyment of the present moment to a possibly mistaken expectation of a happiness which is supposed to be found in health. But even in this case, if the general desire for happiness did not influence his will, and supposing that in his particular case health was not a necessary element in this calculation, there yet remains in this, as in all other cases, this law—namely, that he should promote his happiness not from inclination but from duty, and by this would his conduct first acquire true moral worth.

Now, in a famous, because it is somewhat shocking, passage, Kant turns to the biblical injunction that we should "love our neighbors." But love is an inclination and not rational, not a matter of will. Therefore, Kant suggests that we distinguish two kinds of love, "practical" and "pathological," and only the first has moral worth. (The phrase "pathological love" comes from the Greek word *pathos,* which means "feeling" in general as well as "suffering," from which we get our medical word "pathology.") Pathological love, which includes all of those romantic and family feelings of intimacy and tenderness, is (as inclination) irrelevant to morality. What would this suggest in terms of the moral worth of a person's relationship to his or her spouse and children? What would "marital duty" mean on this account?

It is in this manner, undoubtedly, that we are to understand those passages of Scripture also in which we are commanded to love our neighbor, even our enemy. For love, as an affection, cannot be commanded, but beneficence for duty's sake may, even though we are not impelled to it by any inclination—nay, are even repelled by a natural and unconquerable aversion. This is *practical* love, and not *pathological*—a love which is seated in the will, and not in the propensions of sense—in principles of action and not of tender sympathy; and it is this love alone which can be commanded.

Although Kant did not list it as such, the proposition that to have "moral worth" an action must be done for the sake of duty was the first in a series of propositions which structure this part of the *Groundwork.* The second follows.

The second proposition is: That an action done from duty derives its moral worth, *not from the purpose* which is to be attained by it, but from the maxim by which it is determined, and therefore does not depend on the realization of the object of the action, but merely on the *principle of volition* by which the action has taken place, without regard to any object of desire. It is clear from what precedes that the purposes which we may have in view in our actions, or their effects regarded as ends and springs of the will, cannot give to actions any unconditional or moral worth. In what, then, can their worth lie if it is not to consist in the will and in reference to its expected effect? It cannot lie anywhere but in the *principle of the will* without regard to the ends which can be attained by the action. For the will stands between its *a priori* principle, which is formal, and its *a posteriori* spring, which is material, as between two roads, and as it must be determined by something, it follows that it must be determined by the formal principle of volition when an action is done from duty, in which case every material principle has been withdrawn from it.

The distinction here between purpose and maxim is a bit misleading, but what Kant means by "purpose" is what the various teleological theorists have in mind when they talk about the "aim" of an action, what it is trying to achieve. But not only are the consequences of an action not part of moral considerations, according to Kant, the aim of an action is not either. The aim, like the results of action, is empirical (Kant uses the phrase *a posteriori,* which means "empirical" but is a direct contrast to *a priori* and means literally "after"). The maxim, on the other hand, is not so much an aim but a principle, that is, the general grounds upon which one acts. Thus the grocer might have as his aim satisfying this customer and making a profit on the sale, but the maxim on which he acts is (if he is being moral) that one should be honest.

The third proposition, then, combines the special notion of moral worth and the emphasis on principles and concludes that morality (duty) is acting for the sake of principle (the moral law) as a kind of necessity.

The third proposition, which is a consequence of the two preceding, I would express thus: *Duty is the necessity of acting from respect for the law.* I may have *inclination* for an object as the effect of my proposed action, but I cannot have *respect* for it just for this reason that it is an effect and not an energy of will. Similarly, I cannot have respect for inclination, whether my own or another's; I can at most, if my own, approve it; if another's, sometimes even love it, that is, look on it as favorable to my own interest. It is only what is connected with my will as a principle, by no means as an effect—what does not subserve my inclination, but overpowers it, or at least in case of choice excludes it from its calculation—in other words, simply the law of itself, which can be an object of respect, and hence a command. Now an action done from duty must wholly exclude the influence of inclination, and with it every object of the will, so that nothing remains which can determine the will except objectively the *law,* and subjectively *pure respect* for this practical law, and consequently the maxim that I should follow this law even to the thwarting of all my inclinations.

Kant now gives us what will soon appear more formally as the first formulation of the categorical imperative. It says, act in such a way that one would be willing to have the maxim of one's action a law for everyone. (Thus if I am going to lie, I ask myself whether I would be willing for everyone to act on the principle that lying is OK.) But it is not just the consequences of everyone's so acting that are at stake, and it is not just prudence that should motivate me (if I am moral). The moral consideration here (anticipating the main argument of the following section of the *Groundwork*) is whether such a maxim could be rationally held by everyone (as a "universal law"). Kant insists that it could not be, since if everyone lied, no one would believe anyone. Similarly, if everyone were to break promises, it would make no sense to make a promise, since no one would take it seriously anyway.

Thus the moral worth of an action does not lie in the effect expected from it, nor in any principle of action which requires to borrow its motive from this expected effect. For all these effects—agreeableness of one's condition, and even the promotion of the happiness of others—could have been also brought about by other causes, so that for this there would have been no need of the will of a rational being; whereas it is in this alone that the supreme and unconditional good can be found. The pre-eminent good which we call moral can therefore consist in nothing else than *the conception of law* in itself, *which certainly is only possible in a rational being,* in so far as this conception, and not the expected effect, determines the will. This is a good which is already present in the person who acts accordingly, and we have not to wait for it to appear first in the result.

But what sort of law can that be the conception of which must determine the will, even without paying any regard to the effect expected from it, in order that this will may be called good absolutely and without qualification? As I have deprived the will of every impulse which could arise to it from obedience to any law, there remains nothing but the universal conformity of its actions to law in general, which alone is to serve the will as a principle, that is. I am never to act otherwise than so *that I could also will that my maxim should become a universal law.* Here, now, it is the simple conformity to law in general, without assuming any particular law applicable to certain actions, that serves the will as its principle, and must so serve it if duty is not to be a vain delusion and a chimerical notion. The common reason of men in its practical judgments perfectly coincides with this, and always has in view the principle here suggested. Let the question be, for example: May I when in distress make a promise with the intention not to keep it? I readily distinguish here between the two significations which the question may have: whether it is prudent or whether it is right to make a false promise? The former may undoubtedly often be the case. I see clearly indeed that it is not enough to extricate myself from a present difficulty by means of this subterfuge, but it must be well considered whether there may not hereafter spring from this lie much greater inconvenience than that from which I now free myself, and as, with all my supposed *cunning,* the consequences cannot be so easily foreseen but that credit once lost may be much more injurious to me than any mischief which I seek to avoid at present, it should be considered whether it would not be more *prudent* to act herein according to a universal maxim, and to make it a habit to promise nothing except with the intention of keeping it. But it is soon clear to me that such a maxim will still only be based on the fear of consequences. Now it is a wholly different thing to be truthful from duty, and to be so from apprehension of injurious consequences. In the first case, the very notion of the action already implies a law for me: in the second case, I must first look about elsewhere to see what results may be combined with it which would affect myself. For to deviate from the principle of duty is beyond all doubt wicked; but to be unfaithful to my maxim of prudence may often be very advantageous to me, although to abide by it is certainly safer. The shortest way, however, and an unerring one, to discover the answer to this question whether a lying promise is consistent with duty, is to ask myself, Should I be content that my maxim (to extricate myself from difficulty by a false promise) should hold good as a universal law, for myself as well as for others; and should I be able to say to myself, "Every one may make a deceitful promise when he finds himself in a difficulty from which he cannot otherwise extricate himself"? Then I presently become aware that, while I can will the lie, I can by no means will that lying should be a universal law. For with such a law there would be no promises at all, since it would be in vain to allege my intention in regard to my future actions to those who would not believe this allegation, or if they over-hastily did so, would pay me back in my own coin. Hence my maxim, as soon as it should be made a universal law, would necessarily destroy itself.

I do not, therefore, need any far-reaching penetration to discern what I have to do in order that my will may be morally good. Inexperienced in the course of the world, incapable of being prepared for all its contingencies, I only ask myself: Canst thou also will that thy maxim should be a universal law? If not, then it must be rejected, and that not because of a disadvantage accruing from it to myself or even to others, but because it cannot enter as a principle into a possible universal legislation, and reason extorts from me immediate respect for such legislation. I do not indeed as yet *discern* on what this respect is based (this the philosopher may inquire), but at least I understand this—that it is an estimation of the worth which far outweighs all worth of what is recommended by inclination, and that the necessity of acting from *pure* respect for the practical law is what constitutes duty, to which every other motive must give place because it is the condition of a will being good *in itself,* and the worth of such a will is above everything.

Finally, Kant summarizes the importance of such moral thinking, even though most people do not think of it in such "abstract and universal form." Yet most people implicitly employ such reasoning and philosophers do so as a matter of necessity. (That is what makes them philosophers.) But is all of this necessary? Couldn't people be morally good without this rational apparatus? "Innocence is a glorious thing," Kant responds, but it is lost eventually and "easily seduced." The assurance of morality is that it is based on will power and reason and does not depend upon good feelings and inclinations, which are themselves undependable.

Thus, then, without quitting the moral knowledge of common human reason, we have arrived at its principle. And although, no doubt, common men do not conceive it in such an abstract and universal form, yet they always have it really before their eyes, and use it as the standard of their decision. Here it would be easy to show how, with this compass in hand, men are well able to distinguish, in every case that occurs, what is good, what bad, conformably to duty or inconsistent with it, if, without in the least teaching them anything new, we only, like Socrates, direct their attention to the principle they themselves employ; and that, therefore, we do not need science and philosophy to know what we should do to be honest and good, yea, even wise and virtuous. Indeed we might well have conjectured beforehand that the knowledge of what every man is bound to do, and therefore also to know, would be within the reach of every man, even the commonest. Here we cannot forbear admiration when we see how great an advantage the practical judgment has over the theoretical in the common understanding of men. In the latter, if common reason ventures to depart from the laws of experience and from the perceptions of the senses, it falls into mere inconceivabilities and self-contradictions, at least into a chaos of uncertainty, obscurity, and instability. But in the practical sphere it is just when the common understanding excludes all sensible springs from practical laws that its power of judgment begins to show itself to advantage. It then becomes even subtle, whether it be that it chicanes with its own conscience or with other claims respecting what is to be called right, or whether it desires for its own instruction to determine honestly the worth of actions; and, in the latter case, it may even have as good a hope of hitting the mark as any philosopher whatever can promise himself. Nay, it is almost more sure of doing so, because the philosopher cannot have any other principle, while he may easily perplex his judgment by a multitude of considerations foreign to the matter, and so turn aside from the right way. Would it not therefore be wiser in moral concerns to acquiesce in the judgment of common reason, or at most only to call in philosophy for the purpose of rendering the system of morals more complete and intelligible, and its rules more convenient for use (especially for disputation), but not so as to draw off the common understanding from its happy simplicity, or to bring it by means of philosophy into a new path of inquiry and instruction?

Innocence is indeed a glorious thing, only, on the other hand, it is very sad that it cannot well maintain itself, and is easily seduced. On this account even wisdom—which otherwise consists more in conduct than in knowledge—yet has need of science, not in order to learn from it, but to secure for its precepts admission and permanence. Against all the commands of duty which reason represents to man as so deserving of respect, he feels in himself a powerful counterpoise in his wants and inclinations, the entire satisfaction of which he sums up under the name of happiness. Now reason issues its commands unyieldingly, without promising anything to the inclinations, and, as it were, with disregard and contempt for these claims, which are so impetuous, and at the same time so plausible, and which will not allow themselves to be suppressed by any command. Hence there arises a natural *dialetic,* i.e. a disposition, to argue against these strict laws of duty and to question their validity, or at least their purity and strictness; and, if possible, to make them more accordant with our wishes and inclinations, that is to say, to corrupt them at their very source, and entirely to destroy their worth—a thing which even common practical reason cannot ultimately call good.

Thus is the *common reason of man* compelled to go out of its sphere, and to take a step into the field of a *practical philosophy,* not to satisfy any speculative want (which never occurs to it as long as it is content to be mere sound reason), but even on practical grounds, in order to attain in it information and clear instruction respecting the source of its principle, and the correct determination of it in opposition to the maxims which are based on wants and inclinations, so that it may escape from the perplexity of opposite claims, and not run the risk of losing all genuine moral principles through the equivocation into which it easily falls. Thus, when practical reason cultivates itself, there insensibly arises in it a dialectic which forces it to seek aid in philosophy, just as happens to it in its theoretic use; and in this case, therefore, as well as in the other, it will find rest nowhere but in a thorough critical examination of our reason.

DISCUSSION

Aristotle presented us with an ethics which was extremely specific to a certain kind of society and a particularly privileged class within that society. The good life was for them, and there was no conception of "virtue" which was not tied to specific roles and responsibilities and which did not presuppose certain particular circumstances and skills within which those virtues made sense and served society. In Kant, we see exactly the opposite, a view of virtue in which *all* such particularities are eliminated from consideration and in which all questions of good fortune and fate are neutralized. A person might be miserable, but he or she has as good a chance as anyone else to be morally good. A person might be incapacitated from acting in all but the most nominal ways, but that doesn't stop him or her from having a good will. A person might have all sorts of terrible problems, but that need not and should not interfere with his or her efforts to be rational, to do the right thing even in the most adverse circumstances.

The conditions of morality for Kant are nothing other than being a human being—or, more accurately—being a rational being (on the assumption that we are primarily talking about ourselves). Aristotle insisted on all sorts of preconditions before talking about the good life and virtue would even make sense—a good upbringing, a leisurely life, adequate wealth, health, and social status. For Kant, one only needs a working brain, and not much more. One knows what is right because one is rational, because one knows—presumably without having yet read Kant—that one's duty is what one ought to do, whatever one's personal inclinations. And one knows too that duty is impersonal, in that anyone, in similar circumstances, would have the same duty, whatever their inclinations. We can leave it an open question how much this is simply a matter of certain languages and the concept of "duty" (*pflicht* in German) and, more speculatively, how much reason itself is bound to language and culture and not universal at all. But Kant certainly thought that reason and duty were universal (as did most of the Enlightenment), and, within our society at any rate, duty does seem to have such a meaning, such that duties apply to anyone in certain circumstances, whatever they would rather do.

Furthermore, Kant is surely right in basing his theory on the idea that we value people, at least as moral agents, on the basis of their good intentions. No matter how consistently good he may act, we would certainly never praise a man who did the right thing only because he was always looking askance and worrying about being punished ("shifty-eyed," we would call him). Conversely, we would continue to praise a person who at least always tried to do the right thing (though we would surely lose patience—at least—after consistent failures). Perhaps Kant overplays the emphasis on good intentions ("a good will") and underplays the importance—even the moral importance—of good results. But, then, he is after the "pure" conception of morals, not a diagnosis of our own impatience with human frailty and failure.

What is crucial to morals, he insists, is the will; all else is irrelevant. We might object that this totally ignores the fact that what is most important, to most of us, is not so much people's moral status but the results of their actions. What good is a "good man" if his every action makes us worse off than before? But Kant is not supposing, of course, that a good will will usually have disastrous consequences; the assumption, if anything is being assumed here, is that good intentions do usually lead to beneficial actions, and he even says that concern for duty is, in part, concern for the promotion of happiness. What is crucial to a good will is acting on principle, not on the basis of "sympathy" or any other personal (or interpersonal) feeling. We might object strenuously to this in the context of close family ties or a romantic relationship, but, in a world where so many of our dealings are with strangers (as opposed to Aristotle's *polis*), such a demand at least seems reasonable. (In fact, if we think of an administrative position—giving grants to students, for example—acting on the basis of personal ties and feelings rather than impersonal principles is the height of immorality.)

The emphasis on rationality and a priori considerations exclusively nevertheless yields questionable results even when we limit our concern to the clearly more impersonal cases, in which personal feelings and particular circumstances are excluded. Are there rules which can be applied to everyone, regardless of any attention to particular circumstances? Does this emphasis on rationality in fact only encourage that impersonal and uncaring bureaucratic attitude that so many people deeply resent at least as much as they resent emotional immorality and personal injustice? (In fact, the bureaucracy was a relatively new institution in Kant's day, and, unlike today, it was looked upon with great favor by most people as an impersonal antidote to the personal abuses of power and privilege by the aristocracy.) And for ourselves, are we to consider as most moral those acts which we have to think and deliberate about? Do we in fact have principles (even if implicit and merely subjective) in all our actions, or is it more as Aristotle suggested—that the habitual act comes first, the principles and ability to deliberate later on? What kind of a portrait is Kant giving us here of ourselves as moral beings? Is it a portrait we can recognize, and one which we are willing to accept?

C. The Categorical Imperative

Kant has argued that an act has moral worth insofar as it is done for the sake of duty alone. But do we ever act out of so pure a motive? Kant is perfectly willing to admit that we do not, that even our most dutiful and morally self-conscious actions may still have reference to "the dear self" of self-interest and prudence. Indeed, he is even willing to say that "it is absolutely impossible to make out by experience with complete certainty a single case in which the maxim of an action, however right in itself, rested simply on moral grounds and on the conception of duty." Kant anticipates his future colleague, Sigmund Freud, in speculating on the "secret springs of action," unconscious impulses of which we may not be aware even in the noblest action. But if none of our actions is purely moral, it does not follow (as "those who ridicule all morality" would argue) that all of our actions are selfish either. Acting from pure duty may be an ideal, but it is thereby no less a real ingredient in our behavior. It may be, for example, that none of us has ever made a friend without some self-interested motive (if only that we have a good time together); but this is not to say that none of us has ever been a friend. It is only to say that morality is an ideal, which is never to be found in pure form in the mixed motives of actual human behavior.

SECOND SECTION. TRANSITION FROM POPULAR MORAL PHILOSOPHY TO THE METAPHYSIC OF MORALS

If we have hitherto drawn our notion of duty from the common use of our practical reason, it is by no means to be inferred that we have treated it as an empirical notion. On the contrary, if we attend to the experience of men's conduct, we meet frequent and, as we ourselves allow, just complaints that one cannot find a single certain example of the disposition to act from pure duty. Although many things are done in *conformity* with what *duty* prescribes, it is nevertheless always doubtful whether they are done strictly *from duty,* so as to have a moral worth. Hence there have at all times been philosophers who have altogether denied that this disposition actually exists at all in human actions, and have ascribed everything to a more or less refined self-love. Not that they have on that account questioned the soundness of the conception of morality; on the contrary, they spoke with sincere regret of the frailty and corruption of human nature, which though noble enough to take as its rule an idea so worthy of respect, is yet too weak to follow it, and employs reason, which ought to give it the law only for the purpose of providing for the interest of the inclinations, whether singly or at the best in the greatest possible harmony with one another.

In fact, it is absolutely impossible to make out by experience with complete certainty a single case in which the maxim of an action, however right in itself, rested simply on moral grounds and on the conception of duty. Sometimes it happens that with the sharpest self-examination we can find nothing beside the moral principle of duty which could have been powerful enough to move us to this or that action and to so great a sacrifice; yet we cannot from this infer with certainty that it was not really some secret impulse of self-love, under the false appearance of duty, that was the actual determining cause of the will. We like then to flatter ourselves by falsely taking credit for a more noble motive; whereas in fact we can never, even by the strictest examination, get completely behind the secret springs of action; since, when the question is of moral worth, it is not with the actions which we see that we are concerned, but with those inward principles of them which we do not see.

Moreover, we cannot better serve the wishes of those who ridicule all morality as a mere chimera of human imagination overstepping itself from vanity, than by conceding to them that notions of duty must be drawn only from experience (as from indolence, people are ready to think is also the case with all other notions); for this is to prepare for them a certain triumph. I am willing to admit out of love of humanity that even most of our actions are correct, but if we look closer at them we everywhere come upon the dear self which is always prominent, and it is this they have in view, and not the strict command of duty which would often require self-denial. Without being an enemy of virtue, a cool observer, one that does not mistake the wish for good, however lively, for its reality, may sometimes doubt whether true virtue is actually found anywhere in the world, and this especially as years increase and the judgment is partly made wiser by experience, and partly also more acute in observation. This being so, nothing can secure us from falling away altogether from our ideas of duty, or maintain in the soul a well-grounded respect for its law, but the clear conviction that although there should never have been actions which really sprang from such pure sources, yet whether this or that takes place is not at all the question; but that reason of itself, independent on all experience, ordains what ought to take place, that accordingly actions of which perhaps the world has hitherto never given an example, the feasibility even of which might be very much doubted by one who founds everything on experience, are nevertheless inflexibly commanded by reason; that, *ex. gr.*, even though there might never yet have been a sincere friend, yet not a whit the less is pure sincerity in friendship required of every man, because, prior to all experience, this duty is involved as duty in the idea of a reason determining the will by *à priori* principles.

If morality is an ideal of pure reason, it follows that it applies not just to human beings but to "all rational creatures." And as an ideal of pure reason, morality cannot be understood just on the basis of actual experience, first because we have probably never seen an example of pure dutiful action, but second—and more importantly—because we would need our a priori standard of moral perfection in order to recognize an ideal example if we found one—for example, in Christ as a moral ideal.

When we add further that, unless we deny that the notion of morality has any truth or reference to any possible object, we must admit that its law must be valid, not merely for men, but for all *rational creatures generally,* not merely under certain contingent conditions or with exceptions, but *with absolute necessity,* then it is clear that no experience could enable us to infer even the possibility of such apodictic laws. For with what right could we bring into unbounded respect as a universal precept for every rational nature that which perhaps holds only under the contingent conditions of humanity? Or how could laws of the determination of *our* will be regarded as laws of the determination of the will of rational beings generally, and for us only as such, if they were merely empirical, and did not take their origin wholly *à priori* from pure but practical reason?

Nor could anything be more fatal to morality than that we should wish to derive it from examples. For every example of it that is set before me must be first itself tested by principles of morality, whether it is worthy to serve as an original example, *i.e.* as a pattern, but by no means can it authoritatively furnish the conception of morality. Even the Holy One of the Gospels must first be compared with our ideal of moral perfection before we can recognize Him as such; and so He says of Himself, "Why call ye Me [whom you see] good; none is good [the model of good] but God only [whom ye do not see]?" But whence have we the conception of God as the supreme good? Simply from the *idea* of moral perfection, which reason frames *à priori,* and connects inseparably with the notion of a free will. Imitation finds no place at all in morality, and examples serve only for encouragement, *i.e.* they put beyond doubt the feasibility of what the law commands, they make visible that which the practical rule expresses more generally, but they can never authorize us to set aside the true original which lies in reason, and to guide ourselves by examples.

Thus a pure moral philosophy is necessary, even if it may not be, in the usual sense, a "popular" philosophy.

If then there is no genuine supreme principle of morality but what must rest simply on pure reason, independent on all experience, I think it is not necessary even to put the question, whether it is good to exhibit these concepts in their generality (*in abstracto*) as they are established *à priori* along with the principles belonging to them, if our knowledge is to be distinguished from the *vulgar,* and to be called philosophical. In our times indeed this might perhaps be necessary;

for if we collected votes whether pure rational knowledge separated from everything empirical, that is to say, metaphysic of morals, or whether popular practical philosophy is to be preferred, it is easy to guess which side would preponderate.

This descending to popular notions is certainly very commendable, if the ascent to the principles of pure reason has first taken place and been satisfactorily accomplished. This implies that we first *found* Ethics on Metaphysics, and then, when it is firmly established, procure a *hearing* for it by giving it a popular character. But it is quite absurd to try to be popular in the first inquiry, on which the soundness of the principles depends. It is not only that this proceeding can never lay claim to the very rare merit of a true *philosophical popularity,* since there is no art in being intelligible if one renounces all thoroughness of insight; but also it produces a disgusting medley of compiled observations and half-reasoned principles. Shallow pates enjoy this because it can be used for every-day chat, but the sagacious find in it only confusion, and being unsatisfied and unable to help themselves, they turn away their eyes, while philosophers, who see quite well through this delusion, are little listened to when they call men off for a time from this pretended popularity, in order that they might be rightfully popular after they have attained a definite insight.

We need only look at the attempts of moralists in that favourite fashion, and we shall find at one time the special constitution of human nature (including, however, the idea of a rational nature generally), at one time perfection, at another happiness, here moral sense, there fear of God, a little of this, and a little of that, in marvellous mixture, without its occurring to them to ask whether the principles of morality are to be sought in the knowledge of human nature at all (which we can have only from experience); and, if this is not so; if these principles are to be found altogether *à priori* free from everything empirical, in pure rational concepts only, and nowhere else, not even in the smallest degree; then rather to adopt the method of making this a separate inquiry, as pure practical philosophy, or (if one may use a name so decried) as metaphysic of morals, to bring it by itself to completeness, and to require the public, which wishes for popular treatment to await the issue of this undertaking.

Such a metaphysic of morals, completely isolated, not mixed with any anthropology, theology, physics, or hyperphysics, and still less with occult qualities (which we might call hypophysical), is not only an indispensable substratum of all sound theoretical knowledge of duties, but is at the same time a desideratum of the highest importance to the actual fulfilment of their precepts. For the pure conception of duty, unmixed with any foreign addition of empirical attractions, and, in a word, the conception of the moral law, exercises on the human heart, by way of reason alone (which first becomes aware with this that it can of itself be practical), an influence so much more powerful than all other springs which may be derived from the field of experience, that in the consciousness of its worth, it despises the latter, and can by degrees become their master; whereas a mixed ethics, compounded partly of motives drawn from feelings and inclinations, and partly also of conceptions of reason, must make the mind waver between motives which cannot be brought under any principle, which lead to good only by mere accident, and very often also to evil.

The analysis which follows, therefore, is of the pure conception of duty, based solely on reason. And yet, such a "speculative" endeavor is nevertheless of the greatest practical importance; by gaining such a pure understanding of duty and its principles we can clarify the nature of morality for ourselves (and not only for ourselves but "for every rational creature") and we can teach ourselves and our children the ideal, with an eye to producing "pure moral dispositions, and to engraft them on men's minds to the promotion of the greatest possible good in the world."

From what has been said, it is clear that all moral conceptions have their seat and origin completely *à priori* in the reason, and that, moreover, in the commonest reason just as truly as in that which is in the highest degree speculative; that they cannot be obtained by abstraction from any empirical, and therefore merely contingent knowledge; that it is just this purity of their origin that makes them worthy to serve as our supreme practical principle, and that just in proportion as we add anything empirical, we detract from their genuine influence, and from the absolute value of actions; that it is not only of the greatest necessity, in a purely speculative point of view, but is also of the greatest practical importance, to derive these notions and laws from pure reason, to present them pure and unmixed, and even to determine the compass of this practical or pure rational knowledge, *i.e.* to determine the whole faculty of pure practical reason; and, in doing so, we must not make its principles dependent on the particular nature of human reason, though in speculative philosophy this may be permitted, or may even at times be necessary; but since moral laws ought to hold good for every rational creature, we must derive them from the general concept of a rational being. In this way, although for its *application* to man morality has need of anthropology, yet, in the first instance, we must treat it independently as pure philosophy, *i.e.* as metaphysic, complete in itself (a thing which in such distinct branches of science is easily done); knowing well that unless we are in possession of this, it would not only be vain to determine the moral element of duty in right actions for purposes of speculative criticism, but it would be impossible to base morals on their genuine principles, even for common practical purposes, especially of moral instruction, so as to produce pure moral dispositions, and to engraft them on men's minds to the promotion of the greatest possible good in the world.

But in order that in this study we may not merely advance by the natural steps from the common moral judgment (in this case very worthy of respect) to the philosophical, as has been already done, but also from a popular philosophy, which goes no further than it can reach by groping with the help of examples, to metaphysic (which does not allow itself to be checked by anything empirical, and as it must measure the whole extent of this kind of rational knowledge, goes as far as ideal conceptions, where even examples fail us), we must follow and clearly describe the practical faculty of reason, from the general rules of its determination to the point where the notion of duty springs from it.

The strategy for doing this is to describe the basic rules of practical reason, the laws according to which our duties are prescribed. All of nature operates according to laws, Kant tells us, but only rational beings also have a conception of laws and the will to act according to them. The will is practical reason, Kant says, that is, the ability to choose what is right.

Everything in nature works according to laws. Rational beings alone have the faculty of acting according *to the conception* of laws—that is, according to principles, that is, have a *will*. Since the deduction of actions from principles requires *reason,* the will is nothing but practical reason. If reason infallibly determines the will, then the actions of such a being which are recognized as objectively necessary are subjectively necessary also, that is, the will is a faculty to choose *that only* which reason independent on inclination recognizes as practically necessary, that is, as good. But if reason of itself does not sufficiently determine the will, if the latter is subject also to subjective conditions (particular impulses) which do not always coincide with the objective conditions, in a word, if the will does not *in itself* completely accord with reason (which is actually the case with men), then the actions which objectively are recognized as necessary are subjectively contingent, and the determination of such a will according to objective laws is *obligation,* that is to say, the relation of the objective laws to a will that is not thoroughly good is conceived as the determination of the will of a rational being by principles of reason, but which the will from its nature does not of necessity follow.

Kant now introduces his central notion: the categorical imperative.

The conception of an objective principle, in so far as it is obligatory for a will, is called a command (of reason), and the formula of the command is called an Imperative.

All imperatives are expressed by the word *ought* [*or shall*], and thereby indicate the relation of an objective law of reason to a will which from its subjective constitution is not necessarily determined by it (an obligation). They say that something would be good to do or to forbear, but they say it to a will which does not always do a thing because it is conceived to be good to do it. That is practically *good,* however, which determines the will by means of the conceptions of reason, and consequently not from subjective causes, but objectively, that is, on principles which are valid for every rational being as such. It is distinguished from the *pleasant* as that which influences the will only by means of sensation from merely subjective causes, valid only for the sense of this or that one, and not as a principle of reason which holds for every one.

A perfectly good will would therefore be equally subject to objective laws (viz., laws of good), but could not be conceived as *obliged* thereby to act lawfully, because of itself from its subjective constitution it can only be determined by the conception of good. Therefore no imperatives hold for the Divine will, or in general for a *holy* will; *ought* is here out of place because the volition is already of itself necessarily in unison with the law. Therefore imperatives are only formulae to express the relation of objective laws of all volition to the subjective imperfection of the will of this or that rational being, for example, the human will.

Now all *imperatives* command either *hypothetically* or *categorically*. The former represent the practical necessity of a possible action as means to something else that is willed (or at least which one might possibly will). The categorical imperative would be that which represented an action as necessary of itself without reference to another end, that is, as objectively necessary.

Since every practical law represents a possible action as good, and on this account, for a subject who is practically determinable by reason as necessary, all imperatives are formulae determining an action which is necessary according to the principle of a will good in some respects. If now the action is good only as a means *to something else,* then the imperative is *hypothetical;* if it is conceived as good *in itself* and consequently as being necessarily the principle of a will which of itself conforms to reason, then it is *categorical.*

Thus the imperative declares what action possible by me would be good, and presents the practical rule in relation to a will which does not forthwith perform an action simply because it is good, whether because the subject does not always know that it is good, or because, even if it know this, yet its maxims might be opposed to the objective principles of practical reason.

Accordingly the hypothetical imperative only says that the action is good for some purpose, *possible* or *actual.* In the first case it is a *problematical,* in the second an *assertorial* practical principle. The categorical imperative which declares an action to be objectively necessary in itself without reference to any purpose, that is, without any other end, is valid as an *apodictic* (practical) principle.

In other words, a hypothetical imperative applies to a person only if he or she fulfills the "if . . ." clause, as in "if you want to stay slim, don't drink too much German beer." If you don't care about staying slim, the imperative ("don't drink too much German beer") does not apply to you. On the other hand, a categorical imperative has no such "if . . ." clause and applies to everyone under whatever circumstances. A commandment such as "Honor thy father and thy mother" is a categorical imperative because it does not have any exclusions or conditions, such as "if they were generous with you . . ." or "if you want to get your inheritance. . . ." Everyone is bound by reason to obey, whatever one's parents have been like, whatever one might expect from them in the future.

Most of ethics and practical behavior consists of hypothetical imperatives, that is, acting toward an end. But the number of ends or goals of our activities are almost innumerable.

Whatever is possible only by the power of some rational being may also be conceived as a possible purpose of some will; and therefore the principles of action as regards the means necessary to attain some possible purpose are in fact infinitely numerous. All sciences have a practical part consisting of problems expressing that some end is possible for us, and of imperatives directing how it may be attained. These may, therefore, be called in general imperatives of *skill.* Here there is no question whether the end is rational and good, but only what one must do in order to attain it. The precepts for the physician to make his patient thoroughly healthy, and for a poisoner to ensure certain death, are of equal value in this respect, that each serves to effect its purpose perfectly. Since in early youth it cannot be known what ends are likely to occur to us in the course of life, parents seek to have their children taught a *great many things,* and provide for their *skill* in the use of means for all sorts of arbitrary ends, of none of which can they determine whether it may not perhaps hereafter be an object to their pupil, but which it is at all events *possible* that he might aim at; and this anxiety is so great that they commonly neglect to form and correct their judgment on the value of the things which may be chosen as ends.

But as Aristotle argued too, there is one end that seems to be the end of all of our activities, and that is happiness. Nevertheless, even if we can assume that every action is aimed at happiness, the imperative that says "if you want to be happy . . ." is still hypothetical.

There is *one* end, however, which may be assumed to be actually such to all rational beings (so far as imperatives apply to them, viz., as dependent beings), and, therefore, one purpose which they not merely *may* have, but which we may with certainty assume that they all actually *have* by a natural necessity, and this is *happiness.* The hypothetical imperative which expresses the practical necessity of an action as means to the advancement of happiness is *assertorial.* We are not to present it as necessary for an uncertain and merely possible purpose, but for a purpose which we may presuppose with certainty and *a priori* in every man, because it belongs to his being. Now skill in the choice of means to his own greatest well-being may be called *prudence,* in the narrowest sense. And thus the imperative which refers to the choice of means to one's own happiness, that is, the precept of prudence, is still always *hypothetical;* the action is not commanded absolutely, but only as means to another purpose.

Categorical imperatives command without conditions. Morality thus consists of categorical imperatives which must be obeyed for their own sake, whatever the consequences. Properly speaking, only morality commands. (Skills have rules, prudence has advice or "counsel".)

Finally, there is an imperative which commands a certain conduct immediately, without having as its condition any other purpose to be attained by it. This imperative is *categorical.* It concerns not the matter of the action, or its intended result, but its form and the principle of which it is itself a result: and what is essentially good in it consists in the mental disposition, let the consequence be what it may. This imperative may be called that of *morality.* . . .

The very form of a categorical imperative tells us what it is, namely, the necessity that the maxim of an action should conform to an unconditional, universal law.

When I conceive a hypothetical imperative, in general I do not know beforehand what it will contain until I am given the condition. But when I conceive a categorical imperative, I know at once what it contains. For as the imperative contains besides the law only the necessity that the maxims shall conform to this law, while the law contains no conditions restricting it, there remains nothing but the general statement that the maxim of the action should conform to a universal law, and it is this conformity alone that the imperative properly represents as necessary.

Furthermore, there can be but a single categorical imperative (thus, *the* categorical imperative).

There is therefore but one categorical imperative, namely, this. *Act only on that maxim whereby thou canst at the same time will that it should become a universal law.*

All other categorical imperatives ("thou shalt not kill," "don't lie") are either alternative formulations of this imperative or derived (deduced) from it.

Now if all imperatives of duty can be deduced from this one imperative as from their principle, then, although it should remain undecided whether what is called duty is not merely a vain notion, yet at least we shall be able to show what we understand by it and what this notion means.

One alternative formulation is this:

Since the universality of the law according to which effects are produced constitutes what is properly called *nature* in the most general sense (as to form)—that is, the existence of things so far as it is determined by general laws—the imperative of duty may be expressed thus: *Act as if the maxim of thy action were to become by thy will a universal law of nature.*

The two formulations look the same, but the slight difference in wording makes an enormous difference. The first says, "a universal law." In other words, what if everyone were to adopt this as their maxim? The second says, "a universal law of nature." In Kant's philosophy, the realm of morality (freedom and the will) is radically separated from the world of nature (the world of science and causality). The law of nature formulation is thus concerned not with the maxim of action but rather with the actual results. It is one thing to ask, What if everyone tried to do that?—something quite different to ask, What if everyone actually *did* that?

Kant now gives us four illustrations, a mixed batch of examples whose point is not always clear (but then, we should be delighted to get a few examples; Kant does not give us many of them).

We will now enumerate a few duties, adopting the usual division of them into duties to ourselves and to others, and into perfect and imperfect duties.

1. A man reduced to despair by a series of misfortunes feels wearied of life, but is still so far in possession of his reason that he can ask himself whether it would not be contrary to his duty to himself to take his own life. Now he inquires whether the maxim of his action could become a universal law of nature. His maxim is: From self-love I adopt it as a principle to shorten my life when its longer duration is likely to bring more evil than satisfaction. It is asked then simply whether this principle founded on self-love can become a universal law of nature. Now we see at once that a system of nature of which it should be a law to

destroy life by means of the very feeling whose special nature it is to impel to the improvement of life would contradict itself, and therefore could not exist as a system of nature; hence that maxim cannot possibly exist as a universal law of nature, and consequently would be wholly inconsistent with the supreme principle of all duty.

2. Another finds himself forced by necessity to borrow money. He knows that he will not be able to repay it, but sees also that nothing will be lent to him unless he promises stoutly to repay it in a definite time. He desires to make this promise, but he has still so much conscience as to ask himself: Is it not unlawful and inconsistent with duty to get out of a difficulty in this way? Suppose, however, that he resolves to do so, then the maxim of his action would be expressed thus: When I think myself in want of money I will borrow money and promise to repay it, although I know that I never can do so. Now this principle of self-love or of one's own advantage may perhaps be consistent with my whole future welfare; but the question now is, Is it right? I change then the suggestion of self-love into a universal law, and state the question thus: How would it be if my maxim were a universal law? Then I see at once that it could never hold as a universal law of nature, but would necessarily contradict itself. For supposing it to be a universal law that everyone when he thinks himself in a difficulty should be able to promise whatever he pleases, with the purpose of not keeping his promise, the promise itself would become impossible, as well as the end that one might have in view in it, since no one would consider that anything was promised to him, but would ridicule all such statements as vain pretenses.

3. A third finds in himself a talent which with the help of some culture might make him a useful man in many respects. But he finds himself in comfortable circumstances and prefers to indulge in pleasure rather than to take pains in enlarging and improving his happy natural capacities. He asks, however, whether his maxim of neglect of his natural gifts, besides agreeing with his inclination to indulgence, agrees also with what is called duty. He sees then that a system of nature could indeed subsist with such a universal law, although men (like the South Sea islanders) should let their talents rest and resolve to devote their lives merely to idleness, amusement, and propagation of their species—in a word, to enjoyment; but he cannot possibly *will* that this should be a universal law of nature, or be implanted in us as such by a natural instinct. For, as a rational being, he necessarily wills that his faculties be developed, since they serve him, and have been given him, for all sorts of possible purposes.

4. A fourth, who is in prosperity, while he sees that others have to contend with great wretchedness and that he could help them, thinks: What concern is it of mine? Let everyone be as happy as Heaven pleases, or as he can make himself; I will take nothing from him nor even envy him, only I do not wish to contribute anything to his welfare or to his assistance in distress! Now no doubt, if such a mode of thinking were a universal law, the human race might very well subsist, and doubtless even better than in a state in which everyone talks of sympathy and good-will, or even takes care occasionally to put it into practice, but, on the other side, also cheats when he can, betrays the rights of men, or

otherwise violates them. But although it is possible that a universal law of nature might exist in accordance with that maxim, it is impossible to *will* that such a principle should have the universal validity of a law of nature. For a will which resolved this would contradict itself, inasmuch as many cases might occur in which one would have need of the love and sympathy of others, and in which, by such a law of nature, sprung from his own will, he would deprive himself of all hope of the aid he desires.

Let's look at these examples again.

1. Suppose a man is miserable and is contemplating suicide. The maxim of his intended action is "for my own sake, I will end my life if I am only going to be miserable," Could this be a universal law of nature? No, Kant argues, since nature could not maintain life if living things were unwilling to endure hardship to survive. Notice that it is the "law of nature" formulation that Kant uses here; it is not clear how the "first formulation" (universal law) would work in the same case. Presumably our concern is not whether cabbages and worms would commit suicide but rather the morality of rational creatures doing so.

2. Here we see repeated in more detail the example already used in sect. 1. A person needs money and is forced to borrow, falsely promising to repay when he knows that he cannot. The maxim would be, "If I need money, I will make a false promise to repay it." Universalized, it becomes, "Anyone who needs money can make false promises to get it, even knowing that repayment is impossible." We have already noted the sense in which such a law contradicts itself. Kant puts it with unusual charm, "No one would consider that anything was promised to him, but would ridicule all such statements as vain pretenses," This is the key example. Note again that it is not the inconvenience of the projected universal results that makes the act immoral. It is the logical *inconsistency* of the universalized maxim. Thus the test of a maxim, as an attempted instance of the categorical imperative, is this:

1 State the maxim of your action
2 Universalize it as a law for everyone
3 Ask yourself whether the intended action would still be possible after such universalization

The whole process is not much different in strategy than the grandmotherly admonition, "What if everyone did that?" The difference, of course, is that Kant has a theory about why it matters to ask such a question which does not so easily allow the usual reply, "But everyone *won't* do it!" Since it is a logical condition and not merely speculation on the results of mass conformity, Kant is not so easily answered as grandmother (who is probably worried about actual consequences).

3. The third example again returns to the second formulation. But notice too that Kant here appeals to his overall teleological vision, the idea that our talents have been given to us for a purpose. In fact, the usual test of the categorical imperative seems *not* to work here, for Kant even admits that we could universalize our laziness as a law of nature and all be like (what Kant fantasizes as) the South Pacific natives who do little but lie in the sun and enjoy themselves. The argument, then, is not that the universalized maxim contradicts itself but rather that it contradicts nature's purposes—a very different matter.

4. The fourth example is, ironically, a conservative political philosophy which has become (but has always been) popular in the United States, usually under the all-purpose banner of "liberty." It is the view that everyone should make his or her own

way in the world and be as happy as he or she can be, but without expecting help from anyone else. It is a philosophy, not surprisingly, usually espoused by those who are already rich and well-off, or soon plan to be. Could such an attitude by universalized as law? (Kant remarks that the resulting world might not be as bad as a world in which everyone liberally espoused sympathetic platitudes about the poor but never did a damned thing themselves about it.) Notice that here again it is primarily the law of nature formulation (why?) and notice again that the contradiction involved is less than convincing. The argument (which has been made into the basis of an elaborate theory of justice by American Kantian philosopher John Rawls[1], is that none of us no matter how rich or well-off, would be willing to universalize the attitude that "each person should get what he or she can, but without expecting any help from others" because one never knows when he or she might *need* the help of others. (Rawls sets up the conditions of the just society such that everyone could agree to its conditions without knowing their own role or place. It is an immensely expanded version of the childhood lesson in justice, in which the older child is asked to cut the cake, with the understanding that the other children will get the first choices.) As Kant presents the case, however, justice is not the issue. It is rather whether one might oneself claim just the help that this attitude now denies to others and thus contradict oneself. One might well argue, however, that one could consistently hold this position, even, when—unhappily—one finds oneself in precisely the downtrodden position that one never before considered (though not every conservative carries this through in practice).

Out of four examples, only one fully employs the first and primary formulation of the categorical imperative, and, perhaps not coincidentally, it is the only one of the examples that seems to illustrate adequately the thesis that Kant has been arguing. Nevertheless, Kant seems contented with the argument, even commenting that "it has been completely shown by these examples how all duties depend . . . on the same principle."

These are a few of the many actual duties, or at least what we regard as such, which obviously fall into two classes on the one principle that we have laid down. We must be *able to will* that a maxim of our action should be a universal law. This is the canon of the moral appreciation of the action generally. Some actions are of such a character that their maxim cannot without contradiction be even *conceived* as a universal law of nature, far from it being possible that we should *will* that it *should* be so. In others, this intrinsic impossibility is not found, but still it is impossible to *will* that their maxim should be raised to the universality of a law of nature, since such a will would contradict itself. It is easily seen that the former violate strict or rigorous (inflexible) duty; the latter only laxer (meritorious) duty. Thus it has been completely shown by these examples how all duties depend as regards the nature of the obligation (not the object of the action) on the same principle.

If what Kant says about the categorical imperative is true, then how is it possible that we ever do anything knowingly wrong? (This is very much the kind of question asked by Socrates, Plato, and Aristotle under the name "incontinence." See pages 102 to 107.) But the problem is not that we do not know the moral principle in question or that we (conveniently) forget it. Nor is it the kind of incontinence focused on by Plato and

[1]*A Theory of Justice* (Cambridge: Harvard University Press, 1971).

Aristotle, when desire or passion blinds us to what we ought to do. It is rather that, as rationalizing as well as rational beings, we make *exceptions* of ourselves.

If now we attend to ourselves on occasion of any transgression of duty, we shall find that we in fact do not will that our maxim should be a universal law, for that is impossible for us; on the contrary, we will that the opposite should remain a universal law, only we assume the liberty of making an *exception* in our own favor or (just for this time only) in favor of our inclination. Consequently, if we considered all cases from one and the same point of view, namely, that of reason, we should find a contradiction in our own will namely, that a certain principle should be objectively necessary as a universal law, and yet subjectively should not be universal, but admit of exceptions. As, however, we at one moment regard our action from the point of view of a will wholly conformed to reason, and then again look at the same action from the point of view of a will affected by inclination, there is not really any contradiction, but an antagonism of inclination to the precept of reason, whereby the universality of the principle is changed into a mere generality, so that the practical principle of reason shall meet the maxim half way. Now, although this cannot be justified in our own impartial judgment, yet it proves that we do really recognize the validity of the categorical imperative and (with all respect for it) only allow ourselves a few exceptions which we think unimportant and forced from us.

Kant now returns to the teleological perspective and asks once again how we can know that there is such a law, a categorical imperative, such as he has just explained.

We have thus established at least this much—that if duty is a conception which is to have any import and real legislative authority for our actions, it can only be expressed in categorical, and not at all in hypothetical, imperatives. We have also, which is of great importance, exhibited clearly and definitely for every practical application the content of the categorical imperative, which must contain the principle of all duty if there is such a thing at all. We have not yet, however, advanced so far as to prove a priori that there actually is such an imperative, that there is a practical law which commands absolutely of itself and without any other impulse, and that the following of this law is duty.

With the view of attaining to this it is of extreme importance to remember that we must not allow ourselves to think of deducing the reality of this principle from the *particular attributes of human nature.* For duty is to be a practical, unconditional necessity of action: it must therefore hold for all rational beings (to whom an imperative can apply at all), and *for this reason only* be also a law for all human wills. On the contrary, whatever is deduced from the particular natural characteristics of humanity, from certain feelings and propensions, nay, even, if possible, from any particular tendency proper to human reason, and which need not necessarily hold for the will of every rational being—this may indeed supply us with a maxim but not with a law; with a subjective principle on which we may have a propension and inclination to act, but not with an objective principle on which we should be *enjoined* to act, even though all our propensions, inclinations, and natural dispositions were opposed to it. In fact, the sublimity and intrinsic dignity of the command in duty are so much the more evident, the less the subjective impulses favor it and the more they oppose it, without being able in the slightest degree to weaken the obligation of the law or to diminish its validity.

Here then we see philosophy brought to a critical position, since it has to be firmly fixed, notwithstanding that it has nothing to support it in heaven or earth. Here it must show its purity as absolute director of its own laws, not the herald of those which are whispered to it by an implanted sense or who knows what tutelary nature. Although these may be better than nothing, yet they can never afford principles dictated by reason, which must have their source wholly *a priori* and thence their commanding authority, expecting everything from the supremacy of the law and the due respect for it, nothing from inclination, or else condemning the man to self-contempt and inward abhorrence.

And again the distinction between the empirical and the essential a priori questions of morality is discussed.

Thus every empirical element is not only quite incapable of being an aid to the principle of morality, but is even highly prejudicial to the purity of morals; for the proper and inestimable worth of an absolutely good will consists just in this that the principle of action is free from all influence of contingent grounds, which alone experience can furnish. We cannot too much or too often repeat our warning against this lax and even mean habit of thought which seeks for its principle among empirical motives and laws; for human reason in its weariness is glad to rest on this pillow, and in a dream of sweet illusions (in which, instead of Juno, it embraces a cloud) it substitutes for morality a bastard patched up from limbs of various derivation, which looks like anything one chooses to see in it; only not like virtue to one who has once beheld her in her true form.

The question then is this: Is it a necessary law *for all rational beings* that they should always judge of their actions by maxims of which they can themselves will that they should serve as universal laws? If it is so, then it must be connected (altogether *a priori*) with the very conception of the will of a rational being generally. . . .

Two terms often employed by Kant, and by many philosophers and philosophy students, are the words "subjective" and "objective." The maxim of an action, for example, is described as a "subjective" principle, as opposed to a law, which is "objective." Similarly, in his first critique, Kant is concerned to show that our subjective experiences and beliefs are in fact objective knowledge. "Subjective" means literally "pertaining to the subject," the individual person. Subjective experience therefore includes personal biases and misinformation, and the maxims (that is, subjective principles) of our actions inevitably contain selfish or at least self-centered concerns. Moral laws are free from any selfish or self-referential concerns, just as objective knowledge is free from such biases and misinformation. In the following passage, Kant also distinguishes between the subjective "springs" of action and the objective "motive." (We will see much more of these terms in the pages to follow.)

The will is conceived as a faculty of determining oneself to action *in accordance with the conception of certain laws*. And such a faculty can be found only in rational beings. Now that which serves the will as the objective ground of its self-determination is the *end,* and if this is assigned by reason alone, it must hold for all rational beings. On the other hand, that which merely contains the ground of possibility of the action of which the effect is the end, this is called the *means*. The subjective ground of the desire is the *spring,* the objective ground of the volition is the *motive;* hence the distinction between subjective ends which rest on springs, and objective ends which depend on motives valid for every rational being. Practical principles are *formal* when they abstract from all subjective ends; they are *material* when they assume these, and therefore particular, springs of action. The ends which a rational being proposes to himself at pleasure as *effects* of his actions (material ends) are all only relative, for it is only their relation to the particular desires of the subject that gives them their worth, which therefore cannot furnish principles universal and necessary for all rational beings and for every volition, that is to say, practical laws. Hence all these relative ends can give rise only to hypothetical imperatives.

We are now ready to introduce a third formulation of the categorical imperative, one that is as important as the first. The principle is that we should always treat people as ends, never (merely) as means. In other words, don't "use" people. We have already seen that Kant considers the concern for (our own) happiness to be only a hypothetical imperative. But the concern for happiness in general (which includes us) is nevertheless the basis for this categorical imperative. (Notice that Kant uses the word "humanity" to refer to individual human beings as well as the human species in general.)

Supposing, however, that there were something *whose existence* has *in itself* an absolute worth, something which, being *an end in itself,* could be a source of definite laws, then in this and this alone would lie the source of a possible categorical imperative, that is, a practical law.

Now I say: man and generally any rational being *exists* as an end in himself, *not merely as a means* to be arbitrarily used by this or that will, but in all his actions, whether they concern himself or other rational beings, must be always regarded at the same time as an end. All objects of the inclinations have only a conditional worth; for if the inclinations and the wants founded on them did not exist, then their object would be without value, But the inclinations themselves, being sources of want, are so far from having an absolute worth for which they should be desired that, on the contrary, it must be the universal wish of every rational being to be wholly free from them. Thus the worth of any object which is *to be acquired* by our action is always conditional. Beings whose existence depends not on our will but on nature's, have nevertheless, if they are irrational beings, only a relative value as means, and are therefore called *things;* rational beings, on the contrary, are called *persons,* because their very nature points them out as ends in themselves, that is, as something which must not be used merely as means, and so far therefore restricts freedom of action (and is an object of respect). These, therefore, are not merely subjective ends whose existence has a worth *for us* as an effect of our action, but *objective* ends, that is, things whose existence is an end in itself—an end, moreover, for which no other can be substituted, which they should subserve *merely* as means, for otherwise nothing whatever would possess *absolute worth;* but if all worth were conditioned and therefore contingent, then there would be no supreme practical principle of reason whatever.

If then there is a supreme practical principle or, in respect of the human will, a categorical imperative, it must be one which, being drawn from the conception of that which is necessarily an end for everyone because it is *an end in itself,* constitutes an *objective* principle of will, and can therefore serve as a universal practical law. The foundation of this principle is: *rational nature exists as an end in itself.* Man necessarily conceives his own existence as being so; so far then this is a *subjective* principle of human actions. But every other rational being regards its existence similarly, just on the same rational principle that holds for me; so that it is at the same time an objective principle from which as a supreme practical law all laws of the will must be capable of being deduced. Accordingly the practical imperative will be as follows: *So act as to treat humanity, whether in thine own person or in that of any other, in every case as an end withal, never as means only.* We will now inquire whether this can be practically carried out.

Kant now returns to his previous examples and tests them according to this new formulation.

To abide by the previous examples:

First, under the head of necessary duty to oneself: He who contemplates suicide should ask himself whether his action can be consistent with the idea of humanity *as an end in itself.* If he destroys himself in order to escape from painful circumstances, he uses a person merely as *a mean* to maintain a tolerable condition up to the end of life. But a man is not a thing, that is to say, something which can be used merely as means, but must in all his actions be always considered as an end in himself. I cannot, therefore, dispose in any way of a man in my own person so as to mutilate him, to damage or kill him. (It belongs to ethics proper to define this principle more precisely, so as to avoid all misunderstanding, for example, as to the amputation of the limbs in order to preserve myself; as to exposing my life to danger with a view to preserve it, etc. This question is therefore omitted here.)

Secondly, as regards necessary duties, or those of strict obligation, towards others: He who is thinking of making a lying promise to others will see at once that he would be using another man *merely as a mean,* without the latter containing at the same time the end in himself. For he whom I propose by such a promise to use for my own purposes cannot possibly assent to my mode of acting towards him, and therefore cannot himself contain the end of this action. This violation of the principle of humanity in other men is more obvious if we take in examples of attacks on the freedom and property of others. For then it is clear that he who transgresses the rights of men intends to use the person of others merely as means, without considering that as rational beings they ought always to be esteemed also as ends, that is, as beings who must be capable of containing in themselves the end of the very same action.

Thirdly, as regards contingent (meritorious) duties to oneself: It is not enough that the action does not violate humanity in our own person as an end in itself, it must also *harmonize* with it. Now there are in humanity capacities of greater perfection which belong to the end that nature has in view in regard to humanity in ourselves as the subject; to neglect these might perhaps be consistent with the *maintenance* of humanity as an end in itself, but not with the *advancement* of this end.

Fourthly, as regards meritorious duties towards others: The natural end which all men have is their own happiness. Now humanity might indeed subsist although no one should contribute anything to the happiness of others, provided he did not intentionally withdraw anything from it; but after all, this would only harmonize negatively, not positively, with *humanity as an end in itself,* if everyone does not also endeavor, as far as in him lies, to forward the ends of others. For the ends of any subject which is an end in himself ought as far as possible to be *my* ends also, if that conception is to have its *full* effect with me.

Again there are oddities, (1) A man who commits suicide is said to be "using himself," an odd argument at the least. (We might be using someone else as a mere means if we kill him in order to help our career or steal his valuables, but it is hard to argue that killing oneself is on a logical par.) (2) Here again, the case is more convincing. It is using someone in a malicious and immoral way to make false promises. (3) Again he invokes the teleological viewpoint (in this case, the "advancement" of humanity). (4) Again he invokes the principle of harmony (from part 3), but it is not clear that neglecting other people's welfare (or rationalizing it as their own responsibility) is a violation of people as "ends" or treating them merely as "means."

What happens now has been interpreted by some Kant scholars as a fourth formulation of the categorical imperative. It is not stated as such, but it clearly has some of the same features as the first three formulations. The actual formulation might read, "Act as a universal legislator."

This principle that humanity and generally every rational nature is *an end in itself* (which is the supreme limiting condition of every man's freedom of action), is not borrowed from experience, *first,* because it is universal, applying as it does to all rational beings whatever, and experience is not capable of determining anything about them; *secondly,* because it does not present humanity as an end to men (subjectively), that is, as an object which men do of themselves actually adopt as an end; but as an objective end which must as a law constitute the supreme limiting condition of all our subjective ends, let them be what we will; it must therefore spring from pure reason. In fact the objective principle of all practical legislation lies (according to the first principle) in *the rule* and its form of universality which makes it capable of being a law (say, for example, a law of nature); but the *subjective* principle is in the *end;* now by the second principle, the subject of all ends is each rational being inasmuch as it is an end in itself. Hence follows the third practical principle of the will, which is the ultimate condition of its harmony with the universal practical reason, viz., the idea of *the will of every rational being as a universally legislative will.*

On this principle all maxims are rejected which are inconsistent with the will being itself universal legislator. Thus the will is not subject to the law, but so subject that it must be regarded *as itself giving the law,* and on this ground only subject to the law (of which it can regard itself as the author).

In the previous imperatives, namely, that based on the conception of the conformity of actions to general laws, as in a *physical system of nature,* and that based on the universal *prerogative* of rational beings as *ends* in themselves— these imperatives just because they were conceived as categorical excluded from any share in their authority all admixture of any interest as a spring of action; they were, however, only *assumed* to be categorical, because such an assumption was necessary to explain the conception of duty. But we could not prove independently that there are practical propositions which command categorically, nor can it be proved in this section; one thing, however, could be done, namely, to indicate in the imperative itself, by some determinate expression, that in the case of volition from duty all interest is renounced, which is the specific criterion of categorical as distinguished from hypothetical imperatives. This is done in the present (third) formula of the principle, namely, in the idea of the will of every rational being as a *universally legislating will.*

For although a will *which is subject to laws* may be attached to this law by means of an interest, yet a will which is itself a supreme lawgiver, so far as it is such, cannot possibly depend on any interest, since a will so dependent would itself still need another law restricting the interest of its self-love by the condition that it should be valid as universal law.

Thus the *principle* that every human will is *a will which in all its maxims gives universal laws,* provided it be otherwise justified, would be very *well adapted* to be the categorical imperative, in this respect, namely, that just because of the idea of universal legislation it is *not based on any interest,* and therefore it alone among all possible imperatives can be *unconditional.* Or still better, converting the proposition, if there is a categorical imperative (that is, a law for the will of every rational being), it can only command that everything be done from maxims of one's will regarded as a will which could at the same time will that it should itself give universal laws, for in that case only the practical principle and the imperative which it obeys are unconditional, since they cannot be based on any interest.

Kant now introduces—somewhat late in the discussion—his central insistence on *autonomy,* which is not part of the categorical imperative as such but rather its precondition.

Looking back now on all previous attempts to discover the principle of morality, we need not wonder why they all failed. It was seen that man was bound to laws by duty, but it was not observed that the laws to which he is subject are *only those of his own giving,* though at the same time they are *universal,* and that he is only bound to act in conformity with his own will—a will, however, which is designed by nature to give universal laws. For when one has conceived man only as subject to a law (no matter what), then this law required some interest, either by way of attraction or constraint, since it did not originate as a law from *his own will,* but this will was according to a law obliged by *something else* to act in a certain manner. Now by this necessary consequence all the labor spent in finding a supreme principle of *duty* was irrevocably lost. For men never elicited duty, but only a necessity of acting from a certain interest. Whether this interest was private or otherwise, in any case the imperative must be conditional, and could not by any means be capable of being a moral command. I will therefore call this the principle of *Autonomy* of the will, in contrast with every other which I accordingly reckon as *Heteronomy.*

And finally, a fifth formulation of the categorical imperative, a somewhat utopian vision which says, in effect, that we should act as if we were all members of the perfectly moral community.

The conception of every rational being as one which must consider itself as giving in all the maxims of its will universal laws, so as to judge itself and its actions from this point of view—this conception leads to another which depends on it and is very fruitful, namely, that of a *kingdom of ends.*

By a "kingdom" I understand the union of different rational beings in a system by common laws. Now since it is by laws that ends are determined as regards their universal validity, hence, if we abstract from the personal differences of rational beings, and likewise from all the content of their private ends, we shall be able to conceive all ends combined in a systematic whole (including both rational beings as ends in themselves, and also the special ends which each may propose to himself), that is to say, we can conceive a kingdom of ends, which on the preceding principles is possible.

For all rational beings come under the *law* that each of them must treat itself and all others *never merely as means,* but in every case *at the same time as ends in themselves.* Hence results a systematic union of rational beings by common objective laws, that is, a kingdom which may be called a kingdom of ends, since what these laws have in view is just the relation of these beings to one another as ends and means. It is certainly only an ideal.

A rational being belongs as a *member* to the kingdom of ends when, although giving universal laws in it, he is also himself subject to these laws. He belongs to it *as sovereign* when, while giving laws, he is not subject to the will of any other.

A rational being must always regard himself as giving laws either as member or as sovereign in a kingdom of ends which is rendered possible by the freedom of will. He cannot, however, maintain the latter position merely by the maxims of his will, but only in case he is a completely independent being without wants and with unrestricted power adequate to his will.

Morality consists then in the reference of all action to the legislation which alone can render a kingdom of ends possible. This legislation must be capable of existing in every rational being, and of emanating from his will, so that the principle of this will is never to act on any maxim which could not without contradiction be also a universal law, and accordingly always so to act *that the will could at the same time regard itself as giving in its maxims universal laws.* If now the maxims of rational beings are not by their own nature coincident with this objective principle, then the necessity of acting on it is called practical necessitation that is, *duty.* Duty does not apply to the sovereign in the kingdom of ends, but it does to every member of it and to all in the same degree.

What is so "perfect" about the kingdom of ends (which is sometimes interpreted as Heaven) is not just that everyone wills and does what is right but that everyone *respects* everyone else. This is the point of the third formulation ("people as ends, not merely means") as well, but it can be summarized in a very different word—"dignity." Dignity, however, is not to be considered a mere "value," for it has no market price; it cannot be bought or sold. Kant is here reacting to early capitalism in Europe (the market society was just beginning to go strong, at the end of the eighteenth century[2]). He is saying, in modern terms, that "human life and dignity do not have a price. They are absolute and have intrinsic worth."

The practical necessity of acting on this principle, that is, duty, does not rest at all on feelings, impulses, or inclinations, but solely on the relation of rational beings to one another, a relation in which the will of a rational being must always be regarded as *legislative,* since otherwise it could not be conceived as *an end in itself.* Reason then refers every maxim of the will, regarding it as legislating universally, to every other will and also to every action towards oneself; and this not on account of any other practical motive or any future advantage, but from the idea of the *dignity* of a rational being, obeying no law but that which he himself also gives.

In the kingdom of ends everything has either *value* or *dignity.* Whatever has a value can be replaced by something else which is *equivalent;* whatever, on the other hand, is above all value, and therefore admits of no equivalent, has a dignity.

Whatever has reference to the general inclinations and wants of mankind has a *market value;* whatever, without presupposing a want, corresponds to a certain taste, that is, to a satisfaction in the mere purposeless play of our faculties, has a *fancy value;* but that which constitutes the condition under which alone anything can be an end in itself, this has not merely a relative worth, that is, value, but an intrinsic worth, that is, *dignity.*

Now morality is the condition under which alone a rational being can be an end in himself, since by this alone it is possible that he should be a legislating member in the kingdom of ends. Thus morality, and humanity as capable of it, is that which alone has dignity. Skill and diligence in labor have a market value; wit, lively imagination, and humor have fancy value; on the other hand, fidelity to promises, benevolence from principle (not from instinct), have an intrinsic worth. Neither nature nor art contains anything which in default of these it could put in their place, for their worth consists not in the effects which spring from them, not in the use and advantage which they secure, but in the disposition of

[2]Adam Smith wrote *Wealth of Nations* in 1776.

mind, that is, the maxims of the will which are ready to manifest themselves in such actions, even though they should not have the desired effect. These actions also need no recommendation from any subjective taste or sentiment, that they may be looked on with immediate favor and satisfaction; they need no immediate propension or feeling for them; they exhibit the will that performs them as an object of an immediate respect, and nothing but reason is required to *impose* them on the will; not to *flatter* it into them, which, in the case of duties, would be a contradiction. This estimation therefore shows that the worth of such a disposition is dignity, and places it infinitely above all value, with which it cannot for a moment be brought into comparison or competition without as it were violating its sanctity.

What then is it which justifies virtue or the morally good disposition, in making such lofty claims? It is nothing less than the privilege it secures to the rational being of participating in the giving of universal laws, by which it qualifies him to be a member of a possible kingdom of ends, a privilege to which he was already destined by his own nature as being an end in himself, and on that account legislating in the kingdom of ends; free as regards all laws of physical nature, and obeying those only which he himself gives, and by which his maxims can belong to a system of universal law to which at the same time he submits himself. For nothing has any worth except what the law assigns it. Now the legislation itself which assigns the worth of everything must for that very reason possess dignity, that is, an unconditional incomparable worth; and the word *respect* alone supplies a becoming expression for the esteem which a rational being must have for it. *Autonomy* then is the basis of the dignity of human and of every rational nature. . . .

must have for it. *Autonois of the dignity of human and of every rational nature. . . .*

The Autonomy of the Will as the Supreme Principle of Morality

Autonomy of the will is that property of it by which it is a law to itself (independently of any property of the objects of volition). The principle of autonomy then is: Always so to choose that the same volition shall comprehend the maxims of our choice as a universal law. . . . That the principle of autonomy in question is the sole principle of morals can be readily shown by mere analysis of the conceptions of morality. For by this analysis we find that its principle must be a categorical imperative, and that what this commands is neither more nor less than this very autonomy.

DISCUSSION

The categorical imperative is the true key to Kant's philosophy. In two words, it summarizes the deontological orientation of his ethics: a moral principle is an "unconditional command." The categorical imperative is also the condensed statement of morality in general, particularly in its first formulation which commands us to always act as we would will others to act too ("Act as if the maxim of your action were to be a universal law for everyone.") The resemblance to the biblical Golden Rule is more than superficial, and Kant himself comments on the kinship between the two.

The role of the categorical imperative in ethics, however, is something more specific as well. It is a *test* of moral principles, a kind of criterion. The conditions Kant imposes on the categorical imperative—not only its unconditional nature but its form as a universal principle—also mark the conditions which any moral principle—any particular categorical imperative—must fulfill. A moral maxim must be universalizable as moral law. What determines a moral law, Kant argues, are purely formal conditions. That is, one need not (and should not) look at the particular circumstances or consequences or feelings of the agent, nor should one consult authorities or the customs of the locale. A maxim which has the wrong form cannot be universalized, and a maxim which is not moral cannot be universalized without inconsistency. Inconsistency or contradiction is a purely formal flaw in principles and thus appropriate, as Kant's analysis demands, for a purely rational test of a purely rational endeavor, morality.

There are a great many problems here, needless to say. What Kant demands is clear enough; moral principles are a priori principles of reason and so must be established independent of empirical concerns (such as the feelings or fortunes of the participants). But what he means by "inconsistency" or "contradiction" is not at all clear, as evidenced by his hardly adequate four examples. And whether the categorical imperative test will work for even a small subsection of what we consider the moral realm, as one tries it out on more and more examples, becomes increasingly doubtful.

Consider, for example, the moral question of adultery. Suppose one is considering having an illicit affair and, following Kant's test, universalizes his or her maxim. What is the result? One might argue that the institution of marriage as we know it would be changed considerably; sexual fidelity would no longer be a part of it (not even the pretense of fidelity). But would this count as an inconsistency? A contradiction? It does not seem so. Consider also the troublesome example of a shoplifter, about to steal a gadget from a department store. He or she being Kantian universalizes the maxim and asks, What if everyone would steal? A plausible answer would be that, if everyone would take whatever he or she wanted, without considering who owned anything, then the very notion of ownership would seem to collapse, and ownership would be nothing but possession ("ten-tenths of the law," one might say). Stealing would therefore be impossible, for stealing is a violation of ownership, which would no longer exist.

This imagined consequence, however, is more problematic than it looks at first. It does seem as if we have a contradiction of just the sort Kant envisioned, but now suppose that we present our deliberations to a Marxist, who believes that private property is itself illegitimate and immoral. The Marxist will say, "good, then everyone ought to steal." Kant would reply that this is an illicit appeal to consequences, namely, the Marxist's hoped-for improvement of the human lot with the abolition of private property. But suppose the Marxist, ready for this reply, responds as follows, "If that is a contradiction, it is only because you begin by *assuming* the legitimacy of the institution of private property. In other words, the categorical imperative has the result, no matter how 'formal' its appearance, of protecting already established institutions, whatever they may be." The real question, we can then imagine our Marxist insisting, is whether those institutions themselves are good. The categorical imperative simply begs the ethical question.

Perhaps the most troublesome objection to Kant's categorical imperative is aimed at the one part of the theory that we have so far taken at face value—the maxim itself. What is the maxim of a particular action? It is not, Kant insists, the *end* of the action, its purpose or desired result. It is not the desire or the "spring" of action. It is rather its implicit principle, its subjective characterization. But how is this determined? Consider an example: a man cannot afford medicine for his sick wife. The pharmacy has refused him credit; the pharmicist has just left the prescription desk to answer the telephone. The man spies the medicine on the inside counter, within an easy stretch. A Kantian, he pauses a moment to deliberate, What if everyone were to . . .? To what? To steal? To steal medicine? To steal medicine that is desperately needed? To steal medicine desperately needed that one cannot afford? To steal this particular medicine which one's wife desperately needs and which one cannot afford? Which is the correct implicit principle of the intended action? Which is the maxim?

Part of the problem is the fact that the maxim is implicit; it does not appear in consciousness fully articulated but is rather formulated afterward, as a description of one's intention. But even leaving aside the psychological nuances of unconscious and deceptive maxims (for example, "to steal medicine from this bastard who turned me down in my hour of need") the variety of alternative maxims is bewildering. The maxim might include only the most general, value-neutral description of the action, "to take medicine from a pharmacy without paying for it," or it might be extremely detailed and specific, "to take this medicine from this pharmacy under the nose of this pharmacist who had just turned down a request for credit in the face of this desperate situation in which one's wife has this disease with these symptoms. . . ." In the process of universalization, of course, one would presumably take out all of the particular references (to "this" pharmacy and pharmacist, for instance), but one might retain their substance, neverthe- less, with a detailed description ("a pharmacist about 40 years old, slightly balding at the top, wearing tortoise-shell glasses"). The first step of Kant's test of a moral principle, "take the maxim of your action," is extremely problematic. How specific—or how general—should a maxim be?

This objection, that the maxim does not appear fully articulated and can be characterized in any of a variety of ways, is not just a technical difficulty. It undermines the whole point of the categorical imperative. This becomes evident as soon as we take several of these competing maxims and universalize them. If the man in the pharmacy asks, "What if everyone were to take medicine without paying for it?" the economic consequences for the drug companies might be disturbing, but the consistency of the universal law does not seem to be called into question. Even with the more loaded description, "to steal medicine," one can presume that the free market system and the institution of private property do not depend upon the pharmaceuticals industry and no contradiction is even on the horizon. Generalized to the description, "to steal," of course, the contradiction does arise in Kant's sense, but why is "to steal" a more accurate description of the intended act than "to steal medicine which one desperately needs." If we universalize the latter, it is hard to imagine anything remotely resembling a contradiction in Kant's sense. But what this means is that the logical or formal consequences of universalizing the maxim of one's action depend on the detail and nature of the characterization of the maxim. This, however, requires just that attention to empirical elements that Kant tried to eliminate, an attention to circumstances and personal need, for example. The man might settle for the general description, "to steal," and then try to make an exception of himself, as Kant suggested. But he need not do this, and if he is a clever Kantian, he will rather alter his description of his intended action such that he is not an exception at all. Thus it is possible, by way of a suitable framing of one's universal principles, to always find or create a principle that passes Kant's test and, nevertheless, is wholly designed to satisfy one's personal inclinations.

The purely formal test devised by Kant seems to collapse against the force of this objection. This is not, however, an argument against Kant's deontological ethics or against the categorical imperative (as Mill charges, for instance). It is only an argument against the adequacy of the categorical imperative alone as a standard for what—specifically—we ought to do. The general theory of morality as formal and a priori has not thus been refuted; what has been shown—barring a successful reply—is that the general theory by itself has no fixed rule of application to particular cases. (If there were such a rule, would we need a rule for the application of rules? This question worried Kant and has worried many of his critics since.) Even if we accept the moral principle that one should not steal, it still remains open for us to decide, in each particular case, what counts as stealing and whether all kinds of stealing are equally prohibited.

Suppose two categorical imperatives contradict one another. Suppose you have to decide whether to lie about your friend's whereabouts to the Nazis, the alternative being to have a hand in your friend's death. Even if we agree on the proper characterization of the alternative maxims and principles involved, how can we decide which takes (a priori) priority? The well-being of the friend is not a permissible consideration (nor is the question how you will be able to live with yourself later). If the decision—as a moral decision—must rest on purely formal criteria, what could they be?

One suggestion that Kant makes is the distinction between "perfect" and "imperfect" duties. A perfect duty is one which cannot be violated universally. (Lying is the usual example, since universal lying makes impossible the very act of lying.) An imperfect duty is one whose violation one cannot *will* universally, but nevertheless it might be possible for everyone to violate it. Complicity to murder (or even murder) would, on this account, not be a violation of a perfect duty (since everyone might try to murder each other in a way that everyone could not try to lie to one another). But this has an intolerable consequence for our example above; the perfect duty not to lie takes priority over the imperfect duty not to be an accomplice in your friend's death.

One Kantian reply which bears more consideration than it is usually given is the insistence that the first formulation of the categorical imperative alone is not meant to provide the test of morality; only the various formulations together do this. Thus the lying versus murder example above may not be decided in a palatable way by the first formulation, but the second ("law of nature") formulation does give us our preferred answer. The "ends not merely means" formulation further provides an important set of considerations not included in the first two, most importantly some (formal) concern for the well-being of the people involved. Together, the various formulations give us a much more complete moral picture, and a more complete moral test.

D. Freedom and Autonomy

It is in the third and last section of the *Groundwork* that Kant actually takes up the metaphysics of his moral philosophy, the basic principles which form the foundations of morality. In his earlier *Critique of Pure Reason,* Kant had summarized the basic concerns of metaphysics in a phrase, "God, Freedom and Immortality." The first and last of these—God and immortality—are a brief summary of what in fact is the essence of Christianity: the belief in an all-powerful, all-knowing, and beneficent God who is also our ultimate moral judge, and belief in the immortality of the human soul, which will survive the death of the body and be able to reap the rewards—or punishments—which we have earned here in life.[3] The second metaphysical principle—freedom—is the condition without which the very concept of morality would make no sense at all. "Ought implies can," writes Kant, meaning that it makes no sense to say that a person ought to do something unless he or she is free to do it—or not to do it. It would make no sense to say that a person ought to break the law of gravity, for example, but neither would it make sense to tell a person that he or she ought to obey it. Where there is no freedom to choose, there are no moral considerations. Freedom, Kant tells us, is "the key to the explanation of the autonomy of the will."

In *The Critique of Pure Reason,* Kant had argued that every event in the universe must have its sufficient natural cause; in other words, it had to happen in a certain way because of all of the other events and conditions preceding it. But this idea of universal causality—though undeniable in science—is intolerable in the realm of human action, where we would like to think (and must think, if we are to make sense of moral freedom) that *we* are the cause of our behavior, however influenced we may be by our circumstances, our upbringing, and any number of other causal factors. Thus Kant makes a sharp distinction in his philosophy between the "sensible" world of nature, which is ruled by causality, and the "intelligible" world of freedom, which is the world of the will, our autonomous choices, which are not determined by anything foreign to the will itself.

But freedom from external determination of our choices and actions is only part of the meaning of this all-important condition of morality; Kant calls this a "negative" sense of freedom, freedom from external causes of our actions. But there is also a "positive" concept of freedom, which is the freedom to will in accordance with the moral law. Here Kant again distinguishes between the moral law—which is central to the world of freedom and morality—and the laws of nature—which are within the domain of causality. It is of the utmost importance for Kant to keep these always separate, for it is the separation of freedom from nature (and our inclinations) which forms the foundation of his entire moral philosophy.

THIRD SECTION.

Transition from the Metaphysic of Morals to the Critique of Pure Practical Reason.

The Concept of Freedom is the Key that explains the Autonomy of the The Will. The *will* is a kind of causality belonging to living beings in so far as they are rational, and *freedom* would be this property of such causality that it can be efficient, independently on foreign causes *determining* it; just as *physical necessity* is the property that the causality of all irrational beings has of being determined to activity by the influence of foreign causes.

The preceding definition of freedom is *negative,* and therefore unfruitful for the discovery of its essence; but it leads to a *positive* conception which is so much the more full and fruitful. Since the conception of causality involves that of laws,

---

[3]Kant discusses the connection between morality and religion in *The Critique of Practical Reason* and in his later work, *Religion within the Bounds of Reason Alone* (1794).

according to which, by something that we call cause, something else, namely, the effect, must be produced; hence, although freedom is not a property of the will depending on physical laws, yet it is not for that reason lawless; on the contrary, it must be a causality acting according to immutable laws, but of a peculiar kind; otherwise a free will would be an absurdity. Physical necessity is a heteronomy of the efficient causes, for every effect is possible only according to this law, that something else determines the efficient cause to exert its causality. What else then can freedom of the will be but autonomy, that is the property of the will to be a law to itself? But the proposition: The will is in every action a law to itself, only expresses the principle, to act on no other maxim than that which can also have as an object itself as a universal law. Now this is precisely the formula of the categorical imperative and is the principle of morality, so that a free will and a will subject to moral laws are one and the same. . . .

Freedom

Must Be Presupposed as a Property of the Will of all Rational Beings   It is not enough to predicate freedom of our own will, from whatever reason, if we have not sufficient grounds for predicating the same of all rational beings. For as morality serves as a law for us only because we are *rational beings,* it must also hold for all rational beings; and as it must be deduced simply from the property of freedom, it must be shown that freedom also is a property of all rational beings. It is not enough, then, to prove it from certain supposed experiences of human nature (which indeed is quite impossible, and it can only be shown *à priori*), but we must show that it belongs to the activity of all rational beings endowed with a will. Now I say every being that cannot act except *under the idea of freedom* is just for that reason in a practical point of view really free, that is to say, all laws which are inseparably connected with freedom have the same force for him as if his will had been shown to be free in itself by a proof theoretically conclusive. Now I affirm that we must attribute to every rational being which has a will that it has also the idea of freedom and acts entirely under this idea. For in such a being we conceive a reason that is practical, that is, has causality in reference to its objects. Now we cannot possibly conceive a reason consciously receiving a bias from any other quarter with respect to its judgments, for then the subject would ascribe the determination of its judgment not to its own reason, but to an impulse. It must regard itself as the author of its principles independent of foreign influences. Consequently as practical reason or as the will of a rational being it must regard itself as free, that is to say, the will of such a being cannot be a will of its own except under the idea of freedom. This idea must therefore in a practical point of view be ascribed to every rational being.

Of the Interest Attaching to the Ideas of Morality   We have finally reduced the definite conception of morality to the idea of freedom. This latter, however, we could not prove to be actually a property of ourselves or of human nature; only we saw that it must be presupposed if we would conceive a being as rational and conscious of its causality in respect of its actions, *i.e.,* as endowed with a will; and so we find that on just the same grounds we must ascribe to every being endowed with reason and will this attiibute of determining itself to action under the idea of its freedom.

Now it resulted also from the presupposition of this idea that we became aware of a law that the subjective principles of action, *i.e.* maxims, must also be so assumed that they can also hold as objective, that is, universal principles, and so serve as universal laws of our own dictation. But why, then, should I subject myself to this principle and that simply as a rational being, thus also subjecting to it all other beings endowed with reason? I will allow that no interest *urges* me to this, for that would not give a categorical imperative, but I must *take* an interest in it and discern how this comes to pass; for this "I ought" is properly an "I would," valid for every rational being, provided only that reason determined his actions without any hindrance. But for beings that are in addition affected as we are by springs of a different kind, namely sensibility, and in whose case that is not always done which reason alone would do, for these that necessity is expressed only as an "ought," and the subjective necessity is different from the objective.

It seems, then, as if the moral law, that is, the principle of autonomy of the will, were properly speaking only presupposed in the idea of freedom, and as if we could not prove its reality and objective necessity independently. In that case we should still have gained something considerable by at least determining the true principle more exactly than had previously been done; but as regards its validity and the practical necessity of subjecting oneself to it, we should not have advanced a step. For if we were asked why the universal validity of our maxim as a law must be the condition restricting our actions, and on what we ground the worth which we assign to this manner of acting—a worth so great that there cannot be any higher interest; and if we were asked further how it happens that it is by this alone a man believes he feels his own personal worth, in comparison with which that of an agreeable or disagreeable condition is to be regarded as nothing, to these questions we could give no satisfactory answer.

DISCUSSION

When Kant calls the realm of morality "the world of freedom," he is clearly stating, once again, the basic proposition of his entire conception of morality. Morality means acting *willfully* and not because one is in any way compelled to act, whether by external forces or by one's own inclinations. And morality means *autonomy,* that is, accepting the moral law for oneself and by oneself, on the basis of reason alone. The impetus behind this radical emphasis on fredom is the entire Enlightenment, as well as the independent spirit of Kant's Pietist Lutheranism. But the philosophical emphasis is clearly directed against that whole history of ethics, from Aristotle to Hume, that would reduce morals to a matter of inclination—to the search for happiness and the satisfaction of desires. For Aristotle and Hume, nothing is more essential to morality than participation in a community, which sets the customs and expectations, which cultivates in us the proper sentiments and gives moral behavior both its purpose and sanction. (A similar view is defended by

Hegel—against Kant—only a few years later.) But for Kant, participation in a community —has nothing to do with morality. Moral principles are a matter of the rational will, which means that we must be free to see beyond and even reject the customs and expectations we have learned. We must sometimes fight our sentiments and inclinations in general; indeed, our moral worth is tested in our ability to do so. The purpose of moral behavior, Kant insists, is not utility but rationality itself, in which freedom and autonomy are the key ingredients. As for sanctions, it is not a matter of morality if we behave correctly because of fear of censure or embarrassment. This too is a denial of freedom, that is, the freedom to do what we will independently of any causal influences, of which punishment is a primary example. (Kant and his German followers, including Hegel, were very concerned with the nature of punishment, which they felt turned a person into an "object" and denied his or her free will.)

It is important to ask, however, whether Kant goes too far in the direction of freedom and autonomy. Even if there are universal moral principles, for example, does it make sense to suppose that we can discover them through reason alone, without the context (as well as the education) of some particular community? And is freedom really the essence of morals? Why so dismiss the Aristotelian vision of a society of people who are "naturally" good just because they have been taught to be good, not because they "will" it, perhaps against all inclination? Is "moral worth" so important? Is autonomy really the inescapable basis of ethics? Or is it possible that Kant's ideal ultimately leaves us in a moral vacuum, with a sense of ourselves devoid of any ethos, attachment, or belonging?

STUDY QUESTIONS

1 What is the "categorical imperative"? How is a categorical imperative distinguished from a "hypothetical" imperative? Why does Kant talk about *the* categorical imperative rather than simply talking about categorical imperatives ("don't lie," "don't cheat") in general?

2 What is "duty"? How do we distinguish duties from other acts that we think we should do? What does Kant mean by "acting for the sake of duty" (rather than "in accordance with duty")?

3 Why are *principles* so central to Kant's conception of morality? Why does he talk so little about "good character" and "personal merit," as Aristotle and Hume do? Why does he dismiss consequences as irrelevant to moral worth?

4 What is "moral worth"? Can an act be good in any sense but not show moral worth? Can a person be good in any sense if he or she does not have moral worth? A person who wants to do what is right, but for reasons of inclination rather than a sense of duty, does not thereby have moral worth; why does Kant insist on this? Is he saying that we are not acting morally unless we do not want to do what we ought to do, but do it because we have to?

5 Why does Kant call his ethical treatise a work on "the metaphysics of morals"? Why does he call it a "metaphysics"?

6 Why does Kant reject Hume's moral skepticism? How does he reject it? What role do the sentiments play in Kant's ethics?

7 Why is freedom a presupposition of morality (a "postulate of practical reason")? Does the development of good habits and "character"—as in Aristotle—mean that we are not acting freely? Does "freedom" in Kant mean that we are free to choose anything? What restrictions does he place on this freedom?

8 What does it mean to say that morality is a function of "practical reason"? As opposed to what? What does this mean about the form of moral principles?

9 Why must there be a God and an immortal soul in order for there to be morality? In what sense are these presuppositions of duty? In what ways do these two "postulates of practical reason" threaten the central thesis of Kant's moral philosophy?

10 What is a "deontological" theory of morals? How is Kant's ethics an example of such a moral theory?

11 What is "autonomy"? What is necessary for a being to be autonomous? If a person accepts the idea that the Ten Commandments are the direct commandments of God, does that make him or her less autonomous? If a person resolves to obey the law and defend his or her country, ("right or wrong") does that mean less autonomy?

12 Is seeking the advice and opinions of other people acting in accordance with Kant's moral philosophy? Should we do this? Must we do this?

13 Why does Kant say that the only thing good "without qualification" is a good will? Why is being born rich not good "without qualification"? Why not being in good health or successful?

14 Do religious commandments tell us our duty because they are given by God? Or has God given them to us because they do in fact tell us what is good? What moral and religious questions depend on the answer to this question?

15 Is God rational? Why or why not?

16 Are we rational? In what senses? In what senses not? What does Kant mean by rationality?

17 Why not lie? Is it ever right to lie? How does Kant's categorical imperative act as a test in cases in which we are tempted to lie (even for good reasons)? In what sense is it inconsistent to will that everyone, in similar circumstances, ought to lie?

18 What is the connection—if any—between the various formulations of the categorical imperative? Which formulations are most important? Or are they all of equal importance? Why not just stick with the first (and best known) formulation, and treat the others as corollaries or subsidiary principles?

19 Is Kant a teleologist? In what sense? What purpose does reason serve, and why does it not primarily serve to make us happy, according to Kant?

20 What are "inclinations" and why are they of no moral worth?

21 What does it mean to urge love as "practical" (as opposed to "pathological")? Why does Kant insist on this?

22 Why should one not commit suicide, according to Kant, even if life is very painful and unpromising and seems much more trouble than it's worth?

23 In what peculiar sense does Kant claim to have a "popular philosophy"? (Nietzsche wrote: "Kant's joke; he defended the common man in language which the common man could not possibly understand.")

24 Why should we help other people, according to Kant? What should motivate us, if our actions are morally worthy? What is the place of sympathy?

25 What is a "maxim"? Give some examples of maxims of actions. When does a maxim become a moral law?

26 What is the "kingdom of ends"? What ideal role does it play in Kant's ethics? In his religious vision of the *summum bonum?*

27 If I promised my friend that I would go to the movies with him, but my brother gets ill and asks me to stay with him, what should I do, according to Kant? How do I decide what to do?

CHAPTER 7

JOHN STUART MILL

While the concept of "utility" has been employed by any number of modern authors in ethics (David Hume, for instance), the name "utilitarianism" is inevitably associated with one author more than any other, John Stuart Mill. (He also made up the word, though he admits adopting it "from a passing expression" in a popular book of the time.) The idea that happiness (or pleasure) and the general well-being should be the basis and the ultimate aim of ethics has been prominent since at least Aristotle, but, nevertheless, it was Mill who took this teleological (that is, goal-oriented) ethical standard and turned it into a precise contemporary viewpoint. Indeed, many moral philosophers would insist that utilitarianism is one of the very few commonly agreed upon candidates for a general ethical theory. Whether or not one believes that it can overcome certain now standard objections, utilitarianism—in much the form that Mill defended it over a century ago—is one of the most plausible and prominent ethical viewpoints.

Utilitarianism was, in more primitive form, the ethical philosophy of the Enlightenment, particularly in England and France, during most of the seventeenth and eighteenth centuries. (It is worth noting that it had comparatively little influence in Germany, where Kant was the foremost defender of Enlightenment thinking.) Hume was only one of many secular, business-minded reformers who insisted that utility—what is useful—is the only reasonable general standard for social rules, laws, and moral principles, and by the time of Jeremy Bentham, at the end of the eighteenth century, this idea was generally accepted among the liberal-minded. It was Bentham who turned the idea into a rigorous decision procedure, however, and, with Mill's father—James Mill—initiated a kind of movement aimed primarily at legal reform in England. By the time John Stuart joined this movement (he always rejected the idea of utilitarianism as a single sectarian viewpoint), it was, on the one hand, already well established but, on the other hand, it was being profoundly challenged by an antithetical countermovement from Germany. That counter-movement was Kant's deontological (that is, duty-based) ethics, which rejected the premise of the utilitarian philosophy, the so-called "principle of utility" (named by

Bentham)—"the principle which approves or disapproves of every action whatsoever, according to the tendency which it appears to have to augment or diminish the happiness of the party whose interest is in question" [Bentham, *An Introduction to the Principles of Morals and Legislation* (New York: Hafner, 1948), Prop. II].

Not surprisingly, therefore, Mill begins his classic treatise defining and defending utilitarianism (simply entitled *Utilitarianism,* published in 1861) with a few general remarks about the obviousness of the principle of utility and the fact that even Kant felt compelled to recognize it in his ethics. The argument between Kant and Mill is one of the most basic arguments in ethics—if not *the* basic argument in ethical theory—but it involves several dimensions, not just "duty versus utility," and so the confrontation between them is often based on misunderstandings and failure to address the same question. First of all, as the very names tell us, Mill's ethics of utility is a teleological ethics concerned with human happiness and desires, while Kant's deontological ethics explicitly rejects utility as a measure of moral worth and instead emphasizes duty *even to the exclusion of utility and happiness.* But this head-on collision is not as it seems. Notice that what Kant rejects is the idea that moral worth is measured by utility; that is, the moral goodness of the person is not a question of how useful he or she is but rather how good his or her intentions are and the morality of the principles (maxims) which define those intentions. Kant does not reject the idea that the goodness of the action (not the person) may be measured by utility; indeed, he would be willing to admit that, in such a context, the very meaning of a "good" act is its contribution to happiness, *so long as it is not also taken as a measure of moral worth.* And Mill, on his side, does not reject the idea that we do evaluate persons according to their intentions as well as according to the utility of their actions. What he rejects is the Kantian emphasis on intentions instead of usefulness, as if a person could be perfectly good even if his or her good intentions consistently resulted in the most awful consequences. (Dostoevsky wrote a novel, about the same time, about just such a fellow; the novel was appropriately called *The Idiot.)* The collision thus seems more of a sideswipe; there is certainly a deep disagreement in emphasis but not the wholesale contradiction suggested by many proponents of one view or the other.

The same might be said of the utilitarian emphasis on *consequences,* which Kant rejects as being irrelevant to morality. It is not that Mill is unconcerned with the intentions (or the goodwill) behind a person's actions, but he is concerned with such intentions only insofar as these too have a bearing on utility. Would we be so concerned about a misanthrope's malicious intentions, for example, if every expression of his contempt was in fact a great boon to everyone? And it is not as if Kant is unconcerned with happiness in his emphasis on duty alone as the measure of moral worth. Indeed, some of his arguments even suggest that one justification of the emphasis on duty is the promotion of happiness (for example, in the "kingdom of ends" formulation of the categorical imperative, page 277). Moreover, Kant both begins and ends his *Groundwork* with the observation that we find it intolerable that virtue should not be commensurate with happiness, and it is on this basis that Mill considers him, in effect, a closet utilitarian, for whom "utilitarian arguments are indispensable." (You will notice that Mill intentionally misunderstands Kant's insistence that it is the logical inconsistency of universalized maxims, not their consequences, that is the test of the categorical imperative. See page 276.)

Jeremy Bentham's version of utilitarianism was a purely quantitative calculus ("the happiness calculus") in which the sheer amounts of pleasure and pain were the measure of the goodness or badness of an action. Mill rejects this purely quantitative calculus, insisting that the *quality* of pleasure and pain is equally important. He recognized that, as a general ethical theory (as opposed to a theory of punishment, for example), there had to be some essential distinction made between the indulgent pleasures of gluttons and libertines and the more-"refined" pleasures of artists, philosophers, and saints. (Note the agreement here with Kant's third example, concerned with developing one's talents rather than lying around naked and contented in the sun.) The revision tended to take some of the "vulgarity" out of utilitarianism, but at a considerable cost. The primary virtue of Bentham's theory was its simplicity, the fact that all ethical decisions could be appealed to a single standard—the *summum bonum* of pleasure and pain. But as Mill adds the dimension of quality to the utilitarian calculus, we find ourselves with two standards instead of just one: the *amount* of pleasure and pain and the *quality* of the pleasures and pains. But where there are two standards, one must have a way of weighing them against one another. How much artistic suffering—Rembrandt agonizing over an unfinished portrait—is balanced by how much pleasure? (A trip to southern France? Dinner at the luxurious Shwarte Shaep restaurant?) Or are we comparing apples and bananas? Can one compare the joys of reading Joyce with the pleasures of a good glass of wine? The problem with adding a conception of the quality of pleasure is that it destroys just that simple evaluation device which seemed to be the most obvious virtue of utilitarianism. And, in deciding the relative quality of pleasures, is there not also the tendency to slip into just that a priori mode of thinking which Mill was so concerned to reject? (For example: "It doesn't matter what the consequences are, art is good in itself." Or in the lingo of the late nineteenth century, "Art for art's sake.")

In *Utilitarianism,* Mill first defines what he means by the name of his theory, but then he also goes on to "prove" and defend it. The "proof" is qualified by the fact that—as Mill tells us—one cannot actually prove ultimate principles. Bentham had claimed this too, that defending the principle of utility was "as impossible as it is needless." It was a simple fact of nature, Bentham had argued, that everything we do was governed by "the two sovereign masters, pleasure and pain." ["In words a man may pretend to abjure their empire; but in reality he will remain subject to it all the while" (Bentham, *Introduction to the Principles of Morals and Legislation,* 1948, Prop. I).] Nevertheless, Mill does provide us with a proof, and it has become perhaps the single most controversial element of his ethics. We will encounter and discuss it in Section D (Chapter 4, "Of What Sort of Proof the Principle of Utility Is Susceptible"). Finally, Mill takes on one of the most damaging objections to utilitarianism, its apparent inability to adequately account for justice. After all, if the only measures of right and wrong are the amounts and qualities of pleasure and pain, what grounds are there for people's rights (for example, the right to a fair share, or the right not to be tortured) when these do not promote "the greatest good for the greatest number"? (See Section E, Mill's Chapter 5.)

JOHN STUART MILL

Mill was born in 1806 into a hard-driving, intellectual family. His accomplishments by the age of 10 would have been admirable in a 60-year-old scholar; he learned languages and higher mathematics; he studied the sciences and could discuss the latest theories and discoveries in science with the most brilliant academicians in London. But he pushed himself and was pushed so hard that he suffered a nervous breakdown at the age of 20 and turned his attention from the hard sciences to the "softer" and more emotionally expressive study of poetry. He also became involved in political reform and the early feminist movement, with his wife Harriet Taylor. He is best known for his ethical and political writings, particularly *On Liberty* (1859) and *Utilitarianism* (1863), but his works on logic, mathematics, and the philosophy of science represent the best efforts of the British empiricist tradition in the nineteenth century. John Stuart Mill died in 1873.

A. Happiness and the *Summum Bonum*

In his General Remarks, Mill addresses the question of the *summum bonum,* the "foundation of morality." He points out that utilitarianism has been a viable candidate for that exalted conceptual position ever since Socrates and the Sophists, but it has often been confused. He asserts the resolutely teleological orientation of his ethics: "All action is for the sake of some end." "Rules of action," he adds, "take their whole character and color from the end to which they are subservient." Having thus attacked Kant's position (though not yet Kant by name) he then goes on to claim that "all those *a priori* moralists" ("who deem it necessary to argue at all") in fact find utilitarian arguments "indispensable" to them, whether or not they admit this. Finally referring to Kant with great respect, Mill points out that even he could not defend an ethic of pure duty which would allow him to deduce any substantial specific conclusion.

CHAPTER I. GENERAL REMARKS

There are few circumstances among those which make up the present condition of human knowledge more unlike what might have been expected, or more significant of the backward state in which speculation on the most important subjects still lingers, than the little progress which has been made in the decision of the controversy respecting the criterion of right and wrong. From the dawn of philosophy, the question concerning the *summum bonum,* or, what is the same thing, concerning the foundation of morality, has been accounted the main problem in speculative thought, has occupied the most gifted intellects and divided them into sects and schools, carrying on a vigorous warfare against one another. And after more than two thousand years the same discussions continue, philosophers are still ranged under the same contending banners, and neither thinkers nor mankind at large seem nearer to being unanimous on the subject than when the youth Socrates listened to the old Protagoras, and asserted (if Plato's dialogue be grounded on a real conversation) the theory of utilitarianism against the popular morality of the so-called sophist.

It is true that similar confusion and uncertainty and, in some cases, similar discordance exist respecting the first principles of all the sciences, not excepting that which is deemed the most certain of them—mathematics, without much impairing, generally indeed without impairing at all, the trustworthiness of the

J. S. Mill, *Utilitarianism* (1863).

conclusions of those sciences. An apparent anomaly, the explanation of which is that the detailed doctrines of a science are not usually deduced from, nor depend for their evidence upon, what are called its first principles. Were it not so, there would be no science more precarious, or whose conclusions were more insufficiently made out, than algebra, which derives none of its certainty from what are commonly taught to learners as its elements, since these, as laid down by some of its most eminent teachers, are as full of fictions as English law, and of mysteries as theology. The truths which are ultimately accepted as the first principles of a science are really the last results of metaphysical analysis, practised on the elementary notions with which the science is conversant; and their relation to the science is not that of foundations to an edifice, but of roots to a tree, which may perform their office equally well though they be never dug down to and exposed to light. But though in science the particular truth precede the general theory, the contrary might be expected to be the case with a practical art, such as morals or legislation. All action is for the sake of some end, and rules of action, it seems natural to suppose, must take their whole character and color from the end to which they are subservient. When we engage in a pursuit, a clear and precise conception of what we are pursuing would seem to be the first thing we need, instead of the last we are to look forward to. A test of right and wrong must be the means, one would think, of ascertaining what is right or wrong, and not a consequence of having already ascertained it.

The difficulty is not avoided by having recourse to the popular theory of a natural faculty, a sense or instinct, informing us of right and wrong. For—besides that the existence of such a moral instinct is itself one of the matters in dispute—those believers in it who have any pretensions to philosophy have been obliged to abandon the idea that it discerns what is right or wrong in the particular case in hand, as our other senses discern the sight or sound actually present. Our moral faculty, according to all those of its interpreters who are entitled to the name of thinkers, supplies us only with the general principles of moral judgments; it is a branch of our reason, not of our sensitive faculty; and must be looked to for the abstract doctrines of morality, not for perception of it in the concrete. The intuitive, no less than what may be termed the inductive, school of ethics insists on the necessity of general laws. They both agree that the morality of an individual action is not a question of direct perception, but of the application of a law to an individual case. They recognize also, to a great extent, the same moral laws, but differ as to their evidence and the source from which they derive their authority. According to the one opinion, the principles of morals are evident *a priori*, requiring nothing to command assent except that the meaning of the terms be understood. According to the other doctrine, right and wrong, as well as truth and falsehood, are questions of observation and experience. But both hold equally that morality must be deduced from principles; and the intuitive school affirm as strongly as the inductive that there is a science of morals. Yet they seldom attempt to make out a list of the *a priori* principles which are to serve as the premises of the science; still more rarely do they make any effort to reduce those various principles to one first principle, or common ground of obligation. They either assume the ordinary precepts of morals as of *a priori* authority, or they lay down as the common groundwork of those maxims, some generality much less obviously authoritative than the maxims themselves, and which has never succeeded in gaining popular acceptance. Yet to support their pretensions there ought either to be some one fundamental principle or law at the root of all morality, or, if there be several, there should be a determinate order of precedence among them; and the one principle, or the rule for deciding between the various principles when they conflict, ought to be self-evident.

To inquire how far the bad effects of this deficiency have been mitigated in practice, or to what extent the moral beliefs of mankind have been vitiated or made uncertain by the absence of any distinct recognition of an ultimate standard, would imply a complete survey and criticism of past and present ethical doctrine. It would, however, be easy to show that whatever steadiness or consistency these moral beliefs have attained has been mainly due to the tacit influence of a standard not recognized. Although the non-existence of an acknowledged first principle has made ethics not so much a guide as a consecration of men's actual sentiments, still, as men's sentiments, both in favor and of aversion, are greatly influenced by what they suppose to be the effect of things upon their happiness, the principle of utility, or, as Bentham latterly called it, the greatest happiness principle, has had a large share in forming the moral doctrines even of those who most scornfully reject its authority. Nor is there any school of thought which refuses to admit that the influence of actions on happiness is a most material and even predominant consideration in many of the details, of morals, however unwilling to acknowledge it as the fundamental principle of morality and the source of moral obligation. I might go much further and say that to all those *a priori* moralists who deem it necessary to argue at all, utilitarian arguments are indispensable. It is not my present purpose to criticize these thinkers; but I cannot help referring, for illustration, to a systematic treatise by one of the most illustrious of them, the *Metaphysics of Ethics* by Kant. This remarkable man, whose system of thought will long remain one of the landmarks in the history of philosophical speculation, does, in the treatise in question, lay down a universal first principle as the origin and ground of moral obligation; it is this: "So act that the rule on which thou actest would admit of being adopted as a law by all rational beings." But when he begins to deduce from this precept any of the actual duties of morality, he fails, almost grotesquely, to show that there would be any contradiction, any logical (not to say physical) impossibility, in the adoption by all rational beings of the most outrageously immoral rules of conduct. All he knows is that the *consequences* of their universal adoption would be such as no one would choose to incur.

On the present occasion, I shall, without further discussion of the other theories, attempt to contribute something towards the understanding and appreciation of the "utilitarian" or "happiness" theory, and towards such proof as it is susceptible of. It is evident that this cannot be proof in the ordinary and popular meaning of the term. Questions of ultimate ends are not amenable to direct proof. Whatever can be proved to be good must be so by being shown to be a means to something admitted to be good without proof. The medical art is proved to be good by its conducing to health; but how is it possible to prove that health is good? The art of music is good, for the reason, among others, that it produces pleasure; but what proof is it possible to give that pleasure is good? If, then, it is asserted that there is a comprehensive formula, including all things which are in themselves good, and that whatever else is good is not so as an end but as a means, the formula may be accepted or rejected, but is not a subject of what is commonly understood by proof. We are not, however, to infer that its acceptance or rejection must depend on blind impulse, or arbitrary choice. There is a larger meaning of the word "proof," in which this question is as amenable to it as any other of the disputed questions of philosophy. The subject is within the cognizance of the rational faculty; and neither does that faculty deal with it solely in the way of intuition. Considerations may be presented capable of determining the intellect either to give or withhold its assent to the doctrine; and this is equivalent to proof.

We shall examine presently of what nature are these considerations; in what manner they apply to the case, and what rational grounds, therefore, can be given for accepting or rejecting the utilitarian formula. But it is a preliminary condition of rational acceptance or rejection, that the formula should be correctly understood. I believe that the very imperfect notion ordinarily formed of its meaning, is the chief obstacle which impedes its reception; and that could it be cleared, even from only the grosser misconceptions, the question would be greatly simplified, and a proportion of its difficulties removed. Before, therefore, I attempt to enter into the philosophical grounds which can be given for assenting to the utilitarian standard, I shall offer some illustrations of the doctrine itself; with the view of showing more clearly what it is, distinguishing it from what it is not, and disposing of such of the practical objections to it as either originate in, or are closely connected with, mistaken interpretations of its meaning. Having thus prepared the ground, I shall afterwards endeavour to throw such light as I can upon the question, considered as one of philosophical theory.

DISCUSSION

Mill, like Aristotle, begins his ethics with a clear statement of a teleological position. There is an ultimate good—a *summum bonum*—and all of our actions are aimed (well or foolishly) toward that good. Like Aristotle too, Mill insists that this good is happiness, but for Mill and most modern thinkers, happiness refers more to a state of mind than to achievements or circumstances. It is essential, Mill insists, that we look to the actual consequences of our actions, but the value of these consequences depends upon their effect on us, whether we are satisfied or frustrated, pleased or displeased, caused pleasure or pain. How can Mill prove that the ultimate goal of all of our actions is happiness? He does appeal to the general agreement that this is so (as Aristotle does), but this does not constitute a proof. He considers the a priori views of such moral philosophers as Kant, but these are acceptable only insofar as they too advance happiness. Finally, Mill acknowledges that there may be no proper "proof" of an ultimate principle, but nevertheless he is confident that he can give us good reasons for accepting it. In fact, he offers us a very famous "proof" (in Chapter 4) which philosophers have been picking apart ever since. But whether or not it is provable, the happiness principle—that what we all want and what all ethics is aimed at is happiness—is well established as the starting point of Mill's utilitarianism.

B. What Utilitarianism Is

In Chapter 2, Mill presents his doctrine concerning the *quality* of pleasures, attacking those who say that utilitarianism celebrates only the vulgar pleasures and ignores the "higher" values in life. Mill's model here is the ancient philosopher Epicurus (from whose name we get our word "epicurean" for someone fond of luxury and the good life). Epicurus (341–270 B.C.) also taught that the good life is the life of pleasure, but he too had to convince his critics that he did not mean only the bodily pleasures but intellectual and spiritual pleasures as well. Indeed, Epicurus spent considerable time lecturing his students on the abuses of hedonism (the life of pleasure) and the dangers of excess, and he spent equal time lauding the pleasures of philosophy and the arts. Mill makes the same point, that those who accuse utilitarianism of vulgarity are themselves degrading human life by supposing that only the "lower" pleasures are indeed pleasurable.

It is here too that Mill provides us with his actual criterion for deciding the quality of pleasures: "It is better to be a human being dissatisfied than a pig satisfied: better to be a Socrates dissatisfied than a fool satisfied." But how can we know this? Isn't this just a fraternal expression of support of one philosopher by another? But Mill gives us a test; Socrates knows *both* the life of bodily pleasure and the more difficult life of the mind, and *chooses* the latter. The fool and the pig, however, "know only their own side of the question." The test, in other words, is which pleasure is to be chosen by those who know both of them.

The problem is *why* they choose. When Socrates chooses the pleasures of the mind—however dissatisfying—over the pleasures of the body, on what grounds does he do so? If the former are simply more pleasurable, then we are back to a purely quantitative measure, not a qualitative test. Does Socrates's choice reflect a difference in the quality of pleasures or only his (and Mill's) preference? And is it true that Socrates (or Mill, or we) have a choice, or are we abstract-minded creatures just as caught up in our life of reflection (however modest in its quality) as the fool and the pig are caught up in their life of vulgar hedonism?

Notice that Mill—in direct opposition to Kant—denies that there is any particular virtue to acting "for the sake of duty"; it is only important that our actions are *in accordance with* duty. It is results that count, and though the motive may be relevant to our opinion of the agent, it is irrelevant to the worth of the action.

Mill begins, briefly and sarcastically, by attacking those critics who, on the other side, object that utility is a concept opposed to pleasure (as in the emphasis on mere efficiency demanded by some people, to the exclusion of any enjoyment). Mill essentially calls them stupid and not worth attending to, and then goes on to pronounce his quality of pleasure doctrine, finally turning once again to his critics (including Thomas Carlyle, one of the great writers and thinkers of the time).

A passing remark is all that needs be given to the ignorant blunder of supposing that those who stand up for utility as the test of right and wrong use the term in that restricted and merely colloquial sense in which utility is opposed to pleasure. An apology is due to the philosophical opponents of utilitarianism, for even the momentary appearance of confounding them with anyone capable of so absurd a misconception; which is the most extraordinary, inasmuch as the contrary accusation, of referring everything to pleasure, and that, too, in its grossest form, is another of the common charges against utilitarianism: and, as has been pointedly remarked by an able writer, the same sort of persons, and often the very same persons, denounce the theory "as impracticably dry when the word 'utility' precedes the word 'pleasure,' and as too practically voluptuous when the word 'pleasure' precedes the word 'utility'." Those who know anything about the matter are aware that every writer, from Epicurus to Bentham, who maintained the theory of utility, meant by it, not something to be contradistin-guished from pleasure, but pleasure itself, together with exemption from pain; and instead of opposing the useful to the agreeable or the ornamental, have always declared that the useful means these, among other things. Yet the common herd, including the herd of writers, not only in newspapers and periodicals, but in books of weight and pretension, are perpetually falling into this shallow mistake. Having caught up the word "utilitarian" while knowing nothing whatever about it but its sound they habitually express by it the rejection or the neglect of pleasure in some of its forms: of beauty, of ornament or of amusement. Nor is the term thus ignorantly misapplied solely in disparagement, but occasionally in compliment, as though it implied superiority to frivolity and the mere pleasures of the moment. And this perverted use is the only one in which the word is popularly known, and the one from which the new generation are acquiring their sole notion of its meaning. Those who introduced the word, but who had for many years discontinued it as a distinctive appellation, may well feel themselves called upon to resume it if by doing so they can hope to contribute anything towards rescuing it from this utter degradation.[1]

The creed which accepts as the foundation of morals "utility" or the "greatest happiness principle" holds that actions are right in proportion as they tend to promote happiness, wrong as they tend to produce the reverse of happiness. By happiness is intended pleasure, and the absence of pain; by unhappiness, pain, and the privation of pleasure. To give a clear view of the moral standard set up

---

[1]The author of this essay has reason for believing himself to be the first person who brought the word "utilitarian" into use. He did not invent it, but adopted it from a passing expression in Mr. Galt's *Annals of the Parish*. After using it as a designation for several years, he and others abandoned it from a growing dislike to anything resembling a badge or watchword of sectarian distinction. But as a name for one single opinion, not a set of opinions—to denote the recognition of utility as a standard, not any particular way of applying it—the term supplies a want in the language, and offers, in many cases, a convenient mode of avoiding tiresome circumlocution.

by the theory, much more requires to be said; in particular, what things it includes in the ideas of pain and pleasure; and to what extent this is left an open question. But these supplementary explanations do not affect the theory of life on which this theory of morality is grounded—namely, that pleasure and freedom from pain are the only things desirable as ends; and that all desirable things (which are as numerous in the utilitarian as in any other scheme) are desirable either for the pleasure inherent in themselves, or as means to the promotion of pleasure and the prevention of pain.

Now such a theory of life excites in many minds, and among them in some of the most estimable in feeling and purpose, inveterate dislike. To suppose that life has (as they express it) no higher end than pleasure—no better and nobler object of desire and pursuit—they designate as utterly mean and groveling; as a doctrine worthy only of swine, to whom the followers of Epicurus were, at a very early period, contemptuously likened; and modern holders of the doctrine are occasionally made the subject of equally polite comparisons by its German, French, and English assailants.

When thus attacked, the Epicureans have always answered that it is not they, but their accusers, who represent human nature in a degrading light, since the accusation supposes human beings to be capable of no pleasures except those of which swine are capable. If this supposition were true, the charge could not be gainsaid, but would then be no longer an imputation; for if the sources of pleasure were precisely the same to human beings and to swine, the rule of life which is good enough for the one would be good enough for the other. The comparison of the Epicurean life to that of beasts is felt as degrading, precisely because a beast's pleasures do not satisfy a human being's conceptions of happiness. Human beings have faculties more elevated than the animal appetites and, when once made conscious of them, do not regard anything as happiness which does not include their gratification. I do not, indeed, consider the Epicureans to have been by any means faultless in drawing out their scheme of consequences from the utilitarian principle. To do this in any sufficient manner, many Stoic, as well as Christian, elements require to be included. But there is no known Epicurean theory of life which does not assign to the pleasures of the intellect, of the feelings and imagination, and of the moral sentiments, a much higher value of pleasures than to those of mere sensation. It must be admitted, however, that utilitarian writers in general have placed the superiority of mental over bodily pleasures chiefly in the greater permanency, safety, uncostliness, etc., of the former—that is, in their circumstantial advantages rather than in their intrinsic nature. And on all these points utilitarians have fully proved their case; but they might have taken the other and, as it may be called, higher ground with entire consistency. It is quite compatible with the principle of utility to recognize the fact that some kinds of pleasure are more desirable and more valuable than others. It would be absurd that, while, in estimating all other things, quality is considered as well as quantity, the estimation of pleasures should be supposed to depend on quantity alone.

If I am asked what I mean by difference of quality in pleasures, or what makes one pleasure more valuable than another, merely as a pleasure, except its being greater in amount, there is but one possible answer. Of two pleasures, if there be one to which all or almost all who have experience of both give a decided preference, irrespective of a feeling of moral obligation to prefer it, that is the more desirable pleasure. If one of the two is, by those who are competently acquainted with both, placed so far above the other that they prefer it, even though knowing it to be attended with a greater amount of discontent, and would not resign it for any quantity of the other pleasure which their nature is capable of, we are justified in ascribing to the preferred enjoyment a superiority in quality so far outweighing quantity as to render it, in comparison, of small account.

Now it is an unquestionable fact that those who are equally acquainted with and equally capable of appreciating and enjoying both, do give a most marked preference to the manner of existence which employs their higher faculties. Few human creatures would consent to be changed into any of the lower animals for a promise of the fullest allowance of a beast's pleasures; no intelligent human being would consent to be a fool, no instructed person would be an ignoramus, no person of feeling and conscience would be selfish and base, even though they should be persuaded that the fool, the dunce, or the rascal is better satisfied with his lot than they are with theirs. They would not resign what they possess more than he for the most complete satisfaction of all the desires which they have in common with him. If they ever fancy they would, it is only in cases of unhappiness so extreme that to escape from it they would exchange their lot for almost any other, however undesirable in their own eyes. A being of higher faculties requires more to make him happy, is capable probably of more acute suffering, and certainly accessible to it at more points, than one of an inferior type; but in spite of these liabilities, he can never really wish to sink into what he feels to be a lower grade of existence. We may give what explanation we please of this unwillingness; we may attribute it to pride, a name which is given indiscriminately to some of the most and to some of the least estimable feelings of which mankind are capable: we may refer it to the love of liberty and personal independence, an appeal to which was with the Stoics one of the most effective means for the inculcation of it; to the love of power or to the love of excitement, both of which do really enter into and contribute to it; but its most appropriate appellation is a sense of dignity, which all human beings possess in one form or other, and in some, though by no means in exact, proportion to their higher faculties, and which is so essential a part of the happiness of those in whom it is strong that nothing which conflicts with it could be otherwise than momentarily an object of desire to them. Whoever supposes that this preference takes place at a sacrifice of happiness—that the superior being, in anything like equal circumstances, is not happier than the inferior—confounds the two very different ideas of happiness and content. It is indisputable that the being whose capacities of enjoyment are low has the greatest chance of having them fully satisfied; and a highly endowed being will always feel that any happiness which he can look for, as the world is constituted, is imperfect. But he can learn to bear its imperfections, if they are at all bearable; and they will not make him envy the being who is indeed unconscious of the imperfections, but only because he feels not at all the good which those imperfections qualify. It is better to be a human being dissatisfied than a pig satisfied: better to be Socrates dissatisfied than a fool satisfied. And if the fool, or the pig, are of a different opinion, it is because they only know their own side of the question. The other party to the comparison knows both sides.

It may be objected that many who are capable of the higher pleasures occasionally, under the influence of temptation, postpone them to the lower. But this is quite compatible with a full appreciation of the intrinsic superiority of the higher. Men often, from infirmity of character, make their election for the nearer good, though they know it to be the less valuable; and this no less when the choice is between two bodily pleasures than when it is between bodily and mental. They pursue sensual indulgences to the injury of health, though perfectly aware that health is the greater good. It may be further objected that many who begin with youthful enthusiasm for everything noble, as they advance in years, sink into indolence and selfishness. But I do not believe that those who undergo this very common change voluntarily choose the lower description of pleasures in preference to the higher. I believe that, before they devote themselves exclusively to the one, they have already become incapable of the other. Capacity for the nobler feelings is in most natures a very tender plant, easily killed, not only by hostile influences, but by mere want of sustenance; and in the majority of young persons it speedily dies away if the occupations to which their position in life has devoted them, and the society into which it has thrown them, are not favorable to keeping that higher capacity in exercise. Men lose their high aspirations as they lose their intellectual tastes, because they have not time or opportunity for indulging them; and they addict themselves to inferior pleasures, not because they deliberately prefer them, but because they are either the only ones to which they have access, or the only ones which they are any longer capable of enjoying. It may be questioned whether any one who has remained equally susceptible to both classes of pleasures, ever knowingly and calmly preferred the lower, though many, in all ages, have broken down in an ineffectual attempt to combine both.

From this verdict of the only competent judges, I apprehend there can be no appeal. On a question which is the best worth having of two pleasures, or which of two modes of existence is the most grateful to the feelings, apart from its moral attributes and from its consequences, the judgment of those who are qualified by knowledge of both, or, if they differ, that of the majority of them, must be admitted as final. And there needs be the less hesitation to accept this judgment respecting the quality of pleasures, since there is no other tribunal to be referred to even on the question of quantity. What means are there of determining which is the acutest of two pains, or the intensest of two pleasurable sensations, except the general suffrage of those who are familiar with both? Neither pains nor pleasures are homogeneous, and pain is always heterogeneous with pleasure. What is there to decide whether a particular pleasure is worth purchasing at the cost of a particular pain, except the feelings and judgment of the experienced? When, therefore, those feelings and judgment declare the pleasures derived from the higher faculties to be preferable *in kind,* apart from the question of intensity, to those of which the animal nature, disjoined from the higher faculties, is susceptible, they are entitled on this subject to the same regard.

I have dwelt on this point, as being a necessary part of a perfectly just conception of utility or happiness considered as the directive rule of human conduct. But it is by no means an indispensable condition to the acceptance of the utilitarian standard; for that standard is not the agent's own greatest happiness, but the greatest amount of happiness altogether; and if it may possibly be doubted whether a noble character is always the happier for its nobleness, there can be no doubt that it makes other people happier, and that the world in general is immensely a gainer by it. Utilitarianism, therefore, could only attain its end by the general cultivation of nobleness of character, even if each individual were only benefited by the nobleness of others, and his own, so far as happiness is concerned, were a sheer deduction from the benefit. But the bare enunciation of such an absurdity as this last, renders refutation superfluous.

According to the Greatest Happiness Principle, as above explained, the ultimate end, with reference to and for the sake of which all other things are desirable (whether we are considering our own good or that of other people), is an existence exempt as far as possible from pain, and as rich as possible in enjoyments, both in point of quantity and quality; the test of quality, and the rule for measuring it against quantity, being the preference felt by those who, in their opportunities of experience, to which must be added their habits of self-consciousness and self-observation, are best furnished with the means of comparison. This, being, according to the utilitarian opinion, the end of human action, is necessarily also the standard of morality; which may accordingly be defined, the rules and precepts for human conduct, by the observance of which an existence such as has been described might be, to the greatest extent possible, secured to all mankind; and not to them only, but, so far as the nature of things admits, to the whole sentient creation.

Against this doctrine, however, rises another class of objectors, who say that happiness, in any form, cannot be the rational purpose of human life and action; because, in the first place, it is unattainable: and they contemptuously ask, What right hast thou to be happy? a question which Mr. Carlyle clenches by the addition, What right, a short time ago, hadst thou even *to be?* Next, they say, that men can do *without* happiness; that all noble human beings have felt this, and could not have become noble but by learning the lesson of *Entsagen,* or renunciation; which lesson, thoroughly learnt and submitted to, they affirm to be the beginning and necessary condition of all virtue.

The first of these objections would go to the root of the matter were it well founded; for if no happiness is to be had at all by human beings, the attainment of it cannot be the end of morality, or of any rational conduct. Though, even in that case, something might still be said for the utilitarian theory; since utility includes not solely the pursuit of happiness, but the prevention or mitigation of unhappiness; and if the former aim be chimerical, there will be all the greater scope and more imperative need for the latter, so long at least as mankind think fit to live, and do not take refuge in the simultaneous act of suicide recommended under certain conditions by Novalis. When, however, it is thus positively asserted to be impossible that human life should be happy, the assertion, if not something like a verbal quibble, is at least an exaggeration. If by happiness be meant a continuity of highly pleasurable excitement, it is evident enough that this is impossible. A state of exalted pleasure lasts only moments, or in some cases, and with some intermissions, hours or days, and is the occasional brilliant flash of enjoyment, not its permanent and steady flame. Of this the philosophers who have taught that happiness is the end of life were as fully aware as those who taunt them. The happiness which they meant was not a life of rapture; but moments of such, in an existence made up of few and transitory pains, many and various pleasures, with a decided predominance of the active over the passive, and having as the foundation of the whole, not to expect more from life than it is capable of bestowing. A life thus composed, to those who have been fortunate enough to obtain it, has always appeared worthy of the name of happiness. And such an existence is even now the lot of many, during some considerable portion of their lives. The present wretched education, and wretched social arrangements, are the only real hindrance to its being attainable by almost all.

The objectors perhaps may doubt whether human beings, if taught to consider happiness as the end of life, would be satisfied with such a moderate share of it. But great numbers of mankind have been satisfied with much less. The main constituents of a satisfied life appear to be two, either of which by itself is often found sufficient for the purpose: tranquillity, and excitement. With much tranquillity, many find that they can be content with very little pleasure: with much excitement, many can reconcile themselves to a considerable quantity of pain. There is assuredly no inherent impossibility in enabling even the mass of mankind to unite both; since the two are so far from being incompatible that they are in natural alliance, the prolongation of either being a preparation for, and exciting a wish for, the other. It is only those in whom indolence amounts to a vice, that do not desire excitement after an interval of repose; it is only those in whom the need of excitement is a disease, that feel the tranquillity which follows excitement dull and insipid, instead of pleasurable in direct proportion to the excitement which preceded it. When people who are tolerably fortunate in their outward lot do not find in life sufficient enjoyment to make it valuable to them, the cause generally is, caring for nobody but themselves. To those who have neither public nor private affections, the excitements of life are much curtailed, and in any case dwindle in value as the time approaches when all selfish interests must be terminated by death: while those who leave after them objects of personal affection, and especially those who have also cultivated a fellow-feeling with the collective interests of mankind, retain as lively an interest in life on the eve of death as in the vigour of youth and health. Next to selfishness, the principal cause which makes life unsatisfactory, is want of mental cultivation. A cultivated mind—I do not mean that of a philosopher, but any mind to which the fountains of knowledge have been opened, and which has been taught, in any tolerable degree, to exercise its faculties—finds sources of inexhaustible interest in all that surrounds it; in the objects of nature, the achievements of art, the imaginations of poetry, the incidents of history, the ways of mankind past and present, and their prospects in the future. It is possible, indeed, to become indifferent to all this, and that too without having exhausted a thousandth part of it; but only when one has had from the beginning no moral or human interest in these things and has sought in them only the gratification of curiosity.

Now there is absolutely no reason in the nature of things why an amount of mental culture sufficient to give an intelligent interest in these objects of contemplation, should not be the inheritance of every one born in a civilised country. As little is there an inherent necessity that any human being should be a selfish egotist, devoid of every feeling or care but those which centre in his own miserable individuality. Something far superior to this is sufficiently common even now, to give ample earnest of what the human species may be made. Genuine private affections, and a sincere interest in the public good, are possible, though in unequal degrees, to every rightly brought up human being. In a world in which there is so much to interest, so much to enjoy, and so much also to correct and improve, everyone who has this moderate amount of moral and intellectual requisites is capable of an existence which may be called enviable, and unless such a person, through bad laws, or subjection to the will of others, is denied the liberty to use the sources of happiness within his reach, he will not fail to find this enviable existence, if he escape the positive evils of life, the great sources of physical and mental suffering—such as indigence, disease, and the unkindness, worthlessness, or premature loss of objects of affection. The main stress of the problem lies, therefore, in the contest with these calamities, from which it is a rare good fortune entirely to escape; which, as things now are cannot be obviated, and often cannot be in any material degree mitigated. Yet no one whose opinion deserves a moment's consideration can doubt that most of the great positive evils of the world are in themselves removable, and will, if human affairs continue to improve, be in the end reduced within narrow limits. Poverty, in any sense implying suffering, may be completely extinguished by the wisdom of society, combined with the good sense and providence of individuals. Even that most intractable of enemies, disease, may be indefinitely reduced in dimensions by good physical and moral education, and proper control of noxious influences; while the progress of science holds out a promise for the future of still more direct conquests over this detestable foe. And every advance in that direction relieves us from some, not only of the chances which cut short our own lives, but, what concerns us still more, which deprive us of those in whom our happiness is wrapt up. As for vicissitudes of fortune, and other disappointments connected with worldly circumstances, these are principally the effect either of gross imprudence, of ill-regulated desires, or of bad or imperfect social institutions. All the grand sources, in short, of human suffering are in a great degree, many of them almost entirely, conquerable by human care and effort; and though their removal is grievously slow—though a long succession of generations will perish in the breach before the conquest is completed, and this world becomes all that, if will and knowledge were not wanting, it might easily be made—yet every mind sufficiently intelligent and generous to bear a part, however small and inconspicuous, in the endeavour, will draw a noble enjoyment from the contest itself, which he would not for any bribe in the form of selfish indulgence consent to be without.

And this leads to the true estimation of what is said by the objectors concerning the possibility and the obligation, of learning to do without happiness. Unquestionably it is possible to do without happiness; it is done involuntarily by nineteen-twentieths of mankind, even in those parts of our present world which are least deep in barbarism; and it often has to be done voluntarily by the hero or the martyr, for the sake of something which he prizes more than his individual happiness. But this something, what is it, unless the happiness of others, or some of the requisites of happiness? It is noble to be capable of resigning entirely one's own portion of happiness, or chances of it: but, after all, this self-sacrifice must be for some end; it is not its own end; and if we are told that its end is not happiness, but virtue, which is better than happiness, I ask, would the sacrifice be made if the hero or martyr did not believe that it would earn for others immunity from similar sacrifices? Would it be made, if he thought that his renunciation of happiness for himself would produce no fruit for any of his fellow creatures, but to make their lot like his, and place them also in the condition of persons who have renounced happiness? All honour to those who can abnegate for themselves the personal enjoyment of life, when by such renunciation they contribute worthily to increase the amount of happiness in the world; but he who does it, or professes to do it, for any other purpose, is no more deserving of admiration than the ascetic mounted on his pillar. He may be an inspiring proof of what men *can* do, but assuredly not an example of what they *should*.

Though it is only in a very imperfect state of the world's arrangements that any one can best serve the happiness of others by the absolute sacrifice of his own, yet so long as the world is in that imperfect state, I fully acknowledge that the readiness to make such a sacrifice is the highest virtue which can be found in man. I will add, that in this condition of the world, paradoxical as the assertion may be, the conscious ability to do without happiness gives the best prospect of realising such happiness as is attainable. For nothing except that consciousness can raise a person above the chances of life, by making him feel that, let fate and fortune do their worst, they have not power to subdue him: which, once felt, frees him from excess of anxiety concerning the evils of life, and enables him, like many a Stoic in the worst times of the Roman Empire, to cultivate in tranquillity the sources of satisfaction accessible to him, without concerning himself about the uncertainty of their duration, any more than about their inevitable end.

Meanwhile, let utilitarians never cease to claim the morality of self-devotion as a possession which belongs by as good a right to them, as either to the Stoic or to the Transcendentalist. The utilitarian morality does recognise in human beings the power of sacrificing their own greatest good for the good of others. It only refuses to admit that the sacrifice is itself a good. A sacrifice which does not increase, or tend to increase, the sum total of happiness, it considers as wasted. The only self-renunciation which it applauds, is devotion to the happiness, or to some of the means of happiness, of others; either of mankind collectively, or of individuals within the limits imposed by the collective interests of mankind.

I must again repeat, what the assailants of utilitarianism seldom have the justice to acknowledge, that the happiness which forms the utilitarian standard of what is right in conduct, is not the agent's own happiness, but that of all concerned. As between his own happiness and that of others, utilitarianism requires him to be as strictly impartial as a disinterested and benevolent spectator. In the golden rule of Jesus of Nazareth, we read the complete spirit of the ethics of utility. To do as one would be done by, and to love one's neighbour as oneself constitute the ideal perfection of utilitarian morality. As the means of making the nearest approach to this ideal, utility would enjoin, first, that laws and social arrangements should place the happiness, or (as speaking practically it may be called) the interest, of every individual, as nearly as possible in harmony with the interest of the whole; and secondly, that education and opinion, which have so vast a power over human character, should so use that power as to establish in the mind of every individual an indissoluble association between his own happiness and the good of the whole; especially between his own happiness and the practice of such modes of conduct, negative and positive, as regard for the universal happiness prescribes: so that not only he may be unable to conceive the possibility of happiness to himself, consistently with conduct opposed to the general good, but also that a direct impulse to promote the general good may be in every individual one of the habitual motives of action, and the sentiments connected therewith may fill a large and prominent place in every human being's sentient existence. If the impugners of the utilitarian morality represented it to their own minds in this its true character, I know not what recommendation possessed by any other morality they could possibly affirm to be wanting to it: what more beautiful or more exalted developments of human nature any other ethical system can be supposed to foster, or what springs of action, not accessible to the utilitarian, such systems rely on for giving effect to their mandates.

The objectors to utilitarianism cannot always be charged with representing it in a discreditable light. On the contrary, those among them who entertain anything like a just idea of its disinterested character, sometimes find fault with its standard as being too high for humanity. They say it is exacting too much to require that people shall always act from the inducement of promoting the general interests of society. But this is to mistake the very meaning of a standard of morals, and to confound the rule of action with the motive of it. It is the business of ethics to tell us what are our duties, or by what test we may know them; but no system of ethics requires that the sole motive of all we do shall be a feeling of duty; on the contrary, ninety-nine hundredths of all our actions are done from other motives, and rightly so done, if the rule of duty does not condemn them. It is the more unjust to utilitarianism that this particular misapprehension should be made a ground of objection to it, inasmuch as utilitarian moralists have gone beyond almost all others in affirming that the motive has nothing to do with the morality of the action, though much with the worth of the agent. He who saves a fellow creature from drowning does what is morally right, whether his motive be duty, or the hope of being paid for his trouble: he who betrays the friend that trusts him, is guilty of a crime, even if his object be to serve another friend to whom he is under greater obligations.[2] But to speak only of actions done from the motive of duty, and in direct obedience to principle: it is a misapprehension of the utilitarian mode of thought, to conceive it as implying that people should fix their minds upon so wide a generality as the world, or society at large. The great majority of good actions are intended, not for the benefit of the world, but for that of individuals, of which the good of the world is made up; and the thoughts of the most virtuous man need not on these occasions travel beyond the particular persons concerned, except so far as is necessary to assure himself that in benefiting them he is not violating the rights—that is, the legitimate and authorized expectations—of any one else. The multiplication of happiness is, according to the utilitarian ethics, the object of virtue: the occasions on which any person (except one in a thousand) has it in his power to do this on an extended scale, in other words, to be a public benefactor, are but exceptional; and on these occasions alone is he called on to consider public utility; in every other case, private utility, the interest or happiness of some few persons, is all he has to attend to. Those alone the influence of whose actions extends to society in general, need concern themselves habitually about so large an object. In the case of abstinences indeed—of things which people forbear to do, from moral considerations, though the consequences in the particular case might be beneficial—it would be unworthy of an intelligent agent

[2]An opponent, whose intellectual and moral fairness it is a pleasure to acknowledge (the Rev. J. Llewelyn Davies), has objected to this passage, saying, "Surely the rightness or wrongness of saving a man from drowning does depend very much upon the motive with which it is done. Suppose that a tyrant, when his enemy jumped into the sea to escape from him, saved him from drowning simply in order that he might inflict upon him more exquisite tortures, would it tend to clearness to speak of that rescue as 'a morally right action?' Or suppose again, according to one of the stock illustrations of ethical inquiries, that a man betrayed a trust received from a friend, because the discharge of it would fatally injure that friend himself or some one belonging to him, would utilitarianism compel one to call the betrayal 'a crime' as much as if it had been done from the meanest motive?"

I submit, that he who saves another from drowning in order to kill him by torture afterwards, does not differ only in motive from him who does the same thing from duty or benevolence; the act itself is different. The rescue of the man is, in the case supposed, only the necessary first step of an act far more atrocious than leaving him to drown would have been. Had Mr. Davies said, "The rightness or wrongness of saving a man from drowning does depend very much"—not upon the motive, but— "upon the *intention*," no utilitarian would have differed from him. Mr. Davies, by an oversight too common not to be quite venial, has in this case confounded the very different ideas of Motive and Intention. There is no point which utilitarian thinkers (and Bentham pre-eminently) have taken more pains to illustrate than this. The morality of the action depends entirely upon the intention—that is, upon what the agent *wills* to do. But the motive, that is, the feeling which makes him will so to do, when it makes no difference in the act, makes none in the morality: though it makes a great difference in our moral estimation of the agent, especially if it indicates a good or a bad habitual *disposition*—a bent of character from which useful, or from which hurtful actions are likely to arise.

not to be consciously aware that the action is of a class which, if practised generally, would be generally injurious, and that this is the ground of the obligation to abstain form it. The amount of regard for the public interest implied in this recognition, is no greater than is demanded by every system of morals; for they all enjoin to abstain form whatever is manifestly pernicious to society.

The same considerations dispose of another reproach against the doctrine of utility, founded on a still grosser misconception of the purpose of a standard of morality, and of the very meaning of the words right and wrong. It is often affirmed that utilitarianism renders men cold and unsympathizing; that it chills their moral feelings towards individuals; that it makes them regard only the dry and hard consideration of the consequences of actions, not taking into their moral estimate the qualities from which those actions emanate. If the assertion means that they do not allow their judgment respecting the rightness or wrongness of an action to be influenced by their opinion of the qualities of the person who does it, this is a complaint not against utilitarianism, but against any standard of morality at all; for certainly no known ethical standard decides an action to be good or bad because it is done by a good or a bad man, still less because done by an amiable, a brave, or a benevolent man, or the contrary. These considerations are relevant, not to the estimation of actions, but of persons; and there is nothing in the utilitarian theory inconsistent with the fact that there are other things which interest us in persons besides the rightness and wrongness of their actions. The Stoics, indeed, with the paradoxical misuse of language which was part of their system, and by which they strove to raise themselves above all concern about anything but virtue, were fond of saying that he who has that has everything; that he, and only he, is rich, is beautiful, is a king. But no claim of this description is made for the virtuous man by the utilitarian doctrine. Utilitarians are quite aware that there are other desirable possessions and qualities besides virtue, and are perfectly willing to allow to all of them their full worth. They are also aware that a right action does not necessarily indicate a virtuous character, and that actions which are blameable often proceed from qualities entitled to praise. When this is apparent in any particular case, it modifies their estimation, not certainly of the act, but of the agent. I grant that they are, notwithstanding, of opinion, that in the long run the best proof of a good character is good actions; and resolutely refuse to consider any mental disposition as good, of which the predominant tendency is to produce bad conduct. This makes them unpopular with many people; but it is an unpopularity which they must share with every one who regards the distinction between right and wrong in a serious light; and the reproach is not one which a conscientious utilitarian need be anxious to repel.

If no more be meant by the objection than that many utilitarians look on the morality of actions, as measured by the utilitarian standard, with too exclusive a regard, and do not lay sufficient stress upon the other beauties of character which go towards making a human being loveable or admirable, this may be admitted. Utilitarians who have cultivated their moral feelings, but not their sympathies nor their artistic perceptions, do fall into this mistake; and so do all other moralists under the same conditions. What can be said in excuse for other moralists is equally available for them, namely, that if there is to be any error, it is better that it should be on that side. As a matter of fact, we may affirm that among utilitarians as among adherents of other systems, there is every imaginable degree of rigidity and of laxity in the application of their standard: some are even puritanically rigorous, while others are as indulgent as can possibly be desired by sinner or by sentimentalist. But on the whole, a doctrine which brings prominently forward the interest that mankind have in the repression and prevention of conduct which violates the moral law is likely to be inferior to no other in turning the sanctions of opinion against such violations. It is true, the question, What does violate the moral law? is one on which those who recognise different standards of morality are likely now and then to differ. But difference of opinion on moral questions was not first introduced into the world by utilitarianism, while that doctrine does supply, if not always an easy, at all events a tangible and intelligible mode of deciding such differences.

It may not be superfluous to notice a few more of the common misapprehensions of utilitarian ethics, even those which are so obvious and gross that it might appear impossible for any person of candour and intelligence to fall into them: since persons, even of considerable mental endowments, often give themselves so little trouble to understand the bearings of any opinion against which they entertain a prejudice, and men are in general so little conscious of this voluntary ignorance as a defect, that the vulgarest misunderstandings of ethical doctrines are continually met with in the diliberate writings of persons of the greatest pretensions both to high principle and to philosophy. We not uncommonly hear the doctrine of utility inveighed against as a *godless* doctrine. If it be necessary to say anything at all against so mere an assumption, we may say that the question depends upon what idea we have formed of the moral character of the Deity. If it be a true belief that God desires, above all things, the happiness of his creatures, and that this was his purpose in their creation, utility is not only not a godless doctrine, but more profoundly religious than any other. If it be meant that utilitarianism does not recognize the revealed will of God as the supreme law of morals, I answer, that an utilitarian who believes in the perfect goodness and wisdom of God, necessarily believes that whatever God has thought fit to reveal on the subject of morals, must fulfil the requirements of utility in a supreme degree. But others besides utilitarians have been of opinion that the Christian revelation was intended, and is fitted, to inform the hearts and minds of mankind with a spirit which should enable them to find for themselves what is right, and incline them to do it when found, rather than to tell them, except in a very general way, what it is: and that we need a doctrine of ethics, carefully followed out, to *interpret* to us the will of God. Whether this opinion is correct or not, it is superfluous here to discuss; since whatever aid religion, either natural or revealed, can afford to ethical investigation, is as open to the utilitarian moralist as to any other. He can use it as the testimony of God to the usefulness or hurtfulness of any given course of action, by as good a right as others can use it for the indication of a transcendental law, having no connection with usefulness or with happiness.

Again, Utility is often summarily stigmatized as an immoral doctrine by giving it the name of Expediency, and taking advantage of the popular use of that term to contrast it with Principle. But the Expedient, in the sense in which it is opposed to the Right, generally means that which is expedient for the particular interest of the agent himself; as when a minister sacrifices the interests of his country to keep himself in place. When it means anything better than this, it means that which is expedient for some immediate object, some temporary purpose, but which violates a rule whose observance is expedient in a much higher degree. The Expedient, in this sense, instead of being the same thing with the useful, is a branch of the hurtful. Thus, it would often be expedient, for the purpose of getting over some momentary embarrassment, or attaining some object immediately useful to ourselves or others, to tell a lie. But inasmuch as the cultivation in ourselves of a sensitive feeling on the subject of veracity, is one of the most useful, and the enfeeblement of that feeling one of the most hurtful, things to which our conduct can be instrumental; and inasmuch as any, even unintentional, deviation from truth, does that much towards weakening the trustworthiness of human assertion, which is not only the principal support of all present social well-being, but the insufficiency of which does more than any one thing that can be named to keep back civilisation, virtue, everything on which human happiness on the largest scale depends; we feel that the violation, for a present advantage, of a rule of such transcendent expediency, is not expedient, and that he who, for the sake of convenience to himself or to some other individual, does what depends on him to deprive mankind of the good, and inflict upon them the evil, involved in the greater or less reliance which they can place in each other's word, acts the part of one of their worst enemies. Yet that even this rule, sacred as it is, admits of possible exceptions, is acknowledged by all moralists; the chief of which is when the withholding of some fact (as of information from a malefactor, or of bad news from a person dangerously ill) would preserve some one (especially a person other than oneself) from great and unmerited evil, and when the withholding can only be effected by denial. But in order that the exception may not extend itself beyond the need, and may have the least possible effect in weakening reliance on veracity, it ought to be recognised, and, if possible, its limits defined; and if the principle of utility is good for anything, it must be good for weighing these conflicting utilities against one another, and marking out the region within which one or the other preponderates.

Again, defenders of utility often find themselves called upon to reply to such objections as this—that there is not time, previous to action, for calculating and weighing the effects of any line of conduct on the general happiness. This is exactly as if any one were to say that it is impossible to guide our conduct by Christianity, because there is not time, on every occasion on which anything has to be done, to read through the Old and New Testaments. The answer to the objection is, that there has been ample time, namely, the whole past duration of the human species. During all that time mankind have been learning by experience the tendencies of actions; on which experience all the prudence, as well as all the morality of life, is dependent. People talk as if the commencement of this course of experience had hitherto been put off, and as if, at the moment when some man feels tempted to meddle with the property or life of another, he had to begin considering for the first time whether murder and theft are injurious to human happiness. Even then I do not think that he would find the question very puzzling; but, at all events, the matter is now done to his hand. It is truly a whimsical supposition, that if mankind were agreed in considering utility to be the test of morality, they would remain without any agreement as to what *is* useful, and would take no measures for having their notions on the subject taught to the young, and enforced by law and opinion. There is no difficulty in proving any ethical standard whatever to work ill, if we suppose universal idiocy to be conjoined with it, but on any hypothesis short of that, mankind must by this time have acquired positive beliefs as to the effects of some actions on their happiness; and the beliefs which have thus come down are the rules of morality for the multitude, and for the philosopher until he has succeeded in finding better. That philosophers might easily do this, even now, on many subjects; that the received code of ethics is by no means of divine right; and that mankind have still much to learn as to the effects of actions on the general happiness, I admit, or rather, earnestly maintain. The corollaries from the principle of utility, like the precepts of every practical art, admit of indefinite improvement, and, in a progressive state of the human mind, their improvement is perpetually going on. But to consider the rules of morality as improvable, is one thing; to pass over the intermediate generalisations entirely, and endeavour to test each individual action directly by the first principle, is another. It is a strange notion that the acknowledgment of a first principle is inconsistent with the admission of secondary ones. To inform a traveller respecting the place of his ultimate destination, is not to forbid the use of landmarks and direction-posts on the way. The proposition that happiness is the end and aim of morality, does not mean that no road ought to be laid down to that goal, or that persons going thither should not be advised to take one direction rather than another. Men really ought to leave off talking a kind of nonsense on this subject, which they would neither talk nor listen to on other matters of practical concernment. Nobody argues that the art of navigation is not founded on astronomy, because sailors cannot wait to calculate the Nautical Almanack. Being rational creatures, they go to sea with it ready calculated; and all rational creatures go out upon the sea of life with their minds made up on the common questions of right and wrong, as well as on many of the far more difficult questions of wise and foolish. And this, as long as foresight is a human quality, it is to be presumed they will continue to do. Whatever we adopt as the fundamental principle of morality, we require subordinate principles to apply it by: the impossibility of doing without them, being common to all systems, can afford no argument against any one in particular: but gravely to argue as if no such secondary principles could be had, and as if mankind had remained till now, and always must remain, without drawing any general conclusions from the experience of human life, is as high a pitch, I think, as absurdity has ever reached in philosophical controversy.

The remainder of the stock arguments against utilitarianism mostly consists in laying to its charge the common infirmities of human nature, and the general difficulties which embarrass conscientious persons in shaping their course through life. We are told that an utilitarian will be apt to make his own particular case an exception to moral rules, and, when under temptation, will see an utility in the breach of a rule greater than he will see in its observance. But is utility the only creed which is able to furnish us with excuses for evil doing, and means of cheating our own conscience? They are afforded in abundance by all doctrines which recognise as a fact in morals the existence of conflicting considerations; which all doctrines do, that have been believed by sane persons. It is not the fault of any creed, but of the complicated nature of human affairs, that rules of conduct cannot be so framed as to require no exceptions, and that hardly any kind of action can safely be laid down as either always obligatory or always condemnable. There is no ethical creed which does not temper the rigidity of its laws, by giving a certain latitude, under the moral responsibility of the agent, for accommodation to peculiarities of circumstances; and under every creed, at the opening thus made, self-deception and dishonest casuistry get in. There exists no moral system under which there do not arise unequivocal cases of conflicting obligation. These are the real difficulties, the knotty points both in the theory of ethics, and in the conscientious guidance of personal conduct. They are overcome practically with greater or with less success according to the intellect and virtue of the individual; but it can hardly be pretended that any one will be the less qualified for dealing with them, from possessing an ultimate standard to which conflicting rights and duties can be referred. If utility is the ultimate source of moral obligations, utility may be invoked to decide between them when their demands are incompatible. Though the application of the standard may be difficult, it is better than none at all: while in other systems, the moral laws all claiming independent authority, there is no common umpire entitled to interfere between them; their claims to precedence one over another rest on little better than sophistry, and unless determined, as they generally are, by the unacknowledged influence of considerations of utility, afford a free scope for the action of personal desires and partialities. We must remember that only in these cases of conflict between secondary principles is it requisite that first principles should be appealed to. There is no case of moral obligation in which some secondary principle is not involved; and if only one, there can seldom be any real doubt which one it is, in the mind of any person by whom the principle itself is recognised.

DISCUSSION

It was David Hume who argued that "utility" was the sole basis of ethics, the foundation of justice and benevolence as well as our more self-interested actions. Bentham turned the concept into the full-fledged philosophy of "utilitarianism." His colleague was James

Mill, John Stuart Mill's father, and Mill literally grew up with the idea. But "utility" is not the central concept of utilitarianism, as it was in Hume's ethics; pleasure is the crucial concept (which Hume discusses only in a casual way). It is here that Mill differs most from Aristotle, who emphatically denied that what he called "happiness" (*eudaimonia*) was to be identified with pleasure. Mill's harsh rebuttal of those who try to make utilitarianism sound vulgar or voluptuous because of its emphasis on pleasure reflects the disapproval of hedonism throughout the history of ethics, and the heart of Mill's theory is his attempt to make the notion of "pleasure" (which he equates with happiness) more respectable.

It is with this in mind that he introduces his novel theory of the "quality" of pleasure to supplement Bentham's quantitative theory. It is worth noting how negligible a role "utility" plays in Mill's discussion. He does not suggest that some pleasures are more "useful" than others; in fact the utility of pleasure seems not to be at all in question, particularly since the "higher" pleasures typically consist of such activities as reading and thinking and enjoying the arts, which may be laudable but hardly useful. By contrast, Mill hardly discusses at all the pleasures of physical work and economic production, although he was, we might add, one of the leading economists of the nineteenth century. He seems to have viewed physical labor as relentless drudgery (a view much more extreme than that of Karl Marx—who was in London about the same time).

There can be no mistaking what Mill means by "higher" pleasures; these are those enjoyments which are more intellectual, artistic, or spiritual (although Mill was basically an atheist) as opposed to those which are more physical and physiological. The pleasures of good food, sex, and other physical activities are not excluded, but they are given a distinctly lower value on Mill's "quality" scale of pleasures. He does not exclude or ignore noble actions as sources of pleasure, but he clearly suggests that nobility and intellect go hand in hand, and that "men lose their high aspirations as they lose their intellectual tastes." It is Socrates who supplies Mill with his most prominent example of the "higher" pleasures—however dissatisfied the great philosopher may have been with his own intellectual accomplishments, and it is a pig who provides the paradigm of enjoyment of the "lower" pleasures, thus setting up the scale in the most biased possible way. But are all pleasures of the intellect so noble? And must we consider all physical pleasures as piglike? Is enjoying an excellent bottle of Bordeaux really on a par with wallowing in the mud? And are the joys of abstruse metaphysics necessarily "higher" (that is, better) than the simple physical pleasure of receiving—or giving—an effective back rub?

The real problem with Mill's conception of "quality" of pleasures is not the bias of his scale in favor of the intellectual and against the physical, however. We can still readily agree to some distinction between quality of pleasures—for example, we would agree that the pleasure one gets from having cooked and served a good dinner to one's friends is much better than the pleasures of a sadist, even if the sadist should get more enjoyment out of his or her perversions. And isn't there something debatably "better" about enjoying Mozart than "picking one's toes in Poughkeepsie"? But it is Mill's *criterion* for distinguishing the qualities of pleasures that is dubious; he says that the former is preferred to the latter by all or most competent judges who have experienced both kinds of pleasure. But is it all that clear that we would or do choose the higher pleasures? And what do we mean by "choose"? Public television often broadcasts Shakespearean plays opposite network series of undeniable worthlessness, and a vast audience of those who have experienced both choose to watch the worthlessness. What does this mean? If questioned, surely most people who have read, seen, and appreciated Shakespeare will say that they prefer the "higher" pleasure of Shakespeare. What they do, however, is watch "Mork and Mindy" or "Three's Company." Which counts as a choice? And how does either succeed as a plausible test of quality? Indeed, isn't the (indisputable) difference in quality assumed beforehand? And don't people choose in part because of that difference? The sad fact seems to be that most people choose on the basis of the quantity of simple pleasure (or the simplicity of quantity of pleasure), but the philosophic point is that the choice—on whatever grounds—is not the test of quality; if anything, quality survives despite the majority choices.

What Mill has tried to do is to reduce the vulgarity and "voluptuousness" of Bentham's quantitative pleasure model of ethics and replace it with a two-dimensional model of both quantity and quality. But the beauty of Bentham's ethics was that it reduced all ethical calculations to a single dimension, and this is just what Mill has undone. How will we tell when one pleasure is of a greater quality than another? How can we tell when quality overrides quantity, or vice versa? When is extravagant physical pleasure more desirable than a modest intellectual or artistic pleasure? When is a good philosophy lecture worth more than a day at the beach? And since "utility" is not even mentioned as a criterion—and would be implausible as a defense of most of Mill's preferred "higher" pleasures anyway—have we not moved back to square one, and opened up—rather than solved—the question of the *summum bonum* all over again?

C. The Ultimate Sanction

A *sanction* is a motive for action which we otherwise might not perform (though it often has a more negative meaning—as a threat of punishment for wrongdoing). Mill distinguishes two kinds of sanctions, *external* and *internal.* External sanctions are the law, social disapproval, and punishment (including divine punishment); the internal sanction is one's conscience—feeling good when you do right and feeling guilty when you do wrong. It is this internal sanction, Mill argues, that is the ultimate sanction, and Mill suggests that conscience be cultivated precisely in order to make wrongdoing painful and correct behavior additionally pleasurable.

CHAPTER III. OF THE ULTIMATE SANCTION OF THE PRINCIPLE OF UTILITY

The question is often asked, and properly so, in regard to any supposed moral standard—What is its sanction? what are the motives to obey? or, more specifically, what is the source of its obligation? whence does it derive its binding force? It is a necessary part of moral philosophy to provide the answer to this question, which, though frequently assuming the shape of an objection to the utilitarian morality, as if it had some special applicability to that above others, really arises in regard to all standards. It arises, in fact, whenever a person is called on to *adopt* a standard, or refer morality to any basis on which he has not been accustomed to rest it. For the customary morality, that which education and opinion have consecrated, is the only one which presents itself to the mind with the feeling of being *in itself* obligatory; and when a person is asked to believe that this morality *derives* its obligation from some general principle round which custom has not thrown the same halo, the assertion is to him a paradox; the supposed corollaries seem to have a more binding force than the original theorem; the superstructure seems to stand better without than with what is represented as its foundation. He says to himself, I feel that I am bound not to rob or murder, betray or deceive; but why am I bound to promote the general happiness? If my own happiness lies in something else, why may I not give that the preference?

If the view adopted by the utilitarian philosophy of the nature of the moral sense be correct, this difficulty will always present itself until the influences which form moral character have taken the same hold of the principle which they have taken of some of the consequences—until, by the improvement of education, the feeling of unity with our fellow creatures shall be (what it cannot be denied that Christ intended it to be) as deeply rooted in our character, and to our own consciousness as completely a part of our nature, as the horror of crime is in an ordinarily well-brought-up young person. In the meantime, however, the difficulty has no peculiar application to the doctrine of utility, but is inherent in every attempt to analyze morality and reduce it to principles; which, unless the principle is already in men's minds invested with as much sacredness as any of its applications, always seems to divest them of a part of their sanctity.

The principle of utility either has, or there is no reason why it might not have, all the sanctions which belong to any other system of morals. Those sanctions are either external or internal. Of the external sanctions it is not necessary to speak at any length. They are the hope of favor and the fear of displeasure from our fellow creatures or from the Ruler of the universe, along with whatever we may have of sympathy or affection for them, or of love and awe of Him, inclining us to do His will independently of selfish consequences. There is evidently no reason why all these motives for observance should not attach themselves to the utilitarian morality as completely and as powerfully as to any other. Indeed, those of them which refer to our fellow creatures are sure to do so, in proportion to the amount of general intelligence; for whether there be any other ground of moral obligation than the general happiness or not, men do desire happiness; and however imperfect may be their own practice, they desire and commend all conduct in others toward themselves by which they think their happiness is promoted. With regard to the religious motive, if men believe, as most profess to do, in the goodness of God, those who think that conduciveness to the general happiness is the essence or even only the criterion of good must necessarily believe that it is also that which God approves. The whole force therefore of external reward and punishment, whether physical or moral, and whether proceeding from God or from our fellow men, together with all that the capacities of human nature admit of disinterested devotion to either, become available to enforce the utilitarian morality, in proportion as that morality is recognized; and the more powerfully, the more the appliances of education and general cultivation are bent to the purpose.

So far as to external sanctions. The internal sanction of duty, whatever our standard of duty may be, is one and the same—a feeling in our own mind; a pain, more or less intense, attendant on violation of duty, which in properly cultivated moral natures rises, in the more serious cases, into shrinking from it as an impossibility. This feeling, when disinterested and connecting itself with the pure idea of duty, and not with some particular form of it, or with any of the merely accessory circumstances, is the essence of conscience; though in that complex phenomenon as it actually exists, the simple fact is in general all encrusted over with collateral associations derived from sympathy, from love, and still more from fear; from all the forms of religious feeling; from the recollections of childhood and of all our past life; from self-esteem, desire of the esteem of others, and occasionally even self-abasement. This extreme complication is, I apprehend, the origin of the sort of mystical character which, by a tendency of the human mind of which there are many other examples, is apt to be attributed to the idea of moral obligation, and which leads people to believe that the idea cannot possibly attach itself to any other objects than those which, by a supposed mysterious law, are found in our present experience to excite it. Its binding force, however, consists in the existence of a mass of feeling which must be broken through in order to do what violates our standard of right, and which, if we do nevertheless violate that standard, will probably have to be encountered afterwards in the form of remorse. Whatever theory we have of the nature or origin of conscience, this is what essentially constitutes it.

The ultimate sanction, therefore, of all morality (external motives apart) being a subjective feeling in our own minds, I see nothing embarrassing to those whose standard is utility in the question, What is the sanction of that particular standard? We may answer, the same as of all other moral standards—the conscientious feelings of mankind. Undoubtedly this sanction has no binding efficacy on those who do not possess the feelings it appeals to; but neither will these persons be more obedient to any other moral principle than to the utilitarian one. On them morality of any kind has no hold but through the external sanctions. Meanwhile the feelings exist, a fact in human nature, the reality of which, and the great power with which they are capable of acting on those in whom they have been duly cultivated, are proved by experience. No reason has ever been shown why they may not be cultivated to as great intensity in connection with the utilitarian as with any other rule of morals.

There is, I am aware, a disposition to believe that a person who sees in moral obligation a transcendental fact, an objective reality belonging to the province of "things in themselves," is likely to be more obedient to it than one who believes it to be entirely subjective, having its seat in human consciousness only. But whatever a person's opinion may be on this point of ontology, the force he is really urged by is his own subjective feeling, and is exactly measured by its strength. No one's belief that duty is an objective reality is stronger than the belief that God is so; yet the belief in God, apart from the expectation of actual reward and punishment, only operates on conduct through, and in proportion to, the subjective religious feeling. The sanction, so far as it is disinterested, is always in the mind itself; and the notion, therefore, of the transcendental moralists must be that this sanction will not exist *in* the mind unless it is believed to have its root out of the mind; and that if a person is able to say to himself, "That which is restraining me and which is called my conscience is only a feeling in my own mind," he may possibly draw the conclusion that when the feeling ceases the obligation ceases, and that if he find the feeling inconvenient, he may disregard it and endeavor to get rid of it. But is this danger confined to the utilitarian morality? Does the belief that moral obligation has its seat outside the mind make the feeling of it too strong to be got rid of? The fact is so far otherwise that all moralists admit and lament the ease with which, in the generality of minds, conscience can be silenced or stifled. The question, "Need I obey my conscience?" is quite as often put to themselves by persons who never heard of the principle of utility as by its adherents. Those whose conscientious feelings are so weak as to allow of their asking this question, if they answer it affirmatively, will not do so because they believe in the transcendental theory, but because of the external sanctions.

It is not necessary, for the present purpose, to decide whether the feeling of duty is innate or implanted. Assuming it to be innate, it is an open question to what objects it naturally attaches itself; for the philosophic supporters of that theory are now agreed that the intuitive perception is of principles of morality and not of the details. If there be anything innate in the matter, I see no reason why the feeling which is innate should not be that of regard to the pleasures and pains of others. If there is any principle of morals which is intuitively obligatory, I should say it must be that. If so, the intuitive ethics would coincide with the utilitarian, and there would be no further quarrel between them. Even as it is, the intuitive moralists, though they believe that there are other intuitive moral obligations, do already believe this to be one; for they unanimously hold that a large *portion* of morality turns upon the consideration due to the interests of our fellow creatures. Therefore, if the belief in the transcendental origin of moral obligation gives any additional efficacy to the internal sanction, it appears to me that the utilitarian principle has already the benefit of it.

On the other hand, if, as is my own belief, the moral feelings are not innate but acquired, they are not for that reason the less natural. It is natural to man to speak, to reason, to build cities, to cultivate the ground, though these are acquired faculties. The moral feelings are not indeed a part of our nature in the sense of being in any perceptible degree present in all of us; but this, unhappily, is a fact admitted by those who believe the most strenuously in their transcendental origin. Like the other acquired capacities above referred to, the moral faculty, if not a part of our nature, is a natural outgrowth from it; capable, like them, in a certain small degree, of springing up spontaneously; and susceptible of being brought by cultivation to a high degree of development. Unhappily it is also susceptible, by a sufficient use of the external sanctions and of the force of early impressions, of being cultivated in almost any direction so that there is hardly anything so absurd or so mischievous that it may not, by means of these influences, be made to act on the human mind with all the authority of conscience. To doubt that the same potency might be given by the same means to the principle of utility, even if it had no foundation in human nature, would be flying in the face of all experience.

But moral associations which are wholly of artificial creation, when the intellectual culture goes on, yield by degrees to the dissolving force of analysis; and if the feeling of duty, when associated with utility, would appear equally arbitrary; if there were no leading department of our nature, no powerful class of sentiments, with which that association would harmonize, which would make us feel it congenial and incline us not only to foster it in others (for which we have abundant interested motives), but also to cherish it in ourselves—if there were not, in short, a natural basis of sentiment for utilitarian morality, it might well happen that this association also, even after it had been implanted by education, might be analyzed away.

But there *is* this basis of powerful natural sentiment; and this it is which, when once the general happiness is recognized as the ethical standard, will constitute the strength of the utilitarian morality. This firm foundation is that of the social feelings of mankind—the desire to be in unity with our fellow creatures, which is already a powerful principle in human nature, and happily one of those which tend to become stronger, even without express inculcation, from the influences of advancing civilization. The social state is at once so natural, so necessary, and so habitual to man, that, except in some unusual circumstances or by an effort of voluntary abstraction, he never conceives himself otherwise than as a member of a body; and this association is riveted more and more, as mankind are further removed from the state of savage independence. Any condition, therefore, which is essential to a state of society becomes more and more an inseparable part of every person's conception of the state of things which he is born into, and which is the destiny of a human being. Now society between human beings, except in the relation of master and slave, is manifestly impossible on any other footing than that the interests of all are to be consulted. Society between equals can only exist on the understanding that the interests of all are to be regarded equally. And since in all states of civilization, every person, except an absolute monarch, has equals, everyone is obliged to live on these terms with somebody; and in every age some advance is made toward a state in which it will be impossible to live permanently on other terms with anybody. In this way people grow up unable to conceive as possible to them a state of total disregard of other people's interests. They are under a necessity of conceiving themselves as at least abstaining from all the grosser injuries, and (if only for their own protection) living in a state of constant protest against them. They are also familiar with the fact of co-operating with others and proposing to themselves a collective, not an individual, interest as the aim (at least for the time being) of their actions. So long as they are co-operating, their ends are identified with those of others; there is at least a temporary feeling that the interests of others are their own interests. Not only does all strengthening of social ties, and all healthy growth of society, give to each individual a stronger personal interest in practically consulting the welfare of others, it also leads him to identify his *feelings* more and more with their good, or at least with an even greater degree of practical consideration for it. He comes, as though instinctively, to be conscious of himself as a being who *of course* pays regard to others. The good of others becomes to him a thing naturally and necessarily to be attended to, like any of the physical conditions of our existence. Now, whatever amount of this feeling a person has, he is urged by the strongest motives both of interest and of sympathy to demonstrate it, and to the utmost of his power encourage it in others; and even if he has none of it himself, he is as greatly interested as anyone else that others should have it. Consequently, the smallest germs of the feeling are laid hold of and nourished by the contagion of sympathy and the influences of education; and a complete web of corroborative association is woven round it by the powerful agency of the external sanctions. This mode of conceiving ourselves and human life, as civilization goes on, is felt to be more and more natural. Every step in political improvement renders it more so, by removing the sources of opposition of interest and leveling those inequalities of legal privilege between individuals or classes, owing to which there are large portions of mankind whose happiness it is still practicable to disregard. In an improving state of the human mind, the influences are constantly on the increase which tend to generate in each individual a feeling of unity with all the rest; which, if perfect, would make him never think of, or desire, any beneficial condition for himself in the benefits of which they are not included. If we now suppose this feeling of unity to be taught as a religion, and the whole force of education, of institutions, and of opinion directed, as it once was in the case of religion, to make every person grow up from infancy surrounded on all sides both by the profession and the practice of it, I think that no one who can realize this conception will feel any misgiving about the sufficiency of the ultimate sanction for the happiness morality. To any ethical student who finds the realization difficult, I recommend, as a means of facilitating it, the second of M. Comte's two principal works, the *Traité de politique positive*. I entertain the strongest objections to the system of politics and morals set forth in that treatise, but I think it has superabundantly shown the possibility of giving to the service of humanity, even without the aid of belief in a Providence, both the psychological power and the social efficacy of a religion, making it take hold of human life, and color all thought, feeling, and action in a manner of which the greatest ascendancy ever exercised by any religion may be but a type and foretaste; and of which the danger is, not that it should be insufficient, but that it should be so excessive as to interfere unduly with human freedom and individuality.

Neither is it necessary to the feeling which constitutes the binding force of the utilitarian morality on those who recognize it to wait for those social influences which would make its obligation felt by mankind at large. In the comparatively early state of human advancement in which we now live, a person cannot, indeed, feel that entireness of sympathy with all others which would make any real discordance in the general direction of their conduct in life impossible, but already a person in whom the social feeling is at all developed cannot bring himself to think of the rest of his fellow creatures as struggling rivals with him for the means of happiness, whom he must desire to see defeated in their object in order that he may succeed in his. The deeply rooted conception which every individual even now has of himself as a social being tends to make him feel it one of his natural wants that there should be harmony between his feelings and aims and those of his fellow creatures. If differences of opinion and of mental culture make it impossible for him to share many of their actual feelings—perhaps make him denounce and defy those feelings—he still needs to be conscious that his real aim and theirs do not conflict; that he is not opposing himself to what they really wish for, namely, their own good, but is, on the contrary, promoting it. This feeling in most individuals is much inferior in strength to their selfish feelings, and is often wanting altogether. But to those who have it, it possesses all the characters of a natural feeling. It does not present itself to their minds as a superstition of education or a law despotically imposed by the power of society, but as an attribute which it would not be well for them to be without. This conviction is the ultimate sanction of the greatest happiness morality. This it is which makes any mind of well-developed feelings work with, and not against, the outward motives to care for others, afforded by what I have called the external sanctions; and, when those sanctions are wanting or act in an opposite direction, constitutes in itself a powerful internal binding force, in proportion to the sensitiveness and thoughtfulness of the character, since few but those whose mind is a moral blank could bear to lay out their course of life on the plan of paying no regard to others except so far as their own private interest compels.

DISCUSSION

Mill is surely right that, for most of us, "pangs of conscience" serve as an effective deterrent, causing a pain of sorts that offsets the pleasure gained from many a minor indiscretion. But there is a problem in treating the pain of a bad conscience as a pain in the sense that is important to utilitarianism. Pangs of conscience are not just pain and not just internal punishment. If we think about it, the pain of guilt is rather difficult to specify; it is unpleasant, to be sure, and one might note the discomfort of that choked-up, flushed feeling that often accompanies guilt. But this would hardly seem to be a deterrent to self-interested action, and, because it is internal, it would be easy enough to assuage the guilt by taking certain drugs or having a stiff martini. Why doesn't this work? It is not because the guilty feelings last so long (one can always take another drink). It is rather because guilt is not just a pain; it is a much more pervasive aspect of our lives. Guilt is painful because it reflects an intolerable view of ourselves, as a rotten person or, at least, as a person who has done something rotten. Eliminating the pain of guilt is not yet to eliminate the guilt, and the pain of a pang of conscience is not a sanction so much as it is part and parcel of our moral sense itself. Does this mean that guilt cannot play the role that Mill thinks it does—as an internal punishment? The suggestion that it is the ultimate sanction of our actions may be circular; we do not come to believe that what we did was wrong because we feel guilty; we feel guilty because we know that what we did was wrong.

D. The "Proof" of Utilitarianism

Although he began *Utilitarianism* with the reminder that there can be no "proof" of ultimate ends, Mill now proceeds to give us a proof of sorts. The methodological premise is that the only possible proof that something is an ultimate end is that it is in fact desirable. The conclusion is that (general) happiness, and only (general) happiness, is desirable as an ultimate end. The steps of the argument are not entirely clear, and generations of critics and defenders of Mill have struggled to recast the argument in its strongest form. Mill's own attention, however, is not focused on the formal validity of the argument so much as it is on the most common objections to its first premise, in particular, the question whether such desirable goods as virtue, power, and fame must be considered as distinct from happiness or rather desirable components of it.

CHAPTER IV. OF WHAT SORT OF PROOF THE PRINCIPLE OF UTILITY IS SUSCEPTIBLE

It has already been remarked that questions of ultimate ends do not admit of proof, in the ordinary acceptation of the term. To be incapable of proof by reasoning is common to all first principles, to the first premises of our knowledge, as well as to those of our conduct. But the former, being matters of fact, may be the subject of a direct appeal to the faculties which judge of fact—namely, our senses and our internal consciousness. Can an appeal be made to the same faculties on questions of practical ends? Or by what other faculty is cognizance taken of them?

Questions about ends are, in other words, questions about what things are desirable. The utilitarian doctrine is that happiness is desirable, and the only thing desirable, as an end; all other things being only desirable as means to that end. What ought to be required of this doctrine, what conditions is it requisite that the doctrine should fulfill—to make good its claim to be believed?

The only proof capable of being given that an object is visible is that people actually see it. The only proof that a sound is audible is that people hear it; and so of the other sources of our experience. In like manner, I apprehend, the sole evidence it is possible to produce that anything is desirable is that people do actually desire it. If the end which the utilitarian doctrine proposes to itself were not, in theory and in practice, acknowledged to be an end, nothing could ever convince any person that it was so. No reason can be given why the general happiness is desirable, except that each person, so far as he believes it to be attainable, desires his own happiness. This, however, being a fact, we have not only all the proof which the case admits of, but all which it is possible to require, that happiness is a good; that each person's happiness is a good to that person, and the general happiness, therefore, a good to the aggregate of all persons. Happiness had made out its title as *one* of the ends of conduct, and consequently one of the criteria of morality.

But it has not, by this alone, proved itself to be the sole criterion. To do that, it would seem, by the same rule, necessary to show, not only that people desire happiness, but that they never desire anything else. Now it is palpable that they do desire things which, in common language, are decidedly distinguished from happiness. They desire, for example, virtue and the absence of vice, no less really than pleasure and the absence of pain. The desire of virtue is not as universal, but it is as authentic a fact as the desire of happiness. And hence the opponents of the utilitarian standard deem that they have a right to infer that there are other ends of human action besides happiness, and that happiness is not the standard of approbation and disapprobation.

But does the utilitarian doctrine deny that people desire virtue, or maintain that virtue is not a thing to be desired? The very reverse. It maintains not only that virtue is to be desired, but that it is to be desired disinterestedly, for itself. Whatever may be the opinion of utilitarian moralists as to the original conditions by which virtue is made virtue, however they may believe (as they do) that actions and dispositions are only virtuous because they promote another end than virtue, yet this being granted, and it having been decided, from considerations of this description, what *is* virtuous, they not only place virtue at the very head of the things which are good as means to the ultimate end, but they also recognize as a psychological fact the possibility of its being, to the individual, a good in itself, without looking to any end beyond it; and hold that the mind is not in a right state, not in a state conformable to utility, not in the state most conducive to the general happiness, unless it does love virtue in this manner—as a thing desirable in itself, even although, in the individual instance, it should not produce those other desirable consequences which it tends to produce, and on account of which it is held to be virtue. This opinion is not, in the smallest degree, a departure from the happiness principle. The ingredients of happiness are very various, and each of them is desirable in itself, and not merely when considered as swelling an aggregate. The principle of utility does not mean that any given pleasure, as music, for instance, or any given exemption from pain, as for example health, is to be looked upon as means to a collective something termed happiness, and to be desired on that account. They are desired and desirable in and for themselves; besides being means, they are a part of the end. Virtue, according to the utilitarian doctrine, is not naturally and originally part of the end, but it is capable of becoming so; and in those who love it disinterestedly it has become so, and is desired and cherished, not as a means to happiness, but as a part of their happiness.

To illustrate this further, we may remember that virtue is not the only thing originally a means, and which if it were not a means to anything else would be and remain indifferent, but which by association with what it is a means to comes to be desired for itself, and that too with the utmost intensity. What, for example, shall we say of the love of money? There is nothing originally more desirable about money than about any heap of glittering pebbles. Its worth is solely that of the things which it will buy; the desires for other things than itself, which it is a means of gratifying. Yet the love of money is not only one of the strongest moving forces of human life, but money is, in many cases, desired in and for itself; the desire to possess it is often stronger than the desire to use it, and goes on increasing when all the desires which point to ends beyond it, to be compassed by it, are falling off. It may, then, be said truly that money is desired not for the sake of an end, but as part of the end. From being a means to happiness, it has come to be itself a principal ingredient of the individual's conception of happiness. The same may be said of the majority of the great objects of human life: power, for example, or fame, except that to each of these there is a certain amount of immediate pleasure annexed, which has at least the semblance of being naturally inherent in them—a thing which cannot be said of money. Still, however, the strongest natural attraction, both of power and of fame, is the immense aid they give to the attainment of our other wishes; and it is the strong association thus generated between them and all our objects of desire which gives to the direct desire of them the intensity it often assumes, so as in some characters to surpass in strength all other desires. In these cases the means have become a part of the end, and a more important part of it than any of the things which they are means to. What was once desired as an instrument for the attainment of happiness has come to be desired for its own sake. In being desired for its own sake it is, however, desired as *part* of happiness. The person is made, or thinks he would be made, happy by its mere possession; and is made unhappy by failure to obtain it. The desire of it is not a different thing from the desire of happiness any more than the love of music or the desire of health. They are included in happiness. They are some of the elements of which the desire of happiness is made up. Happiness is not an abstract idea but a concrete whole; and these are some of its parts. And the utilitarian standard sanctions and approves their being so. Life would be a poor thing, very ill provided with sources of happiness, if there were not this provision of nature by which things originally indifferent, but conducive to, or otherwise associated with, the satisfaction of our primitive desires, become in themselves sources of pleasure more valuable than the primitive pleasures, both in permanency, in the space of human existence that they are capable of covering, and even in intensity.

Virtue, according to the utilitarian conception, is a good of this description. There was no original desire of it, or motive to it, save its conduciveness to pleasure, and especially to protection from pain. But through the association thus formed it may be felt a good in itself, and desired as such with as great intensity as any other good; and with this difference between it and the love of money, of power, or of fame, that all of these may, and often do, render the individual noxious to the other members of the society to which he belongs, whereas there is nothing which makes him so much a blessing to them as the cultivation of the disinterested love of virtue. And consequently, the utilitarian standard, while it tolerates and approves those other acquired desires, up to the point beyond which they would be more injurious to the general happiness than promotive of it, enjoins and requires the cultivation of the love of virtue up to the greatest strength possible, as being above all things important to the general happiness.

It results from the preceding considerations that there is in reality nothing desired except happiness. Whatever is desired otherwise than as a means to some end beyond itself, and ultimately to happiness, is desired as itself a part of happiness, and is not desired for itself until it has become so. Those who desire virtue for its own sake desire it either because the consciousness of it is a pleasure, or because the consciousness of being without it is a pain, or for both reasons united; as in truth the pleasure and pain seldom exist separately, but almost always together—the same person feeling pleasure in the degree of virtue attained, and pain in not having attained more. If one of these gave him no pleasure, and the other no pain, he would not love or desire virtue, or would desire it only for the other benefits which it might produce to himself or to persons whom he cared for.

We have now, then, an answer to the question, of what sort of proof the principle of utility is susceptible. If the opinion which I have now stated is psychologically true—if human nature is so constituted as to desire nothing which is not either a part of happiness or a means of happiness, we can have no other proof, and we require no other, that these are the only things desirable. If so, happiness is the sole end of human action, and the promotion of it the test by which to judge of all human conduct; from whence it necessarily follows that it must be the criterion of morality, since a part is included in the whole.

And now to decide whether this is really so, whether mankind do desire nothing for itself but that which is a pleasure to them, or of which the absence is a pain, we have evidently arrived at a question of fact and experience, dependent, like all similar questions, upon evidence. It can only be determined by practised self-conciousness and self-observation, assisted by observation of others. I believe that these sources of evidence, impartially consulted, will declare that desiring a thing and finding it pleasant, aversion to it and thinking of it as painful, are phenomena entirely inseparable or rather two parts of the same phenomenon; in strictness of language, two different modes of naming the same psychological fact; that to think of an object as desirable (unless for the sake of its consequences) and to think of it as pleasant are one and the same thing; and that to desire anything except in proportion as the idea of it is pleasant, is a physical and metaphysical impossibility.

So obvious does this appear to me that I expect it will hardly be disputed; and the objection made will be, not that desire can possibly be directed to anything ultimately except pleasure and exemption from pain, but that the will is a different thing from desire; that a person of confirmed virtue or any other person whose purposes are fixed carries out his purposes without any thought of the pleasure he has in contemplating them or expects to derive from their fulfill-ment, and persists in acting on them, even though these pleasures are much diminished by changes in his character or decay of his passive sensibilities, or are outweighed by the pains which the pursuit of the purposes may bring upon him. All this I fully admit and have stated it elsewhere as positively and emphatically as anyone. Will, the active phenomenon, is a different thing from desire, the state of passive sensibility, and, though originally an offshoot from it, may in time take root and detach itself from the parent stock, so much so that in the case of a habitual purpose, instead of willing the thing because we desire it, we often desire it only because we will it. This, however, is but an instance of that familiar fact, the power of habit, and is nowise confined to the case of virtuous actions. Many indifferent things which men originally did from a motive of some sort they continue to do from habit. Sometimes this is done unconsciously, the consciousness coming only after the action; at other times with conscious volition, but volition which has become habitual and is put in operation by the force of habit, in opposition perhaps to the deliberate preference, as often happens with those who have contracted habits of vicious or hurtful indulgence. Third and last comes the case in which the habitual act of will in the individual instance is not in contradiction to the general intention prevailing at other times, but in fulfillment of it, as in the case of the person of confirmed virtue and of all who pursue deliberately and consistently any determinate end. The distinction between will and desire thus understood is an authentic and highly important psychological fact; but the fact consists solely in this—that will, like all other parts of our constitution, is amenable to habit, and that we may will from habit what we no longer desire for itself, or desire only because we will it. It is not the less true that will, in the beginning, is entirely produced by desire, including in that term the repelling influence of pain as well as the attractive one of pleasure. Let us take into consideration no longer the person who has a confirmed will to do right, but him in whom that virtuous will is still feeble, conquerable by temptation, and not to be fully relied on; by what means can it be strengthened? How can the will to be virtuous, where it does not exist in sufficient force, be implanted or awakened? Only by making the person *desire* virtue—by making him think of it in a pleasurable light, or of its absence in a painful one. It is by associating the doing right with pleasure, or the wrong with pain, or by eliciting and impressing and bringing home to the person's experience the pleasure naturally involved in the one or the pain in the other, that it is possible to call forth that will to be virtuous which, when confirmed, acts without any thought of either pleasure or pain. Will is the child of desire, and passes out of the dominion of its parents only to come under that of habit. That which is the result of habit affords no presumption of being intrinsically good; and there would be no reason for wishing that the purpose of virtue should become independent of pleasure and pain were it not that the influence of the pleasurable and painful associations which prompt to virtue is not sufficiently to be depended on for unerring constancy of action until it has acquired the support of habit. Both in feeling and in conduct, habit is the only thing which imparts certainty; and it is because of the importance to others of being able to rely absolutely on one's feelings and conduct, and to oneself of being able to rely on one's own, that the will to do right ought to be cultivated into this habitual independence. In other words, this state of the will is a means to good, not intrinsically a good; and does not contradict the doctrine that nothing is a good to human beings but in so far as it is either itself pleasurable or a means of attaining pleasure or averting pain.

But if this doctrine be true, the principle of utility is proved. Whether it is so or not must now be left to the consideration of the thoughtful reader.

DISCUSSION

Despite Mill's disclaimers, his "proof" certainly has the appearance of a standard deductive argument, and it has been interpreted as such by many moral philosophers. There are many reformulations of the argument, some of them more flattering and more generous than others. One of the most common reformulations, in more straightforward deductive form, is this:

1 One's own happiness (pleasure) is the only thing desired by each person.
2 (Therefore) the general happiness (the happiness of all) is the only thing desired for itself by all.
3 The only test of something's being desirable is its being desired.
4 (Therefore) the general happiness is the only thing desired in itself.
5 (Therefore) the only test of the rightness and wrongness of actions is their tendency to promote the general happiness ("the greatest good for the greatest number").

Mill takes statement 1 to be a "metaphysical necessity," in fact, a simple statement of psychological egoism and hedonism—that each person desires his or her own happiness. In response to the obvious objection that other goods are wanted for themselves (for example, virtue), Mill says that such goods are part of (or a means to) happiness, and not distinct from it. But even so, Mill's first premise betrays what many critics have pointed out as a serious confusion: it may be true that each person wants to be happy and is in fact made happier by the satisfaction of each desire (including desires to be virtuous, to have power, fame, money, and so on). But is it true that what each person wants is therefore happiness (or satisfaction) *alone*? If a man wants to be virtuous and is made happier by his being virtuous, does it follow that he really wanted happiness? Perhaps what he wanted was the virtue. Thus even if being virtuous produces happiness, it does not follow that it is a means to happiness. People do not just desire happiness (pleasure), even if getting what they desire always (or usually) makes them happier.

Statement 2 is an inference from statement 1. It too betrays a fallacy, which logicians call "the fallacy of composition." The confusion is in Mill's so easily slipping from a statement that

2a All individuals want their own happiness,

to

2b All individuals want everyone's happiness.

The phrase "the general happiness" is ambiguous between these two very different statements, and a sentence such as "everyone desires the happiness of all" only makes things more confusing. Notice that so far we have argued only a *fact* about people; no mention has been made of what they *should* desire.

Statement 3 is the focus of the most frequent criticisms and discussions of Mill's proof; it too contains a suspicious ambiguity. Statement 3 functions as a premise, but it is also an argument that

The sole evidence it is. possible to produce that anything is desirable is that people actually do desire it.

Mill argues by analogy that just as an object is visible only if people see it, a thing is desirable only if people desire it. But "visible" means *able to be seen;* "desirable" does not mean *able to be desired.* It means *should be desired.* One might alter the wording cautiously and suggest that "desirable" does mean *worthy* of being desired. We should also remember that Mill himself does not exactly say that "desirable" *means* "desired"; he just points out that the *test* of desirability must have something to do with being desired. But no matter how it is argued—the critics claim—this crucial premise involves the unwarranted leap from the simple fact that people desire something to the value judgment that it is worth desiring. (This is often taken as an illustration of the "naturalistic fallacy," the inference of a value judgment from a strictly factual statement.) But, on the other hand, could one possibly say that people's desires are *irrelevant* to what is good?

What are we to make of this flawed attempt, about which Mill himself clearly had reservations? The logical inadequacy of the "proof" does not end its obvious appeal. There is something undeniable in the claim that any doctrine about what we ought to want has to be based on what we actually want. And there is something equally undeniable—perhaps even trivial—in the claim each of us wants to be happy, that is, wants his or her own happiness. Mill is right, no doubt, that our individual happiness is not incompatible with the happiness of others, and it is equally clear that the happiness of others is often bound up with our own. (It is much easier to have fun at a party when everyone else is enjoying themselves too.) But how can these plausible claims be put together in a valid argument? Or is "the principle of utility," for all of its initial appeal, an inadequate principle of ethics because it cannot be proved?

E. Justice and Utility

Justice and utility are typically placed opposite one another, as in the following example: a wealthy neighborhood finds itself the occasional victim of a small crime wave, the perpetrators of which are found to live in a small pocket of poor minority families. To stop the crime and to prevent any likelihood of further criminal activity, the wealthy majority band together and quite easily—and by means of the law—force the minority families out of their homes. The action succeeds; the crime wave stops. And the suffering of the few evicted families is exceeded by the relief of the wealthy majority. In terms of utility ("the greatest happiness of the greatest number") the right thing has been done; the amount of pleasure now exceeds the amount of suffering, and the balance of pleasure under the new arrangement now exceeds the balance of pleasure had things remained as they were. Nevertheless, we feel quite strongly that justice has been violated. Some innocent people—even if they were a poor minority—have been unfairly treated. They have *rights* which have been violated, and no argument for utility can compensate them for that. The "greatest good for the greatest number" is not the same thing as *justice*.

John Stuart Mill was, as a matter of fact, one of the great defenders of individual rights; his essay *On Liberty* (published a few years before *Utilitarianism*) established the doctrine of individual liberty—including the rights of the minority in the face of an overwhelming majority—more persuasively than any other modern document. It is of the utmost importance to him, therefore, to show that justice and utility are not incompatible, for his whole ethics is committed to the proposition that there is only one *summum bonum*—the happiness of all, and his whole life was dedicated to the importance of individual rights and justice.

CHAPTER V. ON THE CONNECTION BETWEEN JUSTICE AND UTILITY

In all ages of speculation one of the strongest obstacles to the reception of the doctrine that utility or happiness is the criterion of right and wrong has been drawn from the idea of justice. The powerful sentiment and apparently clear perception which that word recalls with a rapidity and certainty resembling an instinct have seemed to the majority of thinkers to point to an inherent quality in things; to show that the just must have an existence in nature as something absolute, generically distinct from every variety of the expedient and, in idea, opposed to it, though (as is commonly acknowledged) never, in the long run, disjoined from it in fact.

In the case of this, as of our other moral sentiments, there is no necessary connection between the question of its origin and that of its binding force. That a feeling is bestowed on us by nature does not necessarily legitimate all its promptings. The feeling of justice might be a peculiar instinct, and might yet require, like our other instincts, to be controlled and enlightened by a higher reason. If we have intellectual instincts leading us to judge in a particular way, as well as animal instincts that prompt us to act in a particular way, there is no necessity that the former should be more infallible in their sphere than the latter in theirs; it may as well happen that wrong judgments are occasionally suggested by those, as wrong actions by these. But though it is one thing to believe that we have natural feelings of justice, and another to acknowledge them as an ultimate criterion of conduct, these two opinions are very closely connected in point of fact. Mankind are always predisposed to believe that any subjective feeling, not otherwise accounted for, is a revelation of some objective reality. Our present object is to determine whether the reality to which the feeling of justice corresponds is one which needs any such special revelation, whether the justice or injustice of an action is a thing intrinsically peculiar and distinct from all its other qualities or only a combination of certain of those qualities presented under a peculiar aspect. For the purpose of this inquiry it is practically important to consider whether the feeling itself, of justice and injustice, is *sui generis* like our sensations of color and taste or a derivative feeling formed by a combination of others. And this it is the more essential to examine, as people are in general willing enough to allow that objectively the dictates of justice coincide with a part of the field of general expediency; but inasmuch as the subjective mental feeling of justice is different from that which commonly attaches to simple expediency, and, except in the extreme cases of the latter, is far more imperative in its demands, people find it difficult to see in justice only a particular kind or branch of general utility, and think that its superior binding force requires a totally different origin.

To throw light upon this question, it is necessary to attempt to ascertain what is the distinguishing character of justice, or of injustice; what is the quality, or whether there is any quality, attributed in common to all modes of conduct designated as unjust (for justice, like many other moral attributes, is best defined by its opposite), and distinguishing them from such modes of conduct as are disapproved, but without having that particular epithet of disapprobation applied to them. If in everything which men are accustomed to characterize as just or unjust some one common attribute or collection of attributes is always present, we may judge whether this particular attribute or combination of attributes would be capable of gathering round it a sentiment of that peculiar character and intensity by virtue of the general laws of our emotional constitution, or whether the sentiment is inexplicable and requires to be regarded as a special provision of nature. If we find the former to be the case, we shall, in resolving this question, have resolved also the main problem; if the latter, we shall have to seek for some other mode of investigating it:

To find the common attributes of a variety of objects, it is necessary to begin by surveying the objects themselves in the concrete. Let us therefore advert successively to the various modes of action and arrangements of human affairs which are classed, by universal or widely spread opinion, as just or as unjust. The things well known to excite the sentiments associated with those names are of a very multifarious character. I shall pass them rapidly in review, without studying any particular arrangement.

In the first place, it is mostly considered unjust to deprive anyone of his personal liberty, his property, or any other thing which belongs to him by law. Here, therefore, is one instance of the application of the terms "just" and "unjust" in a perfectly definite sense, namely, that it is just to respect, unjust to violate, the *legal rights* of anyone. But this judgment admits of several exceptions, arising from the other forms in which the notions of justice and injustice present themselves. For example, the person who suffers the deprivation may (as the phrase is) have *forfeited* the rights which he is so deprived of—a case to which we shall return presently. But also—

Secondly, the legal rights of which he is deprived may be rights which *ought* not to have belonged to him; in other words, the law which confers on him these rights may be a bad law. When it is so or when (which is the same thing for our purpose) it is supposed to be so, opinions will differ as to the justice or injustice of infringing it. Some maintain that no law, however bad, ought to be disobeyed by an individual citizen; that his opposition to it, if shown at all, should only be shown in endeavoring to get it altered by competent authority. This opinion (which condemns many of the most illustrious benefactors of mankind, and would often protect pernicious institutions against the only weapons which, in the state of things existing at the time, have any chance of succeeding against them) is defended by those who hold it on grounds of expediency, principally on that of the importance to the common interest of mankind, of maintaining inviolate the sentiment of submission to law. Other persons, again, hold the directly contrary opinion that any law, judged to be bad, may blamelessly be disobeyed, even though it be not judged to be unjust but only inexpedient, while others would confine the license of disobedience to the case of unjust laws; but, again, some say that all laws which are inexpedient are unjust, since every law imposes some restriction on the natural liberty of mankind, which restriction is an injustice unless legitimated by tending to their good. Among these diversities of opinion it seems to be universally admitted that there may be unjust laws, and that law, consequently, is not the ultimate criterion of justice, but may give to one person a benefit, or impose on another an evil, which justice condemns. When, however, a law is thought to be unjust, it seems always to be regarded as being so in the same way in which a breach of law is unjust, namely, by infringing somebody's right, which, as it cannot in this case be a legal right, receives a different appellation and is called a moral right. We may say, therefore, that a second case of injustice consists in taking or withholding from any person that to which he has a *moral right.*

Thirdly, it is universally considered just that each person should obtain that (whether good or evil) which he *deserves,* and unjust that he should obtain a good or be made to undergo an evil which he does not deserve. This is, perhaps, the clearest and most emphatic form in which the idea of justice is conceived by the general mind. As it involves the notion of desert, the question arises what constitutes desert? Speaking in a general way, a person is understood to deserve good if he does right, evil if he does wrong; and in a more particular sense, to deserve good from those to whom he does or has done good, and evil from those to whom he does or has done evil. The precept of returning good for evil has never been regarded as a case of the fulfillment of justice, but as one in which the claims of justice are waived, in obedience to other considerations.

Fourthly, it is confessedly unjust to *break faith* with anyone: to violate an engagement, either express or implied, or disappoint expectations raised by our own conduct, at least if we have raised those expectations knowingly and voluntarily. Like the other obligations of justice already spoken of, this one is not regarded as absolute, but as capable of being overruled by a stronger obligation of justice on the other side, or by such conduct on the part of the person concerned as is deemed to absolve us from our obligation to him and to constitute a *forfeiture* of the benefit which he has been led to expect.

Fifthly, it is, by universal admission, inconsistent with justice to be *partial*—to show favor or preference to one person over another in matters to which favor and preference do not properly apply. Impartiality, however, does not seem to be regarded as a duty in itself, but rather as instrumental to some other duty; for it is admitted that favor and preference are not always censurable, and, indeed, the cases in which they are condemned are rather the exception than the rule. A person would be more likely to be blamed than applauded for giving his family or friends no superiority in good offices over strangers when he could do so without violating any other duty; and no one thinks it unjust to seek one person in preference to another as a friend, connection, or companion. Impartiality where rights are concerned is of course obligatory, but this is involved in the more general obligation of giving to everyone his right. A tribunal, for example, must be impartial because it is bound to award, without regard to any other consideration, a disputed object to the one of two parties who has the right to it. There are other cases in which impartiality means being solely influenced by desert, as with those who, in the capacity of judges, preceptors, or parents, administer reward and punishment as such. There are cases, again, in which it means being solely influenced by consideration for the public interest, as in making a selection among candidates for a government employment. Impartiality, in short, as an obligation of justice, may be said to mean being exclusively influenced by the considerations which it is supposed ought to influence the particular case in hand, and resisting solicitation of any motives which prompt to conduct different from what those considerations would dictate.

Nearly allied to the idea of impartiality is that of *equality,* which often enters as a component part both into the conception of justice and into the practice of it, and, in the eyes of many persons, constitutes its essence. But in this, still more than in any other case, the notion of justice varies in different persons, and always conforms in its variations to their notion of utility. Each person maintains that equality is the dictate of justice, except where he thinks that expediency requires inequality. The justice of giving equal protection to the rights of all is maintained by those who support the most outrageous inequality in the rights themselves. Even in slave countries it is theoretically admitted that the rights of the slave, such as they are, ought to be as sacred as those of the master, and that a tribunal which fails to enforce them with equal strictness is wanting in justice; while, at the same time, institutions which leave to the slave scarcely any rights to enforce are not deemed unjust because they are not deemed inexpedient. Those who think that utility requires distinctions of rank do not consider it unjust that riches and social privileges should be unequally dispensed; but those who think this inequality inexpedient think it unjust also. Whoever thinks that government is necessary sees no injustice in as much inequality as is constituted by giving to the mágistrate powers not granted to other people. Even among those who hold leveling doctrines, there are differences of opinion about expediency. Some communists consider it unjust that the produce of the labor of the community should be shared on any other principle than that of exact equality; others think it just that those should receive most whose wants are greatest; while others hold that those who work harder, or who produce more, or whose services are more valuable to the community, may justly claim a larger quota in the division of the produce. And the sense of natural justice may be plausibly appealed to in behalf of every one of these opinions.

Among so many diverse applications of the term "justice," which yet is not regarded as ambiguous, it is a matter of some difficulty to seize the mental link which holds them together, and on which the moral sentiment adhering to the term essentially depends. Perhaps, in this embarrassment, some help may be derived from the history of the word, as indicated by its etymology.

In most if not in all languages, the etymology of the word which corresponds to "just" points distinctly to an origin connected with the ordinances of law. *Justum* is a form of *jussum,* that which has been ordered. *Dikaion* comes directly from *dike,* a suit at law. *Recht,* from which came *right* and *righteous,* is synonymous with law. The courts of justice, the administration of justice, are the courts and the administration of law. *La justice,* in French, is the established term for judicature. I am not committing the fallacy, imputed with some show of truth to Horne Tooke,[3] of assuming that a word must still continue to mean what it originally meant. Etymology is slight evidence of what the idea now signified is, but the very best evidence of how it sprang up. There can, I think, be no doubt that the *idée mère,* the primitive element, in the formation of the notion of justice was conformity to law. It constituted the entire idea among the Hebrews, up to the birth of Christianity; as might be expected in the case of a people whose laws attempted to embrace all subjects on which precepts were required, and who believed those laws to be a direct emanation from the Supreme Being. But other nations, and in particular the Greeks and Romans, who knew that their laws had been made originally, and still continued to be made, by men, were not afraid to admit that those men might make bad laws; might do, by law, the same things, and from the same motives, which if done by individuals without the sanction of law would be called unjust. And hence the sentiment of injustice came to be attached, not to all violations of law, but only to violations of such laws as *ought* to exist, including such as ought to exist but do not, and to laws themselves if supposed to be contrary to what ought to be law. In this manner the idea of law and of its injunctions was still predominant in the notion of justice, even when the laws actually in force ceased to be accepted as the standard of it.

It is true that mankind consider the idea of justice and its obligations as applicable to many things which neither are, nor is it desired that they should be, regulated by law. Nobody desires that laws should interfere with the whole detail of private life; yet everyone allows that in all daily conduct a person may and does show himself to be either just or unjust. But even here, the idea of the breach of what ought to be law still lingers in a modified shape. It would always give us pleasure, and chime in with our feelings of fitness, that acts which we deem unjust should be punished, though we do not always think it expedient that this should be done by the tribunals. We forego that gratification on account of incidental inconveniences. We should be glad to see just conduct enforced and injustice repressed, even in the minutest details, if we were not, with reason, afraid of trusting the magistrate with so unlimited an amount of power over individuals. When we think that a person is bound in justice to do a thing, it is an ordinary form of language to say that he ought to be compelled to do it. We should be gratified to see the obligation enforced by anybody who had the power. If we see that its enforcement by law would be inexpedient, we lament the impossibility, we consider the impunity given to injustice as an evil, and strive to make amends for it by bringing a strong expression of our own and the public disapprobation to bear upon the offender. Thus the idea of legal constraint is still the generating idea of the notion of justice, though undergoing

---

[3]Reference is to John Horne (1736–1812), who in 1782 adopted the name of his friend, William Tooke. He was cofounder of the Constitutional Society, a club of radical writers whose endorsement of the French Revolution, incidentally, was severely criticized by Burke in his *Reflections on the Revolution in France.* In his later years he was a close friend of Bentham, Coleridge, and Tom Paine.

several transformations before that notion as it exists in an advanced state of society becomes complete.

The above is, I think, a true account, as far as it goes, of the origin and progressive growth of the idea of justice. But we must observe that it contains as yet nothing to distinguish that obligation from moral obligation in general. For the truth is that the idea of penal sanction, which is the essence of law, enters not only into the conception of injustice, but into that of any kind of wrong. We do not call anything wrong unless we mean to imply that a person ought to be punished in some way or other for doing it—if not by law, by the opinion of his fellow creatures; if not by opinion, by the reproaches of his own conscience. This seems the real turning point of the distinction between morality and simple expediency. It is a part of the notion of duty in every one of its forms that a person may rightfully be compelled to fulfill it. Duty is a thing which may be *exacted* from a person, as one exacts a debt. Unless we think that it may be exacted from him, we do not call it his duty. Reasons of prudence, or the interest of other people, may militate against actually exacting it, but the person himself, it is clearly understood, would not be entitled to complain. There are other things, on the contrary, which we wish that people should do, which we like or admire them for doing, perhaps dislike or despise them for not doing, but yet admit that they are not bound to do; it is not a case of moral obligation; we do not blame them, that is, we do not think that they are proper objects of punishment. How we come by these ideas of deserving and not deserving punishment will appear, perhaps, in the sequel; but I think there is no doubt that this distinction lies at the bottom of the notions of right and wrong; that we call any conduct wrong, or employ, instead, some other term of dislike or disparagement, according as we think that the person ought, or ought not, to be punished for it; and we say it would be right to do so and so, or merely that it would be desirable or laudable, according as we would wish to see the person whom it concerns compelled, or only persuaded and exhorted, to act in that manner.[4]

This, therefore, being the characteristic difference which marks off, not justice, but morality in general from the remaining provinces of expediency and worthiness, the character is still to be sought which distinguishes justice from other branches of morality. Now it is known that ethical writers divide moral duties into two classes, denoted by the ill-chosen expressions, duties of perfect and of imperfect obligation; the latter being those in which, though the act is obligatory, the particular occasions of performing it are left to our choice, as in the case of charity or beneficence, which we are indeed bound to practice but not toward any definite person, nor at any prescribed time. In the more precise language of philosophic jurists, duties of perfect obligation are those duties in virtue of which a correlative *right* resides in some person or persons; duties of imperfect obligation are those moral obligations which do not give birth to any

---

[4]See this point enforced and illustrated by Professor Bain, in an admirable chapter (entitled "The Ethical Emotions, or the Moral Sense"), of the second of the two treatises composing his elaborate and profound work on the Mind (*The Emotions and the Will,* 1859).

right. I think it will be found that this distinction exactly coincides with that which exists between justice and the other obligations of morality. In our survey of the various popular acceptations of justice, the term appeared generally to involve the idea of a personal right—a claim on the part of one or more individuals, like that which the law gives when it confers a proprietary or other legal right. Whether the injustice consists in depriving a person of a possession, or in breaking faith with him, or in treating him worse than he deserves, or worse than other people who have no greater claims—in each case the supposition implies two things: a wrong done, and some assignable person who is wronged. Injustice may also be done by treating a person better than others; but the wrong in this case is to his competitors, who are also assignable persons. It seems to me that this feature in the case—a right in some person, correlative to the moral obligation—constitutes the specific difference between justice and generosity or beneficence. Justice implies something which it is not only right to do, and wrong not to do, but which some individual person can claim from us as his moral right. No one has a moral right to our generosity or beneficence because we are not morally bound to practice those virtues toward any given individual. And it will be found with respect to this as to every correct definition that the instances which seem to conflict with it are those which most confirm it. For if a moralist attempts, as some have done, to make out that mankind generally, though not any given individual, have a right to all the good we can do them, he at once, by that thesis, includes generosity and beneficence within the category of justice. He is obliged to say that our utmost exertions are *due* to our fellow creatures, thus assimilating them to a debt; or that nothing less can be a sufficient *return* for what society does for us, thus classing the case as one of gratitude; both of which are acknowledged cases of justice, and not of the virtue of beneficence; and whoever does not place the distinction between justice and morality in general, where we have now placed it, will be found to make no distinction between them at all, but to merge all morality in justice.

Having thus endeavored to determine the distinctive elements which enter into the composition of the idea of justice, we are ready to enter on the inquiry whether the feeling which accompanies the idea is attached to it by a special dispensation of nature, or whether it could have grown up, by any known laws, out of the idea itself; and, in particular, whether it can have originated in considerations of general expediency.

I conceive that the sentiment itself does not arise from anything which would commonly or correctly be termed an idea of expediency, but that, though the sentiment does not, whatever is moral in it does.

We have seen that the two essential ingredients in the sentiment of justice are the desire to punish a person who has done harm and the knowledge or belief that there is some definite individual or individuals to whom harm has been done.

Now it appears to me that the desire to punish a person who has done harm to some individual is a spontaneous outgrowth from two sentiments, both in the highest degree natural and which either are or resemble instincts: the impulse of self-defense and the feeling of sympathy.

It is natural to resent and to repel or retaliate any harm done or attempted against ourselves or against those with whom we sympathize. The origin of this sentiment it is not necessary here to discuss. Whether it be an instinct or a result of intelligence, it is, we know, common to all animal nature; for every animal tries to hurt those who have hurt, or who it thinks are about to hurt, itself or its young. Human beings, on this point, only differ from other animals in two particulars. First, in being capable of sympathizing, not solely with their offspring, or, like some of the more noble animals, with some superior animal who is kind to them, but with all human, and even with all sentient, beings; secondly, in having a more developed intelligence, which gives a wider range to the whole of their sentiments, whether self-regarding or sympathetic. By virtue of his superior intelligence, even apart from his superior range of sympathy, a human being is capable of apprehending a community of interest between himself and the human society of which he forms a part, such that any conduct which threatens the security of the society generally is threatening to his own, and calls forth his instinct (if instinct it be) of self-defense. The same superiority of intelligence, joined to the power of sympathizing with human beings generally, enables him to attach himself to the collective idea of his tribe, his country, or mankind in such a manner that any act hurtful to them raises his instinct of sympathy and urges him to resistance.

The sentiment of justice, in that one of its elements which consists of the desire to punish, is thus, I conceive, the natural feeling of retaliation or vengeance, rendered by intellect and sympathy applicable to those injuries, that is, to those hurts, which wound us through, or in common with, society at large. This sentiment, in itself, has nothing moral in it; what is moral is the exclusive subordination of it to the social sympathies, so as to wait on and obey their call. For the natural feeling would make us resent indiscriminately whatever anyone does that is disagreeable to us; but, when moralized by the social feeling, it only acts in the directions conformable to the general good: just persons resenting a hurt to society, though not otherwise a hurt to themselves, and not resenting a hurt to themselves, however painful, unless it be of the kind which society has a common interest with them in the repression of.

It is no objection against this doctrine to say that, when we feel our sentiment of justice outraged, we are not thinking of society at large or of any collective interest, but only of the individual case. It is common enough, certainly, though the reverse of commendable, to feel resentment merely because we have suffered pain; but a person whose resentment is really a moral feeling, that is, who considers whether an act is blamable before he allows himself to resent it—such a person, though he may not say expressly to himself that he is standing up for the interest of society, certainly does feel that he is asserting a rule which is for the benefit of others as well as for his own. If he is not feeling this, if he is regarding the act solely as it affects him individually, he is not consciously just; he is not concerning himself about the justice of his actions. This is admitted even by anti-utilitarian moralists. When Kant (as before remarked) propounds as the fundamental principle of morals, "So act that thy rule of conduct might be adopted as a law by all rational beings," he virtually acknowledges that the interest of mankind collectively, or at least of mankind indiscriminately, must be in the mind of the agent when conscientiously deciding on the morality of the act. Otherwise he uses words without a meaning; for that a rule even of utter selfishness could not *possibly* be adopted by all rational beings—that there is any insuperable obstacle in the nature of things to its adoption—cannot be even plausibly maintained. To give any meaning to Kant's principle, the sense put upon it must be that we ought to shape our conduct by a rule which all rational beings might adopt *with benefit to their collective interest.*

To recapitulate: the idea of justice supposes two things—a rule of conduct and a sentiment which sanctions the rule. The first must be supposed common to all mankind and intended for their good. The other (the sentiment) is a desire that punishment may be suffered by those who infringe the rule. There is involved, in addition, the conception of some definite person who suffers by the infringement, whose rights (to use the expression appropriated to the case) are violated by it. And the sentiment of justice appears to me to be the animal desire to repel or retaliate a hurt or damage to oneself or to those with whom one sympathizes, widened so as to include all persons, by the human capacity of enlarged sympathy and the human conception of intelligent self-interest. From the latter elements the feeling derives its morality; from the former, its peculiar impressiveness and energy of self-assertion.

I have, throughout, treated the idea of a *right* residing in the injured person and violated by the injury, not as a separate element in the composition of the idea and sentiment, but as one of the forms in which the other two elements clothe themselves. These elements are a hurt to some assignable person or persons, on the one hand, and a demand for punishment, on the other. An examination of our own minds, I think, will show that these two things include all that we mean when we speak of violation of a right. When we call anything a person's right, we mean that he has a valid claim on society to protect him in the possession of it, either by the force of law or by that of education and opinion. If he has what we consider a sufficient claim, on whatever account, to have something guaranteed to him by society, we say that he has a right to it. If we desire to prove that anything does not belong to him by right, we think this done as soon as it is admitted that society ought not to take measures for securing it to him, but should leave him to chance or to his own exertions. Thus a person is said to have a right to what he can earn in fair professional competition, because society ought not to allow any other person to hinder him from endeavoring to earn in that manner as much as he can. But he has not a right to three hundred a year, though he may happen to be earning it; because society is not called on to provide that he shall earn that sum. On the contrary, if he owns ten thousand pounds three-per-cent stock, he *has* a right to three hundred a year because society has come under an obligation to provide him with an income of that amount.

To have a right, then, is, I conceive, to have something which society ought to defend me in the possession of. If the objector goes on to ask why it ought, I can give him no other reason than general utility. If that expression does not seem to convey a sufficient feeling of the strength of the obligation, nor to account for the peculiar energy of the feeling, it is because there goes to the composition of the sentiment, not a rational only but also an animal element—the thirst for retaliation; and this thirst derives its intensity, as well as its moral justification, from the extraordinarily important and impressive kind of utility which is concerned. The interest involved is that of security, to everyone's feelings the most vital of all interests. All other earthly benefits are needed by one person, not needed by another; and many of them can, if necessary, be cheerfully foregone or replaced by something else; but security no human being can possibly do without; on it we depend for all our immunity from evil and for the whole value of all and every good, beyond the passing moment, since nothing but the gratification of the instant could be of any worth to us if we could be deprived of everything the next instant by whoever was momentarily stronger than ourselves. Now this most indispensable of all necessaries, after physical nutriment, cannot be had unless the machinery for providing it is kept unintermittedly in active play. Our notion, therefore, of the claim we have on our fellow creatures to join in making safe for us the very groundwork of our existence gathers feelings around it so much more intense than those concerned in any of the more common cases of utility that the difference in degree (as is often the case in psychology) becomes a real difference in kind. The claim assumes that character of absoluteness, that apparent infinity and incommensurability with all other considerations which constitute the distinction between the feeling of right and wrong and that of ordinary expediency and inexpediency. The feelings concerned are so powerful, and we count so positively on finding a responsive feeling in others (all being alike interested) that *ought* and *should* grow into *must,* and recognized indispensability becomes a moral necessity, analogous to physical, and often not inferior to it in binding force.

If the preceding analysis, or something resembling it, be not the correct account of the notion of justice—if justice be totally independent of utility, and be a standard *per se,* which the mind can recognize by simple introspection of itself—it is hard to understand why that internal oracle is so ambiguous, and why so many things appear either just or unjust, according to the light in which they are regarded.

We are continually informed that utility is an uncertain standard, which every different person interprets differently, and that there is no safety but in the immutable, ineffaceable, and unmistakable dictates of justice, which carry their evidence in themselves and are independent of the fluctuations of opinion. One would suppose from this that on questions of justice there could be no controversy; that, if we take that for our rule, its application to any given case could leave us in as little doubt as a mathematical demonstration. So far is this from being the fact that there is as much difference of opinion, and as much discussion, about what is just as about what is useful to society. Not only have different nations and individuals different notions of justice, but in the mind of one and the same individual, justice is not some one rule, principle, or maxim, but many which do not always coincide in their dictates, and, in choosing between which, he is guided either by some extraneous standard or by his own personal predilections.

For instance, there are some who say that it is unjust to punish anyone for the sake of example to others, that punishment is just only when intended for the good of the sufferer himself. Others maintain the extreme reverse, contending that to punish persons who have attained years of discretion, for their own benefit, is despotism and injustice, since, if the matter at issue is solely their own good, no one has a right to control their own judgment of it; but that they may justly be punished to prevent evil to others, this being the exercise of the legitimate right of self-defense. Mr. Owen,[5] again, affirms that it is unjust to punish at all, for the criminal did not make his own character; his education and the circumstances which surrounded him have made him a criminal, and for these he is not responsible. All these opinions are extremely plausible; and so long as the question is argued as one of justice simply, without going down to the principles which lie under justice and are the source of its authority, I am unable to see how any of these reasoners can be refuted. For in truth every one of the three builds upon rules of justice confessedly true. The first appeals to the acknowledged injustice of singling out an individual and making him a sacrifice, without his consent, for other people's benefit. The second relies on the acknowledged justice of self-defense and the admitted injustice of forcing one person to conform to another's notions of what constitutes his good. The Owenite invokes the admitted principle that it is unjust to punish anyone for what he cannot help. Each is triumphant so long as he is not compelled to take into consideration any other maxims of justice than the one he has selected; but as soon as their several maxims are brought face to face, each disputant seems to have exactly as much to say for himself as the others. No one of them can carry out his own notion of justice without trampling upon another equally binding. These are difficulties; they have always been felt to be such; and many devices have been invented to turn rather than to overcome them. As a refuge from the last of the three, men imagined what they called the freedom of the will— fancying that they could not justify punishing a man whose will is in a thoroughly hateful state unless it be supposed to have come into that state through no influence of anterior circumstances. To escape from the other difficulties, a favorite contrivance has been the fiction of a contract whereby at some unknown period all the members of society engaged to obey the laws and consented to be punished for any disobedience to them, thereby giving to their legislators the right, which it is assumed they would not otherwise have had, of punishing them, either for their own good or for that of society. This happy thought was considered to get rid of the whole difficulty and to legitimate the infliction of punishment, in virtue of another received maxim of justice, *volenti non fit injuria*—that is not unjust which is done with the consent of the person who is

---

[5]Reference is to Robert Owen (1771–1858), British reformer and a pioneer of the co-operative movement in Great Britain and the United States. His major work, *A New View of Society, or Essay on the Principle of the Formation of the Human Character,* expounds the theory that man's character is wholly determined by environment.

supposed to be hurt by it. I need hardly remark that, even if the consent were not a mere fiction, this maxim is not superior in authority to the others which it is brought in to supersede. It is, on the contrary, an instructive specimen of the loose and irregular manner in which supposed principles of justice grow up. This particular one evidently came into use as a help to the coarse exigencies of courts of law, which are sometimes obliged to be content with very uncertain presumptions, on account of the greater evils which would often arise from any attempt on their part to cut finer. But even courts of law are not able to adhere consistently to the maxim, for they allow voluntary engagements to be set aside on the ground of fraud, and sometimes on that of mere mistake or misinformation.

Again, when the legitimacy of inflicting punishment is admitted, how many conflicting conceptions of justice come to light in discussing the proper apportionment of punishments to offenses. No rule on the subject recommends itself so strongly to the primitive and spontaneous sentiment of justice as the *lex talionis,* an eye for an eye and a tooth for a tooth. Though this principle of the Jewish and of the Mohammedan law has been generally abandoned in Europe as a practical maxim, there is, I suspect, in most minds, a secret hankering after it; and when retribution accidentally falls on an offender in that precise shape, the general feeling of satisfaction evinced bears witness how natural is the sentiment to which this repayment in kind is acceptable. With many, the test of justice in penal infliction is that the punishment should be proportioned to the offense, meaning that it should be exactly measured by the moral guilt of the culprit (whatever be their standard for measuring moral guilt), the consideration what amount of punishment is necessary to deter from the offense having nothing to do with the question of justice, in their estimation; while there are others to whom that consideration is all in all, who maintain that it is not just, at least for man, to inflict on a fellow creature, whatever may be his offenses, any amount of suffering beyond the least that will suffice to prevent him from repeating, and others from imitating, his misconduct.

To take another example from a subject already once referred to. In co-operative industrial association, is it just or not that talent or skill should give a title to superior remuneration? On the negative side of the question it is argued that whoever does the best he can deserves equally well, and ought not in justice to be put in a position of inferiority for no fault of his own; that superior abilities have already advantages more than enough, in the admiration they excite, the personal influence they command, and the internal sources of satisfaction attending them, without adding to these a superior share of the world's goods; and that society is bound in justice rather to make compensation to the less favored for this unmerited inequality of advantages than to aggravate it. On the contrary side it is contended that society receives more from the more efficient laborer; that, his services being more useful, society owes him a larger return for them; that a greater share of the joint result is actually his work, and not to allow his claim to it is a kind of robbery; that, if he is only to receive as much as others, he can only be justly required to produce as much, and to give a smaller amount of time and exertion, proportioned to his superior efficiency. Who shall decide between these appeals to conflicting principles of justice? Justice has in this case two sides to it, which it is impossible to bring into harmony, and the two disputants have chosen opposite sides; the one looks to what it is just that the individual should receive, the other to what it is just that the community should give. Each, from his own point of view, is unanswerable; and any choice between them, on grounds of justice, must be perfectly arbitrary. Social utility alone can decide the preference.

How many, again, and how irreconcilable are the standards of justice to which reference is made in discussing the repartition of taxation. One opinion is that payment to the state should be in numerical proportion to pecuniary means. Others think that justice dictates what they term graduated taxation—taking a higher percentage from those who have more to spare. In point of natural justice a strong case might be made for disregarding means altogether, and taking the same absolute sum (whenever it could be got) from everyone; as the subscribers to a mess or to a club all pay the same sum for the same privileges, whether they can all equally afford it or not. Since the protection (it might be said) of law and government is afforded to and is equally required by all, there is no injustice in making all buy it at the same price. It is reckoned justice, not injustice, that a dealer should charge to all customers the same price for the same article, not a price varying according to their means of payment. This doctrine, as applied to taxation, finds no advocates because it conflicts so strongly with man's feelings of humanity and of social expediency; but the principle of justice which it invokes is as true and as binding as those which can be appealed to against it. Accordingly it exerts a tacit influence on the line of defense employed for other modes of assessing taxation. People feel obliged to argue that the state does more for the rich man than for the poor, as a justification for its taking more from them, though this is in reality not true, for the rich would be far better able to protect themselves, in the absence of law or government, than the poor, and indeed would probably be successful in converting the poor into their slaves. Others, again, so far defer to the same conception of justice as to maintain that all should pay an equal capitation tax for the protection of their persons (these being of equal value to all), and an unequal tax for the protection of their property, which is unequal. To this others reply that the all of one man is as valuable to him as the all of another. From these confusions there is no other mode of extrication than the utilitarian.

Is, then, the difference between the just and the expedient a merely imaginary distinction? Have mankind been under a delusion in thinking that justice is a more sacred thing than policy, and that the latter ought only to be listened to after the former has been satisfied? By no means. The exposition we have given of the nature and origin of the sentiment recognizes a real distinction; and no one of those who profess the most sublime contempt for the consequences of actions as an element in their morality attaches more importance to the distinction than I do. While I dispute the pretensions of any theory which sets up an imaginary standard of justice not grounded on utility, I account the justice which is grounded on utility to be the chief part, and incomparably the most sacred and binding part, of all morality. Justice is a name for certain classes of moral rules which concern the essentials of human well-being more nearly, and are therefore of more absolute obligation, than any other rules for the guidance of life; and the notion which we have found to be of the essence of the idea of justice—that of a right residing in an individual—implies and testifies to this more binding obligation.

The moral rules which forbid mankind to hurt one another (in which we must never forget to include wrongful interference with each other's freedom) are more vital to human well-being than any maxims, however important, which only point out the best mode of managing some department of human affairs. They have also the peculiarity that they are the main element in determining the whole of the social feelings of mankind. It is their observance which alone preserves peace among human beings; if obedience to them were not the rule, and disobedience the exception, everyone would see in everyone else an enemy against whom he must be perpetually guarding himself. What is hardly less important, these are the precepts which mankind have the strongest and the most direct inducements for impressing upon one another. By merely giving to each other prudential instruction or exhortation, they may gain, or think they gain, nothing; in inculcating on each other the duty of positive beneficence, they have an unmistakable interest, but far less in degree; a person may possibly not need the benefits of others, but he always needs that they should not do him hurt. Thus the moralities which protect every individual from being harmed by others, either directly or by being hindered in his freedom of pursuing his own good, are at once those which he himself has most at heart and those which he has the strongest interest in publishing and enforcing by word and deed. It is by a person's observance of these that his fitness to exist as one of the fellowship of human beings is tested and decided; for on that depends his being a nuisance or not to those with whom he is in contact. Now it is these moralities primarily which compose the obligations of justice. The most marked cases of injustice, and those which give the tone to the feeling of repugnance which characterizes the sentiment, are acts of wrongful aggression or wrongful exercise of power over someone; the next are those which consist in wrongfully withholding from him something which is his due—in both cases inflicting on him a positive hurt, either in the form of direct suffering or of the privation of some good which he had reasonable ground, either of a physical or of a social kind, for counting upon.

The same powerful motives which command the observance of these primary moralities enjoin the punishment of those who violate them; and as the impulses of self-defense, of defense of others, and of vengeance are all called forth against such persons, retribution, or evil for evil, becomes closely connected with the sentiment of justice, and is universally included in the idea. Good for good is also one of the dictates of justice; and this, though its social utility is evident, and though it carries with it a natural human feeling, has not at first sight that obvious connection with hurt or injury which, existing in the most elementary cases of just and unjust, is the source of the characteristic intensity of the sentiment. But the connection, though less obvious, is not less real. He who accepts benefits and denies a return of them when needed inflicts a real hurt by disappointing one of the most natural and reasonable of expectations, and one which he must at least tacitly have encouraged, otherwise the benefits would seldom have been conferred. The important rank, among human evils and wrongs, of the disappointment of expectation is shown in the fact that it constitutes the principal criminality of two such highly immoral acts as a breach of friendship and a breach of promise. Few hurts which human beings can sustain are greater, and none wound more, than when that on which they habitually and with full assurance relied fails them in the hour of need; and few wrongs are greater than this mere withholding of good; none excite more resentment, either in the person suffering or in a sympathizing spectator. The principle, therefore, of giving to each what they deserve, that is, good for good as well as evil for evil, is not only included within the idea of justice as we have defined it, but is a proper object of that intensity of sentiment which places the just in human estimation above the simply expedient.

Most of the maxims of justice current in the world, and commonly appealed to in its transactions, are simply instrumental to carrying into effect the principles of justice which we have now spoken of. That a person is only responsible for what he has done voluntarily, or could voluntarily have avoided, that it is unjust to condemn any person unheard; that the punishment ought to be proportioned to the offense, and the like, are maxims intended to prevent the just principle of evil for evil from being perverted to the infliction of evil without that justification. The greater part of these common maxims have come into use from the practice of courts of justice, which have been naturally led to a more complete recognition and elaboration than was likely to suggest itself to others, of the rules necessary to enable them to fulfill their double function—of inflicting punishment when due, and of awarding to each person his right.

That first of judicial virtues, impartiality, is an obligation of justice, partly for the reason last mentioned, as being a necessary condition of the fulfillment of other obligations of justice. But this is not the only source of the exalted rank, among human obligations, of those maxims of equality and impartiality, which, both in popular estimation and in that of the most enlightened, are included among the precepts of justice. In one point of view, they may be considered as corollaries from the principles already laid down. If it is a duty to do to each according to his deserts, returning good for good, as well as repressing evil by evil, it necessarily follows that we should treat all equally well (when no higher duty forbids) who have deserved equally well of *us,* and that society should treat all equally well who have deserved equally well of *it,* that is, who have deserved equally well absolutely. This is the highest abstract standard of social and distributive justice, toward which all institutions and the efforts of all virtuous citizens should be made in the utmost possible degree to converge. But this great moral duty rests upon a still deeper foundation, being a direct emanation from the first principle of morals, and not a mere logical corollary from secondary or derivative doctrines. It is involved in the very meaning of utility, or the greatest happiness principle. That principle is a mere form of words without rational signification unless one person's happiness, supposed equal in degree (with the proper allowance made for kind), is counted for exactly as much as another's. Those conditions being supplied, Bentham's dictum, "everybody to count for one, nobody for more than one," might be written under the principle of utility as an explanatory commentary.[6] The equal claim of everybody to happiness, in the estimation of the moralist and of the legislator, involves an equal claim to all the means of happiness except in so far as the inevitable conditions of human life and the general interest in which that of every individual is included set limits to the maxim; and those limits ought to be strictly construed. As every other maxim of justice, so this is by no means applied or held applicable universally; on the contrary, as I have already remarked, it bends to every person's ideas of social expediency. But in whatever case it is deemed applicable at all, it is held to be the dictate of justice. All persons are deemed to have a *right* to equality of treatment, except when some recognized social expediency requires the reverse. And hence all social inequalities which have ceased to be considered expedient assume the character, not of simple inexpediency, but of injustice, and appear so tyrannical that people are apt to wonder how they ever could have been tolerated—forgetful that they themselves, perhaps, tolerate other inequalities under an equally mistaken notion of expediency, the correction of which would make that which they approve seem quite as monstrous as what they have at last learned to condemn. The entire history of social improvement has been a series of transitions by which one custom or institution after another, from being a

[6]This implication, in the first principle of the utilitarian scheme, of perfect impartiality between persons is regarded by Mr. Herbert Spencer (in his *Social Statics*) as a disproof of the pretensions of utility to be a sufficient guide to right; since (he says) the principle of utility presupposes the anterior principle that everybody has an equal right to happiness. It may be more correctly described as supposing that equal amounts of happiness are equally desirable, whether felt by the same or different persons. This, however, is not a *pre*supposition, not a premise needful to support the principle of utility, but the very principle itself; for what is the principle of utility if it be not that "happiness" and "desirable" are synonymous terms? If there is any anterior principle implied, it can be no other than this, that the truths of arithmetic are applicable to the valuation of happiness, as of all other measurable quantities.

[8](Mr. Herbert Spencer, in a private communication on the subject of the preceding note, objects to being considered an opponent of utilitarianism and states that he regards happiness as the ultimate end of morality; but deems that end only partially attainable by empirical generalizations from the observed results of conduct, and completely attainable only by deducing, from the laws of life and the conditions of existence, what kinds of action necessarily tend to produce happiness, and what kinds to produce unhappiness. With the exception of the word "necessarily," I have no dissent to express from this doctrine; and (omitting that word) I am not aware that any modern advocate of utilitarianism is of a different opinion. Bentham, certainly, to whom in the *Social Statics* Mr. Spencer particularly referred, is, least of all writers, chargeable with unwillingness to deduce the effect of actions on happiness from the laws of human nature and the universal conditions of human life. The common charge against him is of relying too exclusively upon such deductions and declining altogether to be bound by the generalizations from specific experience which Mr. Spencer thinks that utilitarians generally confine themselves to. My own opinion (and, as I collect, Mr. Spencer's) is that in ethics, as in all other branches of scientific study, the consilience of the results of both these processes, each corroborating and verifying the other, is requisite to give to any general proposition the kind and degree of evidence which constitutes scientific proof.)

supposed primary necessity of social existence, has passed into the rank of a universally stigmatized injustice and tyranny. So it has been with the distinctions of slaves and freemen, nobles and serfs, patricians and plebeians; and so it will be, and in part already is, with the aristocracies of color, race, and sex.

It appears from what has been said that justice is a name for certain moral requirements which, regarded collectively, stand higher in the scale of social utility, and are therefore of more paramount obligation, than any others, though particular cases may occur in which some other social duty is so important as to overrule any one of the general maxims of justice. Thus, to save a life, it may not only be allowable, but a duty, to steal or take by force the necessary food or medicine, or to kidnap and compel to officiate the only qualified medical practitioner. In such cases, as we do not call anything justice which is not a virtue, we usually say, not that justice must give way to some other moral principle, but that what is just in ordinary cases is, by reason of that principle, not just in the particular case. By this useful accommodation of language, the character of indefeasibility attributed to justice is kept up, and we are saved from the necessity of maintaining that there can be laudable injustice.

The considerations which have now been adduced resolve, I conceive, the only real difficulty in the utilitarian theory of morals. It has always been evident that all cases of justice are also cases of expediency; the difference is in the peculiar sentiment which attaches to the former, as contradistinguished from the latter. If this characteristic sentiment has been sufficiently accounted for; if there is no necessity to assume for it any peculiarity of origin; if it is simply the natural feeling of resentment, moralized by being made co-extensive with the demands of social good; and if this feeling not only does but ought to exist in all the classes of cases to which the idea of justice corresponds—that idea no longer presents itself as a stumbling block to the utilitarian ethics. Justice remains the appropriate name for certain social utilities which are vastly more important, and therefore more absolute and imperative, than any others are as a class (though not more so than others may be in particular cases); and which, therefore, ought to be, as well as naturally are, guarded by a sentiment, not only different in degree, but also in kind; distinguished from the milder feeling which attaches to the mere idea of promoting human pleasure or convenience at once by the more definite nature of its commands and by the sterner character of its sanctions.

DISCUSSION

Mill's argument here resembles in its strategy the arguments he presents earlier concerning virtue; he attempts to show that justice is not a "peculiar and distinct" moral quality but rather a particularly important aspect of utility. He begins by tracing the notion of justice to the concept of law (for example, among the ancient Hebrews, Greeks, and Romans) but then insists that justice is something other than law, first because there are bad laws, second because it is unthinkable that every aspect of our lives in which there is justice and injustice (for example, giving and getting grades in school) should be regulated by law. He further distinguishes justice from morality, on the grounds that justice involves rights, and then he presents us with a general argument to show that rights and justice serve social utility.

Mill examines a number of ingredients in justice, among them legal rights, moral rights, "merit," what a person deserves, and impartiality; but the ingredient in justice to which he gives the most attention is that of *equality.* Mill does not mean by "equality" that everyone should receive the same out of life, nor does he even mean that everyone ought to have "equal opportunities" without regard to the overall well-being of everyone else. He means that, so far as happiness is concerned, each person's happiness (though not necessarily his or her deserving happiness) counts the same as everyone else's, or, in Bentham's words, "everybody to count for one, nobody more than one." Indeed, by the end of the chapter Mill is convinced that this principle of equality virtually follows from the principle of utility ("might be written as an explanatory commentary"). But the qualification that "all persons . . . have a *right* to equality of treatment, *except when some recognized social expediency requires the reverse,*" already includes the loophole in which the majority can persecute the minority, and in which those who already have the more advantageous positions in society can convincingly claim that social expediency overrides the rights of the protesting poor.

Why should Mill—the champion of minority rights—endorse such a loophole? Because he clearly wants flexibility in his concept of justice; just as he has rejected a priori moral thinking all along, it is particularly important for him to do so here. To allow for an absolute principle of equality, for example, might under any number of circumstances lead to great unhappiness, just as to insist that all contractual rights must be upheld or all laws obeyed leaves too much room for the enforcement of deceptive agreements and bad laws.

Consider taxation, for example, a topic which is central to most discussions of justice. One suggestion which at first sounds fair is that everyone should pay exactly the same. But it then becomes clear that in some circumstances—for example, when the need to tax is great and the distribution of income is extremely unequal—the misery thus caused those less well-off will be considerable. On the other hand, so-called "progressive" taxation—taxing people a higher percentage of their earnings as they earn more—strikes many people as unfair for a very different reason. One deserves what he or she earns, they say, and being taxed more leads people to work less and grumble more, thus adding to the national misery and detracting from utility considerably. In the name of equality, one might propose the more radical suggestion that everyone should be taxed so they are left with equal shares (the policy of some socialist governments), but the net resentment and inefficiency here are undeniable. And yet, one can easily imagine a small society—for example, a religious brotherhood—in which this scheme is of the greatest utility and acceptable to everyone. One might also imagine taxation by lottery, such that everyone's share is determined by chance; but the lack of both utility and justice in this suggestion—even if it might sound fair—is obvious.

How are we to choose among these alternatives, each of which has some claim to our attention? Rejecting easy and a priori answers, Mill insists that we look only to the consequences, that we actually look and see which will promote the general happiness and which will not. That is the essence of his utilitarianism, even in that "vastly more important," even "more absolute and imperative" social utility called "justice." Justice too, whatever more noble claims have been made for it, is nothing other than a means to promote the greatest happiness of the greatest number.

STUDY QUESTIONS

1 What is utilitarianism? How does Mill's conception of it differ from Bentham's conception? What is "the principle of utility"?

2 What is the justification for identifying happiness and pleasure? What role does pain play in utilitarianism? Is the avoidance of pain always the ultimate goal in utilitarianism?

3 In what sense is Mill's utilitarianism "teleological"?

4 Why does Mill say that even Kant had to appeal to the principle of utility? Is this true of Kant, would you say?

5 Does Mill ignore the question of "moral worth"? What relevance would moral worth have to the promotion of good consequences, according to the principle of utility?

6 Why does Mill think that the principle of utility entails a principle of equality? Does the one principle entail the other? What happens if one accepts the principle of utility but does not accept the principle of equality? (What happens if one accepts the principle of equality but does not accept the principle of utility?)

7 Can justice be accounted for in terms of utility alone? What problems arise in an utilitarian account of justice?

8 Why can one not "prove" ultimate ends? Why does Mill reject the idea of proof?

9 How does Mill proceed to give support (if not "proof") to the principle of utility? Outline the various steps in the argument and explain their justification. What justifies the move from "everyone wants his or her own happiness" to "everyone wants the happiness of all"?

10 Is it the test of something's being desirable that it is in fact desired? What qualifications must be added to make this plausible? Does the fact that something is desired thereby make it desirable?

11 What is meant by "quality" of pleasures? What new problems does this introduce into utilitarianism?

CHAPTER 8

FRIEDRICH NIETZSCHE

If ethics is the understanding of good and evil, it is not surprising that the great moral philosophers should have spent so much of their efforts trying to clarify what is good and what is evil. But Nietzsche had something quite different in mind when he began his radical research on the nature and origins of morals, toward the end of the nineteenth century. Other philosophers—Kant most famously—took morality to be something of a given, to be clarified and justified but not questioned. Nietzsche, however, does not take morality to be a given but rather a very human—he would say "all-too-human"—invention, and, what is more, a tyrannical and destructive invention at that.

"Beyond good and evil" is one of the phrases Nietzsche frequently uses to mark his radical divorce from traditional ethics. He also calls himself an "immoralist," and he has often been called an "irrationalist." His works contain passages apparently condoning cruelty and callousness, and he writes long diatribes against such Christian virtues as pity, humility, and charity. But Nietzsche's reputation as a fanatic and as the *enfant terrible* or "bad boy" of ethics has been vastly exaggerated. As a person, he was by all accounts gentle and considerate, soft-spoken and witty. And though he rejects the religiously loaded concepts of "good and evil," he accepts the importance of values and is not hesitant about defending what he considers good against what he considers bad.

What is the difference between "good and evil" and "good and bad"? The first refers to that ancient conception (Nietzsche traces it to Zoroastrianism) in which good and evil are objective forces in the world, defined in the Judeo-Christian tradition by God and the devil, and culminating in the concept of *sin*—which Nietzsche despised. ("To rid the world of the concepts of Sin and Guilt: that is my goal.") "Good and bad," by contrast, refer to the strictly *psychological* question of the strength and satisfaction of our desires. What is good, Nietzsche proclaims, is what is strongest, most alive, and creative. He is not so much an immoralist or an irrationalist as he is an enthusiast. His passion radiates from his writings, and it is passion that he celebrates throughout them. On the other hand, what Nietzsche despises most is weakness and impotence, and it is on this ground that he rejects the whole of Judeo-Christian morality and the moral emphasis on reason. In Christian morality, "only the emasculated man is the good man," he complains, as opposed to the ancient Greek warrior he idealizes. It is in this context that his comments on cruelty and suffering should be understood; it is not that Nietzsche urges cruelty, but he is concerned that the inhibitions of morality have had the effect of deadening our passions and spirit. It is not that Nietzsche likes suffering (though he had enough of it himself), but the good life, he insists, has to be created out of suffering as well as pleasure. "What does not overcome me," he writes, "makes me stronger," and—of the ancient Greeks—"how much these people must have suffered to be so beautiful."

Nietzsche's emphasis on the psychology of morals is not original (he believed that it was, even though he had already read John Stuart Mill). But, together with his vehement rejection of all objective moral standards ("there are no moral phenomena, only moralistic interpretations of phenomena"), his psychologizing clearly marks him as an ethical teleologist, who believes that the good must be defined in terms of our goals rather than in terms of any categorical principles of morals imposed from the outside (for example, the Ten Commandments). But for Nietzsche the ultimate human goal—the *summum bonum*—is not happiness. (Indeed, he calls Mill "vulgar" for his emphasis on pleasure and happiness.) He sometimes says that it is "the will to power," by which he means self-assertion and expression, or what we might call "inner strength" rather than power over other people. He sometimes says that the goal is life itself (and he then defines "life" in terms of the quest for strength and "self-overcoming," that is, growth). But we would not misunderstand Nietzsche if we took his ethics to be aimed primarily at reinstating that ancient pagan ideal—the hero—in place of the bloodless bourgeois bureaucrat who in modern times represents "the good man." Nietzsche is not interested in the normal "good man" but rather in the *great* man, the more than human *übermensch* (literally, "overman"). But if Napoleon and Caesar are mentioned as possible *übermenschen,* it is important to note that Mozart and the great German poet Goethe are too. The vitality that Nietzsche so celebrates need not be physical but may be spiritual as well. Like Aristotle and the ancients, Nietzsche's ethics is primarily concerned with *character,* emphasizing individual virtue, and not only ignoring but rejecting universal moral rules which inhibit character and treat everyone as equal.

What is morality, that Nietzsche despises it so? He takes it to be, as we mentioned above, a universal set of commandments which treat us all the same. What's wrong with that? Nietzsche's answer is that morality *appears* to benefit and protect everyone, but this in fact is not true. What it does is benefit the weakest members of society and protect them. It is the expression of their *resentment* of the strong and successful. Therefore, it does not benefit but inhibits the strongest members of society. And if one also believes—as Nietzsche clearly does—that a society flourishes and is valuable because of the great individuals it produces, then this is a serious objection indeed. Morality is in fact the protection of the weak—a "slave" or "herd" morality.

The only good is to be found in life, in this world, in the satisfaction of our desires, in the realization of our "will to power," according to Nietzsche. He rejects all "other worldly" values and all authority but one's self. Is Nietzsche therefore an egoist? He would say, "no"; in fact one of the most repeated arguments of his philosophy is his rejection of the ego, insisting that our actions are not to be understood that way (for example, "a thought comes when 'it' will, not when 'I' will"). If what we mean by "egoism" is satisfying one's own interests, then Nietzsche would say that morality itself is egoistic—the expression of the resentment of the weaker members of society whose main interest it is to be protected from the strong. Furthermore, he says, it is not just a question of self-interest but rather of *whose* self-interest is in question. Nietzsche, unlike most other modern philosophers, does not believe in universal human equality. Some people are better, more alive, and more creative than others, he says, and they deserve more too (and will take it for themselves). He is an unabashed elitist, much like the ancient philosophers Plato and Aristotle. His philosophy is "for the few," he insists, that is, for those who find themselves unhealthily inhibited by the strictures of morality and have much more to offer the world than being merely good citizens and morally proper neighbors.

FRIEDRICH NIETZSCHE

Nietzsche was born in 1844, in a small town in Germany. Yet he despised Germany ("there's too much beer in the German intellect") and spent most of his adult life in Italy and Switzerland, where he became a citizen. He was trained in the classics and promised to be one of the most brilliant philologists in Basel; he was made a professor at the age of 25. Bad health (caused by an illness he caught while a medic in the Franco-Prussian War of 1870) forced him to resign his professorship, and he spent the rest of his conscious life suffering from a number of ailments. But it was during this time too that he wrote virtually all of his astonishingly cheerful and energetic works. In 1889, Nietzsche became hopelessly insane. He died in 1900.

The following selections have been taken from a number of Nietzsche's published and unpublished works, including *Beyond Good and Evil, Genealogy of Morals, Twilight of the Idols, The Antichrist,* and *The Will to Power.*

A. *Beyond Good and Evil*

THE NATURAL HISTORY OF MORALS

186. The moral sentiment in Europe at present is perhaps as subtle, belated, diverse, sensitive, and refined, as the "Science of Morals" belonging thereto is recent, initial, awkward, and coarse-fingered:—an interesting contrast, which sometimes becomes incarnate and obvious in the very person of a moralist. Indeed, the expression, "Science of Morals" is, in respect to what is designated thereby, far too presumptuous and counter to *good* taste,—which is always a foretaste of more modest expressions. One ought to avow with the utmost fairness *what* is still necessary here for a long time, *what* is alone proper for the present: namely, the collection of material, the comprehensive survey and classification of an immense domain of delicate sentiments of worth, and distinctions of worth, which live, grow, propagate, and perish—and perhaps attempts to give a clear idea of the recurring and more common forms of these living crystallisations—as preparation for a *theory of types* of morality. To be sure, people have not hitherto been so modest. All the philosophers, with a

From *Beyond Good and Evil,* translated by Helen Zimmern, 3rd ed. (The Macmillan Co., 1911), pp. 103–131, 223–241. Reprinted, with the permission of the publisher.

pedantic and ridiculous seriousness, demanded of themselves something very much higher, more pretentious, and ceremonious, when they concerned themselves with morality as a science: they wanted to *give a basis* to morality—and every philosopher hitherto has believed that he has given it a basis; morality itself, however, has been regarded as something "given." How far from their awkward pride was the seemingly insignificant problem—left in dust and decay—of a description of forms of morality, notwithstanding that the finest hands and senses could hardly be fine enough for it! It was precisely owing to moral philosophers knowing the moral facts imperfectly, in an arbitrary epitome, or an accidental abridgement—perhaps as the morality of their environment, their position, their church, their *Zeitgeist,* their climate and zone—it was precisely because they were badly instructed with regard to nations, eras, and past ages, and were by no means eager to know about these matters, that they did not even come in sight of the real problems of morals—problems which only disclose themselves by a comparison of *many* kinds of morality. In every "Science of Morals" hitherto, strange as it may sound, the problem of morality itself has been *omitted;* there has been no suspicion that there was anything problematic there! That which philosophers called "giving a basis to morality," and endeavoured to realise, has, when seen in a right light, proved merely a learned form of good *faith* in prevailing morality, a new means of its *expression,* consequently just a matter-of-fact within the sphere of a definite morality, yea, in its ultimate motive, a sort of denial that it is *lawful* for this morality to be called in question—and in any case the reverse of the testing, analysing, doubting, and vivisecting of this very faith. Hear, for instance, with what innocence—almost worthy of honour—Schopenhauer represents his own task, and draw your conclusions concerning the scientificalness of a "Science" whose latest master still talks in the strain of children and old wives: "The principle," he says (page 136 of the *Grundprobleme der Ethik*), "the axiom about the purport of which all moralists are *practically* agreed: 'Do not hurt anyone, but help everyone, as much as you can.'—is *really* the proposition which all moral teachers strive to establish, . . . the *real* basis of ethics which has been sought, like the philosopher's stone, for centuries."—The difficulty of establishing the proposition referred to may indeed be great—it is well known that Schopenhauer also was unsuccessful in his efforts; and whoever has thoroughly realised how absurdly false and sentimental this proposition is, in a world whose essence is Will to Power, may be reminded that Schopenhauer, although a pessimist, *actually*—played the flute . . . daily after dinner: one may read about the matter in his biography. A question by the way: a pessimist, a repudiator of God and of the world, who *makes a halt* at morality—who assents to morality, and plays the flute to "do not hurt anyone" morals, what? Is that really—a pessimist?

187. Apart from the value of such assertions as "there is a categorical imperative in us," one can always ask: What does such an assertion indicate about him who makes it? There are systems of morals which are meant to justify their author in the eyes of other people; other systems of morals are meant to tranquillise him, and make him self-satisfied; with other systems he wants to crucify and humble himself; with others he wishes to take revenge; with others to conceal himself; with others to glorify himself and gain superiority and distinction;—this system of morals helps its author to forget, that system makes him, or something of him, forgotten; many a moralist would like to exercise power and creative arbitrariness over mankind; many another, perhaps, Kant especially, gives us to understand by his morals that "what is estimable in me, is that I know how to obey—and with you it *shall* not be otherwise than with me!" In short, systems of morals are only a *sign-language of the emotions.*

188. In contrast to *laisser-aller,* every system of morals is a sort of tyranny against "nature" and also against "reason"; that is, however, no objection, unless one should again decree by some system of morals, that all kinds of tyranny and unreasonableness are unlawful. What is essential and invaluable in every system of morals, is that it is a long constraint. In order to understand Stoicism, or Port-Royal, or Puritanism, one should remember the constraint under which every language has attained to strength and freedom—the metrical constraint, the tyranny of rhyme and rhythm. How much trouble have the poets and orators of every nation given themselves!—not excepting some of the prose writers of today, in whose ear dwells an inexorable conscientiousness—"for the sake of a folly," as utilitarian bunglers say, and thereby deem themselves wise—"from submission to arbitrary laws," as the anarchists say, and thereby fancy themselves "free," even free-spirited. The singular fact remains, however, that everything of the nature of freedom, elegance, boldness, dance, and masterly certainty, which exists or has existed, whether it be in thought itself, or in administration, or in speaking and persuading, in art just as in conduct, has only developed by means of the tyranny of such arbitrary law; and in all seriousness, it is not at all improbable that precisely this is "nature" and "natural"—and *not laisser-aller!* Every artist knows how different from the state of letting himself go, is his "most natural" condition, the free arranging, locating, disposing, and constructing in the moments of "inspiration"—and how strictly and delicately he then obeys a thousand laws, which, by their very rigidness and precision, defy all formulation by means of ideas (even the most stable idea has, in comparison therewith, something floating, manifold, and ambiguous in it). The essential thing "in heaven and in earth" is, apparently (to repeat it once more), that there should be long *obedience* in the same direction; there thereby results, and has always resulted in the long run, something which has made life worth living; for instance, virtue, art, music, dancing, reason, spirituality—anything whatever that is transfiguring, refined, foolish, or divine. The long bondage of the spirit, the distrustful constraint in the communicability of ideas, the discipline which the thinker imposed on himself to think in accordance with the rules of a church or a court, or conformable to Aristotelian premises, the persistent spiritual will to interpret everything that happened according to a Christian scheme, and in every occurrence to rediscover and justify the Christian God:—all this violence, arbitrariness, severity, dreadfulness, and unreasonableness, has proved itself the disciplinary means whereby the European spirit has attained its strength, its remorseless curiosity and subtle mobility; granted also that much irrecoverable strength and spirit had to be stifled, suffocated, and spoiled in the process (for here, as everywhere, "nature" shows herself as she is, in all her extravagant and *indifferent* magnificence, which is shocking, but nevertheless noble). That for centuries European thinkers only thought in order to prove something—nowadays, on the contrary, we are suspicious of every thinker who "wishes to prove something"—that it was always settled beforehand what *was to be* the result of their strictest thinking, as it was perhaps in the Asiatic astrology of former times, or as it is still at the present day in the innocent, Christian-moral explanation of immediate personal events "for the glory of God," or "for the good of the soul":—this tyranny, this arbitrariness, this severe and magnificent stupidity, has *educated* the spirit; slavery, both in the coarser and the finer sense, is apparently an indispensable means even of spiritual education and discipline. One may look at every system of morals in this light: it is "nature" therein which teaches to hate the *laisser-aller,* the too great freedom, and implants the need for limited horizons, for immediate duties—it teaches the *narrowing of perspectives,* and thus, in a certain sense, that stupidity is a condition of life and development. "Thou must obey some one, and for a long time; *otherwise* thou wilt come to grief, and lose all respect for thyself"—this seems to me to be the moral imperative of nature, which is certainly neither "categorical," as old Kant wished (consequently the "otherwise"), nor does it address itself to the individual (what does nature care for the individual!), but to nations, races, ages, and ranks, above all, however, to the animal "man" generally, to *mankind. . . .*

190. There is something in the morality of Plato which does not really belong to Plato, but which only appears in his philosophy, one might say, in spite of him: namely, Socratism, for which he himself was too noble. "No one desires to injure himself, hence all evil is done unwittingly. The evil man inflicts injury on himself; he would not do so, however, if he knew that evil is evil. The evil man, therefore, is only evil through error; if one free him from error one will necessarily make him—good."—This mode of reasoning savours of the *populace,* who perceive only the unpleasant consequences of evil-doing, and practically judge that "it is *stupid* to do wrong"; while they accept "good" as identical with "useful and pleasant," without further thought. As regards every system of utilitarianism, one may at once assume that it has the same origin, and follow the scent: one will seldom err.—Plato did all he could to interpret something refined and noble into the tenets of his teacher, and above all to interpret himself into them—he, the most daring of all interpreters, who lifted the entire Socrates out of the street, as a popular theme and song, to exhibit him in endless and impossible modifications—namely, in all his own disguises and multiplicities. In jest, and in Homeric language as well, what is the Platonic Socrates, if not—

"Plato in front, Plato in back, but in the middle a Chimaera."

191. The old theological problem of "Faith" and "Knowledge," or more plainly, of instinct and reason—the question whether, in respect to the valuation of things, instinct deserves more authority than rationality, which wants to appreciate and act according to motives, according to a "Why," that is to say, in conformity to purpose and utility—it is always the old moral problem that first appeared in the person of Socrates, and had divided men's minds long before Christianity. Socrates himself, following, of course, the taste of his talent—that of a surpassing dialectician—took first the side of reason: and, in fact, what did he do all his life but laugh at the awkward incapacity of the noble Athenians, who were men of instinct, like all noble men, and could never give satisfactory answers concerning the motives of their actions? In the end, however, though silently and secretly, he laughed also at himself: with his finer conscience and introspection, he found in himself the same difficulty and incapacity. "But why"—he said to himself—"should one on that account separate oneself from the instincts! One must set them right, and the reason *also*—one must follow the instincts, but at the same time persuade the reason to support them with good arguments." This was the real *falseness* of that great and mysterious ironist: he brought his conscience up to the point that he was satisfied with a kind of self-outwitting: in fact, he perceived the irrationality in the moral judgment.— Plato, more innocent in such matters, and without the craftiness of the plebeian, wished to prove to himself, at the expenditure of all his strength—the greatest strength a philosopher had ever expended—that reason and instinct lead spontaneously to one goal, to the good, to "God"; and since Plato, all theologians and philosophers have followed the same path—which means that in matters of morality, instinct (or as Christians call it, "Faith," or as I call it, "the herd") has hitherto triumphed. Unless one should make an exception in the case of Descartes, the father of rationalism (and consequently the grandfather of the Revolution), who recognised only the authority of reason: but reason is only a tool, and Descartes was superficial. . . .

197. The beast of prey and the man of prey (for instance, Caesar Borgia) are fundamentally misunderstood, "nature" is misunderstood, so long as one seeks a "morbidness" in the constitution of these healthiest of all tropical monsters and growths, or even an innate "hell" in them—as almost all moralists have done hitherto. Does it not seem that there is a hatred of the virgin forest and of the tropics among moralists? And that the "tropical man" must be discredited at all costs, whether as disease and deterioration of mankind, or as his own hell and self-torture? And why? In favour of the "temperate zones"? In favour of the temperate men? The "moral"? The mediocre?—This for the chapter: "Morals as Timidity."

198. All the systems of morals which address themselves with a view to their "happiness," as it is called—what else are they but suggestions for behaviour adapted to the degree of *danger* from themselves in which the individuals live; recipes for their passions, their good and bad propensities, in so far as such have the Will to Power and would like to play the master; small and great expediencies and elaborations, permeated with the musty odour of old family medicines and old-wife wisdom: all of them grotesque and absurd in their form—because they address themselves to "all," because they generalise where generalisation is not authorised; all of them speaking unconditionally, and taking themselves unconditionally; all of them flavoured not merely with one grain of salt, but rather endurable only, and sometimes even seductive, when they are over-spiced and begin to smell dangerously, especially of "the other world?" That is all of little value when estimated intellectually, and is far from being "science," much less "wisdom"; but, repeated once more, and three times repeated, it is expediency, expediency, expediency, mixed with stupidity, stupidity, stupidity—whether it be the indifference and statuesque coldness towards the heated folly of the emotions, which the Stoics advised and fostered; or the no-more-laughing and no-more-weeping of Spinoza, the destruction of the emotions by their analysis and vivisection, which he recommended so naively; or the lowering of the emotions to an innocent mean at which they may be satisfied, the Aristotelianism of morals; or even morality as the enjoyment of the emotions in a voluntary attenuation and spiritualisation by the symbolism of art, perhaps as music, or as love of God, and of mankind for God's sake—for in religion the passions are once more enfranchised, provided that . . . ; or, finally, even the complaisant and wanton surrender to the emotions, as has been taught by Hafis and Goethe, the bold letting-go of the reins, the spiritual and corporeal moral license in the exceptional cases of wise old codgers and drunkards, with whom it "no longer has much danger."—This also for the chapter: "Morals as Timidity."

199. Inasmuch as in all ages, as long as mankind has existed, there have also been human herds (family alliances, communities, tribes, peoples, states, churches), and always a great number who obey in proportion to the small number who command—in view, therefore, of the fact that obedience has been most practised and fostered among mankind hitherto, one may reasonably suppose that, generally speaking, the need thereof is now innate in every one, as a kind of *formal conscience* which gives the command: "Thou shalt uncondition-ally do something, unconditionally refrain from something"; in short, "Thou shalt." This need tries to satisfy itself and to fill its form with a content; according to its strength, impatience, and eagerness, it at once seizes as an omnivorous appetite with little selection, and accepts whatever is shouted into its ear by all sorts of commanders—parents, teachers, laws, class prejudices, or public opinion. The extraordinary limitation of human development, the hesitation, protractedness, frequent retrogression, and turning thereof, is attrib-utable to the fact that the herd-instinct of obedience is transmitted best, and at the cost of the art of command. If one imagine this instinct increasing to its greatest extent, commanders and independent individuals will finally be lacking altogether; or they will suffer inwardly from a bad conscience, and will have to impose a deception on themselves in the first place in order to be able to command: just as if they also were only obeying. This condition of things actually exists in Europe at present—I call it the moral hypocrisy of the commanding class. They know no other way of protecting themselves from their bad conscience than by playing the role of executors of older and higher orders (of predecessors, of the constitution, of justice, of the law, or of God himself), or they even justify themselves by maxims from the current opinions of the herd, as "first servants of their people," or "instruments of the public weal." On the other hand, the gregarious European man nowadays assumes an air as if he were the only kind of man that is allowable; he glorifies his qualities, such as public spirit, kindness, deference, industry, temperance, modesty, indulgence, sympathy, by virtue of which he is gentle, endurable, and useful to the herd, as the peculiarly human virtues. In cases, however, where it is believed that the leader and bellwether cannot be dispensed with, attempt after attempt is made nowadays to replace commanders by the summing together of clever gregarious men: all representative constitutions, for example, are of this origin. In spite of all, what a blessing, what a deliverance from a weight becoming unendurable, is the appearance of an absolute ruler for these gregarious Europeans—of this fact the effect of the appearance of Napoleon was the last great proof: the history of the influence of Napoleon is almost the history of the higher happiness to which the entire century has attained in its worthiest individuals and periods. . . .

201. As long as the utility which determines moral estimates is only gregarious utility, as long as the preservation of the community is only kept in view, and the immoral is sought precisely and exclusively in what seems dangerous to the maintenance of the community, there can be no "morality of love to one's neighbour." Granted even that there is already a little constant exercise of consideration, sympathy, fairness, gentleness, and mutual assistance, granted that even in this condition of society all those instincts are already active which are latterly distinguished by honourable names as "virtues," and eventually almost coincide with the conception "morality": in that period they do not as yet belong to the domain of more valuations—they are still *ultra-moral*. A sympathetic action, for instance, is neither called good nor bad, moral nor immoral, in the best period of the Romans; and should it be praised, a sort of resentful disdain is compatible with this praise, even at the best, directly the sympathetic action is compared with one which contributes to the welfare of the whole, to the *res publica*. After all, "love to our neighbour" is always a secondary matter, partly conventional and arbitrarily manifested in relation to our *fear of our neighbour*. After the fabric of society seems on the whole established and secured against external dangers, it is this fear of our neighbour which again creates new perspectives of moral valuation. Certain strong and dangerous instincts, such as the love of enterprise, foolhardiness, revengefulness, astuteness, rapacity, and love of power, which up till then had not only to be honoured from the point of view of general utility—under other names, of course, than those here given—but had to be fostered and cultivated (because they were perpetually required in the common danger against the common enemies), are now felt in their dangerousness to be doubly strong—when the outlets for them are lacking—and are gradually branded as immoral and given over to calumny. The contrary instincts and inclinations now attain to moral honour; the gregarious instinct gradually draws its conclusions. How much or how little dangerousness to the community or to equality is contained in an opinion, a condition, an emotion, a disposition, or an endowment—that is now the moral perspective; here again fear is the mother of morals. It is by the loftiest and strongest instincts, when they break out passionately and carry the individual far above and beyond the average, and the low level of the gregarious conscience, that the self-reliance of the community is destroyed; its belief in itself, its backbone, as it were, breaks; consequently these very instincts will be most branded and defamed. The lofty independent spirituality, the will to stand alone, and even the cogent reason, are felt to be dangers; everything that elevates the individual above the herd, and is a source of fear to the neighbour, is henceforth called *evil;* the tolerant, unassuming, self-adapting, self-equalising disposition, the *mediocrity* of desires, attains to moral distinction and honour. Finally, under very peaceful circumstances, there is always less opportunity and necessity for training the feelings to severity and rigour; and now every form of severity, even in justice, begins to disturb the conscience; a lofty and rigourous nobleness and self-responsibility almost offends, and awakens distrust, "the lamb," and still more "the sheep," wins respect. There is a point of diseased mellowness and effeminacy in the history of society, at which society itself takes the part of him who injures it, the part of the *criminal,* and does so, in fact, seriously and honestly. To punish, appears to it to be somehow unfair—it is certain that the idea of "punishment" and "the obligation to punish" are then painful and alarming to people. "Is it not sufficient if the criminal be rendered *harmless?* Why should we still punish? Punishment itself is terrible!"—with these questions gregarious morality, the morality of fear, draws its ultimate conclusion. If one could at all do away with danger, the cause of fear, one would have done away with this morality at the same time, it would no longer be necessary, it *would not consider itself* any longer necessary!—Whoever examines the conscience of the present-day European, will always elicit the same imperative from its thousand moral folds and hidden recesses, the imperative of the timidity of the herd: "we wish that some time or other there may be *nothing more to fear!*" Some time or other—the will and the way *thereto* is nowadays called "progress" all over Europe.

202. Let us at once say again what we have already said a hundred times, for people's ears nowadays are unwilling to hear such truths—*our* truths. We know well enough how offensively it sounds when any one plainly, and without metaphor, counts man amongst the animals; but it will be accounted to us almost a *crime,* that it is precisely in respect to men of "modern ideas" that we have constantly applied the terms "herd," "herd-instincts," and such like expressions. What avail is it? We cannot do otherwise, for it is precisely here that our new insight is. We have found that in all the principal moral judgments Europe has become unanimous, including likewise the countries where European influence prevails: in Europe people evidently *know* what Socrates thought he did not know, and what the famous serpent of old once promised to teach—they "know" to-day what is good and evil. It must then sound hard and be distasteful to the ear, when we always insist that that which here thinks it knows, that which here glorifies itself with praise and blame, and calls itself good, is the instinct of the herding human animal: the instinct which has come and is ever coming more and more to the front, to preponderance and supremacy over other instincts, according to the increasing physiological approximation and resemblance of which it is the symptom. *Morality in Europe at present is herding-animal morality;* and therefore, as we understand the matter, only one kind of human morality, beside which, before which, and after which many other moralities, and above all *higher* moralities, are or should be possible. Against such a "possibility," against such a "should be," however, this morality defends itself with all its strength; it says obstinately and inexorably: "I am morality itself and nothing else is morality!" Indeed, with the help of a religion which has humoured and flattered the sublimest desires of the herding-animal, things have reached such a point that we always find a more visible expression of this morality even in political and social arrangements: the *democratic* movement is the inheritance of the Christian movement. That its *tempo,* however, is much too slow and sleepy for the more impatient ones, for those who are sick and distracted by the herding-instinct, is indicated by the increasingly furious howling, and always less disguised teeth-gnashing of the anarchist dogs, who are now roving through the highways of European culture. Apparently in opposition to the peacefully industrious democrats and Revolution-ideologues, and still more so to the awkward philosophasters and fraternity-visionaries who call themselves Socialists and want a "free society," those are really at one with them all in their thorough and instinctive hostility to every form of society other than that of the *autonomous* herd (to the extent even of repudiating the notions "master" and "servant"— *ni Dieu ni maître,* says a socialist formula); at one in their tenacious opposition to every special claim, every special right and privilege (this means ultimately opposition to *every* right, for when all are equal, no one needs "rights" any longer); at one in their distrust of punitive justice (as though it were a violation of the weak, unfair to the *necessary* consequences of all former society); but equally at one in their religion of sympathy, in their compassion for all that feels, lives, and suffers (down to the very animals, up even to "God"—the extravagance of "sympathy for God" belongs to a democratic age); altogether at one in the cry and impatience of their sympathy, in their deadly hatred of suffering generally, in their almost feminine incapacity for witnessing it or *allowing* it; at one in their involuntary beglooming and heart-softening, under the spell of which Europe seems to be threatened with a new Buddhism; at one in their belief in the morality of *mutual* sympathy, as though it were morality in itself, the climax, the *attained* climax of mankind, the sole hope of the future, the consolation of the present, the great discharge from all the obligations of the past; altogether at one in their belief in the community as the *deliverer,* in the herd, and therefore in "themselves."

203. We, who hold a different belief—we, who regard the democratic movement, not only as a degenerating form of political organisation, but as equivalent to a degenerating, a waning type of man, as involving his medio-crising and depreciation: where have *we* to fix our hopes? In *new philosophers*—there is no other alternative: in minds strong and original enough to initiate opposite estimates of value, to transvalue and invert "eternal valuations"; in forerunners, in men of the future, who in the present shall fix the constraints and fasten the knots which will compel millenniums to take *new* paths. To teach man the future of humanity as his *will,* as depending on human will, and to make preparation for vast hazardous enterprises and collective attempts in rearing and educating, in order thereby to put an end to the frightful rule of folly and chance which has hitherto gone by the name of "history" (the folly of the "greatest number" is only its last form)—for that purpose a new type of philosophers and commanders will some time or other be needed, at the very idea of which everything that has existed in the way of occult, terrible, and benevolent beings might look pale and dwarfed. The image of such leaders hovers before *our* eyes:—is it lawful for me to say it aloud, ye free spirits? The conditions which one would partly have to create and party utilise for their genesis; the presumptive methods and tests by virtue of which a soul should grow up to such an elevation and power as to feel a *constraint* to these tasks; a transvaluation of values, under the new pressure and hammer of which a conscience should be steeled and a heart transformed into brass, so as to bear the weight of such responsibility; and on the other hand the necessity for such leaders, the dreadful danger that they might be lacking, or miscarry and degenerate:—these are *our* real anxieties and glooms, ye know it well, ye free spirits! these are the heavy distant thoughts and storms which sweep across the heaven of *our* life. There are few pains so grievous as to have seen, divined, or experienced how an exceptional man has missed his way and deteriorated; but he who has the rare eye for the universal danger of "man" himself *deteriorating,* he who like us has recognised the extraordinary fortuitousness which has hitherto played its game in respect to the future of mankind—a game in which neither the hand, nor even a "finger of God" has participated!—he who divines the fate that is hidden under the idiotic unwariness and blind confidence of "modern ideas," and still more under the whole of Christo-European morality—suffers from an anguish with which no other is to be compared. He sees at a glance all that could still *be made out of man* through a favourable accumulation and augmentation of human powers and arrangements; he knows with all the knowledge of his conviction how unexhausted man still is for the greatest possibilities, and how often in the past the type man has stood in presence of mysterious decisions and new paths:—he knows still better from his painfulest recollections on what wretched obstacles promising developments of the highest rank have hitherto usually gone to pieces, broken down, sunk, and become contemptible. The *universal degeneracy of mankind* to the level of the "man of the future"—as idealised by the sociolistic fools and shallow-pates—this degeneracy and dwarfing of man to an absolutely gregarious animal (or as they call it, to a man of "free society"), this brutalising of man into a pigmy with equal rights and claims, is undoubtedly *possible!* He who has thought out this possibility to its ultimate conclusion knows *another* loathing unknown to the rest of mankind—and perhaps also a new *mission!*

WHAT IS NOBLE?

257. Every elevation of the type "man," has hitherto been the work of an aristocratic society and so it will always be—a society believing in a long scale of gradations of rank and differences of worth among human beings, and requiring slavery in some form or other. Without the *pathos of distance,* such as grows out of the incarnated difference of classes, out of the constant outlooking and downlooking of the ruling caste on subordinates and instruments, and out of their equally constant practice of obeying and commanding, of keeping down and keeping at a distance—that other more mysterious pathos could never have arisen, the longing for an ever new widening of distance within the soul itself, the formation of ever higher, rarer, further, more extended, more comprehensive states, in short, just the elevation of the type "man," the continued "self-surmounting of man," to use a moral formula in a supermoral sense. To be sure, one must not resign oneself to any humanitarian illusions about the history of the origin of an aristocratic society (that is to say, of the preliminary condition for the elevation of the type "man"): the truth is hard. Let us acknowledge unprejudicedly how every higher civilisation hitherto has *originated!* Men with a still natural nature, barbarians in every terrible sense of the word, men of prey, still in possession of unbroken strength of will and desire for power, threw themselves upon weaker, more moral, more peaceful races (perhaps trading or cattle-rearing communities), or upon old mellow civilisations in which the final vital force was flickering out in brilliant fireworks of wit and depravity. At the commencement, the noble caste was always the barbarian caste: their superiority did not consist first of all in their physical, but in their psychical power—they were more *complete* men (which at every point also implies the same as "more complete beasts").

258. Corruption—as the indication that anarchy threatens to break out among the instincts, and that the foundation of the emotions, called "life," is convulsed—is something radically different according to the organisation in which it manifests itself. When, for instance, an aristocracy like that of France at the beginning of the Revolution, flung away its privileges with sublime disgust and sacrificed itself to an excess of its moral sentiments, it was corruption:—it was really only the closing act of the corruption which had existed for centuries, by virtue of which that aristocracy had abdicated step by step its lordly prerogatives and lowered itself to a *function* of royalty (in the end even to its decoration and parade-dress). The essential thing, however, in a good and healthy aristocracy is that it should *not* regard itself as a function either of the kingship or the commonwealth, but as the *significance* and highest justification thereof—that it should therefore accept with a good conscience the sacrifice of a legion of individuals, who, *for its sake,* must be suppressed and reduced to imperfect men, to slaves and instruments. Its fundamental belief must be precisely that society is *not* allowed to exist for its own sake, but only as a foundation and scaffolding, by means of which a select class of beings may be able to elevate themselves to their higher duties, and in general to a higher *existence:* like those sun-seeking climbing plants in Java—they are called *Sipo Matador,*— which encircle an oak so long and so often with their arms, until at last, high above it, but supported by it, they can unfold their tops in the open light, and exhibit their happiness.

259. To refrain mutually from injury, from violence, from exploitation, and put one's will on a par with that of others: this may result in a certain rough sense in good conduct among individuals when the necessary conditions are given (namely, the actual similarity of the individuals in amount of force and degree of worth, and their co-relation within one organisation). As soon, however, as one wished to take this principle more generally, and if possible even as *the fundamental principle of society,* it would immediately disclose what it really is—namely, a Will to the *denial* of life, a principle of dissolution and decay. Here one must think profoundly to the very basis and resist all sentimental weakness: life itself is *essentially* appropriation, injury, conquest of the strange and weak, suppression, severity, obtrusion of peculiar forms, incorporation, and at the least, putting it mildest, exploitation;—but why should one for ever use precisely these words on which for ages a disparaging purpose has been stamped? Even the organisation within which, as was previously supposed, the individuals treat each other as equal—it takes place in every healthy aristocracy—must itself, if it be a living and not a dying organisation, do all that towards other bodies, which the individuals within it refrain from doing to each other: it will have to be the incarnated Will to Power, it will endeavour to grow, to gain ground, attract to itself and acquire ascendency—not owing to any morality or immorality, but because it *lives,* and because life *is* precisely Will to Power. On no point, however, is the ordinary consciousness of Europeans more unwilling to be corrected than on this matter; people now rave everywhere, even under the guise of science, about coming conditions of society in which "the exploiting character" is to be absent:—that sounds to my ears as if they promised to invent a mode of life which should refrain from all organic functions. "Exploitation" does not belong to a depraved, or imperfect and primitive society: it belongs to the *nature* of the living being as a primary organic function; it is a consequence of the intrinsic Will to Power, which is precisely the Will to Life.—Granting that as a theory this is a novelty—as a reality it is the *fundamental fact* of all history: let us be so far honest towards ourselves!

260. In a tour through the many finer and coarser moralities which have hitherto prevailed or still prevail on the earth, I found certain traits recurring regularly together, and connected with one another, until finally two primary types revealed themselves to me, and a radical distinction was brought to light. There is *master-morality* and *slave-morality;*—I would at once add, however, that in all higher and mixed civilisations, there are also attempts at the reconciliation of the two moralities; but one finds still oftener the confusion and mutual misunderstanding of them, indeed, sometimes their close juxtaposition—even in the same man, within one soul. The distinctions of moral values have either originated in a ruling caste, pleasantly conscious of being different from the ruled—or among the ruled class, the slaves and dependents of all sorts. In the first case, when it is the rulers who determine the conception "good," it is the exalted, proud disposition which is regarded as the distinguishing feature, and that which determines the order of rank. The noble type of man separates from himself the beings in whom the opposite of this exalted, proud disposition displays itself: he despises them. Let it at once be noted that in this first kind of morality the antithesis "good" and "bad" means practically the same as "noble" and "despicable";—the antithesis "good" and *"evil"* is of a different origin. The cowardly, the timid, the insignificant, and those thinking merely of narrow utility are despised; moreover, also, the distrustful, with their constrained glances, the self-abasing, the dog-like kind of men who let themselves be abused, the mendicant flatterers, and above all the liars:—it is a fundamental belief of all aristocrats that the common people are untruthful. "We truthful ones"—the nobility in ancient Greece called themselves. It is obvious that everywhere the designations of moral value were at first applied to *men,* and were only derivatively and at a later period applied to *actions;* it is a gross mistake, therefore, when historians of morals start questions like, "Why have sympathetic actions been praised?" The noble type of man regards *himself* as a determiner of values; he does not require to be approved of; he passes the judgment: "What is injurious to me is injurious in itself"; he knows that it is he himself only who confers honour on things; he is a *creator of values.* He honours whatever he recognises in himself: such morality is self-glorification. In the foreground there is the feeling of plentitude, of power, which seeks to overflow, the happiness of high tension, the consciousness of a wealth which would fain give and bestow:— the noble man also helps the unfortunate, but not—or scarcely—out of pity, but rather from an impulse generated by the super-abundance of power. The noble man honours in himself the powerful one, him also who has power over himself, who knows how to speak and how to keep silence, who takes pleasure in subjecting himself to severity and hardness, and has reverence for all that is severe and hard. "Wotan placed a hard heart in my breast," says an old Scandinavian Saga: it is thus rightly expressed from the soul of a proud Viking. Such a type of man is even proud of *not* being made for sympathy; the hero of the Saga therefore adds warningly: "He who has not a hard heart when young, will never have one." The noble and brave who think thus are the furthest removed from the morality which sees precisely in sympathy, or in acting for the good of others, or in *désintéressement,* the characteristic of the moral; faith in oneself, pride in oneself, a radical enmity and irony towards "selflessness," belong as definitely to noble morality, as do a careless scorn and precaution in presence of sympathy and the "warm heart."—It is the powerful who *know* how to honour, it is their art, their domain for invention. The profound reverence for age and for tradition—all law rests on this double reverence,—the belief and prejudice in favour of ancestors and unfavourable to newcomers, is typical in the morality of the powerful; and if, reversely, men of "modern ideas" believe almost instinctively in "progress" and the "future," and are more and more lacking in respect for old age, the ignoble origin of these "ideas" has complacently betrayed itself thereby. A morality of the ruling class, however, is more especially foreign and irritating to present-day taste in the sternness of its principle that one has duties only to one's equals; that one may act towards beings of a lower rank, towards all that is foreign, just as seems good to one, or "as the heart desires," and in any case "beyond good and evil": it is here that sympathy and similar sentiments can have a place. The ability and obligation to exercise prolonged gratitude and prolonged revenge—both only within the circle of equals,—artfulness in retaliation, *raffinement* of the idea in friendship, a certain necessity to have enemies (as outlets for the emotions of envy, quarrelsomeness, arrogance—in fact, in order to be a good *friend*): all these are typical characteristics of the noble morality, which, as has been pointed out, is not the morality of "modern ideas," and is therefore at present difficult to realise, and also to unearth and disclose.—It is otherwise with the second type of morality, *slave-morality*. Supposing that the abused, the oppressed, the suffering, the unemancipated, the weary, and those uncertain of themselves, should moralise, what will be the common element in their moral estimates? Probably a pessimistic suspicion with regard to the entire situation of man will find expression, perhaps a condemnation of man, together with his situation. The slave has an unfavourable eye for the virtues of the powerful; he has a scepticism and distrust, a *refinement* of distrust of everything "good" that is there honoured—he would fain persuade himself that the very happiness there is not genuine. On the other hand, *those* qualities which serve to alleviate the existence of sufferers are brought into prominence and flooded with light; it is here that sympathy, the kind, helping hand, the warm heart, patience, diligence, humility, and friendliness attain to honour; for here these are the most useful qualities, and almost the only means of supporting the burden of existence. Slave-morality is essentially the morality of utility. Here is the seat of the origin of the famous antithesis "good" and "evil":— power and dangerousness are assumed to reside in the evil, a certain dreadfulness, subtlety, and strength, which do not admit of being despised. According to slave-morality, therefore, the "evil" man arouses fear; according to master-morality, it is precisely the "good" man who arouses fear and seeks to arouse it, while the bad man is regarded as the despicable being. The contrast attains its maximum when, in accordance with the logical consequences of slave-morality, a shade of depreciation—it may be slight and well-intentioned—at last attaches itself to the "good" man of this morality; because, according to the servile mode of thought, the good man must in any case be the *safe* man: he is good-natured, easily deceived, perhaps a little stupid, *un bonhomme*. Everywhere that slave-morality gains the ascendency, language shows a tendency to approximate the significations of the words "good" and "stupid."—At last fundamental difference: the desire for *freedom*, the instinct for happiness and the refinements of the feeling of liberty belong as necessarily to slave-morals and morality, as artifice and enthusiasm in reverence and devotion are the regular symptoms of an aristocratic mode of thinking and estimating.—Hence we can understand without further detail why love *as a passion*—it is our European specialty—must absolutely be of noble origin; as is well known, its invention is due to the Provençal poet-cavaliers, those brilliant, ingenious men of the *"gai saber,"* to whom Europe owes so much, and almost owes itself.

261. Vanity is one of the things which are perhaps most difficult for a noble man to understand: he will be tempted to deny it, where another kind of man thinks he sees it self-evidently. The problem for him is to represent to his mind beings who seek to arouse a good opinion of themselves which they themselves do not possess—and consequently also do not "deserve,"—and who yet *believe* in this good opinion afterwards. This seems to him on the one hand such bad taste and so self-disrespectful, and on the other hand so grotesquely unreasonable, that he would like to consider vanity an exception, and is doubtful about it in most cases when it is spoken of. He will say, for instance: "I may be mistaken about my value, and on the other hand may nevertheless demand that my value should be acknowledged by others precisely as I rate it:—that, however, is not vanity (but self-conceit, or, in most cases, that which is called 'humility,' and also 'modesty')." Or he will even say: "For many reasons I can delight in the good opinion of others, perhaps because I love and honour them, and rejoice in all their joys, perhaps also because their good opinion endorses and strengthens my belief in my own good opinion, perhaps because the good opinion of others, even in cases where I do not share it, is useful to me, or gives promise of usefulness:—all this, however, is not vanity." The man of noble character must first bring it home forcibly to his mind, especially with the aid of history, that, from time immemorial, in all social strata in any way dependent, the ordinary man *was* only that which he *passed for:*—not being at all accustomed to fix values, he did not assign even to himself any other value than that which his master assigned to him (it is the peculiar *right of masters* to create values). It may be looked upon as the result of an extraordinary atavism, that the ordinary man, even at present, is still always *waiting* for an opinion about himself, and then instinctively submitting himself to it; yet by no means only to a "good" opinion, but also to a bad and unjust one (think, for instance, of the greater part of the self-appreciations and self-depreciations which believing women learn from their confessors, and which in general the believing Christian learns from his Church).

. . . The vain person rejoices over *every* good opinion which he hears about himself (quite apart from the point of view of its usefulness, and equally regardless of its truth or falsehood), just as he suffers from every bad opinion: for he subjects himself to both, he *feels* himself subjected to both, by that oldest instinct of subjection which breaks forth in him.—It is "the slave" in the vain man's blood, the remains of the slave's craftiness. . . .

262. A *species* originates, and a type becomes established and strong in the long struggle with essentially constant *unfavourable* conditions. On the other hand, it is known by the experience of breeders that species which receive superabundant nourishment, and in general a surplus of protection and care, immediately tend in the most marked way to develop variations, and are fertile in prodigies and monstrosities (also in monstrous vices). Now look at an aristocratic commonwealth, say an ancient Greek *polis,* or Venice, as a voluntary or involuntary contrivance for the purpose of *rearing* human beings; there are there men beside one another, thrown upon their own resources, who want to make their species prevail, chiefly because they *must* prevail, or else run the terrible danger of being exterminated. The favour, the superabundance, the protection are there lacking under which variations are fostered; the species needs itself as species, as something which, precisely by virtue of its hardness, its uniformity, and simplicity of structure, can in general prevail and make itself permanent in constant struggle with its neighbours, or with rebellious or rebellion-threatening vassals. The most varied experience teaches it what are the qualities to which it principally owes the fact that it still exists, in spite of all gods and men, and has hitherto been victorious: these qualities it calls virtues, and these virtues alone it develops to maturity. It does so with severity, indeed it desires severity; every aristocratic morality is intolerant in the education of youth, in the control of women, in the marriage customs, in the relations of old and young, in the penal laws (which have an eye only for the degenerating): it counts intolerance itself among the virtues, under the name of "justice." A type with few, but very marked features, a species of severe, warlike, wisely silent, reserved and reticent men (and as such, with the most delicate sensibility for the charm and *nuances* of society) is thus established, unaffected by the vicissitudes of generations; the constant struggle with uniform *unfavourable* conditions is, as already remarked, the cause of a type becoming stable and hard. Finally, however, a happy state of things results, the enormous tension is relaxed; there are perhaps no more enemies among the neighbouring peoples, and the means of life, even of the enjoyment of life, are present in superabundance. With one stroke the bond and constraint of the old discipline severs: it is no longer regarded as necessary, as a condition of existence—if it would continue, it can only do so as a form of *luxury,* as an archaïsing *taste.* Variations, whether they be deviations (into the higher, finer, and rare), or deteriorations and monstrosities, appear suddenly on the scene in the greatest exuberance and splendour; the individual dares to be individual and detach himself. At this turning-point of history there manifest themselves, side by side, and often mixed and entangled together, a magnificent, manifold, virgin-forest-like up-growth and up-striving, a kind of *tropical tempo* in the rivalry of growth, and an extraordinary decay and self-destruction, owing to the savagely opposing and seemingly exploding egoisms, which strive with one another "for sun and light," and can no longer assign any limit, restraint, or forbearance for themselves by means of the hitherto existing morality. It was this morality itself which piled up the strength so enormously, which bent the bow in so threatening a manner:—it is now "out of date," it is getting "out of date." The dangerous and disquieting point has been reached when the greater, more manifold, more comprehensive life *is lived beyond* the old morality; the "individual" stands out, and is obliged to have recourse to his own law-giving, his own arts and artifices for self-preservation, self-elevation, and self-deliverance. Nothing but new "Whys," nothing but new "Hows," no common formulas any longer, misunderstanding and disregard in league with each other, decay, deterioration, and the loftiest desires frightfully entangled, the genius of the race overflowing from all the cornucopias of good and bad, a portentous simultaneousness of Spring and Autumn, full of new charms and mysteries peculiar to the fresh, still inexhausted, still unwearied corruption. Danger is again present, the mother of morality, great danger; this time shifted into the individual, into the neighbour and friend, into the street, into their own child, into their own heart, into all the most personal and secret recesses of their desires and volitions. What will the moral philosophers who appear at this time have to preach? They discover, these sharp onlookers and loafers, that the end is quickly approaching, that everything around them decays and produces decay, that nothing will endure until the day after tomorrow, except one species of man, the incurably *mediocre*. The mediocre alone have a prospect of continuing and propagating themselves—they will be the men of the future, the sole survivors; "be like them! become mediocre!" is now the only morality which has still a significance, which still obtains a hearing.—But it is difficult to preach this morality of mediocrity! it can never avow what it is and what it desires! it has to talk of moderation and dignity and duty and brotherly love—it will have difficulty *in concealing its irony!*

263. There is an *instinct for rank*, which more than anything else is already the sign of a *high* rank; there is a *delight* in the *nuances* of reverance which leads one to infer noble origin and habits. The refinement, goodness, and loftiness of a soul are put to a perilous test when something passes by that is of the highest rank, but is not yet protected by the awe of authority from obtrusive touches and incivilities: something that goes its way like a living touchstone, undistinguished, undiscovered, and tentative, perhaps voluntarily veiled and disguised. He whose task and practice it is to investigate souls, will avail himself of many varieties of this very art to determine the ultimate value of a soul, the unalterable, innate order of rank to which it belongs: he will test it by its *instinct for reverence*. "Difference breeds hatred:" the vulgarity of many a nature spurts up suddenly like dirty water, when any holy vessel, any jewel from closed shrines, any book bearing the marks of great destiny, is brought before it; while on the other hand, there is an involuntary silence, a hesitation of the eye, a cessation of all gestures, by which it is indicated that a soul *feels* the nearness of what is worthiest of respect. The way in which, on the whole, the reverence for the *Bible* has hitherto been maintained in Europe, is perhaps the best example of discipline and refinement of manners which Europe owes to Christianity: books of such profoundness and supreme significance require for their protection an external tyranny of authority, in order to acquire the *period* of thousands of years which is necessary to exhaust and unriddle them. Much has been achieved when the sentiment has been at last instilled into the masses (the shallow-pates and the boobies of every kind) that they are not allowed to touch everything, that there are holy experiences before which they must take off their shoes and keep away the unclean hand—it is almost their highest advance towards humanity. On the contrary, in the so-called cultured classes, the believers in "modern ideas," nothing is perhaps so repulsive as their lack of shame, the easy insolence of eye and hand with which they touch, taste, and finger everything; and it is possible that even yet there is more *relative* nobility of taste, and more tact for reverence among the people, among the lower classes of the people, especially among peasants, than among the newspaper-reading *demimonde* of intellect, the cultured class. . . .

265. At the risk of displeasing innocent ears, I submit that egoism belongs to the essence of a noble soul, I mean the unalterable belief that to a being such as "we," other beings must naturally be in subjection, and have to sacrifice themselves. The noble soul accepts the fact of his egoism without question, and also without consciousness of harshness, constraint, or arbitrariness therein, but rather as something that may have its basis in the primary law of things:—if he sought a designation for it he would say: "It is justice itself." He acknowledges under certain circumstances, which made him hesitate at first, that there are other equally privileged ones; as soon as he has settled this question of rank, he moves among those equals and equally privileged ones; with the same assurance, as regards modesty and delicate respect, which he enjoys in intercourse with himself—in accordance with an innate heavenly mechanism which all the stars understand. It is an *additional* instance of his egoism, this artfulness and self-limitation in intercourse with his equals—every star is a similar egoist; he honours *himself* in them, and in the rights which he concedes to them, he has no doubt that the exchange of honours and rights, as the *essence* of all intercourse, belongs also to the natural condition of things. The noble soul gives as he takes, prompted by the passionate and sensitive instinct of requital, which is at the root of his nature. The notion of "favour" has, among equals, neither significance nor good repute; there may be a sublime way of letting gifts as it were light upon one from above, and of drinking them thirstily like dew-drops but for those arts and displays the noble soul has no aptitude. His egoism hinders him here: in general, he looks "aloft" unwillingly—he looks either *forward*, horizontally and deliber-ately, or downwards—*he knows that he is on a height.*

ASSORTED "MAXIMS AND ARROWS"

To pose questions here with a *hammer,* and, perhaps to hear as a reply that famous hollow sound which speaks of bloated entrails—what a delight for one who has ears even behind his ears, for me, an old psychologist and pied piper before whom just that which would remain silent must become outspoken. . . .

Regarding the sounding out of idols, this time they are not just idols of the age, but eternal idols, which are here touched with a hammer as with a tuning fork: there are altogether no older, no more convinced, no more puffed-up idols—and none more hollow. That does not prevent them from being those in which people have the most faith; nor does one ever say "idol," especially not in the most distinguished instance.

When stepped on, a worm doubles up. That is clever. In that way he lessens the probability of being stepped on again. In the language of morality: *humility.*

You run *ahead?* Are you doing it as a shepherd? Or as an exception? A third case would be the fugitive. *First* question of conscience.

Are you genuine? Or merely an actor? A representative? Or that which is represented? In the end, perhaps you are merely a copy of an actor. *Second* question of conscience.

The disappointed one speaks. I searched for great human beings; I always found only the *apes* of their ideals.

[From *Human All-Too-Human,* 1878–1880.]

The sad truth is that we remain necessarily strangers to ourselves, we don't understand our own substance, we *must* mistake ourselves; the axiom, "Each man is farthest from himself," will hold for us to all eternity. . . .
[From *Genealogy of Morals*, 1887.]

And there he lay, sick, miserable, malevolent against himself: full of hatred against the springs of life, full of suspicion against all that was still strong and happy. In short, a "Christian." . . .
[From *Twilight of the Idols*, 1889.]

B. "Good and Evil," "Good and Bad"

1. The English psychologists to whom we owe the only attempts that have thus far been made to write a genealogy of morals are no mean posers of riddles, but the riddles they pose are themselves, and being incarnate have one advantage over their books—they are interesting. What are these English psychologists really after? One finds them always, whether intentionally or not, engaged in the same task of pushing into the foreground the nasty part of the psyche, looking for the effective motive forces of human development in the very last place we would wish to have them found, e.g., in the inertia of habit, in forgetfulness, in the blind and fortuitous association of ideas: always in something that is purely passive, automatic, reflexive, molecular, and, moreover, profoundly stupid. What drives these psychologists forever in the same direction? A secret, malicious desire to belittle humanity, which they do not acknowledge even to themselves? A pessimistic distrust, the suspiciousness of the soured idealist? Some petty resentment of Christianity (and Plato) which does not rise above the threshold of consciousness? Or could it be a prurient taste for whatever is embarrassing, painfully paradoxical, dubious and absurd in existence? Or is it, perhaps, a kind of stew—a little meanness, a little bitterness, a bit of anti-Christianity, a touch of prurience and desire for condiments? . . . But, again, people tell me that these men are simply dull old frogs who hop and creep in and around man as in their own element—as though man were a bog. However, I am reluctant to listen to this, in fact I refuse to believe it; and if I may express a wish where I cannot express a conviction, I do wish wholeheartedly that things may be otherwise with these men—that these microscopic examiners of the soul may be really courageous, magnanimous, and proud animals, who know how to contain their emotions and have trained themselves to subordinate all wishful thinking to the truth—any truth, even a homespun, severe, ugly, obnoxious, un-Christian, unmoral truth. For such truths do exist.

2. All honor to the beneficent spirits that may motivate these historians of ethics! One thing is certain, however, they have been quite deserted by the true spirit of history. They all, to a man, think unhistorically, as is the age-old custom among philosophers. The amateurishness of their procedure is made plain from the very beginning, when it is a question of explaining the provenance of the concept and judgment *good*. "Originally," they decree, "altruistic actions were praised and approved by their recipients, that is, by those to whom they were useful. Later on, the origin of that praise having been forgotten, such actions were felt to be good simply because it was the habit to commend them." We notice at once that this first derivation has all the earmarks of the English psychologists' work. Here are the key ideas of utility, forgetfulness, habit, and, finally, error, seen as lying at the root of that value system which civilized man had hitherto regarded with pride as the prerogative of all men. This pride must now be humbled, these values devalued. Have the debunkers succeeded?

Now it is obvious to me, first of all, that their theory looks for the genesis of the concept *good* in the wrong place: the judgment *good* does not originate with those to whom the good has been done. Rather it was the "good" themselves, that is to say the noble, mighty, highly placed, and high-minded who decreed themselves and their actions to be good, i.e., belonging to the highest rank, in contradistinction to all that was base, low-minded and plebeian. It was only this *pathos of distance* that authorized them to create values and name them—what was utility to them? The notion of utility seems singularly inept to account for such a quick jetting forth of supreme value judgments. Here we come face to face with the exact opposite of that lukewarmness which every scheming prudence, every utilitarian calculus presupposes—and not for a time only, for the rare, exceptional hour, but permanently. The origin of the opposites *good* and *bad* is to be found in the pathos of nobility and distance, representing the dominant temper of a higher, ruling class in relation to a lower, dependent one. (The lordly right of bestowing names is such that one would almost be justified in seeing the origin of language itself as an expression of the rulers' power. They say, "This *is* that or that"; they seal off each thing and action with a sound and thereby take symbolic possession of it.) Such an origin would suggest that there is no *a priori* necessity for associating the word *good* with altruistic deeds, as those moral psychologists are fond of claiming. In fact, it is only after aristocratic values have begun to decline that the egotism-altruism dichotomy takes possession of the human conscience; to use my own terms, it is the herd instinct that now asserts itself. Yet it takes quite a while for this instinct to assume such sway that it can reduce all moral valuations to that dichotomy—as is currently happening throughout Europe, where the prejudice equating the terms *moral, altruistic,* and *disinterested* has assumed the obsessive force of an *idée fixe.*

10. The slave revolt in morals begins by rancor turning creative and giving birth to values—the rancor of beings who, deprived of the direct outlet of action, compensate by an imaginary vengeance. All truly noble morality grows out of triumphant self-affirmation. Slave ethics, on the other hand, begins by saying *no* to an "outside," an "other," a non-self, and that *no* is its creative act. This reversal of direction of the evaluating look, this invariable looking outward instead of inward, is a fundamental feature of rancor. Slave ethics requires for its inception a sphere different from and hostile to its own. Physiologically speaking, it requires an outside stimulus in order to act at all; all its action is reaction. The opposite is true of aristocratic valuations; such values grow and act spontaneously, seeking out their contraries only in order to affirm themselves even more gratefully and delightedly. Here the negative concepts, *humble, base, bad,* are late, pallid counterparts of the positive, intense and passionate credo, "We noble, good, beautiful, happy ones." Aristocratic valuations may go amiss and do violence to reality, but this happens only with regard to spheres which they do not know well, or from the knowledge of which they austerely guard themselves: the aristocrat will, on occasion, misjudge a sphere which he holds in contempt, the sphere of the common man, the people. On the other hand we should remember that the emotion of contempt, of looking down, provided that it falsifies at all, is as nothing compared with the falsification which suppressed hatred, impotent vindictiveness, effects upon its opponent, though only in effigy. There is in all contempt too much casualness and nonchalance, too much blinking of facts and impatience, and too much inborn gaiety for it ever to make of its object a downright caricature and monster.

. . . All this stands in utter contrast to what is called happiness among the impotent and oppressed, who are full of bottled-up aggressions. Their happiness is purely passive and takes the form of drugged tranquillity, stretching and yawning, peace, "sabbath," emotional slackness. Whereas the noble lives before his own conscience with confidence and frankness (*gennaīos* "nobly bred" emphasizes the nuance "truthful" and perhaps also "ingenuous"), the rancorous person is neither truthful nor ingenuous nor honest and forthright with himself. His soul squints; his mind loves hide-outs, secret paths, and back doors; everything that is hidden seems to him his own world, his security, his comfort; he is expert in silence, in long memory, in waiting, in provisional self-depreciation, and in self-humiliation. A race of such men will, in the end, inevitably be cleverer than a race of aristocrats, and it will honor sharp-wittedness to a much greater degree, i.e., as an absolutely vital condition for its existence. Among the noble, mental acuteness always tends slightly to suggest luxury and overrefinement. The fact is that with them it is much less important than is the perfect functioning of the ruling, unconscious instincts or even a certain temerity to follow sudden impulses, court danger, or indulge spurts of violent rage, love, worship, gratitude, or vengeance. When a noble man feels resentment, it is absorbed in his instantaneous reaction and therefore does not poison him. Moreover, in countless cases where we might expect it, it never arises, while with weak and impotent people it occurs without fail. It is a sign of strong, rich temperaments that they cannot for long take seriously their enemies, their misfortunes, their *misdeeds;* for such characters have in them an excess of plastic curative power, and also a power of oblivion. (A good modern example of the latter is Mirabeau, who lacked all memory for insults and meannesses done him, and who was unable to forgive because he had forgotten.) Such a man simply shakes off vermin which would get beneath another's skin—and only here, if anywhere on earth, is it possible to speak of "loving one's enemy." The noble person will respect his enemy, and respect is already a bridge to love. . . . Indeed he requires his enemy for himself, as his mark of distinction, nor could he tolerate any other enemy than one in whom he finds nothing to despise and much to esteem. Imagine, on the other hand, the "enemy" as conceived by the rancorous man! For this is his true creative achievement: he has conceived the "evil enemy," the Evil One, as a fundamental idea, and then as a pendant he has conceived a Good One—himself.

11. The exact opposite is true of the noble-minded, who spontaneously creates the notion *good,* and later derives from it the conception of the *bad.* How ill-matched these two concepts look, placed side by side: the bad of noble origin, and the *evil* that has risen out of the cauldron of unquenched hatred! The first is a by-product, a complementary color, almost an afterthought; the second is the beginning, the original creative act of slave ethics. But neither is the conception of good the same in both cases, as we soon find out when we ask ourselves who it is that is really evil according to the code of rancor. The answer is: precisely the good one of the opposite code, that is the noble, the powerful—only colored, reinterpreted, reenvisaged by the poisonous eye of resentment. And we are the first to admit that anyone who knew these "good" ones only as enemies would find them evil enemies indeed. For these same men who, amongst themselves, are so strictly constrained by custom, worship, ritual, gratitude, and by mutual surveillance and jealousy, who are so resourceful in consideration, tenderness, loyalty, pride and friendship, when once they step outside their circle become little better than uncaged beasts of prey. Once abroad in the wilderness, they revel in the freedom from social constraint and compensate for their long confinement in the quietude of their own community. They revert to the innocence of wild animals: we can imagine them returning from an orgy of murder, arson, rape, and torture, jubilant and at peace with themselves as though they had committed a fraternity prank—convinced, moreover, that the poets for a long time to come will have something to sing about and to praise. Deep within all these noble races there lurks the beast of prey, bent on spoil and conquest. This hidden urge has to be satisfied from time to time, the beast let loose in the wilderness. This goes as well for the Roman, Arabian, German, Japanese nobility as for the Homeric heroes and the Scandinavian vikings. The noble races have everywhere left in their wake the catchword "barbarian." And even their highest culture shows an awareness of this trait and a certain pride in it (as we see, for example, in Pericles' famous funeral oration, when he tells the Athenians: "Our boldness has gained us access to every land and sea, and erected monuments to itself *for both good and evil.* ") This "boldness" of noble races, so headstrong, absurd, incalculable, sudden, improbable (Pericles commends the Athenians especially for their *rathumia*), their utter indifference to safety and comfort, their terrible pleasure in destruction, their taste for cruelty—all these traits are embodied by their victims in the image of the "barbarian," the "evil enemy," the Goth or the Vandal. The profound and icy suspicion which the German arouses as soon as he assumes power (we see it happening again today) harks back to the persistent horror with which Europe for many centuries witnessed the raging of the blond Teutonic beast. If it were true, as passes current nowadays, that the real meaning of culture resides in its power to domesticate man's savage instincts, then we might be justified in viewing all those rancorous machinations by which the noble tribes, and their ideals, have been laid low as the true instruments of culture. But this would still not amount to saying that the *organizers* themselves represent culture. Rather, the exact opposite would be true, as is vividly shown by the current state of affairs. These carriers of the leveling and retributive instincts, these descendants of every European and extra-European slavedom, and especially of the pre-Aryan populations, represent human retrogression most flagrantly. Such "instruments of culture" are a disgrace to man and might make one suspicious of culture altogether. One might be justified in fearing the wild beast lurking within all noble races and in being on one's guard against it, but who would not a thousand times prefer fear when it is accompanied with admiration to security accompanied by the loathsome sight of perversion, dwarfishness, degeneracy? And is not the latter our predicament today? What accounts for our repugnance to man—for there is no question that he makes us suffer? Certainly not our fear of him, rather the fact that there is no longer anything to be feared from him; that the vermin "man" occupies the entire stage; that, tame, hopelessly mediocre, and savorless, he considers himself the apex of historical evolution; and not entirely without justice, since he is still somewhat removed from the mass of sickly and effete creatures whom Europe is beginning to stink of today.

16. Let us conclude. The two sets of valuations, good/bad and good/evil, have waged a terrible battle on this earth, lasting many millennia; and just as surely as the second set has for a long time now been in the ascendant, so surely are there still places where the battle goes on and the issue remains in suspension. It might even be claimed that by being raised to a higher plane the battle has become much more profound. Perhaps there is today not a single intellectual worth his salt who is not divided on that issue, a battleground for those opposites.

C. "Guilt," "Bad Conscience," and Related Matters

1. To breed an animal with the right to make promises—is not this the paradoxical problem nature has set itself with regard to man? and is it not man's true problem? That the problem has in fact been solved to a remarkable degree will seem all the more surprising if we do full justice to the strong opposing force, the faculty of oblivion. Oblivion is not merely a *vis inertiae,* as is often claimed, but an active screening device, responsible for the fact that what we experience and digest psychologically does not, in the stage of digestion, emerge into consciousness any more than what we ingest physically does. The role of this active oblivion is that of a concierge: to shut temporarily the doors and windows of consciousness; to protect us from the noise and agitation with which our lower organs work for or against one another; to introduce a little quiet into our consciousness so as to make room for the nobler functions and functionaries of our organism which do the governing and planning. This concierge maintains order and etiquette in the household of the psyche; which immediately suggests that there can be no happiness, no serenity, no hope, no pride, no *present,* without oblivion. A man in whom this screen is damaged and inoperative is like a dyspeptic (and not merely *like* one): he can't be done with anything. . . . Now this naturally forgetful animal, for whom oblivion represents a power, a form of strong health, has created for itself an opposite power, that of remembering, by whose aid, in certain cases, oblivion may be suspended—specifically in cases where it is a question of promises. By this I do not mean a purely passive succumbing to past impressions, the indigestion of being unable to be done with a pledge once made, but rather an active not wishing to be done with it, a continuing to will what has once been willed, a veritable "memory of the will"; so that, between the original determination and the actual performance of the thing willed, a whole world of new things, conditions, even volitional acts, can be interposed without snapping the long chain of the will. But how much all this presupposes! A man who wishes to dispose of his future in this manner must first have learned to separate necessary from accidental acts; to think causally; to see distant things as though they were near at hand; to distinguish means from ends. In short, he must have become not only calculating but himself calculable, regular even to his own perception, if he is to stand pledge for his own future as a guarantor does.

2. This brings us to the long story of the origin or genesis of responsibility. The task of breeding an animal entitled to make promises involves, as we have already seen, the preparatory task of rendering man up to a certain point regular, uniform, equal among equals, calculable. The tremendous achievement which I have referred to in *Daybreak* as "the custom character of morals," that labor man accomplished upon himself over a vast period of time, receives its meaning and justification here—even despite the brutality, tyranny, and stupidity associated with the process. With the help of custom and the social strait-jacket, man was, in fact, made calculable. However, if we place ourselves at the terminal point of this great process, where society and custom finally reveal their true aim, we shall find the ripest fruit of that tree to be the sovereign individual, equal only to himself, all moral custom left far behind. This autonomous, more than moral individual (the terms *autonomous* and *moral* are mutually exclusive) has developed his own, independent, long-range will, which dares to make promises; he has a proud and vigorous consciousness of what he has achieved, a sense of power and freedom, of absolute accomplishment. This fully emancipated man, master of his will, who dares make promises—how should he not be aware of his superiority over those who are unable to stand security for themselves? Think how much trust, fear, reverence he inspires (all three fully *deserved*), and how, having that sovereign rule over himself, he has mastery too over all weaker-willed and less reliable creatures! Being truly free and possessor of a long-range, pertinacious will, he also possesses a scale of values. Viewing others from the center of his own being, he either honors or disdains them. It is natural to him to honor his strong and reliable peers, all those who promise like sovereigns: rarely and reluctantly; who are chary of their trust; whose trust is a mark of distinction; whose promises are binding because they know that they will make them good in spite of all accidents, in spite of destiny itself. Yet he will inevitably reserve a kick for those paltry windbags who promise irresponsibly and a rod for those liars who break their word even in uttering it. His proud awareness of the extraordinary privilege responsibility confers has penetrated deeply and become a dominant instinct. What shall he call that dominant instinct, provided he ever feels impelled to give it a name? Surely he will call it his *conscience.*

D. *Twilight of the Idols*

MORALITY AS ANTI-NATURE

All passions have a phase when they are merely disastrous, when they drag down their victim with the weight of stupidity—and a later, very much later phase when they wed the spirit, when they "spiritualize" themselves. Formerly, in view of the element of stupidity in passion, war was declared on passion itself, its destruction was plotted; all the old moral monsters are agreed on this: *il faut tuer les passions.*[1] The most famous formula for this is to be found in the New Testament, in that Sermon on the Mount, where, incidentally, things are by no means looked at from a height. There it is said, for example, with particular reference to sexuality: "If thy eye offend thee, pluck it out." Fortunately, no Christian acts in accordance with this precept. *Destroying* the passions and cravings, merely as a preventive measure against their stupidity and the unpleasant consequences of this stupidity—today this itself strikes us as merely another acute form of stupidity. We no longer admire dentists who "pluck out" teeth so that they will not hurt any more.

To be fair, it should be admitted, however, that on the ground out of which Christianity grew, the concept of the "spiritualization of passion" could never have been formed. After all the first church, as is well known, fought *against* the "intelligent" in favor of the "poor in spirit." How could one expect from it an

---

[1] "One must kill the passions."

From *Twilight of the Idols,* translated by Walter Kaufmann in *The Viking Portable Nietzsche* (New York: Viking, 1954). Reprinted with permission.

intelligent war against passion? The church fights passion with excision in every sense: its practice, its "cure," is *castratism.* It never asks: "How can one spiritualize, beautify, deify a craving?" It has at all times laid the stress of discipline on extirpation (of sensuality, of pride, of the lust to rule, of avarice, of vengefulness). But an attack on the roots of passion means an attack on the roots of life: the practice of the church is *hostile to life.*

The same means in the fight against a craving—castration, extirpation—is instinctively chosen by those who are too weak-willed, too degenerate, to be able to impose moderation on themselves; by those who are so constituted that they require *La Trappe,* to use a figure of speech, or (without any figure of speech) some kind of definitive declaration of hostility, a *cleft* between themselves and the passion. Radical means are indispensable only for the degenerate; the weakness of the will—or, to speak more definitely, the inability *not* to respond to a stimulus—is itself merely another form of degeneration. The radical hostility, the deadly hostility against sensuality, is always a symptom to reflect on: it entitles us to suppositions concerning the total state of one who is excessive in this manner. . . .

I reduce a principle to a formula. Every naturalism in morality—that is, every healthy morality—is dominated by an instinct of life; some commandment of life is fulfilled by a determinate canon of "shalt" and "shalt not"; some inhibition and hostile element on the path of life is thus removed. *Anti-natural* morality— that is, almost every morality which has so far been taught, revered, and preached—turns, conversely, *against* the instincts of life: it is *condemnation* of these instincts, now secret, now outspoken and impudent. When it says, "God looks at the heart," it says No to both the lowest and the highest desires of life, and posits God as the *enemy of life.* The saint in whom God delights is the ideal eunuch. Life has come to an end where the "kingdom of God" begins.

Once one has comprehended the outrage of such a revolt against life as has become almost sacrosanct in Christian morality, one has, fortunately, also comprehended something else: the futility, apparentness, absurdity, and *mendaciousness* of such a revolt. A condemnation of life by the living remains in the end a mere symptom of a certain kind of life: the question whether it is justified or unjustified is not even raised thereby. One would require a position *outside* of life, and yet have to know it as well as one, as many, as all who have lived it, in order to be permitted even to touch the problem of the *value* of life: reasons enough to comprehend that this problem is for us an unapproachable problem. When we speak of values, we speak with the inspiration, with the way of looking at things, which is part of life: life itself forces us to posit values; life itself values through us when we posit values. From this it follows that even that anti-natural morality which conceives of God as the counterconcept and condemnation of life is only a value judgment of life—but of what life? of what kind of life? I have already given the answer: of declining, weakened, weary, condemned life. Morality, as it has so far been understood—as it has in the end been formulated once more by Schopenhauer, as "negation of the will to life"—is the very *instinct of decadence,* which makes an imperative of itself. It says: "Perish!" It is a condemnation pronounced by the condemned.

Let us finally consider how naive it is altogether to say: "Man *ought* to be such and such!" Reality shows us an enchanting wealth of types, the abundance of a lavish play and change of forms—and some wretched loafer of a moralist comments: "No! Man ought to be different." He even knows what man should be like, this wretched bigot and prig: he paints himself on the wall and comments, *"Ecce homo!"* But even when the moralist addresses himself only to the single human being and says to him, "You ought to be such and such!" he does not cease to make himself ridiculous. The single human being is a piece of *fatum* from the front and from the rear, one law more, one necessity more for all that is yet to come and to be. To say to him, "Change yourself!" is to demand that everything be changed, even retroactively. And indeed there have been consistent moralists who wanted man to be different, that is, virtuous—they wanted him remade in their own image, as a prig: to that end, they *negated* the world! No small madness! No modest kind of immodesty!

Morality, insofar as it *condemns* for its own sake, and *not* out of regard for the concerns, considerations, and contrivances of life, is a specific error with which one ought to have no pity—an *idiosyncrasy of degenerates* which has caused immeasurable harm.

We others, we immoralists, have, conversely, made room in our hearts for every kind of understanding, comprehending, and *approving.* We do not easily negate; we make it a point of honor to be *affirmers.* More and more, our eyes have opened to that economy which needs and knows how to utilize all that the holy witlessness of the priest, of the *diseased* reason in the priest, rejects—that economy in the law of life which finds an advantage even in the disgusting species of the prigs, the priests, the virtuous. *What* advantage? But we ourselves, we immoralists, are the answer.

What alone can be *our* doctrine? That no one *gives* man his qualities—neither God, nor society, nor his parents and ancestors, nor he himself. (The nonsense of the last idea was taught as "intelligible freedom" by Kant—perhaps by Plato already.) No one is responsible for man's being there at all, for his being such-and-such, or for his being in these circumstances or in this environment. The fatality of his essence is not to be disentangled from the fatality of all that has been and will be. Man is not the effect of some special purpose, of a will, and end; nor is he the object of an attempt to attain an "ideal of humanity" or an "ideal of happiness" or an "ideal of morality." It is absurd to wish to devolve one's essence on some end or other. We have invented the concept of "end": in reality there is no end.

One is necessary, one is a piece of fatefulness, one belongs to the whole, one is in the whole; there is nothing which could judge, measure, compare, or sentence our being, for that would mean judging, measuring, comparing, or sentencing the whole. But there is nothing besides the whole. That nobody is held responsible any longer, that the mode of being may not be traced back to a *causa prima,* that the world does not form a unity either as a sensorium or as "spirit"—that alone is the great liberation; with this alone is the innocence of becoming restored. The concept of "God" was until now the greatest objection to existence. We deny God, we deny the responsibility in God: only thereby do we redeem the world.

My demand upon the philosopher is known, that he take his stand *beyond* good and evil and leave the illusion of moral judgment *beneath* himself. This demand follows from an insight which I was the first to formulate: that *there are altogether no moral facts.* Moral judgments agree with religious ones in believing in realities which are no realities. Morality is merely an interpretation of certain phenomena—more precisely, a misinterpretation. Moral judgments, like religious ones, belong to a stage of ignorance at which the very concept of the real and the distinction between what is real and imaginary, are still lacking; thus "truth," at this stage, designates all sorts of things which we today call "imaginings." Moral judgments are therefore never to be taken literally: so understood, they always contain mere absurdity. Semeiotically, however, they remain invaluable: they reveal, at least for those who know, the most valuable realities of cultures and inwardnesses which did not know enough to "understand" themselves. Morality is mere sign language, mere symptomatology; one must know what it is all about to be able to profit from it.

E. The Antichrist

REVALUATION OF ALL VALUES

What is good? Everything that heightens the feeling of power in man, the will to power, power itself.

What is bad? Everything that is born of weakness.

What is happiness? The feeling that power is *growing,* that resistance is overcome.

Not contentedness but more power; not peace but war; not virtue but fitness (Renaissance virtue, *virtù,* virtue that is moraline-free).

The weak and the failures shall perish: first principle of *our* love of man. And they shall even be given every possible assistance.

What is more harmful than any vice? Active pity for all the failures and all the weak: Christianity. . . .

It is a painful, horrible spectacle that has dawned on me: I have drawn back the curtain from the *corruption* of man. In my mouth, this word is at least free from one suspicion: that it might involve a moral accusation of man. It is meant—let me emphasize this once more—*moraline-free.* So much so that I experience this corruption most strongly precisely where men have so far aspired most deliberately to "virtue" and "godliness." I understand corruption, as you will guess, in the sense of decadence: it is my contention that all the values in which mankind now sums up its supreme desiderata are *decadence-values.*

I call an animal, a species, or an individual corrupt when it loses its instincts, when it chooses, when it prefers, what is disadvantageous for it. A history of "lofty sentiments," of the "ideals of mankind"—and it is possible that I shall have to write it—would almost explain too *why* man is so corrupt. Life itself is to my mind the instinct for growth, for durability, for an accumulation of forces, for *power:* where the will to power is lacking there is decline. It is my contention that all the supreme values of mankind *lack* this will—that the values which are symptomatic of decline, *nihilistic* values, are lording it under the holiest names.

F. The Will to Power

I

Whose Will to Power Is Morality? The *common factor* of all European history since the time of *Socrates* is the attempt to make the *moral values* dominate all other values, in order that they should not be only the leader and judge of life, but also of: (1) knowledge, (2) Art, (3) political and social aspirations. . . .

What is the meaning of this *will to power on the part of moral values,* which has played such a part in the world's prodigious evolutions?

Answer: Three powers lie concealed behind it: (1) the instinct of the *herd* opposed to the strong and independent; (2) the instinct of all *sufferers* and all *abortions* opposed to the happy and well-constituted; (3) the instinct of the mediocre opposed to the exceptions. . . .

II

The Tendency of Moral Evolution. Every one's desire is that there should be no other teaching and valuation of things than those by means of which he himself succeeds. Thus the *fundamental tendency* of the *weak* and *mediocre* of all times, has been to *enfeeble the strong and to reduce them to the level of the weak: their chief weapon in this process* was the *moral principle.* The attitude of the strong towards the weak is branded as evil: the higher states of the strong become bad bywords. . . .

III

The instinct of the herd values the *juste milieu* and the *average* as the highest and most precious of all things: the spot where the majority is to be found, and the air that it breathes there. In this way it is the opponent of all order of rank; it regards a climb from the level to the heights in the same light as a descent from the majority to the minority. The herd regards the *exception,* whether it be above or beneath its general level, as something which is antagonistic and dangerous to itself. Their trick in dealing with the exceptions above them, the strong, the mighty, the wise, and the fruitful, is to persuade them to become guardians, herdsmen, and watchmen—in fact, to become their *head-servants:* thus they convert a danger into a thing which is useful. In the middle, fear ceases: here a man is alone with nothing; here there is not much room even for misunderstandings; here there is equality; here a man's individual existence is not felt as a reproach, but as the *right* existence; here contentment reigns supreme. Mistrust is active only towards the exceptions; to be an exception is to be a sinner.

IV

The whole of the morality of Europe is based upon the values *which are useful to the herd;* the sorrow of all higher and exceptional men is explained by the fact that everything which distinguishes them from others reaches their consciousness in the form of a feeling of their own smallness and egregiousness. It is the *virtues* of modern men which are the causes of pessimistic gloominess; the mediocre, like the herd, are not troubled much with questions or with conscience—they are cheerful. (Among the gloomy strong men, Pascal and Schopenhauer are noted examples.)

    The more dangerous a quality seems to the herd, the more completely it is condemned. . . .

VI

My teaching is this, that the herd seeks to maintain and preserve one type of man, and that it defends itself on two sides—that is to say, against those which are decadents from its ranks (criminals, etc.), and against those who rise superior to its dead level. The instincts of the herd tend to a stationary state of society; they merely preserve. They have no creative power. . . .

DISCUSSION

Unlike most other philosophers, Nietzsche does not try to *justify* morality; instead, he tries to *explain* it through psychology. What we call "morality," he argues, is in fact a "herd" or "slave morality," which was invented for the protection of the weak and coerces and inhibits those who could do more than merely "be moral." Thus he insists that there are "no moral facts" and no objective moral order, but rather a "tyranny against nature" invented by those whose natures are weak and insecure. A virtue such as humility, for example, inhibits our natural tendency to be proud and outspoken about our own accomplishments—which of course does not bother those who have nothing to be proud about. There is nothing "right" about humility, or, for that matter, about pride.

But pride is "natural"; humility is not. Pride is a manifestation of strength and accomplishment; humility is a mark of meekness and self-denial.

Accordingly, Nietzsche distinguishes his two kinds of moral perspectives—master and slave moralities. Master morality is the nobility of great desires, expressing what one feels, without the inhibitions of universal rules. This is not to say that masters must be cruel or inconsiderate; Nietzsche even says at one point that the strong have a *duty* to help the weak, but this as a mark of character rather than a moral obligation. Slave morality is prompted not by desire and passion, however, but by fear and a sense of inadequacy. For the slave, "good" comes to mean just the opposite of what it means to the master—self-denial instead of self-fulfillment. In turn, the master's "good" becomes slave morality's "evil" and the Christian concept of sin. Denying one's passions becomes morally imperative for everyone; expressing or pursuing one's passion is universally prohibited—which is no inconvenience, of course, to those of little passion.

Nietzsche claims that he is giving us a "genealogy" when he traces the origins of "slave morality" to the literal slaves of ancient Egypt and early Rome. Similarly, he claims that he is simply explaining two types of morality when he distinguishes master and slave moral concepts. But it is clear that the terms "master" and "slave" are anything but neutral and that Nietzsche obviously prefers and defends the former and despises the latter. Furthermore, Nietzsche spends so much of his philosophical energy attacking (slave) morality and its metaphysical supports in Christianity that his ethics too often appears to be simply negative—or what he calls "nihilism"—a brutal attack which leaves nothing in its place. But Nietzsche would have been offended by this view of his work, which he repeatedly called a "Yea-saying" to life and an expression of the ultimate freedom and "cheerfulness." He saw nihilism rather as a product of morality itself and he saw his rejection of (slave) morality and religion ("God is dead") as a liberating force in our lives, an opening up of infinite possibilities: "Every hazard is permitted. . . . The sea, *our sea,* lies open there. Perhaps there has never been so open a sea."

STUDY QUESTIONS

1 What does Nietzsche mean by "will to power"? If he were in an argument with John Stuart Mill about utilitarianism, what would Nietzsche say about Mill's basic premise, that everyone desires his or her own happiness (pleasure)?

2 What is "slave morality" and why is our own morality a version of it? What is the origin of slave morality? What is its motivation?

3 Why does Nietzsche so vehemently reject the general principle that "you shouldn't ever hurt anyone"? Does he thereby defend the desirability of cruelty?

4 In what sense does Nietzsche claim to be a "psychologist in the matter of morals"? What is he looking for when he asks, "What does such an assertion [for example, "there is a categorical imperative"] indicate about the person who makes it?

5 Why is every morality "tyranny against nature"? Why does Nietzsche attack the dominance of reason in morals? In what way does he thus resemble Hume? In what ways does he differ from Hume? What would Nietzsche say about the role of the "moral sentiments" in ethics?

6 Why does Nietzsche so despise Christianity and Judeo-Christian morality? Could one defend Christianity and morality without invoking the considerations Nietzsche rejects? Is Christian morality based fundamentally on resentment and weakness? Does Nietzsche insist that *all* Christians are so motivated?

7 What does Nietzsche have against Socrates? Why does he link Socrates with Christianity?

8 Nietzsche credits the ancient Hebrew for "the miracle of the inversion of valuations" that defines slave morality. What is this "inversion" and how does it work? How does slave morality translate the values of "master morality" into its own terms?

9 What is the *"übermensch"*? Why and in what way is he (or she) "more than human"? What kind of ideal is Nietzsche holding up to us here?

10 What's wrong with weakness?

11 What is so bad about socialism and democracy (which Nietzsche links together as a single phenomenon)?

12 What is "noble"? In what ways does Nietzsche's morality agree with that of Plato and Aristotle? In what ways is it clearly different?

13 What's wrong with "humility"? (Would Aristotle agree?)

14 What is wrong with taking the main terms of morality as essentially impersonal or "disinterested"? Isn't this the very essence of morals?

15 How is morality a symptom of "decadence"? What particular features of morality make it "life-denying," according to Nietzsche?

16 "There are altogether no moral facts." What does this mean?

17 What is wrong with trying to "improve mankind"?

18 Is Nietzsche a teleologist in ethics? Why does he insist that "man is not the effect of some special purpose, of a will, an end; nor is he the object of an attempt to attain an 'ideal of humanity' or an 'ideal of happiness' or an 'ideal of morality'?" What does he mean when he writes, "We have invented the concept of 'end'; in reality there is no end?"

CHAPTER 9

ALBERT CAMUS

Although he repudiated the label "existentialist" after a notorious fight with his one-time friend Jean-Paul Sartre in 1955, Albert Camus is rightly included as a central figure of existentialism, the philosophy that captured the French imagination after World War II and has been popular in the United States ever since. Camus was much more a novelist and a journalist than a philosopher as such. His ethical attention was directed at the violent politics and moral dilemmas of his times, rather than to the abstract theories about the justification of morals or the nature of the good. Nevertheless, in his first philosophical essay, *The Myth of Sisyphus,* and in his great short novel, *The Stranger,* Camus expounds a very definite ethical theory, despite its literary presentation.

The theory centers around the concept of "the Absurd," by which Camus means the overall absurdity of human existence. He is an atheist, but an atheist with old-fashioned expectations about the world—for example, that it should make sense and that life ought to be fair. But the world is "indifferent" to our rational demands of it, and herein lies "the absurd." We do not really understand the world, nor do we understand ourselves. Life is not fair, and against the injustice of life we have no moral choice but to *rebel.* This means that, if it is true that life has no meaning, we refuse to accept that life has no meaning and we *make* it meaningful. It also means that we refuse to accept wishful rationalizations that might make life seem meaningful—by believing in God or in some utopian vision about the distant future. Camus calls such escape fantasies "philosophical suicide." The significance of our lives exists precisely in this spirit of revolt; it is life itself that becomes our sole value, nothing else.

The metaethics Camus loosely presents to us is a version of what Nietzsche called "nihilism"—the theory that none of our values are justifiable. The reasons are not easily specified: the absence of a God is surely his main reason for our plight, although Camus indicates that, even if there were a God, our lives would still be absurd. Our awareness of time and of our own death is also a reason. (Camus does not spell this out, but the view is largely borrowed from the very difficult German existentialist Martin Heidegger.) But most of all, it is that simple chain of reasoning—starting with "Why?"—that is our undoing. We ask, What's the point? and there is no answer. That is "the Absurd," that silence where we expect and demand an answer.

Camus's ethics, therefore, does not contain any concrete rules or prescriptions for our behavior; there is no categorical imperative, and there is no list of virtues. Nevertheless, Camus has a very definite morality in mind, despite his emphasis on the unjustifiability of values and the meaninglessness of life. He is self-consciously a *humanist,* and his insistence on life itself as the only value leads him to insist that it is obligatory for all of us to respect the lives of others, not to sacrifice them to some abstract or distant cause.' Accordingly, much of his moral and political life was caught up between the violence of the left and the violence of the right, both of which he deplored. (It was his refusal to side with the left, preferring to insist on the purity of his position and his more abstract sense of revolt, that prompted his disagreement with Sartre.) He argued that our values are without justification, but at the same time he emerged as one of the great moralists of the twentieth century. Indeed, the whole basis of his moralizing was precisely his insistence that morality could not be based on anything but our own stubborn insistence on living to the fullest.

ALBERT CAMUS

Camus was born in French colonial Algeria, a *pied noir,* into a poor working-class family. His father died when he was an infant, and a childhood of illness and poverty set the stage for the celebration of life that was the core of his philosophy. He never felt completely comfortable in Paris with Sartre and his sophisticated friends, though both men had achieved considerable literary success. Sartre moved more and more to the left, embracing Marxism and defending the notion of violent revolution as a vehicle of social change; Camus could not accept the idea, and in the bloody fight to free Algeria from French rule he could not bring himself to choose sides. After publication of Camus's *The Rebel* in 1955, the two friends split for good. In 1960, Camus was killed in a car crash, an "absurd death," his ex-friend Sartre wrote in a reverent obituary.

The following selections are from *The Myth of Sisyphus* and *The Stranger.*

A. *The Myth of Sisyphus*

AN ABSURD REASONING

There is but one truly serious philosophical problem, and that is suicide. Judging whether life is or is not worth living amounts to answering the fundamental question of philosophy. All the rest—whether or not the world has three dimensions, whether the mind has nine or twelve categories—comes afterwards. These are games; one must first answer. And if it is true, as Nietzsche claims, that a philosopher, to deserve our respect, must preach by example, you can appreciate the importance of that reply, for it will precede the definitive act.

These are facts the heart can feel; yet they call for careful study before they become clear to the intellect.

If I ask myself how to judge that this question is more urgent than that, I reply that one judges by the actions it entails. I have never seen anyone die for the ontological argument. Galileo, who held a scientific truth of great importance, abjured it with the greatest ease as soon as it endangered his life. In a certain sense, he did right.[1] That truth was not worth the stake. Whether the earth or the sun revolves around the other is a matter of profound indifference. To tell the truth, it is a futile question. On the other hand, I see many people die because they judge that life is not worth living. I see others paradoxically getting killed for the ideas or illusions that give them a reason for living (what is called a reason for living is also an excellent reason for dying). I therefore conclude that the meaning of life is the most urgent of questions. How to answer it? On all essential problems (I mean thereby those that run the risk of leading to death or those that intensify the passion of living) there are probably but two methods of thought: the method of La Palisse and the method of Don Quixote. Solely the balance between evidence and lyricism can allow us to achieve simultaneously emotion and lucidity. In a subject at once so humble and so heavy with emotion, the learned and classical dialectic must yield, one can see, to a more modest attitude of mind deriving at once and the same time from common sense and understanding.

Suicide has never been dealt with except as a social phenomenon. On the contrary, we are concerned here, at the outset, with the relationship between individual thought and suicide. An act like this is prepared within the silence of the heart, as is a great work of art. The man himself is ignorant of it. One evening he pulls the trigger or jumps. Of an apartment-building manager who had killed himself I was told that he had lost his daughter five years before, that he had changed greatly since, and that that experience had "undermined" him. A more exact word cannot be imagined. Beginning to think is beginning to be undermined. Society has but little connection with such beginnings. The worm is in man's heart. That is where it must be sought. One must follow and understand this fatal game that leads from lucidity in the face of existence to flight from light.

There are many causes for a suicide, and generally the most obvious ones were not the most powerful. Rarely is suicide committed (yet the hypothesis is not excluded) through reflection. What sets off the crisis is almost always unverifiable. Newspapers often speak of "personal sorrows" or of "incurable illness." These explanations are plausible. But one would have to know whether a friend of the desperate man had not that very day addressed him indifferently. He is the guilty one. For that is enough to precipitate all the rancors and all the boredom still in suspension.[2]

But if it is hard to fix the precise instant, the subtle step when the mind opted

---

[1] *From the point of view of the relative value of truth. On the other hand, from the point of view of virile behavior, this scholar's fragility may well make us smile.*

[2] *Let us not miss this opportunity to point out the relative character of this essay. Suicide may indeed be related to much more honorable considerations—for example, the political suicides of protest, as they were called, during the Chinese revolution.*

for death, it is easier to deduce from the act itself the consequences it implies. In a sense, and as in melodrama, killing yourself amounts to confessing. It is confessing that life is too much for you or that you do not understand it. Let's not go too far in such analogies, however, but rather return to everyday words. It is merely confessing that that "is not worth the trouble." Living, naturally, is never easy. You continue making the gestures commanded by existence for many reasons, the first of which is habit. Dying voluntarily implies that you have recognized, even instinctively, the ridiculous character of that habit, the absence of any profound reason for living, the insane character of that daily agitation, and the uselessness of suffering.

What, then, is that incalculable feeling that deprives the mind of the sleep necessary to life? A world that can be explained even with bad reasons is a familiar world. But, on the other hand, in a universe suddenly divested of illusions and lights, man feels an alien, a stranger. His exile is without remedy since he is deprived of the memory of a lost home or the hope of a promised land. This divorce between man and his life, the actor and his setting, is properly the feeling of absurdity. All healthy men having thought of their own suicide, it can be seen, without further explanation, that there is a direct connection between this feeling and the longing for death. . . .

All great deeds and all great thoughts have a ridiculous beginning. Great works are often born on a streetcorner or in a restaurant's revolving door. So it is with absurdity. The absurd world more than others derives its nobility from that abject birth. In certain situations, replying "nothing" when asked what one is thinking about may be pretense in a man. Those who are loved are well aware of this. But if that reply is sincere, if it symbolizes that odd state of soul in which the void becomes eloquent, in which the chain of daily gestures is broken, in which the heart vainly seeks the link that will connect it again, then it is as it were the first sign of absurdity.

It happens that the stage sets collapse. Rising, streetcar, four hours in the office or the factory, meal, streetcar, four hours of work, meal, sleep, and Monday Tuesday Wednesday Thursday Friday and Saturday according to the same rhythm—this path is easily followed most of the time. But one day the "why" arises and everything begins in that weariness tinged with amazement. "Begins"—this is important. Weariness comes at the end of the acts of a mechanical life, but at the same time it inaugurates the impulse of consciousness. It awakens consciousness and provokes what follows. What follows is the gradual return into the chain or it is the definitive awakening. At the end of the awakening comes, in time, the consequence: suicide or recovery. In itself weariness has something sickening about it. Here, I must conclude that it is good. For everything begins wih consciousness and nothing is worth anything except through it. There is nothing original about these remarks. But they are obvious; that is enough for a while, during a sketchy reconnaissance in the origins of the absurd. Mere "anxiety," as Heidegger says, is at the source of everything.

Likewise and during every day of an unillustrious life, time carries us. But a moment always comes when we have to carry it. We live on the future:

"tomorrow," "later on," "when you have made your way," "you will understand when you are old enough." Such irrelevancies are wonderful, for, after all,
it's a matter of dying. Yet a day comes when a man notices or says that he is
thirty. Thus he asserts his youth. But simultaneously he situates himself in
relation to time. He takes his place in it. He admits that he stands at a certain
point on a curve that he acknowledges having to travel to its end. He belongs to
time, and by the horror that seizes him, he recognizes his worst enemy.
Tomorrow, he was longing for tomorrow, whereas everything in him ought to
reject it. That revolt of the flesh is the absurd.[3]

A step lower and strangeness creeps in: perceiving that the world is "dense,"
sensing to what a degree a stone is foreign and irreducible to us, with what
intensity nature or a landscape can negate us. At the heart of all beauty lies
something inhuman, and these hills, the softness of the sky, the outline of these
trees at this very minute lose the illusory meaning with which we had clothed
them, henceforth more remote than a lost paradise. The primitive hostility of
the world rises up to face us across millennia. For a second we cease to
understand it because for centuries we have understood in it solely the images
and designs that we had attributed to it beforehand, because henceforth we lack
the power to make use of that artifice. The world evades us because it becomes
itself again. That stage scenery masked by habit becomes again what it is. It
withdraws at a distance from us. Just as there are days when under the familiar
face of a woman, we see as a stranger her we had loved months or years ago,
perhaps we shall come even to desire what suddenly leaves us so alone. But the
time has not yet come. Just one thing: that denseness and that strangeness of the
world is the absurd.

Men, too, secrete the inhuman. At certain moments of lucidity, the mechanical aspect of their gestures, their meaningless pantomime makes silly everything
that surrounds them. A man is talking on the telephone behind a glass partition;
you cannot hear him, but you see his incomprehensible dumb show: you wonder
why he is alive. This discomfort in the face of man's own inhumanity, this
incalculable tumble before the image of what we are, this "nausea," as a writer
of today calls it, is also the absurd. Likewise the stranger who at certain seconds
comes to meet us in a mirror, the familiar and yet alarming brother we encounter
in our own photographs is also the absurd. . . .

Now I can broach the notion of suicide. It has already been felt what solution
might be given. At this point the problem is reversed. It was previously a
question of finding out whether or not life had to have a meaning to be lived. It
now becomes clear, on the contrary, that it will be lived all the better if it has no
meaning. Living an experience, a particular fate, is accepting it fully. Now, no
one will live this fate, knowing it to be absurd, unless he does everything to keep
before him that absurd brought to light by consciousness. Negating one of the
terms of the opposition on which he lives amounts to escaping it. To abolish

[3]*But not in the proper sense. This is not a definition, but rather an enumeration of the feelings that
may admit of the absurd. Still, the enumeration finished, the absurd has nevertheless not been
exhausted.*

conscious revolt is to elude the problem. The theme of permanent revolution is thus carried into individual experience. Living is keeping the absurd alive. Keeping it alive is, above all, contemplating it. Unlike Eurydice, the absurd dies only when we turn away from it. One of the only coherent philosophical positions is thus revolt. It is a constant confrontation between man and his own obscurity. It is an insistence upon an impossible transparency. It challenges the world anew every second. Just as danger provided man the unique opportunity of seizing awareness, so metaphysical revolt extends awareness to the whole of experience. It is that constant presence of man is his own eyes. It is not aspiration, for it is devoid of hope. That revolt is the certainty of a crushing fate, without the resignation that ought to accompany it.

This is where it is seen to what a degree absurd experience is remote from suicide. It may be thought that suicide follows revolt—but wrongly. For it does not represent the logical outcome of revolt. It is just the contrary by the consent it presupposes. Suicide, like the leap, is acceptance at its extreme. Everything is over and man returns to his essential history. His unique and dreadful future—he sees and rushes toward it. In its way, suicide settles the absurd. It engulfs the absurd in the same death. But I know that in order to keep alive, the absurd cannot be settled. It escapes suicide to the extent that it is simultaneously awareness and rejection of death. It is, at the extreme limit of the condemned man's last thought, that shoelace that despite everything he sees a few yards away, on the very brink of his dizzying fall. The contrary of suicide, in fact, is the man condemned to death.

That revolt gives life its value. Spread out over the whole length of a life, it restores its majesty to that life. To a man devoid of blinders, there is no finer sight than that of the intelligence at grips with a reality that transcends it. The sight of human pride is unequaled. No disparagement is of any use. That discipline that the mind imposes on itself, that will conjured up out of nothing, that face-to-face struggle have something exceptional about them. To impoverish that reality whose inhumanity constitutes man's majesty is tantamount to impoverishing him himself. I understand then why the doctrines that explain everything to me also debilitate me at the same time. They relieve me of the weight of my own life, and yet I must carry it alone. At this juncture, I cannot conceive that a skeptical metaphysics can be joined to an ethics of renunciation.

Consciousness and revolt, these rejections are the contrary of renunciation. Everything that is indomitable and passionate in a human heart quickens them, on the contrary, with its own life. It is essential to die unreconciled and not of one's own free will. Suicide is a repudiation. The absurd man can only drain everything to the bitter end, and deplete himself. The absurd is his extreme tension, which he maintains constantly by solitary effort, for he knows that in that consciousness and in that day-to-day revolt he gives proof of his only truth, which is defiance. . . .

But what does life mean in such a universe? Nothing else for the moment but indifference to the future and a desire to use up everything that is given. Belief in the meaning of life always implies a scale of values, a choice, our preferences.

Belief in the absurd, according to our definitions, teaches the contrary. But this is worth examining.

Knowing whether or not one can live *without appeal* is all that interests me. I do not want to get out of my depth. This aspect of life being given me, can I adapt myself to it? Now, faced with this particular concern, belief in the absurd is tantamount to substituting the quantity of experiences for the quality. If I convince myself that this life has no other aspect than that of the absurd, if I feel that its whole equilibrium depends on that perpetual opposition between my conscious revolt and the darkness in which it struggles, if I admit that my freedom has no meaning except in relation to its limited fate, then I must say that what counts is not the best living but the most living. It is not up to me to wonder if this is vulgar or revolting, elegant or deplorable. Once and for all, value judgments are discarded here in favor of factual judgments. I have merely to draw the conclusions from what I can see and to risk nothing that is hypothetical. Supposing that living in this way were not honorable, then true propriety would command me to be dishonorable.

The most living; in the broadest sense, that rule means nothing. It calls for definition. It seems to begin with the fact that the notion of quantity has not been sufficiently explored. For it can account for a large share of human experience. A man's rule of conduct and his scale of values have no meaning except through the quantity and variety of experiences he has been in a position to accumulate. Now, the conditions of modern life impose on the majority of men the same quantity of experiences and consequently the same profound experience. To be sure, there must also be taken into consideration the individual's spontaneous contribution, the "given" element in him. But I cannot judge of that, and let me repeat that my rule here is to get along with the immediate evidence. I see, then, that the individual character of a common code of ethics lies not so much in the ideal importance of its basic principles as in the norm of an experience that it is possible to measure. To stretch a point somewhat, the Greeks had the code of their leisure just as we have the code of our eight-hour day. But already many men among the most tragic cause us to foresee that a longer experience changes this table of values. They make us imagine that adventurer of the everyday who through mere quantity of experiences would break all records (I am purposely using this sports expression) and would thus win his own code of ethics. Yet let's avoid romanticism and just ask ourselves what such an attitude may mean to a man with his mind made up to take up his bet and to observe strictly what he takes to be the rules of the game.

Breaking all the records is first and foremost being faced with the world as often as possible. How can that be done without contradictions and without playing on words? For on the one hand the absurd teaches that all experiences are unimportant, and on the other it urges toward the greatest quantity of experiences. How, then, can one fail to do as so many of those men I was speaking of earlier—choose the form of life that brings us the most possible of that human matter, thereby introducing a scale of values that on the other hand one claims to reject?

But again it is the absurd and its contradictory life that teaches us. For the mistake is thinking that that quantity of experiences depends on the circumstances of our life when it depends solely on us. Here we have to be over-simple. To two men living the same number of years, the world always provides the same sum of experiences. It is up to us to be conscious of them. Being aware of one's life, one's revolt, one's freedom, and to the maximum, is living, and to the maximum. Where lucidity dominates, the scale of values becomes useless. Let's be even more simple. Let us say that the sole obstacle, the sole deficiency to be made good, is constituted by premature death. Thus it is that no depth, no emotion, no passion, and no sacrifice could render equal in the eyes of the absurd man (even if he wished it so) a conscious life of forty years and a lucidity spread over sixty years. Madness and death are his irreparables. Man does not choose. The absurd and the extra life it involves *therefore do not depend on man's will,* but on its contrary, which is death. Weighing words carefully, it is altogether a question of luck. One just has to be able to consent to this. There will never be any substitute for twenty years of life and experience.

By what is an odd inconsistency in such an alert race, the Greeks claimed that those who died young were beloved of the gods. And that is true only if you are willing to believe that entering the ridiculous world of the gods is forever losing the purest of joys, which is feeling, and feeling on this earth. The present and the succession of presents before a constantly conscious soul is the ideal of the absurd man. But the word "ideal" rings false in this connection. It is not even his vocation, but merely the third consequence of his reasoning. Having started from an anguished awareness of the inhuman, the meditation on the absurd returns at the end of its itinerary to the very heart of the passionate flames of human revolt.

Thus I draw from the absurd three consequences, which are my revolt, my freedom, and my passion. By the mere activity of consciousness I transform into a rule of life what was an invitation to death—and I refuse suicide. I know, to be sure, the dull resonance that vibrates throughout these days. Yet I have but a word to say: that it is necessary. . . .

The preceding merely defines a way of thinking. But the point is to live.

THE MYTH OF SISYPHUS (Told by Camus)

The gods had condemned Sisyphus to ceaselessly rolling a rock to the top of a mountain, whence the stone would fall back of its own weight. They had thought with some reason that there is no more dreadful punishment than futile and hopeless labor. . . .

You have already grasped that Sisyphus is the absurd hero. He *is,* as much through his passions as through his torture. His scorn of the gods, his hatred of death, and his passion for life won him that unspeakable penalty in which the whole being is exerted toward accomplishing nothing. This is the price that must be paid for the passions of this earth. . . .

If this myth is tragic, that is because its hero is conscious. Where would his torture be, indeed, if at every step the hope of succeeding upheld him? The workman of today works every day in his life at the same tasks, and this fate is no less absurd. But it is tragic only at the rare moments when it becomes conscious. Sisyphus, proletarian of the gods, powerless and rebellious, knows the whole extent of his wretched condition: it is what he thinks of during his descent. The lucidity that was to constitute his torture at the same time crowns his victory. There is no fate that cannot be surmounted by scorn. . . .

All Sisyphus' silent joy is contained therein. His fate belongs to him. His rock is his thing. Likewise, the absurd man, when he contemplates his torment, silences all the idols. In the universe suddenly restored to its silence, the myriad wondering little voices of the earth rise up. Unconscious, secret calls, invitations from all the faces, they are the necessary reverse and price of victory. There is no sun without shadow, and it is essential to know the night. The absurd man says yes and his effort will henceforth be unceasing. If there is a personal fate, there is no higher destiny, or at least there is but one which he concludes is inevitable and despicable. For the rest, he knows himself to be the master of his days. At that subtle moment when man glances backward over his life, Sisyphus returning toward his rock, in that slight pivoting he contemplates that series of unrelated actions which becomes his fate, created by him, combined under his memory's eye and soon sealed by his death. Thus, convinced of the wholly human origin of all that is human, a blind man eager to see who knows that the night has no end, he is still on the go. The rock is still rolling.

I leave Sisyphus at the foot of the mountain! One always finds one's burden again. But Sisyphus teaches the higher fidelity that negates the gods and raises rocks. He too concludes that all is well. This universe henceforth without a master seems to him neither sterile nor futile. Each atom of that stone, each mineral flake of that night-filled mountain, in itself forms a world. The struggle itself toward the heights is enough to fill a man's heart. One must imagine Sisyphus happy.

B. *The Stranger*

Then all day there was my appeal to think about. I made the most of this idea, studying my effects so as to squeeze out the maximum of consolation. Thus, I always began by assuming the worst; my appeal was dismissed. That meant, of course, I was to die. Sooner than others, obviously. "But," I reminded myself, "it's common knowledge that life isn't worth living, anyhow." And, on a wide view, I could see that it makes little difference whether one dies at the age of thirty or threescore and ten—since, in either case, other men and women will continue living, the world will go on as before. Also, whether I died now or forty years hence, this business of dying had to be got through, inevitably. Still, somehow this line of thought wasn't as consoling as it should have been; the idea of all those years of life in hand was a galling reminder! However, I could argue myself out of it, by picturing what would have been my feelings when my term was up, and death had cornered me. Once you're up against it, the precise manner of your death has obviously small importance. Therefore—but it was hard not to lose the thread of the argument leading up to that "therefore"—I should be prepared to face the dismissal of my appeal. . . .

The chaplain gazed at me with a sort of sadness. I now had my back to the wall and light was flowing over my forehead. He muttered some words I didn't catch; then abruptly asked if he might kiss me. I said, "No." Then he turned, came up to the wall, and slowly drew his hand along it.

"Do you really love these earthly things so very much?" he asked in a low voice.

I made no reply.

For quite a while he kept his eyes averted. His presence was getting more and more irksome, and I was on the point of telling him to go, and leave me in peace, when all of a sudden he swung around on me, and burst out passionately:

"No! No! I refuse to believe it. I'm sure you've often wished there was an afterlife."

Of course I had, I told him. Everybody has that wish at times. But that had no more importance than wishing to be rich, or to swim very fast, or to have a better-shaped mouth. It was in the same order of things. I was going on in the same vein, when he cut in with a question. How did I picture the life after the grave?

I fairly bawled out at him: "A life in which I can remember this life on earth. That's all I want of it." And in the same breath I told him I'd had enough of his company.

But, apparently, he had more to say on the subject of God. I went close up to him and made a last attempt to explain that I'd very little time left, and I wasn't going to waste it on God.

Then he tried to change the subject by asking me why I hadn't once addressed him as "Father," seeing that he was a priest. That irritated me still more, and I told him he wasn't my father; quite the contrary, he was on the others' side.

"No, no, my son," he said, laying his hand on my shoulder. "I'm on *your* side, though you don't realize it—because your heart is hardened. But I shall pray for you."

Then, I don't know how it was, but something seemed to break inside me, and I started yelling at the top of my voice. I hurled insults at him, I told him not to waste his rotten prayers on me; it was better to burn than to disappear. I'd taken him by the neckband of his cassock, and, in a sort of ecstasy of joy and rage, I poured out on him all the thoughts that had been simmering in my brain. He seemed so cocksure, you see. And yet none of his certainties was worth one strand of a woman's hair. Living as he did, like a corpse, he couldn't even be sure of being alive. It might look as if my hands were empty. Actually, I was sure of myself, sure about everything, far surer than he; sure of my present life and of the death that was coming. That, no doubt, was all I had; but at least that certainty was something I could get my teeth into—just as it had got its teeth into me. I'd been right, I was still right, I was always right. I'd passed my life in a certain way, and I might have passed it in a different way, if I'd felt like it. I'd acted thus, and I hadn't acted otherwise; I hadn't done *x*, whereas I had done *y* or *z*. And what did that mean? That, all the time, I'd been waiting for this present moment, for that dawn, tomorrow's or another day's, which was to justify me. Nothing, nothing had the least importance, and I knew quite well why. He, too, knew why. From the dark horizon of my future a sort of slow, persistent breeze had been blowing toward me, all my life long, from the years that were to come. And on its way that breeze had leveled out all the ideas that people tried to foist on me in the equally unreal years I then was living through. What difference could they make to me, the deaths of others, or a mother's love, or his God; or the way a man decides to live, the fate he thinks he chooses, since one and the same fate was bound to "choose" not only me but thousands of millions of privileged people who, like him, called themselves my brothers. Surely, surely he must see that? Every man alive was privileged; there was only one class of men, the privileged class. All alike would be condemned to die one day; his turn, too, would come like the others'. And what difference could it make if, after being charged with murder, he were executed because he didn't weep at his mother's funeral, since it all came to the same thing in the end? The same thing for Salamano's wife and for Salamano's dog. That little robot woman was as "guilty" as the girl from Paris who had married Masson, or as Marie, who wanted me to marry her. What did it matter if Raymond was as much my pal as Céleste, who was a far worthier man? What did it matter if at this very moment Marie was kissing a new boy friend? As a condemned man himself, couldn't he grasp what I meant by that dark wind blowing from my future? . . .

I had been shouting so much that I'd lost my breath, and just then the jailers rushed in and started trying to release the chaplain from my grip. One of them made as if to strike me. The chaplain quietened them down, then gazed at me for a moment without speaking. I could see tears in his eyes. Then he turned and left the cell.

Once he'd gone, I felt calm again. But all this excitement had exhausted me and I dropped heavily on to my sleeping plank. I must have had a longish sleep, for, when I woke, the stars were shining down on my face. Sounds of the countryside came faintly in, and the cool night air, veined with smells of earth and salt, fanned my cheeks. The marvelous peace of the sleepbound summer night flooded through me like a tide. Then, just on the edge of daybreak, I heard a steamer's siren. People were starting on a voyage to a world which had ceased to concern me forever. Almost for the first time in many months I thought of my mother. And now, it seemed to me, I understood why at her life's end she had taken on a "fiancé"; why she'd played at making a fresh start. There, too, in that Home where lives were flickering out, the dusk came as a mournful solace. With death so near, Mother must have felt like someone on the brink of freedom, ready to start life all over again. No one, no one in the world had any right to weep for her. And I, too, felt ready to start life all over again. It was as if that great rush of anger had washed me clean, emptied me of hope, and, gazing up at the dark sky spangled with its signs and stars, for the first time, the first, I laid my heart open to the benign indifference of the universe. To feel it so like myself, indeed, so brotherly, made me realize that I'd been happy, and that I was happy still. For all to be accomplished, for me to feel less lonely, all that remained to hope was that on the day of my execution there should be a huge crowd of spectators and that they should greet me with howls of execration.

DISCUSSION

The absurd should not be confused with mere absurdities—tragic or ridiculous setbacks in life. It is life itself that is without a given meaning, without a God, in particular, to give it meaning. But it is just as important to appreciate that the absurd is not the *conclusion* of Camus's argument (insofar as it can be called an argument) but rather the inescapable *problem* with which all philosophizing begins. His opening comment about suicide being the only philosophical question is hyperbole, but the point is intended to force us to overcome our sense of absurdity (which Camus says in his preface to the *Myth* is "a widespread sensibility of our age"). Camus emerges as the ultimate defender of the value of life—in fact it is the *only* value. Love of life alone gives life meaning and is its meaning. Meursault ("the stranger") displays this enthusiasm even when he is about to lose his life; in fact, a recurrent image in Camus's writing (he inherited it from André Gide) is "the pure flame of life itself," which is most appreciated, needless to say, by someone who has been condemned to death.

The "Myth of Sisyphus" itself, as Camus tells it, however, casts some doubt on that optimistic picture. What makes Sisyphus "the absurd hero," according to Camus, is his *consciousness* of the absurdity of his task. And how does he overcome the despair that would seem to follow his awareness? It is not just through his absorption in his task ("his rock is his thing"), it is also through *scorn*. ("There is no fate that cannot be surmounted by scorn.") But this is hardly the same thing as "love of life" (and note that Sisyphus also has gods to scorn, which is exactly what Camus denies to us). Indeed, to what extent is Camus's celebration of "the rebel" and "revolt" an expression not of exuberance but of resentment, precisely the passion that Nietzsche found most ignoble and the undoing of ethics?

STUDY QUESTIONS

1 What is "the Absurd"? What does it mean to say that "life is absurd"? Why would someone think such a thing?

2 Why does Camus deny that all moral systems lack justification? How would he respond, respectively, to Aristotle, to Kant, to Mill? How would they respond, in turn, to him?

3 Why does Meursault ("the stranger") get so angry when the prison chaplain insists on telling him about "the afterlife"? What is Meursault's own conception of the afterlife ("if there is one")? Why does his anger "wash him clean"?

4 Is Sisyphus in fact an apt model for life for all of us? In what ways do our lives resemble the "futile labor" of rolling a rock up a mountain, only to have it inevitably roll back down again? Is scorn and defiance our answer too? Against what or whom? If you reject Camus's Sisyphusian model, what would you put in its place?

5 Is Sisyphus happy?

6 What kind of answer should one expect to that awesome "Why?" that Camus says starts off our "absurd reasoning"? Need it always be absurd? Is there a way of ending it satisfactorily which is not also an example of what Camus calls "philosophical suicide"?

7 What is the ultimate, undisputed value *summum bonum* of Camus's philosophy, despite his emphasis on "the Absurd" and the meaninglessness of life? Is there any way of defending this value?

CHAPTER 10

JEAN-PAUL SARTRE

Jean-Paul Sartre is generally recognized as *the* "existentialist." The word is his, and the dozens of other philosophers associated with existentialism—including many who have disclaimed their association—are judged to be more or less "existential" philosophers by their proximity to Sartre's ideas. One can summarize those ideas in two words—"freedom" and "responsibility." Freedom, Sartre tells us, is the primary condition of human existence, the brute fact that we can and must make choices and, consequently, "make ourselves" into what we will be. Responsibility follows freedom; to have choices and to be able to make a difference is to be responsible for what one chooses and the difference one makes. This includes, of course, *not* choosing, since—Sartre keeps reminding us—not to choose is to *choose* not to choose, whether through willful ignorance, or indecision, or any number of other devices for denying responsibility—which he calls "bad faith" *(mauvaise foi)*.

Like Nietzsche and Camus, Sartre rejects the whole history of ethical justifications. The world is not rational, and we have no reason to expect it to conform to our demands. There is no God, Sartre insists, and therefore no one and nothing to give purpose to the universe or meaning to life. Furthermore, he argues in his popular 1947 lecture, *Existentialism Is a Humanism* (reprinted in part here), there is no one or nothing to give an "essence"—a distinctive purpose or reason—to our existence. There is no human nature, in other words, just our freedom, which it is our responsibility to use as we will. *We* give purpose and meaning to our lives, and there is no one and nothing to assure us that it is the "right" purpose or meaning. This is the human condition, and it is the point of Sartre's philosophy, not to give us an ethical code or rules to live by, but to keep reminding us of this frightening but inescapable freedom and the responsibility that goes along with it.

Sartre started in philosophy as a student of *phenomenology*—a method formulated by the German-Czech philosopher Edmund Husserl at the beginning of this century. The key to phenomenology is the careful investigation of human experience itself, and it is there that Sartre grounds his ethical views. Our basic freedom is first of all a phenomenological finding; that is, a careful examination of our every practical experience shows that the possibility of choice is always there. (A similar point had been argued by Kant—who was decidedly not an existentialist—when he argued that freedom was the necessary "postulate" of practical reason.)

Sartre divides the world into two kinds of "being," which he calls "being-in-itself" (être-en-soi) and "being-for-itself" (être-pour-soi). The first is the being of things. Things simply are what they are; they don't worry about what they ought to be. The second is the being of human consciousness; it is incomplete, aware of the future and the various possibilities for the future. Accordingly, we have a "double property," the facts about ourselves and our denial of those facts—which Sartre calls facticity and transcendence, respectively (p.400). Human beings are always worried about what they will be and what they ought to be. But, because there is no God and because we are endowed (or cursed) with continuous choices, we have no basis for choosing one course of action, one way of life, rather than another. Our basic emotion, accordingly, is anxiety—about what we are, what we will do, what we will be. (In an early novel, Sartre says that our most basic philosophical feeling is rather nausea, but his outlook improves at least slightly later on.)

Our lives, according to Sartre, are always incompletely formed, "indeterminate." Not only can we change our plans for the future, we also change our past. Suppose you are a pre-med student, working hard to get into medical school and remembering with pride how long you have wanted to be a doctor and the various jobs and responsibilities you have had with that end in mind. But when you flunk your organic chemistry course, your view drastically changes. Not only do you give up your plan to go to medical school, you stop thinking about your past in pre-med terms. Now you have decided to be an architect, and so you weave a tale of continued creativity and interest in buildings. The facts of the past may stay the same, but the stories we create around them—and what facts are deemed relevant or not—change significantly.

What we would like, according to Sartre, is to be both free and determined, that is, to be able to choose but at the same time "know who we are." But there is no "knowing who we are," for we are not yet anything or anyone in particular, and one cannot be free and at the same time determined. This ideal of being both free and determined is, as a matter of fact, the conception of God that many medieval philosophers (notably Augustine) defended, which leads Sartre to say, somewhat blasphemously, that what we all really want is to be God. But Sartre is not really interested in theology here; what concerns him is the fact that our lives embody an impossible, ultimate wish. There is no summum bonum; there is only frustration and the illusion of temporary happiness. "Man is a useless passion," he writes in one of the bleaker passages of Being and Nothingness, his most important existentialist treatise.

It would be a mistake, however, to see Sartre as a pessimist, with a tragic and gloomy picture of human life. Shortly before he died in 1980, Sartre insisted in an interview that he had "never had an unhappy day in his life." His plays and novels exude a mischievous sense of humor, and he claims throughout his works that (his) existentialism is in fact the most optimistic philosophy, because it gives each of us the freedom and responsibility to take charge of our own lives and frees us from the impositions and constraints falsely imposed on us by authoritative appeals to "human nature," what is natural "or God's Will."

JEAN-PAUL SARTRE

Sartre was born in Paris in 1905, and he continued to live there for virtually the whole of his life. He studied philosophy and for a short time taught in the provinces, which he hated. He joined the army at the outbreak of World War II, was captured and spent some time in a German prison camp, reading the German philosophers (Hegel and Heidegger) and resolving to dedicate his life writing in the cause of freedom. *Being and Nothingness* was published in 1943 and quickly became the classic text of the new fashion, "existentialism." Sartre's politics moved further and further to the left, but though a Marxist he never joined the Communist party, which he considered dogmatic and immoral. He spent his life with Simone de Beauvoir, herself an accomplished novelist and journalist. He died in 1980, at the age of 75.

A. Existentialism Is a Humanism

. . . For in truth this is of all teachings the least scandalous and the most austere: it is intended strictly for technicians and philosophers. All the same, it can easily be defined.

The question is only complicated because there are two kinds of existentialists. There are, on the one hand, the Christians, amongst whom I shall name Jaspers and Gabriel Mercel, both professed Catholics; and on the other the existential atheists, amongst whom we must place Heidegger as well as the French existentialists and myself. What they have in common is simply the fact that they believe that *existence* comes before *essence*—or, if you will, that we must begin from the subjective. What exactly do we mean by that?

If one considers an article of manufacture—as for example, a book or a paper-knife—one sees that it has been made by an artisan who had a conception of it; and he has paid attention, equally, to the conception of a paper-knife and to the pre-existent technique of production which is a part of that conception and is, at bottom, a formula. Thus the paper-knife is at the same time an article producible in a certain manner and one which, on the other hand, serves a definite purpose, for one cannot suppose that a man would produce a paper-knife without knowing what it was for. Let us say, then, of the paper-knife that its essence—that is to say the sum of the formulae and the qualities which made its production and its definition possible—precedes its existence. The presence of such-and-such a paper-knife or book is thus determined before my eyes. Here, then, we are viewing the world from a technical standpoint, and we can say that production precedes existence.

When we think of God as the creator, we are thinking of him, most of the time, as a supernatural artisan. Whatever doctrine we may be considering, whether it be a doctrine like that of Descartes, or of Leibnitz himself, we always imply that the will follows, more or less, from the understanding or at least accompanies it, so that when God creates he knows precisely what he is creating. Thus, the conception of man in the mind of God is comparable to that of the paper-knife in the mind of the artisan: God makes man according to a procedure and a conception, exactly as the artisan manufactures a paper-knife, following a definition and a formula. Thus each individual man is the realisation of a certain conception which dwells in the divine understanding. In the philosophic atheism of the eighteenth century, the notion of God is suppressed, but not, for all that, the idea that essence is prior to existence; something of that idea we still find everywhere, in Diderot, in Voltaire and even in Kant. Man possesses a human nature; that "human nature," which is the conception of human being, is found in every man; which means that each man is a particular example of an universal conception, the conception of Man. In Kant, this universality goes so far that the wild man of the woods, man in the state of nature and the bourgeois are all contained in the same definition and have the same fundamental qualities. Here again, the essence of man precedes that historic existence which we confront in experience.

Atheistic existentialism, of which I am a representative, declares with greater consistency that if God does not exist there is at least one being whose existence comes before its essence, a being which exists before it can be defined by any conception of it. That being is man or, as Heidegger has it, the human reality. What do we mean by saying that existence precedes essence? We mean that man first of all exists, encounters himself, surges up in the world—and defines himself afterwards. If man as the existentialist sees him is not definable, it is because to begin with he is nothing. He will not be anything until later, and then he will be what he makes of himself. Thus, there is no human nature, because there is no God to have a conception of it. Man simply is. Not that he is simply what he conceives himself to be, but he is what he wills, and as he conceives himself after already existing—as he wills to be after that leap towards existence. Man is nothing else but that which he makes of himself. That is the first principle of existentialism. . . .

Before that projection of the self nothing exists; not even in the heaven of intelligence: man will only attain existence when he is what he purposes to be. Not, however, what he may wish to be. For what we usually understand by wishing or willing is a conscious decision taken—much more often than not—after we have made ourselves what we are. I may wish to join a party, to write a book or to marry—but in such a case what is usually called my will is probably a manifestation of a prior and more spontaneous decision. If, however, it is true that existence is prior to essence, man is responsible for what he is. Thus, the first effect of existentialism is that it puts every man in possession of himself as he is, and places the entire responsibility for his existence squarely upon his own shoulders. And, when we say that man is responsible for himself, we do not mean that he is responsible only for his own individuality, but that he is responsible for all men. The word "subjectivism" is to be understood in two senses, and our adversaries play upon only one of them. Subjectivism means, on the one hand, the freedom of the individual subject and, on the other, that man cannot pass beyond human subjectivity. It is the latter which is the deeper meaning of existentialism. When we say that man chooses himself, we do mean that every one of us must choose himself; but by that we also mean that in choosing for himself he chooses for all men. For in effect, of all the actions a man may take in order to create himself as he wills to be, there is not one which is not creative, at the same time, of an image of man such as he believes he ought to be. To choose between this or that is at the same time to affirm the value of that which is chosen; for we are unable ever to choose the worse. What we choose is always the better; and nothing can be better for us unless it is better for all. If, moreover, existence precedes essence and we will to exist at the same time as we fashion our image, that image is valid for all and for the entire epoch in which we find ourselves. Our responsibility is thus much greater than we had supposed, for it concerns mankind as a whole. If I am a worker, for instance, I may choose to join a Christian rather than a Communist trade union. And if, by that membership, I choose to signify that resignation is, after all, the attitude that best becomes a man, that man's kingdom is not upon this earth, I do not commit myself alone to that view. Resignation is my will for everyone, and my action is, in consequence, a commitment on behalf of all mankind. Or if, to take a more personal case, I decide to marry and to have children, even though this decision proceeds simply from my situation, from my passion or my desire, I am thereby committing not only myself, but humanity as a whole, to the practice of monogamy. I am thus responsible for myself and for all men, and I am creating a certain image of man as I would have him to be. In fashioning myself I fashion man.

This may enable us to understand what is meant by such terms—perhaps a little grandiloquent—as anguish, abandonment and despair. As you will soon see, it is very simple. First, what do we mean by anguish? The existentialist frankly states that man is in anguish. His meaning is as follows—When a man commits himself to anything, fully realising that he is not only choosing what he will be, but is thereby at the same time a legislator deciding for the whole of mankind—in such a moment a man cannot escape from the sense of complete and profound responsibility. There are many, indeed, who show no such anxiety. But we affirm that they are merely disguising their anguish or are in flight from it. Certainly, many people think that in what they are doing they commit no one but themselves to anything: and if you ask them, "What would happen if everyone did so?" they shrug their shoulders and reply, "Everyone does not do so." But in truth, one ought always to ask oneself what would happen if everyone did as one is doing; nor can one escape from that disturbing thought except by a kind of self-deception. The man who lies in self-excuse, by saying "Everyone will not do it," must be ill at ease in his conscience, for the act of lying implies the universal value which it denies. By its very disguise his anguish reveals itself. This is the anguish that Kierkegaard called "the anguish of Abraham." You know the story: An angel commanded Abraham to sacrifice his son: and obedience was obligatory, if it really was an angel who had appeared and said, "Thou, Abraham, shalt sacrifice thy son." But anyone in such a case would wonder, first, whether it was indeed an angel and secondly, whether I am really Abraham. Where are the proofs? A certain mad woman who suffered from hallucinations said that people were telephoning to her, and giving her orders. The doctor asked, "But who is it that speaks to you?" She replied: "He says it is God." And what, indeed, could prove to her that it was God? If an angel appears to me, what is the proof that it is an angel; or, if I hear voices, who can prove that they proceed from heaven and not from hell, or from my own subconsciousness or some pathological condition? Who can prove that they are really addressed to me?

Who, then, can prove that I am the proper person to impose, by my own choice, my conception of man upon mankind? I shall never find any proof whatever; there will be no sign to convince me of it. If a voice speaks to me, it is still I myself who must decide whether the voice is or is not that of an angel. If I regard a certain course of action as good, it is only I who choose to say that it is good and not bad. There is nothing to show that I am Abraham: nevertheless I also am obliged at every instant to perform actions which are examples. Everything happens to every man as though the whole human race had its eyes fixed upon what he is doing and regulated its conduct accordingly. So every man ought to say, "Am I really a man who has the right to act in such a manner that humanity regulates itself by what I do?" If a man does not say that, he is dissembling his anguish. Clearly, the anguish with which we are concerned here is not one that could lead to quietism or inaction. It is anguish pure and simple, of the kind well known to all those who have borne responsibilities. When, for instance, a military leader takes upon himself the responsibility for an attack and sends a number of men to their death, he chooses to do it and at bottom he alone chooses. No doubt he acts under a higher command, but its orders, which are more general, require interpretation by him and upon that interpretation depends the life of ten, fourteen or twenty men. In making the decision, he cannot but feel a certain anguish. All leaders know that anguish. It does not prevent their acting, on the contrary it is the very condition of their action, for the action presupposes that there is a plurality of possibilities, and in choosing one of these, they realise that it has value only because it is chosen. Now it is anguish of that kind which existentialism describes, and moreover, as we shall see, makes explicit through direct responsibility towards other men who are concerned. Far from being a screen which could separate us from action, it is a condition of action itself.

And when we speak of "abandonment"—a favourite word of Heidegger—we only mean to say that God does not exist, and that it is necessary to draw the consequences of his absence right to the end. The existentialist is strongly opposed to a certain type of secular moralism which seeks to suppress God at the least possible expense. Towards 1880, when the French professors endeavoured to formulate a secular morality, they said something like this:—God is a useless and costly hypothesis, so we will do without it. However, if we are to have morality, a society and a law-abiding world, it is essential that certain values should be taken seriously; they must have an *a priori* existence ascribed to them. It must be considered obligatory *a priori* to be honest, not to lie, not to beat one's wife, to bring up children and so forth; so we are going to do a little work on this subject, which will enable us to show that these values exist all the same, inscribed in an intelligible heaven although, of course, there is no God. In other words—and this is, I believe, the purport of all that we in France call radicalism—nothing will be changed if God does not exist; we shall re-discover the same norms of honesty, progress and humanity, and we shall have disposed of God as an out-of-date hypothesis which will die away quietly of itself. The existentialist, on the contrary, finds it extremely embarrassing that God does not exist, for there disappears with Him all possibility of finding values in an intelligible heaven. There can no longer be any good *a priori,* since there is no infinite and perfect consciousness to think it. It is nowhere written that "the good" exists, that one must be honest or must not lie, since we are now upon the plane where there are only men. Dostoievsky once wrote "If God did not exist, everything would be permitted"; and that, for existentialism, is the starting point. Everything is indeed permitted if God does not exist, and man is in consequence forlorn, for he cannot find anything to depend upon either within or outside himself. He discovers forthwith, that he is without excuse. For if indeed existence precedes essence, one will never be able to explain one's action by reference to a given and specific human nature; in other words, there is no determinism—man is free, man *is* freedom. Nor, on the other hand, if God does not exist, are we provided with any values or commands that could legitimise our behaviour. Thus we have neither behind us, nor before us in a luminous realm of values, any means of justification or excuse. We are left alone, without excuse. That is what I mean when I say that man is condemned to be free. Condemned, because he did not create himself, yet is nevertheless at liberty, and from the moment that he is thrown into this world he is responsible for everything he does. The existentialist does not believe in the power of passion. He will never regard a grand passion as a destructive torrent upon which a man is swept into certain actions as by fate, and which, therefore, is an excuse for them. He thinks that man is responsible for his passion. Neither will an existentialist think that a man can find help through some sign being vouchsafed upon earth for his orientation: for he thinks that the man himself interprets the sign as he chooses. He thinks that every man, without any support or help whatever, is condemned at every instant to invent man. . . .

As an example by which you may the better understand this state of abandonment, I will refer to the case of a pupil of mine, who sought me out in the following circumstances. His father was quarrelling with his mother and was also inclined to be a "collaborator"; his elder brother had been killed in the German offensive of 1940 and this young man, with a sentiment somewhat primitive but generous, burned to avenge him. His mother was living alone with him, deeply afflicted by the semi-treason of his father and by the death of her eldest son, and her one consolation was in this young man. But he, at this moment, had the choice between going to England to join the Free French

Forces or of staying near his mother and helping her to live. He fully realised that this woman lived only for him and that his disappearance—or perhaps his death—would plunge her into despair. He also realised that, concretely and in fact, every action he performed on his mother's behalf would be sure of effect in the sense of aiding her to live, whereas anything he did in order to go and fight would be an ambiguous action which might vanish like water into sand and serve no purpose. For instance, to set out for England he would have to wait indefinitely in a Spanish camp on the way through Spain; or, on arriving in England or in Algiers he might be put into an office to fill up forms. Consequently, he found himself confronted by two very different modes of action: the one concrete, immediate but directed towards only one individual; and the other an action addressed to an end infinitely greater, a national collectivity, but for that very reason ambiguous—and it might be frustrated on the way. At the same time, he was hesitating between two kinds of morality; on the one side the morality of sympathy, of personal devotion and, on the other side, a morality of wider scope but of more debatable validity. He had to choose between those two. What could help him to choose? Could the Christian doctrine? No. Christian doctrine says: Act with charity, love your neighbour, deny yourself for others, choose the way which is hardest, and so forth. But which is the harder road? To whom does one owe the more brotherly love, the patriot or the mother? Which is the more useful aim, the general one of fighting in and for the whole community, or the precise aim of helping one particular person to live? Who can give an answer to that *a priori?* No one. Nor is it given in any ethical scripture. The Kantian ethic says, Never regard another as a means, but always as an end. Very well; if I remain with my mother, I shall be regarding her as the end and not as a means: but by the same token I am in danger of treating as means those who are fighting on my behalf; and the converse is also true, that if I go to the aid of the combatants I shall be treating them as the end at the risk of treating my mother as a means.

If values are uncertain, if they are still too abstract to determine the particular, concrete case under consideration, nothing remains but to trust in our instincts. That is what this young man tried to do; and when I saw him he said, "In the end it is feeling that counts; the direction in which it is really pushing me is the one I ought to choose. If I feel that I love my mother enough to sacrifice everything else for her—my will to be avenged, all my longings for action and adventure—then I stay with her. If, on the contrary, I feel that my love for her is not enough, I go." But how does one estimate the strength of a feeling? The value of his feeling for his mother was determined precisely by the fact that he was standing by her. I may say that I love a certain friend enough to sacrifice such or such a sum of money for him, but I cannot prove that unless I have done it. I may say, "I love my mother enough to remain with her," if actually I have remained with her. I can only estimate the strength of this affection if I have performed an action by which it is defined and ratified. But if I then appeal to this affection to justify my action, I find myself drawn into a vicious circle. . . .

What is at the very heart and centre of existentialism is the absolute character of the free commitment, by which every man realises himself in realising a type of humanity—a commitment always understandable, to no matter whom in no matter what epoch—and its bearing upon the relativity of the cultural pattern which may result from such absolute commitment. One must observe equally the relativity of Cartesianism and the absolute character of the Cartesian commitment. In this sense you may say, if you like, that every one of us makes the absolute by breathing, by eating, by sleeping or by behaving in any fashion whatsoever. There is no difference between free being—being as self-committal, as existence choosing its essence—and absolute being. And there is no difference whatever between being as an absolute, temporarily localised—that is, localised in history—and universally intelligible being. . . .

. . . Existentialism is nothing else but an attempt to draw the full conclusions from a consistently atheistic position. . . . Not that we believe God does exist, but we think that the real problem is not that of His existence; what man needs is to find himself again and to understand that nothing can save him from himself, not even a valid proof of the existence of God. In this sense existentialism is optimistic, it is a doctrine of action, and it is only by self-deception, by confusing their own despair with ours that Christians can describe us as without hope.

B. *Being and Nothingness*

BAD FAITH

. . . What are we to say is the being of man who has the possibility of denying himself? . . . It is best to choose and to examine one determined attitude which is essential to human reality and which is such that consciousness instead of directing its negation outward turns it toward itself. This attitude, it seems to me, is *bad faith (mauvaise foi)*. . . .

Take the example of a woman who has consented to go out with a particular man for the first time. She knows very well the intentions which the man who is speaking to her cherishes regarding her. She knows also that it will be necessary sooner or later for her to make a decision. But she does not want to realize the urgency; she concerns herself only with what is respectful and discreet in the attitude of her companion. She does not apprehend this conduct as an attempt to achieve what we call "the first approach"; that is, she does not want to see possibilities of temporal development which his conduct presents. She restricts this behavior to what is in the present; she does not wish to read in the phrases which he addresses to her anything other than their explicit meaning. If he says to her, "I find you so attractive!" she disarms this phrase of its sexual background; she attaches to the conversation and to the behavior of the speaker,

By permission. From Jean-Paul Sartre, *Being and Nothingness,* trans. by Hazel Barnes, Philosophical Library, New York, and Literary Masterworks, Inc., New York, 1956.

the immediate meanings, which she imagines as objective qualities. The man who is speaking to her appears to be sincere and respectful as the table is round or square, as the wall coloring is blue or gray. The qualities thus attached to the person she is listening to are in this way fixed in a permanence like that of things, which is no other than the projection of the strict present of the qualities into the temporal flux. This is because she does not quite know what she wants. She is profoundly aware of the desire which she inspires, but the desire cruel and naked would humiliate and horrify her. Yet she would find no charm in a respect which would be only respect. In order to satisfy her, there must be a feeling which is addressed wholly to her *personality*—*i.e.,* to her full freedom—and which would be a recognition of her freedom. But at the same time this feeling must be wholly desire; that is, it must address itself to her body as object. This time then she refuses to apprehend the desire for what it is; she does not even give it a name; she recognizes it only to the extent that it transcends itself toward admiration, esteem, respect and that it is wholly absorbed in the more refined forms which it produces, to the extent of no longer figuring anymore as a sort of warmth and density. But then suppose he takes her hand. This act of her companion risks changing the situation by calling for an immediate decision. To leave the hand there is to consent in herself to flirt, to engage herself. To withdrew it is to break the troubled and unstable harmony which gives the hour its charm. The aim is to postpone the moment of decision as long as possible. We know what happens next; the young woman leaves her hand there, but she *does not notice* that she is leaving it. She does not notice because it happens by chance that she is at this moment all intellect. She draws her companion up to the most lofty regions of sentimental speculation; she speaks of Life, of her life, she shows herself in her essential aspect—a personality, a consciousness. And during this time the divorce of the body from the soul is accomplished; the hand rests inert between the warm hands of her companion—neither consenting nor resisting—a thing.

We shall say that this woman is in bad faith. But we see immediately that she uses various procedures in order to maintain herself in this bad faith. She has disarmed the actions of her companion by reducing them to being only what they are; that is, to existing in the mode of the in-itself. But she permits herself to enjoy his desire, to the extent that she will apprehend it as not being what it is, will recognize its transcendence. Finally while sensing profoundly the presence of her own body—to the degree of being disturbed perhaps—she realizes herself as *not being* her own body, and she contemplates it as though from above as a passive object to which events can *happen* but which can neither provoke them nor avoid them because all its possibilities are outside of it. What unity do we find in these various aspects of bad faith? It is a certain art of forming contradictory concepts which unite in themselves both an idea and the negation of that idea. The basic concept which is thus engendered utilizes the double property of the human being, who is at once a *facticity* and a *transcendence*. These two aspects of human reality are and ought to be capable of a valid coordination. But bad faith does not wish either to coordinate them or to surmount them in a synthesis. Bad faith seeks to affirm their identity while preserving their differences. It must affirm facticity as *being* transcendence and transcendence as *being* facticity, in such a way that at the instant when a person apprehends the one, he can find himself abruptly faced with the other. . . .

If man is what he is, bad faith is forever impossible and candor ceases to be his ideal and becomes instead his being. But is man what he is? And more generally, how can he *be* what he is when he exists as consciousness of being? If candor or sincerity is a universal value, it is evident that the maxim "one must be what one is" does not serve solely as a regulating principle for judgments and concepts by which I express what I am. It posits not merely an ideal of knowing but an ideal of *being;* it proposes for us an absolute equivalence of being with itself as a prototype of being. In this sense it is necessary that we *make ourselves* what we are. But what *are we* then if we have the constant obligation to make ourselves what we are, if our mode of being is having the obligation to be what we are?

Let us consider this waiter in the café. His movement is quick and forward, a little too precise, a little too rapid. He comes toward the patrons with a step a little too quick. He bends forward a little too eagerly; his voice, his eyes express an interest a little too solicitous for the order of the customer. Finally there he returns, trying to imitate in his walk the inflexible stiffness of some kind of automaton while carrying his tray with the recklessness of a tight-rope-walker by putting it in a perpetually unstable, perpetually broken equilibrium which he perpetually re-establishes by a light movement of the arm and hand. All his behavior seems to us a game. He applies himself to chaining his movements as if they were mechanisms, the one regulating the other; his gestures and even his voice seem to be mechanisms; he gives himself the quickness and pitiless rapidity of things. He is playing, he is amusing himself. But what is he playing? We need not watch long before we can explain it: he is playing at *being* a waiter in a café. There is nothing there to surprise us. The game is a kind of marking out and investigation. The child plays with his body in order to explore it, to take inventory of it; the waiter in the café plays with his condition in order to *realize* it. This obligation is not different from that which is imposed on all tradesmen. Their condition is wholly one of ceremony. The public demands of them that they realize it as a ceremony; there is the dance of the grocer, of the tailor, of the auctioneer, by which they endeavor to persuade their clientele that they are nothing but a grocer, an auctioneer, a tailor. A grocer who dreams is offensive to the buyer, because such a grocer is not wholly a grocer. Society demands that he limit himself to his function as a grocer, just as the soldier at attention makes himself into a soldier-thing with a direct regard which does not see at all, which is no longer meant to see, since it is the rule and not the interest of the moment which determines the point he must fix his eyes on (the sight "fixed at ten paces"). There are indeed many precautions to imprison a man in what he is, as if we lived in perpetual fear that he might escape from it, that he might break away and suddenly elude his condition.

In a parallel situation, from within, the waiter in the café can not be immediately a café waiter in the sense that this inkwell *is* an inkwell, or the glass is a glass. It is by no means that he can not form reflective judgments or concepts concerning his condition. He knows well what it "means"; the obligation of getting up at five o'clock, of sweeping the floor of the shop before the restaurant opens, of starting the coffee pot going, *etc*. He knows the rights which it allows: the right to tips, the right to belong to a union, *etc*. But all these concepts, all these judgments refer to the transcendent. It is a matter of abstract possibilities, of rights and duties conferred on a "person possessing rights." And it is precisely this person *who I have to be* (if I am the waiter in question) and who I am not. It is not that I do not wish to be this person or that I want this person to be different. But rather there is no common measure between his being and mine. It is a "representation" for others and for myself, which means that I can be he only in *representation*. But if I represent myself as him, I am not he; I am separated from him as the object from the subject, separated *by nothing,* but this nothing isolates me from him. I cannot be he, I can only play *at being* him; that is, imagine to myself that I am he. And thereby I affect him with nothingness. In vain do I fulfill the functions of a café waiter. I can be he only in the neutralized mode, as the actor is Hamlet, by mechanically making the *typical gestures* of my state and by aiming at myself as an imaginary café waiter through those gestures taken as an "analogue." What I attempt to realize is a being-in-itself of the café waiter, as if it were not just in my power to confer their value and their urgency upon my duties and the rights of my position, as if it were not my free choice to get up each morning at five o'clock or to remain in bed, even though it meant getting fired. As if from the very fact that I sustain this role in existence I did not transcend it on every side, as if I did not constitute myself as one *beyond* my condition. Yet there is no doubt that I *am* in a sense a café waiter—otherwise could I not just as well call myself a diplomat or a reporter? But if I am one, this cannot be in the mode of being in-itself. I am a waiter in the mode of *being what I am not.*

Furthermore we are dealing with more than mere social positions; I am never any one of my attitudes, any one of my actions. The good speaker is the one who *plays at* speaking, because he cannot *be speaking.* The attentive pupil who wishes to *be* attentive, his eyes riveted on the teacher, his ears open wide, so exhausts himself in playing the attentive role that he ends up by no longer hearing anything. . . .

Under these conditions what can be the significance of the ideal of sincerity except as a task impossible to achieve, of which the very meaning is in contradiction with the structure of my consciousness. To be sincere, we said, is to be what one is. That supposes that I am not originally what I am. But here naturally Kant's "You ought, therefore you can" is implicitly understood. I can *become* sincere; this is what my duty and my effort to achieve sincerity imply. But we definitely establish that the original structure of "not being what one is" renders impossible in advance all movement toward being in itself or "being what one is." And this impossibility is not hidden from consciousness; on the contrary, it is the very stuff of consciousness; it is the embarrassing constraint which we constantly experience; it is our very incapacity to recognize ourselves, to constitute ourselves as being what we are. It is this necessity which means that, as soon as we posit ourselves as a certain being, by a legitimate judgment, based on inner experience or correctly deduced from *a priori* or empirical premises, then by that very positing we surpass this being—and that not toward another being but toward emptiness, toward *nothing*.

How then can we blame another for not being sincere or rejoice in our own sincerity since this sincerity appears to us at the same time to be impossible? How can we in conversation, in confession, in introspection, even attempt sincerity since at the very time when we announce it we have a prejudicative comprehension of its futility? Let us take an example: A homosexual frequently has an intolerable feeling of guilt, and his whole existence is determined in relation to this feeling. One will readily foresee that he is in bad faith. In fact it frequently happens that this man, while recognizing his homosexual inclination, while avowing each and every particular misdeed which he has committed, refuses with all his strength to consider himself *"a paederast."* His case is always "different," peculiar; there enters into it something of a game, of chance, of bad luck; the mistakes are all in the past; they are explained by a certain conception of the beautiful which women cannot satisfy; we should see in them the results of a restless search, rather than the manifestations of a deeply rooted tendency, *etc., etc.* Here is assuredly a man in bad faith who borders on the comic since, acknowledging all the facts which are imputed to him, he refuses to draw from them the conclusion which they impose. His friend, who is his most severe critic, becomes irritated with this duplicity. The critic asks only one thing—and perhaps then he will show himself indulgent: that the guilty one recognize himself as guilty, that the homosexual declare frankly—whether humbly or boastfully matters little—"I am a paederast." We ask here: Who is in bad faith? The homosexual or the champion of sincerity?

The homosexual recognizes his faults, but he struggles with all his strength against the crushing view that his mistakes constitute for him a *destiny*. He does not wish to let himself be considered as a thing. He has an obscure but strong feeling that a homosexual is not a homosexual as this table is a table or as this red-haired man is red-haired. It seems to him that he has escaped from each mistake as soon as he has posited it and recognized it; he even feels that the psychic duration by itself cleanses him from each misdeed, constitutes for him an undetermined future, causes him to be born anew. Is he wrong? Does he not recognize in himself the peculiar, irreducible character of human reality? His attitude includes then an undeniable comprehension of truth. But at the same time he needs this perpetual rebirth, this constant escape in order to live; he must constantly put himself beyond reach in order to avoid the terrible judgment of collectivity. Thus he plays on the word *being*. He would be right actually if he understood the phrase "I am a paederast" in the sense of "I am not what I am." That is, if he declared to himself, "To the extent that a pattern of conduct is defined as the conduct of a paederast and to the extent that I have adopted this conduct, I am a paederast. But to the extent that human reality cannot be finally defined by patterns of conduct, I am not one." But instead he slides surreptitiously toward a different connotation of the word "being." He understands "not being a paederast" in the sense in which this table *is not* an inkwell. He is in bad faith.

But the champion of sincerity is not ignorant of the transcendence of human reality, and he knows how at need to appeal to it for his own advantage. He makes use of it even and brings it up in the present argument. Does he not wish, first in the name of sincerity, then of freedom, that the homosexual reflect on himself and acknowledge himself as a homosexual? Does he not let the other understand that such a confession will win indulgence for him? What does this mean if not that the man who will acknowledge himself as a homosexual will no longer be *the same* as the homosexual whom he acknowledges being and that he will escape into the region of freedom and of good will? The critic asks the man then to be what he is in order no longer to be what he is. It is the profound meaning of the saying, "A sin confessed is half pardoned." The critic demands of the guilty one that he constitute himself as a thing, precisely in order no longer to treat him as a thing. And this contradiction is constitutive of the demand of sincerity. Who cannot see how offensive to the Other and how reassuring for me is a statement such as, "He's just a paederast," which removes a disturbing freedom from a trait and which aims at henceforth constituting all the acts of the Other as consequences following strictly from his essence. That is actually what the critic is demanding of his victim—that he constitute himself as a thing, that he should entrust his freedom to his friend as a fief, in order that the friend should return it to him subsequently—like a suzerain to his vassal. The champion of sincerity is in bad faith to the degree that in order to reassure himself, he pretends to judge, to the extent that he demands that freedom as freedom constitute itself as a thing. We have here only one episode in that battle to the death of consciousnesses which Hegel calls "the relation of the master and the slave." A person appeals to another and demands that in the name of his nature as consciousness he should radically destroy himself as consciousness, but while making this appeal he leads the other to hope for a rebirth beyond this destruction. . . .

Bad faith is possible only because sincerity is conscious of missing its goal inevitably, due to its very nature. I can try to apprehend myself as *not being cowardly,"* when I *am* so, only on condition that the "being cowardly" is itself "in question" at the very moment when it exists, on condition that it is itself *one* question, that at the very moment when I wish to apprehend it, it escapes me on all sides and annihilates itself. The condition under which I can attempt an effort in bad faith is that in one sense, I *am not* this coward which I do not wish to be. But if I *were not* cowardly in the simple mode of not-being-what-one-is-not, I would be "in good faith" by declaring that I am not cowardly. Thus this inapprehensible coward is evanescent; in order for me not to be cowardly, I must in some way also be cowardly. That does not mean that I must be "a little" cowardly, in the sense that "a little" signifies "to a certain degree cowardly—and not cowardly to a certain degree." No. I must at once both be and not be totally and in all respects a coward. Thus in this case bad faith requires that I should not be what I am; that is, that there be an imponderable difference separating being from non-being in the mode of being of human reality.

But bad faith is not restricted to denying the qualities which I possess, to not seeing the being which I am. It attempts also to constitute myself as being what I am not. It apprehends me positively as courageous when I am not so. And that is possible, once again, only if I am what I am not. . . .

FREEDOM AND RESPONSIBILITY

Although the considerations which are about to follow are of interest primarily to the ethicist, it may nevertheless be worthwhile after these descriptions and arguments to return to the freedom of the for-itself and try to understand what the fact of this freedom represents for human destiny.

The essential consequence of our earlier remarks is that man being condemned to be free carries the weight of the whole world on his shoulders; he is responsible for the world and for himself as a way of being. We are taking the word "responsibility" in its ordinary sense as "consciousness (of) being the incontestable author of an event or of an object." In this sense the responsibility of the for-itself is overwhelming since he is the one by whom it happens that *there is* a world; since he is also the one who makes himself be, then whatever may be the situation in which he finds himself, the for-itself must wholly assume this situation with its peculiar coefficient of adversity, even though it be insupportable. He must assume the situation with the proud consciousness of being the author of it, for the very worst disadvantages or the worst threats which can endanger my person have meaning only in and through my project; and it is on the ground of the engagement which I am that they appear. It is therefore senseless to think of complaining since nothing foreign has decided what we feel, what we live, or what we are.

Furthermore this absolute responsibility is not resignation; it is simply the logical requirement of the consequences of our freedom. What happens to me happens through me, and I can neither affect myself with it nor revolt against it nor resign myself to it. Moreover everything which happens to me is *mine*. By this we must understand first of all that I am always equal to what happens to me *qua* man, for what happens to a man through other men and through himself can be only human. The most terrible situations of war, the worst tortures do not create a non-human state of things; there is no non-human situation. It is only through fear, flight, and recourse to magical types of conduct that I shall decide on the non-human, but this decision is human, and I shall carry the entire responsibility for it. But in addition the situation is *mine* because it is the image of my free choice of myself, and everything which it presents to me is *mine* in that this represents me and symbolizes me. Is it not I who decide the coefficient of adversity in things and even their unpredictability by deciding myself?

Thus there are no *accidents* in life; a community event which suddenly bursts forth and involves me in it does not come from the outside. If I am mobilized in a war, this war is *my* war; it is in my image and I deserve it. I deserve it first because I could always get out of it by suicide or by desertion; these ultimate possibles are those which must always be present for us when there is a question of envisaging a situation. For lack of getting out of it, I have *chosen* it. This can be due to inertia, to cowardice in the face of public opinion, or because I prefer certain other values to the value of the refusal to join in the war (the good opinion of my relatives, the honor of my family, *etc.*). Any way you look at it, it is a matter of a choice. This choice will be repeated later on again and again without a break until the end of the war. Therefore we must agree with the statement by J. Romains, "In war there are no innocent victims." If therefore I have preferred war to death or to dishonor, everything takes place as if I bore the entire responsibility for this war. Of course others have declared it, and one might be tempted perhaps to consider me as a simple accomplice. But this notion of complicity has only a juridical sense, and it does not hold here. For it depended on me that for me and by me this war should not exist, and I have decided that it does exist. There was no compulsion here, for the compulsion could have got no hold on a freedom. I did not have any excuse; . . . the peculiar character of human-reality is that it is without excuse. Therefore it remains for me only to lay claim to this war.

But in addition the war is *mine* because by the sole fact that arises in a situation which I cause to be and that I can discover it there only be engaging myself for or against it, I can no longer distinguish at present the choice which I make of myself from the choice which I make of the war. To live this war is to choose myself through it and to choose it through my choice of myself. There can be no question of considering it as "four years of vacation" or as a "reprieve," as a "recess," the essential part of my responsibilities being elsewhere in my married, family, or professional life. In this war which I have chosen I choose myself from day to day, and I make it mine by making myself. If it is going to be four empty years, then it is I who bear the responsibility for this.

Finally, . . . each person is an absolute choice of self from the standpoint of a world of knowledges and of techniques which this choice both assumes and illumines; each person is an absolute upsurge at an absolute date and is perfectly unthinkable at another date. It is therefore a waste of time to ask what I should have been if this war had not broken out, for I have chosen myself as one of the possible meanings of the epoch which imperceptibly led to war. I am not distinct from this same epoch; I could not be transported to another epoch without contradiction. Thus I *am* this war which restricts and limits and makes comprehensible the period which preceded it. In this sense we may define more precisely the responsibility of the for-itself if to the earlier quoted statement, "There are no innocent victims," we add the words, "We have the war we deserve." Thus, totally free, undistinguishable from the period for which I have chosen to be the meaning, as profoundly responsible for the war as if I had myself declared it, unable to live without integrating it in *my* situation, engaging myself in it wholly and stamping it with my seal, I must be without remorse or regrets as I am without excuse; for from the instant of my upsurge into being, I carry the weight of the world by myself alone without anything or any person being able to lighten it.

Yet this responsibility is of a very particular type. Someone will say, "I did not ask to be born." This is a naïve way of throwing greater emphasis on our facticity. I am responsible for everything, in fact, except for my very responsibility, for I am not the foundation of my being. Therefore everything takes place as if I were compelled to be responsible. I am *abandoned* in the world, not in the sense that I might remain abandoned and passive in a hostile universe like a board floating on the water, but rather in the sense that I find myself suddenly alone and without help, engaged in a world for which I bear the whole responsibility without being able, whatever I do, to tear myself away from this responsibility for an instant. For I am responsible for my very desire of fleeing responsibilities. To make myself passive in the world, to refuse to act upon things and upon Others is still to choose myself, and suicide is one mode among others of being-in-the-world. Yet I find an absolute responsibility for the fact that my facticity (here the fact of my birth) is directly inapprehensible and even inconceivable, for this fact of my birth never appears as a brute fact but always across a projective reconstruction of my for-itself. I am ashamed of being born or I am astonished at it or I rejoice over it, or in attempting to get rid of my life I affirm that I live and I assume this life as bad. Thus in a certain sense I *choose* being born. This choice itself is integrally affected with facticity since I am not able not to choose, but this facticity in turn will appear only in so far as I surpass it toward my ends. Thus facticity is everywhere but inapprehensible; I never encounter anything except my responsibility. That is why I can not ask, "*Why was I born?*" or curse the day of my birth or declare that I did not ask to be born, for these various attitudes toward my birth—*i.e.,* toward the *fact* that I realize a presence in the world—are absolutely nothing else but ways of assuming this birth in full responsibility and of making it *mine.* Here again I encounter only myself and my projects so that finally my abandonment—*i.e.,* my facticity— consists simply in the fact that I am condemned to be wholly responsible for myself. I am the being which *is* in such a way that in its being its being is in question. And this "is" of my being *is* as present and inapprehensible.

Under these conditions since every event in the world can be revealed to me only as an *opportunity* (an opportunity made use of, lacked, neglected, *etc.*), or better yet since everything which happens to us can be considered as a *chance* (*i.e.,* can appear to us only as a way of realizing this being which is in question in our being) and since others as transcendences-transcended are themselves only *opportunities* and *chances,* the responsibility of the for-itself extends to the entire world as a peopled-world. It is precisely thus that the for-itself apprehends itself in anguish; that is, as a being which is neither the foundation of its own being nor of the Other's being nor of the in-itselfs which form the world, but a being which is compelled to decide the meaning of being—within it and everywhere outside of it. The one who realizes in anguish his condition as *being* thrown into a responsibility which extends to his very abandonment has no longer either remorse or regret or excuse; he is no longer anything but a freedom which perfectly reveals itself and whose being resides in this very revelation. But as we pointed out . . . , most of the time we flee anguish in bad faith.

DISCUSSION

The central claim of Sartre's existentialist philosophy is the fact that we are free to choose what we are and what we will be. But it is essential that we do not take him to be saying what is clearly nonsense, that a person can do anything he or she chooses to do. A person raised in Detroit cannot choose to have been raised in Marseilles, and a person born to be five-foot-eight cannot choose to be six-foot-ten. We have all wished—after a moment of tragedy—that we could relive the last few hours and act differently; but that is impossible. What we can do, however, is to choose what we are to make out of the circumstances in which we find ourselves. A Jew in France during the Nazi occupation could not change the fact that he or she was a Jew but could and had to choose whether to hide that fact, or flee the country, or join the underground resistance forces, or sacrifice oneself as a possible example of Nazi atrocities. We cannot choose to succeed in what we try to do, but we can always choose to try. That is Sartre's basic point, and it is the one point that he relentlessly refuses to let us forget.

To forget, to pretend that one has no choice in the matter or cannot do anything about it, is bad faith. Bad faith is, first of all, pretending that there is nothing to be done or nothing one can do; at the extreme limits (which were the daily condition during the war) one can always choose to risk or sacrifice one's life to make a point. In more modest circumstances, one can always quit a job rather than do what one disapproves of (for example, resigning as contractor because the assignment is to destroy a neighborhood) or drop a class if one disapproves of the way it is taught. Of course there is always a cost; the contractor may have trouble getting another job, and the student may have trouble getting another course (or getting out of this one). But cost does not eliminate choice. The choice remains; it is just a question of what one chooses.

Bad faith can also be appealing one's decisions to something outside of oneself. Insisting that one did something because "God willed it" is a way of not taking responsibility for one's own actions; so is appealing an action to the law, as in, "it's the law" or "I'm just doing my job." One can always break the law, protesting as one does so that it is a bad law. Appeals to morality may also be instances of bad faith; sometimes we decide to lie (for example, when it is a "white" lie); other times we do not. It is bad faith, therefore, to insist that, when one does not lie, it is because of a moral principle. One supports the principle by refusing to lie, but one does not refuse to lie because of the principle. (What would Immanuel Kant and John Stuart Mill say about this?)

It is in this context that we are to understand Sartre's celebrated example about the young man who must choose to join the army or stay with his grieving mother. Appeal to principles will not help him; he must choose. But this dramatic case, in which the two sides are evenly balanced, is no different from our every choice, according to Sartre. We are always in a position where, in addition to choosing our particular course of action, we are also choosing to exemplify a kind of character and to support a principle of some sort, whether implicit in our actions or explicit in our explanations of our actions. It is with this in mind that Sartre evokes the very Kantian image of our always acting not just for ourselves but for all of humanity. We, in our every action, try to demonstrate what we think humanity ought to be.

There is a problem with bad faith, however, no matter how morally moving that concept. Sartre seemingly portrays bad faith as if anything we do, other than acknowledge our responsibility for choosing—and the facts of the case—is going to be bad faith. But according to Sartre's own arguments, the facts of the case are in part determined by our choices, and our choices—needless to say—are circumscribed by the facts. This makes it look as if there is no escaping bad faith, that we are guilty of manipulating the facts or rationalizing our choices no matter what we do. The example of the homosexual (p. 403) displays this difficulty. Our decisions (our *transcendence*) shape the facts; thus it is not clear exactly what the facts that we must accept should be. How do we avoid bad faith—as Sartre is clearly urging us? And what is "bad" about bad faith?

This problem raises another, more fundamental to the entire outlook of Sartre's philosophy. In his emphasis on freedom of choice, Sartre neglects one of the main ingredients—if not the main ingredient—in any ethics—what we have called an ethos, a community of shared values and interests. The entire thrust of Sartre's philosophy is precisely to separate ourselves from any such uncritical participation in a community and to stress the picture of each individual in isolation, facing the world and having to make his or her choices—alone. It is a vision of life that is quite common in the late twentieth century, but the question is whether an ethics is possible in light of it. Indeed, Sartre himself had doubts about this, and his later work—especially his massive *Critique of Dialectical Reason* in 1960—is very much an attempt to redefine the nature of community and say how it is possible.

STUDY QUESTIONS

1 What is "existentialism"? Sartre defines his position by insisting that there is no God. How, then, is religious or theistic existentialism possible? Could "existence (still) precede essence"?

2 Is Sartre a teleologist? A deontologist? Explain.

3 In what sense are we *always* free, according to Sartre? Is this plausible? To what extent is it an (a priori) conclusion based on Sartre's division of the world into consciousness (being-for-itself) and the being of things (being-in-itself)? To what extent is it a reasonable observation about people's actual behavior and motivation?

4 What is "bad faith"? Why is it bad?

5 Why are we a "useless passion"? How can Sartre insist that he is an "optimist"?

6 Why should we always act as if we were acting for all of humanity? Is Sartre here repeating the categorical imperative? What are the differences? What are the similarities?

7 Why is there no "human nature"? Is Sartre denying that we have instincts and other "natural" inclinations and motives? Give an example in which a clearly "natural" desire is nevertheless a matter of self-conscious choice. Give an example in which a supposed feature of "human nature" is a matter of self-conscious choice.

8 What is "abandonment"? What is "despair"?

9 What should Sartre's student have done? Why?

10 "The genius of Proust is the sum of Proust's works." What does this mean?

11 Can one rationally choose to be dishonest, for Sartre? How would he disagree with Kant on this issue?

12 Sartre says that everyone is responsible for the war (written during World War II). He also said that "we were never more free than during the German occupation (of Paris)." How would you make sense of these two extreme and conscientiously perverse statements?